USHER
iBT TOEFL
INTERMEDIATE TEST
READING 02

어셔 iBT 토플 인터미디어트 테스트 리딩 02

어셔 어학 연구소

USHER
iBT TOEFL INTERMEDIATE TEST
READING 02
어셔 iBT 토플 인터미디어트 테스트 리딩 02

초판 1쇄 발행 · 2023년 5월 1일

지은이 · 어셔토플연구소
펴낸곳 · (주) 어셔어학연구소
펴낸이 · 어셔어학연구소
주　소 · 서울시 서초구 잠원로3길 40 태남빌딩 2층 어셔 어학연구소
전　화 · 02) 595-5679
홈페이지 · www.usher.co.kr
ISBN · 979-11-85317-26-7

정　가 · 24,000원

저작권자 · ⓒ2019, 어셔어학연구소

이 책 및 mp3 내용의 저작권은 저자에게 있습니다.
서면에 의한 저자와 출판사의 허락없이 내용의 일부 혹은 전부를 인용하거나, 발췌하는 것을 금합니다.

COPYRIGHT ⓒ 2019 by Usher Language Research Institute
All rights reserved including the rights of reproduction In whole or part in any form Printed in Korea

PREFACE I

본 토플(TOEFL) 교재는 iBT토플을 공부하는 학생들의 다음과 같은 요청에서 제작 동기를 찾습니다.

☞ 급하게 토플(TOEFL)은 해야 하는데, 문제 유형조차 파악이 안 되는 경우

- 토플 시험에 임박했는데, 토플 유형조차 파악이 안되었지만, 급하게 토플 유형파악 및 기초와 더불어 토플 실전 문제를 다뤄보고 싶은 학생들은 본 토플 교재의 문제지 부분만을 집중적으로 풀어보면 충분합니다.
- 총 **6회 분량**의 문제지가 들어 있으므로, 이 부분을 매일 1회씩 풀어보고, 문제에 대한 **유형과 난이도를 파악** 및 **시간 배분을** 연습한다면, **실전 시험 대비서**로서 확실한 몫을 담당해 줄 것입니다.

☞ 토플 기초일 경우,

☞ 실제 토플 시험에 임박해서, 문제 풀이는 해야 하는데, 자세한 설명이 필요한 경우

1. **기본적인 문장을 볼 줄 안다는 가정 하**에 본 토플 교재를 통해 부족한 부분을 채워 주시기 바랍니다.
2. 문제 풀이와 유형은 물론 **단어와 구문**부터 약하다면 지문의 모든 토플 **단어와 구문**을,
3. 문장의 **구조 파악**이 약하다면 **묶기 부분**을,
4. 문장의 단어, 구문, 문장 구조는 다 파악되지만 **매끄럽지 못하다면, 열 번 읽기**를 통해 확실한 마무리를 해 두시기 바랍니다.
   - 토플점수 올리는것은 실력 올리면 쉽게, 당연히 따라옵니다. 오랜 시간이 걸리는 일이 아닙니다. 확신을 갖고 열심히 해 주시기 바랍니다.

☞ 오답 패턴 정리가 필요한사람 / 위의 모든 것을 함과 더불어, 실전 iBT토플 경향 파악이 필요한 경우

- 오답 패턴정리는 실상 시험문제 푸는데 별로 큰 어려움이 없습니다. 토플은 기본적으로 해석만 잘해도 기본점수 20점 이상은 나오고, 조금만 더 매끄럽다면 25점 확보는 기본으로 하고 들어가야 하는 시험입니다. 오답 패턴만을 생각 하시는 분들은, 문제 6회를 푼 뒤 각 설명 중에서 **답 근거와 문단 정리** 부분만을 확실히 해두신다면, 기본이 되는 오답 패턴 때문에 어려움을 느끼시지는 않으시리라 생각합니다.

☞ 토플 독학해야 하는데, 문제유형뿐만 아니라, 자세한 문장 설명과 공부방법까지 필요한 경우

☞ 토플 고득점을 위한 탄탄한 준비를 필요로 하는 경우

- 토플 독학을 하는 분들, 토플 고득점을 위한 탄탄한 준비를 필요로 하는 분들도, 공부하는 과정 중에서 부족함이 느껴지신다면, 그 부분이 앞서 말한 부분 중 어디인지(1~4)를 우선 파악해주시고, 그리고 나서, 필요한 부분을 집중 정리 공략해 두시면, 큰 효용을 보실 수 있음을 확신합니다.

☞ 토플 고득점을 위한 토플 학원 추천 교재를 찾으시는 경우

PREFACE II

학생들이 가장 많이 하는 질문을 서문에서 정리해 볼까 합니다.

질문 1 토플 시험 성적표를 보니, 독해, 듣기, 쓰기, 말하기 네 부분으로 되어 있던데 어떤 과목부터 해야 할까요?

유학생들의 현지에서의 학업을 위한 준비여부를 파악하기 위해 만들어진 시험인 토플에서의 독해부분은 수능 영어나, 비즈니스 영어인 토익 등과 비교해서 볼 때 어휘나, 문장의 복잡성 등이 아무래도 어려운 경향이 있습니다.

많은 학생들이 TOEFL LISTENING(토플 리스닝)을 먼저 걱정하곤 하는데, 이런 학생들에게 스크립트를 주고 문제를 풀어보라고 했을 때 파악되는 것은 결국 못 들어서가 아닌 기초적인 독해조차 안돼서 못하는 경우가 많습니다.

뿐만 아니라 TOEFL WRITING(토플 라이팅)에 대해서라면 무언가를 창작하고 싶다면 모방이 우선입니다. 글을 쓸 때도 마찬가지로 모방의 대상은 글을 읽는 것이기에 쓰기보다는 당연히 독해가 우선입니다.

나아가 천천히 생각하며 문장조차 만들어 내지 못하는 학생들이 짧은 순간 문장을 만드는 것은 물론 발음과 엑센트와 억양까지 신경 써 가며 해야 하는 TOEFL SPEAKING(토플 스피킹)은 더욱 더 설명하기 힘든 일입니다.

이런 점에서 이 iBT 토플 책을 보시는 여러분들은, 다음 순서를 꼭 기억해 주시기 바랍니다.

토플 단어암기 → 토플 문법 (문장보기) → 토플 독해 → 듣기, 쓰기, 말하기

혹시, 외국 생활이 먼저인 학생들은(중·고등학교 생활을 영어권 국가에서 한 학생들) 듣기, 쓰기, 말하기가 더 편할 수도 있을 것입니다. 하지만 만약 토플시험을 즉시 봐서 점수를 넘길 수 없는 학생이라면, 결국 외국 나가서 학교 다니며 기본 되는 영어실력을 충분히 쌓지 않아서 성적을 따지 못하는 경우라고 해도 틀린 말은 아닐 것입니다. 이런 경우 다른 과목에 비해서 귀찮은 토플 단어 암기와 독해, 특히 주로 문제로 나오는 어려운 문장을 보는 것에 취약할 것이고 이는 해외에서 살았었다는 이유만으로 어느 정도 해결되는 듣기나 말하기와는 달리 별도의 노력이 필요한 부분이므로 국내에서 새로이 공부하는 학생들과 크게 달라질 것 없이, 위의 순서대로 「토플 단어암기 → 토플 문법 (문장보기) → 토플 독해」라는 순서는 따라야 할 것입니다.

이 토플 교재를 보시기 전의 여러분은 꼭 단어 암기는 기본으로 되어 있어야 하며 문장도 기본적인 틀은 잡혀있는 상태 이어야 할 것입니다. 꼭 이 순서를 기억해서 토플 공부를 해 주시기 바랍니다.

질문 2 문제 풀 때, 시간이 모자라요…….

TOEFL (토플) 시험 섹션 이름에서 알 수 있듯이, 토플 리딩과 리스닝은 정확히 (READING / LISTENING COMPREHENSION) 입니다. 묻고자 하는 것이 단순한 읽고 들을 수 있느냐 (READING / LISTENING) 가 아닌, 이해 (COMPREHENSION) 를 했느냐를 파악하는데 초점을 맞췄습니다.

단어와 문법이라는 기본이 닦여있다는 가정하에 독해력을 향상시키기 위해서는,
"빨리보다는 먼저 정확히" 에 초점을 맞춰 주시기 바랍니다. 점수는 이 두 가지가 잘되면 자연히 따라오게 됩니다. 많은 학생들이 얘기합니다. 시간이 모자라서 문제를 풀지 못한다고… 하지만, 이런 학생들에게 시간을 아무리 줘도 네 개의 선택지 중에서 두 개는 제끼더라도 결국 둘 중에 하나를 선택할 때는 여지없이 오답을 찍는 경우가 많습니다.

이유는 간단히 문장 해석이 정확히 되지 않으니 이런 어려움을 50년 동안 알고 있는 ETS가 낸 오답패턴을 결국 벗어나지 못해 답을 선택할 수 없는 것입니다.

그러므로 우선은 많은 문제를 풀지 못하더라도 푼 문제는 다 맞힌다는 생각으로 먼저 임해주시기 바랍니다. 만약 14문제 중 다 풀고도 시간이 모자라지 않지만 5문제 밖에 못 맞힌 학생과 시간이 없어 5문제 밖에 못 풀었지만 5문제를 다 맞힌 두 학생이 있다면 발전 가능성은 후자 쪽에 더 많습니다. 정확성을 키운 학생은 하던 방식대로 조금만 더 반복하면 시간은 자연히 줄지만 전자의 학생의 경우에는 실력 자체를 늘리는 일을 해야 하므로 문제 해결이 훨씬 어렵습니다.

그러므로, 꼭 「정확성 → 속도 → 그리고 토플 점수」를 기대하시기 바랍니다.

질문 3 본문 읽고, 문제 푸는 게 나을까요? vs 문제 풀며 본문을 읽는 게 나을까요?

두 방법 모두 장단점이 있습니다. 결론부터 실력을 기준으로 설명한다면, 대체로 전자는 실력이 있는 학생들이 푸는 방법이고, 후자는 실력이 약한 학생들이 쓰는 방법인 경우가 많습니다.

	본문 읽고 문제풀기	문제 풀며 본문 읽기(※44p 따라가며 풀기 참조)
실력 기준	실력있는 학생들이 할 수 있습니다.	실력이 약한 학생들이 점수를 내려 할 때 잘 쓰는 방법입니다.
장점	대체로 어려운 문제인 Summary, Infer, Purpose를 잘 풀 수 있습니다.	대체로 쉬운 문제인 Fact 를 잘푸는 경향이 있습니다.
단점	덤벙대다 오히려 쉬운 문제인 Fact 문제를 잘 틀리는 경향이 있습니다.	실력이 되지 않아 어려운 문제인 Infer, Purpose, Summary 문제를 잘 풀지 못합니다.
보완 방법	문단정리 + 답근거 꼼꼼히 하는 연습을 많이 합니다.	문단정리 + 답근거 꼼꼼히 하는 것은 당연하고, 이러한 학생들의 문제는 실력이므로, 실력을 키워야 합니다. 많은 문제를 푸는 것보다 적은 지문이더라도 성확히 반복적으로 읽어서 읽는 실력 자체를 많이 늘릴 수 있도록 합니다.
공통점	* 외우지 않은 이상 단어 문제는 둘 다 어려울 수도, 쉬울 수도 있습니다. * 30점중 25점까지 맞는 것은 둘 다 할 수 있습니다. 하지만, 그 점수가 한계로 굳어지는 경향이 있습니다.	
결론	결국 25점을 넘어 30점으로 가기 위해서는 기초 실력 쌓는 것은 당연하고, 꼼꼼하게 풀어서 실수를 줄이는 것도 해야 하기에 두 가지를 합칠 수 있는 상황이 되어야 합니다. 즉, 문제를 다 풀고 5분 정도 남아서 미심쩍은 문제들은 다시 한 번 훑어볼 수 있도록 만들 수 있어야 합니다. (정확도 + 속도 둘 다 가질 것)	

토플은 어려운 시험이 아닙니다. 간단히 한글로 해석해 주고 풀어보라고 했는데도 못 풀만큼 내용이 어렵거나, 문제를 꼬아서 수험생을 힘들게 하는 시험이 아닙니다. **그저 해석이 되지 않고 이해가 되지 않아 힘들어한다고 해도 과언이 아닙니다.** 그러므로 토플 공부 순서는 문제를 많이 풀려고 하지 말고, **본문 이해를 정확히 하는 연습**을 우선하시기 바랍니다. 그림자를 잡아서 움직이려 하지 말고, 그림자를 만드는 몸을 움직이시기 바랍니다.

PREFACE II

질문 4 토플 독해 공부할 때, 꼭 해야 하는 것은 무엇일까요?

긴장감있는 문제풀이 + (문제 푼 직후의 확실한 분석, 즉) 정확한 해석 + 문단정리 + 답근거는 필수사 입니다.

문제를 풀 때, 정신 놓고 편안히 풀면 1시간이면 풀 세 지문을 두 시간이 넘게 풀고도 실수는 실수대로 많이 하곤 합니다. 게다가 실제 토플 시험을 준비하는 입장에서는 전혀 도움이 되지 않습니다. 아울러, 해설지는 그저 문제의 답을 적어 두고 해석만을 적어둔 것이 아닙니다. 여러분이 iBT 토플 공부하는 과정 중 꼭 해야 할 내용들을 체크해 놓은 것이므로 답근거와 문단정리를 한 후 해설지에서 꼭 두 가지를 비교해 보시기 바랍니다.

아직 스스로 생각할 때 실력이 모자라다고 생각되는 학생의 경우에는 위의 내용을 충분히 따른 후 그 외에 본문을 씹어 먹는다는 생각으로 분해 분석해야 합니다. 그러기 위해서는

틀린 문제를 왜 틀렸는지 분석 후, 단어 찾는 것은 당연하고 구문암기, 열 번 읽기 등을 통한 적용까지 마쳐야 합니다.

질문 5 토플 시험이 얼마 안 남았어요. 가장 빨리 토플 독해 점수를 올릴 수 있는 방법은 무엇일까요?

토플 시험이 급박한 학생들이 가장 많이 하는 질문입니다. 이 질문은 두 가지로 나눠서 생각해봐야 합니다.
실력이 충분히 쌓은 경우와 그렇지 못한 경우.
실력이 충분치 못한 경우에는 답이 없습니다. 해석도, 내용 이해도 안되는 상태에서 이해를 묻는 시험문제를 풀 수 있다고 말할 수 없는 것은 당연할 것입니다. 하지만 실력은 기본이 된다는 가정하에서는 마무리 방법으로서 두가지를 해 볼만합니다.

1. 모니터 적응

대부분의 경우 학생들이 공부할 때는 종이로 공부를 하던 버릇이 있어서 모니터로, 시험을 보는 것이 특히나 모국어가 아닌 영어의 경우에는 더욱 더 문제가 될 경우가 적지 않습니다. 권하는 내용은 실제 시험을 보기 전, 모의고사를 두세 번 더 보는 것으로 실제 점수를 5점까지 끌어 올린 경우를 드물지 않게 보곤 합니다. 나름 자신이 있는 분들께 권해 드립니다.

2. 오답 정리

본인이 푼 문제지를 다 모아서 틀린 문제유형을 파악하고, 본인이 자주 낚이는 패턴을 분석해 보면, 본인만의 독특한 실수를 찾을 수 있습니다. 이것은 같은 반에서 공부했다고, 같은 수준이라고, 틀리는 문제가 같지는 않기 때문에 가르쳐 주는 선생님도 주변의 친구들도 심지어는 본인도 모르고 지나치는 경우가 많습니다. 하지만 당연히 풀어놓은 문제지가 없는 학생들의 경우에는 파악할 '재료'가 없기 때문에 시도조차 기대할 수는 없습니다. 실제점수로 대략 3점 내지 5점 정도까지도 올릴 수 있습니다. 이때 주의할 것은 실수를 줄이도록 노력하는 것입니다. 더 나은 기술, 더 나은 실력보다는 내가 어이없이 한 실수만 줄여도 이 정도의 점수 향상 폭은 충분히 가능합니다.

3. 모의토플시험을 신청해서 본다.

실제토플 가격은 $200(약 23만원)입니다. 가격도 가격인 만큼, 실제 토플을 보기 전에 모의토플 보는 것을 추천합니다. 모의토플은 실제 토플과는 똑같은 시험 형식으로, 컴퓨터로 진행이 됩니다. 4과목을 다 응시 될 경우, full, 49,000원, reading, listening, 2과목을 응시할 경우 25,000원 정도 듭니다.

질문이 끝난후에 : 모니터 적응까지 마무리 지어야 합니다. 사설이 많이 길지만 장황한 문제지의 장점에 대한 설명보다는 당장 문제지를 선택해야 하는 학생들이 궁금해 할 내용들로 서문을 채웠습니다. 본 문제지는 이런 생각을 바탕으로 만들었기에 학생들에게 어떤 모습으로든 도움이 될 것이라 생각합니다. 하지만 그저 안다는 점과 아는 것을 행하는 점은 전혀 다른 문제입니다. 마지막으로 잘 해야 하는 점은 지금까지 설명한 것을 잘 실행하는 것입니다. 꼭 실행해서 좋은 결과를 이루시기 바랍니다.

질문 6 토플 독해 실력을 키울 때, 순서가 어떻게 되나요?

step 1 단어

일단, 단어가 안되면, 아무것도 안됩니다. 이건 독해라서가 아니라 **리딩, 리스닝, 스피킹 라이팅 모두에 해당**되는 내용이고, 그 중에서 특히, 독해 지문에서 모르는 단어가 지문당 10개가 넘으면 위험 신호이고, 20개가 넘는다면, 판 끝났다고 생각하시면 됩니다.

step 2 구문 암기

단어가 마무리 되면, 그 단어만 가지고는 **단어 나열식 영어로만 때려 맞출 수 밖에** 없습니다. 그땐 단어끼리 같이 뭉치는 아이들의 **패턴을 파악해야 합니다.** 그래서 어셔어학원에서는 단어가 마무리 된 이후, 인터반(전체 5단계 중 3단계)부터 구문암기를 집중관리합니다. 이 부분이 진행되어야, 정확도가 확실히 늘어나기 시작합니다.

step 3 묶기

단어와 구문이 눈에 익힐때 쯤엔 문법파트에서 배운 대로 문장 구조는, 쉽게는 아니어도, 실수를 최소화 하면서 읽을 만큼은 되어야 합니다. 하지만, 학생들은 스스로 본인이 읽은 문장이 올바른지도 알지 못한 채, (특히, **절 처리와 분사처리**) 계속 진행하는 것은 도움되지 않습니다. 정확히 보는 것 쉽습니다. 그러니, **추측하지 말고 정확히 접근하는 버릇**만 잠시 들여 주시기 바랍니다. **답은 묶기입니다.** 영어로 된 모든 문장을 묶어두는 버릇이 생기면, 나중엔, 눈으로도 자연스레 처리되고, 정확도와 속도가 같이 늘 때 즈음엔 신경 쓰지 않아도 됩니다. 억지로 떼어내지 마시기 바랍니다. 너무 많이 해서 당연히 되었기 때문에 손을 떼어도 잘 될 때까지 (열심히 하면 두 달 내외면 됩니다) 모든 영어문장 (모든 과목)에서 해두시기 바랍니다.

step 4 열번 읽기

묶기까지 모두 되면 여러분들의 자신감은 상당히 늘어날 것입니다. 이 때만 되어도 20점은 무난히 넘길 수 있습니다. 하지만 아직 점수를 받은 것도, 끝난 것도 아니기에 점수 25점을 당연히 지나 30점이 될 때까지 긴장 풀지 말고, 앞의 세가지 단계를 지속적으로 반복해 두시기 바랍니다. 그 이후, **"이건 내가 모를 수가 없다"** 라는 생각이 들 때까지 **"열 번 읽기"** 하시기 바랍니다. 그리고 잘 되었는지 스스로 궁금하면, 초시계를 두고 지문을 읽어 보시기 바랍니다. 7분 내에 끊었나를 파악 바랍니다.

step 5 약간의 요령

25점이 넘어서면, 30점으로 가는데 약간의 요령이 필요합니다. 가령, insertion문제의 경우, 한국과는 다르게 두괄식을 선호하는 영어권 문화에 따라 해석으로도 안 풀리는 문제들은 따로 정리해두어야 할 내용들이 있습니다. 하지만 분명한 건 이런 내용들 **전부 설명하는데 30분도 걸리지 않습니다.** 이런 내용들을 몰라서 점수 25점 안 나오는 게 아니고 28점 안 나오는 게 아니므로, 이하 단계는 너무 신경 쓰지 마시기 바랍니다. 여기까지 오신 여러분들은 관성으로도 30점까지 갈 확률이 높습니다.

PREFACE II

step 6 실전연습

실전 연습이 마지막입니다. 이제 25점은 확실하고 28점도 종종 넘는 여러분들은 정말 **실전 연습**이 필요한 단계입니다. 시간이 문제된다고들 하는 경우가 가장 많은데, 의외의 내용은 25점 이하의 실력을 가진 학생들이 그런 얘기를 하는 경우가 많지 28점 이상들은 대체로 시간이 남습니다. (3지문 60분 줬을 때, 심하게는 17분만에 풀고 잤음에도 28점 나오는 학생도 있었습니다) 이 때의 문제는 꼼꼼함입니다.

어이없게 fact 문제에서 실수해서 한 두 개씩 틀리는 게 만점을 방해합니다. **꼼꼼해야** 합니다. 그리고 의외의 변수, 종이가 아닌 **모니터 적응**까지 마무리 지어야 합니다.

이상을 정리하면 다음과 같은 내용을 파악하실 수 있으리라 생각합니다.

〈독해 실력 향상 및 점수 향상의 필수단계〉

	step1	step2	step3	step4	step5	step6
	단어암기	구문	묶기	열번읽기	요령습득	실전연습
매일 과정 - 어셔에서 이뤄지는, 매일 시험으로, 확인해야 하는 내용입니다.	매일 200	묶기 시험	구문 시험	해석테스트	문제풀이및 시간조절	컴퓨터사용 모의시험
각 단계별 개념만 잡는 소요시간 (체화과정 제외)	2주	1일	1일	1일	30분	1일
체화과정 (적용과정) - 아는 것과 적용은 다릅니다.	2개월	1개월	2개월	1개월	1주	1주
어셔 과정 (어셔 커리큘럼과 연계 시)	완초1	완초2	인터	K1	K2	K1 이상
단계별 가능 점수 (30점 만점 중)	15	18	20	25	28	30

PREFACE III

반도에 흔한 고민 모음 (= 개념장착)

토플 리딩 노하우를 알려주세요. 리딩 문제 푸는 요령을 알려주세요.

먼저 묻습니다.
본문을 읽을 수나 있습니까?

예 vs 아니오
➡ "예" 라고 했다면 : 실력이 맞다면 현재 당신의 점수는 25점은 나왔어야 합니다.
➡ "아니오" 라고 했다면 : 다른 생각은 접어두시고, 본문부터 잘 읽으세요.

한글로 준다면?
- 문제 못 풀 수가 없습니다. 문제에 트릭도 없고, 너무 쉬운 문제입니다.

이렇게 쉬운 문제 푸는 요령?
- 묻습니다. 한글로 줬을 때, 다 푸는 당신에게 무엇을 가르쳐 줘야 하나요?
  '실수네요..' 인 당신에게 무엇을 가르쳐 줄까요?

반면, 그건 '한글이니까 그렇죠' 라고 말하는 당신에게 무엇을 가르쳐줄까요?
해석이 안되서 그러는 거라면,
'해석부터 하세요' 가 정답입니다.

결론 25점 이하는 다른 것에 신경 쓰지 마시고, 해석에만 집중하십시오.

시간이 문제인데요 ……

푼 곳까지 채점했을 때 25점이 나옵니까?

예 VS 아니오.
➡ "예" 라고 했다면 : 3일내로 시간 모자라지 않게 해줄 수 있습니다.
➡ "아니오" 라고 했다면 : 앞서 언급한 순서 무조건 따라 주시기 바랍니다.

속도로 고민할 만큼 정확도가 따라주지 않는 것입니다.
정확도 ➡ 속도

결론 정확도가 완성되면 속도는 전혀 문제 안됩니다.
정확도 올리는데 3개월이라면 (완초2~K1), 그래서 당신이 해냈다면, 속도는 3일내에 올려주겠습니다.

뭐가 됐든 25점 이상은 되야 합니다.

다 풀고 25점과, 다 못 풀고 25점 둘이 있다면,
다 못 풀고 25점이 훨씬 유리합니다.

PREFACE III

같은 반 애들이 오르는 것보다 너무 느려서 화가 나요.

하지만 같은 반, 같은 교실에 앉아 있어도 변수는 다음과 같습니다.
1. 같은 반을 두 번이상 듣는 학생 (이미 암기는 해두었지만, 적용이 안 되는 상태입니다.)
2. 중고등학교 때, 수능공부 때, 때려 맞추는 감은 있는 학생 (뭐든 해둔 건 티가 납니다.)
3. 외국에서 살다가 온 학생(외국에서 몇 년 살고, 한국 와서 추천받아 토플학원 다니는 것 자체가 이미 이상한 겁니다. 그런 학생들은 화가 나도 됩니다. 그런 학생들처럼 외국 나가서도 살아보고 같이 못한 뒤에는 그런 생각 가져도 됩니다. 그런데 그 학생들이 외국 살다 온 덕에 잘하는 것에 대한 열등의식은 버려도 됩니다.)
4. 초·중고등학교 때, 열성 부모님 덕분에 미리 뭘 해둔 학생들(체계는 없는데, 완전 못하지는 않습니다. 그렇다고 점수가 확 나버릴 만큼도 아닌 어정쩡한 상태)
5. 외고, 특목고, 영문과, 영어 교육과 학생들(외국에서 산 것만큼이나, 외고 학생들이 같이 앉아있는 것 자체가 이상한 것입니다.)

위에 어느 것에도 해당되지 않아서, 힘들어 하는 학생들이 많습니다.
하지만 위의 경우에 해당하지 않아서, 없는 것을 자책한다고, 아쉬워한다고, 부모님 탓해봐야 달라지는 것 없고, 아쉬워할 일도, 자책할 일도, 탓할 일도 아닙니다. 맘먹고 덤비면, 오래 걸릴 일도 아니기 때문입니다.

단어부터 중고등학교 과정 마치는 데까지 3개월이면, 충분합니다. 읽기에 집중되어 있는 수능 정도의 수준은 아무것도 없는 상태에서, 제대로만 붙으면, 3개월이면 충분히 해볼 만하고, 예체능이라서, 정말 I my me mine도 모른다 해도, 한 두달만 더 붙이면 됩니다.

그런데, 되도 않게 토플 한 두 달에 마쳤다는 주변 얘기를 시작으로, (물론, 와서 해보니 그건 아니더라지만) 옆에 같은 반에서 시작했던 학생들에게마저 떨어진다는 느낌을 받는 순간, 그냥 여러분은 말린 겁니다.

결론부터 말하면 문제 푸는데 전혀 도움 안됩니다.

문제는 문제가 있는 곳에서 풀어야 하고, 하나하나 차근차근 잡아내고 골라내고, 다듬으면, 금방 좋아질 수 있는 내용인데, 인생에서 무슨 거대한 숙적을 만난 듯 몇 달째, 상담만……. 상담만 하지 말고, 담백하게 질문 바랍니다.

"(반배치 등의 상태가) 이런데, 뭐부터 해야 할까요?"
그러면, 답변도 담백하게 갑니다.

"단어부터 / 문법부터 / 구문부터 / 묶기부터 / 해태부터 / 통딕테부터 / 쉐도잉부터 / 노트테이킹부터 / 문제풀이부터 / 발음부터 / 타이핑부터 / 기본 표현부터 / brainstorming부터 / 시간 내 쓰는 연습부터 / 전체 모의고사 보면서 마무리 / 중에 하나를 하세요…." 라고.

위의 것 중에서 하나씩만 잡아나가면 됩니다.

전부 잡으면, 110점 이상 나옵니다.
이 글을 읽는 분들 중에서 다수가 80점이면 끝납니다.
높아 봐야 100점이고, 극상들만 110점 이상입니다.

위의 것 중에서, 반만 해도 80점은 나옵니다.

절대로 감정소모 하지 않아야 합니다.

시간이 없어요. 단어도 안 되는 것 같은데, 문법, 독해, 듣기도 해야 하고, 말하기 듣기는 답도 없어요. 근데 다 해야 해요.

꼭 기억 바랍니다.
적은, 한번에 많이 만들면 상황이 힘들어집니다.

나폴레옹과 히틀러 둘 다, 전 유럽을 다 삼켜놓고도 결국 패한 이유는
적을 동시에 많이 두어서 입니다.

답은 춘추 전국시대 때부터 있습니다.
중국에서 나라가 많을 때 동맹 성립과 깨짐이 반복적으로 생겼는데 이때 핵심은,

1. 나를 도와주는 상대냐 (아군이냐)
2. 나를 도와주지는 않더라도, 내게 해를 끼치면 안 되는 상대에게는 일단 화친을 맺었습니다.

즉, 동시에 적을 여럿 만들지 않는다는 것입니다.

나폴레옹과 히틀러 둘 다, 유럽 대륙 좌측엔 영국을, 우측엔 러시아를 적으로 두고 싸웠습니다. 문제는 화력을 한군데 모아야 하는데, 그걸 실행하지 못한 게 문제였습니다. (나폴레옹과 히틀러가 이기기를 바라는 건 아닙니다. ^^;)

동시에 싸움대상으로 놓아도 되는 경우는 하나입니다.
월등히 높은 실력 차.
그래서 동시 상대가 될 때.
스스로에게 물어봐 주시기 바랍니다.
위의 단계 중, 동시에 세 네 과목씩 동시 처리 가능한 게 어디까지인지. (동그라미 쳐보기)

PREFACE III

그럼에도, 수업 정도는 들어두면 좋은 이유

집에 부모님이 차를 운전하는 집 자녀들과, 그렇지 않은 집 자녀들 사이에서
운전 면허증 따기 쉬워하는 사람은 어렸을 때부터 당연하게, 봐온 사람입니다.
차 운전에 있어 기본 순서 정도는 그냥 압니다.
차에 타면, 일단, P에 기어가 들어가 있는지, (이것 모르고, 그냥 시동 키를 켜도 작동 않는다고 하는 사람 의외로 많습니다.)
차 시동을 켜는 스위치가 무엇인지 (키를 돌리는 것인지, 누르는 것인지)
이후에도, 비가 올땐 뭘 만져야 하는지,
어두울 땐 뭘 돌려야 하는지,
방향지시는 어떻게 하는지,
브레이크는 뭔지,
엑셀은 뭔지.
무엇 하나 가르쳐 주지 않아도 기본적으로 아는 사람과,
브레이크와 엑셀도 모르고 그냥 배우는 사람은 당연히 배우는 속도도, 숙지 속도도 다르게 된 이유는,
설명하지 않아도 명확할 것입니다.

미리 봐두시기 바랍니다.
옆에 사람들이 같은 실력이 아닌 것은 인정하더라도
배울 것은 배워두는 게 좋습니다.

노출은 잦을수록,
다면적 일수록 좋습니다.

옆에서 늘 같이 공부하던 사람들이,
어떤 점들을 해결하니, 어떤 결과가 나오는지,
어떤 단계에서 힘들어 하고,
그 단계를 지나는 사람들의 공통점이 무엇인지 찾아두면,
스스로 공부하며 방법에 대한 확신을 찾는 동안의 불안함과,
방법을 찾으며 소비하는 시간을 아껴둘 수 있습니다.
방법을 강사 샘에게 그냥 말로만, 전달받는 것과,
옆에 사람들이 하면서 해결하는 것을 본 뒤의 확신은
차원을 달리합니다.

많이 봐두시기 바랍니다. 그리고 긍정적 자극 받으시기 바랍니다.

부정적인 스트레스 받지 말고.

이하의 글은, 열심히 잘 따라주는 학생들의 성적 변화 패턴을 확인하여, 정리한 내용입니다.
잘 따라오는 학생들과 못 따라 오는 학생들로 나누겠습니다.

	빠른 학생의 패턴	느린 학생의 패턴	비고
	전제 - 한 지문 내에서 모르는 단어 10개 이상은 위험, 5개 이하로 떨어뜨릴 것. (어셔 단어장 암기 필수 - 중고등, 토플 단어 둘다 해두면 되는 양입니다.) - 항상 180개 이상일 것.	단어 안되면, 그냥 엉망이나 기대 버릴 것	-
1주차	구문 암기 시작	구문 암기 시작	-
2주차	구문 **반복 확인**(빠른 사람들)	구문 암기 진행	-
3주차	구문 암기 - **적용** 거의 같이됨	구문 **반복 확인** 시작	-
4주차	제대로 된 해태 시작 - 적용되면 **정확도** 늘기 시작 - 20점대 진입	구문 반복 확인만 되고 적용 안됨	-
5주차	문제풀이 시작 - 정확도(푼 건 거의 맞을 시) - **시간 내** 풀이 목표 시작 - 이미 25	구문 적용 시작	-
6주차	문풀 12-28 굳히기	구문 적용 진행	-
7주차	문풀 28 굳히기	구문 **적용**하고, 슬슬 정확도 오르기 시작	-
8주차	**시간 줄이기** - 15분내 - 30목표	**정확도** 자신감 생기기 시작 - 20점대 내외	리스닝 병행 시작(선택)
9주차	-	시간에 대한 욕심 내기 시작	-
10주차	-	**시간내** 풀이 가능 시작 - 25 진입	무조건 리스닝 병행 시작
11주차	-	문풀 12-28 굳히기	-
12주차	-	문풀 28 굳히기	-
13주차	-	**시간 줄이기** - 15분내 - 30목표	-

※ 다분히 개인차가 있지만, 단어 180개 전제 상태입니다. 단어 180개 이하는 더 늦어집니다.

<u>**수능 1등급은 토플 RC 23내외 나옵니다.**</u>
6년 똑바로 공부해서 바로 나오던가, 두 달에 이 정도 나오면 짧은 거 아닐까요?

PREFACE III

정확도를 올리고 싶으신가요?
리딩을 잘 하고 싶으신가요?
다음을 꼭 지켜주세요.

Reading

가장 중요
1. 동사가 나오기 전까지는 문장이 아무리 길어도 '은', '는', '이', '가'로 잡고 기다릴 것
2. 문장 속에서 '~ 이다.'는 주절 동사 한번만 (등위접속사가 붙는 경우 제외)
   즉, 종속 접속사가 있으면, 그에 맞게, '~ 이지만', '~ 이므로' 등으로 해석
3. 해석은 앞에서부터 치고 나갈 것 (리스닝 대비도 가능)

위의 목록 완료 후,
4. 절 처리 / 분사 처리
5. 명사 처리 중요성 (전치사 뒤, 동사 뒤, 아무리 길어도 명사부터 볼 것)

→ 이에 대한 해결 방법-묶기
묶기 참고 (p.34)

Comprehension

되감기 (p.31)
문장 내 (단어 단위-구 단위-절 단위) → 문단 내 (문장 단위) → 지문 내 (문단 단위)
문장 내 중에서, 구 단위만 잘해도 20점
문단 내 중에서, 문장 단위만 잘해도 25점
지문 내 중에서, 문단 단위까지 잘하면 28점 이상!

느린 학생 패턴 (실력이 워낙 없어서 못하는 학생 말고)

자기 고집이 강한 학생 구체적으로,
단어 안 외우는 학생
구문 단어 안 외우는 학생
문법 안 되는 학생 (안되면서, 묶기도 안 하는 학생)
열 번 읽기 안 하는 학생

위의 패턴에 걸리는 학생은, 각 단계별 처방을 했음에도, 따라주지 않는다면, 시간이 지체될 수 밖에 없습니다.

TABLE OF CONTENTS

USHER iBT TOEFL INTERMEDIATE TEST READING 02
어셔 iBT 토플 인터미디어트 테스트 리딩 02

Introduction

Preface I. II. III. ★	3
Table of contents	15
1. 본 IBT 토플 교재의 특징 ★	16
2. 본 iBT 토플 교재의 구성	18
3. 계획표 짤 준비	22
4. 실력별 학습 계획	24
5. 토플 공부 방법 및 순서 ★	26
6. iBT TOEFL(iBT 토플) 소개	38
7. iBT TOEFL READING 소개	40
8. READING STRATEGIES ★	44
잔소리	55

문제집

TEST 1 — 61
Costs of Quitting a Job — 63
Cell Theory — 67
Mating Songs of Frogs — 71

TEST 2 — 77
Milankovitch Cycles and Glaciation — 79
The Making of Calendars — 83
The Decline of the Ottoman Empire — 87

TEST 3 — 93
Geographic Isolation of Species — 95
The Empire of Alexander the Great — 99
Early Maize Cultivation in the American Southwest — 103

TEST 4 — 109
Temperature Regulation in Marine Organisms — 111
The Upper Paleolithic Revolution — 115
Nineteenth-Century Theories of Mountain Formation — 119

TEST 5 — 125
Colonial America and the Navigation Acts — 127
The Most Common Bird on Earth — 131
National Parks in the Western United States — 135

TEST 6 — 141
The Role of Dress in Africa — 143
Evidence of an Asteroid Impact — 147
Native Americans and European Trade Goods — 151
Vocabulary / 구문 정리 — 157
묶기 — 195
열번 읽기 — 233

Practice Tests 6회

TEST 1 — 272
답안 & 문제 유형 분석표 — 273
TEST 1 해석 및 해설 — 274

TEST 2 — 294
답안 & 문제 유형 분석표 — 295
TEST 2 해석 및 해설 — 296

TEST 3 — 316
답안 & 문제 유형 분석표 — 317
TEST 3 해석 및 해설 — 318

TEST 4 — 338
답안 & 문제 유형 분석표 — 339
TEST 4 해석 및 해설 — 340

TEST 5 — 362
답안 & 문제 유형 분석표 — 363
TEST 5 해석 및 해설 — 364

TEST 6 — 384
답안 & 문제 유형 분석표 — 385
TEST 6 해석 및 해설 — 386

본 iBT 토플 교재의 특징

USHER iBT TOEFL INTERMEDIATE TEST READING(어셔 iBT 토플 인터미디어트 테스트 리딩)

1 토플 리딩 실력을 늘리는 "공부 버릇" 안내

서문 강화
- 문제지 본문을 건드리기 전에 서문에 있는 개념 정리를 잘 봐두고, 잘 적용 바랍니다. 문제지에서만 얻어간다면, 이미 실력이 있는 학생들입니다. 약한 실력이 문제라면, 서문 내용과 각 단계별 주의 사항을 잘 따라 주시기 바랍니다.

2 실제 iBT 토플 시험과 가장 유사한 실전서

최신 바뀐 본문 반영
- 최신 출제 경향을 반영하여 학생들이 어려워하는 과학 주제는 물론 인문, 사회, 역사, 인물 등 지문의 다양화 및 상향된 난이도를 반영하였으며, 각 분야별 빈도를 참고하여 내용을 구성하였습니다.

최신 경향, 문제 반영
- 문제 역시 좀더 어려워진 최신 경향에 맞게 하였기에 효과적인 iBT토플 리딩 시험을 공략하기에 좋은 점을 모아두었습니다.

3 실력 향상을 위한 실전 문제 설명서

실전
- 중급이라해도, 실력 향상과 실제 시험 적용을 위해 실전 난이도 문제들로 구성하였습니다. 그리고 보다 자세히, 꼼꼼히 파고 들어 설명하였습니다.

유형별 제시전략
- 각 문제별 유형 전략을 제시하여 기본 실력을 전제로 가장 빠르고 효과적인 문제 접근을 가능케 하였습니다.

4 자세한 iBT 토플 공부방법 설명

공부 방법 설명
- 대부분의 여타 토플 교재들이 소홀히 하고 있는 해석에만 초점을 맞춘 것이 아닌 학생들이 공부하는 방법 자체를 설명해 두었습니다.

방법 활용
- 이를 잘 활용하기 위해 서문과 독해 학습방법, 독해 문제 풀이 전략(오답 패턴) 부분을 잘 활용해 주시기 바랍니다.

5 묶기

공부 과정 중에서 문제 풀이 방법에 대해 고민하지 말고, 본문 내용 파악 우선 바랍니다
- 그때 가장 우선 해야할 것이 문장구조 파악입니다.
  문장 구조를 파악할 때, 가장 도움 되는 방법으로 어셔에서 진행하는 것이 묶기입니다.
  문장 해석 안되면 일단 묶기부터 하시기 바랍니다.
  묶기가 다 되면, 해석의 탄탄한 기본이 닦입니다.

6 토플 독학하기 쉽게 설명된 해설서 (토플 학원 못다니는 학생들을 위한 추천서)

답근거 찾기
- 정확한 지문 해석은 물론, 해설 시에도 정답만을 짚어주는 기존의 해설서의 방식을 탈피하여, 답근거를 명확히 하는 연습을 할 수 있도록, 본문과 오답에 각각 답이 되는 이유와, 틀린 이유를 표시해 두었습니다. 토플 독학을 하는 학생들에게 큰 도움이 되도록 하였습니다.

해설서 활용법
- 꼭 먼저 문제를 풀고, 고민한 후, 정답지의 내용과 하나하나 비교하며 확인하시기 바랍니다.

7 체계적인 학습관리

일정표
- 스스로의 실력과 여건에 맞는 일정표를 작성하여 목표를 갖고 토플 공부에 임하여 더 좋은 결과를 가질 수 있도록 하였습니다.

리딩전략
- 모든 ETS문제는 정답과 오답을 만드는데 패턴이 있습니다. 이런 패턴들을 모아 정리하였습니다. 본인이 공부 중에 자꾸 틀리는 문제가 있다면, 그 문제의 오답 패턴 중 어떤 것 때문인지를 파악하여 빠른 효과를 기대할 수 있도록 하였습니다.

수준별 학습
- 학생 별로 공부를 해 본 학생과 해보지 않은 학생들간의 공부 법에 차이를 두어 본 토플책에 설명해 두었습니다. 목표를 어디까지 잡아야 할지를 잘 파악해서 무리한 계획을 세워, 중도 포기하는 일을 없도록 추천 계획표를 잘 이용 하시기 바랍니다.

8 잔소리

- 잔소리를 작성하여 각 TEST 사이에 적어두었습니다. 중복되는 내용이더라도, 한번 더 참고 및 적용 바랍니다. 하는 척만 하는 게 아닌, 해야 실력이 늡니다.

본 iBT 토플 교재의 구성

USHER iBT TOEFL INTERMEDIATE TEST READING(어셔 iBT 토플 인터미디어트 테스트 리딩)

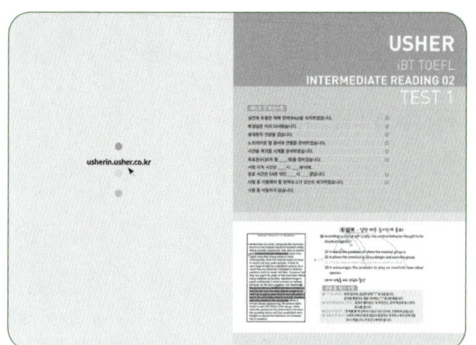

1. 시험 전 준비 사항

토플 시험 시작 전 시험칠 수 있는 환경인지 여부부터 파악하기 위해, 준비사항을 적어 놓았습니다. 토플 어학원에선 담당 매니저 선생님들이 챙겨주시지만, 혼자 공부할 때는 중간에 끊김이 생길 수 있으므로 특히 주의해서 지켜주시기 바랍니다.

2. Test

실전 감각유지 및 실제 iBT 토플 시험에서의 확실한 효과를 위해서 6회분의 문제를 구성하였습니다. 실제 시험과 같은 형식의 문제지로 주의해서 문제를 풀어주시기 바랍니다.

3. 시험 직후 체크 리스트 + 문제 유형 분석
   (나의 취약점 분석)

iBT 토플 시험 직후 주의 사항과, 단순한 채점이 아닌, 스스로의 문제점을 점검할 수 있도록 유형 분석표를 만들어 놓았습니다. 답만 먼저 확인하지 말고, 어떤 유형에서 반복적으로 틀리는지, 어떤 유형이 어렵고 혼란스러운지 스스로 체크해 보면서 스스로 문제가 무엇인지 꼭 점검해 주시기 바랍니다. 서문에 있는 READING STRATEGIES(p.44)를 참고해 각각 유형별로 어떻게 접근해야 할지도 파악해 주시길 바랍니다.

4. 잔소리

토플 리딩 뿐만 아니라 토플을 공부하면서 잊지 말아야 할 것들을 잔소리 형식으로 적어 놓았습니다. 누구나 잔소리를 듣기 싫어하지만, 항상 들어보면 틀린 말은 아닌, 나에게 이득이 되는 말들 뿐입니다. 아무리 알고 있다 해도 실천하는 것과는 다르기에, 계속 리마인드 시켜주고 실제로 실천하여 좋은 결과, 좋은 동기 부여가 되도록 꼭 다시 한번 참고하시기 바랍니다.

| 토플 공부도우미 | usherin.usher.co.kr

5. VOCABULARY + 구문정리
본문에 나온 토플 단어 정리와 구문을 각각 한페이지씩 정리해 두었습니다. 열번 읽기 위해서는 필히 단어와 구문암기를 먼저 한 후 넘어가시기 바랍니다.

6. 묶기
주어, 동사, 문장구조 파악을 정확하게 하기 위해 필수인 묶기를 지문 모든 문장에 적용시켰습니다. 스스로 1차적으로 묶기를 한 후, 처리가 안되는 부분을 참고하시기 바랍니다.

7. 열 번 읽기
문제지 맨 뒤에는 간단한 정답과 더불어, 각 본문만 주요 구문 표시만을 해두어 반복할 수 있도록 추가페이지를 만들었습니다. 그냥 버리지 말고, 꼭 들고 다니면서 반복적으로 읽어두시기 바랍니다

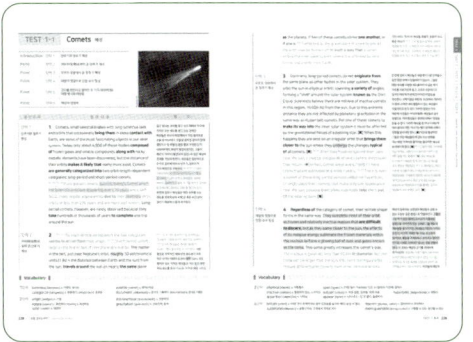

8. 정답 및 해석 + 해설
매회 문제를 푼 뒤, 이를 정확히 알기 위해 해석과 자세한 해설, 지문의 구조, 토플 단어 정리 뿐만 아니라, 토플 독학 하시는 분들을 위해 문제 초이스 내에 오답이유 표시 및 본문에 정답 근거 등의 공부 편의성을 위한 부가 내용을 넣었습니다.

2 본 iBT 토플교재의 구성

해석 · 해설 추가설명

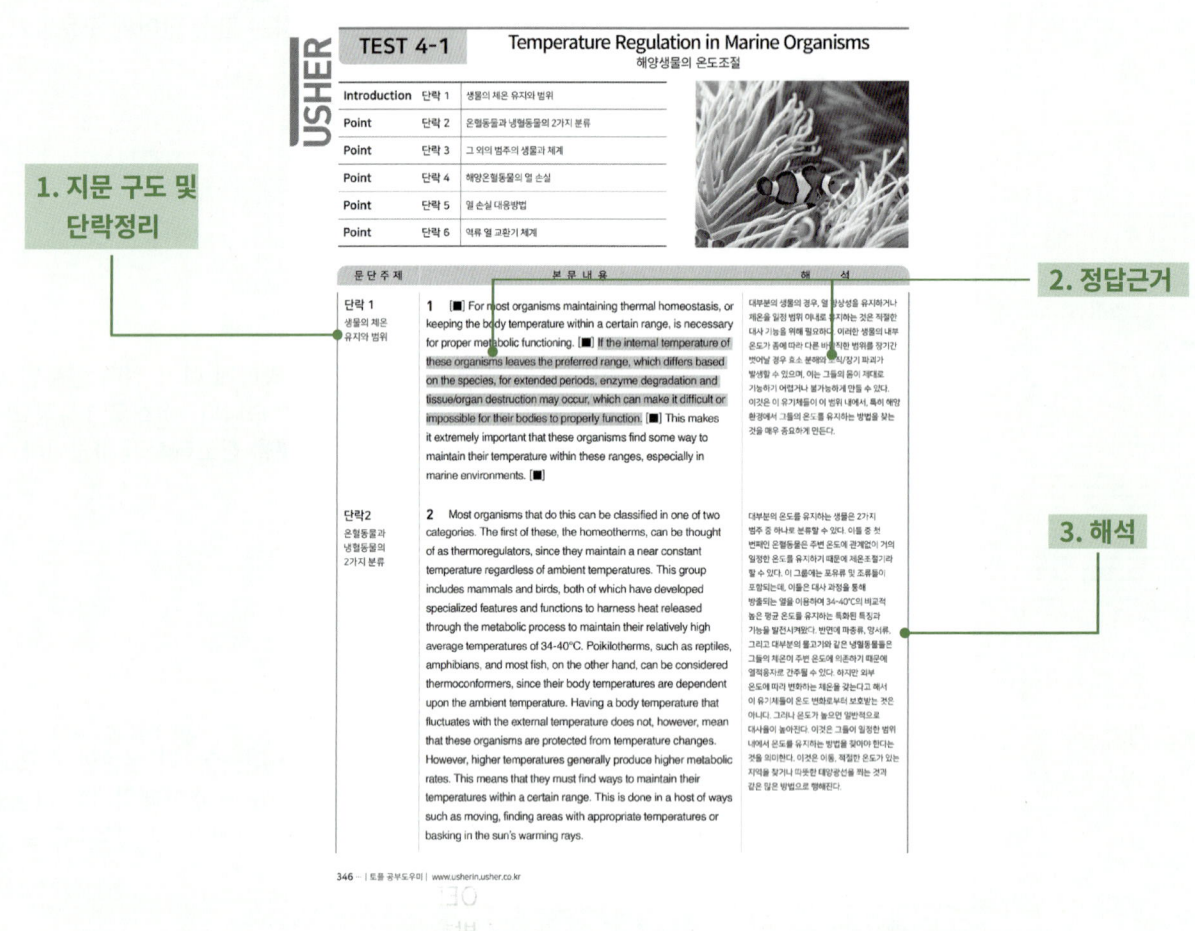

1. 지문 구조 및 단락정리
단락의 내용을 알아볼 수 있도록 도표화한 내용정리를 제공하였습니다. 내용정리와 더불어 제공한 사진을 보시면서 내용을 충분히 이해하시기 바랍니다.

2. 정답 근거
모든 문제는 정답근거가 없이는 문제를 만들지 않습니다. 꼭 정답 근거를 찾아가며 문제 푸는 버릇을 들이시기 바랍니다. 그냥 감으로 '어딘가에서..' 라는 식의 답 근거 제공은 ETS가 쉽게 엮어버리는 오답채택 확률을 높일 뿐입니다. 꼭, 본인이 답 근거라고 지목한 부분과, 답지의 부분이 맞는지 파악하는 습관을 들이시길 바랍니다.

3. 해석
지문 이해를 위해선 꼭 필요한 내용입니다. 하지만, 문장 해석에 급급해서 내용을 놓치는 일이 없도록 주의해서 '되감기' 를 많이 해두시기 바랍니다. (p.31 참고)

| 토플 공부도우미 | usherin.usher.co.kr

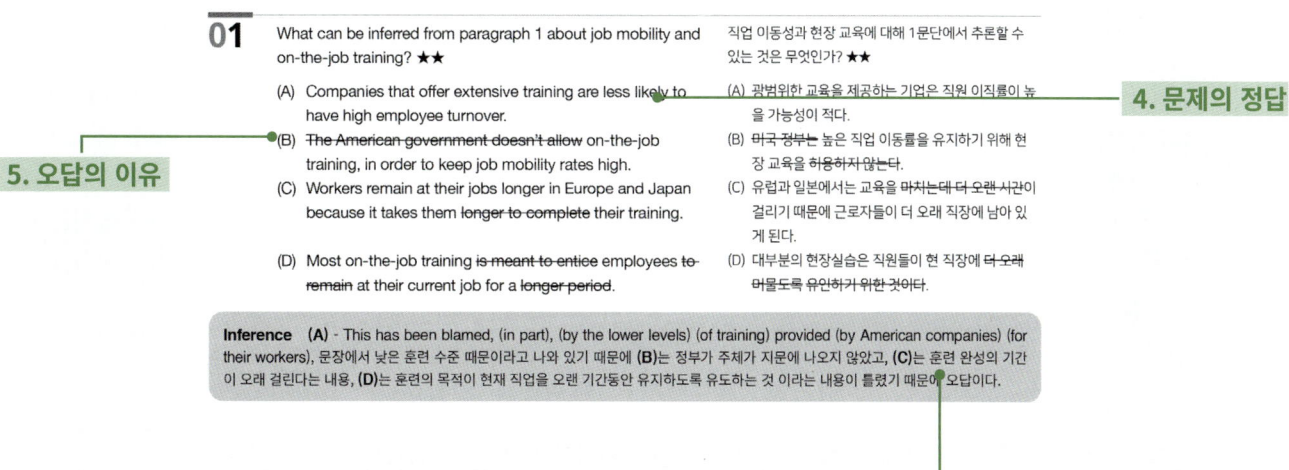

4. 문제의 정답

문제의 정답에 색을 넣어 표시해 쉽게 알 수 있도록 하였고, 옆의 해석 부분과 가급적 찾기 쉽도록 위치를 맞추어 두었습니다.

5. 오답이유

일반 문제지들이 정답 근거만 제시하는 것에 반해, USHER iBT TOEFL INTERMEDIATE TEST READING (어셔 iBT 토플 인터미디어트 테스트 리딩) 에서는, 오답의 이유도 밝혀두어 혼자 공부하는 토플 독학생들에게 도움이 될 수 있도록 하였습니다.

6. 해설

답이 되는 이유와 오답 이유를 좀더 필요로 하는 학생들을 위해, 하나하나 풀어 더욱더 자세히 설명해 두었습니다. 하지만, 만약 정답 근거와 오답 표시를 보고 금방 이해가 간다면 굳이 다 읽으실 필요는 없습니다.

3 계획표 짤 준비

USHER iBT TOEFL INTERMEDIATE TEST READING(어셔 iBT 토플 인터미디어트 테스트 리딩)

1 난 왜 토플 공부 할까? = 토플 점수 따서 뭐할까? Know-why

많은 학생들이 주로 고민하는 것은 늘 know-how에 대한 연구입니다. 물론 효율적인 토플 공부방법 참 중요합니다. 하지만, 그보다 먼저 해야 할 것은 과연 내가 왜 이 짓(?!!!)을 하고 있는가를 분명히 하는 것입니다. 즉, 다른 말로 목적이 뚜렷해야 한다는 뜻입니다. 공부하는 다수의 학생들이 공부하면서 매우 지겨워 하는 이유는 간단히 아직 내가 왜 해야 하는지가 명확하지 않기 때문입니다. 당장 4개월 뒤 외국에 공부하러 나가야 한다거나, 외국으로 이민 수속을 준비하고 있고 2개월 뒤 비행기표를 끊어놓은 상황 또는 국내에서라면 과외자리를 얻기 위해선 보여줄 점수가 필요 하다면 당장 써먹어야 한다는 생각 때문에 하루하루를 정말 꽉꽉 채워서 공부할 수밖에 없습니다. 하지만, 배워봐야 언제 써먹을까 싶은 학생들에게, 특히나 공부의 목적이 단순히 점수를 위해서라면 대부분 공부할 때의 목적은 저먼 나라의 이야기처럼 별 관심이 없습니다. (물론 중요하지 않다는 것은 아닙니다) 이런 상황이라면 공부하다가 도중에 그만두기 딱 입니다. 싫다면? 이유부터 생각해 봅시다.

< 나는 토플공부해서 ( )점 따면, ( ) 하겠다 >

2 위의 목표에서 ( ) 달 내에라는 말은 뺐습니다. 이유는 누구나 공부를 질질 끌면서 하기는 싫어합니다.

하지만, 그렇다고 내 능력은 생각지도 않고 시간 계획을 짜버리면 중간에 포기하기 쉽습니다.
남들은 1 → 2 → 3 → 4 → 5 단계를 가는 것이 정석이라고들 할 때, 왠지 나는 1 → 3 → 5 로 갈 수 있을 것 같은 근거 없는 자신감? 이런 계획은 수시로 고칠 일만 더 만들 뿐 별로 도움 되진 않습니다.
지금은 시간을 생각하지 마십시오. 일단 샘플로 해보고 시간 계산해도 늦지 않습니다.
그리고 다음 단계도 생각하지 마십시오.
단어, 문법, 독해, 듣기, 쓰기, 말하기 어느 하나 다 안 중요한 것이 없다고 생각하는 순간,
무리한 계획을 세우게 되고, 그 후엔 스스로 질려 포기하기 쉽습니다.
하지만, 확실한 것은 지금 앞 단계를 확실히 끝내면 다음 단계로의 과정이 자연스레 이뤄진다는 점이고,
지금 확실치 않게 해두면,
두고두고 발목 잡는 일이 된다는 점입니다.

3 현재 나의 공부를 방해하는 요소 파악 - 뇌구조 놀이 (p.23)

다들 익숙한 놀이 이지만, 정말 잘 이용하는 것이 어려운 이유는 오직 한가지 솔직하지 못해서입니다.
솔직하게 적어보십시오.

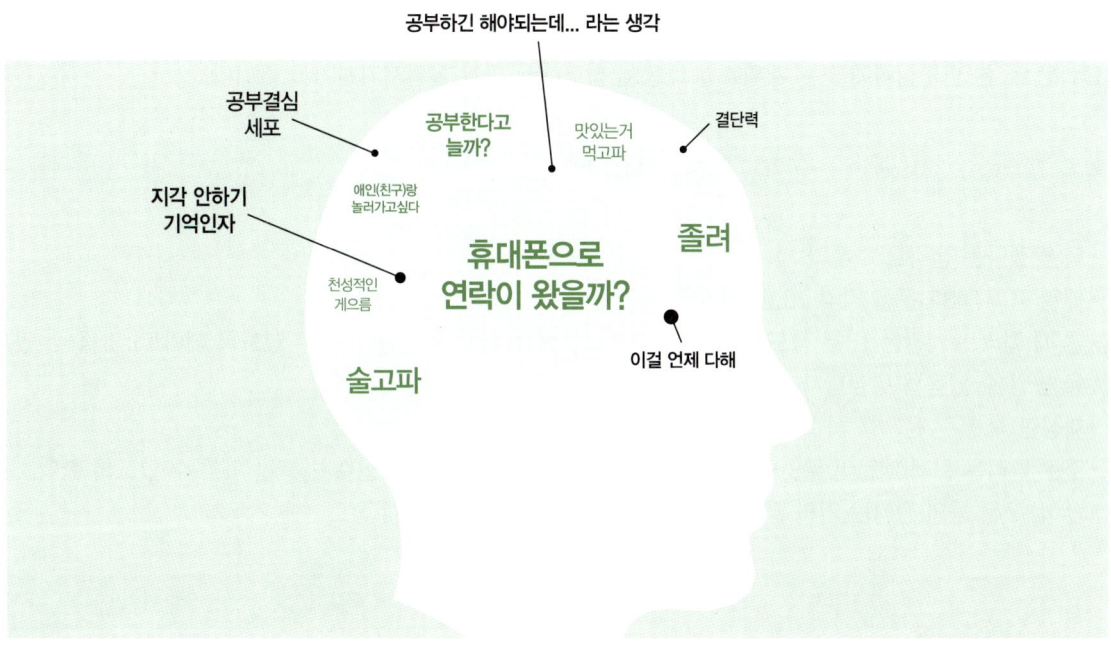

4 1번부터 3번까지의 내용들을 정리하고 나서 이제 본격적인 스스로의 공부방법을 짜보십시오.

실력별 학습 계획

USHER iBT TOEFL INTERMEDIATE TEST READING(어셔 iBT 토플 인터미디어트 테스트 리딩)

Test 1을 푼 뒤, 본인의 실력에 맞는 계획표를 다음을 참고해서 짜서 실행시키시기 바랍니다.

1 맞은 개수 25개 이상 out of 30 : 목표 - 매일 1회 (3지문씩 푼다)

- 다 맞겠다는 생각으로 푼다.
- 매일 정해진 3지문을 각각 20분씩 1시간 동안 푼다.
- 풀 때 걸리는 시간은 13분 정도로 하고, 나머지 5분은 실수 여부를 체크할 수 있도록 해야 다 맞을 수 있는 확률을 높일 수 있음을 명심하자.
- 채점한 후 틀린 문제를 꼭 확인한 뒤, 실수를 줄이려 노력한다.
- 주로 틀리는 문제 패턴이 무엇인지 꼭 알아내서 다음 시험에선 같은 실수 반복을 피할 수 있도록 한다.
- 단어, 구문 등의 정리는 거의 끝났어야 하므로, 간단히 빠진 것 몇 개 정도는 챙겨두자.

1주	1일차	2일차	3일차	4일차	5일차	6일차
	Test 1	Test 2	Test 3	Test 4	Test 5	Test 6

2 맞은 개수 21개 이상 out of 30 : 목표 - 매일 2 지문씩 푼다

- 매일 정해진 지문을 각각 18분씩 36분 동안 푼다.
- 채점한 후 틀린 문제를 꼭 확인한 뒤, (스터디가 가능하다면, 스터디를 통해서 확인 후) 실수를 줄이려 노력한다.
- 아직 시간계산 등의 어려움이 극복되지 않았을 것이고, 다 풀기도 빠듯할 것이지만, 시험 시간 동안 최선을 다하는 자세를 가져야 한다.
- 매일매일 꾸준히 2지문을 소화하되, 꼭 확실히 짚고 넘어간다.
- 아직 중간중간 처리되지 않는 문장, 단어, 구문 등은 필히 꼭 챙겨서 다음 시험에선 같은 실수 반복하지 않게 하여야 한다.
- 아직, 기본 실력 부분에서 밀리는 것이므로, 반복적으로 읽는 것을 게을리하지 않는다.

	1일차	2일차	3일차	4일차	5일차
1주	지문 2 out of 18	지문 4 out of 18	지문 6 out of 18	지문 8 out of 18	지문 10 out of 18
	6일차	7일차	8일차	9일차	
2주	지문 12 out of 18	지문 14 out of 18	지문 16 out of 18	지문 18 out of 18	

3 맞은 개수 20개 이하 out of 30 : **목표 - 매일 1 지문씩 푼다**

- 매일 정해진 1지문을 18분 동안 푼다.
- 시간 내에 다 푸는 것은 아직 염두에 둘 때가 아니다.
  그저 편하게, 열심히 풀되, 풀었던 문제는 다 맞힌다는 생각으로 진지할 필요는 있다.
- 아직은 시험에 충분한 준비가 되어있지 않으므로, 반드시 문제보다는 본문에 초점을 맞추어 본문 이해에 노력을 하고, 모든 단어와 구문 등은 반드시 암기한다.
- 틀린 문제 중에 기초적인 단어 등이 많이 포함되어 있다면, 무조건 USHER iBT TOEFL VOCABULARY 를 병행 암기하며 진도를 나가야 한다.
- 문제의 실수 여부보다는 실력 자체에 초점을 맞춰 노력한다.
- 아무리 시간이 많이 걸려도, 풀었던 문제지는 꼭 반복적으로 읽는 것을 많이 하여야 실력 향상을 이룰 수 있다.

	1일차	2일차	3일차	4일차	5일차
1주	지문 1 out of 15	지문 2 out of 15	지문 3 out of 15	지문 4 out of 15	지문 5 out of 15
	6일차	7일차	8일차	9일차	10일차
2주	지문 6 out of 15	지문 7 out of 15	지문 8 out of 15	지문 9 out of 15	지문 10 out of 15
	11일차	12일차	13일차	14일차	15일차
3주	지문 11 out of 15	지문 12 out of 15	지문 13 out of 15	지문 14 out of 15	지문 15 out of 15
	16일차	17일차	18일차		
4주	지문 16 out of 16	지문 17 out of 17	지문 18 out of 18		

토플 공부 방법 및 순서

USHER iBT TOEFL INTERMEDIATE TEST READING(어셔 iBT 토플 인터미디어트 테스트 리딩)

복습

수업 중 얻은 내용을 다 이해한다는 생각으로 반드시 반복 복습해둔다.

i) 확실한 수업 내용 확인을 수업직후 이후 한번 더 적어보고(백지시험),
ii) 이 내용들에 포함된 모든 단어와 표현을 암기 후,
iii) 마지막으로는
　㉠ 눈으로 읽다가,
　㉡ 문장구조가 확실해지면, 입으로 내가 아나운서가 된것처럼 shadowing을 할 수 있을 만큼 반복적으로 읽는다. (10번)
iv) 많이 듣는 것은 이 과정들이 다 된 후 노래 듣듯이 편하게~^^

예습

수업준비 잘 할 것

= "잘" 이라 함은, 모든 수업내용을 모두 아는 것이 아닌, 수업시간에 내가 어디서 집중해야 하는가를 알 수 있게 "아는 것과 모르는 것을 구별" 해두는 정도!

= (즉, 혼자 할 수 있는 것까지만 해두는 것!!! 모르는 단어 찾아 두는 것은 기본 중 기본)

수업직후!

수업 "끝나자마자" 바로 그 자리 에서 수업 내용을

i) 모두 같이 훑어보고
ii) 모든 내용 정리 후
iii) 모르는 것은 옆에 학생에게 물어서라도 알아둔다!
iv) 같이 스터디를 하는 학생들간에는 반드시 집에 가기 전에 정리한 암기사항들을 자체 시험을 통해 철저히 암기한다.

수업

예습 한 것을 근거로, 모르는 것을 집중적으로 확인한다.
(= 그럼으로써, 수업의 수준이 좌우된다)

| 토플 공부도우미 | usherin.usher.co.kr

다음 순서를 반드시 지켜 주시기 바랍니다. 순서는 다음과 같습니다.

예습

1. 시험 전 지시사항 체크
2. 시험 중 체크사항
3. 시험 직후 스터디
4. 개인 준비 시작 (단어 암기, 모르는 문장 표시, 묶기)

1. 시험 전 지시사항 체크

실전에 유용한 독해 전략(44p)을 숙지하였습니다. ○
화장실은 미리 다녀왔습니다. ○
휴대폰의 전원을 껐습니다. ○
노트테이킹 할 종이와 연필을 준비하였습니다. ○
시간을 체크할 시계를 준비하였습니다. ○
목표점수(30개 중 ___개)를 정하였습니다. ○
시험 시작 시간은 ___시 ___분이며, 종료 시간은 54분 뒤인 ___시 ___분입니다. ○
시험 중 이동해야 할 방해요소가 있는지 체크하였습니다. ○
시험 중 이동하지 않습니다. ○

2. 시험 중 체크사항

Sentinel Behavior in Meerkats

1.→ Meerkats are small, mongoose-like mammals that live in the Kalahari Desert of Southern Africa. Being primarily insectivores, they feed on beetles and scorpions buried underground, which they locate using their strong sense of smell. Unfortunately, when the meerkat lowers its head to search out prey under grasses, it limits its own range of sight by a significant amount. As a result they are extremely vulnerable to airborne predators such as hawks and owls. To ensure that they can reach the safety of their bolt-holes before being snatched up by birds, meerkats forage in packs and partake in what is known as sentinel behavior. As the term suggests, one meerkat in the group acts as a sentinel and does not look for food like the rest, but rather stands upright on its hind legs to gain a wider field of view with which it scans the surrounding area for possible predators and other threats to the community. When it senses danger approaching, the sentinel barks loudly to warn the others of the danger. Many scientists questioned this phenomenon because the revealing stance and loud vocalization were thought to expose the meerkat to an increased risk of predation.

폭 넓게 – 일단 버릇 들이는게 중요!

32 According to paragraph 1, why was sentinel behavior thought to be disadvantageous?
(A) It warns the predator of where the meerkat group is.
(B) It allows the meerkat to sense danger and warn the group.
(C) It helps the predators locate the sentinel meerkat.
(D) It encourages the predator to prey on meerkats over other species.

스터디 자료들 미리 수집해 둘것!

2.1 "?" 표시하기

- 궁금한 걸 건드려야 실력이 늘어 납니다. 중요한 건, 시험 문제를 풀면서 다 기록을 남길 순 없으니 본문을 읽으며, 궁금한 곳에만 남겨 두는 겁니다. 표시 안 해두면, 나중에 기억도 안 납니다. 시간 없지만, 체크해 둬서 나중에 확인대상 정리라는 중요한 과정입니다.
- 문제에도 물음표 해둡니다. ? 결국 질문꺼리는 많을수록 실력 높이기 좋습니다. 귀중한 시간 투자해서 내가 모르는 것을 골라두는 작업은 절대 소홀히 하지 않습니다.

5 토플 공부 방법 및 순서

2.2 문제 핵심 단어에 동그라미
- 묻는 말에 대답합니다. 별거 아닌 것 같아도 중요합니다. 묻는 말에 대답합니다.
  그래야 i) 읽어야 할 범위가 줄어들고, ii) 쓸데없이 고민하는 일 줄입니다.

2.3 답근거 날리기
- 멍하게 문제 푸는 학생들 참 많습니다. 생각하며 틀린 이유 단어로 날리다 보면, 재밌습니다. 그리고, 실력도 늡니다. 간결하게 날려야 합니다. 죽죽 그으면 안됩니다. 실력 키우는데 도움 안됩니다.

2.4 경쟁 문장 표시
- 경쟁 문장 체크 (모든 객관식 문제는 결국, 정답과 경쟁하는 것은, 1개입니다. 만약 4개 모두 모르겠으면 그냥 실력이 아닌 겁니다. 시험장 갈 정도라면, 마지막 하나와 결국 싸워야 맞는 겁니다).

3. 시험 직후 - 이견문제만 스터디 (답은 모른채 해야합니다.)

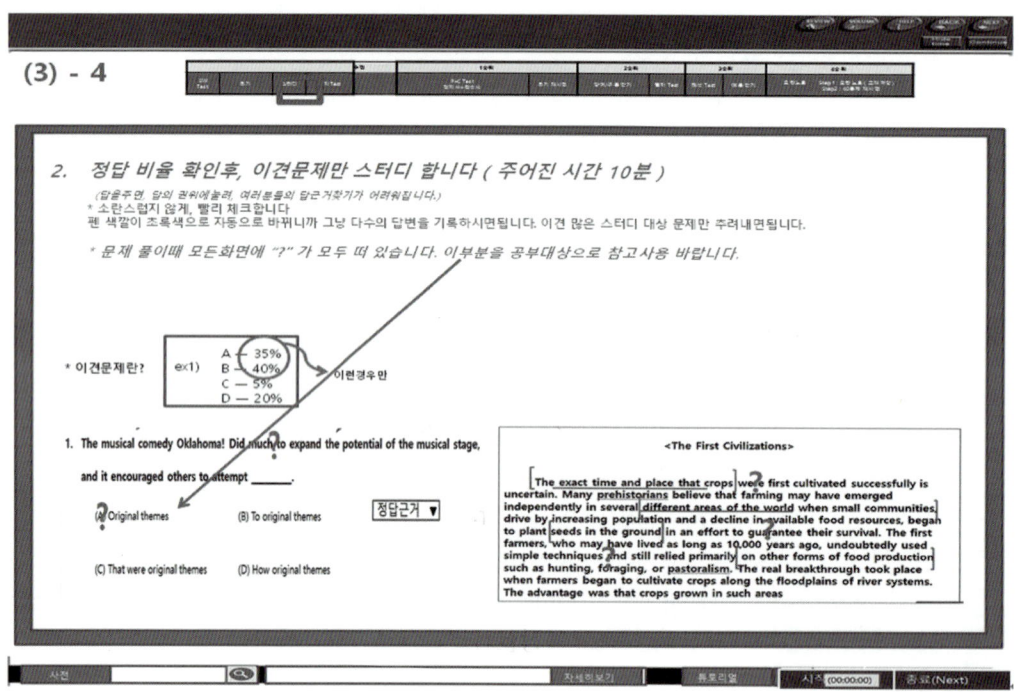

순서 :
i) (답 없이) 조원끼리 답 맞추고
ii) 이견문제 파악 후 (지문당 3-4문제! 넘으면 그 조 해산!), 스터디 (10분내)
iii) 답근거 (모두)
iv) ? 파악해서 서로 질문. 모르겠으면 형광펜 처리

4. 개별 공부 시작
모르는 단어 암기까지 / 모르는 문장 형광 표시 / 묶기 (할 수 있는 데까지)

수업 중

수업의 질은 철저하게 학생들이 예습을 얼마나 잘 해두었나에 달려있다 해도 과언이 아닙니다.
꼭 앞의 과정을 잘 정리해서 확실히 챙겨두시기 바랍니다.
특히, 궁금해서 밑줄 쳐 둔 부분 등은 집중해서 잘 처리해 주시기 바랍니다.

단, 우선 문장 해석 및 내용 정리 위주로 하되, 문제 푸는 나름의 요령은 어느 정도 실력에 신경 쓸 것!
세가지만 잘 지켜주시기 바랍니다.

1. 등 떼고
2. 펜 잡고
3. 멍 때리지 말고

세가지 안 하면, 할게 없습니다. 공부밖에.

수업 직후

수업시간에 적은 내용은 즉시 확인 + 정리해야 합니다.
보통 수업시간 50분 분량을 한번 훑어보는데 걸리는 시간은 많지 않습니다.
잘 집중했다면, 한번 다 보고, 화장실 다녀와도 될 만큼이니까, 꼭 해두시기 바랍니다. 한번 귀찮은 5분을 투자하면,
집에 가서 한 시간은 아낄 수 있고,
덤으로, 공부하는 것이 그렇게 어렵지만은 않다는 걸 알게 될 겁니다.

- 문제를 푼 곳까지 표시합니다. (잔소리1)
- 조원들과 수업시간 내용을 한번 확인합니다. 편의점으로, 화장실로 즉시 나가지 말고, 5분내로 잠시 검토하고 일어섭니다.

스터디 그룹 조원 중 한 명이 처음부터 중요내용이라고 짚어준 내용을 훑어 나갈 때, 나머지 조원들은 틀리거나 빠진 내용들을 채워주며 정리하면 됩니다. 시간은 5분 내외면 충분합니다.

** 학생들이 문장은 이해를 하되, 글 내용(문단)을 모르고 가는 경우가 많으므로, 반드시 간단히 문단 정리할 때, 내가 이해한 것 인지 꼭 스스로를 의심하며 읽어야 합니다. 가끔씩은 스터디 때, 또는 수업시간에 선생님이 정리해 준 내용을 스스로 이해한걸로 착각하고 넘어가는 학생들이 많습니다. (READING **COMPREHENSION**임을 명심!!)

5 토플 공부 방법 및 순서

복습

i) 단어 및 구문 암기 퀴즈 (스스로라도 해야 합니다 - 시험은 인간이 만든 가장 완벽한 시스템!!!) (***백지시험)
ii) 10번 읽기 (열 번 읽고, usher.co.kr/usher_intra.php → '난 오늘' 흔적에 mp3 녹음해서 기록 남기기)
iii) mp3확인 (들으면서 다 알아 들어야 합니다. 이게 쉬운 것이 아니므로 안된다고 실망은 하지 말되, 되도록 노력해 보시기 바랍니다)

예습 - 수업 - 복습 중에서 **가장 중요한 것은 복습입니다.**
밥상 잘 차려놓고 먹지 않는 사람처럼, 예습 수업만 잘 준비하고 복습하지 않는 **"짓"**은 하지 마시기 바랍니다.

1. 반드시 암기합니다.
   단어와 구문은 암기합니다. 이후, 꼭 시험으로 암기 여부 파악 합니다.

2. 암기와 적용은 다릅니다.
   묶기를 통해서, 문장을 바로 파악 하고 있는지 꼭 파악합니다.
   묶기의 중요성은, 다음 내용에서 확인 바랍니다.
   꼭 합니다. 실력을 올리는데 꼭 필요합니다.

■ 복습 부분에 대한 재강조

1. 백지시험 (반드시 암기 후 읽기!)

누구나 시험 보는 것은 싫어합니다.
하지만, 시험은 인간이 만든 가장 좋은 확인 방법입니다. 본인이 안다고 생각했던 내용들도 정작 확인 시에는 잘 모르고 있다는 점을 파악할 일이 있을 것입니다. 이런 경우, 스스로 문제점이 있다고 생각할 일이 아니고, 원래 공부과정 중 하나 로서 당연하게 받아들이되, 분발해서 모자란 부분을 잘 채워 나갈 수 있도록 하는 방법으로서 스스로 체크 하는 시험을 권해드립니다.

  ***시험 방법**
   각 지문 별로, 해석하다가 막히는 부분은 단어 아니면, 구문에서 막혔을 것입니다.
   이런 경우, 혼자 공부할 경우에는, 시험지를 우선 작성해서 여러 장 복사해 놓거나, 여러 명이 같이 할 경우에는 한 명씩 돌아가면서 시험을 봐서 90% 이상 맞지 못하면,
   통과시키지 않는 연습을 미리 해두면, 그날 부분은 확실한 복습을
   하게 될 것입니다.

다시 한번!! 예습, 수업, 복습 중에서 **가장 중요한 것은 복습이라는 점**을 기억해 두시기 바랍니다. 그저 수업 시간에 앉아 있었다는 사실만으로, 노트에 적어놓았다는 사실만으로는 실력이 늘지 않습니다. 어떻게든, 그 내용들을 잘 정리해서 써 먹을 수 있을 만큼 만들어 두어야 진짜 본인 실력이 되는 것입니다.

2. 되감기
  i) 문장 단위
  ii) 문단 단위
  iii) 글 단위

전체에서 두루 쓰이는 방법으로, 긴 문장일 경우에는 문장 내에서, 문단의 경우에는 문장과 문장 사이의 전개를, 글 전체라면, 각 문단별의 연결 관계를 생각하며 읽는 것을 말합니다.

되감기 방법

i) 문장
묶기 형식의 문장에서 문장을 완전히 파악하기 위해 주어, 동사, 구, 절 단위로 나누어 되감기를 합니다.

가장 중요한 건,

> 1. 동사가 나오기 전까지는 문장이 아무리 길어도 '은', '는', '이', '가' 로 잡고 기다려야 한다.
> 2. 문장 속에서 'rv이다' 는 주절 동사 한번만 나온다. (등위접속사가 붙는 경우 제외) 즉, 종속 접속사가 있으면, 그에 맞게, '~이지만', '~이므로' 등으로 해석한다.
> 3. 해석은 앞에서부터 치고 나가야 한다.

위에 것을 다 완료하면,

> 4. 절처리, 분사처리까지 신경써야 한다.
> 5. 전치사 뒤, 동사 뒤, 아무리 길어도 명사부터 보고 처리해야 한다.

Ex)

```
    1.          2.              3.                    4.              5.          6.
A situation [[in which) an economic market is dominated (by a single seller) (of a product)] is known (as a monopoly)
```

1. **상황은**
2. 상황은, **이 상황내에서**
3. 상황은, 이 상황내에서 **경제시장이 지배되어지는 상황은**
4. 상황은, 이 상황내에서, 경제시장이 **하나의 상품이 하나의 판매자에 의해** 경제시장이 지배되어지는 상황은
5. 상황은, 이 상황내에서, 경제시장이 하나의 상품이 하나의 판매자에 의해 경제시장이 지배되어지는 상황은, **알려진다.**
6. 상황은, 이 상황내에서, 경제시장이 하나의 상품이 하나의 판매자에 의해 경제시장이 지배되어지는 상황은, 알려진다, **독점으로써**.
7. 경제 시장이 하나의 상품이 하나의 판매자에 의해 지배되어 지는 상황은 독점으로써 알려진다.

5 토플 공부 방법 및 순서

ii) 문단

문장 되감기 후, 문장이 모두 파악되면, 각 문단의 내용을 더욱 이해하기 위해 문단 안에 세부적인 내용을 나누어 되감기 합니다.

→ 1. Even before the Venetian Senate's act of 1474, isolated monopolies were granted in Europe. For example, in England the monarchs would grant letters patent, or "letters that lie open", to people in their graces, granting them a monopoly to produce or provide specific goods and services. This tradition of granting monopolies eventually led to the term 'patents' we use today. / 2. It was not, however, until the Venetian Act that the standardized process of granting patents occurred. Britain, influenced by this new concept, eventually implemented such a system as a kind of mercantilist instrument to attract emigrants with skills that could possibly aid Britain's industry with the guarantee of exclusive monopoly, after the significant economic drain caused by the War of the Roses. / 3. By the early 17th century, patents had become royal favors to subjects of loyalty or wealth, with monopolies being granted on products and services such as running ale-houses. This led to inefficiency and left room for the corruption that brought about the Statute of Monopolies of 1624, which required courts to outlaw all monopolies but those based on true inventive intentions. / 4. When the Industrial Revolution spurred an explosive number of new inventions, patents became an increasingly important component of the socioeconomic machine. This era marks a change in the perception of the role of patents in society, in that they were no longer given only for the introduction of a new finished product, but also for the introduction of technological know-how or processes. /

1. Venetian Senate 법령 이전에도 주어졌던 독점.
2. Venetian Senate 법령 이후 특허 수요의 표준화.
3. 특허의 비효율성과 부패를 막기 위해 생긴 Statute of Monopolies.
4. 산업화 이후, 특허의 역할 변화.

iii) 글

각각 문단 안에 내용까지 완전히 이해한 후, 전체적인 글의 흐름과 정리를 위해 글을 문단 별로 나누어 되감기 합니다.

TEST 2-1 1. 날짜: ___년 ___월 ___일 2. 구문 암기 여부: ☐ YES / ☐ NO 3. 읽기 횟수 (목표: 열 번 읽기) 1회 2회 3회 4회 5회 6회 7회 8회 9회 10회

Milankovitch Cycles and Glaciation

1   Scientists have ⁽⁰¹⁾**pieced together** a relatively detailed timeline of the twenty glacial cycles that ⁽⁰²⁾**took place** during the Pleistocene Epoch (10,000-2,000,000 years ago). During these frigid periods, glaciers up to 3,900m thick covered 30% of Earth's surface. These were most prevalent in the higher-latitude regions of both hemispheres, which ⁽⁰³⁾**were covered by** glaciers as far south as Germany in the Northern Hemisphere and as far north as the Andes in the Southern Hemisphere. However, despite 100+ years of ⁽⁰⁴⁾**research into** these periods, researchers ⁽⁰⁵⁾**are unable to explain** their cause.

2   Over the years, diverse factors, such as continental location, oceanic circulation and solar energy fluctuation, have been cited as possible causes of these glaciations. One of the most interesting was ⁽⁰⁶⁾**put forth** by Scottish scientist James Croll who ⁽⁰⁷⁾**used** the previously known fact that cyclic ⁽⁰⁸⁾**changes in** Earth's orbit affect how solar radiation impacts Earth's surface **to deduce** that they could also affect the global climate. Using this theory, Yugoslavian mathematician Milutin Milankovitch developed an equation that showed how these cyclic changes in Earth's orbit, now known as Milankovitch cycles, could cause climatic changes and ⁽⁰⁹⁾**lead to** continental glaciations.

3   Milankovitch ⁽¹⁰⁾**based** his equation on three cyclic changes in Earth's position ⁽¹¹⁾**relative to** the Sun that he thought could collectively ⁽¹²⁾**have an effect on** the solar radiation that is incident on Earth's surface: eccentricity, obliquity, and precession. The first of these, eccentricity, is the elliptical variation in the Earth's orbit that sometimes ⁽¹³⁾**brings** it **closer to** the Sun and slightly changes every revolution in a 96,000-year cycle. The second of these, obliquity, ⁽¹⁴⁾**is concerned with** the annual changes in the tilt of Earth's axis that causes seasonal variation. As this tilt changes, in a 41,000-year cycle, the temperature difference between winter and summer becomes extreme and more mild as the tilt is respectively higher or lower. The final of the Milankovitch cycles, precession, is the circular wobble that Earth performs on its axis every 12,700 years, in a movement that resembles the wobble of a slowly moving top. Although these three cycles do not affect the amount of solar radiation that reaches the Earth, they greatly affect its distribution. Milankovitch's equation showed that every 40,000 years these three cycles would perfectly synchronize ⁽¹⁵⁾**in a way that** would greatly reduce the difference between winter and summer temperatures and ⁽¹⁶⁾**prevent** the winter ice **from** melting during the summer, thereby ⁽¹⁷⁾**allowing** it **to build up**, and causing an overall glacial growth.

4   Despite developing this theory in the 1920s, Milankovitch was limited in his ⁽¹⁸⁾**ability to test** it extensively, since the timeline of the Pleistocene Epoch temperature changes ⁽¹⁹⁾**necessary for** testing it was not developed until the 1970s. After the development of this new chronology, a ⁽²⁰⁾**correlation between** Milankovitch cycles **and** the major climatic changes of the last 65 million years became clearer. Further, core samples ⁽²¹⁾**taken from** the deep-sea floor proved that Milankovitch's equation was incredibly ⁽²²⁾**accurate in** predicting climate changes over the last few hundred thousand years, including the end of the Pleistocene Epoch.

5   Unfortunately, this accuracy and correlation does not fully explain the cause of glaciation throughout history. If Milankovitch's explanation was accurate, it would ⁽²³⁾**require** glaciations **to have occurred** regularly throughout Earth's history, yet they ⁽²⁴⁾**appear to have occurred** only rarely. This has ⁽²⁵⁾**led** scientists **to determine** that there must be another factor that ⁽²⁶⁾**works with** the Milankovitch cycles to cause glaciations. When this mystery factor has sufficiently lowered the average temperature, the cyclic variations of solar radiation caused by the Milankovitch Cycles can ⁽²⁷⁾**throw Earth into and out of** glacial periods ⁽²⁸⁾**with the regularity** predicted by the Milankovitch equation.

6   ⁽²⁹⁾**In the quest to discover** this mystery-cooling factor, ⁽³⁰⁾**a number of** possibilities have been suggested. One of these is that changes in the Sun's luminosity have allowed fluctuations in the solar energy that reaches Earth. However, this is highly unlikely, since ⁽³¹⁾**it is now believed that** the Sun has steadily become stronger over time. Another possible cause of lower temperatures was volcanic dust in the atmosphere ⁽³²⁾**shielding** Earth **from** solar radiation and ⁽³³⁾**causing** temperatures **to drop**. This is also rather unlikely, since the beginning of the last glaciation does not ⁽³⁴⁾**correspond with** known major eruptions. A more recent theory states that ⁽³⁵⁾**differences in** atmospheric carbon dioxide (CO_2) have caused temperature fluctuations on Earth. Since CO_2 traps radiation in the atmosphere, periods of decreased atmospheric CO_2 ⁽³⁶⁾**results in** lower temperatures on Earth's surface, allowing solar radiation to escape. This ⁽³⁷⁾**is especially attractive to** researchers, because studies of the Greenland ice cap show that ⁽³⁸⁾**the number of** CO_2 bubbles found in the different strata changes ⁽³⁹⁾**depending on** when the ice formed. Samples from periods ⁽⁴⁰⁾**known to be** warmer show higher CO_2 levels, while colder periods have significantly less, thereby confirming the correlation between CO_2 levels and Earth's temperature.

---

1. 식물의 성장에서 빛의 중요성
2. 개화가능성을 높이기 위한 식물의 적응
3. 낮의 길이에 대한 반응에 따른 식물의 3가지 분류
4. 식물들이 낮 시간과 밤 시간을 구별하는 방법
5. 어두움의 길이에 따른 다른 반응
6. 신호를 통한 개화

5 토플 공부 방법 및 순서

3. 묶기

근본적으로 크게 토플 성적을 올리거나, 실력을 올릴 때, 가장 필요한 것은, 누가 뭐래도 해석입니다.
하지만, 공부를 하고 싶은 맘은 누구나 있겠지만,
'어떻게' 를 궁금해 할 때,
잘하는 사람들은 '한번에 해석만 잘 하면 돼' 라고 말하는 것을
구분동작으로 나눌 필요가 있습니다.
이때, 당연히 필요한 것은 재료가 되는, 단어, 구문이고,
이 재료를 잘 엮어서 좋은 결과물을 만들어 내는 과정이 묶기라고 생각하시면 됩니다.
그런데, 대부분 단어 구문 암기 하는 것도 귀찮아 할 뿐만 아니라,
이렇게 암기해둔 내용조차 종종, 단어 나열식으로 대충 감으로만 처리하는 경우를 많이 봅니다.
절대 하면 안되는 행동입니다.
그렇다면, 이렇게 대충 감/으로 누구는 해내고 누구는 못해낸다면, 그 부분을 미분할 필요가 있습니다.
대부분 타 학원에서는 / (슬래시) 만으로 대충 끊어 읽게 만드는 경우가 많은데,
어셔에서는 이것을 구체적으로 나눠놓았습니다.

---

01. Comets, small celestial bodies (with long luminous tails and orbits) [that occasionally bring them (in close contact) (with Earth)], are some (of the most fascinating objects) (in our solar system). Today, only about 4,900 (of these bodies) composed (of frozen gases and volatile compounds) (along with rocky metallic elements) have been discovered, but the distance (of their orbits) makes it likely [that many more exist]. Comets are generally categorized (into two orbit length dependent categories): long-period and short-period comets. Short-period comets, (such as Halley's Comet) [which has been documented appearing every 76 years (since 240 B.C.E.,)] make regular appearances (due to their relatively short orbits) (of less than 200 years) and are more well-known. Long-period comets, however, are rarely observed [because they take hundreds or thousands (of years) (to complete) one trip (around the sun)].

02. The main difference (between the two categories) seems (to arrive) (from their origins). Short-period comets begin (in the Kuiper belt) (of non-planetary matter). This field (of matter), just (past Neptune's orbit), roughly 50 50 astronomical units (1 AU=the distance between Earth and the sun) (from the sun), travels (around the sun) (on nearly the same plane) (as the planets). [If two (of these comets) strike one another], or [if one is affected (by the gravitation) (of a nearby planet)], the orbit may be thrown off (in such a way) [that a comet enters the inner solar system] [where it is affected (by solar forces) and visible (from Earth)].

1) 주어,동사
2) 절
3) 전치사구
4) 분사
5) to 부정사

★묶기 방법

1. 주어 동사 표시 - 밑줄로
  ☞ 특히 동사구는 전체 밑줄 (가운데 부사가 껴도 전체 밑줄!!!)
   예 would have done
  ☞ 동사 수동은 "화살표"를 "동사 위에" 뒤집어서 표시해 둘 것!!!
   예 was not normally cut away

2. [종속접속사 + 주어 + 동사] 절처리 예 [that are difficult (to discern)]

3. (p+n) 전치사구 예 (in close contact)

4. Ing/ed 분사 (항상 "박스로" 처리해 둘 것!) ※ 박스처리는 ing , ed , 형용사 만!
  ☞ 현재분사는 그냥 두고, 과거분사는 "화살표"를 "과거분사 위에" 뒤집어서 표시해 둘 것!
  ☞ 후치수식은 모두 후치수식 표시를 해둬야 합니다. 뒤에서 수식에 약한 한국 학생들에게는 필수입니다.
   ing 예 •[which has been documented appearing every 76 years.
   ed 예 •(by the matter) ejected (from the Swift-Tuttle comet)
   형용사 예 •undergo the changes typical (of all comets)

5. to 부정사는 (to do)만 묶을 것 = (전치사 + 동명사까지만)
  예 (to study) math = (by studying) math
   ☞ 만약 학생이 (전치사 + 동명사 + 명사)까지 묶으면 ➔ 이건, 동명사를 형용사로 해석한 경우이므로 잘못 해석됨.

6. 완초 1반은 n 기능까지 표시할 것

7. 채점 뒤, ❶ - 틀린 곳에 번호 적고, 고치고(형광쎈으로)
  ❷ - 오른쪽 페이지에 이유 적을 것
  ❸ - ❷에 적힌 이유 중, 공통되는 것을 잡아낸 뒤
  ❹ - 다음 시험지에서 공통된 것이 또 잡히면, 긴장할 것

★만약, 묶기가 이해되지 않으면 문법기초가 약해서 입니다.
 어서 문법(Grammar)을 통해 꼭 기초를 다져 주시기 바랍니다.

5. 토플 공부 방법 및 순서

4. 10번 읽기

다시 한번, 반드시 **암기 후 읽어야 합니다**. 읽다 보면 암기 되겠지... 란 생각은 통하지 않습니다.
앞선 백지 시험을 다 마쳤을 경우에서 멈추면, 외운 것을 적용할 수 있다고 장담할 수 있는 상황은 아닙니다.
결국, 자연스레 독해를 해둬야 문제가 해결될 수 있는데, 문제는 늘 같은 내용이 같은 문장 형태로 나오지 않는다는 사실입니다.
그렇다고, 막연히 그냥 어떻게 되겠지... 라는 생각으로 손을 놓으면 안되고, 꼭 수업 나간 지문을 반복적으로 읽으시기 바랍니다.
이때, 주의할 것은 그냥 소리 내서 읽으라는 말이 아닙니다.
꼭 내용을 이해하면서 해석하고, 문단문단마다 꼭 내용을 정리하면서 읽으셔야 합니다.
그냥 소리 내서 읽기만 하거나, 문장 해석만을 할 경우에는 많이 읽었더라도 이해 실력을 높이는 데는 도움이 되지 않습니다.
토플이 원하는 것은 READING이 아닌, COMPREHENSION입니다.!!!

▌10번 읽기 방법 ▌

4.1 어려운 문장만 확실해 질때 까지 열번 읽어서 랜덤하게 물어도 확실하게 답변할 수 있게 만들어야 합니다. 그리고 나머지 문장들을 4.2에 따라 진행합니다.

4.2 처음 읽을 때는 상당히 긴 시간이 걸릴 것입니다. 보통 iBT 지문 750자 내외를 기준으로 30분에서 한 시간 이상이 걸리기도 합니다. (단어를 다 외우고 구문을 다 외웠음에도) 하지만, 이건 본인의 실력이 나쁜 게 아닌 원래 정상적인 일입니다. 그리고 두 번째 읽을 때도 크게 차이가 나지는 않을 것입니다. 하지만, 세 번째 네 번째로 가면 갈수록 속도도 이해도도 높아지는 것을 느낄 수 있을 것입니다.

읽으면서 수시로 스스로에게 물어보시기 바랍니다. '이 지문을 2주 뒤 갑자기 읽어도 자신 있게 읽을 수 있을까?' 자신 있을 경우에만, 다음 공부로 넘어가시기 바랍니다.
바를 정(正)자를 지문 상단에 체크하면서 읽으시고, 소요되는 시간도 같이 체크해보시기 바랍니다.

항상 긴장하고 점검하며 공부해야 집중력도 유지됩니다. 보통 이렇게 되는 데는 최소 5번은 읽어야 자신감이 생길 것이고, 보수적으로 내용에 따라 열 번을 각오하고 읽으시는 것을 권해드립니다.

스스로 준비가 충분히 되어 있는지를 테스트 할 때는, 공부가 끝난 다음 날 문제지의 제일 뒤에 있는 지문만을 **모아놓은 '열번읽기'를 펴고 읽었을 때,** 막힘없이 잘 이해가 될 만큼 읽히면 일차통과입니다.

이후, 주말마다 메모없는 책 뒤 부분만을 펴고 확인을 반복하시기 바랍니다. 확실히 굳히는 방법이기도 하며, 새로운 내용들이 보이기도 할 것입니다.

5. Api 프로그램 (어셔 재학생 대상)

묶기, 단어, 구문 시험을 Api 프로그램을 사용하여 매일 정기적으로 치르게 되면,
열흘 내에 각 항목의 반복 패턴을 파악할 수 있습니다.
그대로 열흘 내외를 더하면, 상당한 정도의 적용도를 기대할 수 있습니다.
잘 이용해서 좋은 결과 바랍니다.

구문단어

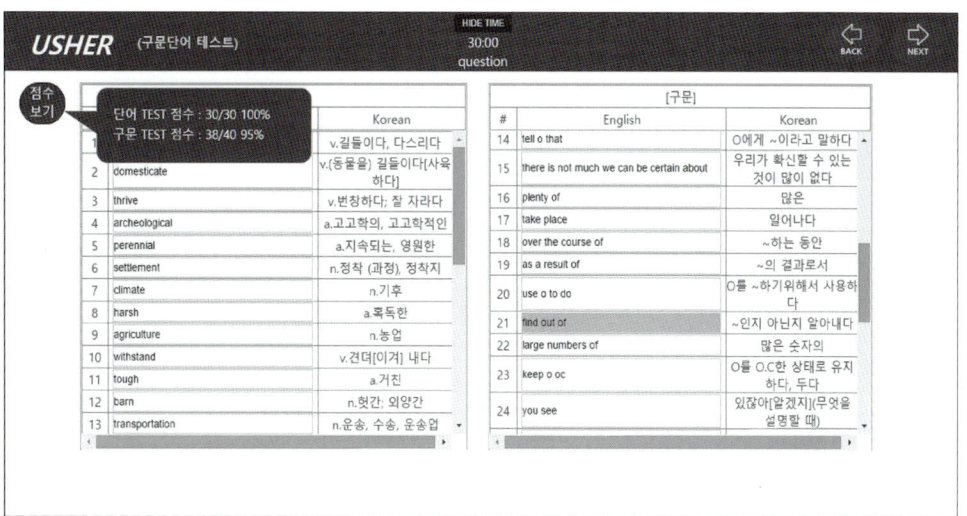

묶기

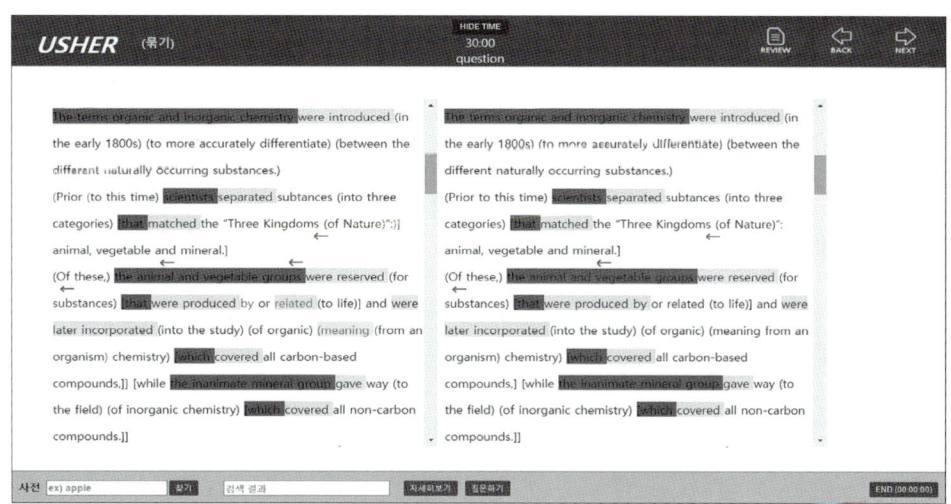

iBT TOEFL(iBT 토플) 소개

USHER iBT TOEFL INTERMEDIATE TEST READING(어셔 iBT 토플 인터미디어트 테스트 리딩)

iBT TOEFL (iBT 토플)이란?

TOEFL(Test of English as a Foreign Language)이란 주로 영어권 국가의 대학교에 진학하는 외국인 학생의 영어실력을 평가하기 위하여 만들어진 시험입니다. 현재 TOEFL (토플)은 iBT(internet-Based Test) TOEFL이라 불리며, PBT(Paper- Based Test) 와 CBT(Computer-Based Test)를 거쳐 채택된 3세대 시험방식입니다. 읽기, 듣기, 말하기, 쓰기의 다양한 분야의 영어실력을 보기 때문에 현재 세계적으로 가장 공신력 있는 영어시험으로 자리 잡았습니다.

iBT TOEFL (iBT 토플) 구성

시험순서	지문 개수	시간	세부사항	*더미 (Dummy)	만점
Reading (상대평가)	Passage 3개 (700단어 X 3개)	60~100분	Passage 당 18분 10문제	Passage 1개 더 출제 가능	30점
Listening (상대평가)	Conversation 2개	60~90분	Conversation 당 3분 5문제	Set 1개 (1Conversation + 2 Lecture) 더 출제 가능	30점
	Lecture 3개		Lecture 당 5분 6문제		
Speaking (절대평가)	Independent 1개 Intergrated 3개	15분 내외	-	없음	30점
Writing (절대평가)	Intergrated 1개 Independent 1개	55분 (25 + 30분)	-	없음	30점
총 약 4시간					총점 120점

*더미 (Dummy)란 원래 '꼭두각시, 연습용 인형'이란 뜻으로, TOEFL (토플)에서는 성적에 포함되지 않는 문제들을 일컫습니다. 원래의 출제 의도는 난이도 조절이었지만, iBT TOEFL (iBT 토플)에 와서 그 의미가 변하였으며, 외형상 실제 문제와 구분할 방법은 없습니다. (더 자세한 내용은 http://usherin.usher.co.kr 참조)

꼭 알아두세요!

접수	시험일정이 나오면 접수 가능 * Late fee(응시 7일 전 시험 신청 시) 40$추가
비용	시험 - 미화 $ 210 (원화결제 가능) 취소한 성적 복원 - 미화 $ 20 성적 전송 - 미화 $ 20 (1개 기관당) 일자 변경 - 미화 $ 60 재채점 - 미화 $ 80 (1개 section당: 성적 불신시 speaking, writing만 가능)

시험	한 달에 3회~5회 (토요일과 일요일에만 실시: http://ets.org/toefl에서 확인 가능)
시험장소	전국 27개 도시에 있는 Test Center 및 세계 각국의 ETS Test Center (안양, 아산, 부천, 부산, 천안, 청주, 춘천, 대구, 대전, 고성, 고양, 군포, 광주, 경기, 경주, 경산, 화성, 인천, 제주, 전주, 진주, 오산, 포천, 성남, 서울, 울산, 용인 등 27개 도시 - 토플 시험장에 대한 자세한 정보는 http://usherin.usher.co.kr 참조)
준비물	토플 web site에 등록되어 있는 신분증 지참
성적 발표일	토플 시험으로부터 최소 8일 ~ 최대 14일
성적 유효기간	2년
토플 시험 등록 취소	시험 등록 후 7일 까지 : 전액환불 시험 등록 후 8일 이후 : 금액의 50% 환불 시험보기 4일전 : 금액의 50% 환불 콜센터에 전화하거나 홈페이지에서 취소 (e-mail로는 불가능)

시험장에서!

1. 시험절차   시험장에 도착하면 여권 확인 후, 성적표에 나올 사진을 찍고 감독관의 안내에 따라 순서대로 시험을 시작한다.

2. 필기도구   연필과 종이는 감독관이 나누어주므로 따로 필요가 없고, 부족하면 얼마든지 더 달라고 할 수 있다. 다만, Section 시작 전에 종이에 필기할 경우, 부정행위로 간주될 수 있으므로 각별히 주의하자.

3. 헤드폰 음량   시험 도중 언제든지 조절할 수 있다.

4. 마이크 음량   시험 시작 직후와 Speaking Section 직전에 조절할 수 있다.

5. 휴식시간   Listening Section과 Speaking Section 사이에 10분의 휴식시간이 주어지고, 화장실에 가거나, 간식을 먹을 수 있다.
이 시간을 잘 활용해 Speaking에 대비하자!

6. 주의사항   각 응시자마다 시험 진행 시간이 다르기 때문에, 내가 Listening이나 Writing Section을 풀고 있을 때, 다른 사람의 목소리가 방해가 되는 경우가 많으니 염두해 두자.

iBT TOEFL READING 소개

USHER iBT TOEFL INTERMEDIATE TEST READING(어셔 iBT 토플 인터미디어트 테스트 리딩)

iBT READING 영역에서는 유학을 나갔을 때, 학생들이 학교생활, 즉, 수업을 따라가는데 필요한 가장 기초적인 수준의 읽기 능력여부를 파악하는데 목적이 있습니다. 그러므로, 다양한 분야의 지문이 있지만, 꼭 배경 지식을 요구하지는 않으므로 시작부터 너무 겁먹을 필요는 없습니다. 하지만, 20분 이내에 1지문을 푸는 것을 대다수의 시험보는 학생들은 힘들어 하므로, 정확하고 빠른 독해 능력은 문제 푸는데 있어 핵심적인 부분이다. 여기서 중요한 것은 정확이 먼저이고 빠름은 다음순서라는 사실은 꼭 기억해야 합니다.

iBT READING 구성

총 지문 개수는 3개에서 4개의 지문으로 나뉘며, 시험 시작 후 **연속되어 지문이 나오므로**, 학생들의 집중력이 1시간 이상 길어야 함을 미리 알고 준비하여야 합니다. **(2019년 8월에 시험 방식 바뀜)**

iBT READING 특징

- **NOTE TAKING**이 허용된다
- 지문에 제목이 주어진다.
- 전문용어 등은 뜻을 알려주는 **GLOSSARY**기능이 있다.

> **GLOSSARY**
> blood poisoning caused by pathogenic microorganisms and their toxic products in the bloodstream.

iBT READING 문제 유형 분석

난이도	문제 유형	문제 유형 설명	배점	지문당 문항 수
쉬움 (기본점수 약 60% 차지함)	VOCABULARY	유의어 찾기	1점	1~2개
	FACT & NEGATIVE FACT	지문 내용과 맞거나, 틀린 내용 찾기	1점	2~4개
어려움 (변별력 목적 약 40% 차지함)	REFERENCE	지시어가 가리키는 대상 찾기	1점	0~1개
	SENTENCE SIMPLICATION	문장 PARAPHRASE	1점	1개
	INSERTION	논리에 맞게 문장 끼워 넣기	1점	1개
	RHETORICAL PURPOSE	작가가 글속의 내용을 넣은 이유 찾기	1점	1~2개
	INFERENCE	제공된 정보로 내용 추론하기	1점	1~2개
	SUMMARY	문단 정리	2점	둘 중 선택적으로 하나만 남. 하지만, 주로 SUMMARY가 많이 나옴
	CATEGORY CHART	문단 속 정보를 알맞게 정렬하기	2~3점	

- 현재 풀고 있는 문제의 위치와, 시간확인 및 뒤로 돌아갈 수 있는 기능들이 우측 상단에 있다. (아래 그림 참조)

iBT READING 화면 구성

화면 상단 우측에 시험 진행 사항을 알려주는 부분이 있다. Question 14 of 30

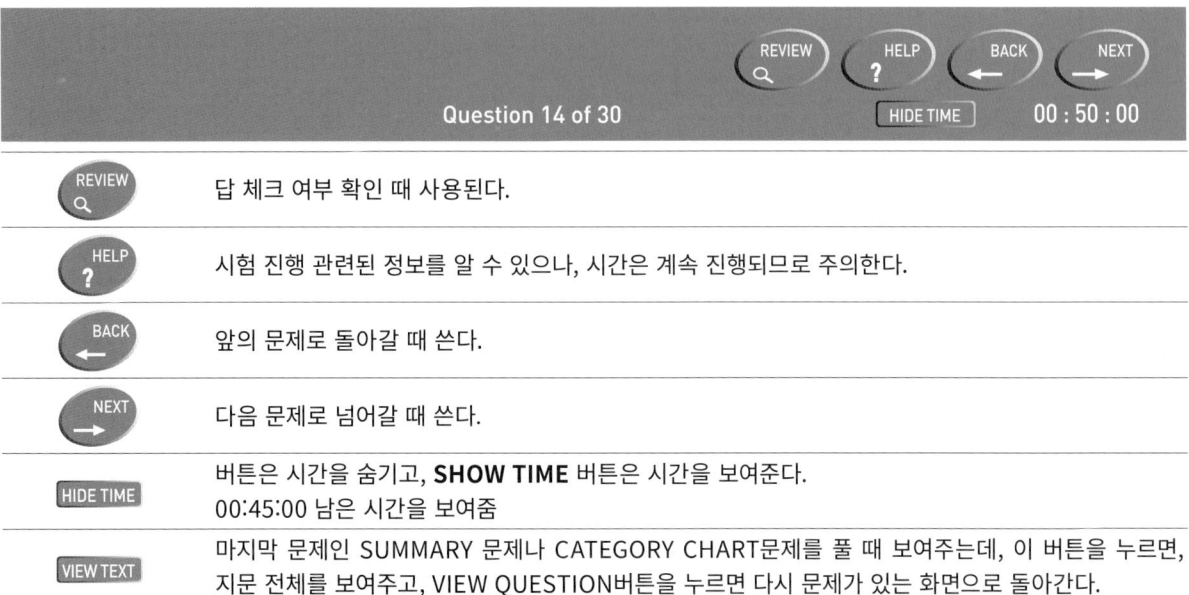

REVIEW	답 체크 여부 확인 때 사용된다.
HELP	시험 진행 관련된 정보를 알 수 있으나, 시간은 계속 진행되므로 주의한다.
BACK	앞의 문제로 돌아갈 때 쓴다.
NEXT	다음 문제로 넘어갈 때 쓴다.
HIDE TIME	버튼은 시간을 숨기고, **SHOW TIME** 버튼은 시간을 보여준다. 00:45:00 남은 시간을 보여줌
VIEW TEXT	마지막 문제인 SUMMARY 문제나 CATEGORY CHART문제를 풀 때 보여주는데, 이 버튼을 누르면, 지문 전체를 보여주고, VIEW QUESTION버튼을 누르면 다시 문제가 있는 화면으로 돌아간다.

READING DIRECTION 화면

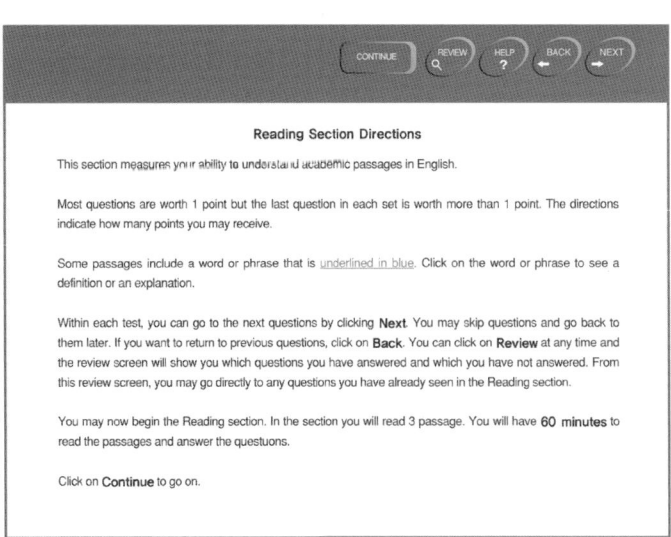

리딩 시험 진행방식을 설명해준다.

7 iBT TOEFL READING 소개

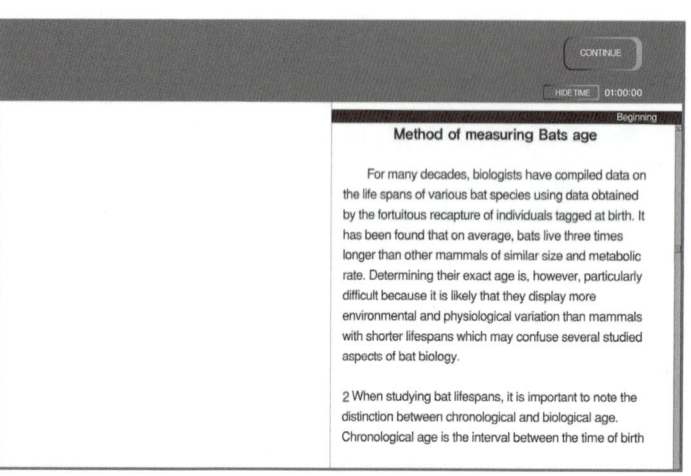

처음엔 문제없이 지문만 보여주는 화면이 있는데, 이때 스크롤을 내려 지문 전체를 봐야만 CONTINUE 버튼을 눌러 본 문제로 넘어갈 수 있다.

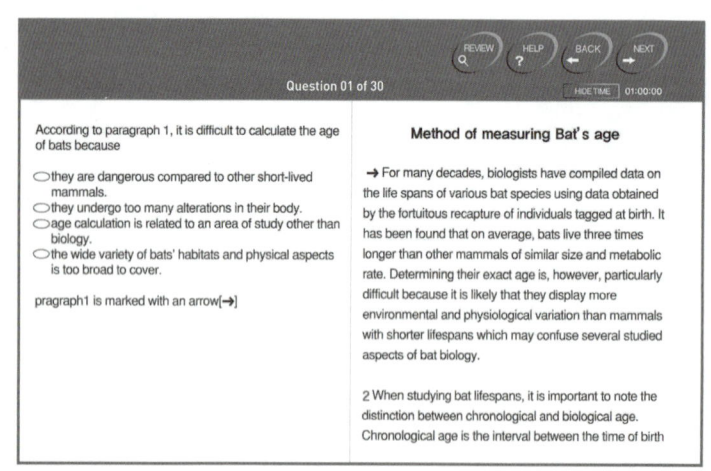

문제로 넘어가면, 문제는 왼쪽에, 지문은 오른쪽에 한 문제씩 보여지며, 우측 상단의 NEXT 버튼을 누르면 다음 문제로 넘어간다. 가끔 본문 속의 파란색 밑줄은 용어해설을 보여줄 때 쓰이며, 누르면 좌측 화면 하단에 나타난다.

SUMMARY 문제 화면

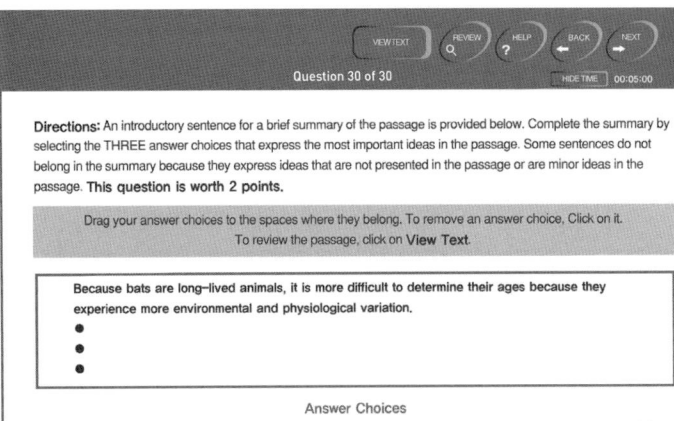

SUMMARY 문제가 나올 때는 화면 속엔 지문없이 문제만 전체 화면으로 보인다. 이때 상단의 VIEW TEXT버튼을 누르면 지문만 다시 보여주며, 다시 문제를 보고 싶을 땐, VIEW QUESTION버튼을 누르면 다시 돌아갈 수 있다. 답을 선택하는 방법은 초이스에 있는 보기를 박스 안에 드래그해서 놓으면 되고, 답을 바꿀 때는 보기를 한번 더 클릭하면 정답자리에서 없어진다.

CATEGORY 문제 화면

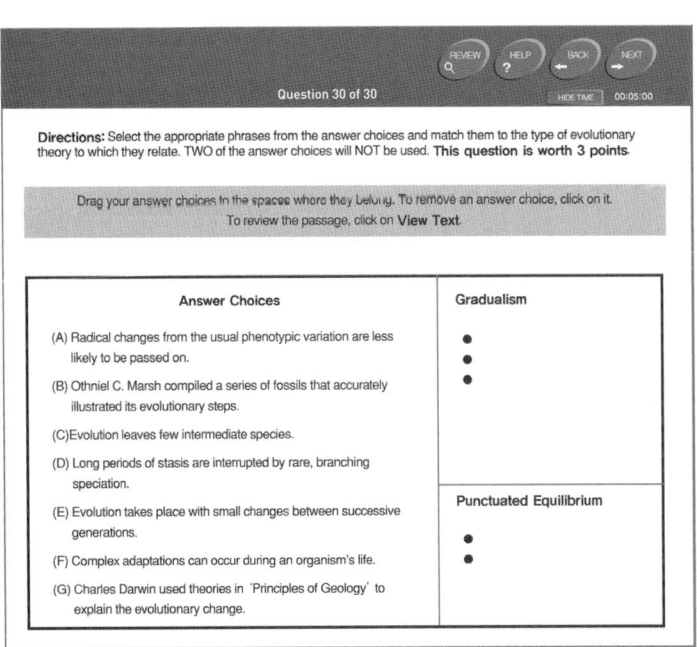

SUMMARY 문제와 같은 화면과 같은 답 선택 방법이 사용된다.

READING STRATEGIES

USHER iBT TOEFL INTERMEDIATE TEST READING(어셔 iBT 토플 인터미디어트 테스트 리딩)

문제 유형을 확인하기 전에 우선, test 1을 풀어보고, 스스로에 대한 평가와 더불어 문제 유형 파악을 해주시기 바랍니다. 먼저 유형을 파악 해보는 것보다는, 일단, 풀어본 뒤 알아가는 것이 훨씬 빠르게 이해할 수 있기에, 각 문제 유형별 전략 뒤에는 test 1을 기준으로 확인 가능한 번호를 적어두었습니다.

쉬운 문제 유형	출제 비율
1. VOCABULARY 2. FACT & NEGATIVE FACT 3. REFERENCE	60%
어려운 문제 유형	출제 비율
4. SENTENCE SIMPLIFICATION 5. INSERTION 6. RHETORICAL PURPOSE 7. INFERENCE 8. SUMMARY 9. CATEGORY CHART	40%

시험이 임박한 학생들을 위한 독해 전략

* 서문에서 이미 학생들의 시간에 대한 수준별 대응책을 적어 놓았습니다. 하지만, 여기선, 대부분의 학생들이 시간이 모자라는 경우가 많으므로 이런 경우에 대해 우선적으로 다루었습니다.

1. 지문은 제목과 각 문단 첫 줄만 읽고, 곧바로 CONTINUE버튼을 눌러 문제로 넘어갑니다.
시간이 없는 경우가 많은데 지문을 다 읽고 넘어가는 경우 시간이 모자라 마지막 문제는 찍지도 못하고 끝나는 경우도 있기 때문에 미리 주의해야 합니다.

2. 문제 풀이하며 본문을 읽습니다. (시간이 없을 경우, 효과가 큼)
토플 문제 번호순서대로, 본문의 답 근거도 순서를 따릅니다. 게다가 중간중간 단어문제나 REFERENCE문제 등이 표시된 경우에는 그 문제보다 앞 문제라면 표시된 곳 앞에서, 뒷 문제라면 표시된 곳 뒤에서 답 근거를 찾으면 됩니다. (뒷 페이지 참조)

3. SKIMMING → SCANNING
대략 훑었어도, 답 근거가 어디쯤이라는 감이 오면, 그때부터는 집중해서 꼼꼼히 내용을 살펴야 합니다. 대부분 문제는 답은 둘 중에 하나로 좁혀지는데 이때 스캐닝 하지 않아 대충 읽고 답을 잡으면 오답에 낚일 확률이 높습니다. 문제 출제 기관인 ETS는 문제만 50년째 만들고 있는 기관입니다. 문제 푸는 여러분을 낚는 데는 상당한 노하우가 있습니다.

4. 문제를 풀며 수시로 내용을 파악해야 합니다.
마지막 SUMMARY문제는 문단 내용을 파악하지 못하면 풀지 못하게 만들어놨습니다. 그런데 문제는 한 문제 한 문제 푸는 데만 급급한 학생들의 경우에는 문단 정리를 하지 못하고, 마지막 SUMMARY문제를 만나는 경우인데, 이땐 대안이 없습니다. 수시로 내용을 정리하며 지나가야 마지막 문제를 잘 풀 수 있습니다. 그러므로 수시로 내용 파악을 해두어야 합니다.

5. 반드시 ① '문제를 똑바로 읽고' ② 핵심 단어에 '동그라미' 를 쳐서 묻는 내용을 명확히 한 후 ③ '답 근거' 를 찾으시길 바랍니다.

*따라가면서 푼다는 말은....

1. **Fact**

2. **Infer**

3. **Purpose**

4. **Fact**

5. **Vocab**

6. **Sentence simplification**

7. **Negative fact**

8. **Vocab**

9. **Insert**

10. **Summary**

3.

5.

6.

8.

위의 ▢▢▢▢ 에 해당하는 문제들은 모두 힌트를 줄 수 있는 내용들입니다.

8 READING STRATEGIES

1 VOCABULARY - 유의어 찾기 문제

▶ **유형 TEST 1-1 > Question 5** (문제집 - 58page)

▶ **질문 형태**

The word " _____ " in the passage is closest in meaning to

The phrase " _____ " in the passage is closet in meaning to

▶ **오답 패턴 (학생들이 잘 낚이는 경우 모음)**
- 선택지 중 두 개의 단어가 모두 사전의 동의어에 있을 경우 (난이도 상)
- 선택지 중 어떤 단어도 사전의 동의어에 없을 경우 (난이도 상)
- 넣어봤을 때, 말은 되지만, 유의어는 아닌 경우
- 단어랑 스펠링이 비슷한 경우

▶ **핵심 전략**
- 무조건 시험장 들어가기 전에 단어 책 한 권은 끝내고 들어가야 합니다. USHER iBT TOEFL VOCABULARY를 마친 후라면 **80%는 처리가 가능합니다.**

- **단어 문제는 무조건 시간을 벌어주는 문제유형입니다.**
  즉, 완전 쉬워서 딱 보고 답이 나왔기 때문에 시간을 벌어주거나, 완전 어렵게 나와서 고민해야 될 상황에서는 절대 고민하지 않고 그냥 콱 찍고 지나가야 합니다. 단어 문제가 어려울 때는 아무리 봐도 어차피 답을 정확히 잡을 수는 없습니다. 본인을 믿고 빨리 체크하고 다음 문제에서 승부를 거는 것이 더 낫습니다.
  그러므로 어려우나 쉬우나, 무조건 단어 문제에서는 시간을 벌어야 하고, 고민하지 않아야 합니다. 단, 아무리 쉬운 문제라도 꼭 문장에 넣어보고 대입 후 체크하도록 함을 잊어서는 안됩니다.

- 만약 단어 문제가 어렵게 난다면, 둘 중 하나입니다. 동의어가 선택지중에서 두 개가 있거나, 동의어 전혀 없을 때
  이 땐, 문맥을 봐서 가장 알맞은 답을 찾아야 합니다.
  단어의 뉘앙스를 정확히 알고 있어야 알 수 있는 문제이므로 앞서 적은 대로 시간을 많이 들이지 않도록 합니다.

- **꼭 집어 넣어서 재확인을 해야 합니다.**
  아무리 동의어라도 문맥상 여러 개의 뜻 중에서 다른 의미로 사용될 수 있기 때문에 반드시 확인을 해봐야 합니다.

2 FACT & NEGATIVE FACT - 지문의 세부 정보를 맞게 적었거나 틀리게 적은 경우를 찾아내는 문제

▶ **유형** Fact - TEST 1-1 > Question 4 (문제집- 58page)
Negative Fact - TEST 1-1 > Question 2 (문제집 - 57page)

▶ **질문 형태**
- Fact
  According to paragraph #, which of the following is true of (about) _____?
  According to paragraph #, _____?
  According to paragraph #, what / when / where / why / how _____?
- Negative fact
  According to paragraph #, all of the following are true of _____ EXCEPT
  According to paragraph #, all of the following statements about _____ EXCEPT
  According to paragraph #, which of the following is NOT true of _____?

▶ **오답 패턴 (학생들이 잘 낚이는 경우 모음)**
- 해석이 안될 경우 (난이도 상)
- 투 클릭(Two click) 문제 (정답 개수로 난이도 중)
- 단어만 사용하고 지문과 무관한 내용
- 언급 안된 내용이 그럴싸하게 적힌 경우
- "EXCEPT" 문제는 꼭 똑바로 묻는대로 대답할 것 (아닌 것 고르라는 얘기는 오답 세 개는 모두 본문에서 맞단 얘기! → 틀린 것 3개를 먼저 배제시켜서 잡는게 확실합니다)
- 상식으로 접근할 경우
- 반만 맞고 반은 틀린 경우 (특히 틀린 부분이 뒷부분일 경우, 학생들은 앞만 보고 답으로 선택하는 경우 주의할 것)
- 본문과 반대 내용을 적어둘 때 (은근히 혼동됨)

▶ **핵심 전략**
- 문제에서 **핵심 되는 단어**를 본문에서 빨리 찾습니다.
  모든 문제를 풀 때는 질문을 잘 읽어야 합니다. 알면서도 틀리는 경우가 많음은 한국어로 내는 시험이나 토플 시험이나 마찬가지입니다. 그러므로, 질문에서 묻는 내용 중 핵심이 되는 단어를 재빨리 지문에서 찾아야 답 근거를 정확히 찾을 수 있습니다. 평상시 문제 풀고 스터디 할 때 조원들과 답 근거 찾기를 열심히 해둔 학생이라면 절대 어렵게 푸는 문제는 아닙니다.
- 지문에서 찾은 내용을 PARAPHRASE한 것을 찾습니다.
  토플시험에는 이런 말이 있습니다. 듣기시험에선 들은 단어가 많은 선택지를 답으로 찍고, 독해시험에선 본문에서 본 단어가 많은 선택지는 피하십시오. 극단적이긴 하지만, 전혀 틀린 말은 아닙니다. 즉, 본문의 내용을 다른 단어로 바꿔서 정답을 내곤 하기 때문에 정보 전달은 올바로 하되, 표현은 모두 바뀌어져 있는 경우가 대부분입니다. 그리고 NEGATIVE FACT의 경우에는 지문과 내용이 다르거나, 언급되어 있지 않는 보기가 정답입니다.
- **너무 강한 표현은 주의해서 봅니다. (절대 답이 안되는 것은 아닙니다)**
  예) never, only.

8 READING STRATEGIES

3 REFERENCE -지문 속의 음영 표시된 지시어가 가리키는 단어가 무엇인지 찾는 문제

▶ **유형 부록 TEST 1-1 > Question 2** (문제집 - 414page)

▶ **질문 형태**

The word " _____ " in the passage refers to

The phrase " _____ " in the passage refers to

▶ **오답 패턴 (학생들이 잘 낚이는 경우 모음)**
- 정답과 (단수 복수의) 수가 일치되는 주변의 명사를 미끼로 쓸 때
- 앞의 내용 중 혼동될만한 내용을 미리 던져두는 경우

▶ **핵심 전략 (앞문장의 주어나 목적어일 가능성이 크다)**
- 평상시 문장을 읽을 때, 인칭대명사 it, they, their나 지시대명사 this, that, those, 그리고 부정대명사 some, others가 무엇을 가리키는지를 늘 확인하며 표시하는 버릇이 필요합니다.
- 답은 앞 문장 또는 같은 문장 앞일 확률이 높습니다.
  지시어가 가리키는 단어는 문장의 뒤, 그리고 두 문장 이상 떨어진 앞 문장에선 찾지 않습니다.
- 답을 찾았다 싶어도 꼭 다시 바뀐 단어로 **집어넣어 보고** 확인합니다.
  자연스러운지 확인하지 않고 찍으면 틀릴 수 있습니다. 쉬운 문제유형이므로 실수하지 않도록 해야 합니다.

4 SENTENCE SIMPLIFICATION
- 본문에서 음영 표시된 한문장의 내용을 그대로 담고 있는 또 다른 문장을 찾아내는 문제

▶ 유형 TEST 1-1 > Question 3 (문제집 - 57page)

▶ 질문 형태

Which of the sentences below best expresses the essential information in the highlighted sentence in the passage? Incorrect choices change the meaning in important ways or leave out essential information.

▶ 오답 패턴 (학생들이 잘 낚이는 경우 모음)
- 일단, 어려운 문장구조이거나, 내용이 복잡하거나, 단어가 어려운 경우라는 것 자체
- 내용 중 일부를 생략하는 경우 (마이너로서 내용은 맞지만, 답이 안됨) (난이도 상)
- 내용은 그럴싸하나 순서나, 인과 등을 반대로 엮는 경우 (난이도 상)
- 논리적으로 비약하는 경우
- 상식으로 내용을 엮은 경우
- 일부는 맞고 일부는 틀린 경우

▶ 핵심 전략
- 평상시 문법부분이 강해야 합니다.
  토플문제의 출제포인트는 뭐든 중간에 막히는 문장입니다. 쉽게 잘 해석되는 부분에서는 문제 출제를 하지 않습니다. 특히나 Sentence Simplification 스타일의 문제는 삭성하고 어려운 문장을 문제로 만든 것입니다. 그러므로, 평상시 대충 내용만 파악하는 독해 습관을 가진 학생들에겐 난감할 수 있는 유형입니다.

- 내용을 잘게 자릅니다. → 꼭 수렴시킵니다.
  문장 속에서 다루고 있는 내용들을 잘게 자른 후, 그 내용들을 어떻게든 수렴시켜야 답이 됩니다. 문제 내용과 다르게 적는 오답 스타일은 쉽게 낸 것입니다. 이런 것은 당연히 오답처리 할 수 있어야 하고, 이보다 더 주의 할 것은 아무리 맞는 내용을 적었다 하더라도 생략된 것은 답이 아닙니다. 그러므로 꼭 잘게 자른 후, 그 내용들을다 포함하였는지 꼼꼼히 따져봐야 합니다.

8 READING STRATEGIES

5 INSERTION – 지문에서 빠진 문장을 알맞은 위치에 넣는 유형

▶ 유형 TEST 1-1 > Question 9 (문제집 - 60page)

▶ 질문 형태

Look at the four squares [■] that indicate where the following sentence could be added to the passage.
삽입문장
Where would the sentence best fit? Click on a square [■] to add the sentence to the passage.
(문제가 뜨면 지문에 4개의 ■가 뜨고 그 중에 하나를 찍으면 문장이 삽입이 됩니다)

▶ 오답 패턴 (학생들이 잘 낚이는 경우 모음)

- 덩어리에서 작은 내용으로 넘어가는 경우 (난이도 상)
- 답이 잘 보이지 않을 때는 끼워넣기 뒤의 문장에서 관련성 있는 단어가 있는지 찾아볼 것. (예 - test 4-13번)
- 중복되는 단어, 지시어 또는 연결어 없이 내용으로만 연결되는 문장 (난이도 상)
- 연결어로 연결되는 경우 (예 - however, moreover, thus) (이어지는 내용은 틀리지만 연결어 보고 단순 선택)
- 지시어나 중복되는 단어로 연결되는 경우 (예 - this, that, 중복단어)
- for example이 끼워넣을 문장에 나오면 앞에 내용보다 뒤에 내용이 훨씬 더 구체적입니다.

▶ 핵심 전략

하
① • 일단 제시된 **끼워 넣을 문장을 읽습니다**.
② • 끼워 넣을 문장 중 IT, THIS, THAT 등 지시어가 나오면 쉬운 문제입니다.
  이런 문제는 지시어가 가리키는 단어를 앞 문장에서 찾을 수 있기만 하면 됩니다. 그러므로 쉽게 풀 수 있는 유형입니다.
  • in fact, indeed가 나오면 끼워넣기 문장은 앞의 문장의 반복입니다. 즉, 같은 내용을 포함한 (약간은 더 클 수 도 있는) 내용이 끼워넣을 문장앞에 와야 합니다.
③ • 끼워 넣을 문장 중, HOWEVER, MOREOVER, ALSO, THEREFORE 등 연결단어가 나오면 쉬운 문제입니다. **연결 어** 역시, 내용을 매끄럽게 이어주기 위해 도움을 주는 단어이므로 이런 단어가 있을 땐 앞뒤 문장의 논리가 매끄러운 곳만 찾아내면 되기에 쉬운 문제입니다.

상
④ • 영어마인드로서 항상 **덩어리**를 먼저 얘기하고, 구체적인 예를 드는 스타일의 문제라면 어려운 문제입니다.
  원어민들은 항상 결론을 던지고 예를 드는 경우가 많습니다.
  하지만, 한글은 예를 들고 결론을 얘기해도 문제되지 않습니다. 예를 들면,
  I) 한국 학생들은 공부를 열심히 한다는 점을 알 수 있습니다.
     지하철에서도, 버스에서도, 도서관에서도, 복도에서도 늘 공부하는 학생들을 많이 만났기 때문입니다.
  II) 지하철에서도, 버스에서도, 도서관에서도, 복도에서도 늘 공부하는 한국 학생들을 많이 만났습니다.
     그렇기 때문에, 한국 학생들은 공부를 열심히 한다는 점을 알 수 있습니다. 답은 I)으로 해야 합니다. 이유는 한국어 처럼, 두괄식, 미괄식, 병렬식, 수미 상관 등의 다양한 글 전개 방법을 취하는 것과 달리, **영어에서는 항상 결론을 먼저 던져놓는 두괄식 형태**의 글 전개가 많기 때문입니다. 한국 학생들에게, 위 두 가지에서 무엇이 맞냐고 묻는다면, 답하지 못하는 경우가 많습니다. 해석해 주고 풀라고 해도 헤매는 유일한 문제 스타일이 될 수 있는 유형이므로 꼭 전제를 먼저 인식해야 합니다.

"덩어리 → 구체적 내용"

극상
⑤ • 답을 체크하기 전에 꼭 문장을 **넣어보고** 확인합니다. 특히 끼어넣은 뒤, 뒤에 나오는 **지시어** it이나 this들을 설명 할 수 있어야 합니다.

6. RHETORICAL PURPOSE - 글쓴이가 글 속의 내용을 넣은 이유 찾기

▶ 유형 TEST 1-1 > Question 8 (문제집 - 59page)

▶ 질문 형태

The phrase "_____" in the passage refers to the explanation why
In paragraph #, what is the author's main purpose in the discussion of _____?
Why does the author mention
In paragraph #, why does the author mention _____ ?
Why does the author include a description of _____ ?

▶ 오답 패턴 (학생들이 잘 낚이는 경우 모음)

- 문단 (paragraph) 전체가 큰 (passage) 전체에서 하는 기능을 물을 때 (난이도 상)
  (문단 정리가 있어야 함 = 서머리 문제)
- 가끔 어려운 문장을 섞은 부분에서 내는 경우 (난이도 상)
- 사실은 맞지만, 묻는 말에 대한 답이 아닌 경우 - 예) 결과를 묻는 질문에 과정은 오답 (난이도 상)
- 예의 특징으로서는 맞으나, 언급 이유는 아닌 경우 (난이도 상)
- 단어만 나열하고 딴소리 한 경우
- 상식으로 접근하는 경우
- 언급 없는 경우

▶ 핵심 전략

- **문제를 똑바로 읽습니다.**
  학생들이 가장 잘 하는 건 달을 보라고 가리켰건만, 달은 안보고 손가락만 보는 경우입니다.
  예를 들어, 국가의 기능이 약하면 국민들이 자구책을 찾습니다. 그 예로는 소말리아 해적과 같이 무정부 상태에서는 잔학하게 활동하는 해적무리들을 우리는 신문지상에서 종종 보곤 합니다. 라는 글에서 왜 해적을 언급했느냐에 대해 보기에는,
  A) 무정부 상태에서의 해적들은 잔학하게 활동 할 수도 있다는 점을 인식시키기 위하여
  B) 무정부 상태에서 국가의 기능이 약할 경우 일어날수 있는 예를 들기 위하여
  답은 당연히 B) 입니다. 하지만, A)를 찍는 경우는 해적이라는 단어의 임팩트와, 본문에서 분명히 해적들이 잔학 하게 활동한다는 내용이 있었기 때문입니다. 하지만, 절대 잊어서는 안 될 일이 질문이 묻는 말에 대답하는 것입니다. 왜 해적을 언급 했느냐 이지, 해적들에 대해 맞는 것을 고르라는 것이 아니므로, 주의해야 합니다

- 문제에서 언급한 부분만 읽지 말고 **앞부분(90%가 여기서 나옵니다.) 또는 뒷부분을 꼭 읽습니다.**
  문제에서 언급한 부분만 읽는 것은 앞서 예를든 것처럼, **예의 특징에 현혹되기 쉽기** 때문입니다.
  꼭 앞부분을 읽어서 흐름상 왜 그 얘기를 집어 넣었는지를 생각해봐야 합니다.

- 문제에 제시된 표현의 기능을 생각해봅니다.(**특히 argue와 explain의 차이를 분명히 구분합니다**)
  다음과 같은 말들이 주로 보기에 나옵니다.
  설명하기 위해서 / 예를 들기 위해서 / 비교, 대조하기 위해서 / 강조하기 위해서 / 주장하기 위해서 / 증명하기 위해서… 등

- 보기 내용을 끝까지 읽습니다.
  앞부분은 맞는 것 같지만, **뒤에서** 지문과 틀린 얘기로 **살짝 뒤트는** 경우가 있습니다.
  그러므로 마지막까지 다 읽고 지문과의 일치성을 꼭 파악하여야 합니다.

8 READING STRATEGIES

7 INFERENCE - 지문에서 콕 집어 얘기하지 않았지만, 충분히 추론할 수 있는 내용 찾기

▶ **유형 TEST 1-1 > Question 1** (문제집 - 57page)

▶ **질문 형태**

Which of the following can be inferred from paragraph # about _____ ?
It can be inferred from the discussion in paragraph # that _____
What can be inferred from paragraph # about _____ ?

> ▶ **오답 패턴 (학생들이 잘 낚이는 경우 모음)**
> - 어려운 문장을 잘못 해석한 경우, 잘못 해석한 것이 꼭 선택지에 있음 (난이도 상)
> - 비약 (난이도 상) * infer문제는 원래 본문에 fact문제처럼 직접적인 답 근거는 없지만, 그렇다고 비약해서는 안됨
> - 언급 없는 경우
> - 상식으로 푼 경우
> - 단어만 사용하고 딴소리 한 경우
> - 반대 사실 언급
> - 반은 맞고 반은 틀린 경우

▶ **핵심 전략**

- **문제의 키워드**를 본문에서 찾습니다.
  FACT 문제에서처럼 문제에서 묻는 핵심적인 키워드를 찾아야 한다는 공통점은 있으나, 대체로 FACT 문제보다는 고민하게 만드는 문장에서 문제를 내는 경우가 많아, 많은 학생들이 어려워하는 문제 유형입니다. 기본 실력이 되어야 하므로, 문장을 읽다가 막힌다 싶으면 그곳이 INFERENCE 문제가 출제될 확률이 높은 곳입니다. 근본적으로 이해가 되지 않으면 풀리지 않으므로 기본 실력이 중요시 되는 유형입니다.

- **지문에서 근거**를 꼭 찾을 것
  문장을 근거로 하든, 문단을 근거로 하든, 결국 항상 본문에 근거를 두고 있으므로, 반드시 지문 내용 중 내용을 연결 지어 답을 찾아야 합니다.

- **상식이나 비약으로 문제를 풀지 않습니다.**
  꼭 주의해야 할 점은 상식이나 비약, 또는 혼자 소설을 써가며 문제를 푸는 경우입니다. 다시 한번, 꼭 본문에서 답 근거를 짚어낼 수 있어야 합니다.

8 SUMMARY - 지문 내용 중 문단 정리를 잘 한 것을 선택하는 문제

▶ 유형 TEST 1-1 > Question 10 (문제집 - 60page)

▶ 질문 형태

Directions: An introductory sentence for a brief summary of the passage is provided below. Complete the summary by selecting the THREE answer choices that express the most important ideas in the passage. Some sentences do not belong in the summary because they express ideas that are not presented in thepassage or are minor ideas in the passage. **This question is worth 2 points.**

Drag your answer choices to the spaces where they belong.
To remove an answer choice, click on it. To review the passage, click **View Text**.

Introductory sentence
-
-
-

(A)	(D)
(B)	(E)
(C)	(F)

▶ 오답 패턴 (학생들이 잘 낚이는 경우 모음)
- 너무 디테일한 내용은 맞아도 답이 아님, 단락급의 덩치가 있는 내용정리이어야 함(난이도 상)
- 상식으로 푼 경우
- 반만 맞고 반은 틀린 경우 (앞부분은 맞았다고 답으로 하면 안됨), 끝까지 다 잘 읽어보고 답을 고를 것
- 전혀 다른 말을 단어만 섞어서 하는 경우
- 완전히 틀린 내용

▶ 핵심 전략 (≒ Fact 문제 처럼)
- 오답부터 제낍니다. (정답 3개를 먼저 잡기가 더 어렵습니다)
- 박스 안의 INTRODUCTORY SENTENCE는 참고만 하고, 문단 급 내용을 고릅니다.
  답이라고 체크할 수 있기 위해선, 그 답이라고 생각한 문단이 과연 몇 문단을 아우를 수 있는지 꼭 생각해봐야 합니다. 즉, 정답들은 모두 몇 문단 내용이라고 짚을 수 있어야 합니다.
- 본문 내용과 맞아도 답이 아닐 수 있습니다.
  문단 급의 내용을 다뤄야 하므로, 비록 본문에서 언급한 맞는 내용이라 하더라도, 너무 디테일해서 틀릴 수도 있음을 주의해야 합니다. 즉, 맞아도(?) 맞지 않을 수(!!!) 있음을 주의해야 합니다.

8 READING STRATEGIES

9 CATEGORY CHART - CATEGORY화 시킬 수 있는 내용일 경우, 맞는 내용들을 짝지어 넣기

▶ **질문 형태**

Directions: Complete the table below by selecting three answer choices that are characteristics of _____ and two answer choices that are characteristics of _____ . **This question is worth 3 points.**

Drag your answer choices to the spaces where they belong.
To remove an answer choice, click on it. To review the passage, click **View Text**.

Answer choice	Category 1
(A)	•
(B)	•
(C)	•
(D)	**Category 2**
(E)	•
(F)	•
(G)	•

▶ **오답 패턴 (학생들이 잘 낚이는 경우 모음)**

FACT 문제를 지문 전반에서 짝짓기로 냈다고 생각하면 편합니다. 그러므로 FACT 문제와 오답 패턴도 상당히 유사합니다. 그러므로 성가시게 시간이 상당히 많이 걸립니다. (다행히 서머리 문제가 많이 나오고 이 유형의 문제는 드물게 나옵니다.)

- 해석이 안될 경우 (난이도 상)
- 단어만 사용하고 지문과 무관한 내용
- 언급 안된 내용을 그럴싸하게 적힌 경우
- 상식으로 접근할 경우
- 반만 맞고 반은 틀린 경우 (특히 틀린 부분이 뒷부분일 경우, 학생들은 앞만 보고 답으로 선택하는 경우 주의할 것)
- 본문과 반대 내용을 적어둘 때 (은근히 혼동됨)

▶ **핵심 전략 (≒ 지문 전체 Fact)**

- 우선 대부분의 마지막 문제는 SUMMARY가 나오므로 **이 유형의 문제는 많이 나오지 않습니다.**

- 하지만 만약 나온다면 시간을 많이 잡아먹는 유형입니다.
  그러므로 본문을 읽을 때 왠지 유형화 시킬 수 있는 본문 내용이라면 미리부터 지문에서 확인하기 쉽도록 비슷한 내용이라 생각되는 것들을 노트테이킹 해놓을 필요가 있습니다.

- 내용이 일치하는지를 꼭 재검토합니다.
  기억으로 문제를 풀면 틀리기 쉬운 문제유형입니다. 비록 시간은 많이 잡아 먹지만 FACT 문제처럼 꼼꼼만 시간을 가지고 보면 어려운 문제만은 아닙니다. 하지만, 시간이 없어서 또는 귀찮아서라는 이유로 확인하지 않으면 틀릴 확률이 상당히 높은 문제유형입니다. 주의해야 합니다.

시간 내 못 푸는 것에 대해서 스트레스 받지 마십시오.

- 문제 풀고 푼데까지, 기록 남겨야 합니다.
14개중 8, 9개 풀던 학생이 12개 풀어가는 것도 발전,
서머리 문제 못 풀던 학생이 손대보려 시도하는 것도
발전입니다.

앞서 얘기했지만, 중요한 건, 정확도 입니다.
정확도 올라간 학생은, 지금 당장은 느려도, 계속 돌리면,
금방 시간이 줄어들 수밖에 없습니다.
당장 만들어 주길 원한다면,
K2 수업 마지막 주에 들어오십시오.
그때, 원하는 정확도가 있으면, 무슨 말인지 알 겁니다.
(원하는 정확도가 없으면? 나쁜 버릇과, '난 왜 안될까?'
라는 패배감만 가지게 될겁니다.)

정확한 사람은, 마무리가 쉽습니다.
왜? 정확하니까, 감으로 해도 될 만큼 정확하니까…

감으로 하는 것 자체를 뭐라 하는 게 아닙니다.
감으로, 하고 싶습니까?
대충 읽어도, 다 내용 파악하고 싶습니까?

한글로는 대충 읽어도 다 파악이 되는 이유는,
많이 읽어서 그렇고,
대충 읽어도 파악될 만큼
정확히 읽는게 되니까 가능한 겁니다.
그리고 대충 읽다가,
이해가 안 되는 부분이 있으면,
그걸 감지하고,
다시 천천히 읽어보면 됩니다.

문제는 영어로 읽을 때는, 자기가 잘 읽고 있는지도 모르고
읽는 경우가 많습니다.
한참 가다가, 중간에 멈추고, '그래서 뭐래?' 그러면
대답하질 못합니다.
대충 읽었으니까…

지문을 읽을 때도, 해석을 할때도, 꼼꼼히 해야만 합니다.
내가 잘 따라가고 있는지 의심하면서,
내용을 정리 해가면서.

정독도 못하는 학생이 속독 하겠다고 한다면,
'건너뛰고싶고,
빨리 완성시키고 싶으면,
더욱 더 단계별로 밟고 지나가라.'
가 답입니다.

USHER

문제풀이 전 체크 사항
묶었나?
? 찍었나?
문제 동그라미 했나?
날렸나?

잔소리 둘!

시험볼 때 무조건 묶어야 합니다.

이유 - 집중력 / 명확성
문제 풀기에 시간이 부족하다고 생각하는데,
절대 늦지 않습니다.
오히려, 묶고, 다 풀고도 시간이 남습니다.
묶다가 다 못 푼다고 하는 건, 묶는 과정이 들어가서가 아니라
실력부족인 겁니다.

어서 문법책을 보면,
묶기를 해야 하는 이유를 적어 뒀지만,
여기서는 다른 이유 하나를 더하려 합니다.
이유는 문법을 위해서가 아닌, 독해를 위해서니까…

누차 말하지만,
독해점수 25점 이하까지는 이유불문 무조건 묶어야 합니다.
25이상은?
시키지 않더라도 구조가 안보이는 문장은 묶어야 합니다.

이유는 간단합니다.
문장 보는 건 점수 터질 때까지도, 계속 발목을 잡는 이유가
되기 때문입니다. 나중에 25점을 넘어도, 단어, 구문,
묶기(문장구조파악)는 여전히 문제됩니다.
그런데, 정말 말 안듣는 학생들을 많이 봤습니다.

일찍 끝내고 싶으신가요? 그럼 더 하십시오.
싫은 만큼 더 하십시오.
연습이란 건, 하면 할수록 시간은 짧아지고,
나중엔 눈으로도 할 수 있게 만들어줍니다.

이 상황은,
기어가지도 못하면서,
뛰는 게 부러워서,
걷는걸 생략하고,
뛰려고 노력하는 것과 다를 게 없습니다.

충분히 기어야 합니다.
그러다 보면, 일어설 것이고,
충분히 걸어야지만,
뛰게 됩니다.
되지도 않았으면서 뛰려 말고…
스스로 지나가다, 어떤 문장이든 안 묶고 그저 공부만 하려면
그냥 다른 책을 푸셔도 좋습니다.
도움이 되지 않는다면 절대 시키지 않습니다.
시간 투자를 하는 건, 다 이유가 있어서 입니다.

누구보다 빨리 마치게 해줄 자신 있습니다.
누구보다 정확하게 만들어줄 수 있습니다.
그러려면, 묶으십시오.
이것을 안 하면, 일반 책 푸는 것과 다른 효과를 낼 수
없습니다.

문제 풀이시간에, 감독하며 지나가다 안 묶는 것을 발견하고,
물으면 가장 잘 하는 대답은
"눈으로 푸는 것 연습 하려구요."
"시험장에선 손을 댈 수 없잖아요."
"버릇될 것 같아서요."

눈으로 풀게 만들어 줄려고 시키는 겁니다.
시험장에서 손 안대게 하려고 시키는 거고
버릇 안 들일려고 하는 겁니다.

시험장가서 같은 부분만 계속 읽고 또 읽고 앉아있기
싫으시다면,
무조건 묶으십시오.

잔소리 셋!

궁금한 것을 잘 이용하는게, 가장 재밌고 효율적으로 공부하는 방법입니다.

관심도 없으면, 질문도 없고, 궁금한 것도 없기 마련 입니다.

하지만 흥미로운 것은, 아무리 싫어하는 과목도, 중간고사 기말고사 때는, 시험이 끝난 뒤, 10분밖에 없는 쉬는 시간을 굳이 전 시간에 본 시험을 가채점 하면서 보내는 학생들이 있습니다.
왜그런지는 저도 모르지만 가끔 저도 그러긴 했습니다.
궁금해서..

그걸 잘 이용하면 됩니다.
궁금할 땐, 사전 한번 찾아보고, 옆 사람이랑 답이 왜 되는지 얘기만 해봐도 팍! 팍!! 머리 속에 박히게 됩니다.

이정도로 공부할 때 확실하고 효과적인 원동력도 없습니다.
정말 이것만 잘 이용해도 대박입니다.
하지만 문제는 이런 궁금점이 늘 있지 않다는 점,
아니, 늘 없다는 점이 문제입니다.

심지어 이렇게까지나 궁금했던 내용조차
오전 시험 다 끝나고, 점심시간 되면 별로 관심 없어집니다.
그냥 피곤할 뿐이고, 난 이미 시험 망친걸 알 뿐이고...
저녁이 되면? 시험때 뭘 본지 기억조차 안납니다.
다음날이면? 담당 선생님이 답지 들고 와서 가르쳐 준다 해도, 별로 관심 없습니다.
그렇게나 궁금해했던 내용인데도 말입니다.

그러니, 시험 즉시 가장 궁금해 할때,
그 때 즉시 건드려야 합니다.
시간은 오래일 필요 없습니다.
딱 서로 이견있는 문제만 골라낸 뒤,
그것만 집중적으로 얘기해보면 됩니다.
싸워도 됩니다. 우겨도 됩니다. 혼자 다굴 당해도 좋고,
그게 혼자만 맞아도 좋고, 혼자만 틀려도 좋습니다.

중요한 건, 자신의 답을 얘기할 때는 분명한 근거가 있어야 한다는 겁니다.
잘된 근거 제시라면, 실력이 늘어가는 과정이고,
잘못된 근거 제시라도, 실력을 올바르게 늘려가는데 어떤 도움보다 큰 도움이 될 것입니다.

꼭 자기 주장을 강하게 어필하면서,
내 주장이 맞는지를 꼭 확인 해봐야 합니다.

결론부터!! 묻는 말에 대답해야 합니다.

심각하게는, 수업시간에 예, 아니오라는
답이 나올 수 없는 질문조차도, 이상하게
예, 아니오로 대답하는 경우가 많습니다.

질문을 정확히 파악하면 유리한 점.
1. 시간을 아낄 수 있다.
2. 정확도를 높일 수 있다.
3. 읽을 부분을 줄여도 된다.
4. 고민하지 않아도 될 내용은 과감히 생략이 가능하다.

이런 이유들이라면, 무조건 해야 하지 않을까요?

그런데도, 질문을 파악하지 않은 채 자기 고집대로 문제를 풀려 합니다.

물론 결과도 좋지 않습니다.
지나친 반복을 봐 왔고, 같은 실수를 안하셨으면 합니다.
이것을 피하는 방법은 간단합니다.
문제에 핵심단어에 동그라미만 치면 됩니다.
얘가 나한테 뭘 묻는지만 파악하면 된다는 겁니다.
어렵지도 않습니다.

꼭 동그라미 쳐둬야 합니다.

USHER

문제풀이 전 체크 사항
묶었나?
? 찍었나?
문제 동그라미 했나?
날렸나?

잔소리 넷!

본문에서 오답근거는 꼭 날려야 합니다.

학생들에게 문제를 풀면서, 답 근거를 찾으라고 그렇게도 많이 얘기 해왔습니다.
그럼에도, 정답 근거조차 잘 안 찾아옵니다.
하지만, 오답 근거까지 본문에서 날릴 것을 주문합니다.

왜?
그게 더 재밌고, 효과가 좋으니까…
두 가지 모두 좋은 건데 안할 이유가 있을까요?
그냥 멍하게 문제지만 보지 말고,
역시나, 묶고 - 모든 문장은 분명 묶어야 합니다.

묶다 보면, 문제에 나오는 한 단어 한 단어가 의미가 훨씬 세게 다가오고, 그 센 의미 중에서
"나 틀린 답! 나 틀린 답!!"
막 외치고 있는데도 틀리는 경우가 많습니다.
답 알려주면, 늘 같은 탄식, '아~'

체스, 바둑, 장기를 두다 보면, 가장 어이 없을 때가,
딱 상대가 두자마자 움직이려다 너무 쉽게 상대가 주는 게 의심스러워서, 잠시 생각해보면, 딱 함정인게 보입니다.
그리고 그걸 피하겠다고, 엄청 고민합니다.
노인장기의 시작인 거죠.
그리고는 결국?
딱 처음 그 첫번째, 가장 최악의 결정을 내리고 맙니다.
너무 당당하게, 자신 있게, 박력 있게.
그리곤 틀립니다.

내가 모른 것만 틀려도 숫자가 만만치 않습니다.
그러니 적어도 내가 아는 것에서는 절대 실수해서는 안됩니다.
실수를 줄이는 방법으로는 deletion 보다 좋은방법이 없고,
그 지우는 방법에선 "단어로 날리기" 만큼 좋은게 없습니다.

"짧게 쓸 시간이 없어서 길게 쓰겠습니다."
처음에 이 말을 듣고 '뭐래?' 싶었습니다.
결론부터 말하자면, 장황할 예정이라는 말입니다.

생각을 많이 하면, 말은 짧지만, 정수를 짚을 수 있습니다.
그러니, 생각을 많이 한 글은 정말 에센스만 남길 수 있기에 짧아질 수 있는 겁니다.
극과 극은 통한다고 하나요?
그래서 짧게 던진 중요한 말은, 내가 처음 이 말을 들을 때처럼
'뭐래?' 라는 반응을 이끌어 내기도 합니다.
하지만, 반드시 기억해야 합니다.
정리 안된 사람들이 장황하다는 것을…

뭔가 상대방이 설명은 하는데 못 알아 듣겠으면,
뭔가 상대방에게 설명을 하는데, 정리가 잘 안되면,
그땐, 말하는 것과 듣는 것을 멈추고, 묻고 답해보면 됩니다.
수 차례 해보십시오.

그러면, 점점 쓸데없는 말들이 쳐나가질 것이고,
그러면, 문제 풀이에 큰 도움이될것입니다.

반드시 기억해야 합니다.
문제 풀이 요령은, 각 문제 스타일별로 오답을 피하는 노하우보다,
기본이 더 중요합니다.
문제 똑바로 읽기와, 단어로 날리기

이게 핵심입니다.
이것만 똑바로 해도 못 풀 문제는 없습니다.

포기하지 마십시오, 버릇됩니다.

살면서 이런 저런 일이 많을 겁니다.
그런데, 지나온 시간들을 돌아 주변을 살펴보면,
되는 사람은 계속 되고,
안 되는 사람은 계속 안 됩니다.

이유를 살펴보면 간단합니다.
되는 사람은 되는 버릇을 가지고 있고,
안 되는 사람은 안 되는 버릇을 가지고 있기 때문입니다.

방법론을 얘기 하는게 아닙니다.
되는 사람은 될 때까지 포기를 안 했다는 공통점이 있고,
안 되는 사람은 안 되면 놓을 줄 안다는 점이 있습니다.

되고 안 되고의 가장 큰 차이는,
실력이나,
타고난 것이나,
물려받은 것이나,
주어진 환경보다,

그냥 스스로 놓느냐, 아니냐의 차이인 듯 합니다.
그냥 놓는 사람은 계속 놓기 마련이고,
안 놓는 사람은 그냥 될 때까지 안 놓습니다.

어셔에서의 시간이
될 이유를 만들어 보는 시간이었으면 좋겠습니다.

다 왔다고 긴장을 풀어버리지도 마십시오.
아직 끝나지 않았습니다.
딱 봐도 힘들어 보이는 학생이 안 된다고 놔버릴 때는,
'그럴수도 있겠다.' 싶습니다.
이겨본 적도 많지 않고,
지금 상태도 좋은 건 아니니…

하지만,
가르치는 입장에서 가장 아쉬울 때는,
전혀 안될 이유도 없고,
지금 상태도 절대 나쁘지 않은데,
어떤 이유 때문인지,
그냥 일찍 놔버려서 결국 목표지점 앞에서 관성이 떨어져
주저 앉는 경우입니다.
여긴 우주가 아닙니다.
한번 생긴 관성이 계속 가게 만들어 주지 않습니다.
빗속에서 축구공을 차본 적이 있으십니까?
일단, 물을 먹어 잘 나가지도 않습니다.
공을 차다 보면, 내 발목도 조심해야 합니다.
공을 차도 공중으로 뜨지도 않습니다.
최악은, 드리블을 할 때, 공을 패스할 때,
공이 물 웅덩이에 빠지면,
그냥 서있습니다. 탁! 섭니다.
그렇게 자신의 점수를 탁 서게 만들 일이 없다고 믿지 마십시오.
마지막까지 몰고 가서, 딱 목표된 지점을 지나야지만 끝난
겁니다.

끝날 때까진 끝난 게 아닙니다.
마지막까지 긴장을 풀어선 안됩니다.

usherin.usher.co.kr

USHER

iBT TOEFL
INTERMEDIATE READING 02
TEST 1

테스트 전 확인사항

실전에 유용한 독해 전략(44p)을 숙지하였습니다. ○
화장실은 미리 다녀왔습니다. ○
휴대폰의 전원을 껐습니다. ○
노트테이킹 할 종이와 연필을 준비하였습니다. ○
시간을 체크할 시계를 준비하였습니다. ○
목표점수(30개 중 ___개)를 정하였습니다. ○
시험 시작 시간은 ___시 ___분이며,
종료 시간은 54분 뒤인 ___시 ___분입니다. ○
시험 중 이동해야 할 방해요소가 있는지 체크하였습니다. ○
시험 중 이동하지 않습니다.

Sentinel Behavior in Meerkats

1. → Meerkats are small, mongoose-like mammals that live in the Kalahari Desert of Southern Africa. Being primarily insectivores, they feed on beetles and scorpions buried underground, which they locate using their strong sense of smell. Unfortunately, when the meerkat lowers its head to search out prey under grasses, it limits its own range of sight by a significant amount. As a result they are extremely vulnerable to airborne predators such as hawks and owls. To ensure that they can reach the safety of their bolt-holes before being snatched up by birds, meerkats forage in packs and partake in what is known as sentinel behavior. As the term suggests, one meerkat in the group acts as a sentinel and does not look for food like the rest, but rather stands upright on its hind legs to gain a wider field of view with which it scans the surrounding area for possible predators and other threats to the community. When it senses danger approaching, the sentinel barks loudly to warn the others of the danger. Many scientists questioned this phenomenon because the revealing stance and loud vocalization were thought to expose the meerkat to an increased risk of predation.

폭 넓게 - 일단 버릇 들이는게 중요!

32. According to paragraph 1, why was sentinel behavior thought to be disadvantageous?

(A) It warns the predator of where the meerkat group is.
(B) It allows the meerkat to sense danger and warn the group.
(C) It helps the predators locate the sentinel meerkat.
(D) It encourages the predator to prey on meerkats over other species.

스터디 자료들 미리 수집해 둘것!

시험 중 체크 사항

❶ "?" 표시하기 : 본문 읽으며, 궁금한 곳에 "?" 표시를 합니다.
　　　　　　　문제를 풀면서도 질문 거리에는 "?" 표시를 해둡니다.
❷ 문제 핵심에 동그라미 : 문제가 물어보는 게 무엇인지, 문제 핵심에 동그라미 표시를 합니다.
❸ 답근거 날리기 : 문제를 풀 때 선택지가 틀린 이유 단어로, 간결하게 날립니다.
❹ 경쟁 문장 표시 : 4개의 선택지 중에 정답과 경쟁하는 마지막 1개의 선택지를 표시 해둡니다. 무조건 1개여야 합니다.

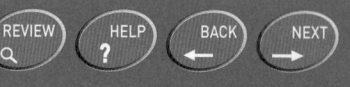

Reading Section Directions

This section measures your ability to understand academic passages in English.

Most questions are worth 1 point but the last question in each set is worth more than 1 point. The directions indicate how many points you may receive.

Some passages include a word or phrase that is underlined in blue. Click on the word or phrase to see a definition or an explanation.

Within each test, you can go to the next questions by clicking **Next**. You may skip questions and go back to them later. If you want to return to previous questions, click on **Back**. You can click on **Review** at any time and the review screen will show you which questions you have answered and which you have not answered. From this reviewscreen, you may go directly to any questions you have already seen in the Reading section.

You may now begin the Reading section. In the section you will read 3 passages. You will have **54 minutes** to read the passages and answer thequestions.

Click on **Continue** to go on.

Next 버튼을 이용하여 다음 문제로 이동하고 **Back** 버튼을 이용하여 이전문제로 이동할 수 있습니다. 문제에 답을 하지 않더라도 다음 문제로 이동할 수 있으며, **Review** 버튼을 이용하여 각 문제별로 답을 체크했는지의 여부를 확인할 수 있습니다. 이번 테스트에서는 세 지문을 읽게 됩니다. 54분 동안 지문을 읽고 문제에 답을 하세요.

Costs of Quitting a Job

1 High job mobility has long been held as a hallmark of the American economy. In contrast to employees in Japan and Europe, American employees appear to switch jobs much more readily. On average, American workers have been with their current employer for a shorter period and have had a larger number of employers than those in other regions. This has been blamed, in part, by the lower levels of training provided by American companies for their workers, but this is likely an oversimplified explanation. In reality, many diverse factors influence American employees' decisions to switch jobs more frequently than their counterparts in Europe and Japan.

2 While economic theories posit that mobility is most likely in prosperous times, when the costs and risks of changing jobs are low, a number of logistical differences make it more likely. [■] One of the most surprising of these is the location of the job. [■] Those employed in urban areas are more likely to change jobs, likely due to the easy availability of other jobs in the city, which means that the employee will not have to relocate his or her home to take another job. [■] Those who live in non-urban areas who quit their jobs will have more difficulty in finding another job due to the limited number available in the region. [■]

3 In addition to logistical and monetary factors, psychological factors also play a large role in job mobility. Individuals with more adventurous personalities and fewer familial responsibilities are more likely to switch jobs easily, as they can overcome the fear of the unknown and are more willing to risk the consequences of job change. In fact, studies have shown that 13% of workers who have switched jobs more than 3 times are responsible for about half of all permanent employment separations. On the other hand, fear and cultural norms can keep employees in their current positions. One of these, the Japanese "lifetime employment" system, has made job

---

01. What can be inferred from paragraph 1 about job mobility and on-the-job training?

(A) Companies that offer extensive training are less likely to have high employee turnover.
(B) The American government doesn't allow on-the-job training, in order to keep job mobility rates high.
(C) Workers remain at their jobs longer in Europe and Japan because it takes them longer to complete their training.
(D) Most on-the-job training is meant to entice employees to remain at their current job for a longer period.

02. According to paragraph 2, which of the following is NOT true about the location of a job?

(A) The site of a job has little bearing on job mobility.
(B) Those who work in urban areas have higher rates of job mobility.
(C) Having to relocate for a job discourages job mobility.
(D) There are limited job opportunities in rural areas.

03. Which of the sentences below best expresses the essential information in the highlighted sentence in the passage? Incorrect choices change the meaning in important ways or leave out essential information.

This system, which was meant to limit the ability of companies to lay off employees, has also built a strong sense of employee loyalty, which makes it societally undesirable for employees to switch jobs without good reason.

(A) Increasing employee loyalty was the main goal of the Japanese "lifetime employment," which discourages companies from laying off employees.
(B) The Japanese employment loyalty scheme had the unintended impact of complicating the process of changing jobs and causing workers to remain in one job.
(C) The Japanese scheme for ensuring that employers didn't fire employees built such a strong sense of allegiance in employees that job mobility began to be frowned upon.
(D) Japanese companies that lay off workers violate the country's "lifetime employment" system for maintaining loyal employees.

04. According to paragraph 3 which of the following is most likely to change jobs?

(A) A married father with several children.
(B) A young, single recent college graduate.
(C) A Japanese office worker.
(D) Someone who has never left a previous job.

05. The term "loath" in the passage is closest in meaning to:

(A) Overjoyed
(B) Likely
(C) Unwilling
(D) Unable

06. According to paragraph 4, all of the following are mentioned regarding real estate's impact on job mobility EXCEPT

(A) Rent controls have a negative effect on the job mobility rate.
(B) People receiving rental subsidies are less likely to take jobs that require them to move.
(C) High rents are only common in areas with high average salaries.
(D) Hefty relocation expenses discourage people from changing jobs.

07. According to paragraph 5, which of the following is true regarding the effect of history on job mobility rates?

(A) Younger nations tend to have high job mobility than countries established long ago.
(B) Countries that were founded by immigrant populations display higher job mobility rates.
(C) Former British colonies have some of the highest job mobility rates in the world.
(D) Nations that were set up in rather isolated locations have lower job mobility.

switching almost unheard of in Japanese society. This system, which was meant to limit the ability of companies to lay off employees, has also built a strong sense of employee loyalty, which makes it societally undesirable for employees to switch jobs without good reason.

4   Interestingly, real estate prices have also been linked to the incidence of job change. Housing policies in Japan and Europe often make residential relocation an expensive prospect, which discourages job mobility in much the same way that non-urban locations do. In many of these countries, rental subsidies are more widely available than in the United States, which makes workers loath to relocate for a job change. In addition, rent control schemes that limit the increase in rent between consecutive rental contracts reduce job and residential mobility, because landlords can negotiate any rental amount for new contracts. This means that any job move that requires relocation could result in an astronomical increase in housing cost.

5   Some researchers also point to history as an indicator of the propensity for job change. The United States, Canada, and Australia are all large, rather sparsely populated countries that show much lower job tenures than most European countries and Japan. They hypothesize that these country's long history of attracting international immigration and their citizens' willingness to undertake long-distance relocation have made job change much less unusual. In a country where people have previously moved thousands of miles from their homeland, pulling up stakes and moving for another job is much less of an event than in countries with more stable populations.

6   With all of these possible explanations for the differences in job mobility rates, another question arises: what is the societal impact of increased job mobility? Some believe that increased job mobility has a positive impact because it increases worker satisfaction and worker-

08. Why does the author mention "employees who they constantly fear will jump ship"?

(A) To show that job mobility makes overseas immigration more likely.
(B) To explain the reason for one of the detriments of high job mobility.
(C) To point out that the shipping industry has the highest rate of job mobility.
(D) To give an example of what happens when companies skimp on training.

job matches. Economists also point to larger numbers of workers and employers seeking matches as a sign of the economic flexibility that makes economic adaptation possible. Conversely, higher mobility with lower costs can cause employers to skimp on training for employees who they constantly fear will jump ship. Whatever the societal cost of job mobility, employers must try to balance job mobility and its associated costs in order to succeed.

09. Look at the four squares [■] that indicate where the following sentence could be added to the passage.

This could cause them to need to make a costly, life-altering move to another region.

Where would the sentence best fit?

Click on a square [■] to add the sentence to the passage.

10. Directions: An introductory sentence for a brief summary of the passage is provided below. Complete the summary by selecting the THREE answer choices that express the most important ideas in the passage. Some sentences do not belong in the summary because they express ideas that are not presented in the passage or are minor ideas in the passage. **This question is worth 2 points.**

> **A number of factors influence mobility in today's job market.**
>
> •
>
> •
>
> •

Answer Choices

(A) American job mobility has traditionally been much higher than that of other industrialized countries such as those in Europe and Japan.

(B) Countries with large immigrant numbers are more likely to have higher job mobility because the population is less averse to major changes and movements.

(C) It is believed that expensive real estate markets can make job changes more unlikely.

(D) Japan's "lifetime employment" system guarantees workers a job if they decide to leave the company they have been working for.

(E) Personality and culture are both factors that can make job changes more or less likely depending on the individual and where they are from.

(F) Businesses encourage job mobility because it reduces their training costs, since employees that have been trained by other companies can easily be hired.

Cell Theory

1   The three main tenets of cell theory, that cells are the basic unit of life, that all organisms are composed of cells, and that cells arise only from other cells, are some of the most basic principles in the field of biology. From this theory scientists have been able to extrapolate a great deal of other scientific knowledge. In fact, our understanding of the role of cells in sexual reproduction and the discovery of our genetic building blocks, DNA, are direct results of this. Cell theory has also allowed medical researchers to better understand illnesses, such as cancer, as well as the cause of viral and bacterial infections. While the theory is now commonly accepted, and may seem like common sense, its development took hundreds of years.

2   In fact, the earliest discoveries in the field took place in the middle of the 17th century when light microscopy began to be regularly used on living creatures. It was during this time that physicist Robert Hooke melted glass into lenses with which he could study fish scales, feathers, and the bodies of various insects, however his greatest discovery was that he noticed a series of chambers in a sample of cork oak, which he felt resembled cubicles and named "cells". Antoine van Leeuwenhoek who created even stronger lenses would later trump this discovery. Using his microscopes he studied the tartar from his teeth and noticed that it contained microscopic organisms he called "aminalcules". Over time he was able to view microorganisms, such as bacteria, that were previously unknown. Leeuwenhoek was able to accurately describe microorganisms and microscopic parts of larger organisms, including the red blood cell. He did not, unfortunately, observe the reproduction of these animalcules or organisms, so he erroneously believed, as did most others of the time, that they simply spontaneously generated.

---

11. Why does the author mention "the role of cells in sexual reproduction and the discovery of our genetic building blocks, DNA"?

(A) To show two of the main points of the cell theory.
(B) To give examples of discoveries made because of cell theory.
(C) To explain how scientists discovered the basic tenets of cell theory.
(D) To offer later discoveries that validated the cell theory.

12. According to paragraph 1, which of the following is NOT a major facet of cell theory?

(A) Complex organisms are composed of cells.
(B) The basic unit of all life is the cell.
(C) All biological discoveries are cell-based.
(D) Cells are produced by previous living cells.

13. Which of the sentences below best expresses the essential information in the highlighted sentence in the passage? Incorrect choices change the meaning in important ways or leave out essential information.

(A) Cells were first discovered by a physicist who used melted glass to study the minute cellular structures of living material such as the small features of insects and fish, as well as material from some plants, such as the cork oak.
(B) Robert Hooke made many important discoveries about insects, fish, and birds, however, he is best known for his botanical discoveries, such as the discovery that they also contained small chambers called cells.
(C) The discovery of cellular structures occurred when Robert Hooke used homemade magnifying glasses to note that scales, feathers, and insect samples all had structures that resembled the chambers of the cork oak, which he called "cells".
(D) Robert Hooke called the compartmentalized structures "cells" found in plants because he thought they bore small rooms when using the glass lenses he made to scrutinize small objects.

14. According to paragraph 3, which of the following is NOT a reason for the slow progress on the cell theory from the 17th-19th centuries?

(A) The equipment of the time was rudimentary and did not provide researchers enough data.
(B) It was nearly impossible to collect and store samples of living material in a way that did not damage it.
(C) Most early biologists did not believe that the cell was the basic building block of living organisms.
(D) Researchers did not perform enough research into, or documentation of, the cells that they were studying.

15. What can be inferred about Robert Brown's 1831 discovery of the cellular nucleus from paragraph 4?

(A) His discovery was possible because of scientific advances that took over the previous two centuries.
(B) Brown was the first researcher to use a microscope to view the nucleus of a cell.
(C) The discovery of the nucleus disproved the earlier theory of spontaneous generation of cells.
(D) Brown was the first researcher to identify DNA as the central component of cells that allows them to reproduce.

16. The term "frequency" in the passage is closest in meaning to:

(A) Irregularity
(B) Number
(C) Density
(D) Rhythm

3   Over the next two centuries a great deal of additional observations would accumulate, but a true cell theory would not emerge until the middle of the 19th century. Today scientists blame this great delay on the inferior scientific equipment, such as microscopes, and techniques, such as preserving samples of living material without destroying it, of 17th & 18th century researchers, which hindered their discoveries. In addition, the early observations of Hooke and Leeuwenhook did not address larger issues, such as cells making up all larger organisms. Hooke had simply noticed the cellular imprint, not the actual cell itself, while Leeuwenhoek observed the actual cell, but failed to provide an accurate description or categorization of its common structures.

4   As the 19th century progressed, these problems were solved through the invention of stronger microscopes, more diligent recording of findings, and increased cooperation by scientists. [■] One of the first to take advantage of these was Scottish surgeon Robert Brown, who noted in 1831 that a circular object was present in all of the orchid cells he studied. [■] Using this finding, he researched other types of cells and found the same structure, which he then posited was a common cellular feature that he named the nucleus. [■] Today, we know that the nucleus is the carrier of our genetic material. [■]

5   By the late 1830s these discoveries only increased in frequency and the cell theory truly began to take hold. In 1838 and 1839, German biologists Matthias Schleiden and Theodor Schwann respectively discovered that all plants and animals were composed of cells. The discovery of cells with nuclei in both types of organisms allowed them to conclude that the cell was the basic unit of life. It also helped them understand that microscopic bacteria had something in common with larger organisms; they were both made up of cells, which were the building blocks of all organisms. These two discoveries were the basic premises for the cell theory.

17. According to paragraph 5, which of the following is true regarding the cell theory?

(A) Robert Brown developed it prior to the discovery of the nucleus.
(B) Researchers who found that plants and animals had similarities at the microscopic level developed it.
(C) Schleiden and Schwann proved that microscopic bacteria could form larger organisms.
(D) The three tenets of the theory were developed at the same time.

18. According to paragraph 6, which of the following can be inferred regarding the theories of Rudolph Virchow?

(A) They were so groundbreaking that they contributed to scientific discoveries by other, later scientists in a variety of fields.
(B) They were opposed by later scientists, such as Pasteur, who believed that Virchow did not understand the true cause of human illnesses.
(C) They caused scientists to change the main rules of theory, since he had proven that they were in accurate.
(D) They proved that cells when a nucleus forms in a cell body, not when a cell body forms around a nucleus, as was previously believed.

6   Later, other cellular biologists expanded on these findings. Perhaps the most important of these was German pathologist Rudolf Virchow who contributed the third tenet of the cell theory in 1855: All cells come from other living cells. This contradicted most common understanding of the time, as it was thought that cells could spontaneously generate when a nucleus was able to form and grow the remainder of the cell body around itself. His explanation allowed later scientists to observe and describe cell division in the late 1880s. His theories also acted as the basic principle behind Pasteur's germ theory of disease, despite Virchow's personal objection to such a theory. He felt that diseases were caused by internal cellular abnormalities and not outside pathogens, which he thought were simply attracted to the abnormal cells as a habitat. While germ theory discounts this for most diseases, he did correctly suggest that abnormal cells could cause some diseases that affect the rest of the body, such as leukemia.

19. Look at the four squares [■] that indicate where the following sentence could be added to the passage.

Although Brown discovered this core component of the cell, he did not know the true significance of his discovery.

Where would the sentence best fit?

Click on a square [■] to add the sentence to the passage.

20. Directions: An introductory sentence for a brief summary of the passage is provided below. Complete the summary by selecting the THREE answer choices that express the most important ideas in the passage. Some sentences do not belong in the summary because they express ideas that are not presented in the passage or are minor ideas in the passage. **This question is worth 2 points.**

> Cells were discovered in the 1600s, but it took over 200 years before the cell theory explained their true importance and nature.
>
> •
> •
> •

Answer Choices

(A) Robert Hooke first described the cell during the 17th century after viewing a series of chambers in a magnified sample of the cork oak.

(B) Leeuwenhook developed more powerful microscopes so that he could confirm the earlier discoveries of Robert Hooke.

(C) Robert Brown was the first researcher to identify the central portion of the cell, which he named the nucleus.

(D) Delays in developing the cell theory were caused by the rudimentary tools used in the 17th and 18th centuries and scientists' insistence upon hiding their discoveries.

(E) Refinements in tools and practices by the 19th century allowed scientists to more accurately and systematically study cells.

(F) Our current understanding of cells states that they are the basic biological units, which make up larger organisms, and that they must propagate through division.

Mating Songs of Frogs

1   Most species of frogs rely upon auditory signals to communicate with one another. This occurs because auditory communication is much more efficient than visual forms of communication. This is because auditory signaling, unlike visual communication, does not require a specific orientation to receive a message. The recipient need not be facing the sender to receive the signal. [■] They also allow signals to be sent over greater distances than visual communication methods. [■] Instead of being blocked by physical barriers, the auditory signal can be transmitted. [■] In fact, auditory communication allows frogs to broadcast their messages through the air, underwater, and even through the substrate. [■] Further, since most frog and toad species are nocturnal, auditory messages have the advantage of being usable even in complete darkness. Due to these advantages, male frogs have developed a complex system of communication that allows them to attract potential mates.

2   Male frogs are able to produce these signs due to a series of adaptations, the most notable being the vocal sacs located beneath the floor of the mouth. To create their distinctive croaking sounds, frogs seal off their nostrils and mouths and use the muscles along their body wall to force air back-and-forth from the lungs through the larynx and into the vocal sac. This air movement across the larynx causes the vocal cords to vibrate and the sound is then amplified by the vocal sacs to produce a loud, clear croaking sound. These sounds attract females, which may respond by approaching the male or even by calling back to the male. This can even lead to duets between receptive couples. Unfortunately, they can also increase the mortality risk, since predators can also recognize the croaking.

3   To human ears these croaks may all sound the same, but they are actually a complex system that allows frogs

---

21. According to paragraph 1, which of the following is NOT a benefit of auditory communication?

(A) It makes communication over long distances easier.
(B) It allows communication between physically separated individuals.
(C) It reduces the importance of the sense of vision.
(D) It can be used in low light situations.

22. Why does the author mention that "hybridization usually produces non-viable offspring"?

(A) To give an example of a reason that male frogs croak in order to attract females.
(B) To show the reader that there is a biological reason that female frogs only understand croaks from their own species.
(C) To help readers understand why female frogs are attracted to the croaking of males.
(D) To explain why recognizing the species is the most important aspect of discerning the male's croaking.

23. According to paragraph 3, which of the following is true regarding the pattern of croaks made by male frogs?

(A) Species of related frogs have similar patterns, which leads to interbreeding.
(B) Frogs use different patterns to communicate with frogs from other areas.
(C) Female frogs do not seem to be able to recognize patterns in the croaking.
(D) Distinctive patterns increase the reproductive efficiency of the frog species.

24. Which of the sentences below best expresses the essential information in the highlighted sentence in the passage? Incorrect choices change the meaning in important ways or leave out essential information.

(A) Female frogs select older male partners because they produce larger offspring that will be more able to endure risks and predators in the natural environment.
(B) To ensure that her brood has genetic advantages, female frogs are innately attracted to older males whose ages denote that they have survived danger in the ecosystem.
(C) Older male frogs have been able to withstand environmental hazards, which gives them an inherent genetic advantage that attracts female frogs to them.
(D) To have stronger offspring, avoiding predators and other threats in the natural environment makes males more attractive to females.

25. What can be inferred about the croaks of young frogs from paragraph 4?

(A) They are generally higher than older frogs because they need to travel longer, since younger frog territories are generally farther from the population center.
(B) They can sometime confuse female frogs and lead them to mate with younger males.
(C) They sometimes mimic those of older frogs in order to disguise their relative youth and inexperience.
(D) They do not initially sound like those of older males since it takes time for them to learn the most productive amplitude and pitch.

26. The term "eschew" in the passage is closest in meaning to:

(A) Embrace
(B) Postpone
(C) Forgo
(D) Dislike

to learn a great deal about the croaking frog. Perhaps the most important information that a female frog can discern from the croaking is the temporal pattern and frequency, both of which are species specific. Although some frog species can interbreed, hybridization usually produces non-viable offspring; therefore female frogs are attracted to the call of males from their species. Frogs are so attuned to differentiating calls that they can even determine if the caller is from the same region. In much the same way that human languages have developed dialects, frog calls vary slightly amongst different geographic populations and can be used to determine whether the call is from a male in a neighboring territory, or if an intruder has appeared.

4 Another key piece of information that females glean from the croaking is the relative size and age of the croaker. Many frog species undergo indeterminate growth, meaning they continuously grow larger as they age. This provides them with larger vocal sacs and larynxes that produce louder and lower tones as they age. Females, which are generally attracted to older frogs, recognize the differences in amplitude and pitch of the caller and are attracted to them. This inherent bias of female frogs toward older males is a method of selecting genetically superior mates, since their age and size indicate that the male frogs have survived environmental and predatory hazards, two traits that would be beneficial for her offspring. However, these two aspects can be ambiguous, as both temperature and distance can cause the calls of younger males to seem louder and lower than older specimens.

5 Female frogs can determine the relative health and territorial safety of the male though his calls as well. Because of the continuous muscle contractions required to push air through the vocal mechanisms, some of which make up 15% of the frogs overall mass, croaking requires a considerable energy expenditure of part of the male. Some studies show tree frog croaking is the most energy intensive activity of any vertebrate. Therefore, it can only

27. According to paragraph 5, which of the following is NOT true regarding frogs that croak during mating season?

(A) They wander around the area croaking until they find a receptive female.
(B) Their continued croaking is a sign that they are relatively safe.
(C) They expend a great deal of energy to produce the noises.
(D) They do not hunt for food while they are croaking.

28. According to paragraph 6, which of the following can be inferred regarding the frog chorus?

(A) Female frogs join the chorus when they have found a suitable mate.
(B) Members of the chorus learn to croak from the other males in adjacent territories.
(C) They do not display aggressive behavior to other frogs within the chorus.
(D) The chorus is generally set up to protect the territory of the local males.

be performed by males that are healthy enough to eschew feeding in order to search for a mate. Further, the ability to continually croak indicates to the female that the male has a secure territory in which he is safe from predation, since he is calling so much attention to himself.

6 Interestingly, male-female interaction is not the only use of auditory communication in frogs. Male frogs also communicate with one another to establish a territory. This is especially important because during the mating season when the males form large 'choruses,' they learn the croaking of their direct neighbors. When they hear these croaks they are not alarmed, but when they hear an unfamiliar call they croak aggressively to warn the intruder that they are encroaching upon another frog's territory.

29. Look at the four squares [■] that indicate where the following sentence could be added to the passage.

This ability allows frogs to broadcast their messages no matter where they are located.

Where would the sentence best fit?

Click on a square [■] to add the sentence to the passage.

30. Directions: An introductory sentence for a brief summary of the passage is provided below. Complete the summary by selecting the THREE answer choices that express the most important ideas in the passage. Some sentences do not belong in the summary because they express ideas that are not presented in the passage or are minor ideas in the passage. **This question is worth 2 points.**

> **Although frog croaking seems basic to our ears, it is a complex communication system.**
>
> •
>
> •
>
> •

Answer Choices

(A) Frogs utilize a system of auditory communication due to its ability to be transmitted over long distances, through barriers, and in the darkness.

(B) Despite auditory communication requiring great energy expenditure, male frogs cannot forage for good while they are engaged in croaking.

(C) Croaking transmits information regarding the size and age of the frog croaking, both of which are important factors in mate selection for female frogs.

(D) Female frogs are naturally attracted to older males because they tend to have larger territories that can support more offspring.

(E) Most frog species cannot recognize the croaking patterns of other species, so they often interbreed, which causes hybridization and lower reproductive efficiency.

(F) Differences in croaks allow frogs to identify members of their chorus and outsiders that may be attempting to horn in to their territory.

You have seen all of the questions in this part of the Reading section. You have time left to review.
As long as there is time remaining, you can check your work.

Click on **Return** to go back to the previous question.
Click on **Review** to see the review screen for this section.
Click on **Continue** to go on.
Once you leave this part of the Reading section, you WILL NOT be able to return to it.

이제 Reading Section이 끝났습니다.
Continue 버튼을 누르면 다시 문제를 검토할 수 없으므로 유의하세요.

시험보고 난 후 ... 체크 리스트 및 스터디 디렉션

1. 내가 불안했던 문제만 재빨리 다시 보고, 불안하게 만든, 즉, 경쟁 초이스를 찾아서 왜 내가 헷갈려 했는지를 파악할 수 있는 메모를 해두시기 바랍니다. 시간이 지나거나, 다른 학생들과 스터디를 하면서는, 자신이 왜 낚였는지 이유조차 기억나지 않아 본인의 실수 패턴 파악이 힘들기 때문입니다.

2. 답지를 확인하지 않고 스터디를 하시기 바랍니다. (그래서, 답지를 문제지 뒤에 붙이지 않고, 본 설명만을 붙여 두었습니다.) 답지를 확인하지 않고 하는 이유는 답을 아는 순간, 답에 끼워 맞춰 설명하려 하고, 이런 태도는 본인 실력 향상에 도움이 되지 않기 때문입니다. 스터디 팀원들간에 대략적인 답을 맞춰보면, 대부분 답안의 윤곽이 나옵니다. 이럴 경우, 이견이 있는 문제만 집중적으로 다루고, 나머지는 개별로 처리하시기 바랍니다.

3. 문제를 끝까지 다 풀었나요? 네 □ / 아니오 □
   다 못 풀었다면, 전체 30 문제 중 푼 문제는? _____ / 30
   시간 모자란 것에 대해서는 크게 신경 쓰지 않아도 됩니다. 무엇보다 중요한 것은 정확도 입니다.
   우선은 풀은 문제를 맞출 확률을 높이고, 그 다음 시간을 걱정해도 늦지 않습니다.

4. 어려웠다고 느껴지는 지문은? 과학 □ / 예술 □ / 인문 □ / 인물 □ / 사회 □
   과학지문이 현격히 다른 분야보다 많지만, 그래도, 공부하다 보면 자신만 어려워하는 분야는 모두 각각입니다. 그러므로, 혹시 배경지식 부분에서 필요한 것이 있다면, usherin.usher.co.kr 에 방문하셔서, 공부가 안될 때, 배경지식 부분을 쉬엄쉬엄 들러서 봐 두시길 바랍니다. 쉬엄쉬엄 입니다. 누가 뭐래도 실력있는 사람은 배경지식이 큰 영향을 끼치지는 않습니다.

5. (채점 후) 문제 풀 때 어렵다고 느낀 지문이 틀리는 개수와 쉬웠다고 느껴졌던 지문의 틀린 개수차이가 있나요? 예 □ / 아니오 □
   어느 순간 깨닫게 됩니다. 내가 잘 아는 내용이 나와서 자신 있게 푸나, 내가 모르는 지문이 나와서 겁먹고 푸나, 틀린 개수가 큰 차이가 나지 않는 것을…. 혹시 그걸 못 느끼신다면, 더욱더 열심히 하시기 바랍니다. ^^

6. 틀린 문제의 번호를 다음의 문제 유형 분석표와 비교해서 파악해 두시기 바랍니다.
   문제 유형을 파악해서 주의하는 것은, 누가 뭐래도 실력이 기본은 받쳐 줄 때 얘기입니다. 문제 푸는 스킬이나, 기타 문제 유형 파악 등은 기본적으로 본문 내용을 이해하고, 해석이 웬만큼 될 때 얘기입니다. 만약, 너무 힘들다면 너무 스트레스 받지 말고, 그냥 '아~ 그렇구나' 정도로 넘기셔도 됩니다. 단, 본문 이해는 절대 양보해서는 안됩니다.

문제 유형 분석표

TEST 1-1	TEST 1-2	TEST 1-3
01 Inference	11 Purpose	21 Fact
02 Fact	12 Fact	22 Purpose
03 Inference	13 Highlight	23 Fact
04 Fact	14 Fact	24 Highlight
05 Vocabulary	15 Fact	25 Inference
06 Fact	16 Vocabulary	26 Vocabulary
07 Fact	17 Fact	27 Fact
08 Purpose	18 Fact	28 Inference
09 Insertion	19 Insertion	29 Insertion
10 Summary	20 Summary	30 Summary

USHER

iBT TOEFL
INTERMEDIATE READING 02
TEST 2

테스트 전 확인사항

실전에 유용한 독해 전략(44p)을 숙지하였습니다.　　　　　○
화장실은 미리 다녀왔습니다.　　　　　　　　　　　　　　○
휴대폰의 전원을 껐습니다.　　　　　　　　　　　　　　　○
노트테이킹 할 종이와 연필을 준비하였습니다.　　　　　　○
시간을 체크할 시계를 준비하였습니다.　　　　　　　　　　○
목표점수(30개 중＿＿＿개)를 정하였습니다.　　　　　　　○
시험 시작 시간은 ＿＿＿시 ＿＿＿분이며,
종료 시간은 54분 뒤인 ＿＿＿시 ＿＿＿분입니다.　　　　○
시험 중 이동해야 할 방해요소가 있는지 체크하였습니다.　○
시험 중 이동하지 않습니다.

Sentinel Behavior in Meerkats

1. → Meerkats are small, mongoose-like mammals that live in the Kalahari Desert of Southern Africa. Being primarily insectivores, they feed on beetles and scorpions buried underground, which they locate using their strong sense of smell. Unfortunately, when the meerkat lowers its head to search out prey under grasses, it limits its own range of sight by a significant amount. As a result they are extremely vulnerable to airborne predators such as hawks and owls. To ensure that they can reach the safety of their bolt-holes before being snatched up by birds, meerkats forage in packs and partake in what is known as sentinel behavior. As the term suggests, one meerkat in the group acts as a sentinel and does not look for food like the rest, but rather stands upright on its hind legs to gain a wider field of view with which it scans the surrounding area for possible predators and other threats to the community. When it senses danger approaching, the sentinel barks loudly to warn the others of the danger. Many scientists questioned this phenomenon because the revealing stance and loud vocalization were thought to expose the meerkat to an increased risk of predation.

폭 넓게 - 일단 버릇 들이는게 중요!

32 According to paragraph 1, why was sentinel behavior thought to be disadvantageous?

　(A) It warns the predator of where the meerkat group is.
　(B) It allows the meerkat to sense danger and warn the group.
　(C) It helps the predators locate the sentinel meerkat.
　(D) It encourages the predator to prey on meerkats over other species.

스터디 자료들 미리 수집해 둘것!

시험 중 체크 사항

❶ "?"표시하기 : 본문 읽으며, 궁금한 곳에 "?" 표시를 합니다.
　　　　　　　문제를 풀면서도 질문 거리에는 "?" 표시를 해둡니다.
❷ 문제 핵심에 동그라미 : 문제가 물어보는 게 무엇인지, 문제 핵심에 동그라미 표시를 합니다.
❸ 답근거 날리기 : 문제를 풀 때 선택지가 틀린 이유 단어로, 간결하게 날립니다.
❹ 경쟁 문장 표시 : 4개의 선택지 중에 정답과 경쟁하는 마지막 1개의 선택지를 표시 해둡니다. 무조건 1개여야 합니다.

Reading Section Directions

This section measures your ability to understand academic passages in English.

Most questions are worth 1 point but the last question in each set is worth more than 1 point. The directions indicate how many points you may receive.

Some passages include a word or phrase that is underlined in blue. Click on the word or phrase to see a definition or an explanation.

Within each test, you can go to the next questions by clicking **Next**. You may skip questions and go back to them later. If you want to return to previous questions, click on **Back**. You can click on **Review** at any time and the review screen will show you which questions you have answered and which you have not answered. From this reviewscreen, you may go directly to any questions you have already seen in the Reading section.

You may now begin the Reading section. In the section you will read 3 passages. You will have **54 minutes** to read the passages and answer thequestions.

Click on **Continue** to go on.

Next 버튼을 이용하여 다음 문제로 이동하고 **Back** 버튼을 이용하여 이전문제로 이동할 수 있습니다. 문제에 답을 하지 않더라도 다음 문제로 이동할 수 있으며, **Review** 버튼을 이용하여 각 문제별로 답을 체크했는지의 여부를 확인할 수 있습니다.
이번 테스트에서는 세 지문을 읽게 됩니다. 54분 동안 지문을 읽고 문제에 답을 하세요.

Milankovitch Cycles and Glaciation

1 Scientists have pieced together a relatively detailed timeline of the twenty glacial cycles that took place during the Pleistocene Epoch (10,000-2,000,000 years ago). During these frigid periods, glaciers up to 3,900m thick covered 30% of Earth's surface. These were most prevalent in the higher-latitude regions of both hemispheres, which were covered by glaciers as far south as Germany in the Northern Hemisphere and as far north as the Andes in the Southern Hemisphere. However, despite 100+ years of research into these periods, researchers are unable to explain their cause.

2 Over the years, diverse factors, such as continental location, oceanic circulation and solar energy fluctuation, have been cited as possible causes of these glaciations. One of the most interesting was put forth by Scottish scientist James Croll who used the previously known fact that cyclic changes in Earth's orbit affect how solar radiation impacts Earth's surface to deduce that they could also affect the global climate. Using this theory, Yugoslavian mathematician Milutin Milankovitch developed an equation that showed how these cyclic changes in Earth's orbit, now known as Milankovitch cycles, could cause climatic changes and lead to continental glaciations.

3 Milankovitch based his equation on three cyclic changes in Earth's position relative to the Sun that he thought could collectively have an effect on the solar radiation that is incident on Earth's surface: eccentricity, obliquity, and precession. The first of these, eccentricity, is the elliptical variation in the Earth's orbit that sometimes brings it closer to the Sun and slightly changes every revolution in a 96,000-year cycle. The second of these, obliquity, is concerned with the annual changes in the tilt of Earth's axis that causes seasonal variation. As this tilt changes, in a 41,000-year cycle, the temperature difference between winter and summer becomes extreme

---

01. What can be inferred from paragraph 1 about the glaciations of the Pleistocene Epoch?

(A) The frigid temperatures of the last glaciation had relatively little effect on the regions surrounding Earth's equator.
(B) During the glaciations, the entire Earth was exposed to frigid temperatures that formed large glaciers.
(C) Geologists and climatologists have pieced together a great deal of information related to the causes of glaciations.
(D) The glaciers that covered the Northern Hemisphere were much thicker than those in the Southern Hemisphere.

02. The term "incident" in the passage is closest in meaning to:

(A) Concentrated
(B) Insinuated
(C) Burning
(D) Striking

03. Why does the author mention "a slowly moving top"?

(A) To help children understand the theory by explaining it with a toy.
(B) To give the reader a common image that can help them understand an abstract idea.
(C) To show that Earth's rotation is slowing as it continues to wobble on its axis.
(D) To imply that Earth will eventually stop wobbling and fall to one side.

04. Which of the sentences below best expresses the essential information in the highlighted sentence in the passage? Incorrect choices change the meaning in important ways or leave out essential information.

(A) The glaciations that occur every 40,000 years were shown by the Milankovitch equation which showed how the temperature differential between summer and winter allowed more ice growth because of higher winter temperatures.

(B) Lower overall temperatures prevented ice from melting during the summer 40,000 years ago, which allowed increased glacial growth to occur, just as was predicted by the equation Milankovitch developed to explain changes in the three aspects of Earth's orbit.

(C) Milankovitch developed an equation showing that glaciations occurred when the glaciers grew as the seasonal temperature gradient decreased and they remained intact through the summer when the three cycles of Earth's orbit line up every 40,000 years.

(D) The three Milankovitch cycles equalize every 40,000 years in such a way that allows glacial growth because the summer temperatures are closer to the winter temperatures, so the glaciers do not melt during the summer.

05. According to paragraph 3, which of the following is NOT true about the Milankovitch Cycles?

(A) Eccentricity in Earth's orbit can cause it to be closer to the Sun during some of its annual orbits.

(B) The reduction in the obliquity of Earth's axis causes fewer extreme temperatures in winter and summer.

(C) Precession is the most rapid of the Milankovitch cycles that affect Earth's orientation with regard to the sun during its orbit.

(D) Variations in certain aspects of Earth's orbit cause differences in the amount of solar radiation that reaches Earth's surface.

and more mild as the tilt is respectively higher or lower. The final of the Milankovitch cycles, precession, is the circular wobble that Earth performs on its axis every 12,700 years, in a movement that resembles the wobble of a slowly moving top. Although these three cycles do not affect the amount of solar radiation that reaches the Earth, they greatly affect its distribution. Milankovitch's equation showed that every 40,000 years these three cycles would perfectly synchronize in a way that would greatly reduce the difference between winter and summer temperatures and prevent the winter ice from melting during the summer, thereby allowing it to build up, and causing an overall glacial growth.

4   Despite developing this theory in the 1920s, Milankovitch was limited in his ability to test it extensively, since the timeline of the Pleistocene Epoch temperature changes necessary for testing it was not developed until the 1970s. After the development of this new chronology, a correlation between Milankovitch cycles and the major climatic changes of the last 65 million years became clearer. Further, core samples taken from the deep-sea floor proved that Milankovitch's equation was incredibly accurate in predicting climate changes over the last few hundred thousand years, including the end of the Pleistocene Epoch.

5   [■] Unfortunately, this accuracy and correlation does not fully explain the cause of glaciation throughout history. [■] If Milankovitch's explanation was accurate, it would require glaciations to have occurred regularly throughout Earth's history, yet they appear to have occurred only rarely. [■] This has led scientists to determine that there must be another factor that works with the Milankovitch cycles to cause glaciations. [■] When this mystery factor has sufficiently lowered the average temperature, the cyclic variations of solar radiation caused by the Milankovitch Cycles can throw Earth into and out of glacial periods with the regularity predicted by the Milankovitch equation.

06. According to paragraph 4, which of the following is true regarding the timeline of the Pleistocene Epoch?

(A) Milankovitch was never able to verify his theory because he did not have enough information about the climate of the Pleistocene Epoch.
(B) Scientists were unaware of existence of glaciations during the Pleistocene Epoch until the 1970s.
(C) The dawn of the Pleistocene Epoch 65 million years ago was verified by Milankovitch's equation.
(D) Core samples from the sea floor confirmed the timeline of the Pleistocene Epoch that Milankovitch had put forth.

07. What can be inferred about the accuracy of the Milankovitch equation from paragraph 5?

(A) Inaccuracies in the Milankovitch equation caused more recent scientists to disregard his findings.
(B) The equation that Milankovitch developed overestimated the frequency of large scale glaciations throughout history.
(C) The mystery-cooling feature Milankovitch included in his equation caused inaccuracies in the prediction of past glacial periods.
(D) Milankovitch's equation was only accurate for recent glaciations and could not be used to predict glaciations before the Pleistocene Epoch.

08. According to paragraph 6, which of the following is true regarding the search for the mystery-cooling factor?

(A) Scientists have determined that an increase in CO_2 levels in the environment caused the glaciations of the Pleistocene Epoch.
(B) Volcanic eruptions likely clouded the environment and trapped colder temperatures in Earth's environment.
(C) Earth's surface has become warmer since the last glaciation due to an increase in the Sun's luminosity over time.
(D) Scientists have found a correspondence between the fluctuations in environmental CO_2 levels and the temperatures of the Earth's surface.

6 In the quest to discover this mystery-cooling factor, a number of possibilities have been suggested. One of these is that changes in the Sun's luminosity have allowed fluctuations in the solar energy that reaches Earth. However, this is highly unlikely, since it is now believed that the Sun has steadily become stronger over time. Another possible cause of lower temperatures was volcanic dust in the atmosphere shielding Earth from solar radiation and causing temperatures to drop. This is also rather unlikely, since the beginning of the last glaciation does not correspond with known major eruptions. A more recent theory states that differences in atmospheric carbon dioxide (CO_2) have caused temperature fluctuations on Earth. Since CO_2 traps radiation in the atmosphere, periods of decreased atmospheric CO_2 results in lower temperatures on Earth's surface, allowing solar radiation to escape. This is especially attractive to researchers, because studies of the Greenland ice cap show that the number of CO_2 bubbles found in the different strata changes depending on when the ice formed. Samples from periods known to be warmer show higher CO_2 levels, while colder periods have significantly less, thereby confirming the correlation between CO_2 levels and Earth's temperature.

09. Look at the four squares [■] that indicate where the following sentence could be added to the passage.

This can be understood if one looks back at Earth's climate since its formation approximately 4.5 billion years ago.

Where would the sentence best fit?

Click on a square [■] to add the sentence to the passage.

10. Directions: An introductory sentence for a brief summary of the passage is provided below. Complete the summary by selecting the THREE answer choices that express the most important ideas in the passage. Some sentences do not belong in the summary because they express ideas that are not presented in the passage or are minor ideas in the passage. **This question is worth 2 points.**

Scientists such as Milankovitch have long tried to explain the glaciations of the Pleistocene Epoch.

-
-
-

Answer Choices

(A) Scientists previously believed that dust produced by volcanic eruptions blocked out the sun's solar energy and led to a rapid cooling of the planet, resulting in glaciations.

(B) Milankovitch furthered claims by James Croll that cyclical changes in Earth's orbit led to environmental changes that allowed Pleistocene Glaciations to occur.

(C) Milankovitch used variations in Earth's orbit, which bring it closer to the sun, and the wobble and tilt of its axis to determine that at certain times Earth's seasons are milder, making glaciations more likely.

(D) Milankovitch lacked the scientific knowledge and tools to test his theory, so it remained unconfirmed for more than fifty years.

(E) The theory proposed by Milankovitch showed that the Earth has undergone a period of glaciation every 40,000 years since the end of the Pleistocene Epoch.

(F) Modern scientists believe that Milankovitch Cycles do not cause glaciations, but they coincide with another factor that lowers overall temperatures and together they cause them.

11. What can be inferred from paragraph 1 about calendars?

    (A) They evolved from earlier systems that involved memorizing celestial occurrences.
    (B) They were developed because moon phases were unreliable time markers.
    (C) They were initially used to predict the upcoming seasonal changes.
    (D) They allowed people to keep track of past events for the first time.

12. According to paragraph 2, which of the following is NOT true about early calendars based upon lunar and solar data?

    (A) They were based on actual observations of the sun and moon.
    (B) They contained errors due to misunderstandings of the lunisolar cycle.
    (C) They could be thrown off by the weather.
    (D) They were only accurate in the location where they were developed.

13. The term "inept" in the passage is closest in meaning to:

    (A) Dishonest
    (B) Unreasonable
    (C) Clumsy
    (D) Unskilled

14. Which of the sentences below best expresses the essential information in the highlighted sentence in the passage? Incorrect choices change the meaning in important ways or leave out essential information.

    (A) The reign of Julius Caesar was responsible for inaccuracies in the calendar because cycles of interluding wars were not aligned by the calendar year during his time, causing a disturbance with the natural world.
    (B) Intercalation cycle became a problem when people forgot to add days under the reign of Julius Caesars so that wars could throw off the annual calendar's synchronization with the natural world.
    (C) The calendar and natural world were out of an agreement under the rule of Julius Caesar on account of ongoing wars as the incorrect sequences for a time in the calendar were made out.
    (D) Many leaders, like Julius Caesar, felt that was more important than intercalations, so they refused to perform them, which led to widespread inaccuracies in the calendar.

The Making of Calendars

1   Even before the invention of the modern calendar, people were able to keep track of events in their lives using the phases of the moon and the seasons. In this way, one could explain that something would occur two days after the next full moon or that one was born 25 winters ago. This reliance upon the moon may seem quite rudimentary, but it also allowed them to count the days between the moons phases and the equinoxes (when the duration of the days and nights are approximately equal) and the solstices (the longest and shortest days of the year), which mark the traditional beginning of each of the seasons. As knowledge and understanding of these events increased, calendars as we now know them began to come together.

2   As these empirical lunar- and solar-based calendars became more popular, their flaws became more evident. [■] For one, they were extremely dependent upon the weather. [■] While it does not affect the actual movement of either of the celestial bodies, it can obscure them and cause inaccuracies in the calendar. [■] The calendars were also dependent upon the location, since the timing of the moon's phases and the solstices and equinoxes change over distances. [■] For instance, the timing of the rise of the new moon would be earlier in eastern locations. It may not even occur on the same day if the second observer is far enough west. This is also problematic for observers in extreme northern latitudes where the sun remains below the horizon for 4.5 months during winter and remains overhead for an equal amount of time in the summer.

3   Secondary problems arose due to the fact that the basic unit of the calendar, the day, does not evenly fit in the calendric concept of either the month or the year. Over time, this causes the calendar day to fall out of line with both the lunar and solar cycle. This basic inaccuracy

15. What can be inferred about intercalation during Julius Caesar's reign from paragraph 3?

(A) It was abandoned during the period because of the constant warfare.
(B) It was rendered unnecessary by the lengthening of the year.
(C) It caused great inaccuracies in the calendar of the time.
(D) It could not be done some years because of the changes in the lunisolar patterns.

16. According to paragraph 4, which of the following is NOT true about the new Julian calendar?

(A) It remained synchronized with lunisolar events better than previous calendars.
(B) It contained systematic intercalations that made their misapplication less likely.
(C) It became widely used across Europe and the Middle East.
(D) It made it easier to determine the dates of Eastern religious and cultural events.

17. According to paragraph 5, which of the following can be inferred regarding lunisolar calendars?

(A) The problems inherent in lunisolar calendars are very similar to those that exist in calendars based on calculations.
(B) They are less accurate than arithmetic calendars because their months all have 29 days.
(C) Inappropriate manipulation is more difficult with lunisolar calendars because they are self-syncing.
(D) The year is shorter under this system because of the lower number of days in each lunar cycle.

---

required that days or months be intercalated, or added to the calendar. Unfortunately, this process was overseen by government officials or holy men who could be corrupt, inept, or both. This problem came to a head during the reign of Julius Caesar, when the intercalation cycle was thrown off by war and were observed in some consecutive years and forgotten in others, causing the calendar year to fall out of sync. To solve this problem, the Julian calendar was introduced around 50 BCE and the Roman Empire's year was officially lengthened to 365.25 days.

4   The new Julian calendar could be easily calculated and remained better synchronized with the cycles of the sun and moon over time. This removed the chance for abuse by laying out a systematic method for intercalations. Surprisingly, calendars in the East and West diverged at this time. Those in the East, namely China and India, depended upon the exact timing of lunar and solar events, because of the importance of these in the society's religions and traditions. But those in the West and Middle East followed rigid arithmetical rules that kept them synchronized with the natural world without the need for constant observations and calculations of astronomical events.

5   Both lunisolar and arithmetic calendar systems still suffered from the problem mentioned earlier, the impossibility of the larger units of time to be divided evenly by the basic unit of measure, the day. Calendar's based on lunation, or the period between new moons, are inherently self-adjusting and will synchronize with the cycles, but arithmetical calendars will only remain synchronized on average. However, this does not mean that the lunar calendar is more accurate, because the cycles of the moon are still not easily divisible by days as each lunation takes approximately 29.53 days.

6   Today, all but a handful of countries have settled on the use of one civil arithmetically based calendar, the

18. Why does the author mention that "1700, 1800, and 1900 would be common (non-leap) years, but 2000 would be a leap year"?

(A) To help the reader understand that the Gregorian calendar adds leap years every 400 years.
(B) To clarify the intercalation system that was used under the Gregorian calendar.
(C) To show that most leap years occur in years that are divisible by 400.
(D) To provide an explanation of why the Gregorian calendar was adopted globally.

Gregorian calendar, which Pope Gregory XIII introduced in 1582. Under the Gregorian calendar, the problem with the uneven number of days in the year was solved through the use of leap years, which contain an extra day, every four years, except those that are divisible by 100, but not by 400. This means that 1700, 1800, and 1900 would be common (non-leap) years, but 2000 would be a leap year. This new calculation effectively brought the average length of the year to 365.2425 years, more in line with the actual time it takes for earth to revolve around the sun. The new calendar system also dropped 10 days to realign the yearly equinoxes, since the accumulated errors in the calendar over the previous 1000-1200 years had moved them forward by 10 days. This does not, however, mean that the Gregorian calendar is without its flaws. The system is estimated to have an error of one day every 3,300 years.

19. Look at the four squares [■] that indicate where the following sentence could be added to the passage.

This was not likely to cause problems in the desert regions of Egypt or Mesopotamia, but it could easily throw off the calendar in regions prone to large storm systems.

Where would the sentence best fit?

Click on a square [■] to add the sentence to the passage.

20. Directions: An introductory sentence for a brief summary of the passage is provided below. Complete the summary by selecting the THREE answer choices that express the most important ideas in the passage. Some sentences do not belong in the summary because they express ideas that are not presented in the passage or are minor ideas in the passage. **This question is worth 2 points.**

> **Since their invention, calendars have undergone a number of changes.**
>
> -
> -
> -

Answer Choices

(A) Prior to the invention of the modern calendar, people relied upon lunar and solar events in order to keep track of time.

(B) Because months and years are not evenly divided by days, early calendars required periodic adjustments to stay in line with lunisolar events.

(C) Intercalations, or adding days to the calendar, were used to synchronize lunar and solar events such as the full moon and the solstices.

(D) The Julian calendar was particularly problematic, because its intercalations were decided by politicians and priest who could be inept or corrupt.

(E) After the introduction of arithmetical calendars, the types of calendars used in different regions split as Eastern societies held on to the lunisolar calendar and Western societies followed the newer form.

(F) The present-day Gregorian calendar more accurately accounts for time differences using an arithmetical formula and is the most widely used calendar in the modern era.

21. Why does the author mention that Suleyman "took this to another level"?

(A) To indicate that Suleyman declared himself above his predecessors.
(B) To give the reader an impression of how Suleyman expanded the Ottoman territory.
(C) To indicate that Suleyman was wiser, more savage and a better administrator than earlier sultans.
(D) To show that the sultans after Suleyman were quite ineffective comparatively.

22. Which of the sentences below best expresses the essential information in the highlighted sentence in the passage? Incorrect choices change the meaning in important ways or leave out essential information.

(A) To govern the massive empire and to concern its mighty neighbors, military strength and growth became secondary and administration and foreign affairs arose its importance.
(B) Once it reached its largest size by leading armies into battle, the Ottoman Empire shifted its focus to managing the vast territory and defending itself from its neighbors.
(C) Because of the increasingly powerful nations that encircled the Ottoman Empire, its armies were tasked with administrative and diplomatic duties, instead of expansion.
(D) Ottoman Sultan's gave up expanding the Empire because they though that proper governance was more important that increasing territory, which made their neighbors more powerful.

23. According to paragraph 2, which of the following is NOT a reason for the decline of the Ottoman Empire?

(A) Internal changes within the empire
(B) Incompetent leadership
(C) Expansion into hostile territory
(D) The increasing power of European countries

The Decline of the Ottoman Empire

1   After its foundation in 1299, Anatolia's Ottoman Empire enjoyed extensive success and expansion under a series of very powerful leaders. Many agree that the empire reached its apex during the reign of its 10th, and longest serving, sultan, Suleyman the Magnificent. Although his predecessors were known for their wisdom, savage conquests, and administrative ability, Suleyman took this to another level and expanded the empire into central Europe, Persia, to the southern coast of the Arabian Peninsula, and across northern Africa. This gave the Ottoman Empire near total hegemony over Mediterranean trade and this period is considered the "Golden Age" of the empire. Unfortunately, Suleyman's successors lacked initiative and competence and under their leadership the empire suffered. Luckily, some of these incompetent leaders relied upon "viziers," or executive officers, who kept the empire in tact for nearly 400 more years.

2   Unfortunately for the Ottoman Sultans, the end of the 16th century marked not only the end of their territorial expansion and regional dominance, but also the beginning of the empire's slow decline. However, this cannot be completely blamed on the incompetence of the leaders. Changes within the empire and the rise of other regional powers, especially those neighboring the empire's European territories, both played a large role in the decline of the empire. These changes caused the role of the Sultan to change dramatically. Instead of being dedicated to leading armies into battle for territorial expansion, bureaucracy and diplomacy became more important to the Sultans so that they could administer the enormous territory of the empire and to deal with its increasingly powerful neighbors. In addition, large army units needed to be permanently positioned, funded, and controlled to fend off the Russian's in the Crimea, the Persians to the west, and other powers around the Mediterranean region.

Questions 24 ~ 26 of 30

24. What can be inferred about Ottoman leadership from paragraph 3?

(A) The emperor became less important than the Grand Viziers.
(B) If earlier powerful Sultans ruled during this time they would have needed to rely upon advisors as well.
(C) Sultans delegated administrative duties to the Vizier so they could focus on the military.
(D) The defeat by the Habsburgs led to the rise of the Vizier and the Divan.

25. The term "de facto" in the passage is closest in meaning to:

(A) Figurative
(B) Effective
(C) Fictional
(D) Essential

26. According to paragraph 4, which of the following is NOT true about the imperial harem in the Ottoman Empire?

(A) It was a powerful group of women connected to the Sultan.
(B) It could be used by the Grand Vizier to increase his power.
(C) It included the female members of the Sultan's family.
(D) It ran the Ottoman Empire during the time of the inept Sultans.

3 These were new roles that would have been difficult for the empire's early successful sultans, but with the lack of skill and experience of those who followed Suleyman the empire fell behind in military and administrative technology and suffered military defeats, such as the empire's loss to Phillip II of Spain and the stunning loss to the Habsburgs and the Holy League when attempting to capture Vienna. The large territory covered too much area for one person to rule over, forcing the sultans to reply upon the Divan, a group of trusted officers, ministers, and a Grand Vizier. These Viziers and their bureaucratic organizations became very powerful in their own right and later sultans, such as Selim II, began to rely upon them to administer the territory.

4 Surprisingly, another group that greatly reduced the power of the Sultan and increased that of the Grand Vizier was the imperial harem. These women, who were connected to the sultan, became more powerful as time went on. Since the Grand Vizier was generally related to the sultan through marriage, he was directly connected to the harem as well and could use these powerful women to increase his power and affect the Sultan. This was probably most easily accomplished through the most powerful member of the harem, the Valide Sultan, who was the Sultan's mother. These women were so powerful that for over 130 years during the 16th and 17th century they were de facto rulers of the empire due to their influence over their sons, many of who were minors.

5 All of these factors weakened the power of the sultan, and in turn the empire, but perhaps the most detrimental change was the major shift in trade from the Mediterranean to the Atlantic Ocean. The European "Age of Discovery" sent explorers and settlers around the world looking for both colonies and trade routes. When they began sailing around Africa to reach the markets of Asia, they effectively removed the Ottoman Empire's great source of wealth and power, it's ability to act as an

27. According to paragraph 5, which of the following is true regarding the Age of Discovery?

   (A) It was begun by the Ottomans in the Atlantic Ocean.
   (B) It allowed traders to bypass Ottoman outposts when trading.
   (C) It made it more expensive for Ottoman goods to reach new markets.
   (D) It caused the rapid collapse of the Ottoman Empire.

28. According to paragraph 6, which of the following can be inferred regarding the collapse of the Ottoman Empire?

   (A) 200 years of wars caused instability in the empire and it collapsed in the late 1800s.
   (B) The Ottoman Empire remained a powerful, modern nation until it was eventually destroyed by war.
   (C) Large scale illnesses weakened the empire and allowed it to easily be overtaken during World War I.
   (D) Its collapse was brought about by joining the losing side during World War I.

intermediary for trade between Europe and Asia. This was not an immediate loss, but over time it became more detrimental for the Ottoman Empire and without strong leadership and a fractured social and political structure, the empire began to decline more rapidly.

6 Over the next 200 years, these problems continued and the Ottoman Empire continued to fade from its previous position as a world super power. By the late 1800s the empire had lost so much territory and was so dominated by European powers that Tsar Nicholas referred to it as the "sick man of Europe," which needed help from its neighbors. Unfortunately, for the empire, this help would not come fast enough. [■] Despite a push for modernization that moved it in a more secular direction to match the European powers, the empire was doomed. [■] After a series of revolutions and wars, the empire joined WWI's Central Powers. [■] This decision ultimately resulted in the final dissolution of the empire. [■]

29. Look at the four squares [■] that indicate where the following sentence could be added to the passage.

Its territories were divided up by the European powers and the modern country of Turkey rose to replace it on the Anatolian peninsula.

Where would the sentence best fit?

Click on a square [■] to add the sentence to the passage.

30. Directions: An introductory sentence for a brief summary of the passage is provided below. Complete the summary by selecting the THREE answer choices that express the most important ideas in the passage. Some sentences do not belong in the summary because they express ideas that are not presented in the passage or are minor ideas in the passage. **This question is worth 2 points.**

After the rule of Suleyman the Magnificent, the Ottoman Empire began a slow decline until it was eventually dissolved.

-
-
-

Answer Choices

(A) Under Suleyman the Magnificent, the Ottoman Empire reached its peak and was in control of most of the Middle East and the Mediterranean coastal region.

(B) Early expansion left the empire too large to be efficiently ruled, especially by the later inept rulers, and the reliance upon advisors led to a weakening of the Sultan and the Empire.

(C) Economic changes brought about by the exploration of the increasingly powerful European nations caused a great weakening of the Empire and its economy.

(D) Defeat at the hands of Spain, the Hapsburgs, and the Holy league caused the Empire to shrink as it lost important territories, such as Vienna.

(E) By the late 1800s the Empire had weakened greatly and it was eventually absorbed by the Central Powers during World War I.

(F) A series of conflict greatly reduced the empire's territory, but its decision to participate in WWI led to its eventual total destruction.

You have seen all of the questions in this part of the Reading section. You have time left to review.
As long as there is time remaining, you can check your work.

Click on **Return** to go back to the previous question.
Click on **Review** to see the review screen for this section.
Click on **Continue** to go on.
Once you leave this part of the Reading section, you WILL NOT be able to return to it.

이제 Reading Section이 끝났습니다.
Continue 버튼을 누르면 다시 문제를 검토할 수 없으므로 유의하세요.

시험보고 난 후 ... 체크 리스트 및 스터디 디렉션

USHER iBT TOEFL INTERMEDIATE TEST REA

1. 내가 불안했던 문제만 재빨리 다시 보고, 불안하게 만든, 즉, 경쟁 초이스를 찾아서 왜 내가 헷갈려 했는지를 파악할 수 있는 메모를 해두시기 바랍니다. 시간이 지나거나, 다른 학생들과 스터디를 하면서는, 자신이 왜 낚였는지 이유조차 기억나지 않아 본인의 실수 패턴 파악이 힘들기 때문입니다.

2. 답지를 확인하지 않고 스터디를 하시기 바랍니다. (그래서, 답지를 문제지 뒤에 붙이지 않고, 본 설명만을 붙여 두었습니다.) 답지를 확인하지 않고 하는 이유는 답을 아는 순간, 답에 끼워 맞춰 설명하려 하고, 이런 태도는 본인 실력 항상에 도움이 되지 않기 때문입니다. 스터디 팀원들간에 대략적인 답을 맞춰보면, 대부분 답안의 윤곽이 나옵니다. 이럴 경우, 이견이 있는 문제만 집중적으로 다루고, 나머지는 개인별로 처리하시기 바랍니다.

3. 문제를 끝까지 다 풀었나요? 네 □ / 아니오 □
   다 못 풀었다면, 전체 30 문제 중 푼 문제는? _____ / 30
   시간 모자란 것에 대해서는 크게 신경 쓰지 않아도 됩니다. 무엇보다 중요한 것은 정확도 입니다.
   우선은 풀은 문제를 맞출 확률을 높이고, 그 다음 시간을 걱정해도 늦지 않습니다.

4. 어려웠다고 느껴지는 지문은? 과학 □ / 예술 □ / 인문 □ / 인물 □ / 사회 □
   과학지문이 현격히 다른 분야보다 많지만, 그래도, 공부하다 보면 자신만 어려워하는 분야는 모두 각각입니다. 그러므로, 혹시 배경지식 부분에서 필요한 것이 있다면, usherin.usher.co.kr 에 방문하셔서, 공부가 안될 때, 배경지식 부분을 쉬엄쉬엄 들러서 봐 두시길 바랍니다. 쉬엄쉬엄 입니다. 누가 뭐래도 실력있는 사람은 배경지식이 큰 영향을 끼치지는 않습니다.

5. (채점 후) 문제 풀 때 어렵다고 느낀 지문이 틀리는 개수와 쉬웠다고 느껴졌던 지문의 틀린 개수차이가 있나요? 예 □ / 아니오 □
   어느 순간 깨닫게 됩니다. 내가 잘 아는 내용이 나와서 자신 있게 푸나, 내가 모르는 지문이 나와서 겁먹고 푸나, 틀린 개수가 큰 차이가 나지 않는 것을…. 혹시 그걸 못 느끼신다면, 더욱더 열심히 하시기 바랍니다. ^^

6. 틀린 문제의 번호를 다음의 문제 유형 분석표와 비교해서 파악해 두시기 바랍니다.
   문제 유형을 파악해서 주의하는 것은, 누가 뭐래도 실력이 기본은 받쳐 줄 때 얘기입니다. 문제 푸는 스킬이나, 기타 문제 유형 파악 등은 기본적으로 본문 내용을 이해하고, 해석이 웬만큼 될 때 얘기입니다. 만약, 너무 힘들다면 너무 스트레스 받지 말고, 그냥 '아~ 그렇구나' 정도로 넘기셔도 됩니다. 단, 본문 이해는 절대 양보해서는 안됩니다.

문제 유형 분석표

TEST 2-1	TEST 2-2	TEST 2-3
01 Inference	11 Inference	21 Purpose
02 Vocabulary	12 Fact	22 Highlight
03 Purpose	13 Vocabulary	23 Fact
04 Highlight	14 Highlight	24 Inference
05 Fact	15 Fact	25 Vocabulary
06 Fact	16 Fact	26 Fact
07 Inference	17 Inference	27 Fact
08 Fact	18 Purpose	28 Inference
09 Insertion	19 Insertion	29 Insertion
10 Summary	20 Summary	30 Summary

USHER
iBT TOEFL
INTERMEDIATE READING 02
TEST 3

테스트 전 확인사항

실전에 유용한 독해 전략(44p)을 숙지하였습니다. ○
화장실은 미리 다녀왔습니다. ○
휴대폰의 전원을 껐습니다. ○
노트테이킹 할 종이와 연필을 준비하였습니다. ○
시간을 체크할 시계를 준비하였습니다. ○
목표점수(30개 중____개)를 정하였습니다. ○
시험 시작 시간은 ____시 ____분이며,
종료 시간은 54분 뒤인 ____시 ____분입니다. ○
시험 중 이동해야 할 방해요소가 있는지 체크하였습니다. ○
시험 중 이동하지 않습니다.

Sentinel Behavior in Meerkats

1. → Meerkats are small, mongoose-like mammals that live in the Kalahari Desert of Southern Africa. Being primarily insectivores, they feed on beetles and scorpions buried underground, which they locate using their strong sense of smell. Unfortunately, when the meerkat lowers its head to search out prey under grasses, it limits its own range of sight by a significant amount. As a result they are extremely vulnerable to airborne predators such as hawks and owls. To ensure that they can reach the safety of their bolt-holes before being snatched up by birds, meerkats forage in packs and partake in what is known as sentinel behavior. As the term suggests, one meerkat in the group acts as a sentinel and does not look for food like the rest, but rather stands upright on its hind legs to gain a wider field of view with which it scans the surrounding area for possible predators and other threats to the community. When it senses danger approaching, the sentinel barks loudly to warn the others of the danger. Many scientists questioned this phenomenon because the revealing stance and loud vocalization were thought to expose the meerkat to an increased risk of predation.

폭 넓게 - 일단 버릇 들이는게 중요!

32. According to paragraph 1, why was sentinel behavior thought to be disadvantageous?

(A) It warns the predator of where the meerkat group is.
(B) It allows the meerkat to sense danger and warn the group.
(C) It helps the predators locate the sentinel meerkat.
(D) It encourages the predator to prey on meerkats over other species.

스터디 자료들을 미리 수집해 둘것!

시험 중 체크 사항

❶ "?"표시하기 : 본문 읽으며, 궁금한 곳에 "?" 표시를 합니다.
　　　　　　　문제를 풀면서도 질문 거리에는 "?" 표시를 해둡니다.
❷ 문제 핵심에 동그라미 : 문제가 물어보는 게 무엇인지, 문제 핵심에 동그라미 표시를 합니다.
❸ 답근거 날리기 : 문제를 풀 때 선택지가 틀린 이유 단어로, 간결하게 날립니다.
❹ 경쟁 문장 표시 : 4개의 선택지 중에 정답과 경쟁하는 마지막 1개의 선택지를 표시 해둡니다. 무조건 1개여야 합니다.

Reading Section Directions

This section measures your ability to understand academic passages in English.

Most questions are worth 1 point but the last question in each set is worth more than 1 point. The directions indicate how many points you may receive.

Some passages include a word or phrase that is underlined in blue. Click on the word or phrase to see a definition or an explanation.

Within each test, you can go to the next questions by clicking **Next**. You may skip questions and go back to them later. If you want to return to previous questions, click on **Back**. You can click on **Review** at any time and the review screen will show you which questions you have answered and which you have not answered. From this reviewscreen, you may go directly to any questions you have already seen in the Reading section.

You may now begin the Reading section. In the section you will read 3 passages. You will have **54 minutes** to read the passages and answer thequestions.

Click on **Continue** to go on.

Next 버튼을 이용하여 다음 문제로 이동하고 **Back** 버튼을 이용하여 이전문제로 이동할 수 있습니다. 문제에 답을 하지 않더라도 다음 문제로 이동할 수 있으며, **Review** 버튼을 이용하여 각 문제별로 답을 체크했는지의 여부를 확인할 수 있습니다.
이번 테스트에서는 세 지문을 읽게 됩니다. **54분** 동안 지문을 읽고 문제에 답을 하세요.

01. Why does the author mention "selective pressures, genetic drift, and mutations"?

(A) To show how populations become isolated from one another.
(B) To explain how populations diverge after a geographic separation.
(C) To give examples of alternative evolutionary processes.
(D) To point out some of the reasons that isolated populations avoid interbreeding.

02. The term "towering" in the passage is closest in meaning to:

(A) Transient
(B) Newly formed
(C) Lofty
(D) Preeminent

03. According to paragraph 2, which of the following is NOT a cause of allopatric speciation?

(A) The movement of tectonic plates that rearranged Earth's landmasses.
(B) An earthquake wiping out an entire population.
(C) The formation of new mountain ranges.
(D) The appearance of a land bridge between two landmasses.

04. What can be inferred about geographical barriers from paragraph 3?

(A) Small physical barriers can cause speciation just as easily as large ones.
(B) Geographic barriers arise when niches go unfilled in ecosystems.
(C) Animals that can fly are unaffected by the development of physical geographical barriers.
(D) River changes are the cause of most geographical barriers in the natural world.

Geographic Isolation of Species

1 One of the most popular definitions of the word species was provided by renowned evolutionary biologist Ernest Mayr, who described a species as a population with the ability to interbreed, which does not interbreed with other such populations. Today, we are unsure of exactly how many species exist in the world, but we have learned of several ways that new species develop. One of the major discoveries has been that the most common method of speciation, called allopatric or geographic speciation, occurs when a population becomes geographically separated. When the two species are separated, they can no longer interbreed. This allows the two populations to follow separate evolutionary courses due to different selective pressures, genetic drift, and mutations within the isolated populations.

2 It may seem illogical that one population could be split into two or more by geography, but there are actually several methods through which this can occur. A quick look at Earth's topography will give several clues as to how this can occur. The first things one notices is that the continents separated by oceans, but knowing about continental drift tells us that these were not always in their current positions. This movement caused populations to be separated. Further, the rise of towering mountain ranges can also divide populations when they become too much of an obstacle for a population to cross. The formation of the Isthmus of Panama would have had the same effect when it formed 3 million years ago. Before this time, populations of organisms swam freely between the Caribbean Sea and the Pacific Ocean, but as the landmass developed it became a barrier to this and the populations were effectively divided between the two great bodies of water.

3 It may seem that these geographical barriers must be quite formidable to cause speciation, but the size of the

05. Which of the sentences below best expresses the essential information in the highlighted sentence in the passage? Incorrect choices change the meaning in important ways or leave out essential information.

Geographic separation does not necessarily cause speciation, but it creates the opportunity for it when a gene pool changes enough to form a reproductive barrier between the two parts of the population

(A) Genetic changes can cause a reproductive barrier within a population that leads them to separate geographically when the opportunity arises and brings about the evolution of new species.

(B) Speciation is brought about by geographic separation because reproductive barriers arise when genetic changes occur in a population that has had the chance to interbreed.

(C) The division of a population by geography does not cause the formation of new species; rather it allows the two genetic groups to diverge enough that interbreeding becomes impossible.

(D) Genetic changes arise due to reproductive barriers that disallow the breeding of two species that are located within a close proximity to one another, leading to the creation of a new population.

06. According to paragraph 4, which of the following can be inferred regarding the Galapagos Islands?

(A) The islands are filled with animal species that were previously found on the South American mainland.

(B) Geographic separation is required for speciation, as can be seen in Galapagos.

(C) A small isolated population is more likely to go through speciation than larger one with relatively unchanged gene pool.

(D) The organisms that live in the Galapagos do not travel between the islands.

required barrier depends upon the population in question. Animals like birds can easily cross mountain ranges, rivers and large distances, so speciation in bird populations requires rather large barriers. Animals that cannot fly require much smaller barriers to split the populations. This can be seen when a river changes course and small animal populations that cannot swim are divided. An example of this occurred when the Grand Canyon formed and the population of antelope squirrels was separated. Despite being only a few miles apart, the antelope squirrel population evolved into two separate species, the white-tailed antelope squirrel north of the canyon and the Harris' antelope squirrel in the deserts south of the canyon.

4 Geographic separation does not necessarily cause speciation, but it creates the opportunity for it when a gene pool changes enough to form a reproductive barrier between the two parts of the population. Interestingly, this is much more likely in a small isolated population than it is in larger populations because their genetic pools can undergo considerable change. This can be seen in the remote Galapagos Islands, which are over 900 Km from the nearest landmass. In 2 million years, a relatively short period in geographical terms, organisms from the South American mainland reached the islands and colonized them.

5 The distance of the Galapagos from the mainland, but the relatively close proximity of the islands to one another, allows them to serve as an outdoor evolutionary laboratory. Marine volcanism formed the archipelago's 18 main islands, which were eventually colonized by organisms that floated there along oceanic currents or winds and founded new populations on the islands. Some were even brought there by other organisms, such as seeds that were carried in the guts, fur and feathers of animals that made their way to the islands.

07. According to paragraph 5, which of the following is NOT an example of a way that new species arrived in the Galapagos Islands?

(A) Floating over the ocean
(B) Being blown there by winds
(C) Other organisms carry them
(D) Volcanic eruptions placed them there

08. According to paragraph 6, which of the following is true regarding the different finch species found in the Galapagos Islands?

(A) They all evolved from the initial colonizers that arrived from South America.
(B) They were created by the interbreeding of different finch species on the islands.
(C) They live on separate islands because of competition over food sources.
(D) They were introduced to the islands by Charles Darwin.

6   Today, due to the founder effect, the descendants of these original colonizers have evolved into a variety of species, most of which are unique to the island. The 13 finch species that Charles Darwin discovered on the island are a prime example of this. Research has shown that they descended from the same early colonizers, yet they have differing feeding habits and beak types. This likely occurred because the small population that colonized the island underwent genetic changes that set them apart. This continued when some of these individuals somehow found their way to one of the other islands and founded a second new population. As these populations filled niches in the ecosystem and became reliant upon a particular type of food, their bodies became adapted to it. [■] This led to differences in the shapes of beaks of the various types of finches. [■] Eventually, these isolated populations developed an affinity for only their own population and began breeding with only their own kind. [■] This effectively set them apart as separate species. [■]

09. Look at the four squares [■] that indicate where the following sentence could be added to the passage.

Today, each island has distinct species, with some of them having up to 10 separate finch species.

Where would the sentence best fit?

Click on a square [■] to add the sentence to the passage.

10. Directions: An introductory sentence for a brief summary of the passage is provided below. Complete the summary by selecting the THREE answer choices that express the most important ideas in the passage. Some sentences do not belong in the summary because they express ideas that are not presented in the passage or are minor ideas in the passage. **This question is worth 2 points.**

Allopatric speciation occurs when geographic isolation causes the development of new species.

-
-
-

Answer Choices

(A) The introduction of a geographic barrier that divides a population allows the two smaller populations to evolve separately and can eventually lead to two discrete species.

(B) Geographic isolation does not cause speciation on its own, but it sets the scene for evolutionary processes that can lead to major differences between the two populations.

(C) The size of the barrier required to divide and isolate a population is dependent upon the size of the organisms and the number of individuals involved.

(D) Continental drift after the split-up of Pangaea separated early landmasses and allowed different species to evolve from early species.

(E) The Galapagos Islands acts as a natural evolutionary laboratory due to the large number of islands and the many species that inhabit them.

(F) The evolution of a multitude of finch species on the different Galapagos islands from the original founding population occurred because of their isolation.

The Empire of Alexander the Great

1 Despite their centuries long fight against Persian domination, the Classical Greek city-states were not unified in any meaningful way. In fact, squabbling and infighting for power between the city-states marked the period, with power switching between them at different times. By the end of the Classical Period, Philip II of Macedon, in northern Greece, began an expansion of his territory, conquering the other city-states and uniting them under his Macedonian rule. However, this expansion would eventually seem trivial when compared to the expansion that was accomplished by his son, Alexander III, who ascended the throne in 336 BCE upon his assassination. This brash new king, who was only 20 years old at the time, would continue his father's planned invasion of the Persian Empire and eventually control a larger empire than any ruler before him, leading to great changes in the regions he conquered.

2 Within two years of taking the throne, Alexander had begun his campaign of international expansion and by 331 BCE the Macedonian ruler had overtaken the Persian Empire in the Levant, including the ancient city of Babylon, and had established a foothold in Egypt as well. After consolidating this great empire, he continued eastward and reached as far east as modern-day India. The great extent of this empire, along with the strong central control that was exerted by Alexander, caused a great number of changes in the movement of goods, capital and people throughout the empire. The removal of trade barriers and movement restrictions, as well as interconnected markets, made it easier for people to travel and trade with one another, and allowed Greek artisans and traders to seek their fortunes in a greatly expanded region. This expansion of trade and territory had several important consequences for both Classical Greece and the regions conquered in its name.

---

11. What can be inferred from paragraph 1 about Philip II's expansion of Macedonian territory?

(A) He was unable to successfully take over the Persian territories.
(B) He expanded the territory to make Macedon less susceptible to Persian control.
(C) He united the Greek city-states and Persian territory to increase his power.
(D) He created the largest empire that the world had ever known.

12. According to paragraph 2, which of the following is NOT true regarding Greece under Alexander the Great?

(A) It overtook the territory formerly controlled by the Persians.
(B) It expanded its territory as far east as India.
(C) It became the largest power in the Western Mediterranean region.
(D) It experienced increased trade and movement due to the unification of new territories.

13. According to paragraph 3, which of the following is true about the new cities in Alexander the Great's empire?

(A) Intellectual leaders rather than military generals ruled them.
(B) They were built around central libraries.
(C) Many Greek citizens settled in them because they were looking for Greek literature.
(D) They acted as sources of Greek culture and influence in the expanded territory.

14. What can be inferred about urban centers in Greece from paragraph 4?

(A) Their populations increased greatly after the expansion of the empire.
(B) The demise of the city-state led to greater expansion of the empire.
(C) Urban centers on the Greek mainland fell apart as citizens moved into the new territory.
(D) Their specialization allowed Greece to expand its trade network.

15. Which of the sentences below best expresses the essential information in the highlighted sentence in the passage? Incorrect choices change the meaning in important ways or leave out essential information.

(A) Although the Greeks previously relied upon their super-humanoid gods for help and prosperity their faith changed as the territorial grew and eastern ways of thinking had taken hold.
(B) The Eastern Greek religions were greatly changed by the new philosophies that were brought about by Alexander the Great's expansion of the empire and caused the citizens to change their impression of the gods.
(C) After the expansion of the Greek city-state, citizens prayed to human-like gods for good luck on important dates and for protection, so that as they expanded eastern religions and philosophy changed the previous beliefs.
(D) The Greek religion had a great impact on eastern philosophy and religion as they brought their ideas about human-like gods, who helped the citizenry and passed on good luck, as the empire expanded eastward.

16. Why does the author mention "Socrates had previously been executed"?

(A) To emphasize that the imperial expansion had the greatest influence on change in Greek's previous beliefs.
(B) To give an indication of the flourishment of his new philosophy in Greece.
(C) To exemplify the type of new philosophies that came from the East.
(D) To insinuate that expansion is not the only cause for changing their belief.

3 [■] One of the most obvious of these changes in the newly unified empire was the expansion of Greek culture and influence. [■] This occurred because Alexander founded at least 70 new urban centers, many of them named after himself, not so much for military control as for cultural expansion. [■] One of the most important ways that this was done was through the propagation of Greek literature and language through the establishment of Greek libraries, such as those established in Antioch (modern-day Turkey) and Alexandria, Egypt, which was the largest and most significant library in the ancient world. [■]

4 Another major change caused by the empire's expansion was the demise of the Greek city-state. Prior to the imperial period the Greek city-states were sparsely populated and centered around the agoras, marketplaces where the population came together to discuss the important issues of society and make decisions in person. Greek philosophers such as Plato and Aristotle, who had been the teenaged Alexander's tutor, felt that this form of government required a small population (less than 5,000) in order to insure that all citizens knew one another and could share their knowledge to make the best decisions. Further, prior to expansion these city-states lacked specialization, which allowed citizens to engage in various civil and personal activities. After trade and commerce developed across the empire citizens had to develop specializations, which brought about professionalism. This meant that the small populations and "jack-of-all-trades" nature of the city-states' residents were no longer sufficient and Greek cities changed dramatically.

5 Imperial expansion also brought the Greeks into contact with eastern philosophy and religion, which affected their previous belief in human-like gods with superhuman powers who could be counted on to intercede on behalf of the city-states citizens and provided protection and good luck during life's milestones. However, these beliefs had

17. The term "intertwining" in the passage is closest in meaning to:

(A) Untangling
(B) Comparing
(C) Connecting
(D) Destroying

18. According to paragraph 6, which of the following can be inferred regarding the influence of the period?

(A) Alexander's rapid expansion of the Greek territory caused his rule to be known as the Hellenistic Period.
(B) Greek philosophy and advances expanded beyond the territory due to the influence of the large empire.
(C) The advances made during the Hellenistic period were a result of the interactions the Greeks had with other cultures in Asia, Europe and Africa.
(D) The influence of the Greeks allowed other cultures to make great strides in arts, literature and governance.

begun to wane even before Alexander's time as Greek's no longer seemed interested in only serving the city-state. In fact, the Athenian philosopher Socrates had previously been executed for suggesting a new morality based upon personal conscience rather than the traditional gods. This new philosophy, however, did not take the place of religion, but instead made the Classical Greeks receptive to new ideas that allowed the religions of the Middle East to mix with Greek philosophy. This new combined system spread across the world after Alexander's death in 323 BCE, forever intertwining the cultures of Greece and the Levant.

6 This dramatic territorial expansion had such a profound effect on the world that Alexander's death ushered in what is known as the Hellenistic period in Greek history, when its influence was at its peak in Europe, Africa, and Asia. During this period the Greeks made great strides in art, literature, architecture, mathematics, governance, philosophy, and science. Without the influence of Alexander the Great's territorial expansion, these advances may have remained confined to the borders of Classical Greece.

19. Look at the four squares [■] that indicate where the following sentence could be added to the passage.

The new cities were meant to turn the "barbaric" subjects into civilized subjects of the empire.

Where would the sentence best fit?

Click on a square [■] to add the sentence to the passage.

20. Directions: An introductory sentence for a brief summary of the passage is provided below. Complete the summary by selecting the THREE answer choices that express the most important ideas in the passage. Some sentences do not belong in the summary because they express ideas that are not presented in the passage or are minor ideas in the passage. **This question is worth 2 points.**

> **Alexander the Great's territorial expansion had great consequences for Classical Greece and the conquered lands**
>
> •
> •
> •

Answer Choices

(A) The vast territorial expansion removed barriers to trade and movement that allowed people to cover longer distances and trade in interconnected markets through the empire.

(B) The increased trade and commerce of the larger empire led to a need for specialization and larger urban populations, which marked the end of the classical Greek city-state.

(C) Alexander expanded Greek territory from his home region of Macedon by overtaking the Persian Empire and continuing eastward towards India.

(D) Expansion of the empire allowed an interchange of ideas that spread Greek culture, while causing changes in Greek philosophy and religion in the motherland.

(E) Eventually, the religions from the eastern section of the empire supplanted the traditional Greek religion based on human-like gods with superhuman abilities.

(F) The expansion of Alexander's empire increased the number of Greek citizens and allowed them to make many strides in science and math.

Early Maize Cultivation in the American Southwest

1 The North American continent has been blessed with vast areas of arable land that allow extensive agricultural output; yet not all areas are conducive to farming. The American southwest is one of these areas. The region's extremely dry conditions and high temperatures make it unfavorable for most farming. In fact, the largest agricultural crop produced across the region today is hay, which is used to feed livestock. However, this was not always the case. It is believed that the climate was much more stable and less arid from around 2500 to 100 B.C.E. It was during this period that certain food crops were introduced to the area from northern Mexico. Around this time, the native inhabitants began farming crops such as beans, squash, and most importantly maize, which, although not highly productive, enjoyed an advantage over the others, its production was very predictable.

2 Early inhabitants practiced hunting and gathering, which was particularly risky due to their reliance upon weather patterns, such as rainfall and sunlight. Although the populations were generally low and could sustain themselves this way, they may sometimes have grown larger and had trouble doing so. [■] This would be particularly true during the leaner times before the spring rains. [■] The coincidence of larger populations and less available food stock may have been the impetus for the inhabitants to begin growing reliable crops such as maize. [■] Despite its low yield, growing such a crop would have allowed them to have greater control over their food supply even if it did not fully satisfy the populations' nutritional needs. [■]

3 Researchers performing radiocarbon dating on maize cobs and seeds believe their introduction occurred between 2000-1500 B.C.E. and then spread to other areas. While maize eventually becomes the most well

---

21. Which of the sentences below best expresses the essential information in the highlighted sentence in the passage? Incorrect choices change the meaning in important ways or leave out essential information.

(A) Nearly assured crop yields gave an edge over the other tribes that existed during the contemporary period, despite its relatively low productivity.
(B) Southwestern tribes began planting crops like beans and squash to make up for the predictably low yields that maize plants returned at the time.
(C) Squash, beans and maize had a major benefit over other farmed food sources in that their harvests, although small, were very predictable over time.
(D) Because crops were predictable, they gave the native farmers an advantage in times when the others were not productive of the plants they farmed.

22. What can be inferred from paragraph 1 about the American southwest?

(A) It is the major livestock-producing region of the United States.
(B) The region's inhabitants have less livestock diversity due to the environment
(C) It has undergone a major climate change over the past two millennia.
(D) Early inhabitants of the area were the first farmers on the North American continent.

23. According to paragraph 2, which of the following is NOT true about early inhabitants of the American southwest?

(A) They were traditionally hunters and gatherers.
(B) Maize made up the majority of their diets.
(C) Their populations were not very large.
(D) The weather controlled their ability to provide for themselves.

24. What can be inferred about the introduction of maize from paragraph 3?

   (A) Maize's spread to the other areas didn't play a part in the southwest people.
   (B) Had it not been for beans and legumes, Maize would become the most well known crops.
   (C) Beans and legumes were concerned with the success of maize crops.
   (D) It was the first time a new plant species had been planted in the southwest.

25. The term "fruitful" in the passage is closest in meaning to:

   (A) Hardy
   (B) Valuable
   (C) Productive
   (D) Impotent

26. According to paragraph 4, which of the following is NOT true about chapalote?

   (A) It was the first maize species to be purposefully cultivated in the American southwest.
   (B) It needs little water to produce an edible product.
   (C) It remains the most popular species of maize in the United States.
   (D) It was crossbred to form hybrids with even more advantageous characteristics.

27. According to paragraph 5, how did early inhabitants of the American southwest guarantee they would have enough food?

   (A) By developing maize that could be grown in regions with lower temperatures.
   (B) Selecting areas where the soil was able to drain water more effectively.
   (C) Bringing water to areas like the canyon mouths.
   (D) Planting crops in multiple locations.

known of these, the others played great roles not only in the diet of the southwestern people, but also in the success of their maize crops. Beans and legumes were especially important during this time, because they replenish the nitrogen that maize depletes from the soil. By planting these crops together, early farmers were able to ensure that their soil stayed fertile enough to produce crops year after year.

4 The first maize species successfully introduced to the region from northern Mexico was most likely a small, brown kernelled variety called chapalote. This species was important because it matures quickly and requires little irrigation after its initial planting, so it is highly drought resistant. Eventually this species was hybridized with an indigenous grass, teosinte, to produce a more fruitful species with more kernel rows and larger cobs. It is believed that the regions inhabitants continued to crossbreed maize species until they came up with the more productive maiz de ocho. This is likely the result of using selection to produce a maize variety with larger kernels for grinding and an earlier flowering season, since growing seasons are highly unpredictable in the region. The short growing season of maiz de ocho and its adaptability to assorted climates made it particularly valuable to the region's inhabitants.

5 This hybridization was particularly important because maize eventually became a staple across the Americas, including in places that pushed the boundaries of its production. By selective breeding of different varieties of maize, early farmers were able to develop varieties that could be planted in regions with poor soil, short growing seasons, and adverse weather. In fact, the maiz de ocho variety allowed maize production to spread from the arid southwest to regions as far north as Canada, which has temperatures too low for most earlier species to survive. This attention to maize cultivation allowed the local inhabitants to become more adept at farming. They

28. Why does the author mention that "tribes continued to lead nomadic lives for nearly 1000 years"?

(A) To help the reader understand how long it took before maize was introduced to the region.
(B) To show that hunting and gathering were much more important than farming for early inhabitants of the southwestern United States.
(C) To explain how maize production expanded from the American southwest to other regions of the continent.
(D) To reinforce the notion that maize production did not have an immediate effect on the lifestyles of the region's inhabitants.

learned to favor soil that held water better and received adequate sunlight. They also realized that the flood plains and canyon mouths contained better soil because of the water that they were exposed to. However, one of the most important farming skills they developed was irrigation. This allowed them to farm in more locations, which ensured their crops even if one area experienced a poor growing season.

6 Surprisingly, the introduction of maize and the early farming attempts did not spark a great shift in the regions' inhabitants' lifestyles. Since early maize was rather unproductive and required little work, it was planted casually. In fact, most of the area tribes continued to lead nomadic lives for nearly 1000 years after maize was introduced north of the Rio Grande. This could also be attributed to the fact that maize is not a complete grain and lacks certain amino acids. It could only become a staple product when consumed alongside other agricultural products. Luckily, two of those were introduced around the same time, squash and beans.

29. Look at the four squares [■] that indicate where the following sentence could be added to the passage.

It could be said that planting crops did not turn the hunters and gatherers into farmers, but rather allowed them to be better at foraging because they had a supplemental food supply.

Where would the sentence best fit?

Click on a square [■] to add the sentence to the passage.

30. Directions: An introductory sentence for a brief summary of the passage is provided below. Complete the summary by selecting the THREE answer choices that express the most important ideas in the passage. Some sentences do not belong in the summary because they express ideas that are not presented in the passage or are minor ideas in the passage. **This question is worth 2 points.**

The introduction of maize into the American southwest between 2000 BCE and 1500 BCE spurred the regions agricultural development.

-
-
-

Answer Choices

(A) The climate of the American southwest from 2500 BCE to 100 BCE was much more stable than it is now and had more rainfall.

(B) Due to the region's erratic weather patterns reliance upon farming was risky, so the native tribes continued their hunting and gathering activities as well.

(C) Maize allowed it easier for the larger tribes of the region to feed themselves as their populations increased since it supplemented their previous methods of food acquisition.

(D) Maiz de ocho was introduced to the southwestern region from Mexico and eventually hybridized to form more tolerant maize that could be grown in other regions.

(E) Hybridization made maize more drought resistant, productive, and quicker to bloom, however it still lacked an essential nutrient, which could be attained through other agricultural products.

(F) The region's inhabitants became more adept at farming and developed techniques that increased their yield, as maize became an important part of their diets.

You have seen all of the questions in this part of the Reading section. You have time left to review.
As long as there is time remaining, you can check your work.

Click on **Return** to go back to the previous question.
Click on **Review** to see the review screen for this section.
Click on **Continue** to go on.
Once you leave this part of the Reading section, you WILL NOT be able to return to it.

이제 Reading Section이 끝났습니다.
Continue 버튼을 누르면 다시 문제를 검토할 수 없으므로 유의하세요.

시험보고 난 후 ... 체크 리스트 및 스터디 디렉션

1. 내가 불안했던 문제만 재빨리 다시 보고, 불안하게 만든, 즉, 경쟁 초이스를 찾아서 왜 내가 헷갈려 했는지를 파악할 수 있는 메모를 해두시기 바랍니다. 시간이 지나거나, 다른 학생들과 스터디를 하면서는, 자신이 왜 낚였는지 이유조차 기억나지 않아 본인의 실수 패턴 파악이 힘들기 때문입니다.

2. 답지를 확인하지 않고 스터디를 하시기 바랍니다. (그래서, 답지를 문제지 뒤에 붙이지 않고, 본 설명만을 붙여 두었습니다.) 답지를 확인하지 않고 하는 이유는 답을 아는 순간, 답에 끼워 맞춰 설명하려 하고, 이런 태도는 본인 실력 향상에 도움이 되지 않기 때문입니다. 스터디 팀원들간에 대략적인 답을 맞춰보면, 대부분 답안의 윤곽이 나옵니다. 이럴 경우, 이견이 있는 문제만 집중적으로 다루고, 나머지는 개인별로 처리하시기 바랍니다.

3. 문제를 끝까지 다 풀었나요? 네 □ / 아니오 □
   다 못 풀었다면, 전체 30 문제 중 푼 문제는? _____ / 30
   시간 모자란 것에 대해서는 크게 신경 쓰지 않아도 됩니다. 무엇보다 중요한 것은 정확도 입니다.
   우선은 풀은 문제를 맞출 확률을 높이고, 그 다음 시간을 걱정해도 늦지 않습니다.

4. 어려웠다고 느껴지는 지문은? 과학 □ / 예술 □ / 인문 □ / 인물 □ / 사회 □
   과학지문이 현격히 다른 분야보다 많지만, 그래도, 공부하다 보면 자신만 어려워하는 분야는 모두 각각입니다. 그러므로, 혹시 배경 지식 부분에서 필요한 것이 있다면, usherin.usher.co.kr 에 방문하셔서, 공부가 안될 때, 배경지식 부분을 쉬엄쉬엄 들러서 봐 두시길 바랍니다. 쉬엄쉬엄 입니다. 누가 뭐래도 실력있는 사람은 배경지식이 큰 영향을 끼치지는 않습니다.

5. (채점 후) 문제 풀 때 어렵다고 느낀 지문이 틀리는 개수와 쉬웠다고 느껴졌던 지문의 틀린 개수차이가 있나요? 예 □ / 아니오 □
   어느 순간 깨닫게 됩니다. 내가 잘 아는 내용이 나와서 자신 있게 푸나, 내가 모르는 지문이 나와서 겁먹고 푸나, 틀린 개수가 큰 차이가 나지 않는 것을…. 혹시 그걸 못 느끼신다면, 더욱더 열심히 하시기 바랍니다. ^^

6. 틀린 문제의 번호를 다음의 문제 유형 분석표와 비교해서 파악해 두시기 바랍니다.
   문제 유형을 파악해서 주의하는 것은, 누가 뭐래도 실력이 기본은 받쳐 줄 때 얘기입니다. 문제 푸는 스킬이나, 기타 문제 유형 파악 등은 기본적으로 본문 내용을 이해하고, 해석이 웬만큼 될 때 얘기입니다. 만약, 너무 힘들다면 너무 스트레스 받지 말고, 그냥 '아~ 그렇구나' 정도로 넘기셔도 됩니다. 단, 본문 이해는 절대 양보해서는 안됩니다.

문제 유형 분석표

TEST 3-1	TEST 3-2	TEST 3-3
01 Purpose	11 Fact	21 Fact
02 Vocabulary	12 Fact	22 Highlight
03 Fact	13 Fact	23 Fact
04 Inference	14 Fact	24 Fact
05 Highlight	15 Highlight	25 Vocabulary
06 Inference	16 Purpose	26 Fact
07 Fact	17 Vocabulary	27 Fact
08 Fact	18 Fact	28 Purpose
09 Insertion	19 Insertion	29 Insertion
10 Summary	20 Summary	30 Summary

USHER
iBT TOEFL
INTERMEDIATE READING 02
TEST 4

테스트 전 확인사항

실전에 유용한 독해 전략(44p)을 숙지하였습니다. ○
화장실은 미리 다녀왔습니다. ○
휴대폰의 전원을 껐습니다. ○
노트테이킹 할 종이와 연필을 준비하였습니다. ○
시간을 체크할 시계를 준비하였습니다. ○
목표점수(30개 중 ____개)를 정하였습니다. ○
시험 시작 시간은 ____ 시 ____ 분이며,
종료 시간은 54분 뒤인 ____시 ____분입니다. ○
시험 중 이동해야 할 방해요소가 있는지 체크하였습니다. ○
시험 중 이동하지 않습니다.

Sentinel Behavior in Meerkats

1. → Meerkats are small, mongoose-like mammals that live in the Kalahari Desert of Southern Africa. Being primarily insectivores, they feed on beetles and scorpions buried underground, which they locate using their strong sense of smell. Unfortunately, when the meerkat lowers its head to search out prey under grasses, it limits its own range of sight by a significant amount. As a result they are extremely vulnerable to airborne predators such as hawks and owls. To ensure that they can reach the safety of their bolt-holes before being snatched up by birds, meerkats forage in packs and partake in what is known as sentinel behavior. As the term suggests, one meerkat in the group acts as a sentinel and does not look for food like the rest, but rather stands upright on its hind legs to gain a wider field of view with which it scans the surrounding area for possible predators and other threats to the community. When it senses danger approaching, the sentinel barks loudly to warn the others of the danger. Many scientists questioned this phenomenon because the revealing stance and loud vocalization were thought to expose the meerkat to an increased risk of predation.

폭 넓게 - 일단 버릇 들이는게 중요!

32 According to paragraph 1, why was sentinel behavior thought to be disadvantageous?

(A) It warns the predator of where the meerkat group is.
(B) It allows the meerkat to sense danger and warn the group.
(C) It helps the predators locate the sentinel meerkat.
(D) It encourages the predator to prey on meerkats over other species.

스터디 자료들 미리 수집해 둘것!

시험 중 체크 사항

❶ "?"표시하기 : 본문 읽으며, 궁금한 곳에 "?" 표시를 합니다.
　　　　　　　　문제를 풀면서도 질문 거리에는 "?" 표시를 해둡니다.
❷ 문제 핵심에 동그라미 : 문제가 물어보는 게 무엇인지, 문제 핵심에 동그라미 표시를 합니다.
❸ 답근거 날리기 : 문제를 풀 때 선택지가 틀린 이유 단어로, 간결하게 날립니다.
❹ 경쟁 문장 표시 : 4개의 선택지 중에 정답과 경쟁하는 마지막 1개의 선택지를 표시 해둡니다. 무조건 1개여야 합니다.

Reading Section Directions

This section measures your ability to understand academic passages in English.

Most questions are worth 1 point but the last question in each set is worth more than 1 point. The directions indicate how many points you may receive.

Some passages include a word or phrase that is underlined in blue. Click on the word or phrase to see a definition or an explanation.

Within each test, you can go to the next questions by clicking **Next**. You may skip questions and go back to them later. If you want to return to previous questions, click on **Back**. You can click on **Review** at any time and the review screen will show you which questions you have answered and which you have not answered. From this reviewscreen, you may go directly to any questions you have already seen in the Reading section.

You may now begin the Reading section. In the section you will read 3 passages. You will have **54 minutes** to read the passages and answer thequestions.

Click on **Continue** to go on.

Next 버튼을 이용하여 다음 문제로 이동하고 **Back** 버튼을 이용하여 이전문제로 이동할 수 있습니다. 문제에 답을 하지 않더라도 다음 문제로 이동할 수 있으며, **Review** 버튼을 이용하여 각 문제별로 답을 체크했는지의 여부를 확인할 수 있습니다.
이번 테스트에서는 세 지문을 읽게 됩니다. 54분 동안 지문을 읽고 문제에 답을 하세요.

Temperature Regulation in Marine Organisms

1 [■] For most organisms maintaining thermal homeostasis, or keeping the body temperature within a certain range, is necessary for proper metabolic functioning. [■] If the internal temperature of these organisms leaves the preferred range, which differs based on the species, for extended periods, enzyme degradation and tissue/organ destruction may occur, which can make it difficult or impossible for their bodies to properly function. [■] This makes it extremely important that these organisms find some way to maintain their temperature within these ranges, especially in marine environments. [■]

2 Most organisms that do this can be classified in one of two categories. The first of these, the homeotherms, can be thought of as thermoregulators, since they maintain a near constant temperature regardless of ambient temperatures. This group includes mammals and birds, both of which have developed specialized features and functions to harness heat released through the metabolic process to maintain their relatively high average temperatures of 34-40°C. Poikilotherms, such as reptiles, amphibians, and most fish, on the other hand, can be considered thermoconformers, since their body temperatures are dependent upon the ambient temperature. Having a body temperature that fluctuates with the external temperature does not, however, mean that these organisms are protected from temperature changes. However, higher temperatures generally produce higher metabolic rates. This means that they must find ways to maintain their temperatures within a certain range. This is done in a host of ways such as moving, finding areas with appropriate temperatures or basking in the sun's warming rays.

---

01. Which of the sentences below best expresses the essential information in the highlighted sentence in the passage? Incorrect choices change the meaning in important ways or leave out essential information.

(A) Animals must ensure that their bodies' enzymes and tissues remain within a specific range to ensure that their internal temperatures do not fluctuate too wildly that it destroys themselves.

(B) Species must be in the range of the average internal temperatures, which makes it impossible for their bodies to adapt to the temperatures when it is out of specific ranges, causing malfunction.

(C) When the body temperatures change too drastically, many species cannot function properly because their enzymes, organs, and tissues are designed to function only with a certain range.

(D) Proper functioning can become unfeasible when temperatures of intramural species have become out of range, depending on its average range, causing internal damage by enzymes and tissues.

02. According to paragraph 2, which of the following is NOT true regarding poikilotherms?

(A) Their internal temperatures change very quickly and often.
(B) They maintain their temperature within certain ranges.
(C) Their metabolic rates are temperature dependent.
(D) They use external mechanisms for temperature control.

03. According to paragraph 3, which of the following is true regarding animals that display traits of both homeotherms and poikilotherms?

(A) Their metabolisms are not dependent upon their temperature.
(B) They are only found in marine environments.
(C) They can be warmer or cooler than their environments.
(D) They do not regulate their temperatures.

04. The term "peripheral" in the passage is closest in meaning to:

(A) Central
(B) Thinner
(C) Outlying
(D) Auxiliary

05. According to paragraph 4, which of the following can be inferred regarding air and water?

(A) Water is a better conductor of heat than air.
(B) Air and water can be used to maintain thermal homeostasis.
(C) Only air breathing species need to worry about lower water temperatures.
(D) Water reduces internal temperatures, while air increases them.

06. Which of the following is NOT mentioned as a means of maintaining body temperature in paragraph 5?

(A) Thick layers of subcutaneous fat.
(B) Dual-layered coats of fur that trap heat.
(C) Waterproof feathers over soft, warm down.
(D) Increased activity to create more heat than land animals.

07. Why does the author mention "fish, such as skipjack tuna"?

(A) To denote that some fish are actually mammals.
(B) To give an idea of the wide variety of species that use this method.
(C) To explain how countercurrent exchange systems work.
(D) To show that circulatory systems are common in various animal species.

3   Interestingly, not all animals fall into these two categories. Several species fall somewhere in the middle of the two. Some of the most well known examples of this are fast-swimming fish, such as the yellowfin tuna, which has an internal temperature that is several degrees warmer than the relatively cold seawater it inhabits. This occurs because they possess a heat retention mechanism that harnesses the heat produced by their muscular activity while swimming. Scientists believe this is necessary because of their reliance upon heat dependent biochemical reactions for their constant physical exertion. An entirely opposite example can be found in the intertidal zone. Some species in this area maintain their bodies at several degrees cooler than the ambient temperature by harnessing the powers of evaporation and circulation of bodily fluids. This allows them to live in areas where the shallow waters reach high temperatures due to the effects of the suns rays and reflection from the light colored substrate. By absorbing and losing heat directly to the air they are able to remain much cooler than non-living objects with corresponding sizes and shapes.

4   In marine environments, homeotherms have the most difficulty maintaining their internal body temperature, since most oceans average between 1.9 and 27°C. Exposure to these cold water temperatures can cause lower internal temperatures due to heat loss through the skin faster than in air. However, several other factors lead to lower temperatures. One of the biggest is the fact that these animals have closed circulatory systems that pump blood around the body, causing heat loss as it approaches the colder peripheral areas of the body. Further, the body's natural radiation of heat and respiration also lower the temperature, since the evaporation of water from the nasal cavities during exhalation has a natural cooling effect on their bodies.

5   Marine animals have developed an assortment of ways to counteract this heat loss. The most common way

08. What can be inferred about countercurrent circulation from paragraph 6?

(A) It maintains internal temperatures more than surface temperatures.
(B) It is the most common circulatory system in fish species.
(C) It allows more blood to be exchanged than would normally occur.
(D) It can also help cool marine species when the water becomes too hot.

is by developing a layer of insulation, but even this can take different forms. Most cetaceans, such as whales and porpoises, and seals build up a thick layer of fat under the skin, known as blubber. However, this does not work for smaller marine mammals such as sea otters. These nimble, weasel-like sea creatures do not store great fat reserves, but instead constantly preen and fluff their thick dual-layer fur. This allows the outer hairs to prevent water from reaching the softer undercoat and traps warm, dry air around the otter. This process is also used by marine birds, which have waterproof outer feathers covering softer down that traps air and body heat. These methods are enhanced by the fact that marine mammals have higher body temperatures than their terrestrial counterparts.

6 Interestingly, the circulatory systems of some marine species also help conserve body heat by acting as countercurrent heat exchangers. In species, like porpoises, the veins that return the used blood surround the arteries, which pump blood from the warm core. This allows the warmer arteries to heat the blood as it returns from relatively colder areas such as the skin surface and flippers, which are not protected by thick blubber layers. This reduces the amount of heat lost to the water and can even be found in some fish, such as skipjack tuna.

09. Look at the four squares [■] that indicate where the following sentence could be added to the passage.

In extreme cases this can lead to permanent damage, or even death, for the organism.

Where would the sentence best fit?

Click on a square [■] to add the sentence to the passage.

10. Directions: An introductory sentence for a brief summary of the passage is provided below. Complete the summary by selecting the THREE answer choices that express the most important ideas in the passage. Some sentences do not belong in the summary because they express ideas that are not presented in the passage or are minor ideas in the passage. **This question is worth 2 points.**

> **Maintaining body temperature within a certain range is important for many animal species, especially those in marine environments.**
>
> ・
> ・
> ・

Answer Choices

(A) Hometherms have near constant internal temperatures, while poikilotherms internal temperatures fluctuate depending on the environment; however, some species display aspects of both.

(B) Most animals have internal body temperatures that remain between 34 and 40°C, which allows them to survive in frigid oceanic waters.

(C) Animal species can be categorized into either homeotherms or poikilotherms depending on the way in which they can maintain thermal homeostasis.

(D) Marine homeotherms can easily lose their inner warmth due to respiration, circulation, and heat conduction by the cold waters of the marine environments.

(E) Most animals that live in water have developed adaptations such as layered feathers and fur, thick layers of fat, and specially adapted circulatory systems to prevent heat loss.

(F) Fast-swimming fish are able to cope with increased water temperatures because of the way in which their circulatory systems react to changing water temperatures.

The Upper Paleolithic Revolution

1 Around 35 to 40 KYA (thousands of years ago), there was a dramatic change in the archaeological record in Europe that marked the change from the Middle to Upper Paleolithic periods. During this transition, anatomically modern humans (AMH) replaced Neanderthal populations in Europe and brought about great changes in humanity. The rise of the AMH population can be seen through a dramatic increase in the use of tools and the invention of several purely human activities. The changes that occurred during the Upper Paleolithic era are so dramatic that they have been referred to as the Upper Paleolithic Revolution.

2 Archaeological finds in many areas across Europe have supported this revolutionary change. The new population used much more versatile stone implements and animal products, such as bone and antler, to produce much more advanced tools. [■] Barbed reindeer harpoons and spear throwers, known as atlatl, have been discovered in European caves indicating a great leap forward in the understanding of hunting, and even rudimentary concepts in physics, such as torque. [■] Interestingly, this also appears to be the period when humans developed art forms, such as figurative art. [■] However, swan bone pipes with worn finger holes similar to flutes and primitive tattooing kits have been found in other European archaeological sites, indicating that figurative cave art was not the AMH's only artistic endeavor. [■]

3 An interesting aspect of these discoveries is that they were all found in Europe, leading researchers to believe that the advances of early AMH were a purely European occurrence around 40 KYA that eventually spread elsewhere. However, the later discovery of decorated ochre and shell beads, as well as evidence of AMH's ability to fish, in South Africa's Blombos Cave dating to 77 KYA and contemporary bone tools found

---

11. What can be inferred from paragraph 1 about changes that occurred during the Upper Paleolithic?

(A) They were a result of the population of AMH that replaced the Neanderthal.
(B) They remain the most fundamental technological changes that have ever occurred.
(C) They caused the Neanderthal population to evolve into AMH.
(D) They allowed AMH to overpower the Neanderthal and conquer their territory.

12. Why does the author mention "rudimentary concepts in physics, such as torque"?

(A) To indicate that tools were not the only advances made by AMH in Europe.
(B) To give an example of the new fields of study initiated by AMH in Europe.
(C) To show a form of higher knowledge exemplified by the new tools found in Europe.
(D) To explain that the Upper Paleolithic Revolution also led to great strides in science.

13. According to paragraph 2, which of the following is NOT included amongst the archaeological finds from the Upper Paleolithic?

(A) Advanced tools
(B) Cave art
(C) Musical instruments
(D) Early tattoos

14. Which of the sentences below best expresses the essential information in the highlighted sentence in the passage? Incorrect choices change the meaning in important ways or leave out essential information.

(A) Many forms of artifacts that human activities evolved before the "revolution" was found in several sites in Africa, indicating that the "revolution" is all but an example of human behavioral evolution.
(B) Decoration of ochre and shells beads in the Blombos Cave and other African sites in 77 Kya, which indicated that the evolution of human behavior is simply the revolution.
(C) Artifacts from the Blombos Cave showed that many types of human activity had evolved before the "revolution" in Europe 77 KYA, such as decorative beads and evidence of fishing in Africa.
(D) Tools that predate the European "revolution" were found in various archaeological sites in Africa, corroborating that the African people were competent in making tools even before the Europeans.

15. What can be inferred about the tools found in Africa from paragraph 3?

(A) They were superior to the ones believed to be from the Upper Paleolithic Revolution.
(B) Early African populations could not have made them before Europeans visited.
(C) They were as advanced as those from the Upper Paleolithic Revolution.
(D) Modern researchers believe that they are from the Upper Paleolithic Revolution.

16. According to paragraph 4, which of the following is NOT true about the discovery of advanced tools in Africa?

(A) It contradicts the theory of the Upper Paleolithic Revolution in Europe.
(B) The tools were discovered before the Upper Paleolithic Revolution in Europe.
(C) The discoveries were ignored by, or unknown to, the Europeans who developed the Upper Paleolithic Revolution theory.
(D) The tools were likely the precursors for the tools attributed to the Upper Paleolithic Revolution in Europe.

in other African sites indicate that this "revolution" was simply an example of human behavioral evolution that had been occurring for much longer. This led researchers to question why the discovery of modern tools from this period were concentrated in Europe and whether the European discoveries were the start of a new form of human behavior, or if they were simply built upon earlier innovations in other parts of the world.

4 Anthropologists Sally McBrearty and Alison Brooks point to Eurocentric bias and disregard for the extent of the African archaeological record as the most likely causes for the discovery of more tools in Europe. They hold that evidence of more modern tools in Africa, such as blades and microlithic technology, higher geographic ranges, art, and long distance trade networks, predates its appearance in Europe by at least 10,000 years and can be found in archaeological sites separated by both geographical area and time frame, thus suggesting a natural evolution, rather than an immediate revolution such as in Europe. This indicates that AMH behavior was likely formed in Africa and exported to other regions. The myriad forms of early rock art found in Australia further support this idea. Since people arrived in Australia around 60 KYA and were isolated from the "revolution" in Europe 40 KYA, their rock art can be seen to show that creativity was already a part of human cognition when early AMH began migrating out of Africa around 70 KYA.

5 This type of scrutiny has caused theories of a sudden advent of modern behavior and tool making during an "Upper Paleolithic Revolution" in Europe to falter. The most logical reason for its supposed sudden occurrence would be, as McBrearty and Brooks pointed out, deficiencies in the archaeological record in Africa and other regions, while those in Europe are rather well preserved. It may simply turn out that artifacts elsewhere have been lost, or have yet to be found. This can be seen by the recent discovery of pierced shells dating from 43 KYA in Lebanon,

17. According to paragraph 5, which of the following is true regarding the Upper Paleolithic Revolution?

    (A) It is the best explanation for the discovery of advanced tools in other regions that date to this period.
    (B) Recent discoveries make it likely that it occurred in Lebanon and not Europe, as was previously thought.
    (C) It is the most likely explanation for gaps in the archaeological record in other regions that made European advances seem groundbreaking.
    (D) The Upper Paleolithic Revolution has been largely disproven by the discovery of advanced tools elsewhere.

18. According to paragraph 6, which of the following can be inferred about the role of climate change in the Upper Paleolithic Revolution?

    (A) Climate change caused great changes around the world, and forced early AMH to migrate to Europe, which had the world's most hospitable climate at the time.
    (B) Deglaciation of Europe caused people with contemporary tools of Africa to move to inhabitable lands of Europe, causing the sudden appearance of tools in the area.
    (C) Glaciation in Europe preserved the tools of the early AMH, causing it to be the source of most examples of advanced tools from the era.
    (D) The effect of the changing weather patterns caused early AMH to adapt to a new environment and forced them to develop new tools.

suggesting the modernization had occurred prior to the date of the "revolution," but went undetected until recently.

6 However, the presence of tools in other areas does not explain the sudden appearance of tools in the European archaeological record. One theory for this is climate change. Prior to the suggested dates of the Upper Paleolithic Revolution, Europe underwent a major climate change that caused the disappearance of the previous glaciers and an overall warming, which made the continent more hospitable for early AMH. This could have allowed a migration of early AMH to the previously uninhabited area. This sudden appearance of AMH in Europe would have led to an increase in more modern tools in the archaeological record, which could explain why they suddenly appeared around 35 KYA.

19. Look at the four squares [■] that indicate where the following sentence could be added to the passage.

The most famous of these are, doubtlessly, cave paintings, such as those found in the Lascaux caves outside Montignac, France.

Where would the sentence best fit?

Click on a square [■] to add the sentence to the passage.

20. Directions: An introductory sentence for a brief summary of the passage is provided below. Complete the summary by selecting the THREE answer choices that express the most important ideas in the passage. Some sentences do not belong in the summary because they express ideas that are not presented in the passage or are minor ideas in the passage. **This question is worth 2 points.**

> **Researchers have noted a great leap forward in human behavior and knowledge in Europe's archaeological record called the "Upper Paleolithic Revolution"**
>
> -
> -
> -

Answer Choices

(A) The Upper Paleolithic Revolution theory was formed when archaeologists found uses of tools more dramatic than any of the previous record.

(B) The tools found in Europe indicate great changes in human evolution, because they are the oldest tools that archaeologists have ever unearthed.

(C) Artifacts found in the Blombos Cave resembled those found at European archaeological sites allowing scientist to determine that they were created by AMH before they migrated.

(D) Anthropologists believe that the behavioral and technological changes found in Europe likely occurred elsewhere and made their way to Europe.

(E) Aboriginal Australian artwork indicates that the AMH in Europe were much more advanced than those who dispersed to other areas.

(F) Climate change allowed a migration to Europe after the ice age, which caused the sudden appearance of tools and art forms there.

Nineteenth-Century Theories of Mountain Formation

1   Due to several major misconceptions, our understanding of mountain formation is relatively new. As recently as the early 19th century, most geological findings were viewed as a series of catastrophic events that allowed geological knowledge to corroborate a short Earth history that corresponded to biblical narratives. However, during the 19th century, scientists began to offer other explanations for geological features, such as mountain formation. Unfortunately, most of the theories they developed were based upon the idea that Earth had been formed as a superheated mass and had steadily cooled through time. This led them to postulate that Earth's core must be shrinking as it cools, as most objects do. From this, they extrapolated that Earth's crust would be deformed by the shrinkage and mountains would form.

2   One of the first geologists to try to explain this was Eduard Suess. He explained that Earth's crust wrinkled as it contracted, just as a drying apple's peel does. His theory assumed that Earth's crust had begun as a single layer, but separated as the "wrinkles" formed. This led to great depressions that became ocean basins and higher areas that formed the continents. Further, he thought that continued contraction would lead to instability and the two features could alternate, meaning that oceans would become continental land and vice versa. Using this theory, he incorrectly postulated that the Alps had once been at the bottom of a massive ocean, but had risen and left the Mediterranean as its only remnant.

3   This alternation was an important point in his theory, because it helped to explain other geological features that scientists, even the great Leonardo da Vinci, had been unable to interpret, such as the discovery of marine fossils on dry land and the interspersed marine and terrestrial sediment found in the stratigraphic column. It also

---

21. What can be inferred from paragraph 1 about Earth's formation and composition?

(A) The theory that the super-heated core being gradually cooled since Earth's formation was proven inaccurate.
(B) Scientists have been unable to explain the formation of landmasses because they do not understand how Earth was formed.
(C) Earth was a much larger planet at the time of its formation due to the great heat that it contained before the cooling process started.
(D) Compared to 19th century, before that time, the Christian bible was the main source of scientific discovery and exploration.

22. According to paragraph 2, which of the following is NOT true regarding Suess's theory about differences in the Earth's crust?

(A) It was based on the contraction of Earth's core due to its gradual cooling over time.
(B) It attempted to explain the different geological features, such as ocean basins and mountains.
(C) It held that the geological features that we know today are permanent since contraction slows over time.
(D) It inaccurately explained the formation of both the Alps in Southern Europe and the nearby Mediterranean Sea.

23. Which of the sentences below best expresses the essential information in the highlighted sentence in the passage? Incorrect choices change the meaning in important ways or leave out essential information.

(A) The theory of alternation was developed to answer the questions posed by scientists, such as da Vinci, who questioned why terrestrial fossils were found in the stratigraphic column along with marine fossils.

(B) Leonardo da Vinci was unable to understand the presence of marine fossils in terrestrial regions before a theory of alteration was developed that explained why marine and terrestrial fossils are found in the same places.

(C) The discovery of marine fossils in terrestrial regions, and the appearance of the two types of fossils in one region was a mystery until the theory of land alteration definitively proved that the lands and seas shifted location over time.

(D) Finding fossils from sea life on dry land had confused scientists, such as Leonardo, for many years, but the theory or alternation helped to explain it along with other geological conundrums like the mix of land and sea fossils in the soil strata.

24. What can be inferred about Darwin's theory of evolution from paragraph 3?

(A) It was greatly influenced by the concept of contraction that Suess was working on.

(B) Although it was concerned mainly with the evolution of animals it also included theories about geological formation.

(C) Darwin developed the theory after Suess had announced his theory of mountain formation and landmass changes.

(D) It could have posed a great problem for Suess's theory if he had not included the interchangeability of oceanic/continental landmasses.

helped to explain a problem brought about by Darwin's contemporaneous theory of evolution. By the mid-1800s, scientists had noticed similar, or even identical, fossils in distant places, such as South America and Africa. Darwin's theory made this identical evolution of two distant species highly unlikely, but Suess countered this with the theory that changes in Earth's landmasses and oceans made it possible. He developed the theory of an ancient, giant landmass connected by land bridges that he referred to as Gondwanaland.

4   Ironically, acceptance of Suess's theory was geographically split; it gained a greater acceptance in Europe than in North America. On the other side of the Atlantic, geologists like James Dwight Dana developed their own explanations for mountain formation. Dana's theory, known as permanence, was based on the continents and oceans remaining as they are. He theorized that as Earth cooled and contracted, minerals with low melting points, like feldspar and quartz, solidified early on and those with higher melting points, like pyroxene and olivine, became solid later, thereby creating ocean basins. As the contraction continued it put immense pressures on Earth's surface, especially along the oceanic/continental boundaries, which caused the creation of the mountain ranges found along continental edges, such as those on the west coast of both North & South America.

5   [■] Dana's theory led fellow American geologist James Hall to theorize that subsidence, or sinking, of sediment from a former shallow sea formed the Appalachian Mountains. [■] Hall felt that these materials were produced by continental erosion and accumulated in linear troughs along the mountain's edge, called geosynclines. [■] As these troughs filled and began to subside, they became deeper and Earth's inner heat turned the sediment into stone. [■] Eventually, it was uplifted to form mountains. Dana slightly modified this theory to explain that sediment had not caused subsidence, but

25. According to paragraph 4, which of the following is NOT true about J.D. Dana's theory of permanence?

(A) Its acceptance in North America led it to overtake Suess's theory in Europe as well.
(B) It did not allow for changes in the location or position of the continents and oceans.
(C) It was based on the physical properties of the different components of Earth's interior.
(D) It attributed geological changes to the same basic force as Suess's theory.

26. According to paragraph 5, which of the following can be inferred regarding the theory of subsidence?

(A) Subsidence failed to gain widespread acceptance in the scientific community because it could only be applied to one mountain range.
(B) There was not enough evidence to prove the occurrence of subsidence in geosyncline troughs near the Appalachian mountains.
(C) Subsidence can be used to explain the composition of some mountains, but not their actual formation.
(D) Dana realized the importance of the subsidence theory and abandoned his previous theory to work on the new one.

27. Why does the author mention "unexplainable strata shortening and the theory of isostasy"?

(A) To offer two theories for the creation of mountains that were developed in the early 20th century.
(B) To give examples of two discoveries that allowed scientists to invalidate earlier theories about changes in Earth's crust and mountain formation.
(C) To show two new theories that were developed as a result of the discoveries made by scientists in the 19th century, such as Suess.
(D) To allow the reader to understand how earlier theories of mountain formation led to the development of the theory of continental drift.

28. The term "definitively" in the passage is closest in meaning to:

(A) Conclusively
(B) Accurately
(C) Conditionally
(D) Belatedly

was actually the result of it. Unfortunately for both, their explanations of how shallow-water sediment built up did nothing to accurately explain how these thick layers of sediment were uplifted.

6 By the early 1900s, the flaws in these theories became evident. Through the discovery of certain features in the earth's crust, such as unexplainable strata shortening and the theory of isostasy that explained that the crust and its mountains were actually floating on Earth's mantle, and not held in place on their own, scientists were able to disprove Suess's theory of oceanic/continental changeability. However, the most important discovery was radiogenic heating, which definitively negated the theory of contraction, and all theories based on it. All of this caused scientists to look for more accurate explanations of mountain formation. The best of these was Alfred Wegener's theory of continental drift. Unfortunately, this theory was not accepted until the existence of tectonic plates was confirmed nearly 50 years later. Today, we know that the actions of these tectonic plates created Earth's various mountain ranges.

29. Look at the four squares [■] that indicate where the following sentence could be added to the passage.

> **He based this idea on the fact that the mountains were made up of layers of shallow-water sedimentary rocks several thousands of feet thick.**

Where would the sentence best fit?

Click on a square [■] to add the sentence to the passage.

30. Directions: An introductory sentence for a brief summary of the passage is provided below. Complete the summary by selecting the THREE answer choices that express the most important ideas in the passage. Some sentences do not belong in the summary because they express ideas that are not presented in the passage or are minor ideas in the passage. **This question is worth 2 points.**

> **Nineteenth Century Scientists Developed Contrasting Theories Regarding the Formation of Mountains.**
>
> •
>
> •
>
> •

Answer Choices

(A) Nineteenth century geologists found that after the radiogenic heating that caused Earth's formation ceased, the planet gradually cooled and as it did the size shrunk.

(B) In Europe, Eduard Suess developed the most accepted theories of mountain formation which said that Earth's crust buckled in various ways as Earth cooled after its formation.

(C) Eduard Suess discovered that the Alps had once been located under a nearby sea, which eventually shrunk and formed the Mediterranean Basin.

(D) Darwin's theory of evolution caused problems for geologists because similar fossils were found in various distant locations around the world.

(E) American geologists disputed the changeability of oceanic/continental lands and explained mountain formation through mineral differences and sediment accretion.

(F) Discoveries in the twentieth century disproved the contraction theory upon which the earlier theories had been based and revealed the more accurate theory of plate tectonics.

You have seen all of the questions in this part of the Reading section. You have time left to review.

As long as there is time remaining, you can check your work.

Click on **Return** to go back to the previous question.

Click on **Review** to see the review screen for this section.

Click on **Continue** to go on.

Once you leave this part of the Reading section, you WILL NOT be able to return to it.

이제 Reading Section이 끝났습니다.
Continue 버튼을 누르면 다시 문제를 검토할 수 없으므로 유의하세요.

시험보고 난 후 ... 체크 리스트 및 스터디 디렉션

1. 내가 불안했던 문제만 재빨리 다시 보고, 불안하게 만든, 즉, 경쟁 초이스를 찾아서 왜 내가 헷갈려 했는지를 파악할 수 있는 메모를 해두시기 바랍니다. 시간이 지나거나, 다른 학생들과 스터디를 하면서는, 자신이 왜 낚였는지 이유조차 기억나지 않아 본인의 실수 패턴 파악이 힘들기 때문입니다.

2. 답지를 확인하지 않고 스터디를 하시기 바랍니다. (그래서, 답지를 문제지 뒤에 붙이지 않고, 본 설명만을 붙여 두었습니다.) 답지를 확인하지 않고 하는 이유는 답을 아는 순간, 답에 끼워 맞춰 설명하려 하고, 이런 태도는 본인 실력 항상에 도움이 되지 않기 때문입니다. 스터디 팀원들간에 대략적인 답을 맞춰보면, 대부분 답안의 윤곽이 나옵니다. 이럴 경우, 이견이 있는 문제만 집중적으로 다루고, 나머지는 개인별로 처리하시기 바랍니다.

3. 문제를 끝까지 다 풀었나요? 네 □ / 아니오 □
   다 못 풀었다면, 전체 30 문제 중 푼 문제는? _____ / 30
   시간 모자란 것에 대해서는 크게 신경 쓰지 않아도 됩니다. 무엇보다 중요한 것은 정확도 입니다.
   우선은 풀은 문제를 맞출 확률을 높이고, 그 다음 시간을 걱정해도 늦지 않습니다.

4. 어려웠다고 느껴지는 지문은? 과학 □ / 예술 □ / 인문 □ / 인물 □ / 사회 □
   과학지문이 현격히 다른 분야보다 많지만, 그래도, 공부하다 보면 자신만 어려워하는 분야는 모두 각각입니다. 그러므로, 혹시 배경지식 부분에서 필요한 것이 있다면, usherin.usher.co.kr 에 방문하셔서, 공부가 안될 때, 배경지식 부분을 쉬엄쉬엄 들러서 봐 두시길 바랍니다. 쉬엄쉬엄 입니다. 누가 뭐래도 실력있는 사람은 배경지식이 큰 영향을 끼치지는 않습니다.

5. (채점 후) 문제 풀 때 어렵다고 느낀 지문이 틀리는 개수와 쉬웠다고 느껴졌던 지문의 틀린 개수차이가 있나요? 예 □ / 아니오 □
   어느 순간 깨닫게 됩니다. 내가 잘 아는 내용이 나와서 자신 있게 푸나, 내가 모르는 지문이 나와서 겁먹고 푸나, 틀린 개수가 큰 차이가 나지 않는 것을…. 혹시 그걸 못 느끼신다면, 더욱더 열심히 하시기 바랍니다. ^^

6. 틀린 문제의 번호를 다음의 문제 유형 분석표와 비교해서 파악해 두시기 바랍니다.
   문제 유형을 파악해서 주의하는 것은, 누가 뭐래도 실력이 기본은 받쳐 줄 때 얘기입니다. 문제 푸는 스킬이나, 기타 문제 유형 파악 등은 기본적으로 본문 내용을 이해하고, 해석이 웬만큼 될 때 얘기입니다. 만약, 너무 힘들다면 너무 스트레스 받지 말고, 그냥 '아~ 그렇구나' 정도로 넘기셔도 됩니다. 단, 본문 이해는 절대 양보해서는 안됩니다.

문제 유형 분석표

TEST 4-1	TEST 4-2	TEST 4-3
01 Highlight	11 Inference	21 Inference
02 Fact	12 Purpose	22 Fact
03 Fact	13 Fact	23 Highlight
04 Vocabulary	14 Highlight	24 Inference
05 Inference	15 Inference	25 Fact
06 Fact	16 Fact	26 Inference
07 Purpose	17 Fact	27 Purpose
08 Fact	18 Inference	28 Vocabulary
09 Insertion	19 Insertion	29 Insertion
10 Summary	20 Summary	30 Summary

USHER

iBT TOEFL
INTERMEDIATE READING 02
TEST 5

테스트 전 확인사항

실전에 유용한 독해 전략(44p)을 숙지하였습니다.   ○

화장실은 미리 다녀왔습니다.   ○

휴대폰의 전원을 껐습니다.   ○

노트테이킹 할 종이와 연필을 준비하였습니다.   ○

시간을 체크할 시계를 준비하였습니다.   ○

목표점수(30개 중 ____개)를 정하였습니다.   ○

시험 시작 시간은 ____시 ____분이며,
종료 시간은 54분 뒤인 ____시 ____분입니다.   ○

시험 중 이동해야 할 방해요소가 있는지 체크하였습니다.   ○

시험 중 이동하지 않습니다.

Sentinel Behavior in Meerkats

1. → Meerkats are small, mongoose-like mammals that live in the Kalahari Desert of Southern Africa. Being primarily insectivores, they feed on beetles and scorpions buried underground, which they locate using their strong sense of smell. Unfortunately, when the meerkat lowers its head to search out prey under grasses, it limits its own range of sight by a significant amount. As a result they are extremely vulnerable to airborne predators such as hawks and owls. To ensure that they can reach the safety of their bolt-holes before being snatched up by birds, meerkats forage in packs and partake in what is known as sentinel behavior. As the term suggests, one meerkat in the group acts as a sentinel and does not look for food like the rest, but rather stands upright on its hind legs to gain a wider field of view with which it scans the surrounding area for possible predators and other threats to the community. When it senses danger approaching, the sentinel barks loudly to warn the others of the danger. Many scientists questioned this phenomenon because the revealing stance and loud vocalization were thought to expose the meerkat to an increased risk of predation.

폭 넓게 - 일단 버릇 들이는게 중요!

32 According to paragraph 1, why was sentinel behavior thought to be disadvantageous?

(A) It warns the predator of where the meerkat group is.
(B) It allows the meerkat to sense danger and warn the group.
(C) It helps the predators locate the sentinel meerkat.
(D) It encourages the predator to prey on meerkats over other species.

스터디 자료들을 미리 수집해 둘것!

시험 중 체크 사항

❶ "?" 표시하기 : 본문 읽으며, 궁금한 곳에 "?" 표시를 합니다.
　　문제를 풀면서도 질문 거리에는 "?" 표시를 해둡니다.
❷ 문제 핵심에 동그라미 : 문제가 물어보는 게 무엇인지, 문제 핵심에 동그라미
　　표시를 합니다.
❸ 답근거 날리기 : 문제를 풀 때 선택지가 틀린 이유 단어로, 간결하게 날립니다.
❹ 경쟁 문장 표시 : 4개의 선택지 중에 정답과 경쟁하는 마지막 1개의 선택지를
　　표시 해둡니다. 무조건 1개여야 합니다.

Reading Section Directions

This section measures your ability to understand academic passages in English.

Most questions are worth 1 point but the last question in each set is worth more than 1 point. The directions indicate how many points you may receive.

Some passages include a word or phrase that is underlined in blue. Click on the word or phrase to see a definition or an explanation.

Within each test, you can go to the next questions by clicking **Next**. You may skip questions and go back to them later. If you want to return to previous questions, click on **Back**. You can click on **Review** at any time and the review screen will show you which questions you have answered and which you have not answered. From this reviewscreen, you may go directly to any questions you have already seen in the Reading section.

You may now begin the Reading section. In the section you will read 3 passages. You will have **54 minutes** to read the passages and answer thequestions.

Click on **Continue** to go on.

Next 버튼을 이용하여 다음 문제로 이동하고 **Back** 버튼을 이용하여 이전문제로 이동할 수 있습니다. 문제에 답을 하지 않더라도 다음 문제로 이동할 수 있으며, **Review** 버튼을 이용하여 각 문제별로 답을 체크했는지의 여부를 확인할 수 있습니다.
이번 테스트에서는 세 지문을 읽게 됩니다. **54분** 동안 지문을 읽고 문제에 답을 하세요.

Colonial America and the Navigation Acts

1   Mercantilism swept across Europe in the sixteenth century. Under this system governments attempted to regulate and protect their economies by ensuring a positive balance of trade using high tariffs and protective import laws. This was especially true in the British Empire, which was threatened by the rising power of Dutch traders after the Eighty Years' War and the lifting of Spanish embargoes on trade with them. After this time, Dutch traders overwhelmed British trade on the Iberian Peninsula, around the Mediterranean Sea, and into the Levant; however, the most troubling development was their rising power in the British colonies, especially those in the New World. In order to protect its trade power, Parliament passed a series of trade laws known collectively as the Navigation Acts, which effectively controlled all imperial commerce.

2   One of the first of the Navigation Acts was the Navigation Ordinance of 1651. This new ordinance limited imports into the British Empire to those brought by British ships or those from the country in which the product had been manufactured. This severely limited Dutch imports, since they specialized in carrying products from other regions, and mainly exported locally made dairy products. As time went by, more of these types of acts were passed, further increasing restrictions on trade, which greatly affected the colonies. In fact, the passage of the Navigation Acts of 1660 and 1663, forced British colonies to export commodities, like sugar and tobacco, only to England aboard British-flagged vessels. They were not, however, all detrimental to the colonies. For instance, the Molasses Act of 1733 added an import tariff to molasses entering the colonies from outside the empire. This basically created a molasses monopoly for plantation owners in the British West Indies, since it was cheaper than that produced on French Caribbean islands. By the 1750s, the economic impact of these laws had become clear in the North American colonies.

---

01. Why does the author mention that the Dutch "mainly exported locally-made dairy products"?

(A) To show that Dutch products were everyday staple products required by the British.
(B) To give the reader an understanding of the weakness of the Dutch economy.
(C) To point out some products that the Dutch could export to the British Empire.
(D) To explain why the Navigation Acts were particularly detrimental to Dutch traders.

02. According to paragraph 2, which of the following is NOT true about the Navigation Acts?

(A) They effectively limited the import of products from outside the British Empire.
(B) They increased the central governments regulation of colonial trade systems.
(C) They encouraged more trade between colonies located far from Great Britain.
(D) They created monopolies for some products within the empire.

03. What can be inferred about the Navigation Acts' regulations on ships and their crews from paragraph 3?

(A) They were seen as a way of providing jobs to more British subjects in the colonies, where the economy was previously faltering.
(B) They inadvertently encouraged the use of slaves since they were considered British under the regulations.
(C) They led to a reduction in the export of products from the Empire, which caused a general downturn in the global economy.
(D) They established the northern colonies as economic powerhouses and greatly altered the population dispersion of early America.

04. The term "stipulation" in the passage is closest in meaning to:

(A) Implication
(B) Suggestion
(C) Condition
(D) Association

05. According to paragraph 4, which of the following is true regarding the enumeration of goods by the Navigation Acts?

(A) It caused the collapse of several important industries in the colonies.
(B) Most colonists became richer because of the higher prices that could be charged for the products.
(C) The regulations had only a negligible effect on trade in the enumerated goods due to concessions made by Parliament.
(D) It was meant to ensure that the Empire had sufficient supplies of products like tobacco and rice.

06. Which of the sentences below best expresses the essential information in the highlighted sentence in the passage? Incorrect choices change the meaning in important ways or leave out essential information.

(A) Parliament provided the colonists money to add additional elements to their economy that were eventually used to increase the raw materials that were exported to other countries that had signed the Navigation Acts.
(B) Over time, Parliament's payments to colonists for providing unprocessed materials that were previously imported from outside the empire under the Navigation Acts brought about more trade and expanded the colonial economy.
(C) The Navigation Acts were written to increase trade to the colonies and allow them to diversify their economy in such a way that would allow them to produce materials that were not available in the Empire at the time.
(D) The imperial government paid a premium for certain products, since the economic expansion of the Navigation Acts made raw materials, like lumber and metals, more expensive to import from rivals in the mercantile system.

3 The first major condition set forth by the Navigation Acts was the use of only British ships with crews that were 75% British, which included colonists and their slaves. This dramatically reduced imports and foreign shipping into the Empire, which allowed the British fleet to become the world's most powerful. Interestingly, it also encouraged shipbuilding in North America, since the colonists could freely trade within the Empire. This brought about the foundation of an American merchant marine fleet and, by the 1750s, one-third of the British fleet was composed of American ships. The concentration of the shipbuilding and export industries in the northeast led to rapid urbanization in the region as more warehouses, docks, and maintenance firms were built there. By the late 18th century, New York City and Philadelphia had become not only the two largest cities in the colonies, but also two of the busiest ports in the entire empire.

4 Another major stipulation of the Navigation Acts was that certain "enumerated goods," such as tobacco, rice, hides, sugar, and naval supplies, could only be shipped directly to England or Scotland, thus giving the British government control over the respective markets. [■] However, the Navigation Acts did not kill the trade in the enumerated goods. [■] In fact, Parliament blocked the import of foreign tobacco and rice, the two commodities most affected by the Acts. [■] This proved burdensome to British citizens, but helped the tobacco farmers. [■] They also agreed to refund import duties on products that were eventually shipped out of the empire, which accounted for 85% of the North American exports. These measures meant that tobacco and rice producers suffered a less than 3% reduction in their income.

5 Eventually, the Navigation Acts led to economic diversification and increased trade in the colonies, since Parliament paid subsidies to colonists for producing raw materials that would have otherwise have been imported from trade rivals, such as silk, iron, dye, and lumber.

07. According to paragraph 5, which of the following was NOT a change in the colonial economy brought about by the Navigation Acts?

(A) Colonial products were supplanted by those made by the British.
(B) Colonists increased their production of raw materials.
(C) Most American finished goods were produced through cottage industries.
(D) The production of ironworks became a major industry.

08. According to paragraph 6, which of the following can be inferred regarding the effects of the mercantile system in the North American colonies?

(A) Mercantilism greatly changed the lifestyle of the colonists.
(B) American colonists surpassed the British middle-class in terms of personal wealth.
(C) British manufactured goods replaced American made products causing America to develop a trade imbalance.
(D) Colonists became dependent upon the British Empire for finished goods.

They did not, however, allow the large-scale production of manufactured goods, such as clothing, that could affect Britain's large-scale factories. This meant that tailors, milliners, and other clothing manufacturers were restricted to producing their products in small shops. These restrictions allowed British clothing to be sold at much lower prices than locally manufactured goods. Surprisingly, the production of ironworks was not limited by the acts and it became a major industry.

6 The last major effect of these acts was that they created a protected market for lower-priced British goods. Demand for colonial materials remained high and led to prosperity in the colonies. This led to an increased demand for British manufactured goods, such as dishware, tea, and furniture, in addition to clothing. This allowed exports to the American colonies to rise from 5% of all British exports in 1700 to nearly 40% by 1760. The influx of these manufactured goods allowed middle-class colonists to live as comfortably as their British counterparts.

09. Look at the four squares [■] that indicate where the following sentence could be added to the passage.

Luckily for the colonists, the list of enumerated goods did not include livestock, lumber, rum, fish, or grains, which made up 60% of their exports.

Where would the sentence best fit?

Click on a square [■] to add the sentence to the passage.

10. Directions: An introductory sentence for a brief summary of the passage is provided below. Complete the summary by selecting the THREE answer choices that express the most important ideas in the passage. Some sentences do not belong in the summary because they express ideas that are not presented in the passage or are minor ideas in the passage. **This question is worth 2 points.**

> **The American colonies were greatly affected by the passage of the Navigation Acts by the British imperial government.**
>
> •
> •
> •

Answer Choices

(A) The American Parliament passed the Navigation Acts in an effort to control trade within the empire and reduce the influence of foreign powers under mercantilism.

(B) Restrictions in the legislation limited the type of goods colonists could export and the types of industries that could be set up in the colonies.

(C) The Navigation Acts required that the crew of all American ships be British citizens or their slaves.

(D) Because of the Molasses Act of 1733, American colonists could freely import cheap molasses from other British colonies in the West Indies.

(E) The colonial economy was diversified to meet the needs of the empire, since tariffs in the Navigation Acts made importing raw materials expensive and benefitted rivals.

(F) Colonists migrated to urban areas to support the growing shipping industry, while the standard of living increased as the colonists became wealthier from trade with Britain.

11. What can be inferred from paragraph 1 about the red-billed quelea?

(A) They are difficult to spot in their natural environment.
(B) They inhabit remote areas far from human settlements.
(C) They are rarely found outside of their native habitats.
(D) They are the largest species of animals in the world.

12. Which of the sentences below best expresses the essential information in the highlighted sentence in the passage? Incorrect choices change the meaning in important ways or leave out essential information.

(A) From watching Human's saving seeds for poor harvest seasons, the red-billed quelea developed behaviors to cope with famine of grass crops.
(B) The red-billed quelea learned to have special traits because of survival in a famine of cereals, as pre-historic humans hoarded grains of wheat and seeds.
(C) The red-billed quelea developed certain feeding traits that helped them avoid population reduction when crops were bad, much like prehistoric people.
(D) The red-billed quelea has evolved behaviors to allow them to deal with crop fluctuations in the way that prehistoric people stockpiled grain crops for food shortages.

The Most Common Bird on Earth

1 Most people outside of Africa have never heard of the red-billed quelea, but these small African birds are the most common bird species on Earth. A member of the weaver family, they live on the grasslands of sub-Saharan Africa in extremely large colonies that contain up to 30 million individuals. Conservative estimates put the total population of the birds across Africa at more than 1.5 billion breeding pairs, with some saying there may be up to 10 billion of the birds.

2 It may seem illogical that these small birds survive in such a harsh environment, but their extreme success is even more remarkable when one considers that they survive nearly entirely on the annual grasses in the region. Although researchers have noted that they eat some insects, mainly beetles, and a few non-grass seeds, these accounted for less than two percent of their overall diet. One might expect that this great dependence upon annual grasses would lead to regular reduction or extinction of the populations, but, much like early humans learned to hoard wheat and barley seeds to deal with lean times, the red-billed quelea have developed certain behaviors that help them cope with the feast or famine nature of the grass crops.

3 One of the most advantageous adaptations made by the red-billed quelea has been the development of variable annual weather-dependent cycles. [■] During the dry season the bird population must sustain itself with the seeds produced at the end of the rainy season. [■] To do this, they gorge themselves on seeds to gain enough wait to sustain them while they migrate to more productive places. [■] This must be done during the dry season, since monsoon rains cause the remaining seeds to germinate, thereby interrupting the food supply for weeks and instigating the move. [■] Luckily, this does not occur simultaneously across the entire savanna and dry seeds,

13. The term "forbidding" in the passage is closest in meaning to:

    (A) Off-limits
    (B) Barren
    (C) Volatile
    (D) Inhospitable

14. According to paragraph 3, which of the following is NOT an adaptation made by the red-billed quelea?

    (A) Stuffing themselves with seeds during the dry season.
    (B) Searching for regions where food sources are more abundant.
    (C) Establishing colonies 50-200 Km. from the grasslands.
    (D) Relocating to new areas when the rainy season begins.

15. According to paragraph 4, which of the following can be inferred regarding the red-billed quelea's brooding cycle?

    (A) Extended periods of favorable weather can cause large increases in the bird's population.
    (B) The queleas build their nests during the rainy season when they are waiting for seeds to ripen once again.
    (C) The male and female quelea forms a strong pair bond that lasts until the brooding season has ended.
    (D) When the dry season approaches, the adult quelea abandon their offspring who form a large, new colony.

16. Why does the author mention "feathered locusts"?

    (A) To describe a new pest species that competes with the red-billed quelea.
    (B) To indicate that the birds are thought of in a similar way to common pests.
    (C) To introduce a new species that evolved after the quelea became more common.
    (D) To explain that queleas have replaced the local insect populations through competition.

young grasses, and mature ripe grasses are available in different areas. To take advantage of this the quelea make 50-200 km migrations across the savannas, which allows them to survive in such a forbidding environment.

4   By the time the rains have germinated and fresh seeds become available, these early-rain migrations end and the quelea return to the previously abandoned areas. Access to these new seeds stimulates the population's males to weave ovoid grass and straw nests in acacia trees. The females who help them complete the nest and who then lay two to four eggs later join them. These colonies can cover up to 100 hectares with 500 nests in each acacia. With an average of 100,000 fledglings per hectare, up to 10 million offspring are produced by each successful colony. Surprisingly, the entire process of nest weaving, mating, brooding and fledging of the juveniles takes only six weeks, which is much shorter than in other birds, and is incredibly synchronized, as the eggs all hatch on the same day. However, this process is dependent upon weather patterns, as an earlier dry season can cause the quelea to abandon their colony, while an extended green season with abundant seed stock can allow them to produce multiple broods in the same region.

5   Since they rely upon seeds, these large colonies can cause problems for the region's farmers. As more and more grains are planted across sub-Saharan Africa, the birds have turned to the crops for nourishment. This has allowed their numbers to explode in the region. It is estimated that the population of these "feathered locusts" has increased by 10-100 times since the 1970s. With each bird eating its own weight in seeds per day this leaves fields within 30 Km. of the breeding sites highly susceptible. Researchers have estimated that flocks can consume upwards of 50 tons of seeds per day, which allows them to wipe out entire small crops and approximately 20% of the annual production of large commercial farms. Annual losses directly attributable

17. According to paragraph 5, which of the following is true regarding the large red-billed quelea populations?

(A) They threaten the region's farmers ability to produce staple crops.
(B) Local farmers are actively looking for ways to eradicate them.
(C) There are now fewer species of other animals to compete with them.
(D) Their populations have reached a plateau and are likely to decline.

18. According to paragraph 6, which of the following is NOT a reason for concern about the introduction of the red-billed quelea to Australia?

(A) Some regions of the country have climates similar to the quelea's native habitat.
(B) Australian farmers plant large amounts of grain crops that could support a quelea population.
(C) The quelea's large colonies would out-compete native species.
(D) Their import has been banned by the Australian national government.

to these small birds have been calculated at $70m, in a region where agricultural production is already in a precarious state.

6   Their easy adaptability and propensity to migrate in large flocks has made the red-billed quelea a cause for concern in areas where their introduction could allow them to become entrenched as an invasive species. One such region is Australia's northwestern state of Queensland, where the climate resembles the quelea's native habitat. Queensland's $440m annual cereal grain harvest would be devastated if large colonies of quelea became established. Colony establishment would also wreak havoc on the region's native species, such as the endangered Gouldian finch, which could not compete with such massive flocks. This has caused the Australian government to ban the import of the world's most common and destructive bird.

19. Look at the four squares [■] that indicate where the following sentence could be added to the passage.

Although the grasslands of sub-Saharan Africa do not undergo major temperature changes, the weather patterns do change dramatically as part of the year is characterized by arid conditions until the monsoon winds bring heavy rains to the region

Where would the sentence best fit?

Click on a square [■] to add the sentence to the passage.

20. Directions: An introductory sentence for a brief summary of the passage is provided below. Complete the summary by selecting the THREE answer choices that express the most important ideas in the passage. Some sentences do not belong in the summary because they express ideas that are not presented in the passage or are minor ideas in the passage. **This question is worth 2 points.**

The Tiny Seed-eating Red-billed Quelea is the World's Most Common Bird.

-
-
-

Answer Choices

(A) Populations of the quelea on the African savanna can reach up to 10 million individuals and the species population ranges from 1.5 billion breeding pairs to 10 billion individuals.

(B) Although the quelea's diet is composed mainly of wild grass seeds, they have been known to eat other seeds and insects.

(C) Despite being dependent upon grass seeds, they have developed migratory and breeding patterns that allow them to flourish in their harsh ecosystems.

(D) Most of the bird population migrates during the rainy season when more seeds are available to replenish the energy they loose during the journey.

(E) Their massive colonies can devastate human farming efforts and are feared in places with similar climates, where they could thrive as an invasive species, such as Australia.

(F) Red-billed quelea have been blamed for destroying more than $70m of grain fields in Australia and for causing native species like the Gouldian finch to be endangered.

21. What can be inferred from paragraph 1 about the American west prior to the 1850s?

(A) It was being exploited by new settlers.
(B) It was relatively uninhabited.
(C) It was the subject of many disputes.
(D) It was used mainly as farmland.

22. Which of the sentences below best expresses the essential information in the highlighted sentence in the passage? Incorrect choices change the meaning in important ways or leave out essential information.

(A) The eternal preservation of America's abundant uninhabited lands to be in the hands of all people came about because of the idea of landscape democracy.
(B) Landscape democracy led to the acquisition of America's land because the idea that people have rights to any vacant land they could claim was put forth.
(C) Because America is a democracy, all vacant national parkland is considered to belong to all people and people can move there freely if they agree to preserve it.
(D) Many early settlers who moved west preserved the vacant lands they came across because they believed in landscape democracy and thought the land should be protected forever.

23. According to paragraph 2, which of the following is NOT true regarding the establishment of national parks in the United States?

(A) It was the first time a country had reserved large plots of land for preservation.
(B) It included an aspect of competition with European powers.
(C) It was supported by business concerns
(D) It was designed through the meeting hled by business leaders.

National Parks in the Western United States

1   The Treaty of Paris, which ended the revolutionary war between Great Britain and its former colonies in the United States, more than doubled the territory of the 13 original colonies as the crown ceded all lands east of the Mississippi River to the newly formed nation. However, the new country's expansion would not stop there. By the middle of the next century, cessations, purchases and treaties would expand the nation's contiguous territory to its current state. This dramatically increased the amount of land owned by the nation and, before mass immigration and westward movement; much of this land was pristine wilderness with a plethora of different geological formations and ecosystems. With so much vacant land, the theory of "landscape democracy," the idea that scenic landscapes belong to all people, came into play and a movement was put forth to preserve this land in perpetuity as national parkland.

2   [■] This theory was revolutionary for the time, as prior to the establishment of Yellowstone National Park in 1872, no national government had ever set aside large swaths of undeveloped land. [■] However, this was not only done for preservation. [■] A sense of inferiority with regards to old world monuments and the belief that America's unique landscapes were one of its most distinguishing features both had a hand in the desire to set aside western lands. [■] Interestingly, business interests also encouraged the conservation movement. It may seem antithetical, but business leaders, such as railroad barons pushed for and supported these national parks, since they would encourage rich easterners to take long trips on their lines and stay in the hotel they set up on the outskirts of the parks. Their desire for profits also led them to heavily advertise the majesty of western parks and features, such as the Grand Canyon, Yellowstone, and Yosemite, which greatly raised awareness of the parks amongst the general public.

24. What can be inferred about Stephen Mather from paragraph 3?

(A) He underwent a major career change.
(B) He wanted to open the parks to business interests.
(C) He was involved in logging.
(D) He was a lifelong politician.

25. The term "magnate" in the passage is closest in meaning to:

(A) Leader
(B) Representative
(C) Tycoon
(D) Advocate

26. According to paragraph 4, which of the following is NOT true about cross-country trips?

(A) They were often undertaken by families in their automobiles.
(B) They began after the completion of new interstate highways.
(C) They showed the need for a new, improved roadway system.
(D) They often ended at recreational facilities, national parks and resorts.

3 Surprisingly, the adoption of the automobile by American's in the early 20th century also bolstered the national parks movement. As the number of cars rose from 0.11 per 1,000 citizens in 1900 to 86.78/K in 1920 and 217.34/K in 1930, drivers began calling for investment in better roads and highways, especially those in the west. 1916's Federal Aid Road Act paid states to construct or improve rural roadways, including those near parkland. This encouraged people to not only drive more, but also to visit the increasing number of national parks. At around the same time, business magnate Stephen Mather was pushing for an independent agency to oversee the national parks and barely a month after passing the Road Act, President Woodrow Wilson signed a bill setting up such an agency and named Mather its first director. He worked to protect these pristine lands from the business interests that were attempting to have them opened for logging and other business ventures.

4 By the middle of the 20th century, cross-country road trips had become quite popular with families who visited national parks, newly founded amusement parks, and ski resorts. They made the need for better roadways evident. This increased recreational travel helped ensure the passage of 1956's Interstate and Defense Highway Act, which authorized the construction of nearly 66,000 Km of roads around the country. This $25B project was the largest public works project in the country's history and increased mobility by linking urban centers through wide divided highways. A direct side effect of this was easier access to national parks for urban inhabitants, which caused a dramatic increase in park usage. In 1920 only 1M people visited the national parks, but by 1950 that number had risen to 33M. After the completion of the new highways the nation's parks welcomed 172M visitors. This increase vastly outpaced the increase in the nation's population, which had only doubled during that time.

27. According to paragraph 5, which of the following is true regarding John Muir?

(A) He thought people should be banned from the national parks.
(B) He wanted the national park system to be closed down.
(C) He was employed by the National Park System.
(D) He played a large role in changing people's minds about national parks.

28. Why does the author mention "109 current countries"?

(A) To help the reader understand how American national parks influenced the world.
(B) To reinforce the fact that the United States was the first country with national parks.
(C) To give the reader an idea of the great expanse of the American national parks.
(D) To suggest that the American national parks should be a separate country.

5   The increased number of visitors quickly caused degradation in the national parks, causing activists, like Sierra Club founder John Muir, to argue that the parks should be preserved as pristine wilderness and protected from further human destruction. This was important, since early parks, like Yellowstone had been set up as recreational areas. His impassioned writing helped to convince Americans, especially the eastern elite, of the importance or preservation of these unique areas.

6   This movement had a great impact on the national park system. Not only did the park system begin working to preserve the wilderness, but it also greatly expanded the amount of protected land. Today, more than 277M people visit the 210,000 Km2 of land protected by the 59 national parks, an area larger than 109 current countries, each year. The beauty, geological features, ecosystems, and recreational opportunities of the land in these parks are now permanently preserved for all American citizens both now and in the future.

29. Look at the four squares [■] that indicate where the following sentence could be added to the passage.

The fact that America was a relatively young nation interacting with other nations also had a large influence on the establishment of parks.

Where would the sentence best fit?

Click on a square [■] to add the sentence to the passage.

30. Directions: An introductory sentence for a brief summary of the passage is provided below. Complete the summary by selecting the THREE answer choices that express the most important ideas in the passage. Some sentences do not belong in the summary because they express ideas that are not presented in the passage or are minor ideas in the passage. **This question is worth 2 points.**

Territorial expansion in the United States led to the establishment of the world's first national parks.

-
-
-

Answer Choices

(A) Early national parks were established to allow American citizens more recreational opportunities as they moved to the rural western regions.

(B) National parks were set up in America as a means of showcasing the unique geological and environmental characteristics of the land and were promoted by business interests.

(C) The establishment of national parks encouraged people to visit the areas, which led to overall degradation of the natural environment.

(D) 1916's Federal Aid Road Act was meant to increase the amount of rural roads near national parks to allow more people to visit them.

(E) Automobile ownership and the vast road network of the country greatly increased the number of visitors to the US's national parks.

(F) Conservationists like John Muir helped convince the national park system that preservation was more important than recreation in the protected lands.

You have seen all of the questions in this part of the Reading section. You have time left to review.
As long as there is time remaining, you can check your work.

Click on **Return** to go back to the previous question.
Click on **Review** to see the review screen for this section.
Click on **Continue** to go on.
Once you leave this part of the Reading section, you WILL NOT be able to return to it.

이제 Reading Section이 끝났습니다.
Continue 버튼을 누르면 다시 문제를 검토할 수 없으므로 유의하세요.

시험보고 난 후 ... 체크 리스트 및 스터디 디렉션 | USHER iBT TOEFL INTERMEDIATE TEST REA

1. 내가 불안했던 문제만 재빨리 다시 보고, 불안하게 만든, 즉, 경쟁 초이스를 찾아서 왜 내가 헷갈려 했는지를 파악할 수 있는 메모를 해두시기 바랍니다. 시간이 지나거나, 다른 학생들과 스터디를 하면서는, 자신이 왜 낚였는지 이유조차 기억나지 않아 본인의 실수 패턴 파악이 힘들기 때문입니다.

2. 답지를 확인하지 않고 스터디를 하시기 바랍니다. (그래서, 답지를 문제지 뒤에 붙이지 않고, 본 설명만을 붙여 두었습니다.) 답지를 확인하지 않고 하는 이유는 답을 아는 순간, 답에 끼워 맞춰 설명하려 하고, 이런 태도는 본인 실력 향상에 도움이 되지 않기 때문입니다. 스터디 팀원들간에 대략적인 답을 맞춰보면, 대부분 답안의 윤곽이 나옵니다. 이럴 경우, 이견이 있는 문제만 집중적으로 다루고, 나머지는 개별별로 처리하시기 바랍니다.

3. 문제를 끝까지 다 풀었나요? 네 □ / 아니오 □
   다 못 풀었다면, 전체 30 문제 중 푼 문제는? _____ / 30
   시간 모자란 것에 대해서는 크게 신경 쓰지 않아도 됩니다. 무엇보다 중요한 것은 정확도 입니다.
   우선은 풀 문제를 맞출 확률을 높이고, 그 다음 시간을 걱정해도 늦지 않습니다.

4. 어려웠다고 느껴지는 지문은? 과학 □ / 예술 □ / 인문 □ / 인물 □ / 사회 □
   과학지문이 현격히 다른 분야보다 많지만, 그래도, 공부하다 보면 자신만 어려워하는 분야는 모두 각각입니다. 그러므로, 혹시 배경지식 부분에서 필요한 것이 있다면, usherin.usher.co.kr 에 방문하셔서, 공부가 안될 때, 배경지식 부분을 쉬엄쉬엄 들러서 봐 두시길 바랍니다. 쉬엄쉬엄 입니다. 누가 뭐래도 실력있는 사람은 배경지식이 큰 영향을 끼치지는 않습니다.

5. (채점 후) 문제 풀 때 어렵다고 느낀 지문이 틀리는 개수와 쉬웠다고 느껴졌던 지문의 틀린 개수차이가 있나요? 예 □ / 아니오 □
   어느 순간 깨닫게 됩니다. 내가 잘 아는 내용이 나와서 자신 있게 푸나, 내가 모르는 지문이 나와서 겁먹고 푸나, 틀린 개수가 큰 차이가 나지 않는 것을…. 혹시 그걸 못 느끼신다면, 더욱더 열심히 하시기 바랍니다. ^^

6. 틀린 문제의 번호를 다음의 문제 유형 분석표와 비교해서 파악해 두시기 바랍니다.
   문제 유형을 파악해서 주의하는 것은, 누가 뭐래도 실력이 기본은 받쳐 줄 때 얘기입니다. 문제 푸는 스킬이나, 기타 문제 유형 파악 등은 기본적으로 본문 내용을 이해하고, 해석이 웬만큼 될 때 얘기입니다. 만약, 너무 힘들다면 너무 스트레스 받지 말고, 그냥 '아~ 그렇구나' 정도로 넘기셔도 됩니다. 단, 본문 이해는 절대 양보해서는 안됩니다.

문제 유형 분석표

TEST 5-1	TEST 5-2	TEST 5-3
01 Purpose	11 Fact	21 Fact
02 Fact	12 Highlight	22 Highlight
03 Inference	13 Vocabulary	23 Fact
04 Fact	14 Fact	24 Inference
05 Fact	15 Inference	25 Vocabulary
06 Highlight	16 Purpose	26 Fact
07 Fact	17 Fact	27 Fact
08 Inference	18 Fact	28 Purpose
09 Insertion	19 Insertion	29 Insertion
10 Summary	20 Summary	30 Summary

USHER
iBT TOEFL
INTERMEDIATE READING 02
TEST 6

테스트 전 확인사항

실전에 유용한 독해 전략(44p)을 숙지하였습니다. ○
화장실은 미리 다녀왔습니다. ○
휴대폰의 전원을 껐습니다. ○
노트테이킹 할 종이와 연필을 준비하였습니다. ○
시간을 체크할 시계를 준비하였습니다. ○
목표점수(30개 중 ___개)를 정하였습니다. ○
시험 시작 시간은 ___시 ___분이며,
종료 시간은 54분 뒤인 ___시 ___분입니다. ○
시험 중 이동해야 할 방해요소가 있는지 체크하였습니다. ○
시험 중 이동하지 않습니다.

Sentinel Behavior in Meerkats

1. → Meerkats are small, mongoose-like mammals that live in the Kalahari Desert of Southern Africa. Being primarily insectivores, they feed on beetles and scorpions buried underground, which they locate using their strong sense of smell. Unfortunately, when the meerkat lowers its head to search out prey under grasses, it limits its own range of sight by a significant amount. As a result they are extremely vulnerable to airborne predators such as hawks and owls. To ensure that they can reach the safety of their bolt-holes before being snatched up by birds, meerkats forage in packs and partake in what is known as sentinel behavior. As the term suggests, one meerkat in the group acts as a sentinel and does not look for food like the rest, but rather stands upright on its hind legs to gain a wider field of view with which it scans the surrounding area for possible predators and other threats to the community. When it senses danger approaching, the sentinel barks loudly to warn the others of the danger. Many scientists questioned this phenomenon because the revealing stance and loud vocalization were thought to expose the meerkat to an increased risk of predation.

폭 넓게 - 일단 버릇 들이는게 중요!

32 According to paragraph 1, why was sentinel behavior thought to be disadvantageous?

(A) It warns the predator of where the meerkat group is.
(B) It allows the meerkat to sense danger and warn the group.
(C) It helps the predators locate the sentinel meerkat.
(D) It encourages the predator to prey on meerkats over other species.

스터디 자료들 미리 수집해 둘것!

시험 중 체크 사항

❶ "?" 표시하기 : 본문 읽으며, 궁금한 곳에 "?" 표시를 합니다.
　　문제를 풀면서도 질문 거리에는 "?" 표시를 해둡니다.
❷ 문제 핵심에 동그라미 : 문제가 물어보는 게 무엇인지, 문제 핵심에 동그라미 표시를 합니다.
❸ 답근거 날리기 : 문제를 풀 때 선택지가 틀린 이유 단어로, 간결하게 날립니다.
❹ 경쟁 문장 표시 : 4개의 선택지 중에 정답과 경쟁하는 마지막 1개의 선택지를 표시 해둡니다. 무조건 1개여야 합니다.

Reading Section Directions

This section measures your ability to understand academic passages in English.

Most questions are worth 1 point but the last question in each set is worth more than 1 point. The directions indicate how many points you may receive.

Some passages include a word or phrase that is underlined in blue. Click on the word or phrase to see a definition or an explanation.

Within each test, you can go to the next questions by clicking **Next**. You may skip questions and go back to them later. If you want to return to previous questions, click on **Back**. You can click on **Review** at any time and the review screen will show you which questions you have answered and which you have not answered. From this reviewscreen, you may go directly to any questions you have already seen in the Reading section.

You may now begin the Reading section. In the section you will read 3 passages. You will have **54 minutes** to read the passages and answer thequestions.

Click on **Continue** to go on.

Next 버튼을 이용하여 다음 문제로 이동하고 **Back** 버튼을 이용하여 이전문제로 이동할 수 있습니다. 문제에 답을 하지 않더라도 다음 문제로 이동할 수 있으며, **Review** 버튼을 이용하여 각 문제별로 답을 체크했는지의 여부를 확인할 수 있습니다.
이번 테스트에서는 세 지문을 읽게 됩니다. 54분 동안 지문을 읽고 문제에 답을 하세요.

The Role of Dress in Africa

1 When most people think about the concept of dressing, they automatically think of only clothing and accessories and whether they are in the right style. However, dress can actually be a much more complex concept, which can be used to communicate both simple ideas and complex information about the wearer. The type of dress that a person chooses can communicate immediate information about their gender, ethnic group, religion, age or even occupation. A few common examples of these are the burka worn by Muslim women and the yarmulke worn by Jewish men. Both of these items point to the age, religion, and gender of their wearers. This complexity and symbolism is a key feature of African dress, which has fascinated outside viewers with its striking range of styles since Arabic writers first described it in the fourteenth century.

2 African dress, like most forms, is intimately connected to the identity of its wearers and observers, since it acts as a signifier of so many aspects of the societies. Despite the neutrality of the adornment, the way in which it is worn, or simply the fact that it is worn, can become symbolically important to a society. There may be importance assigned to the form, type, adornment, and materials used to form the dress worn and this can cause it to become a sensitive aspect of the society. Since many aspects of dress are tied to tribal or religious identity, their use denotes inclusion with the society, but can also draw the ire or derision of society members if they are inappropriately worn or displayed.

3 In addition to denoting societal and religious identity, African dress can also be seen as an indicator of the wearer's sociopolitical standing in the society. In many African societies leaders wear some sort of insignia or symbolic aspect of dress to denote their leadership. In fact, some of these are made of highly prized materials, such

---

01. What can be inferred from paragraph 1 about the concept of "dressing"?

(A) It is only concerned with the symbolic aspects of clothing used by people in similar religious groups.
(B) It is a complex concept that has different meaning for people of different cultures.
(C) It has nothing to do with the donning of clothes that the wearer thinks are fashionable.
(D) It limits the ability of society members to express themselves because of religious rules.

02. According to paragraph 2, which of the following is NOT true regarding the correlation between dress and identity?

(A) The materials used to adorn the body have no natural importance on their own.
(B) The wearing of certain items, or the way in which they are worn, can denote inclusion in certain social or religious groups.
(C) Certain religions and civil societies can assign importance to some materials or forms of adornment.
(D) Due to their religious and cultural significance, members of certain groups cannot wear some items of dress.

03. Which of the sentences below best expresses the essential information in the highlighted sentence in the passage? Incorrect choices change the meaning in important ways or leave out essential information.

(A) Because tribal dress is so religiously important, the inappropriate uses of the elements can cause anger amongst society members.
(B) The use of particular items of dress can indicate membership in a certain group and their misuse can lead to societal anger and ridicule of them.
(C) Societal members can be upset by inappropriately used items of dress because they signify membership in a tribally or religiously united group.
(D) Anger often occurs when items of dress are worn that do not connote an allegiance to the social groups tribal and religious affiliations.

04. Why does the author mention "horsehair and elephant tail hair"?

(A) To emphasize the number of materials that can be used in flywhisks.
(B) To give examples of materials that were culturally significant.
(C) To illustrate the variety of fibers used in African dress.
(D) To show that even cheap materials could be used to signify royalty.

05. The term "profusion" in the passage is closest in meaning to:

(A) Scarcity
(B) Number
(C) Abundance
(D) Amount

06. According to paragraph 4, which of the following is NOT true about the definition of dress?

(A) Used to denote the garments that people place on their bodies for both bodily coverage and adornment.
(B) It includes both temporary and permanent adornments of the body.
(C) Accessories that are both worn and held, such as flywhisks and umbrellas, are included in the definition of dress.
(D) Tattooing and scarification are not considered part of dress in most western societies.

07. According to paragraph 5, which of the following is true regarding cicatrization in sub-Saharan Africa?

(A) It is so common that many societies have designed pottery to mimic the patterns used on their members.
(B) It is used to quickly identify individual members of a society because their clothing styles are very similar.
(C) It is the most prevalent form of permanent bodily adornment used in most of Southern Africa.
(D) It has different meanings and uses based on the location of the scarification.

as ivory, gold, or decorative beading, that are only worn by the leaders. One example of this is the Oba, or leader, of the Benin people in present-day Nigeria. His official dress includes a coral-beaded smock and crown with coral necklaces and ivory pendants and amulets. Further, he carries a flywhisk made of red coral beads that signify his divine rule. In other societies, other flywhisk materials were used to denote the regal nature of the bearer. Two examples of this are the Fare-Fare and Ashanti people of Ghana, whose respective use of horsehair and elephant tail hair denoted kings or chiefs of the highest importance. These flywhisks are such a strong symbol of power and leadership that they have come to be used by rulers across the continent, including by Jomo Kenyatta, the first leader of the modern state of Kenya.

4   The use of these flywhisks as a symbol of leadership brings up another interesting aspect of "dress." Contrary to the common, narrow interpretation of the term dress, the true definition is much broader and includes more than just the clothing worn. It includes accessories, such as the flywhisks, and other methods of beautifying and adorning the body. Items such as cosmetics, jewelry, and accessories like staffs, parasols, and fans, are all considered aspects of dress. However, not all of these aspects can be easily removed. Some societies use permanent bodily modification to perform the same functions. Tattooing may be the most common form of these in modern day western society, but there are a profusion of other forms, such as scarring, piercings and the use of lip plates.

5   [■] In most of sub-Saharan Africa, the use of purposefully inflicted scars, or cicatrization, is the most common type of permanent body modification. [■] They signify membership and status in the society, but can act as protective devices, in addition to simply being beautiful bodily adornment. [■] These scars are placed on different parts of the body, including the face, abdomen and

08. According to paragraph 6, which of the following can be inferred regarding about tattooing in Africa?

(A) The Ancient Egyptians who resided along the Nile River in northern Africa invented the art form.
(B) Scarification was not widely used in Ancient Egypt because the process was developed much later than tattooing.
(C) The Nubians and the Egyptians shared their knowledge of tattooing with one another.
(D) Tattooing the skin served the same purposes as clothing and scarification in other regions.

extremities, and can sometimes take the form of elaborate patterns that cover most of the body. [■] Oftentimes, the lengthy scarification acts as an initiation process, with the aesthetics of the scars correlating to other important figurative aspects of the society, such as pottery and sculpture.

6   Farther north, along the Nile River, tattooing was the main form of permanent body adornment. Researchers have found evidence of tattoos being used as fertility signals in female Egyptian mummies from 2000 B.C. In addition, the adjacent Nubian civilization appears to have utilized tattoos to adorn their bodies, as well. The tattoos in both of these civilizations served the same purpose as scarification, apparel and accessories in other African tribes, and elsewhere. They were symbols of inclusion, protection and identification for their bearers.

09. Look at the four squares [■] that indicate where the following sentence could be added to the passage.

The permanent scars are culturally important and hold important information for those in the society who know their relevance.

Where would the sentence best fit?

Click on a square [■] to add the sentence to the passage.

10. Directions: An introductory sentence for a brief summary of the passage is provided below. Complete the summary by selecting the THREE answer choices that express the most important ideas in the passage. Some sentences do not belong in the summary because they express ideas that are not presented in the passage or are minor ideas in the passage. **This question is worth 2 points.**

African dress comes in many forms and serves many purposes

-
-
-

Answer Choices

(A) Dress has been used by many African societies to communicate information, such as tribal membership and religious beliefs.

(B) Flywhisks can be found in many African tribes, as well as in modern society, and are made of a variety of different materials.

(C) African tribes developed elaborate costumes and body modifications that allowed them to differentiate themselves from and show power to the colonialists.

(D) Some aspects of tribal dress are meant to denote a higher sociopolitical status of the bearer, such as elaborate clothing, flywhisks, and crowns.

(E) Permanent body modifications, such as scarification, perform the same roles as clothing and accessories and are considered an aspect of African dress.

(F) Tattooing is used in fertility in some regions of Africa, but it is much more common in western cultures as a decorative element.

Evidence of an Asteroid Impact

1 Throughout Earth's history, there have been mass extinctions that permanently altered its biodiversity. The most recent of these occurred at the boundary between the Cretaceous and Paleogene periods, around 65 million years ago. During this time, scientists estimate that 75% of all species perished. By the end of the extinction, all non-avian dinosaurs had died off, allowing mammals to rise to the dominant position in most ecosystems.

2 Since discovering this dramatic change in species diversity in the late 19th century, geologists have attempted to explain why so many species died off concurrently. Some posited that dinosaurs could not adapt to climate change or the lowered sea level, while others thought that a more catastrophic event precipitated the disappearance of so many species. They point to such catastrophes as a massive volcanic eruption, an extraterrestrial body striking Earth's surface (which geologists refer to as a bolide), or the effects of cosmic radiation as possible explanations. Unfortunately, they could not produce concrete evidence to support these theories.

3 This changed in 1977 when geologist Walter Alvarez was studying the strata of the soil near Gubbio, Italy and discovered a layer of unique clay from the Cretaceous–Paleogene boundary. Upon sending it for analysis by his father's physics laboratory, he found that it contained nearly 30 times more iridium than is normally found in the rocks of Earth's crust. This was surprising, because, despite the fact that the earth's core and mantle are believed to contain this metallic element, it is rare in the crust. This led him to question the source of the mineral. [■] While a volcanic eruption could have deposited iridium in Earth's crust, he pointed out that it was more likely that a large (10+ Km in diameter) extraterrestrial body containing iridium forcefully struck the earth and sent up a dense cloud of iridium-filled dust across the atmosphere. [■] He

---

11. What can be inferred from paragraph 1 about the five major mass extinctions?

(A) Without the mass extinction at the end of the Cretaceous Period the existence of mammals would be unlikely.
(B) Although they were quite rare, mass extinctions have occurred with regularity throughout Earth's history.
(C) Mass extinctions have allowed Earth to support a larger number of species because they reduced competition.
(D) Without the effects of the final mass extinction, mammals would not likely have evolved into the apex predators in their habitats.

12. According to paragraph 2, which of the following is NOT true regarding scientists' understanding of the extinction of dinosaurs?

(A) There was little research into the topic before the late 1900s.
(B) Some scientists attributed it to climate change and an inability to adapt.
(C) Several theories blaming the extinction on catastrophes emerged.
(D) The evidence that scientists presented for their theories was disputable.

13. What can be inferred about Walter Alvarez from paragraph 3?

(A) He was looking for a pattern in the soil layers that could explain why mass extinctions historically occurred.
(B) His discovery of the iridium-filled layer of clay was the first incontrovertible evidence to support the theory of a bolide impact causing the dinosaur's extinction.
(C) He was unaware of the presence of iridium in Earth's mantle when he came up with his theory about the cause of the Cretaceous–Paleogene boundary.
(D) He was the first scientist to come up with the theory that the dinosaurs went extinct after a major extraterrestrial body collided with Earth's surface.

14. Why does the author mention the "Barringer Crater in Arizona"?

(A) To propose the location of the impact that caused the extinction at the end of the Cretaceous period.
(B) To inform the reader that bolide impacts have occurred in many regions of the world.
(C) To give an example of a documented impact site where the materials in question were found.
(D) To suggest another source for the materials that were found in the layer of soil corresponding to the Cretaceous–Paleogene boundary.

15. According to paragraph 4, which of the following is true about the materials found in the Cretaceous–Paleogene boundary?

(A) They have not been found in any other soil layers.
(B) They are only found in bolide impact sites.
(C) They can be used to determine the age of the impact site.
(D) They are only formed by the extreme pressure of a bolide impact.

16. The term "telltale" in the passage is closest in meaning to:

(A) Satisfactory
(B) Detracting
(C) Destructive
(D) Indicative

proposed that when this dust mixed with other atmospheric matter, atmospheric circulation pushed it throughout the atmosphere and blocked the sun's rays, thereby causing the extinction of the plants that formed the base of the food chain for most other life forms. [■] Eventually, this dust settled on the ground and entered the soil column. [■] This theory was bolstered when high iridium levels were found in soil from the Cretaceous-Paleogene boundary in locations as distant as Russia, Haiti, and New Zealand, and in layers of sediment under the Pacific and Atlantic Oceans.

4   The theory was further strengthened when geologists studying the Cretaceous-Paleogene Boundary found materials common in proven meteoric impact sites such as the Barringer Crater in Arizona. The first of these, shocked quartz, displays a unique planar pattern that is only created by shockwaves traveling through quartz-filled rock after an intense impact, so it indicates that there was some massive impact at the time. They also found stichovite, a dense compressed silicate uncommon in Earth's crust that is formed only in high-pressure situations, in samples from the period. In addition, the existence of tektites, or tiny glasslike droplets formed when terrestrial material is super heated and thrown into the air during a meteor's impact, in the Cretaceous-Paleogene layer samples from distant locations further supported the theory. The presence of soot in this stratum also points to a meteoric impact, since such an impact would have likely caused widespread wildfires.

5   The missing piece of the puzzle was the lack of a bolide impact site, but the lack of one does not necessarily negate the theory, since Earth's atmosphere can weather and erode geological features over time. However, in 1978, while working for Petróleos Mexicanos, geophysicist Glen Penfield found evidence of an impact crater just off the Yucatan Peninsula, near the town of Chicxulub, that was 180 Km in diameter and 20 km in depth. This

17. Which of the sentences below best expresses the essential information in the highlighted sentence in the passage? Incorrect choices change the meaning in important ways or leave out essential information.

(A) Andesitic rocks similar to tektites from the Cretaceous-Paleogene Boundary in other areas of the Caribbean, which are indicative of an extraterrestrial impact, were discovered at the impact site by researcher Alan Hildebrand as he surveyed the site's soil layers, magnetism and gravitation.

(B) Alan Hildebrand used scientific testing to reveal Andesitic rocks, which are a form of tektite, thereby indicating that a bolide impact had occurred somewhere in the Caribbean.

(C) Scientist Alan Hildebrand used core samples as well as magnetic and gravity surveys to locate the impact site by searching for andesitic rocks, which have a composition like tektites.

(D) The presence of Andesitic rocks in the Caribbean region convinced Alan Hildebrand to conduct further testing on the Cretaceous-Paleogene boundary using core samples and magnetic and gravity surveys to search for the similarly composed tektites which indicated the location of the impact site.

find, although under-reported and appreciated at the time, would make it the impact site of the largest bolide to ever strike Earth, which at 10+ Km in diameter, matched Alvarez's estimate perfectly. Further research by geoscientist Alan Hildebrand used core samples, magnetic and gravity surveys to reveal other telltale signs of a bolide at the supposed impact site, such as the existence of andesitic rocks, which have isotopic and chemical compositions similar to tektites found in the Cretaceous-Paleogene boundary across the Caribbean region.

6 Today, Alvarez's theory is the most widely accepted explanation for the mass extinction. Further testing of the event by the Berkeley Geochronology Center dated the bolide impact to 66-65 million years ago, with the extinction occurring within 33,000 years, thereby confirming Alvarez's time line. Even more convincingly, in 2010 a group of scientists published the results of their two decade long study of the Cretaceous-Paleogene boundary layer and concluded that debris from the Chicxulub bolide would have caused the environmental disturbances required to prompt the mass extinction.

18. According to paragraph 6, which of the following is NOT true regarding Alvarez's explanation for the mass extinction?

(A) It is currently the most commonly accepted explanation for the disappearance of the dinosaurs.

(B) The timing of the impact was confirmed by testing by researchers and coincided with the mass extinction.

(C) It was validated by other scientists and is now accepted as the cause of the extinctions, instead of simply a theory.

(D) It was corroborated by research into the bolide impact at Chicxulub.

19. Look at the four squares [■] that indicate where the following sentence could be added to the passage.

The two best explanations would be the result of volcanism or a major bolide collision.

Where would the sentence best fit?

Click on a square [■] to add the sentence to the passage.

20. Directions: An introductory sentence for a brief summary of the passage is provided below. Complete the summary by selecting the THREE answer choices that express the most important ideas in the passage. Some sentences do not belong in the summary because they express ideas that are not presented in the passage or are minor ideas in the passage. **This question is worth 2 points.**

Geologists have produced evidence that explains Earth's most recent mass extinction.

-
-
-

Answer Choices

(A) Scientists did not discover the existence of a mass extinction after the cretaceous period until the end of the 19th century.

(B) Geologists and researchers thought that the extinction of the dinosaurs was caused by the effects of solar radiation, a volcanic eruption, or the inability of dinosaurs to adapt to change.

(C) Walter Alvarez found a layer of iridium-rich clay that led him to theorize that the mass extinction was caused by the impact of an extraterrestrial mass on Earth's surface.

(D) Later scientists found indicators of a bolide impact, such as soot, tektites, and shocked quartz, in the Cretaceous-Paleogene boundary in locations around the world, bolstering the theory of a massive asteroid impact.

(E) Alan Hildebrand's proposed a competing theory of an asteroid impact at Chicxulub after he conducted extensive testing and found indicators of a large meteor impact just off the coast of the Yucatan Peninsula.

(F) Extensive scientific research has confirmed that Alvarez's theory and time frame accurately describe the event that caused the mass extinction and the Chicxulub crater is the most likely location of the impact.

Native Americans and European Trade Goods

1 Prior to their exploration and settlement by Europeans, the United States and Canada hosted a thriving trade network administered by the various native tribes found there. These Pre-Colombian tribes developed extensive trade routes between themselves that allowed them to trade pelts, shells, pottery and other handicrafts from the Great Lakes to the Gulf of Mexico and as far west as the Rocky Mountains. These interactions changed the individual tribes, by providing them not only new material goods and revenue, but also differing ideas and ways of thinking. These changes would, however, **pale in comparison to the changes brought about by the introduction of Europeans** into the North American economy.

2 Although native tribes had encountered Europeans as early as the 11th Century, when Norse explorers tried to create a settlement in eastern Canada, true economic interactions did not occur until the early 1500s. At this time, French fishermen and Basque whalers were regularly travelling to the Grand Banks off of Newfoundland and began trading with the locals they met when they came ashore to process their catches. The native inhabitants they met were eager to trade their goods for European products, such as metal tools, glassware and cloth, and allowed European explorers and traders to establish settlements and trading posts throughout New England, along the St. Lawrence River, and as far south as Virginia. **This situation provided European explorers a beneficial new trading source, but perhaps the biggest draw for them was the trade in fur, especially that of beaver pelts, which had become a phenomenally popular status symbol in Europe at the time.**

3 The fur trade dominated early European-Native American trade and had a profound impact on many

---

21. Why does the author say that tribal changes will "**pale in comparison to the changes brought about by the introduction of Europeans**"?

(A) Because the European settlers would offer a greater diversity of trade goods.
(B) Because early native tribes were very similar and underwent few changes.
(C) Because trade with Europeans would profoundly change life for the native tribes.
(D) Because European settlers had much lighter skin than the members of the native tribes.

22. Which of the sentences below best expresses the essential information in the highlighted sentence in the passage? Incorrect choices change the meaning in important ways or leave out essential information.

(A) Extended trade networks, especially those involved in animal hides, like beaver, which was considered a signifier of wealth, were an advantage of European settlements.
(B) European explorers first went to America to find a new source of beaver pelts, which had become important fashion accessories in Europe.
(C) Early native traders provided European settlers with beaver fur, which had religious significance in Europe, thereby starting a new trade network in North America.
(D) Explorers introduced the beaver to Europe, because they were attempting to introduce a new trade source for their settlements in North America, where they were very popular.

23. According to paragraph 2, which of the following is NOT true regarding early Europeans in North America?

(A) The first Europeans reached North America during the 11th century.
(B) French fishermen and Basque whalers visited Newfoundland to trade with the natives there.
(C) The goods they brought to N. America were highly sought after by the native inhabitants.
(D) Early European settlers benefited greatly from trading with the N. American natives.

Questions 24 ~ 26 of 30

24. According to paragraph 3, which of the following is true regarding early North American trade?

(A) European explorers and settlers introduced trade to the native tribes they found in North America.
(B) Europeans brought furs to trade with the natives they came across because they were considered valuable in Europe at the time.
(C) The native inhabitants were well versed in long distance travel long before the appearance of Europeans.
(D) Products from the Europeans were revered in the native communities because of their novelty.

25. The term "commemorate" in the passage is closest in meaning to:

(A) Assemble
(B) Remember
(C) Invite
(D) Tell of

26. What can be inferred about the native tribes from paragraph 4?

(A) The Iroquois tribes were the most welcoming of European settlers and created decoratice artwork in their honor.
(B) Interaction with new settlers was so positive that they spread westward to trade with them.
(C) European settlements and the products they brought with them changed the convention of the sedentary tribes.
(D) The introduction of metal tools caused the native tribes to admire the European settlers for their advanced technology.

---

aspects of the native societies including their organization, relationships with one another, and even their art and handicrafts. Prior to their interactions with European explorers and products, these tribes had spent thousands of years procuring and trading materials and refined products that were both precious and symbolically important to their cultures' ideals of leadership, influence, wealth and spirituality. The products they received from trading with the Europeans offered them these same opportunities and were incorporated into the indigenous communities values, crafts, and understanding of the world early on.

4 With the permanent settlements, the native tribes had more interaction with European products and became even more influenced by them. Over time, long held traditions such as pottery and tool making were abandoned in favor of European products such as brass kettles and durable steel and iron tools. This became more pronounced as European settlements spread westward and encroached on tribal lands, which allowed them to trade directly with the local tribes. This can be seen in the early 17th century Dutch settlements in the upper Hudson area of present day New York. [■] Prior to these settlements, the powerful Iroquois tribe used beaver tooth blades to carve moose antlers into rudimentary three or four tine combs, but after the introduction of steel blades by their Dutch neighbors these ornaments became much more ornate. [■] In fact, archaeologists excavated one from a Cayuga village with many narrow tines and an intricate carving of two European's on horseback. [■] It is assumed this was to commemorate the visit of an English dignitary, Wentworth Greenhalgh, in 1699. [■]

5 Although many of the European goods that found their way into the society provided increased productivity and security – guns, metal blades, and brass kettles – their longevity led to market saturation, eventually causing a shift in trading. Over time, native tribes began to favor

27. According to paragraph 5, which of the following is NOT true about the European products that were traded with the natives?

(A) Initially the natives favored products that provided them protection and the ability to produce more.
(B) The type of goods traded changed over time.
(C) Tribespeople incorporated European goods into their traditional customs and practices.
(D) European products were chosen because they had a symbolic value not found in traditional products.

28. According to paragraph 6, which of the following can be inferred regarding the native tribes after European settlement?

(A) New diseases killed many of the native inhabitants of North America.
(B) European settlers purposefully killed off the natives in order to take their lands.
(C) The fur trade made the tribes very wealthy, but they were unable to compete when commercial fur companies entered the market.
(D) Tribes that avoided trading with the Europeans remained powerful because their economies were not dependent upon the fur trade.

raw materials and the trade in cloth, wool, glass beads and decorative silver became more important. Native tribes incorporated items like glass beads into their practices and costumes in place of ornaments made of pipestone, copper, and shell. Some local artisans, usually tribeswomen, used these replacement materials to create elaborate formal attire and regalia. The new products offered the native tribes the correct look and symbolism for their practices, but the 'luxurious' imported products also gave the bearer an air of power, wealth, and success.

6 Unfortunately for the native tribes, these positive trade interactions with European settlers did not last forever. Over time, as the number of settlers and traders in the region increased, they brought with them corporatization of the industry and European diseases. The native population was not immune to the ill effects of either of these and soon began to suffer. By the 1850s, beaver fur had fallen out of favor in Europe and the native tribes lost a major source of income. This, combined with oppression by the settlers, threw them into a state of poverty from which many of the tribes have still not recovered.

29. Look at the four squares [■] that indicate where the following sentence could be added to the passage.

Others found in the region seem to indicate that the natives felt that their new neighbors possessed great wealth and power.

Where would the sentence best fit?

Click on a square [■] to add the sentence to the passage.

30. Directions: An introductory sentence for a brief summary of the passage is provided below. Complete the summary by selecting the THREE answer choices that express the most important ideas in the passage. Some sentences do not belong in the summary because they express ideas that are not presented in the passage or are minor ideas in the passage. **This question is worth 2 points.**

> **From the early 1500s to the mid 1800s Native North American tribes traded extensively with European settlers and traders.**
>
> -
> -
> -

Answer Choices

(A) Norse settlers set up the first permanent settlements in North America, but the did not trade with the native inhabitants until the fifteenth century.

(B) The tribes that inhabited North America before it was colonized allowed European's to settle the land because they wanted access to their goods.

(C) North American beaver pelts were in high demand because the native tribes were unaware of their value and sold them cheaper than their European counterparts.

(D) European products were adopted by the native inhabitants and eventually began to replace traditional products in both everyday life and in spiritual practices.

(E) Native tribes adopted the usage of European goods such as brass kettles and glass beads to more quickly assimilate with the new settlers.

(F) Trade between European settlers and native tribes eventually had a detrimental effect on the tribespeople.

You have seen all of the questions in this part of the Reading section. You have time left to review.
As long as there is time remaining, you can check your work.

Click on **Return** to go back to the previous question.
Click on **Review** to see the review screen for this section.
Click on **Continue** to go on.
Once you leave this part of the Reading section, you WILL NOT be able to return to it.

이제 Reading Section이 끝났습니다.
Continue 버튼을 누르면 다시 문제를 검토할 수 없으므로 유의하세요.

시험보고 난 후 ... 체크 리스트 및 스터디 디렉션

USHER iBT TOEFL INTERMEDIATE TEST REA

1. 내가 불안했던 문제만 재빨리 다시 보고, 불안하게 만든, 즉, 경쟁 초이스를 찾아서 왜 내가 헷갈려 했는지를 파악할 수 있는 메모를 해두시기 바랍니다. 시간이 지나거나, 다른 학생들과 스터디를 하면서는, 자신이 왜 낚였는지 이유조차 기억나지 않아 본인의 실수 패턴 파악이 힘들기 때문입니다.

2. 답지를 확인하지 않고 스터디를 하시기 바랍니다. (그래서, 답지를 문제지 뒤에 붙이지 않고, 본 설명만을 붙여 두었습니다.) 답지를 확인하지 않고 하는 이유는 답을 아는 순간, 답에 끼워 맞춰 설명하려 하고, 이런 태도는 본인 실력 향상에 도움이 되지 않기 때문입니다. 스터디 팀원들간에 대략적인 답을 맞춰보면, 대부분 답안의 윤곽이 나옵니다. 이럴 경우, 이견이 있는 문제만 집중적으로 다루고, 나머지는 개인별로 처리하시기 바랍니다.

3. 문제를 끝까지 다 풀었나요? 네 □ / 아니오 □
   다 못 풀었다면, 전체 30 문제 중 푼 문제는? _____ / 30
   시간 모자란 것에 대해서는 크게 신경 쓰지 않아도 됩니다. 무엇보다 중요한 것은 정확도 입니다.
   우선은 풀은 문제를 맞출 확률을 높이고, 그 다음 시간을 걱정해도 늦지 않습니다.

4. 어려웠다고 느껴지는 지문은? 과학 □ / 예술 □ / 인문 □ / 인물 □ / 사회 □
   과학지문이 현격히 다른 분야보다 많지만, 그래도, 공부하다 보면 자신만 어려워하는 분야는 모두 각각입니다. 그러므로, 혹시 배경지식 부분에서 필요한 것이 있다면, usherin.usher.co.kr 에 방문하셔서, 공부가 안될 때, 배경지식 부분을 쉬엄쉬엄 들러서 봐 두시길 바랍니다. 쉬엄쉬엄 입니다. 누가 뭐래도 실력있는 사람은 배경지식이 큰 영향을 끼치지는 않습니다.

5. (채점 후) 문제 풀 때 어렵다고 느낀 지문이 틀리는 개수와 쉬웠다고 느껴졌던 지문의 틀린 개수차이가 있나요? 예 □ / 아니오 □
   어느 순간 깨닫게 됩니다. 내가 잘 아는 내용이 나와서 자신 있게 푸나, 내가 모르는 지문이 나와서 겁먹고 푸나, 틀린 개수가 큰 차이가 나지 않는 것을…. 혹시 그걸 못 느끼신다면, 더욱더 열심히 하시기 바랍니다. ^^

6. 틀린 문제의 번호를 다음의 문제 유형 분석표와 비교해서 파악해 두시기 바랍니다.
   문제 유형을 파악해서 주의하는 것은, 누가 뭐래도 실력이 기본은 받쳐 줄 때 얘기입니다. 문제 푸는 스킬이나, 기타 문제 유형 파악 등은 기본적으로 본문 내용을 이해하고, 해석이 웬만큼 될 때 얘기입니다. 만약, 너무 힘들다면 너무 스트레스 받지 말고, 그냥 '아~ 그렇구나' 정도로 넘기셔도 됩니다. 단, 본문 이해는 절대 양보해서는 안됩니다.

문제 유형 분석표

TEST 6-1	TEST 6-2	TEST 6-3
01 Inference	11 Fact	21 Purpose
02 Fact	12 Fact	22 Highlight
03 Highlight	13 Inference	23 Fact
04 Purpose	14 Purpose	24 Fact
05 Vocabulary	15 Fact	25 Vocabulary
06 Fact	16 Vocabulary	26 Inference
07 Fact	17 Highlight	27 Fact
08 Inference	18 Fact	28 Inference
09 Insertion	19 Insertion	29 Insertion
10 Summary	20 Summary	30 Summary

USHER
iBT TOEFL
INTERMEDIATE READING 02
VOCABULARY 구문정리

TEST 1-1
VOCABULARY

TEST 1-1 지문의 단어 중 토플 필수 단어를 선별하여 정리하였습니다.

- ☐ job mobility [dʒab moubíləti] — n. 직업 유동성
- ☐ hallmark [haˈlmaˌrk] — n. 특징(전형적인)
- ☐ blame [bleim] — v. 비난하다
- ☐ training [tréiniŋ] — n. 훈련
- ☐ likely [láikli] — ad. 아마도 / a. 그럴듯한
- ☐ oversimplified [òuvərsímpləfàid] — a. 지나치게 단순화 된
- ☐ counterpart [káuntərpàːrt] — n. 상대, 대응물
- ☐ posit [pázit] — v. 상정하다, 사실로 가정하다
- ☐ prosperous [práspərəs] — a. 번영하는, 번창한
- ☐ logistical [loudʒístikəl] — a. 수송의, 물류의
- ☐ employ [implɔ́i] — v. 고용하다, 활용하다
- ☐ availability [əvèiləbíləti] — n. 이용가능성
- ☐ relocate [rilouˈkeit] — v. 이전하다, 이동시키다
- ☐ quit [kwit] — v. 그만두다, 떠나다
- ☐ monetary [mánətèri] — a. 금전의, 화폐의
- ☐ psychological [sàikəládʒikəl] — a. 심리적인
- ☐ adventurous [ædvéntʃərəs] — a. 모험적인
- ☐ personality [pə̀ːrsənǽləti] — n. 성격, 개성
- ☐ familial responsibility [fəmíljə rispànsəbíləti] — n. 가족을 위한 책임감
- ☐ overcome [ouˈvərkəˌm] — v. 극복하다
- ☐ the unknown [ənNouˈn] — n. 미지의 것
- ☐ risk [risk] — v. 위험을 무릅쓰다
- ☐ employment separation [implɔ́imənt sèpəréiʃən] — n. 이직
- ☐ cultural norm [kʌltʃərəl nɔːrm] — n. 문화 규범
- ☐ lifetime employment [laiftaim implɔ́imənt] — n. 종신 고용, 평생 고용

- ☐ employee loyalty [implɔ́imənt lɔ́iəlti] — n. 고용 충성심, 애사심
- ☐ societally [sóuʃətli] — ad. 사회적으로
- ☐ undesirable [ə̀ndizaiˈrəbəl] — a. 바람직하지 않은
- ☐ real estate [ríːəlestèit] — n. 부동산
- ☐ incidence [ínsədəns] — n. 발생, 일어남
- ☐ housing policy [háuziŋ páləsi] — n. 주거 정책
- ☐ prospect [práspekt] — n. 예상, 전망
- ☐ discourage [diskɔ́ːridʒ] — v. 막다, 의욕을 꺾다
- ☐ subsidy [sʌ́bsədi] — n. 보조금
- ☐ loath [louθ] — a. ~하기를 꺼리는
- ☐ scheme [skiːm] — n. 계획, 제도
- ☐ residential mobility [rèzədénʃəl moubíləti] — n. 주거 이동성
- ☐ landlord [lǽndlɔˌrd] — n. 주인, 임대인
- ☐ consecutive [kənsékjutiv] — a. 연이은
- ☐ negotiate [nigóuʃièit] — v. 협상하다
- ☐ astronomical [æstrənámikəl] — a. 천문학적인, 어마어마한
- ☐ tenure [ténjər] — n. 재임기간, 종신 재직권
- ☐ job tenure [dʒab ténjər] — n. 직장 재직 기간
- ☐ hypothesize [haipáθisàiz] — v. 가설을 세우다
- ☐ willingness [wíliŋnis] — n. 기꺼이 하는 마음
- ☐ job match [dʒaːb mætʃ] — n. 직업 연결, 직업 조화
- ☐ economic flexibility [èkənámik flèksəbíləti] — n. 경제적 유동성
- ☐ conversely [kənvɔ́ːrsli] — ad. 정반대로, 역으로
- ☐ skimp [skimp] — v. (돈,시간 등을) 지나치게 아끼다
- ☐ whatever [hwatévər, hwətévər] — pn. 어떤 ~ 이든

구문정리

본문 중 중요 구문 정리한 내용입니다. 우선 암기하고 많이 읽으시기 바랍니다.

TEST 1-1 — Costs of Quitting a Job 퇴사 비용

01	hold A as B	A를 B로 유지하다
02	in contrast to	~와는 반대로, 대조를 이루어
03	appear to do	~처럼 보이다
04	on average	평균적으로
05	be with	~와 함께 하다
06	a larger number of	많은 수의
07	blame A by B	A를 B로 인해 비난하다
08	in part	부분적으로, 어느 정도는
09	in reality	실제로는
10	decision to do	~하는 결정
11	a number of	수 많은
12	be likely to do	~할 것 같다
13	due to	~때문에
14	have to do	~해야 한다
15	take a job	직업을 가지다, 일을 맡다
16	have difficulty in -ing	~하는데 어려움을 가지다
17	in addition to	~뿐만 아니라
18	play a role in	~에서 역할을 하다
19	the fear of the unknown	미지의 것에 대한 두려움
20	be willing to do	기꺼이 ~ 하다
21	more than 3 times	3배 이상
22	be responsible for	~에 책임이 있는
23	unheard of	들어보지 않은
24	be meant to do	~라고 의미가 되다
25	ability of A to do	A의 ~하는 능력
26	lay off	해고하다
27	make it undesirable for A to do	A가 ~하는 것을 바람직하지 않게 만들다 (의미상의 주어)
28	link A to B	A와 B를 연결하다
29	make O O.C	O를 O.C 하게 만들다
30	in the same way that	~와 같은 방법, 방식으로
31	loath to do	~하기를 꺼려하는
32	rent control	임대료 통제
33	the increase in	~에서의 증가
34	result in	~을 야기하다, 초래하다
35	point to	~을 가리키다, 시사하다
36	an indicator of	~의 지표
37	propensity for	~의 경향
38	willingness to do	~를 기꺼이 하는 마음
39	pulling up stake	(살던 집에서) 갑자기 이사를 가다 = up sticks
40	difference in	~라는 점에서의 차이
41	point to A as B	A를 B로 가리키다, 시사하다
42	a sign of	~의 신호
43	cause O to do	O가 ~하는 것을 야기하다
44	skimp on	~을 절약하다
45	jump ship	떠나버리다
46	try to do	~하는 것을 노력하다
47	in order to do	~하기 위해서

※ 다시 한 번 암기 후 → 열 번 읽기로 넘어가자!

TEST 1-2 VOCABULARY

TEST 1-2 지문의 단어 중 토플 필수 단어를 선별하여 정리하였습니다.

- ☐ tenet [ténit] — n. 원리, 교리
- ☐ unit [jú:nit] — n. 구성 단위
- ☐ principle [prínsəpl] — n. 원리, 원칙
- ☐ extrapolate [ikstrǽpəlèit] — v. 추론, 추정하다
- ☐ sexual reproduction [sékʃuəl rìːprədəˈkʃən] — n. 유성[성별 구분]생식
- ☐ viral [váiərəl] — a. 바이러스성의, 바이러스에 의한
- ☐ light microscopy [lait maikráskəpi] — n. 광학 현미경 검사
- ☐ scale [skeil] — n. 비늘;규모;저울
- ☐ chamber [tʃéimbər] — n. 공간, -실
- ☐ cork oak [kɔːrk ouk] — n. 코르크 오크 나무
- ☐ resemble [rizémbl] — v. 닮다, 유사하다
- ☐ cubicle [kjúːbikl] — n. 좁은 칸, 작은 구획
- ☐ trump [trʌmp] — v. 이기다, 능가하다
- ☐ tartar [táːrtər] — n. 치석
- ☐ microscopic [màikrəskápik] — a. 미세한, 현미경으로 봐야 하는
- ☐ erroneously [iróuniəsli] — ad. 틀리게, 잘못 되게
- ☐ spontaneously [spantéiniəsli] — ad. 자발적으로, 자연스럽게
- ☐ accumulate [əkjúːmjulèit] — v. 모으다, 축적하다
- ☐ blame [bleim] — v. 비난하다, 탓하다
- ☐ inferior [infíəriər] — a. 하위의, 질 낮은
- ☐ hinder [híndər] — v. 막다, 저해하다
- ☐ address [ədrés] — v. 다루다, 처리하다, 초점을 맞추다
- ☐ imprint [ímprint] — n. 자국, 흔적
- ☐ categorization [kætəgərizéiʃən] — n. 분류, 범주화
- ☐ progress [prágres] — v. 진행하다, 나아가다
- ☐ finding [fáindiŋ] — n. 결과 (조사, 연구 등의)
- ☐ microscope [máikrəskòup] — n. 현미경
- ☐ cooperation [kouàpəréiʃən] — n. 협력, 협동
- ☐ orchid cell [ɔ́ːrkid sel] — n. 난초 세포, 온실 세포
- ☐ posit [pázit] — v. 상정하다, 사실로 받아들이다
- ☐ genetic material [dʒənétik mətíəriəl] — n. 유전 물질
- ☐ nucleus [njúːkliəs] — n. 세포핵
- ☐ carrier [kǽriər] — n. 보균자, 매개체
- ☐ frequency [fríːkwənsi] — n. 빈도
- ☐ respectively [rispéktivli] — ad. 각자, 각각
- ☐ nuclei [njúːkliài] — n. nucleus의 복수
- ☐ conclude [kənklúːd] — v. 결론을 내리다
- ☐ building block [bíldiŋ blak] — n. 구성 요소
- ☐ premise [prémis] — n. 전제 (주장의)
- ☐ expand [ikspǽnd] — v. 확장하다, 말을 덧붙이다
- ☐ contribute [kəntríbjuːt] — v. 기여하다
- ☐ contradict [kàntrədíkt] — v. 반박하다
- ☐ remainder [riméindər] — n. 잔여물, 나머지
- ☐ cell body [sel bádi] — n. 세포체
- ☐ cell division [sel divíʒən] — n. 세포 분열
- ☐ germ theory [dʒəːrm θíːəri] — n. 배종설 [생명체가 배(胚)나 종(種)으로부터 발생한다는 설]
- ☐ despite [dispáit] — prep. ~에도 불구하고
- ☐ objection [əbdʒékʃən] — n. 반대
- ☐ abnormality [æbnɔːrmǽləti] — n. 이상, 기형
- ☐ pathogen [pǽθədʒən] — n. 병원균, 병원체
- ☐ habitat [hǽbitæt] — n. 서식지
- ☐ discout [dískaunt] — v. 무시하다
- ☐ correctly [kəréktli] — ad. 정확하게
- ☐ affect [əfékt] — v. 영향을 미치다
- ☐ leukemia [ljukíːmiə] — n. 백혈병

구문정리

TEST 1-2   **Cell Theory** 셀 이론

본문 중 중요 구문 정리한 내용입니다. 우선 암기하고 많이 읽으시기 바랍니다.

01	compose A of B	A를 B로 구성하다
02	arise from	~로부터 발생하다
03	in the field of	~의 분야에서
04	be able to do	~할 수 있다
05	a great deal of	다량의, 많은
06	in fact	사실상, 실제로
07	allow O to do	O가 ~하는 것을 가능케 하다
08	common sense	상식
09	take place	일어나다, 발생하다
10	in the middle of	~중반에
11	begin to do	~하는 것을 시작하다
12	melt A into B	A를 녹여 B로 만들다
13	a series of	일련의
14	blame A on B	A의 탓을 B로 돌리다
15	address issue	쟁점을 처리하다, 다루다
16	make up	구성하다; 차지하다
17	fail to do	~하는 것을 실패하다
18	the first to do	~한 첫 번째
19	take advantage of	~을 이용하다
20	be present in	~에 존재하다
21	increase in	~면에서 증가하다
22	take hold	장악하다, 강해지다
23	conclude that	~라고 결론을 내리다
24	in common	공동으로
25	make up A of B	A를 B로 구성하다
26	expand on	~에 대해 더 상세히 말하다
27	come from	~로부터 발생하다
28	of the time	그 당시에
29	act as	~로서 역할을 하다 (=serve as, work as)
30	principle behind	~뒤의 원리
31	objection to	~에 대한 반대
32	attract A to B	A를 B로 이끌다

※ 다시 한 번 암기 후 → 열 번 읽기로 넘어가자!

TEST 1-3 VOCABULARY

TEST 1-3 지문의 단어 중 토플 필수 단어를 선별하여 정리하였습니다.

- auditory [ɔ́:ditɔ̀:ri] — a. 청각의
- face [feis] — v. 직면하다, 마주하다
- block [feis] — v. 막다, 차단하다
- physical barrier [fízikəl bǽriər] — n. 물리적 장벽
- transmit [trænsmít] — v. 전달하다, 전송하다
- broadcast [brɔ́:dkæst] — v. 알리다, 방송하다
- substrate [sʌ́bstreit] — n. 기질, 기저층
- toad [toud] — n. 두꺼비
- nocturnal [naktɔ́:rnl] — a. 야행성의
- vocal sac [vóukəl sæk] — n. 노래 주머니
- distinctive [distíŋktiv] — a. 독특한
- croaking sound [krouk saund] — n. 개굴개굴 우는 소리
- nostril [nástrəl] — n. 콧구멍, 비공
- air movement [ɛər mú:vmənt] — n. 기동, 공기 이동
- larynx [lǽriŋks] — n. 후두 (=voice box)
- vocal cords [vóukəl kɔ:rd] — n. 성대
- vibrate [váibreit] — v. 떨리다, 진동을 주다
- amplify [ǽmpləfài] — v. 증폭시키다
- duet [dju:ét] — n. 이중주, 2부 합주
- receptive [rékrièitiv] — a. 수용하는, 받아 들이는
- mortality risk [mɔ:rtǽləti risk] — n. 사망 위험
- recognize [rékəgnàiz] — v. 인지하다, 인식하다
- discern [disɔ́:rn] — v. 알아차리다, 알아보다
- temporal [témpərəl] — a. 시간의, 일시적인
- frequency [frí:kwənsi] — n. 주파수; 빈도
- species-specific [spí:ʃi:zspisífik] — n. 종의 특성, 특징
- interbreed [intɔ́:rbri:d] — v. 상호 교배하다
- hybridization [hàibridəzéiʃən] — n. 이종 교배
- non-viable [nɑ̀nváiəbl] — a. 생존할 수 없는
- offspring [ɔ́fspriŋ] — n. 자손, 자식
- attune [ətjú:n] — v. 조율하다, 맞추다
- differentiate [dìfərénʃièit] — v. 구별하다, 구분 짓다
- dialect [dáiəlèkt] — n. 사투리, 방언
- intruder [intrú:dər] — n. 침입자
- key piece [ki:pi:s] — n. 주요 부분
- glean [gli:n] — v. 모으다, 얻다
- undergo [ə̀ndərgou] — v. 겪다
- indeterminate [ìnditɔ́:rmənət] — a. 쉽게 가늠할 수 없는
- age [eidʒ] — v. 나이가 들다
- amplitude [ǽmplitjù:d] — n. (파동의) 진폭
- pitch [pitʃ] — n. 음의 높이
- inherent [inhíərənt] — a. 내재하는, 고유의
- bias [báiəs] — n. 편견
- hazard [hǽzərd] — n. 위험
- ambiguous [æmbígjuəs] — a. 애매모호한
- specimen [spésəmən] — n. 표본, 견본
- determine [ditɔ́:rmin] — v. 알아내다, 결정하다
- territorial [tèrətɔ́:riəl] — a. 영토의, 지역의
- contraction [kəntrǽkʃən] — n. 수축, 축소
- intensive [inténsiv] — a. 집중적인, 강렬한
- vertebrate [vɔ́:rtəbrət-brèit] — n. 척추 동물
- eschew [istʃú:] — v. 피하다, 삼가다
- interaction [ìntərǽkʃən] — n. 상호작용
- mating season [méitiŋ sí:zn] — n. 짝짓기철, 교미기
- chorus [kɔ́:rəs] — n. 후렴
- encroach [inkróutʃ] — v. 침범하다, 잠식하다

구문정리

본문 중 중요 구문 정리한 내용입니다. 우선 암기하고 많이 읽으시기 바랍니다.

TEST 1-3 — Mating Songs of Frogs 개구리의 짝짓기 노래

01	rely on	~에 의지하다, 의존하다
02	communicate with	~와 소통하다
03	one another	서로서로
04	instead of	~대신에
05	in fact	실제로, 사실상
06	allow O to do	O가 ~하는것을 가능케하다
07	due to	~때문에
08	be able to do	~할 수 있다
09	seal off	봉쇄하다, 봉인하다
10	force from A into B	A에서 B로 들어가도록 강요하다
11	back-and-forth	앞뒤로, 왔다갔다
12	cause O to do	O가 ~하도록 야기하다
13	call back to	~에 부르는 소리에 답하다
14	lead to	~을 야기하다
15	sound the same	똑같이 들리다
16	a great deal	다량, 상당량
17	attract A to B	A를 B로 이끌다
18	so ~ that	너무~해서 그 결과~하다
19	attune A to B	A를 B에 맞추다
20	in much the same way that	~하는 것과 대체로 똑같이
21	use O to do	O를 ~하기 위해 사용하다
22	glean from	~로부터 모으다
23	provide A with B	A에게 B를 제공하다
24	difference in	~에서의 차이
25	bias toward	~쪽으로의 성향, 경향
26	beneficial for	~에 이로운, 유익한
27	as well	또한
28	make up	구성하다, 차지하다
29	enough to do	~하기에 충분한, 충분히
30	in order to do	~하기 위해서
31	search for	~을 찾다
32	ability to do	~할 수 있는 능력
33	indicate to A that	A에게 ~을 나타내다
34	not A but B	A가 아니라 B
35	warn O that	O에게 ~을 경고하다
36	encroach on	~을 침해하다, 침범하다

※ 다시 한 번 암기 후 → 열 번 읽기로 넘어가자!

TEST 2-1
VOCABULARY

TEST 2-1 지문의 단어 중 토플 필수 단어를 선별하여 정리하였습니다.

☐ timeline [táimlàin]	n. 연대표, 시각표	☐ elliptical [ilíptikəl]	a. 타원형의
☐ frigid [fiːld]	a. 몹시 추운, 냉랭한	☐ tilt [tilt]	n. 기울기
☐ glacier [gléiʃər]	n. 빙하	☐ wobble [wάbl]	n. 흔들림, 동요
☐ prevalent [prévələnt]	a. 만연한, 널리 퍼져 있는	☐ axis [æksis]	n. 축, 중심축
☐ latitude [lǽtətjùːd]	n. 위도	☐ synchronize [síŋkrənàiz]	v. 동시에 발생하다
☐ hemisphere [hémisfìər]	n. 반구	☐ extensively [iksténsivli]	ad. 널리, 광범위하게
☐ despite [dispáit]	prep. ~에도 불구하고	☐ chronology [krənάlədʒi]	n. 연대표
☐ diverse [daivə́ːrs]	a. 다양한	☐ prove [pruːv]	v. 증명하다
☐ oceanic circulation [òuʃiǽnik sə̀ːrkjuléiʃən]	n. 해수 순환	☐ unfortunately [ənfɔˈrtʃənətli]	ad. 불행하게도
☐ cite [sait]	v. 인용하다	☐ throughout [θruːáut]	prep. ~를 걸쳐서
☐ mathematician [mæθəmətíʃən]	n. 수학자	☐ rarely [rɛ́ərli]	ad. 거의 ~않는
☐ equation [ikwéiʒən]	n. 방정식, 등식	☐ throw [θrou]	v. 던지다, 빠뜨리다
☐ incident [ínsədənt]	n. 사건, 일	☐ quest [kwest]	n. 탐구, 탐색
☐ eccentricity [èksəntrísəti]	n. 이심률; 편심률 (물체의 운동이 원운동에서 벗어난 정도)	☐ luminosity [lùːmənάsəti]	n. 발광, 광명
☐ obliquity [əblíkwəti]	n. 황도 경사각 (천구의 적도와 황도가 이루는 각도)	☐ trap [træp]	v. 가두다
☐ precession [priséʃən]	n. 세차 운동 (회전체의 회전축이 움직이지 않는 어떤 축의 둘레를 도는 현상)	☐ strata [strǽ-]	n. 층, 지층

구문정리

본문 중 중요 구문 정리한 내용입니다. 우선 암기하고 많이 읽으시기 바랍니다.

TEST 2-1

Milankovitch Cycles and Glaciation
밀란코비치 사이클스 앤 빙하화

01	piece together	종합하다
02	take place	일어나다, 발생하다
03	cover A by B	A를 B로 덮다
04	research into	~에 대한 연구
05	be unable to do	~할 수 없다
06	put forth	제안하다, 제시하다
07	use O to do	O를 ~하기 위해 사용하다
08	change in	~라는 점에서의 변화
09	lead to	~을 야기하다, 이끌다
10	base A on B	A의 기반을 B에 두다
11	relative to	~와 상대적인, 비례하여
12	have an effect on	~에 영향을 끼치다
13	bring O close to	O를 ~에 가깝게 데려오다
14	concern A with B	A를 B에 관련시키다, 관계시키다
15	in a way that	~하는 방법, 방식으로
16	prevent O from -ing	O가 ~하는 것을 막다
17	allow O to do	O가 ~하는 것을 가능케 하다
18	ability to do	~하는 능력
19	necessary for	~를 위해 필수적인
20	correlation between A and B	A와 B사이의 상관관계
21	take A from B	A를 B로부터 얻다, 채취하다
22	accurate in	~면에서 정확한, 정밀한
23	require O to do	O가 ~하는 것을 요구하다
24	appear to do	~하는 것처럼 보이다
25	lead O to do	O가 ~하도록 이끌다
26	work with	~와 함께 작용하다
27	throw A into and out of	A를 안으로 그리고 바깥으로 빠지게 하다
28	with the regularity	규칙적으로
29	in the quest to do	~하려는 탐색 중에
30	a number of	수 많은
31	it is believed that	~라고 믿어진다
32	shield A from B	A를 B로부터 보호하다
33	cause O to do	O가 ~하도록 야기하다
34	correspond with	~와 일치하다, 부합하다
35	difference in	~에서의 차이
36	result in	~을 야기하다
37	be attractive to	~에 매력적이다
38	the number of	~의 수
39	depending on	~에 따라
40	know A to be B	A를 B로 알다

※ 다시 한 번 암기 후 → 열 번 읽기로 넘어가자!

TEST 2-2 VOCABULARY

TEST 2-2 지문의 단어 중 토플 필수 단어를 선별하여 정리하였습니다.

- ☐ phase [feiz] — n. 위상, 양상, 단계
- ☐ full moon [ful mu:n] — n. 보름달
- ☐ reliance [riláiəns] — n. 의존, 의지
- ☐ rudimentary [rù:dəméntəri] — a. 기초적인, 기본적인
- ☐ equinoxe [í:kwənàks] — n. 주야 평분시, 분점 (천구상에서 천구의 적도와 황도가 만나는 시간)
- ☐ solstice [sálstəs] — n. 태양의 지점
- ☐ empirical [impírikəl] — a. 실증적인, 경험에 의거한
- ☐ flaw [flɔ:] — n. 결점, 결함
- ☐ celestial body [səléstʃəl bádi] — n. 천체
- ☐ obscure [əbskjúər] — v. 가리다, 모호하게 하다
- ☐ problematic [prὰbləmǽtik] — a. 문제가 있는
- ☐ latitude [lǽtətjù:d] — n. 위도
- ☐ horizon [həráizn] — n. 수평선, 지평선
- ☐ overhead [ouˈvərheˌd] — a. 머리 위에, 하늘 높이
- ☐ arise [əráiz] — v. 일어나다, 발생하다
- ☐ unit [jú:nit] — n. 구성 단위
- ☐ evenly [í:vənli] — ad. 균등하게, 균일하게
- ☐ calendric [kǽləndər] — a. 달력의, 달력에 관한
- ☐ intercalate [intə́:rkəlèit] — v. 윤일을 넣다, 사이에 끼워넣다
- ☐ oversee [ouˈvərsiˌ] — v. 관리하다, 감독하다

- ☐ corrupt [kərʌ́pt] — a. 부패한, 타락한
- ☐ inept [inépt] — a. 서투른, 솜씨 없는
- ☐ reign [rein] — n. 통치 기간
- ☐ consecutive [kənsékjutiv] — a. 연이은, 연속적인
- ☐ synchronize [síŋkrənàiz] — v. 동시에 발생하다, 동기화하다
- ☐ abuse [əbjú:z] — v. 남용하다
- ☐ intercalation [intə̀:rkəléiʃən] — n. 윤달(계절과 너무 어긋나는 것을 막기 위해 간간이 넣은 달)
- ☐ diverge [daivə́:rs] — v. 나뉘다, 갈라지다
- ☐ rigid [rídʒid] — a. 엄격한, 융통성 없는
- ☐ astronomical [æstrənámikəl] — a. 천문학적인
- ☐ lunisolar [lù:nisóulər] — a. 달과 태양의, 태음태양의
- ☐ arithmetic [əríθmətik] — n. 산수, 연산
- ☐ impossibility [impὰsəbíləti] — n. 불가능성
- ☐ lunation [lu:néiʃən] — n. 태음월 (초승달부터 다음 초승달까지의 기간)
- ☐ inherently [inhíərəntli] — ad. 본질적으로, 선천적으로
- ☐ divisible [divízəbl] — a. 나눌 수 있는
- ☐ leap years [li:p jiərs] — n. 윤년(2월을 29일로 둔 해)
- ☐ realign [rìəláin] — v. 변경하다, 재편성하다
- ☐ estimate [éstəmèit] — v. 추정하다, 추측하다

구문정리

본문 중 중요 구문 정리한 내용입니다. 우선 암기하고 많이 읽으시기 바랍니다.

TEST 2-2 The Making of Calendars 달력 만들기

#	구문	뜻
01	able to do	~할 수 있다
02	keep track of	~을 기록하다
03	in this way	이러한 방식으로
04	reliance upon	~에 대한 의존
05	allow O to do	O가 ~하는것을 가능케 하다
06	begin to do	~하는 것을 시작하다
07	come together	합치다, 종합하다
08	be dependent upon	~에 의지하다, 의존하다
09	for an equal amount of time	같은 시간 동안에
10	cause O to do	O가 ~하는것을 야기하다
11	out of line with	~의 선 바깥으로
12	both A and B	A와 B 둘 다
13	come to a head	무르익다, 정점에 이르다
14	throw off	벗어나다, 떨쳐버리다
15	out of sync	동시에 일어지지 않는, 조화되지 않는
16	lengthen A to B	A를 B까지 늘리다
17	synchronize with	~와 동시에 발생하다
18	lay out	~을 펼치다, 제시하다
19	at this time	이 때에
20	depend on	~에 의지하다
21	the need for	~에 대한 필요
22	suffer from	~로 고통 받다
23	on average	평균적으로
24	all but a handful of	소수를 제외한 모든
25	settle on	~을 결정하다
26	bring A to B	A를 B로 데려오다
27	in line with	~와 연결된
28	it take time for O to do	O가 to to 하는데 시간이 걸리다
29	revolve around	~을 중심으로 돌다, 회전하다
30	move forward	전진하다, 나아가다
31	estimate O to do	O가 ~한다고 추정하다

※ 다시 한 번 암기 후 → 열 번 읽기로 넘어가자!

TEST 2-3 VOCABULARY

TEST 2-3지문의 단어 중 토플 필수 단어를 선별하여 정리하였습니다.

☐ foundation [faundéiʃən]	n. 설립, 토대	
☐ enjoy [indʒɔ́i]	v. 누리다, 향유하다	
☐ extensive [iksténsiv]	a. 광범위한, 대규모의	
☐ apex [éipeks]	n. 정점, 꼭대기	
☐ longest-serving	a. 오래 집권한	
☐ sultan [sʌ́ltən]	n. 일부 이슬람교국의 왕[술탄]	
☐ the Magnificent [ðə mægnífəsnt]	a. 위대한, 위업을 이룩한(보통 고인의 칭호로 사용)	
☐ hegemony [hidʒémoni]	n. 헤게모니, 패권	
☐ initiative [iníʃiətiv]	n. 진취성, 결단력	
☐ competence [kámpətəns]	n. 능숙함	
☐ imcopetent [inkámpətənt]	a. 무능한	
☐ vizier [vɪˈzɪr]	n. (과거 일부 회교국의) 고관, 대신	
☐ intact [intǽkt]	a. 온전한, 그대로인	
☐ territorial [tèrətɔ́:riəl]	a. 육지의, 지상의	
☐ dominance [dámənəns]	n. 지배	
☐ rise [raiz]	n. 출현; 상승	
☐ neighbor [néibər]	v. 이웃하다, 인접하다	
☐ bureaucracy [bjuərákrəsi]	n. 관료제	
☐ diplomacy [diplóuməsi]	n. 외교(술)	
☐ defeat [difí:t]	n. 패배	
☐ capture [kǽptʃər]	v. 장악하다, 점령하다	

☐ administer [ədmínistər]	v. 통치하다, 관리하다
☐ imperial [impíəriəl]	a. 제국의, 황제의
☐ harem [héərəm]	n. 아내(들), 하렘에 사는 여자들
☐ accomplish [əkámpliʃ]	v. 성취하다
☐ de facto [di: fǽktou]	a. 사실상의, 실질적인
☐ minor [máinər]	n. 미성년자
☐ weaken [wí:kən]	v. 약화시키다
☐ detrimental [dètrəméntl]	a. 해로운, 손해를 입히는
☐ effectively [iféktivli]	ad. 실질적으로
☐ intermediary [ìntərmí:dièri]	n. 중개인, 중재자
☐ immediate [imí:diət]	a. 즉각적인
☐ decline [dikláin]	v. 쇠퇴하다
☐ fade [feid]	v. 서서히 사라지다
☐ superpower [sjú:pərpàuər]	n. 초강대국
☐ lose [lu:z]	v. 잃어버리다
☐ dominate [dámənèit]	v. 지배하다
☐ modernization [màdərnizéiʃən]	v. 현대화
☐ secular [sékjulər]	a. 세속적인
☐ doom [du:m]	v. 불행한 운명을 맞게 하다
☐ ultimately [ʌ́ltəmətli]	ad. 결국, 궁극적으로
☐ dissolution [dìsəlú:ʃən]	n. 해산, 소멸

구문정리

본문 중 중요 구문 정리한 내용입니다. 우선 암기하고 많이 읽으시기 바랍니다.

TEST 2-3

The Decline of the Ottoman Empire
오스만 제국의 쇠퇴

01	a series of	일련의
02	know A for B	A를 B로 알다
03	take O to another level	~를 다른 수준으로 높이다
04	expand A into B	A를 B까지 확장하다
05	hegemony over	~에 대한 통제권, 패권
06	consider A B	A를 B로 여기다, 간주하다
07	rely upon	~에 의지하다, 의존하다
08	mark the end of	~의 끝을 나타내다
09	not only A but also B	A뿐만 아니라 B도
10	blame A on B	A의 탓을 B로 돌리다
11	play a role in	~에서 역할을 하다
12	cause O to do	O가 ~하도록 야기하다
13	instead of	~대신에
14	be dedicated to	~에 헌신하다
15	battle for	~을 위한 전투
16	important to	~에 중요한
17	so that	그 결과 ~하다
18	deal with	~을 다루다, 처리하다
19	need to do	~할 필요가 있다
20	fend off	~을 막아내다, 맞서다
21	lack of	~의 부족
22	fall behind in	~면에서 뒤떨어지다
23	loss to	~에서의 손실
24	attempt to do	~하려고 시도하다
25	too ~ for A to do	너무~해서 A가 ~할 수 없다
26	rule over	~을 지배, 통치하다
27	force O to do	O가 ~하도록 강요하다
28	reply upon	~에 대답하다
29	in one's own right	자기 자신의 권리로, 혼자 힘으로
30	begin to do	~하는 것을 시작하다
31	connect A to B	A를 B에 연결시키다
32	as time went on	시간이 흘러감에 따라
33	relate A to B	A를 B와 연관시키다
34	so~that	너무~해서 그 결과 ~하다
35	influence over	~에 대한 영향력
36	in turn	결국
37	shift in	~에서의 변화
38	look for	~을 찾다
39	both A and B	A와 B 둘 다
40	begin -ing	~하는 것을 시작하다
41	ability to do	~하는 능력
42	act as	~로서 역할을 하다
43	not A but B	A가 아니라 B
44	over time	세월이 흐르면서
45	detrimental for	~에 해로운
46	continue to do	~하는 것을 계속하다
47	position as	~로서의 위치
48	refer to A as B	A를 B라고 언급하다
49	push for	~을 추구, 요구하다
50	result in	~을 야기하다

※ 다시 한 번 암기 후 → 열 번 읽기로 넘어가자!

TEST 3-1 VOCABULARY

TEST 3-1 지문의 단어 중 토플 필수 단어를 선별하여 정리하였습니다.

☐ renowned [rináund]	a. 유명한, 알려진	☐ undergo [ə͵ndərgouˈ]	v. ~을 겪다
☐ interbreed [íntə:rbrì:d]	v. 이종 교배하다	☐ considerable [kənsídərəbl]	a. 상당한
☐ speciation [spì:ʃiéiʃən]	n. 종 형성, 종 분화	☐ remote [rimóut]	a. 먼, 외딴
☐ geographically [dʒì:əgrǽfikəli]	ad. 지리적으로	☐ landmass [læˈndmæ͵s]	n. 대륙, 토지
☐ separate [sépərèit]	v. 분리시키다	☐ colonize [kάlənàiz]	v. 개척하다
☐ selective pressure [siléktiv préʃər]	n. 선택압 (개체군의 선택적 증식을 재촉하는 압박)	☐ mainland [méinlænd]	n. 본토
☐ genetic drift [dʒənétik drift]	n. 유전적 부동 (유전자의 빈도 변화)	☐ proximity [prαksíməti]	n. 근접함, 가까움
☐ mutation [mju:téiʃən]	n. 변이, 변화	☐ outdoor [auˈtdɔ͵r]	a. 야외의
☐ topography [təpάgrəfi]	n. 지형(학)	☐ volcanism [vάlkənìzm]	n. 화산 활동
☐ continental drift [kὰntənéntl drift]	n. 대륙 이동	☐ gut [gʌt]	n. 내장, 소화관
☐ rise [raiz]	n. 증가, 상승	☐ fur [fə:r]	n. 털, 모피
☐ towering [táuəriŋ]	a. 우뚝 솟은	☐ founder effect [fάundər ifékt]	n. 선구자 효과
☐ isthmus [ísməs]	n. 지협 (땅이 좁은 지형)	☐ descendant [diséndənt]	n. 후손, 자손
☐ freely [frí:li]	ad. 자유롭게	☐ colonizer [kάlənàizər]	n. 개척자
☐ effectively [iféktivli]	ad. 실질적으로	☐ prime example [praim igzǽmpl]	n. 주요 예시
☐ formidable [fɔ́:rmidəbl]	a. 어마어마한, 무시무시한	☐ differing	a. 다른, 상이한
☐ despite [dispáit]	prep. ~에도 불구하고	☐ feeding habit [fí:diŋ hǽbit]	n. 섭식 습성
☐ necessarily [nèsəsérəli]	ad. 필수적으로, 무조건	☐ niche [nitʃ]	n. 틈새, 생태적 지위
☐ gene pool [dʒi:n pu:l]	n. 유전자 공급원 (유전자 총체)		

TEST 3-1

Geographic Isolation of Species
종의 지리적 고립

01	describe A as B	A를 B로 묘사하다, 설명하다
02	ability to do	~하는 능력
03	interbreed with	~와 이종 교배하다
04	be unsure of	~에 확신이 없다
05	learn of	~에 대해 배우다
06	no longer	더이상 ~않는
07	follow course	경로를 따르다
08	it may seem illogical that	~하는것이 비논리적으로 보일지 모른다
09	split into	~로 쪼개지다
10	look at	~을 바라봄
11	as to	~에 관해
12	separated by	~에 의해 분리되다
13	tell O that	O에게 ~를 말하다
14	cause O to do	O가 ~하도록 야기하다
15	have the same effect	같은 효과를 가지다
16	between A and B	A와 B 사이
17	barrier to	~의 장벽
18	depend upon	~에 의존하다
19	in question	불확실한, 논의 되고 있는
20	require O to do	O를 ~하기 위해 필요로 하다
21	evolve into	~로 진화하다
22	opportunity for	~의 기회
23	enough to do	~하기에 충분한, 충분히
24	in terms	~의 측면에서
25	allow O to do	O가 ~하는것을 가능케하다
26	serve as	~로서 역할을 하다
27	A be colonized by B	A가 B에 의해 개척되다
28	found population	개체를 확립하다
29	make one's way to	~로 나아가다
30	due to	~때문에
31	a variety of	다양한 = various
32	unique to	~에 특유한
33	descend from	~로부터 내려오다, 자손이다
34	set apart	분리하다
35	find one's way to	~로 나아가다
36	fill the niche	틈새를 채우다
37	reliant upon	~에 의존하는
38	adapted to	~에 적응하는
39	lead to	~를 야기하다
40	affinity for	~에 대한 친밀감, 관련성
41	begin ~ing	~하는것을 시작하다

※ 다시 한 번 암기 후 → 열 번 읽기로 넘어가자!

TEST 3-2
VOCABULARY

TEST 3-2 지문의 단어 중 토플 필수 단어를 선별하여 정리하였습니다.

☐ despite [dispáit]	prep. ~에도 불구하고	
☐ squabble [skwábl]	v. 다투다, 옥신각신하다	
☐ infighting [ínfàitiŋ]	n. 내분	
☐ conquer [káŋkər]	v. 정복하다	
☐ trivial [tríviəl]	a. 사소한, 하찮은	
☐ ascend [əsénd]	v. 오르다, 승격하다	
☐ assassination [əsæsənéiʃən]	n. 암살	
☐ brash [bræʃ]	a. 자신만만한	
☐ compaingn [kæmpéin]	n. 운동, 군사 작전	
☐ overtake [ouˈvərteiˌk]	v. 추월하다, 앞지르다	
☐ foothold [fʊˈthouˌld]	n. 발판, 기반	
☐ consolidate [kənsáládèit]	v. 통합하다, 합치다	
☐ exert [igzə́:rt]	v. 가하다, 행사하다	
☐ found [faund]	v. 설립하다, 확립하다	
☐ propagation [pràpəgéiʃən]	n. 선전, 보급	
☐ demise [dimáiz]	n. 종말, 소멸	

☐ marketplace [maˈrkətpleiˌs]	n. 시장, 장터	
☐ teenated [tiˈneiˌdʒ]	a. 십대의	
☐ specialization [spèʃəl-əzéiʃən]	n. 전문화	
☐ professionalism [prəféʃənəlìzm]	n. 전문성	
☐ jack-of-all trades	n. 팔방미인, 무엇이든지 하는 사람	
☐ imperial [impíəriəl]	a. 제국의, 황제의	
☐ intercede [ìntərsí]	v. 중재하다, 탄원하다	
☐ milestone [maiˈlstouˌn]	n. 획기적인 사건; 이정표	
☐ wane [wein]	v. 줄어들다, 약해지다	
☐ execute [éksikjù:t]	v. 처형하다, 실행하다	
☐ morality [mərǽləti]	n. 도덕성	
☐ conscience [kánʃəns]	n. 양심, 가책	
☐ intertwine [ìntərtwaiˈn]	v. 뒤얽히다, 엮다	
☐ profound [prəfáund]	a. 엄청난, 깊은	
☐ usher [ʌʃər]	v. 안내하다, 인도하다	
☐ border [bɔ́:rdər]	n. 경계, 국경	

TEST 3-2

구문정리

본문 중 중요 구문 정리한 내용입니다. 우선 암기하고 많이 읽으시기 바랍니다.

The Empire of Alexander the Great
알렉산더 대왕 제국

01	fight against	~와의 싸움
02	in a way	~한 방식으로
03	under one's rule	~의 지배하에
04	when compared to	~와 비교해봤을 때
05	ascend the throne	왕위에 오르다
06	lead to	~을 야기하다
07	change in	~에서의 변화
08	take the throne	왕위를 차지하다
09	as well	또한, 역시
10	a great number of	많은 수의
11	make it easier for O to do	O가 ~하는것을 더 쉽게 만들다
12	trade with	~와 거래하다
13	one another	서로서로
14	allow O to do	O가 ~하는것을 가능케 하다
15	seek one's fortune	부를 추구하다
16	both A and B	A와 B 둘 다
17	in one's name	자기 이름으로, 독자적으로
18	at least	적어도, 최소한
19	name A after B	A의 이름을 B를 따서 짓다
20	not so much A as B	A라기 보다는 오히려 B
21	prior to	~이전에
22	come together	합치다, 뭉치다
23	make decision	결정을 내리다
24	in person	직접
25	in order to do	~하기 위해서
26	insure that	~을 보장하다
27	engage in	~에 참여하다
28	have to do	~해야만 하다
29	bring about	~을 야기하다
30	no longer	더이상
31	bring A into contact with B	A를 B와 접촉시키다
32	count on	~을 믿다, 기대하다
33	on behalf of	~의 대표해서, 대신하여
34	begin to do	~하기 시작하다
35	seem interested in~ing	~에 관심이 있는것으로 보이다
36	base A on B	A의 기반을 B에 두다
37	take the place of	~을 대체하다
38	receptive to	~을 잘 받아들이는
39	have an effect on	~에 영향을 미치다
40	such~that	너무~해서 그 결과 ~하다
41	what is known as	~라고 알려져 있는
42	be at the peak	정점에 있다
43	make great strides in	~에서 큰 진전을 이루다
44	confined to	~에 한정된

※ 다시 한 번 암기 후 → 열 번 읽기로 넘어가자!

TEST 3-3
VOCABULARY

TEST 3-3지문의 단어 중 토플 필수 단어를 선별하여 정리하였습니다.

- output [aúˈtpʊˌt] — n. 생산량, 산출량
- conducive [kəndjúːsiv] — a. 도움이 되는
- hay [hei] — n. 건초
- feed [fiːd] — v. 먹이를 주다
- livestock [láiv-] — n. 가축
- squash [skwɑʃ] — n. 호박
- maize [meiz] — n. 옥수수 = Indian corn
- practice [prǽktis] — v. 실행하다, 생활화하다
- risky [ríski] — a. 위험한
- coincidence [kouínsidəns] — n. 동시발생, 우연의 일치
- impetus [ímpətəs] — n. 자극제, 추진력
- radiocarbon dating [réidiòukάːrbən déitiŋ] — n. 방사능 탄소 연대 측정법
- legume [légjuːm] — n. 콩과 식물
- replenish [ripléniʃ] — v. 보충하다
- deplete [diplíːt] — v. 고갈시키다
- kernel [kə́ːrnl] — n. 알맹이, 작은 낱알
- mature [mətjúər] — v. 익다, 성숙해지다
- irrigation [ìrəgéiʃən] — n. 관개, 물을 끌어들임
- drought-resistant [draut rizístənt] — a. 가뭄에 잘 견디는
- hybridize [háibridàiz] — v. 잡종을 만들다, 교배시키다
- indigenous [indídʒənəs] — a. 토종의, 토착의
- fruitful [frúːtfəl] — a. 유익한, 생산적인
- crossbreed [krɔːsbriːd] — v. 이종교배를 하다
- grinding [gráindiŋ] — n. 분쇄, 제분
- flowering season [fláuəriŋ síːzn] — n. 개화기
- adaptability [ədæptəbíləti] — n. 적응성, 순응성
- assorted [əsɔ́ːrtid] — a. 여러가지의
- hybridization [hàibridəzéiʃən] — n. 교배, 혼합
- staple [stéipl] — n. 주요 산물
- selective breeding [siléktiv bríːdiŋ] — n. 선별 사육, 선발 번식
- plant [plænt] — v. (나무 씨앗 등을) 심다
- adverse [ædvə́ːrs] — a. 부정적인, 불리한
- farm [fɑːrm] — v. 경작하다, 사육하다
- surprisingly [sərpráiziŋli] — ad. 놀랍게도
- spark [spɑːrk] — v. 촉발시키다, 유발하다
- unproductive [əˌnprədəˈktiv] — a. 생산적이지 않은
- casually [kǽʒuəli] — ad. 우연히, 가끔, 무심코
- amino acid [əmíːnou ǽsid] — n. 아미노산
- consume [kənsúːm] — v. 먹다, 소비하다
- alongside [əlɔˈŋsaiˈd] — ad. ~와 나란히, 함께

구문정리

본문 중 중요 구문 정리한 내용입니다. 우선 암기하고 많이 읽으시기 바랍니다.

TEST 3-3

Early Maize Cultivation in the American Southwest
미국 남서부의 초기 옥수수 재배

01	be blessed with	~로 축복받다, ~을 누리다
02	conducive to	~에 도움이 되는
03	unfavorable for	~에 적합하지 않은
04	use O to do	O를 ~하기 위해 사용하다
05	introduce A to B	A를 B에 소개하다, 도입하다
06	around this time	대략 같은 시기에
07	begin ~ing	~하는 것을 시작하다
08	enjoy an advantage over	~보다 이점을 누리다
09	hunting and gathering	수렵채집
10	reliance upon	~에 대한 의존성
11	have troubling ~ing	~하는데 어려움을 갖다
12	impetus for A to do	A가 ~하는 자극제
13	allow O to do	O가 ~하는 것을 가능케하다
14	have control over	~에 대한 통제권을 갖다
15	even if	비록 ~일지라도
16	spread to	~로 퍼지다
17	play a role in	~에서 역할을 하다
18	not only A but also B	A뿐만 아니라 B도
19	be able to do	~할 수 있다
20	ensure that	~을 보장하다
21	stay fertile	비옥한 상태를 유지하다
22	enough to do	~하기에 충분히
23	year after year	해마다
24	hybridize A with B	A와 B를 교배시키다
25	continue to do	~하는 것을 지속하다
26	come up with	~을 찾아내다, 생산하다
27	adaptability to	~에 적응하는 능력
28	valuable to	~에 귀중한, 가치 있는
29	attention to	~에 대한 관심, 주목
30	adept at	~에 능숙한
31	learn to do	~하는 것을 배우다
32	favor the soil	땅을 비옥하게 하다
33	realize that	~을 깨닫다, 인지하다
34	expose A to B	A를 B에 노출시키다
35	shift in	~에서의 변화
36	in fact	실제로, 사실상
37	attribute A to B	A의 탓을 B로 돌리다
38	around the same time	대략 같은 시기에

※ 다시 한 번 암기 후 → 열 번 읽기로 넘어가자!

TEST 4-1 VOCABULARY

TEST 4-1 지문의 단어 중 토플 필수 단어를 선별하여 정리하였습니다.

- ☐ homeostasis [hòumiəstéisis] — n. 항상성
- ☐ leave [li:v] — v. 떠나다; 남기다
- ☐ differ [dífər] — v. 다르다
- ☐ preferred range [pri:fə́:rd reindʒ] — n. 바람직한 범위
- ☐ enzyme [énzaim] — n. 효소
- ☐ degradation [dègrədéiʃən] — n. 저하, 악화
- ☐ classify [klǽsəfài] — v. 분류하다
- ☐ homeotherm [hóumiəθə̀:rm] — n. 온혈 동물
- ☐ ambient [ǽmbiənt] — a. 주위의, 주변의
- ☐ metabolic [mètəbɑ́lik] — a. 신진대사의
- ☐ fluctuate [flʌ́ktʃuèit] — v. 변동을 거듭하다
- ☐ bask [bæsk] — v. 햇볕을 쬐다
- ☐ inhabit [inhǽbit] — v. 거주하다, 살다
- ☐ retention [riténʃən] — n. 보유, 유지
- ☐ harness [hɑ́:rnis] — v. 이용하다
- ☐ biochemical [bai̯ou̯keˈməkəl] — a. 생화학의
- ☐ biochemical reaction [bai̯ou̯keˈməkəl riǽkʃən] — n. 생화학 반응
- ☐ exertion [igzə́:rʃən] — n. 노력, 분투
- ☐ physical exertion [fízikəl igzə́:rʃən] — n. 격렬한 신체 운동[활동]
- ☐ intertidal zone [ìntərtáidl zoun] — n. 조간대 [만조와 간조 때의 해안선 사이의 부분]
- ☐ bodily fluid [bɑ́dəli flú:id] — n. 체액
- ☐ substrate [sʌ́bstreit] — n. 기질, 기저층
- ☐ corresponding [kɔ̀:rəspɑ́ndiŋ] — a. 상응하는, 해당하는
- ☐ average [ǽvəridʒ] — v. 평균이 ~이 되다
- ☐ pump [pʌmp] — v. 퍼올리다, 퍼내다
- ☐ circulatory system [sə́:rkjulətɔ̀:ri sístəm] — n. 순환계
- ☐ peripheral [pərífərəl] — a. 주변부의, 말초의
- ☐ natural radiation [nǽtʃərəl rèidiéiʃən] — n. 자연방사선 [인간의 자연환경에 존재하는 방사선]
- ☐ respiration [rèspəréiʃən] — n. 호흡
- ☐ nasal cavity [néizəl kǽvəti] — n. 비강, 콧구멍
- ☐ exhalation [èkshəléiʃən] — n. 발산, 숨을 내쉼
- ☐ cooling effect [kú:liŋ ifékt] — n. 냉각 효과
- ☐ counteract [kàuntərǽkt] — v. 대응하다
- ☐ insulation [ìnsəléiʃən] — n. 절연, 단열
- ☐ cetacean [sitéiʃən] — n. 고래목의 동물
- ☐ seal [si:l] — n. 바다표범, 물개
- ☐ blubber [blʌ́bər] — n. 해양동물의 지방
- ☐ nimble [nímbl] — a. 재빠른, 민첩한
- ☐ weasel [wízl] — n. 족제비
- ☐ fat reserve [fæt rizə́:rv] — n. 지방 축적물
- ☐ preen [pri:n] — v. 단장하다, 몸치장을 하다
- ☐ fluff [flʌf] — v. 솜털을 부풀리다
- ☐ dual-layer [djú:əl léiər] — n. 이중 층
- ☐ fur [fə:r] — n. 모피, 털
- ☐ undercoat [əˈndərkoùt] — n. 속털, 긴털밑에나는 잔털
- ☐ down [daun] — n. 새의 솜털
- ☐ trap [træp] — v. 가두다
- ☐ otter [ɑ́tər] — n. 수달
- ☐ waterproof [wɔˈtərpruːf] — a. 방수가 되는
- ☐ enhance [inhǽns] — v. 향상시키다
- ☐ terrestrial [təréstriəl] — a. 육지의, 지상의
- ☐ counterpart [káuntərpɑ̀:rt] — n. 상대물, 대응물
- ☐ conserve [kənsə́:rv] — v. 보존하다, 보호하다
- ☐ countercurrent [káuntərkə̀:rənt] — n. 역류, 반대방향의
- ☐ vein [vein] — n. 정맥 [몸의 각 부분에서 혈액을 모아 심장으로 보내는 혈관]
- ☐ artery [ɑ́:rtəri] — n. 동맥 [심장 박동에 의해 밀려나온 혈액을 온몸으로 보내는 혈관]
- ☐ flipper [flípər] — n. 지느러미발

구문정리

본문 중 중요 구문 정리한 내용입니다. 우선 암기하고 많이 읽으시기 바랍니다.

TEST 4-1

Temperature Regulation in Marine Organisms
해양생물의 온도조절

01	necessary for	~에 필요한
02	based on	~에 기반된
03	make it difficult for A to do	A가 ~하는 것을 어렵게 만들다
04	make it important that	that절 하는 것을 어렵게 만들다
05	way to do	~하는 방법
06	think of A as B	A를 B로 여기다, 간주하다
07	regardless of	~와 관련 없이
08	be dependent upon	~에 의지하다, 달려있다
09	protect A from B	A를 B로부터 보호하다
10	in a way	~한 방법, 방식으로
11	a host of	다수의, 많은
12	fall into	~로 분류되다
13	muscular activity	근육 활동
14	reliance upon	~에 대한 의존성
15	allow O to do	O가 ~하는 것을 가능케하다
16	lose A to B	A를 B에 잃어버리다
17	be able to do	~할 수 있다
18	have difficulty in ~ing	~하는데 어려움을 갖다
19	exposure to	~에 대한 노출
20	lead to	~을 야기하다
21	have an effect on	~에 영향을 끼치다
22	an assortment of	여러가지의
23	take a form	형태를 취하다
24	bulid up	축적하다
25	prevent O from ~ing	O가 ~하는것으로부터 막다
26	act as	~로서 역할을 하다
27	pump A from B	A를 B로부터 퍼오다
28	return from	~에서 돌아오다
29	such as	~와 같은

※ 다시 한 번 암기 후 → 열 번 읽기로 넘어가자!

TEST 4-2 VOCABULARY

TEST 4-2 지문의 단어 중 토플 필수 단어를 선별하여 정리하였습니다.

- ☐ upper paleolithic [ʌpər pèiliəlíθik] — n. 상부 구석기시대
- ☐ around [əráund] — ad. 대략
- ☐ KYA(kiloyears ago) — ad. thousands years ago
- ☐ dramatic [drəmǽtik] — a. 극적인, 급격한
- ☐ transition [trænzíʃən] — n. 변화, 이동
- ☐ anatomically [ænətámikəli] — ad. 해부학적으로
- ☐ rise [raiz] — n. 출현 ; 증가
- ☐ versatile [vɔ́:rsətl] — a. 다용도의; 다재 다능한
- ☐ implement [ímpləmənt] — n. 도구, 기구 ; 시행하다
- ☐ antler [ǽntlər] — n. (사슴의) 가지진 뿔
- ☐ barb [ba:rb] — n. 가시, 미늘
- ☐ barbed [ba:rbd] — a. 가시가 돋친, 미늘이 있는
- ☐ harpoon [ha:rpú:n] — n. 작살
- ☐ spear thrower [spiər θróuər] — n. 창 발사기
- ☐ indicate [índikèit] — v. 가리키다, 나타내다
- ☐ rudimentary [rù:dəméntəri] — a. 기본적인, 기초적인
- ☐ physics [fíziks] — n. 물리학
- ☐ torque [tɔ:rk] — n. 축의 회전력
- ☐ figurative art [fígjurətiv a:rt] — n. 조형 예술
- ☐ primitive [prímətiv] — a. 초기의, 원시사회의
- ☐ tattooing kit — n. 문신 도구
- ☐ endeavor [indévər] — n. 노력, 시도
- ☐ aspect [ǽspekt] — n. 측면, 양상
- ☐ purely [pjúərli] — ad. 순전히, 오로지
- ☐ ochre [óukər] — n. 오커 [페인트, 그림물감의 원료로 쓰이는 황토]
- ☐ contemporary [kəntémpərèri] — a. 동시대의, 당대의
- ☐ question [kwéstʃən] — v. 의문을 제기하다
- ☐ anthropologist [ænθrəpáləʤist] — n. 인류학자
- ☐ microlithic [màikroulíθik] — n. 세석기 [중석기~신석기 초기에 성행한 소형의 석기]
- ☐ time frame [taim freim] — n. 기간
- ☐ immediate [imí:diət] — a. 즉각적인
- ☐ myriad [míriəd] — n. 무수함, 무수히 많음
- ☐ rock art [rak a:rt] — n. 암면 미술
- ☐ cognition [kagníʃən] — n. 인지, 인식
- ☐ scrutiny [skrú:təni] — n. 정밀조사, 철저한 검토
- ☐ advent [ǽdvent] — n. 출현, 도래
- ☐ falter [fɔ́:ltər] — v. 요동치다, 흔들리다
- ☐ deficiency [difíʃənsi] — n. 부족
- ☐ presence [prézns] — n. 존재, 있음
- ☐ undergo [ʌ̀ndərgoú] — v. 겪다
- ☐ uninhabited [ʌninhǽbitid] — a. 거주 되지 않는

TEST 4-2

The Upper Paleolithic Revolution
구석기 시대 후기 혁명

#	표현	뜻
01	change in	~에서의 변화
02	mark the change	변화를 나타내다
03	bring about	~을 야기하다
04	increase in	~에서의 증가
05	so ~ that	너무~해서 그 결과~하다
06	refer to A as B	A를 B라 언급하다, 지칭하다
07	use O to do	O를 ~하기 위해 사용하다
08	known as	~로 알려진
09	leap forward	~쪽으로의 도약
10	appear to do	~하는 것처럼 보이다
11	similar to	~와 유사한
12	lead O to do	O가 ~하도록 야기하다
13	ability to do	~하는 능력
14	date to	연대를 ~로 추정하다
15	point to A as B	A를 B로 가리키다
16	disregard for	~에 대한 무시, 무관심
17	hold that	~을 주장하다, 생각하다
18	at least	적어도, 최소한
19	export A to B	A를 B로 추출하다, 보내다
20	isolate A from B	A를 B로부터 고립시키다
21	see O to do	O가 ~하는 것으로 보다
22	begin to do	~하는 것을 시작하다
23	migrate out of	~밖으로 이동하다
24	cause O to do	O가 ~하도록 야기하다
25	reason for	~에 대한 이유
26	point out	~을 가리키다, 지적하다
27	it may turn out that	~라고 판명될지도 모른다
28	turn out	판명 나다, 드러나다
29	have yet to do	아직 ~하지 않다
30	prior to	~이전에
31	go undetected	발견되지 않다 [become undetected]
32	hospitable for	~에 살기 적합한, 쾌적한
33	migration to	~로의 이동, 이주

※ 다시 한 번 암기 후 → 열 번 읽기로 넘어가자!

TEST 4-3
VOCABULARY

TEST 4-3지문의 단어 중 토플 필수 단어를 선별하여 정리하였습니다.

☐ misconception [miskənseˈpʃən]	n. 오해	☐ permanence [pə́ːrmənəns]	n. 영구성
☐ findings [fáindiŋ]	n. 연구결과	☐ theorize [θíːəràiz]	v. 이론화 하다
☐ catastrophic [kætəstráfik]	a. 재앙적인	☐ feldspar [féldspɑ̀ːr]	n. 장석
☐ corroborate [kərábərèit]	v. 입증하다	☐ quartz [kwɔːrts]	n. 석영
☐ biblical [bíblikəl]	a. 성경의	☐ solidify [səlídəfài]	v. 굳어지다, 굳히다
☐ postulate [pástʃulèit]	v. 상정하다	☐ pyroxene [Pyroxene]	n. 휘석
☐ shrink [ʃriŋk]	v. 줄어들다, 수축되다	☐ olivine [áləvìːn]	n. 감람석
☐ extrapolate [ikstrǽpəlèit]	v. 추론하다	☐ immense [iméns]	a. 거대한, 엄청난
☐ deform [difɔ́ːrm]	v. 변형시키다	☐ continental edge [kɑ̀ntənéntl edʒ]	n. 대륙붕단, 가장자리
☐ shrinkage [ʃríŋkidʒ]	n. 수축, 줄어듦	☐ subsidence [səbsáidns]	n. 침하, 침강
☐ wrinkle [ríŋkl]	v. 주름지다, 구겨지다	☐ erosion [iróuʒən]	n. 침식
☐ contract [kənˈtrækt]	v. 수축하다	☐ linear [líniər]	a. 직선의
☐ peel [piːl]	n. 껍질	☐ trough [trɔ(ː)f]	n. 기압골(=ridge)
☐ separate [sépərèit]	v. 분리되다	☐ subside [səbsáid]	v. 가라앉다
☐ instability [ìnstəbíləti]	n. 불안정	☐ uplift [əˈplift]	v. 들어올리다, 융기하다
☐ alternate [ɔ́ːltərnèit]	v, 번갈아 일어나다	☐ modify [mádəfài]	v. 수정하다
☐ remnant [rémnənt]	n. 잔여물, 나머지	☐ unexplainable [ʌnikspléinəbl]	a. 설명할 수 없는
☐ alternation [ɔ̀ːltərnéiʃən]	n. 변경, 교체	☐ strata [strǽ-]	n. 지층, 단층
☐ interpret [intə́ːrprit]	v. 해석하다	☐ isostasy [aisástəsi]	n. 지각 균형(설)
☐ intersperse [ìntərspə́ːrs]	v. ~사이에 배치하다	☐ disprove [disprúːv]	v. 틀렸음을 입증하다
☐ stratigraphic column	n. 층서주 [퇴적 분지에 쌓인 지층의 기둥]	☐ changeability [tʃèindʒəbíləti]	n. 가변성
☐ contemporaneous [kəntèmpəréiniəs]	a. 동시에 발생하는	☐ radiogenic [rèidioudʒénik]	a. 방사능에 의한
☐ counter [káuntər]	v. 대응하다, 대처하다	☐ definitively [difínətivli]	ad. 결정적으로, 명확하게
☐ landmass [læˈndmæˌs]	n. 광대한 토지	☐ negate [nigéit]	v. 무효화하다
☐ ironically [airánikəli]	ad. 아이러니하게	☐ continental drift [kɑ̀ntənéntl drift]	n. 대륙 이동(설)
☐ acceptance [ækséptəns]	n. 수용, 승인	☐ tectonic plate [tektánik pleit]	n. 지각 표층
☐ geographically [dʒìːəgrǽfikəli]	ad. 지리적으로		

TEST 4-3

Nineteenth-Century Theories of Mountain Formation
19세기 산형성론

구문정리 — 본문 중 중요 구문 정리한 내용입니다. 우선 암기하고 많이 읽으시기 바랍니다.

01	as recently as	~만큼 최근에
02	view A as B	A를 B로 여기다, 간주하다
03	a series of	일련의, 연속적인
04	allow O to do	O가 ~하는 것을 가능케하다
05	correspond to	~에 일치하다
06	begin to do	~하는 것을 시작하다
07	such as	~와 같은
08	base A upon B	A의 기반을 B에 두다
09	lead O to do	O가 ~하도록 이끌다
10	the first to do	~한 첫 번째
11	try to do	~하려고 노력하다
12	lead to	~을 야기하다
13	vice versa	거꾸로, 반대로
14	at the bottom of	~의 바닥면에
15	leave A as B	A를 B로 남겨두다
16	help to do	~하는 것을 돕다
17	be unable to do	~할 수 없다
18	bring about	~을 야기하다
19	make O O.C	O를 O.C하게 만들다
20	change in	~에서의 변화
21	refer to A as B	A를 B라 언급하다, 지칭하다
22	known as	~로 알려진
23	early on	초기에
24	put pressure on	~에 압박을 가하다
25	turn A into B	A를 B로 바꾸다
26	not A but B	A가 아니라 B
27	build up	축적되다
28	do nothing to do	~하는데 아무것도 하지 않다
29	hold in place	고정시키다
30	on one's own	스스로, 혼자서
31	cause O to do	O가 ~하도록 야기하다
32	look for	~을 찾다

※ 다시 한 번 암기 후 → 열 번 읽기로 넘어가자!

TEST 5-1
VOCABULARY

TEST 5-1 지문의 단어 중 토플 필수 단어를 선별하여 정리하였습니다.

- ☐ mercantilism [mə́ːrkəntilìzm] — n. 상업 주의
- ☐ sweep [swiːp] — v. 휩쓸다
- ☐ tariff [tǽrif] — n. 관세
- ☐ threaten [θrétn] — v. 위협하다
- ☐ lift [lift] — v. 철폐하다; 들어올리다
- ☐ embargo [imbáːrgou] — n. 금수 조치, 통상 금지령
- ☐ overwhelm [òuvərhwélm] — v. 압도하다
- ☐ imperial [impíəriəl] — a. 제국의; 황제의
- ☐ ordinance [ɔ́ːrdənəns] — n. 법령, 조례
- ☐ manufacture [mænjufǽktʃər] — v. 제조하다
- ☐ dairy [dɛ́əri] — a. 유제품의
- ☐ detrimental [dètrəméntl] — a. 해로운
- ☐ molasse — n. 당밀 [사탕수수에 남은 즙액]
- ☐ basically [béisikəli] — ad. 기본적으로
- ☐ plantation [plæntéiʃən] — n. 농장
- ☐ colonist [kálənist] — n. 식민지 주민
- ☐ dramatically [drəmǽtikəli] — ad. 급격하게
- ☐ shipping [ʃípiŋ] — n. 해상운송; 선박
- ☐ fleet [fliːt] — n. 함대
- ☐ encourage [inkə́ːridʒ] — v. 장려하다
- ☐ shipbuilding [ʃiˈpbiˌldiŋ] — n. 조선, 건함
- ☐ freely [fríːli] — ad. 자유롭게
- ☐ foundation [faundéiʃən] — n. 기반, 토대
- ☐ one-third [wʌn-θəːrd] — n. 3분의 1
- ☐ urbanization [əːrbənizeiʃən] — n. 도시화
- ☐ warehouse [weˈrhauˌs] — n. 창고
- ☐ dock [dak] — n. 부두; 조선소
- ☐ maintenance [méintənəns] — n. 유지, 보수
- ☐ stipulation [stìpjuléiʃən] — n. 조항, 조건
- ☐ enumerate [injúːməreit] — v. 열거하다
- ☐ naval [néivəl] — a. 해군의
- ☐ parliament [páːrləmənt] — n. 의회, 국회
- ☐ burdensome [bə́ːrdnsəm] — a. 부담스러운, 힘든
- ☐ refund [rifʌnd] — v. 환불하다
- ☐ duties [djúːti] — n. 세금, 관세
- ☐ suffer [sʌ́fər] — v. 고통받다
- ☐ diversification [divə̀ːrsəfikéiʃən] — n. 다양화
- ☐ subsidy [sʌ́bsədi] — n. 보조금
- ☐ raw material [rɔː mətíəriəl] — n. 원자재
- ☐ otherwise [ʌ́ðərwàiz] — ad. 그렇지 않으면
- ☐ large-scale [laːrdʒ-skeil] — a. 대규모의
- ☐ manufactured goods [mænjufǽktʃər gudz] — n. 제품, 공산품
- ☐ tailor [téilər] — n. 재단사
- ☐ milliner [Milliner] — n. 여성 모자 제작자
- ☐ restriction [ristríkʃən] — n. 제한, 제약
- ☐ ironworks [áiərnwə̀ːrks] — n. 제철소
- ☐ prosperity [praspérəti] — n. 번영, 번성
- ☐ dishware [díʃwɛ̀ər] — n. 접시류, 식기류
- ☐ influx [ínflʌks] — n. 쇄도, 유입
- ☐ middle-class [mídl klæs] — n. 중산층
- ☐ comfortably [kʌ́mfərtəbli] — ad. 편안하게
- ☐ counterpart [káuntərpɑ̀ːrt] — n. 상대, 대응물

TEST 5-1

Colonial America and the Navigation Acts
식민지와 항해에 관한 법률

본문 중 중요 구문 정리한 내용입니다. 우선 암기하고 많이 읽으시기 바랍니다.

01	attempt to do	~하는 것을 시도하다
02	Eighty Years' War	네덜란드 독립전쟁
03	lift embargo on	금수 조치를 철폐하다
04	in order to do	~하기 위해서
05	a series of	일련의
06	known as	~로 알려진
07	limit A to B	A를 B까지 제한하다
08	specialize in	~을 전문화하다
09	locally made	현지 생산된
10	as time went by	시간이 흘러감에 따라
11	restriction on	~에 대한 제한
12	force O to do	O가 ~하도록 강요하다
13	detrimental to	~에 해로운
14	add A to B	A를 B에 추가하다
15	set forth	~을 제시하다
16	allow O to do	O가 ~하는 것을 가능케하다
17	trade with	~와 거래하다
18	bring about	~을 야기하다
19	compose A of B	A를 B로 구성하다
20	lead to	~을 야기하다
21	not only A but also B	A뿐만 아니라 B도
22	such as	~와 같은
23	ship A to B	A를 B로 발송하다
24	agree to do	~하는것에 동의하다
25	refund duty on	~에 대한 관세를 환급해주다
26	out of	~ 밖으로
27	account for	차지하다; 설명하다
28	less than	~보다 적은, 이하의
29	pay A to B	A를 B에 지불하다
30	be restricted to	~로 제한되다
31	at prices	~한 가격으로
32	demand for	~에 대한 수요
33	remain high	높게 남아있다
34	in addition to	~뿐만 아니라
35	export to	~로의 수출

※ 다시 한 번 암기 후 → 열 번 읽기로 넘어가자!

TEST 5-2
VOCABULARY

TEST 5-2 지문의 단어 중 토플 필수 단어를 선별하여 정리하였습니다.

☐ weaver family [wíːvər fǽməli]	n. 멧새과 [집 짓는 새]
☐ grassland [grǽsˌlænd]	n. 풀밭, 초원
☐ sub-saharan [sʌb səhǽrən]	a. 사하라 사막 이남의
☐ colony [káləni]	n. 군집체, 군락
☐ up to [ʌp tu]	prep. 최대~까지
☐ conservative [kənsɔ́ːrvətiv]	a. 보수적인
☐ estimate [éstəmeit]	n. 추정치
☐ breeding pair [bríːdiŋ pɛər]	n. 함께 새끼를 기르는 한 쌍
☐ illogical [ilάdʒikəl]	a. 비논리적인, 터무늬없는
☐ harsh [haːrʃ]	a. 가혹한, 혹독한
☐ remarkable [rimάːrkəbl]	a. 놀랄 만한, 주목할 만한
☐ mainly [méinli]	ad. 주로
☐ overall [ouˈvərɔˌl]	a. 종합적인, 대체로
☐ hoard [hɔːrd]	v. 비축하다
☐ feast [fiːst]	n. 향연, 축제, 포식
☐ advantageous [ædvəntéidʒəs]	a. 이로운, 유리한
☐ adaptation [ædəptéiʃən]	n. 적응(력)
☐ variable [véəriəbl]	a. 가변적인, 변동이 심한
☐ monsoon [mansúːn]	n. 장마, 우기
☐ germinate [dʒɔ́ːrmənèit]	v. 시작되다, 발아하다
☐ interrupt [ìntərʌ́pt]	v. 방해하다, 중단시키다
☐ instigate [ínstəgèit]	v. 부추기다, 선동하다
☐ mature [mətjúər]	a. 성숙한, 다 자란
☐ ripe [raip]	a. 익은, 숙성된
☐ forbidding [fərbídiŋ]	a. 험악한, 으스스한
☐ weave [wiːv]	v. 짜다, 짜서 만들다
☐ ovoid [óuvɔid]	a. 타원형의
☐ straw [strɔː]	n. 짚, 지푸라기
☐ lay [lei]	v. 놓다, 두다
☐ fledgling [flédʒliŋ]	n. 어린 새
☐ seed stock [siːd stak]	n. 종자 비축
☐ hectare [héktɛər]	n. 헥타르 (땅 면적의 단위)
☐ brooding [brúːdiŋ]	n. 사육
☐ synchronize [síŋkrənàiz]	v. 동시에 발생하다
☐ hatch [hætʃ]	v. 부화하다
☐ brood [bruːd]	v. 알을 품다
☐ plant [plænt]	v. 심다
☐ nourishment [nɔ́ːriʃmənt]	n. 영양, 자양분
☐ susceptible [səséptəbl]	a. 취약한, 예민한
☐ loss [lɔːs]	n. 손실
☐ attributable [ətríbjutəbl]	a. 원인인, 기인하는
☐ precarious [prikɛ́əriəs]	a. 불안정한, 위태로운
☐ adaptability [ədæptəbíləti]	n. 적응성
☐ propensity [prəpénsəti]	n. 성향, 경향
☐ flock [flak]	n. 무리, 떼
☐ concern [kənsɔ́ːrn]	n. 걱정, 염려
☐ entrench [intréntʃ]	v. 자리 잡다
☐ resemble [rizémbl]	v. 닮다, 유사하다
☐ habitat [hǽbitæt]	n. 서식지
☐ harvest [hάːrvist]	n. 수확물
☐ devastate [dévəstèit]	v. 완전히 파괴하다
☐ wreak [riːk]	v. (큰 피해등을) 가하다, 입히다
☐ havoc [hǽvək]	n. 대파괴, 큰 혼란
☐ ban [bæn]	v. 금지하다
☐ import [impɔ́ːrt]	n. 수입(품)
☐ destructive [distrʌ́ktiv]	a. 파괴적인

TEST 5-2

The Most Common Bird on Earth
지구상에서 가장 흔한 새

#	구문	뜻
01	outside of	~의 바깥쪽에
02	hear of	~에 대해 듣다
03	put A at B	(나이·무게·양 등에 대해) A를 B로 보다, 추산하다
04	account for	차지하다; 설명하다
05	less than	~이하의
06	dependence upon	~에 대한 의지, 의존
07	lead to	~을 야기하다
08	learn to do	~하는 것을 배우다
09	deal with	~을 다루다, 처리하다
10	cope with	~에 대처하다
11	sustain oneself	자신의 생명을 유지하다
12	gorge on	~을 게걸스럽게 먹다
13	enough to do	~하기에 충분한; 충분히
14	migrate to	~로 이동하다
15	cause O to do	O가 ~하도록 야기하다
16	take advantage of	이용하다
17	allow O to do	O가 ~하는것을 가능케하다
18	by the time	~할 때 즈음, 까지
19	return to	~로 돌아가다
20	access to	~로의 접근(권)
21	stimulate O to do	O가 ~하도록 자극하다
22	on the same day	같은 날에
23	be dependent upon	~에 의지, 의존하다(Be)
24	rely on	~에 의지, 의존하다(R)
25	turn to	~에 의지, 의존하다(T)
26	leave O O.C	O를 O.C 한채로 남겨두다
27	wipe out	~을 없애다
28	attributable to	~가 원인인
29	in a state	~한 상태로
30	propensity to do	~하는 경향
31	wreak havoc on	~을 파괴하다

※ 다시 한 번 암기 후 → 열 번 읽기로 넘어가자!

TEST 5-3
VOCABULARY

TEST 5-3 지문의 단어 중 토플 필수 단어를 선별하여 정리하였습니다.

- treaty [tríːti] — n. 조약
- cede [siːd] — v. 양도하다, 이양하다
- cessation [seséiʃən] — n. 중단, 중지
- dramatically [drəmǽtikəli] — ad. 극적으로
- pristine [prístiːn] — a. 아주 깨끗한
- wilderness [wíldərnis] — n. 황무지
- vacant [véikənt] — a. 비어있는
- democracy [dimάkrəsi] — n. 민주주의
- preserve [prizə́ːrv] — v. 보존하다
- establishment [istǽbliʃmənt] — n. 설립
- swath [swaθ] — n. 베어낸 한 구획, 풀밭
- preservation [prèzərvéiʃən] — n. 보호, 보존
- Old world [ould wəːrld] — n. 구세계 [유럽, 아프리카, 아시아]
- distinguishing [distíŋgwiʃiŋ] — a. 특징적인, 특색있는
- antithetical [æntəθétikəl] — a. 현저하게 대조를 이루는
- baron [bǽrən] — n. 부호, 거물
- heavily [hévili] — ad. 심하게, 세게
- advertise [ǽdvərtàiz] — v. 광고하다, 알리다
- majesty [mǽdʒəsti] — n. 장엄함, 웅장함
- raise [reiz] — v. 들어올리다, 일으키다
- awareness [əwέərnis] — n. 인식, 자각
- adoption [ədάpʃən] — n. 선정, 채택
- bolster [bóulstər] — v. 강화하다, 보강하다
- highway [háiwèi] — n. 고속도로
- act [ækt] — n. 법률
- pay [pei] — v. 지불하다, 지급하다
- oversee [ouˈvərsiˌ] — v. 관리, 감독하다
- logging [lɔ́ːgiŋ] — n. 벌목
- passage [pǽsidʒ] — n. 통과
- authorize [ɔ́ːθəràiz] — v. 권한을 부여하다
- mobility [moubíləti] — n. 유동성
- outpace [auˈtpeiˌs] — v. ~을 능가하다, 앞서다
- cause [kɔːz] — v. 야기하다
- degradation [dègrədéiʃən] — n. 저하, 악화
- impassioned [impǽʃənd] — a. 열정적인, 간절한
- convince [kənvíns] — v. 확신시키다
- wilderness [wíldərnis] — n. 황야, 황무지
- recreational [rèkriéiʃənəl] — a. 휴양의, 오락의
- permanently [pə́ːrmənəntli] — ad. 영구적으로

구문정리

본문 중 중요 구문 정리한 내용입니다. 우선 암기하고 많이 읽으시기 바랍니다.

TEST 5-3

National Parks in the Western United States
미국 서부의 국립공원

01	between A and B	A와 B 사이
02	more than double	두배 이상을 만들다[되다]
03	13 original colonies	독립 13주 [미합중국 독립 당시의 13개 영국 식민지]
04	cede A to B	A를 B에 양도하다
05	by the middle of	~중반에
06	expand A to B	A를 B까지 확장하다
07	mass immigration	대량 이주
08	a plethora of	많은, 과다의
09	belong to	~에 속하다
10	come into play	작동하기 시작하다
11	put forth	제시하다
12	in perpetuity	영원히, 영구적으로
13	prior to	~이전에
14	set aside	제쳐두다, 따로 놓다
15	a sense of inferiority	열등감
16	with regard to	~에 관련하여, 관하여
17	have a hand in	~에 관여하다, 가담하다
18	the desire to do	~하고픈 바람
19	business interests	대사업가들
20	push for	~을 요구하다
21	encourage O to do	O가 ~하도록 장려하다
22	take a trip	여행하다
23	set up	설립하다
24	on the outskirts	시외에, 변두리에
25	raise awareness	의식을 높이다
26	general public	일반 대중
27	rise from A to B	A부터 B까지 올라가다
28	begin -ing	~하는 것을 시작하다
29	call for	~을 요구하다, 필요로 하다
30	Federal Aid Road Act	연방보조 도로법
31	not only A but also B	A뿐만 아니라 B도
32	at around the same time	거의 같은 시기에
33	business magnate	거상, 거물
34	independent agency	독립 기관
35	barely a month after	~이후 한달이 채 지나지 않아서
36	sign a bill	법안에 서명하다
37	name A B	A를 B라고 부르다, 명명하다
38	protect A from B	A를 B로부터 보호하다
39	business interests	대사업가들, 기업
40	attempt to do	~하는 것을 시도하다
41	have O O.C	O를 O.C하게 만들다
42	cross-country	국토 횡단의
43	popular with	~에게 인기있는
44	the need for	~에 대한 필요
45	side effect	부작용
46	access to	~로의 접근권
47	increase in	~에서의 증가
48	argue that	~을 주장하다
49	help to do	~하는 것을 돕다
50	convince A of B	A에게 B를 확신시키다
51	have an impact on	~에 영향을 미치다
52	both A and B	A와 B 둘 다

※ 다시 한 번 암기 후 → 열 번 읽기로 넘어가자!

TEST 6-1 VOCABULARY

TEST 6-1 지문의 단어 중 토플 필수 단어를 선별하여 정리하였습니다.

☐ dressing [drésiŋ]	n. 옷 입기
☐ wearer [wέərər]	n. 착용자
☐ immediate [imíːdiət]	a. 즉각적인
☐ ethnic [éθnik]	a. 인종의, 민족의
☐ occupation [àkjupéiʃən]	n. 직업
☐ key [kiː]	a. 주요한
☐ fascinate [fǽsənèit]	v. 매료시키다
☐ striking [stráikiŋ]	a. 두드러진, 인상적인
☐ intimately [íntəmətli]	ad. 친밀하게, 밀접하게
☐ identity [aidéntəti]	n. 정체성, 신원
☐ signifier [signəfàiər]	n. 기표, 징표
☐ despite [dispáit]	prep. ~에도 불구하고
☐ neutrality [njuːtrǽləti]	n. 중립성
☐ adornment [ədɔ́ːrnmənt]	n. 장식(품)
☐ symbolically [simbάlikəli]	ad. 상징적으로
☐ tribal [tráibl]	a. 부족의, 종족의
☐ denote [dinóut]	v. 나타내다, 가리키다
☐ inclusion [inklúːʒən]	n. 포함
☐ draw [drɔː]	v. 이끌어 내다
☐ ire [aiər]	n. 화, 분노
☐ derision [diríʒən]	n. 조롱, 조소
☐ inappropriately [ìnəpróupriətli]	ad. 부적절하게
☐ indicator [índikèitər]	n. 지표
☐ sociopolitical	a. 사회 정치적인
☐ standing [stǽndiŋ]	n. 직위, 지위
☐ insignia [insígniə]	n. 휘장, 배지 [계급·소속 등을 나타내는]
☐ ivory [áivəri]	n. 상아[로 된 물건]
☐ beading [bíːdiŋ]	n. 구슬 장식
☐ smock [smak]	n. 기다란 셔츠, 겉옷
☐ amulet [ǽmjulit]	n. 부적
☐ flywhisk [flai hwisk]	n. 파리채 [종종 고위·권위의 상징]
☐ signify [sígnəfài]	v. 의미하다, 뜻하다
☐ divine [diváin]	a. 신성한
☐ regal [ríːgəl]	a. 제왕의, 군왕의
☐ bearer [bέərər]	n. 소지자
☐ respective [rispéktiv]	a. 각자의, 각각의
☐ interpretation [intəːrprətéiʃən]	n. 해석
☐ beautify [bjúːtəfài]	v. 아름답게 하다
☐ adorn [ədɔ́ːrn]	v. 꾸미다, 장식하다
☐ cosmetics [kazmétik]	n. 화장품
☐ bodily [bάdəli]	a. 신체의
☐ modification [màdəfikéiʃən]	n. 수정, 변경
☐ tattooing	n. 문신
☐ profusion [prəfjúːʒən]	n. 다량, 풍성함
☐ scarring	n. 흉터
☐ purposefully [pɔ́ːrpəsfəli]	ad. 의도적으로
☐ cicatrization [sìkətrizéiʃən]	n. 반흔, 흉터 형성
☐ abdomen [ǽbdəmən, æbdóumən]	n. 복부
☐ extremity [ikstréməti]	n. 맨 끝, 심장에서 가장 먼 신체 부위[손, 발]
☐ elaborate [ilǽbərət]	a. 정교한, 공들인
☐ oftentimes [ɔ́(ː)fəntàimz]	ad. 자주, 종종
☐ scarification [skærəfikéiʃən]	n. 상처 자국
☐ aesthetics [esθétiks]	n. 심미학
☐ along [əlɔ́ːŋ]	prep. ~을 따라
☐ fertility [fərtíləti]	n. 다산; 비옥함
☐ mummy [mʌmi]	n. 미라
☐ adjacent [ədʒéisnt]	a. 인접한, 가까운
☐ apparel [əpǽrəl]	n. 의류, 의복
☐ identification [aidèntifəkéiʃən]	n. 신원 확인, 신분 증명

구문정리

본문 중 중요 구문 정리한 내용입니다. 우선 암기하고 많이 읽으시기 바랍니다.

TEST 6-1

The Role of Dress in Africa
아프리카에서 드레스의 역할

01	think of	~을 생각하다, 고려하다
02	be in the right	이치에 맞다
03	use O to do	O를 ~하기 위해 사용하다
04	both A and B	A와 B 둘다
05	worn by	~에 의해 입혀진, 착용된
06	point to	~을 가리키다
07	connect A to B	A를 B에 연결시키다
08	act as	~로서 역할을 하다
09	important to	~에 중요한
10	assign A to B	A를 B에 할당하다
11	cause O to do	O가 ~하도록 야기하다
12	tie A to B	A를 B에 결부시키다
13	in addition to	~뿐만 아니라
14	see A as B	A를 B로 여기다, 간주하다
15	in fact	사실상, 실제로
16	make up A of B	A를 B로 구성하다
17	highly prized	높게 평가되는
18	of importance	중요한
19	such ~ that	너무~해서 그 결과 ~하다
20	come to do	~하게 되다
21	bring up	불러 일으키다
22	contrary to	~와는 반대로
23	consider A B	A를 B로 여기다, 간주하다
24	a profusion of	풍부한
25	the use of	~의 사용
26	place A on B	A를 B에 두다, 놓다
27	take the form	형태를 취하다
28	correlate to	~와 연관성이 있다
29	in addition	게다가
30	appear to do	~하는 것처럼 보이다
31	utilize O to do	O를 ~하기 위해 사용하다
32	as well	또한, 마찬가지로
33	serve purpose	목적을 수행하다
34	the same A as B	B와 똑같은 A

※ 다시 한 번 암기 후 → 열 번 읽기로 넘어가자!

TEST 6-2
VOCABULARY

TEST 6-2 지문의 단어 중 토플 필수 단어를 선별하여 정리하였습니다.

☐ throughout [θruːáut]	prep. ~에 걸쳐서, 통틀어	
☐ permanently [pə́ːrmənəntli]	ad. 영구적으로	
☐ mass extinction [mæs ikstíŋkʃən]	n. 대멸종	
☐ biodiversity [bai͵oudaivərˈsəti]	n. 생물의 다양성	
☐ cretaceous [kritéiʃəs]	n. 백악기(중생대 마지막 시기)	
☐ paleogene [péiliədʒìːn]	n. 고제3기(신생대 제3기의 전반부 시기)	
☐ estimate [éstəmèit]	v. 추정하다	
☐ perish [périʃ]	v. 사라지다, 죽다	
☐ non-avian [nan-éiviən]	a. 비-조류의	
☐ since [sins]	prep. ~이래로	
☐ dramatic [drəmǽtik]	a. 극적인	
☐ concurrently [kənkə́ːrəntli]	ad. 동시에	
☐ posit [pázit]	v. 사실로 상정하다	
☐ precipitate [prisípitèit]	v. 침전시키다; 촉발시키다	
☐ catastrophe [kətǽstrəfi]	n. 참사, 재앙	
☐ eruption [irʌ́pʃən]	n. 분출	
☐ strike [straik]	v. 치다, 부딪치다	
☐ extraterrestrial body [ekstrətəˈrestriəl bádi]	n. 외계 물체	
☐ bolide [bóulaid, -lid]	n. 불덩이 유성, 폭발 화구	
☐ cosmic radiation [kázmik rèidiéiʃən]	n. 우주 방사선	
☐ concrete [kánkriːt]	a. 구체적인	
☐ strata [strǽ-]	n. 지층, 단층 [stratum의 복수]	
☐ question [kwéstʃən]	v. 의문을 제기하다	
☐ deposit [dipázit]	v. 침전시키다	
☐ atmospheric circulation [ætməsférik sə̀ːrkjuléiʃən]	n. 대기 순환	
☐ thereby [ðɛərbái]	ad. 그렇게 함으로써, 그것 때문에	
☐ soil column [sɔil káləm]	n. 흙 기둥	
☐ bolster [bóulstər]	v. 강화하다, 북돋우다	
☐ sediment [sédəmənt]	n. 침전물	
☐ strengthen [stréŋkθən]	v. 강화되다, 강화 시키다	
☐ meteoric impact [mìːtiɔ́ːrik]	n. 유성 충돌	
☐ quartz [kwɔːrts]	n. 석영	
☐ planar [pléinər]	a. 평면의	
☐ shockwave [ʃaˈkweiˌv]	n. 충격파	
☐ silicate [sílikət]	n. 규산염	
☐ droplet [drǽplit]	n. 작은 방울	
☐ terrestrial [təréstriəl]	a. 지구의, 지상의	
☐ super-heat [súːpər hiːt]	v. 과열시키다	
☐ soot [sut]	n. 그을음	
☐ wildfire [waiˈldfaiˌər]	n. 들불, 번갯불	
☐ negate [nigéit]	v. 무효화하다, 부인하다	
☐ weather [wéðər]	v. 변하게 하다	
☐ erode [iróud]	v. 침식시키다	
☐ under-reported [ʌ́ndər ripɔ́ːrt]	a. 보고가 덜 된	
☐ under-appreciated [ʌ́ndər əpríːʃièit]	a. 인정을 덜 받은	
☐ bolide [bóulaid, -lid]	n. 불덩이 유성, 화구	
☐ estimate [éstəmèit]	n. 추정치	
☐ telltale [teˈlteiˌl]	a. 명확한, 분명한	
☐ andesitic rock [ændizítik rak]	n. 암산암질 암석	
☐ isotopic [àisətápik]	a. 동위원소의	
☐ time line [taim lain]	n. 연대표, 시각표	
☐ convincingly [kənvínsiŋli]	a. 설득력 있게, 납득이 가도록	
☐ debris [dəbríː]	n. 잔해, 쓰레기	
☐ prompt [prɑːmpt]	v. 촉발시키다, 유도하다	

TEST 6-2

Evidence of an Asteroid Impact
소행성 충돌의 증거

#	표현	뜻
01	the boundary between	~사이의 경계
02	die off	죽다, 소멸되다
03	allow O to do	O가 ~하는 것을 가능케하다
04	rise to the position	위치까지 올라가다
05	attempt to do	~하려고 시도하다
06	adapt to	~에 적응하다
07	point to	~을 가리키다, 나타내다
08	refer to A as B	A를 B라고 언급하다
09	upon ~ing	~하자마자 곧
10	believe O to do	O가 ~한다고 믿다
11	point out	~을 가리키다
12	it is likely that	~할 가능성이 높다
13	in diameter	직경이 ~인
14	send up	보내다
15	mix with	~와 혼합하다
16	settle on	~에 정착하다; ~을 정하다
17	common in	~에 흔한
18	travel through	~을 이동하다
19	throw A into B	A를 B안으로 던지다, 뿌리다
20	the lack of	~의 부족
21	work for	~을 위해 일하다, 연구하다
22	just off	~바로 옆에 떨어져 있는
23	use O to do	O를 ~하기 위해 사용하다
24	similar to	~와 비슷한
25	date A to B	A의 연대를 B로 추정하다
26	conclude that	~라고 결론 내리다
27	required to do	~하기 위해 필요되는

※ 다시 한 번 암기 후 → 열 번 읽기로 넘어가자!

TEST 6-3 VOCABULARY

TEST 6-3 지문의 단어 중 토플 필수 단어를 선별하여 정리하였습니다.

- ☐ exploration [èksplə réiʃən] — n. 탐험, 탐사
- ☐ host [houst] — v. 주최하다, 관리하다
- ☐ thriving [θráiviŋ] — a. 번영하는, 번성하는
- ☐ administer [ədmínistər] — v. 관리하다, 집행하다
- ☐ extensive [iksténsiv] — a. 광범위한
- ☐ pelt [pelt] — n. (짐승의) 생가죽
- ☐ handicraft [hǽndikræft] — n. 수공예(품)
- ☐ interaction [i̇ntəræˈkʃən] — n. 상호작용
- ☐ differing — a. 다른, 상이한
- ☐ pale [peil] — v. 창백해지다, 흐릿해지다
- ☐ encounter [inkáuntər] — v. 만나다, 조우하다
- ☐ fishermen [ˈfiʃərmən] — n. 어민
- ☐ whaler [hwéilər] — n. 고래잡이 배
- ☐ local [lóukəl] — n. 현지인
- ☐ process [práses] — v. 가공하다; 처리하다
- ☐ catches [kǽtʃiz] — n. 잡은 물건들
- ☐ trading post [tréidiŋ poust] — n. 교역소
- ☐ draw [drɔː] — n. 이끌림, 이목을 끄는 것
- ☐ phenomenally [finámənli] — ad. 경이적으로
- ☐ dominate [dámənèit] — v. 지배하다, 장악하다
- ☐ profound [prəfáund] — a. 엄청난, 심오한
- ☐ procure [proukjúər, prə-] — v. 구하다, 입수하다
- ☐ spirituality [spìritʃuǽləti] — n. 정신성, 영성
- ☐ indigenous [indídʒənəs] — a. 원산의, 토종의
- ☐ long-held [lɔ(ː)ŋ held] — a. 오랫동안 간직해온
- ☐ brass kettle [bræs kétl] — n. 놋쇠 주전자

- ☐ pronounced [prənáunst] — a. 확연한, 단호한
- ☐ encroach [inkróutʃ] — v. 잠식하다, 침범하다
- ☐ antler [ǽntlər] — n. (사슴의) 가지진 뿔
- ☐ tine [tain] — n. (사슴뿔 같은 것의) 가지
- ☐ comb [koum] — n. 빗
- ☐ ornate [ɔːrnéit] — a. 화려하게 장식된
- ☐ excavate [ékskəvèit] — v. 발굴하다
- ☐ commemorate [kəmémərèit] — v. 기념하다
- ☐ dignitary [dígnitèri] — n. 고위 관리
- ☐ longevity [landʒévəti] — n. 장수
- ☐ saturation [sætʃəréiʃən] — n. 포화
- ☐ favor [féivər] — v. 선호하다
- ☐ glass beads [glæs biːds] — n. 유리 구슬
- ☐ pipestone [páipstòun] — n. 파이프돌 (아메리칸 인디언이 담뱃대를 만드는 데 쓰는 점토암)
- ☐ artisan [áːrtizən] — n. 장인
- ☐ replacement material [ripléismənt mətíəriəl] — n. 대체 물질
- ☐ attire [ətáiər] — n. 의복, 복장
- ☐ regalia [rigéiliə] — n. 예복, 휘장, 왕권의 상징물들
- ☐ symbolism [símbəlìzm] — n. 상징주의
- ☐ luxurious [lʌgzúəriəs] — a. 호화로운
- ☐ bearer [béərər] — n. 소지자
- ☐ corporatization — n. 민영화
- ☐ immune [imjúːn] — a. 면역성이 있는, 영향을 받지 않는
- ☐ oppression [əpréʃən] — n. 억압, 탄압
- ☐ poverty [pávərti] — n. 빈곤, 가난

TEST 6-3

Native Americans and European Trade Goods
아메리카 원주민 및 유럽 무역 상품

01	prior to	~이전에
02	allow O to do	O가 ~하는 것을 가능케하다
03	not only A but also B	A뿐만 아니라 B도
04	way of thinking	사고 방식
05	pale in comparison to	~앞에서는 무색하다, ~보다 못하다
06	bring about	야기하다
07	try to do	~하려고 노력하다
08	at this time	이때에
09	travel to	~로 여행하다
10	off of	~에서 떨어진
11	begin -ing	~하는것을 시작하다
12	trade with	~와 거래하다
13	be eager to do	~하는 것을 열망하다
14	trade in	~을 거래하다
15	have an impact on	~에 영향을 미치다
16	one another	서로서로
17	interaction with	~와의 상호작용
18	spend O -ing	~ing 하는데 O를 쓰다, 소비하다
19	both A and B	A와 B 둘 다
20	offer A B	A에게 B를 제공하다
21	incorporate A into B	A를 B로 통합하다
22	early on	초기에
23	in favor of	~에 찬성하여
24	encroach on	~로 침범하다
25	use O to do	O를 ~하기 위해 사용하다
26	carve A into B	A를 B로 조각하다
27	on horseback	말을 탄
28	find one's way into	~로 나아가다
29	lead to	~로 이어지다
30	shift in	~에서의 변화
31	begin to do	~하는 것을 시작하다
32	the trade in	~에서의 보상판매
33	incorporate A into B	A를 B로 통합하다
34	in place of	~을 대신해서
35	make A of B	A를 B로 만들다
36	give A B	A에게 B를 주다
37	bring with	~을 데려오다
38	be immune to	~에 영향을 받지 않는
39	ill effect	부작용
40	fall out of favor	인기, 총애를 잃다
41	combined with	~와 결합된
42	throw A into B	A를 B로 빠뜨리다

※ 다시 한 번 암기 후 → 열 번 읽기로 넘어가자!

usherin.usher.co.kr

USHER

iBT TOEFL
INTERMEDIATE READING 02
묶기

TEST 1-1 Costs of Quitting a Job

01.   High job mobility has long been held (as a hallmark) (of the American economy). (In contrast to employees) (in Japan and Europe), American employees appear (to switch) jobs much more readily. (On average), American workers have been (with their current employer) (for a shorter period) and have had a larger number (of employers) (than those) (in other regions). This has been blamed, (in part), (by the lower levels) (of training) provided (by American companies) (for their workers), but this is likely an oversimplified explanation. (In reality), many diverse factors influence American employees' decisions (to switch) jobs more frequently (than their counterparts) (in Europe and Japan).

02.   [While economic theories posit [that mobility is most likely (in prosperous times), [when the costs and risks (of changing) jobs are low]]], a number of logistical differences make it more likely. [■] One (of the most surprising) (of these) is the location (of the job). [■] Those employed (in urban areas) are more likely (to change) jobs, likely (due to the easy availability) (of other jobs) (in the city), [which means [that the employee will not have (to relocate) his or her home (to take) another job]]. [■] Those [who live (in non-urban areas) [who quit their jobs]] will have more difficulty (in finding) another job (due to the limited number) available (in the region). [■].

03.   (In addition to logistical and monetary factors), psychological factors also play a large role (in job mobility). Individuals (with more adventurous personalities and fewer familial responsibilities) are more likely (to switch) jobs easily, [as they can overcome the fear (of the unknown) and are more willing (to risk) the consequences (of job change)]. (In fact), studies have shown [that 13% (of workers) [who have switched jobs more than 3 times] are responsible (for about half) (of all permanent employment separations)]. (On the other hand), fear and cultural norms can keep employees (in their current positions). One (of these), the Japanese "lifetime employment" system, has made job switching almost unheard of (in Japanese society). This system, [which was meant (to limit) the ability (of companies) (to lay off) employees], has also built a strong sense (of employee loyalty), [which makes it societally undesirable (for employees) (to switch) jobs (without good reason)].

04.　Interestingly, real estate prices have also been linked (to the incidence) (of job change). Housing policies (in Japan and Europe) often make residential relocation an expensive prospect, [which discourages job mobility (in much the same way) [that non-urban locations do]]. (In many) (of these countries), rental subsidies are more widely available [than (in the United States), [which makes workers loath (to relocate) (for a job change)]]. (In addition), rent control schemes [that limit the increase (in rent) (between consecutive rental contracts)] reduce job and residential mobility, [because landlords can negotiate any rental amount (for new contracts)]. This means [that any job move [that requires relocation] could result (in an astronomical increase) (in housing cost)].

05.　Some researchers also point (to history) (as an indicator) (of the propensity) (for job change). The United States, Canada, and Australia are all large, rather sparsely populated countries [that show much lower job tenures (than most European countries and Japan)]. They hypothesize [that these country's long history (of attracting) international immigration and their citizens' willingness (to undertake) long-distance relocation have made job change much less unusual. (In a country) [where people have previously moved thousands (of miles) (from their homeland)], pulling up stakes and moving (for another job) is much less (of an event) [than (in countries) (with more stable populations)].

06.　(With all) (of these possible explanations) (for the differences) (in job mobility rates), another question arises: what is the societal impact (of increased job mobility)? Some believe [that increased job mobility has a positive impact [because it increases worker satisfaction and worker-job matches]. Economists also point (to larger numbers) (of workers and employers) seeking matches (as a sign) (of the economic flexibility [that makes economic adaptation possible]. Conversely, higher mobility (with lower costs) can cause employers (to skimp) (on training) (for employees) [who [they constantly fear] will jump ship]. Whatever the societal cost (of job mobility), employers must try (to balance) job mobility and its associated costs (in order to succeed).

[■] This could cause them (to need) (to make) a costly, life-altering move (to another region).

TEST 1-2 Cell Theory

01. The three main tenets (of cell theory), [that cells are the basic unit (of life)], [that all organisms are composed (of cells)], and [that cells arise only (from other cells)], are some (of the most basic principles) (in the field) (of biology). (From this theory) scientists have been able (to extrapolate) a great deal (of other scientific knowledge). (In fact), our understanding (of the role) (of cells) (in sexual reproduction) and the discovery (of our genetic building blocks), DNA, are direct results (of this). Cell theory has also allowed medical researchers (to better understand) illnesses, (such as cancer), as well as the cause (of viral and bacterial infections). [While the theory is now commonly accepted, and may seem (like common sense)], its development took hundreds (of years).

02. (In fact), the earliest discoveries (in the field) took place (in the middle) (of the 17th century) [when light microscopy began (to be regularly used) (on living creatures). It was (during this time) [that physicist Robert Hooke melted glass (into lenses) [(with which) he could study fish scales, feathers, and the bodies (of various insects)], however his greatest discovery was [that he noticed a series (of chambers) (in a sample) (of cork oak), [which [he felt] resembled cubicles and named "cells"]. Antoine van Leeuwenhoek [who created even stronger lenses] would later trump this discovery. Using his microscopes he studied the tartar (from his teeth) and noticed [that it contained microscopic organisms [he called "aminalcules"]]. (Over time) he was able (to view) microorganisms, (such as bacteria), [that were previously unknown]. Leeuwenhoek was able (to accurately describe) microorganisms and microscopic parts (of larger organisms), (including the red blood cell). He did not, unfortunately, observe the reproduction (of these animalcules or organisms), so he erroneously believed, [as did most others (of the time)], [that they simply spontaneously generated].

03. (Over the next two centuries) a great deal (of additional observations) would accumulate, but a true cell theory would not emerge (until the middle) (of the 19th century). Today scientists blame this great delay (on the inferior scientific equipment), (such as microscopes), and techniques), (such as preserving) samples (of living material) (without destroying) it, (of 17th & 18th century researchers), [which hindered their discoveries]. (In addition), the early observations (of Hooke and Leeuwenhoek) did not address larger issues, (such as cells) making up all larger organisms. Hooke had simply noticed the cellular imprint, not the actual cell itself, [while Leeuwenhoek observed the actual cell, but failed (to provide) an accurate description or categorization (of its common structures)].

04. [As the 19th century progressed], these problems were solved (through the invention) (of stronger microscopes, more diligent recording) (of findings), and increased cooperation) (by scientists). [■] One (of the first) (to take) advantage (of these) was Scottish surgeon Robert Brown, [who noted (in 1831) [that a circular object was present (in all) (of the orchid cells) [he studied]]]. [■] Using this finding, he researched other types (of cells) and found the same structure, [which [he then posited] was a common cellular feature [that he named the nucleus]. [■] Today, we know [that the nucleus is the carrier (of our genetic material)]. [■]

05. (By the late 1830s) these discoveries only increased (in frequency) and the cell theory truly began (to take) hold. (In 1838 and 1839), German biologists Matthias Schleiden and Theodor Schwann respectively discovered [that all plants and animals were composed (of cells)]. The discovery (of cells) (with nuclei) (in both types) (of organisms) allowed them (to conclude) [that the cell was the basic unit (of life)]. It also helped them understand [that microscopic bacteria had something (in common) (with larger organisms)]; they were both made up (of cells), [which were the building blocks (of all organisms)]. These two discoveries were the basic premises (for the cell theory).

06. Later, other cellular biologists expanded (on these findings). Perhaps the most important (of these) was German pathologist Rudolf Virchow [who contributed the third tenet (of the cell theory) (in 1855)]: All cells come (from other living cells). This contradicted most common understanding (of the time), [as it was thought [that cells could spontaneously generate [when a nucleus was able (to form and grow) the remainder (of the cell body) around itself]]]. His explanation allowed later scientists (to observe and describe) cell division (in the late 1880s). His theories also acted (as the basic principle) (behind Pasteur's germ theory) (of disease), (despite Virchow's personal objection) (to such a theory). He felt [that diseases were caused (by internal cellular abnormalities) and not (outside pathogens), [which [he thought] were simply attracted (to the abnormal cells) (as a habitat)]]. [While germ theory discounts this (for most diseases)], he did correctly suggest [that abnormal cells could cause some diseases [that affect the rest (of the body), (such as leukemia)]].

[■] [Although Brown discovered this core component (of the cell)], he did not know the true significance (of his discovery).

Mating Songs of Frogs

01. Most species (of frogs) rely (upon auditory signals) (to communicate) (with one another). This occurs [because auditory communication is much more efficient (than visual forms) (of communication)]. This is [because auditory signaling, (unlike visual communication), does not require a specific orientation (to receive) a message]. The recipient need not be facing the sender (to receive) the signal. [■] They also allow signals (to be sent) (over greater distances) (than visual communication methods). [■] (Instead of being blocked) (by physical barriers), the auditory signal can be transmitted. [■] (In fact), auditory communication allows frogs (to broadcast) their messages (through the air, underwater, and even through the substrate). [■] Further, [since most frog and toad species are nocturnal], auditory messages have the advantage (of being) usable even (in complete darkness). (Due to these advantages), male frogs have developed a complex system (of communication) [that allows them (to attract) potential mates].

02. Male frogs are able (to produce) these signs (due to a series) (of adaptations), the most notable being the vocal sacs located (beneath the floor) (of the mouth). (To create) their distinctive croaking sounds, frogs seal off their nostrils and mouths and use the muscles (along their body wall) (to force) air back-and-forth (from the lungs) (through the larynx) and (into the vocal sac). This air movement (across the larynx) causes the vocal cords (to vibrate) and the sound is then amplified (by the vocal sacs) (to produce) a loud, clear croaking sound. These sounds attract females, [which may respond (by approaching) the male or even (by calling back) (to the male)]. This can even lead (to duets) (between receptive couples). Unfortunately, they can also increase the mortality risk, [since predators can also recognize the croaking].

03. (To human ears) these croaks may all sound the same, but they are actually a complex system [that allows frogs (to learn) a great deal (about the croaking frog)]. Perhaps the most important information [that a female frog can discern (from the croaking)] is the temporal pattern and frequency, [both (of which) are species-specific]. [Although some frog species can interbreed], hybridization usually produces non-viable offspring; therefore female frogs are attracted (to the call) (of males) (from their species). Frogs are so attuned (to differentiating) calls [that they can even determine [if the caller is (from the same region)]]. (In much the same way) [that human languages have developed dialects], frog calls vary slightly (amongst different geographic populations) and can be used (to determine) [whether the call is (from a male) (in a neighboring territory)], or [if an intruder has appeared].

04. Another key piece (of information) [that females glean (from the croaking)] is the relative size and age (of the croaker). Many frog species undergo indeterminate growth, meaning [they continuously grow larger [as they age]]. This provides them (with larger vocal sacs and larynxes) [that produce louder and lower tones [as they age]]. Females, [which are generally attracted (to older frogs)], recognize the differences (in amplitude and pitch) (of the caller) and are attracted (to them). This inherent bias (of female frogs) (toward older males) is a method (of selecting) genetically superior mates, [since their age and size indicate [that the male frogs have survived environmental and predatory hazards, two traits [that would be beneficial (for her offspring)]]]. However, these two aspects can be ambiguous, [as both temperature and distance can cause the calls (of younger males) (to seem) louder and lower (than older specimens)].

05. Female frogs can determine the relative health and territorial safety (of the male) (through his calls) as well. (Because of the continuous muscle contractions) required (to push) air (through the vocal mechanisms), [some (of which) make up 15% (of the frogs overall mass)], croaking requires a considerable energy expenditure (of part) (of the male). Some studies show [tree frog croaking is the most energy intensive activity (of any vertebrate)]. Therefore, it can only be performed (by males) [that are healthy enough (to eschew) feeding (in order to search) (for a mate). Further, the ability (to continually croak) indicates (to the female) [that the male has a secure territory [(in which) he is safe (from predation)], [since he is calling so much attention (to himself)]].

06. Interestingly, male-female interaction is not the only use (of auditory communication) (in frogs). Male frogs also communicate (with one another) (to establish) a territory. This is especially important [because (during the mating season) [when the males form large 'choruses,'] they learn the croaking (of their direct neighbors)]. [When they hear these croaks] they are not alarmed, but [when they hear an unfamiliar call] they croak aggressively (to warn) the intruder [that they are encroaching (upon another frog's territory)].

[■] This ability allows frogs (to broadcast) their messages [no matter where they are located].

TEST 2-1 Milankovitch Cycles and Glaciation

01. Scientists have pieced together a relatively detailed timeline (of the twenty glacial cycles) [that took place (during the Pleistocene Epoch) (10,000-2,000,000 years ago)]. (During these frigid periods), glaciers (up to 3,900m thick) covered 30% (of Earth's surface). These were most prevalent (in the higher-latitude regions) (of both hemispheres), [which were covered (by glaciers) as far south (as Germany) (in the Northern Hemisphere) and as far north (as the Andes) (in the Southern Hemisphere)]. However, (despite 100+ years) (of research) (into these periods), researchers are unable (to explain) their cause.

02. (Over the years), diverse factors, (such as continental location, oceanic circulation and solar energy fluctuation), have been cited (as possible causes) (of these glaciations). One (of the most interesting) was put forth (by Scottish scientist James Croll) [who used the previously known fact [that cyclic changes (in Earth's orbit) affect [how solar radiation impacts Earth's surface]] (to deduce) [that they could also affect the global climate]. Using this theory, Yugoslavian mathematician Milutin Milankovitch developed an equation [that showed [how these cyclic changes (in Earth's orbit), now known (as Milankovitch cycles), could cause climatic changes and lead (to continental glaciations)]].

03. Milankovitch based his equation (on three cyclic changes) (in Earth's position) relative (to the Sun) [that [he thought] could collectively have an effect (on the solar radiation) [that is incident (on Earth's surface)]]: eccentricity, obliquity, and precession. The first (of these), eccentricity, is the elliptical variation (in the Earth's orbit) [that sometimes brings it closer (to the Sun) and slightly changes every revolution (in a 96,000-year cycle)]. The second (of these), obliquity, is concerned (with the annual changes) (in the tilt) (of Earth's axis) [that causes seasonal variation]. [As this tilt changes], (in a 41,000-year cycle), the temperature difference (between winter and summer) becomes extreme and more mild [as the tilt is respectively higher or lower]. The final (of the Milankovitch cycles), precession, is the circular wobble [that Earth performs (on its axis) every 12,700 years, (in a movement) [that resembles the wobble (of a slowly moving top)]. [Although these three cycles do not affect the amount (of solar radiation) [that reaches the Earth]], they greatly affect its distribution. Milankovitch's equation showed [that every 40,000 years these three cycles would perfectly synchronize (in a way) [that would greatly reduce the difference (between winter and summer temperatures) and prevent the winter ice (from melting) (during the summer)], thereby allowing it (to build up), and causing an overall glacial growth.

04. (Despite developing) this theory (in the 1920s), Milankovitch was limited (in his ability) (to test) it extensively, [since the timeline (of the Pleistocene Epoch temperature changes) necessary (for testing) it was not developed (until the 1970s)]. (After the development) (of this new chronology), a correlation (between Milankovitch cycles and the major climatic changes) (of the last 65 million years) became clearer. Further, core samples taken (from the deep-sea floor) proved [that Milankovitch's equation was incredibly accurate (in predicting) climate changes (over the last few hundred thousand years), (including the end) (of the Pleistocene Epoch)].

05. [■] Unfortunately, this accuracy and correlation does not fully explain the cause (of glaciation) (throughout history). [■] [If Milankovitch's explanation was accurate], it would require glaciations (to have occurred) regularly (throughout Earth's history), yet they appear (to have occurred) only rarely. [■] This has led scientists (to determine) [that there must be another factor [that works (with the Milankovitch cycles) (to cause) glaciations]. [■] [When this mystery factor has sufficiently lowered the average temperature], the cyclic variations (of solar radiation) caused (by the Milankovitch Cycles) can throw Earth (into and out of glacial periods) (with the regularity) predicted (by the Milankovitch equation).

06. (In the quest) (to discover) this mystery-cooling factor, a number of possibilities have been suggested. One (of these) is [that changes (in the Sun's luminosity) have allowed fluctuations (in the solar energy) [that reaches Earth]. However, this is highly unlikely, [since it is now believed [that the Sun has steadily become stronger (over time)]]. Another possible cause (of lower temperatures) was volcanic dust (in the atmosphere) shielding Earth (from solar radiation) and causing temperatures (to drop). This is also rather unlikely, [since the beginning (of the last glaciation) does not correspond (with known major eruptions)]. A more recent theory states [that differences (in atmospheric carbon dioxide) (CO_2) have caused temperature fluctuations (on Earth)]. [Since CO_2 traps radiation (in the atmosphere)], periods (of decreased atmospheric CO_2) results (in lower temperatures) (on Earth's surface), allowing solar radiation (to escape). This is especially attractive (to researchers), [because studies (of the Greenland ice cap) show [that the number (of CO_2 bubbles) found (in the different strata) changes depending (on [when the ice formed])]]. Samples (from periods) known (to be) warmer show higher CO_2 levels, [while colder periods have significantly less], thereby confirming the correlation (between CO_2 levels and Earth's temperature).

[■] This can be understood [if one looks back (at Earth's climate) (since its formation) approximately 4.5 billion years ago].

TEST 2-2 The Making of Calendars

01. Even (before the invention) (of the modern calendar), people were able (to keep) track (of events) (in their lives) using the phases (of the moon) and the seasons. (In this way), one could explain [that something would occur two days (after the next full moon)] or [that one was born 25 winters ago]. This reliance (upon the moon) may seem quite rudimentary, but it also allowed them (to count) the days (between the moons phases and the equinoxes) (when the duration (of the days) and nights are approximately equal) and the solstices (the longest and shortest days (of the year), [which mark the traditional beginning (of each) (of the seasons)]. [As knowledge and understanding (of these events) increased], calendars [as we now know them] began (to come together).

02. [As these empirical lunar-and solar-based calendars became more popular], their flaws became more evident. [■] (For one), they were extremely dependent (upon the weather). [■] [While it does not affect the actual movement (of either) (of the celestial bodies)], it can obscure them and cause inaccuracies (in the calendar). [■] The calendars were also dependent (upon the location), [since the timing (of the moon's phases and the solstices) and equinoxes change (over distances)]. [■] (For instance), the timing (of the rise) (of the new moon) would be earlier (in eastern locations). It may not even occur (on the same day) [if the second observer is far enough west]. This is also problematic (for observers) (in extreme northern latitudes) [where the sun remains (below the horizon) (for 4.5 months) (during winter) and remains overhead (for an equal amount) (of time) (in the summer)].

03. Secondary problems arose (due to the fact) [that the basic unit (of the calendar), the day, does not evenly fit (in the calendric concept) (of either the month or the year)]. (Over time), this causes the calendar day (to fall) (out of line) (with both the lunar and solar cycle). This basic inaccuracy required [that days or months be intercalated, or added (to the calendar)]. Unfortunately, this process was overseen (by government officials or holy men) [who could be corrupt, inept, or both]. This problem came (to a head) (during the reign) (of Julius Caesar), [when the intercalation cycle was thrown off (by war) and were observed (in some consecutive years) and forgotten (in others), causing the calendar year (to fall) (out of sync)]. (To solve) this problem, the Julian calendar was introduced around 50 BCE and the Roman Empire's year was officially lengthened (to 365.25 days).

04. The new Julian calendar could be easily calculated and remained better synchronized with the cycles of the sun and moon over time. This removed the chance for abuse by laying out a systematic method for intercalations. Surprisingly, calendars in the East and West diverged at this time. Those in the East, namely China and India, depended upon the exact timing of lunar and solar events, because of the importance of these in the society's religions and traditions. But those in the West and Middle East followed rigid arithmetical rules that kept them synchronized with the natural world without the need for constant observations and calculations of astronomical events.

05. Both lunisolar and arithmetic calendar systems still suffered from the problem mentioned earlier, the impossibility of the larger units of time to be divided evenly by the basic unit of measure, the day. Calendar's based on lunation, or the periods between new moons, are inherently self-adjusting and will synchronize with the cycles, but arithmetical calendars will only remain synchronized on average. However, this does not mean that the lunar calendar is more accurate, because the cycles of the moon are still not easily divisible by days as each lunation takes approximately 29.53 days.

06. Today, all but a handful of countries have settled on the use of one civil arithmetically based calendar, the Gregorian calendar, which Pope Gregory XIII introduced in 1582. Under the Gregorian calendar, the problem with the uneven number of days in the year was solved through the use of leap years, which contain an extra day, every four years, except those that are divisible by 100, but not by 400. This means that 1700, 1800, and 1900 would be common (non-leap) years, but 2000 would be a leap year. This new calculation effectively brought the average length of the year to 365.2425 years, more in line with the actual time it takes for earth to revolve around the sun. The new calendar system also dropped 10 days to realign the yearly equinoxes, since the accumulated errors in the calendar over the previous 1000-1200 years had moved them forward by 10 days. This does not, however, mean that the Gregorian calendar is without its flaws. The system is estimated to have an error of one day every 3,300 years.

[■] This was not likely to cause problems in the desert regions of Egypt or Mesopotamia, but it could easily throw off the calendar in regions prone to large storm systems.

TEST 2-3 The Decline of the Ottoman Empire

01. (After its foundation) (in 1299), Anatolia's Ottoman Empire enjoyed extensive success and expansion (under a series) (of very powerful leaders). Many agree [that the empire reached its apex (during the reign) (of its 10th), and longest-serving, sultan, Suleyman the Magnificent)]. [Although his predecessors were known (for their wisdom, savage conquests, and administrative ability)], Suleyman took this (to another level) and expanded the empire (into central Europe, Persia), (to the southern coast) (of the Arabian Peninsula), and (across northern Africa). This gave the Ottoman Empire near total hegemony (over Mediterranean trade) and this period is considered the "Golden Age" (of the empire). Unfortunately, Suleyman's successors lacked initiative and competence and (under their leadership) the empire suffered. Luckily, some (of these incompetent leaders) relied (upon "viziers," or executive officers), [who kept the empire intact (for nearly 400 more years)].

02. Unfortunately (for the Ottoman Sultans), the end (of the 16th century) marked not only the end (of their territorial expansion and regional dominance), but also the beginning (of the empire's slow decline). However, this cannot be completely blamed (on the incompetence) (of the leaders). Changes (within the empire) and the rise (of other regional powers), especially those neighboring the empire's European territories, both played a large role (in the decline) (of the empire). These changes caused the role (of the Sultan) (to change) dramatically. (Instead of being dedicated) (to leading) armies (into battle) (for territorial expansion), bureaucracy and diplomacy became more important (to the Sultans) [so that they could administer the enormous territory (of the empire)] and (to deal) (with its increasingly powerful neighbors). (In addition), large army units needed (to be permanently positioned, funded, and controlled) (to fend off) the Russian's in the Crimea, the Persians (to the west), and other powers (around the Mediterranean region).

03. These were new roles [that would have been difficult (for the empire's early successful sultans)], but (with the lack) (of skill and experience) (of those) [who followed Suleyman] the empire fell behind (in military and administrative technology) and suffered military defeats, (such as the empire's loss) (to Phillip II of Spain) and the stunning loss) (to the Habsburgs and the Holy League) [when attempting (to capture) Vienna]. The large territory covered too much area (for one person) (to rule over), forcing the sultans (to reply) (upon the Divan), a group (of trusted officers, ministers, and a Grand Vizier). These Viziers and their bureaucratic organizations became very powerful (in their own right) and later sultans, (such as Selim II), began (to rely) (upon them) (to administer) the territory.

04. Surprisingly, another group [that greatly reduced the power (of the Sultan) and increased that (of the Grand Vizier)] was the imperial harem. These women, [who were connected (to the sultan)], became more powerful [as time went on]. [Since the Grand Vizier was generally related (to the sultan) (through marriage)], he was directly connected (to the harem) as well and could use these powerful women (to increase) his power and affect) the Sultan. This was probably most easily accomplished (through the most powerful member) (of the harem), the Valide Sultan, [who was the Sultan's mother]. These women were so powerful [that (for over 130 years) (during the 16th and 17th century) they were de facto rulers (of the empire) (due to their influence) (over their sons), [many (of who) were minors]].

05. All (of these factors) weakened the power (of the sultan), and (in turn) the empire, but perhaps the most detrimental change was the major shift (in trade) (from the Mediterranean) (to the Atlantic Ocean). The European "Age of Discovery" sent explorers and settlers (around the world) looking (for both colonies and trade routes). [When they began sailing (around Africa) (to reach) the markets (of Asia)], they effectively removed the Ottoman Empire's great source (of wealth and power), it's ability (to act) (as an intermediary) (for trade) (between Europe and Asia). This was not an immediate loss, but (over time) it became more detrimental (for the Ottoman Empire) and (without strong leadership and a fractured social and political structure), the empire began (to decline) more rapidly.

06. (Over the next 200 years), these problems continued and the Ottoman Empire continued (to fade) (from its previous position) (as a world super power). (By the late 1800s) the empire had lost so much territory and was so dominated (by European powers) [that Tsar Nicholas referred to it (as the "sick man) (of Europe)," [which needed help (from its neighbors)]]. Unfortunately, (for the empire), this help would not come fast enough. [■] (Despite a push) (for modernization) [that moved it (in a more secular direction) (to match) the European powers], the empire was doomed. [■] (After a series) (of revolutions and wars), the empire joined WWI's Central Powers. [■] This decision ultimately resulted (in the final dissolution) (of the empire). [■]

[■] Its territories were divided up (by the European powers) and the modern country (of Turkey) rose (to replace) it (on the Anatolian peninsula).

Geographic Isolation of Species

01. One (of the most popular definitions) (of the word species) was provided (by renowned evolutionary biologist Ernest Mayr), [who described a species (as a population) (with the ability) (to interbreed), [which does not interbreed (with other such populations)]]. Today, we are unsure (of exactly [how many species exist (in the world)]), but we have learned (of several ways) [that new species develop]. One (of the major discoveries) has been [that the most common method (of speciation), called allopatric or geographic speciation, occurs [when a population becomes geographically separated]. [When the two species are separated], they can no longer interbreed. This allows the two populations (to follow) separate evolutionary courses (due to different selective pressures, genetic drift, and mutations) (within the isolated populations).

02. It may seem illogical [that one population could be split (into two or more) (by geography)], but there are actually several methods [(through which) this can occur]. A quick look (at Earth's topography) will give several clues (as to [how this can occur]). The first things [one notices] is [that the continents separated (by oceans)], but knowing (about continental drift) tells us [that these were not always (in their current positions)]. This movement caused populations (to be separated). Further, the rise (of towering mountain ranges) can also divide populations [when they become too much (of an obstacle) (for a population) (to cross)]. The formation (of the Isthmus of Panama) would have had the same effect [when it formed 3 million years ago]. (Before this time), populations (of organisms) swam freely (between the Caribbean Sea and the Pacific Ocean), but [as the landmass developed] it became a barrier (to this) and the populations were effectively divided (between the two great bodies) (of water).

03. It may seem [that these geographical barriers must be quite formidable (to cause) speciation], but the size (of the required barrier) depends (upon the population) (in question). Animals (like birds) can easily cross mountain ranges, rivers and large distances, so speciation (in bird populations) requires rather large barriers. Animals [that cannot fly] require much smaller barriers (to split) the populations. This can be seen [when a river changes course and small animal populations [that cannot swim] are divided]]. An example (of this) occurred [when the Grand Canyon formed and the population (of antelope squirrels) was separated]. (Despite being) only a few miles apart, the antelope squirrel population evolved (into two separate species), the white-tailed antelope squirrel north (of the canyon) and the Harris' antelope squirrel (in the deserts) south of the canyon.

04. Geographic separation does not necessarily cause speciation, but it creates the opportunity (for it) [when a gene pool changes enough (to form) a reproductive barrier (between the two parts) (of the population)]. Interestingly, this is much more likely (in a small isolated population) [than it is (in larger populations) [because their genetic pools can undergo considerable change]]. This can be seen (in the remote Galapagos Islands), [which are over 900 Km (from the nearest landmass)]. (In 2 million years), a relatively short period (in geographical terms), organisms (from the South American mainland) reached the islands and colonized them.

05. The distance (of the Galapagos) (from the mainland), but the relatively close proximity (of the islands) (to one another), allows them (to serve) (as an outdoor evolutionary laboratory). Marine volcanism formed the archipelago's 18 main islands, [which were eventually colonized (by organisms) [that floated there (along oceanic currents or winds)]] and founded new populations (on the islands). Some were even brought there (by other organisms), (such as seeds) [that were carried (in the guts, fur and feathers) (of animals) [that made their way (to the islands)]].

06. Today, (due to the founder effect), the descendants (of these original colonizers) have evolved (into a variety of species), [most (of which) are unique (to the island)]. The 13 finch species [that Charles Darwin discovered (on the island)] are a prime example (of this). Research has shown [that they descended (from the same early colonizers), yet they have differing feeding habits and beak types]. This likely occurred [because the small population [that colonized the island] underwent genetic changes [that set them apart]]. This continued [when some (of these individuals) somehow found their way (to one) (of the other islands) and founded a second new population]. [As these populations filled niches (in the ecosystem) and became reliant (upon a particular type) (of food)], their bodies became adapted (to it). [■] This led (to differences) (in the shapes) (of beaks) (of the various types) (of finches). [■] Eventually, these isolated populations developed an affinity (for only their own population) and began breeding (with only their own kind). [■] This effectively set them apart (as separate species). [■]

[■] Today, each island has distinct species, (with some) of them having (up to 10 separate finch species).

TEST 3-2 The Empire of Alexander the Great

01. (Despite their centuries long fight) (against Persian domination), the Classical Greek city-states were not unified (in any meaningful way). (In fact), squabbling and infighting (for power) (between the city-states) marked the period, (with power) switching (between them) (at different times). (By the end) (of the Classical Period), Philip II (of Macedon), (in northern Greece), began an expansion (of his territory), conquering the other city-states and uniting them (under his Macedonian rule). However, this expansion would eventually seem trivial [when compared (to the expansion) [that was accomplished (by his son), Alexander III, [who ascended the throne (in 336 BCE) (upon his assassination)]]]. This brash new king, [who was only 20 years old (at the time)], would continue his father's planned invasion (of the Persian Empire) and eventually control a larger empire (than any ruler) (before him), leading (to great changes) (in the regions) [he conquered].

02. (Within two years) (of taking) the throne, Alexander had begun his campaign (of international expansion) and (by 331 BCE) the Macedonian ruler had overtaken the Persian Empire (in the Levant), (including the ancient city) (of Babylon), and had established a foothold (in Egypt) as well. (After consolidating) this great empire, he continued eastward and reached as far east (as modern-day India). The great extent (of this empire), (along with the strong central control) [that was exerted (by Alexander)], caused a great number (of changes) (in the movement) (of goods, capital and people) (throughout the empire). The removal (of trade barriers) and movement restrictions, as well as interconnected markets, made it easier (for people) (to travel and trade) (with one another), and allowed Greek artisans and traders (to seek) their fortunes (in a greatly expanded region). This expansion (of trade and territory) had several important consequences (for both Classical Greece and the regions) conquered (in its name).

03. [■] One (of the most obvious) (of these changes) (in the newly unified empire) was the expansion (of Greek culture and influence). [■] This occurred [because Alexander founded (at least) 70 new urban centers, many (of them) named (after himself), not so much (for military control) (as for cultural expansion)]. [■] One (of the most important ways) [that this was done] was (through the propagation) (of Greek literature and language) (through the establishment) (of Greek libraries), (such as those) established (in Antioch (modern-day Turkey) and Alexandria, Egypt), [which was the largest and most significant library (in the ancient world)]. [■]

04. Another major change caused by the empire's expansion was the demise of the Greek city-state. Prior to the imperial period the Greek city-states were sparsely populated and centered around the agoras, marketplaces where the population came together to discuss the important issues of society and make decisions in person. Greek philosophers such as Plato and Aristotle, who had been the teenaged Alexander's tutor, felt that this form of government required a small population (less than 5,000) in order to insure that all citizens knew one another and could share their knowledge to make the best decisions. Further, prior to expansion these city-states lacked specialization, which allowed citizens to engage in various civil and personal activities. After trade and commerce developed across the empire citizens they had to develop specializations, which brought about professionalism. This meant that the small populations and "jack-of-all-trades" nature of the city-states' residents were no longer sufficient and Greek cities changed dramatically.

05. Imperial expansion also brought the Greeks into contact with eastern philosophy and religion, which affected their previous belief in human-like gods with superhuman powers who could be counted on to intercede on behalf of the city-states citizens and provided protection and good luck during life's milestones. However, these beliefs had begun to wane even before Alexander's time as Greeks no longer seemed interested in only serving the city-state. In fact, the Athenian philosopher Socrates had previously been executed for suggesting a new morality based upon personal conscience rather than the traditional gods. This new philosophy, however, did not take the place of religion, but instead made the Classical Greeks receptive to new ideas that allowed the religions of the Middle East to mix with Greek philosophy. This new combined system spread across the world after Alexander's death in 323 BCE, forever intertwining the cultures of Greece and the Levant.

06. This dramatic territorial expansion had such a profound effect on the world that Alexander's death ushered in what is known as the Hellenistic period in Greek history, when its influence was at its peak in Europe, Africa, and Asia. During this period the Greeks made great strides in art, literature, architecture, mathematics, governance, philosophy, and science. Without the influence of Alexander the Great's territorial expansion, these advances may have remained confined to the borders of Classical Greece.

[■] The new cities were meant to turn the "barbaric" subjects into civilized subjects of the empire.

TEST 3-3 Early Maize Cultivation in the American Southwest 묶기

01. The North American continent has been blessed (with vast areas) (of arable land) [that allow extensive agricultural output]; yet not all areas are conducive (to farming). The American southwest is one (of these areas). The region's extremely dry conditions and high temperatures make it unfavorable (for most farming). (In fact), the largest agricultural crop produced (across the region) today is hay, [which is used (to feed) livestock]. However, this was not always the case. It is believed [that the climate was much more stable and less arid (from around 2500) (to 100 B.C.E)]. It was (during this period) [that certain food crops were introduced (to the area) (from northern Mexico)]. Around this time, the native inhabitants began farming crops (such as beans, squash, and most importantly maize), [which, [although not highly productive], enjoyed an advantage (over the others)], its production was very predictable.

02. Early inhabitants practiced hunting and gathering, [which was particularly risky (due to their reliance) (upon weather patterns), (such as rainfall and sunlight)]. [Although the populations were generally low and could sustain themselves this way], they may sometimes have grown larger and had trouble doing so. [■] This would be particularly true (during the leaner times) (before the spring rains). [■] The coincidence (of larger populations and less available food stock) may have been the impetus (for the inhabitants) (to begin) growing reliable crops (such as maize). [■] (Despite its low yield), growing such a crop would have allowed them (to have) greater control (over their food supply) [even if it did not fully satisfy the populations' nutritional needs]. [■]

03. Researchers performing radiocarbon dating (on maize cobs and seeds) believe [that their introduction occurred (between 2000-1500 B.C.E) and then spread (to other areas)]. [While maize eventually becomes the most well known (of these)], the others played great roles not only (in the diet) (of the southwestern people), but also (in the success) (of their maize crops). Beans and legumes were especially important (during this time), [because they replenish the nitrogen [that maize depletes (from the soil)]]. (By planting) these crops together, early farmers were able (to ensure) [that their soil stayed fertile enough (to produce) crops year after year].

04. The first maize species successfully introduced (to the region) (from northern Mexico) was most likely a small, brown kernelled variety called chapalote. This species was important [because it matures quickly and requires little irrigation (after its initial planting)], so it is highly drought resistant. Eventually this species was hybridized (with an indigenous grass, teosinte), (to produce) a more fruitful species (with more kernel rows and larger cobs). It is believed [that the regions inhabitants continued (to crossbreed) maize species [until they came up (with the more productive maiz de ocho)]]. This is likely the result (of using) selection (to produce) a maize variety (with larger kernels) (for grinding and an earlier flowering season), [since growing seasons are highly unpredictable (in the region)]. The short growing season (of maiz de ocho) and its adaptability (to assorted climates) made it particularly valuable (to the region's inhabitants).

05. This hybridization was particularly important [because maize eventually became a staple (across the Americas), (including (in places) [that pushed the boundaries (of its production)])]. (By selective breeding) (of different varieties) (of maize), early farmers were able (to develop) varieties [that could be planted (in regions) (with poor soil, short growing seasons, and adverse weather)]. (In fact), the maiz de ocho variety allowed maize production (to spread) (from the arid southwest) (to regions) as far north (as Canada), [which has temperatures too low (for most earlier species) (to survive)]. This attention (to maize cultivation) allowed the local inhabitants (to become) more adept (at farming). They learned (to favor) soil [that held water better and received adequate sunlight]. They also realized [that the flood plains and canyon mouths contained better soil (because of the water) [that they were exposed to]]. However, one (of the most important farming skills) [they developed] was irrigation. This allowed them (to farm) (in more locations), [which ensured their crops [even if one area experienced a poor growing season]].

06. Surprisingly, the introduction (of maize) and the early farming attempts did not spark a great shift (in the regions' inhabitants' lifestyles). [Since early maize was rather unproductive and required little work], it was planted casually. (In fact), most (of the area tribes) continued (to lead) nomadic lives (for nearly 1000 years) [after maize was introduced north (of the Rio Grande)]. This could also be attributed (to the fact) [that maize is not a complete grain and lacks certain amino acids]. It could only become a staple product [when consumed (alongside other agricultural products)]. Luckily, two (of those) were introduced around the same time, squash and beans.

[■] It could be said [that planting crops did not turn the hunters and gatherers (into farmers), but rather allowed them (to be) better (at foraging) [because they had a supplemental food supply]].

TEST 4-1 Temperature Regulation in Marine Organisms

01. [■] (For most organisms) maintaining thermal homeostasis, or keeping the body temperature (within a certain range), is necessary (for proper metabolic functioning). [■] [If the internal temperature (of these organisms) leaves the preferred range, [which differs based (on the species)], (for extended periods)], enzyme degradation and tissue/organ destruction may occur, [which can make it difficult or impossible (for their bodies) (to properly function)]. [■] This makes it extremely important [that these organisms find some way (to maintain) their temperature (within these ranges), especially (in marine environments)]. [■]

02. Most organisms [that do this] can be classified (in one of two categories). The first (of these), the homeotherms, can be thought of (as thermoregulators), [since they maintain a near constant temperature (regardless of ambient temperatures)]. This group includes mammals and birds, [both (of which) have developed specialized features and functions (to harness) heat released (through the metabolic process) (to maintain) their relatively high average temperatures (of 34-40°C). Poikilotherms, (such as reptiles, amphibians, and most fish), (on the other hand), can be considered thermoconformers, [since their body temperatures are dependent (upon the ambient temperature)]. Having a body temperature [that fluctuates (with the external temperature)] does not, however, mean [that these organisms are protected (from temperature changes)]. However, higher temperatures generally produce higher metabolic rates. This means [that they must find ways (to maintain) their temperatures (within a certain range)]. This is done (in a host of ways) (such as moving), finding) areas (with appropriate temperatures) or basking) (in the sun's warming rays).

03. Interestingly, not all animals fall (into these two categories). Several species fall somewhere (in the middle) (of the two). Some (of the most well known examples) (of this) are fast-swimming fish, (such as the yellowfin tuna), [which has an internal temperature [that is several degrees warmer (than the relatively cold seawater) [it inhabits]]]. This occurs [because they possess a heat retention mechanism [that harnesses the heat produced (by their muscular activity) [while swimming]]]. Scientists believe [this is necessary (because of their reliance) (upon heat dependent biochemical reactions) (for their constant physical exertion)]. An entirely opposite example can be found (in the intertidal zone). Some species (in this area) maintain their bodies (at several degrees) cooler (than the ambient temperature) (by harnessing) the powers (of evaporation and circulation) (of bodily fluids). This allows them (to live) (in areas) [where the shallow

waters reach high temperatures (due to the effects) (of the suns rays and reflection) (from the light colored substrate)]. (By absorbing and losing) heat directly (to the air) they are able (to remain) much cooler (than non-living objects) (with corresponding sizes and shapes).

04. (In marine environments), homeotherms have the most difficulty maintaining their internal body temperature, [since most oceans average (between 1.9 and 27°C)]. Exposure (to these cold water temperatures) can cause lower internal temperatures (due to heat loss) (through the skin) faster [than (in air)]. However, several other factors lead (to lower temperatures). One (of the biggest) is the fact [that these animals have closed circulatory systems [that pump blood (around the body), causing heat loss [as it approaches the colder peripheral areas (of the body)]]]. Further, the body's natural radiation (of heat and respiration) also lower the temperature, [since the evaporation (of water) (from the nasal cavities) (during exhalation) has a natural cooling effect (on their bodies).

05. Marine animals have developed an assortment (of ways) (to counteract) this heat loss. The most common way is (by developing) a layer (of insulation), but even this can take different forms. Most cetaceans, (such as whales and porpoises), and seals build up a thick layer (of fat) (under the skin), known (as blubber). However, this does not work (for smaller marine mammals) (such as sea otters). These nimble, weasel-like sea creatures do not store great fat reserves, but instead constantly preen and fluff their thick dual-layer fur. This allows the outer hairs (to prevent) water (from reaching) the softer undercoat and traps warm, dry air (around the otter). This process is also used (by marine birds), [which have waterproof outer feathers covering softer down [that traps air and body heat]]. These methods are enhanced (by the fact) [that marine mammals have higher body temperatures (than their terrestrial counterparts)].

06. Interestingly, the circulatory systems (of some marine species) also help conserve body heat (by acting) (as countercurrent heat exchangers). (In species), (like porpoises), the veins [that return the used blood (surround the arteries), [which pump blood (from the warm core)]]. This allows the warmer arteries (to heat) the blood [as it returns (from relatively colder areas) (such as the skin surface and flippers), [which are not protected (by thick blubber layers)]]. This reduces the amount (of heat) lost (to the water) and can even be found (in some fish), (such as skipjack tuna).

[■] (In extreme cases) this can lead (to permanent damage, or even death), (for the organism).

TEST 4-2　The Upper Paleolithic Revolution

01.　Around 35 (to 40 KYA) (thousands of years ago), there was a dramatic change (in the archaeological record) (in Europe) [that marked the change (from the Middle) (to Upper Paleolithic periods)]. (During this transition), anatomically modern humans (AMH) replaced Neanderthal populations (in Europe) and brought about great changes (in humanity). The rise (of the AMH population) can be seen (through a dramatic increase) (in the use) (of tools) and the invention) (of several purely human activities). The changes [that occurred (during the Upper Paleolithic era)] are so dramatic [that they have been referred to (as the Upper Paleolithic Revolution)].

02.　Archaeological finds (in many areas) (across Europe) have supported this revolutionary change. The new population used much more versatile stone implements and animal products, (such as bone and antler), (to produce) much more advanced tools. [■] Barbed reindeer harpoons and spear throwers, known (as atlatl), have been discovered (in European caves) indicating a great leap forward (in the understanding) (of hunting), and even rudimentary concepts (in physics), (such as torque). [■] Interestingly, this also appears (to be) the period [when humans developed art forms, (such as figurative art)]. [■] However, swan bone pipes (with worn finger holes) similar (to flutes) and primitive tattooing kits have been found (in other European archaeological sites), indicating [that figurative cave art was not the AMH's only artistic endeavor]. [■]

03.　An interesting aspect (of these discoveries) is [that they were all found (in Europe), leading researchers (to believe) [that the advances (of early AMH) were a purely European occurrence around 40 KYA [that eventually spread elsewhere]]]. However, the later discovery (of decorated ochre and shell beads), as well as evidence (of AMH's ability) (to fish), (in South Africa's Blombos Cave) dating (to 77 KYA) and contemporary bone tools) found (in other African sites) indicate [that this "revolution" was simply an example (of human behavioral evolution) [that had been occurring (for much longer)]]. This led researchers (to question) [why the discovery (of modern tools) (from this period) were concentrated (in Europe)] and [whether the European discoveries were the start (of a new form) (of human behavior)], or [if they were simply built (upon earlier innovations) (in other parts) (of the world)].

04. Anthropologists Sally McBrearty and Alison Brooks point to Eurocentric bias and disregard for the extent of the African archaeological record as the most likely causes for the discovery of more tools in Europe. They hold that evidence of more modern tools in Africa, such as blades and microlithic technology, higher geographic ranges, art, and long distance trade networks, predates its appearance in Europe by at least 10,000 years and can be found in archaeological sites separated by both geographical area and time frame, thus suggesting a natural evolution, rather than an immediate revolution such as in Europe. This indicates that AMH behavior was likely formed in Africa and exported to other regions. The myriad forms of early rock art found in Australia further support this idea. Since people arrived in Australia around 60 KYA and were isolated from the "revolution" in Europe 40 KYA, their rock art can be seen to show that creativity was already a part of human cognition when early AMH began migrating out of Africa around 70 KYA.

05. This type of scrutiny has caused theories of a sudden advent of modern behavior and tool making during an "Upper Paleolithic Revolution" in Europe to falter. The most logical reason for its supposed sudden occurrence would be, as McBrearty and Brooks pointed out, deficiencies in the archaeological record in Africa and other regions, while those in Europe are rather well preserved. It may simply turn out that artifacts elsewhere have been lost, or have yet to be found. This can be seen by the recent discovery of pierced shells dating from 43 KYA in Lebanon, suggesting the modernization had occurred prior to the date of the "revolution," but went undetected until recently.

06. However, the presence of tools in other areas does not explain the sudden appearance of tools in the European archaeological record. One theory for this is climate change. Prior to the suggested dates of the Upper Paleolithic Revolution, Europe underwent a major climate change that caused the disappearance of the previous glaciers and an overall warming, which made the continent more hospitable for early AMH. This could have allowed a migration of early AMH to the previously uninhabited area. This sudden appearance of AMH in Europe would have led to an increase in more modern tools in the archaeological record, which could explain why they suddenly appeared around 35 KYA.

[■] The most famous of these are, doubtlessly, cave paintings, such as those found in the Lascaux caves outside Montignac, France.

TEST 4-3 Nineteenth-Century Theories of Mountain Formation

01. (Due to several major misconceptions), our understanding (of mountain formation) is relatively new. As recently (as the early 19th century), most geological findings were viewed (as a series) (of catastrophic events) [that allowed geological knowledge (to corroborate) a short Earth history [that corresponded (to biblical narratives)]]. However, (during the 19th century), scientists began (to offer) other explanations (for geological features), (such as mountain formation). Unfortunately, most (of the theories) [they developed] were based (upon the idea) [that Earth had been formed (as a superheated mass) and had steadily cooled (through time)]. This led them (to postulate) [that Earth's core must be shrinking [as it cools], [as most objects do]]. (From this), they extrapolated [that Earth's crust would be deformed (by the shrinkage) and mountains would form].

02. One (of the first geologists) (to try) (to explain) this was Eduard Suess. He explained [that Earth's crust wrinkled [as it contracted], [just as a drying apple's peel does]]. His theory assumed [that Earth's crust had begun (as a single layer), but separated [as the "wrinkles" formed]. This led (to great depressions) [that became ocean basins and higher areas [that formed the continents]]. Further, he thought [that continued contraction would lead (to instability) and the two features could alternate, meaning [that oceans would become continental land and vice versa]]. Using this theory, he incorrectly postulated [that the Alps had once been (at the bottom) (of a massive ocean), but had risen and left the Mediterranean (as its only remnant)].

03. This alternation was an important point (in his theory), [because it helped (to explain) other geological features [that scientists, even the great Leonardo da Vinci, had been unable (to interpret)], (such as the discovery) (of marine fossils) (on dry land) and the interspersed marine and terrestrial sediment) found (in the stratigraphic column)]. It also helped (to explain) a problem brought about (by Darwin's contemporaneous theory) (of evolution). (By the mid-1800s), scientists had noticed similar, or even identical, fossils (in distant places), (such as South America and Africa). Darwin's theory made this identical evolution (of two distant species) highly unlikely, but Suess countered this (with the theory) [that changes (in Earth's landmasses and oceans) made it possible]. He developed the theory (of an ancient, giant landmass) connected (by land bridges) [that he referred to (as Gondwanaland)].

04. Ironically, acceptance of Suess's theory was geographically split; it gained a greater acceptance in Europe than in North America. On the other side of the Atlantic, geologists like James Dwight Dana developed their own explanations for mountain formation. Dana's theory, known as permanence, was based on the continents and oceans remaining as they are. He theorized that as Earth cooled and contracted, minerals with low melting points, like feldspar and quartz, solidified early on and those with higher melting points, like pyroxene and olivine, became solid later, thereby creating ocean basins. As the contraction continued it put immense pressures on Earth's surface, especially along the oceanic/continental boundaries, which caused the creation of the mountain ranges found along continental edges, such as those on the west coast of both North & South America.

05. [■] Dana's theory led fellow American geologist James Hall to theorize that subsidence, or sinking, of sediment from a former shallow sea formed the Appalachian Mountains. [■] Hall felt that these materials were produced by continental erosion and accumulated in linear troughs along the mountain's edge, called geosynclines. [■] As these troughs filled and began to subside, they became deeper and Earth's inner heat turned the sediment into stone. [■] Eventually, it was uplifted to form mountains. Dana slightly modified this theory to explain that sediment had not caused subsidence, but was actually the result of it. Unfortunately for both, their explanations of how shallow-water sediment built up did nothing to accurately explain how these thick layers of sediment were uplifted.

06. By the early 1900s, the flaws in these theories became evident. Through the discovery of certain features in the earth's crust, such as unexplainable strata shortening) and the theory of isostasy that explained that the crust and its mountains were actually floating on Earth's mantle, and not held in place on their own, scientists were able to disprove Suess's theory of oceanic/continental changeability. However, the most important discovery was radiogenic heating, which definitively negated the theory of contraction, and all theories based on it. All of this caused scientists to look for more accurate explanations of mountain formation. The best of these was Alfred Wegener's theory of continental drift. Unfortunately, this theory was not accepted until the existence of tectonic plates was confirmed nearly 50 years later. Today, we know that the actions of these tectonic plates created Earth's various mountain ranges.

[■] He based this idea on the fact that the mountains were made up of layers of shallow-water sedimentary rocks several thousands of feet thick.

TEST 5-1 Colonial America and the Navigation Acts

01. Mercantilism swept across Europe in the sixteenth century. Under this system, governments attempted to regulate and protect their economies by ensuring a positive balance of trade using high tariffs and protective import laws. This was especially true in the British Empire, which was threatened by the rising power of Dutch traders after the Eighty Years' War and the lifting of Spanish embargoes on trade with them. After this time, Dutch traders overwhelmed British trade on the Iberian Peninsula, around the Mediterranean Sea, and into the Levant; however, the most troubling development was their rising power in the British colonies, especially those in the New World. In order to protect its trade power, Parliament passed a series of trade laws known collectively as the Navigation Acts, which effectively controlled all imperial commerce.

02. One of the first of the Navigation Acts was the Navigation Ordinance of 1651. This new ordinance limited imports into the British Empire to those brought by British ships or those from the country in which the product had been manufactured. This severely limited Dutch imports, since they specialized in carrying products from other regions, and mainly exported locally-made dairy products. As time went by, more of these types of acts were passed, further increasing restrictions on trade, which greatly affected the colonies. In fact, the passage of the Navigation Acts of 1660 and 1663, forced British colonies to export commodities, like sugar and tobacco, only to England aboard British-flagged vessels. They were not, however, all detrimental to the colonies. For instance, the Molasses Act of 1733 added an import tariff to molasses entering the colonies from outside the empire. This basically created a molasses monopoly for plantation owners in the British West Indies, since it was cheaper than that produced on French Caribbean islands. By the 1750s, the economic impact of these laws had become clear in the North American colonies.

03. The first major condition set forth by the Navigation Acts was the use of only British ships with crews that were 75% British, which included colonists and their slaves. This dramatically reduced imports and foreign shipping into the Empire, which allowed the British fleet to become the world's most powerful. Interestingly, it also encouraged shipbuilding in North America, since the colonists could freely trade within the Empire. This brought about the foundation of an American merchant marine fleet and, by the 1750s, one-third of the British fleet was composed of American ships. The concentration of the shipbuilding and export industries

(in the northeast) led (to rapid urbanization) (in the region) [as more warehouses, docks, and maintenance firms were built there]. (By the late 18th century), New York City and Philadelphia had become not only the two largest cities (in the colonies), but also two (of the busiest ports) (in the entire empire).

04. Another major stipulation (of the Navigation Acts) was [that certain "enumerated goods", (such as tobacco, rice, hides, sugar, and naval supplies), could only be shipped directly (to England or Scotland)], thus giving the British government control (over the respective markets). [■] However, the Navigation Acts did not kill the trade (in the enumerated goods). [■] (In fact), Parliament blocked the import (of foreign tobacco and rice), the two commodities most affected (by the Acts). [■] This proved burdensome (to British citizens), but helped the tobacco farmers. [■] They also agreed (to refund) import duties (on products) [that were eventually shipped (out of the empire), [which accounted (for 85%) (of the North American exports)]]. These measures meant [that tobacco and rice producers suffered a less than 3% reduction (in their income)].

05. Eventually, the Navigation Acts led (to economic diversification) and increased trade (in the colonies), [since Parliament paid subsidies (to colonists) (for producing) raw materials [that would have otherwise have been imported (from trade rivals), (such as silk, iron, dye, and lumber)]]. They did not, however, allow the large-scale production (of manufactured goods), (such as clothing), [that could affect Britain's large-scale factories]. This meant [that tailors, milliners, and other clothing manufacturers were restricted (to producing) their products (in small shops)]. These restrictions allowed British clothing (to be sold) (at much lower prices) (than locally manufactured goods). Surprisingly, the production (of ironworks) was not limited (by the acts) and it became a major industry.

06. The last major effect (of these acts) was [that they created a protected market (for lower-priced British goods)]. Demand (for colonial materials) remained high and led (to prosperity) (in the colonies). This led (to an increased demand) (for British manufactured goods), (such as dishware, tea, and furniture), (in addition to clothing). This allowed exports (to the American colonies) (to rise) (from 5%) (of all British exports) (in 1700) (to nearly 40%) (by 1760). The influx (of these manufactured goods) allowed middle-class colonists (to live) as comfortably (as their British counterparts).

[■] Luckily (for the colonists), the list (of enumerated goods) did not include livestock, lumber, rum, fish, or grains, [which made up 60% (of their exports)].

TEST 5-2 The Most Common Bird on Earth

01. Most people (outside of Africa) have never heard (of the red-billed quelea), but these small African birds are the most common bird species (on Earth). A member (of the weaver family), they live (on the grasslands) (of sub-Saharan Africa) (in extremely large colonies) [that contain (up to 30 million individuals)]. Conservative estimates put the total population (of the birds) (across Africa) (at more than 1.5 billion breeding pairs), (with some) saying [there may be up to 10 billion (of the birds)].

02. It may seem illogical [that these small birds survive (in such a harsh environment)], but their extreme success is even more remarkable [when one considers [that they survive nearly entirely (on the annual grasses) (in the region)]]. [Although researchers have noted [that they eat some insects, mainly beetles, and a few non-grass seeds]], these accounted (for less than two percent) (of their overall diet). One might expect [that this great dependence (upon annual grasses) would lead (to regular reduction or extinction) (of the populations)], but, much (like early humans)[who learned (to hoard) wheat and barley seeds (to deal) (with lean times)], the red-billed quelea have developed certain behaviors [that help them cope (with the feast or famine nature) (of the grass crops)].

03. One (of the most advantageous adaptations) made (by the red-billed quelea) has been the development (of variable annual weather-dependent cycles). [■] (During the dry season) the bird population must sustain itself (with the seeds) produced (at the end) (of the rainy season). [■] (To do) this, they gorge themselves (on seeds) (to gain) enough weight (to sustain) them [while they migrate (to more productive places)]. [■] This must be done (during the dry season), [since monsoon rains cause the remaining seeds (to germinate), thereby interrupting the food supply (for weeks) and instigating the move. [■] Luckily, this does not occur simultaneously (across the entire savanna) and dry seeds, young grasses, and mature ripe grasses are available (in different areas). (To take) advantage (of this) the quelea make 50-200 km migrations (across the savannas), [which allows them (to survive) (in such a forbidding environment)].

04. [By the time the rains have germinated and fresh seeds become available], these early-rain migrations end and the quelea return (to the previously abandoned areas). Access (to these new seeds) stimulates the population's males (to weave) ovoid grass and straw nests (in acacia trees). The females [who help them complete the nest] and [who then lay two to four eggs] later join them. These colonies can cover (up to 100 hectares) (with 500 nests) (in each acacia). (With an average) (of 100,000 fledglings) (per hectare), (up to 10 million) offspring are produced (by each successful colony). Surprisingly, the entire process (of nest weaving, mating, brooding and fledging) (of the juveniles) takes only six weeks, [which is much shorter [than (in other birds)], and is incredibly synchronized, [as the eggs all hatch (on the same day)]]. However, this process is dependent (upon weather patterns), [as an earlier dry season can cause the quelea (to abandon) their colony], [while an extended green season (with abundant seed stock) can allow them (to produce) multiple broods (in the same region)].

05. [Since they rely (upon seeds)], these large colonies can cause problems (for the region's farmers). [As more and more grains are planted (across sub-Saharan Africa)], the birds have turned (to the crops) (for nourishment). This has allowed their numbers (to explode) (in the region). It is estimated [that the population (of these "feathered locusts") has increased (by 10-100 times) (since the 1970s)]. (With each bird) eating its own weight (in seeds) (per day) this leaves fields (within 30 Km) (of the breeding sites) highly susceptible. Researchers have estimated [that flocks can consume upwards (of 50 tons) (of seeds) (per day), [which allows them (to wipe out) entire small crops and approximately 20% (of the annual production) (of large commercial farms)]]. Annual losses directly attributable (to these small birds) have been calculated (at $70m), (in a region) [where agricultural production is already (in a precarious state)].

06. Their easy adaptability and propensity (to migrate) (in large flocks) has made the red-billed quelea a cause (for concern) (in areas) [where their introduction could allow them (to become) entrenched (as an invasive species)]. One such region is Australia's northwestern state (of Queensland), [where the climate resembles the quelea's native habitat]. Queensland's $440m annual cereal grain harvest would be devastated [if large colonies (of quelea) became established]. Colony establishment would also wreak havoc (on the region's native species), (such as the endangered Gouldian finch), [which could not compete (with such massive flocks)]. This has caused the Australian government (to ban) the import (of the world's most common and destructive bird).

[■] [Although the grasslands (of sub-Saharan Africa) do not undergo major temperature changes], the weather patterns do change dramatically [as part (of the year) is characterized (by arid conditions) [until the monsoon winds bring heavy rains (to the region)].

TEST 5-3 National Parks in the Western United States

01. The Treaty of Paris, [which ended the revolutionary war (between Great Britain and its former colonies) (in the United States)], more than doubled the territory (of the 13 original colonies) [as the crown ceded all lands east (of the Mississippi River) (to the newly formed nation)]. However, the new country's expansion would not stop there. (By the middle) (of the next century), cessations, purchases and treaties would expand the nation's contiguous territory (to its current state). This dramatically increased the amount (of land) owned (by the nation) and, (before mass immigration and westward movement); much (of this land) was pristine wilderness (with a plethora) (of different geological formations and ecosystems). (With so much vacant land), the theory (of "landscape democracy,") the idea [that scenic landscapes belong (to all people)], came (into play) and a movement was put forth (to preserve) this land (in perpetuity) (as national parkland).

02. [■] This theory was revolutionary (for the time), [as (prior to the establishment) (of Yellowstone National Park) (in 1872), no national government had ever set aside large swaths (of undeveloped land)]. [■] However, this was not only done (for preservation). [■] A sense (of inferiority) (with regards to old world monuments and the belief) [that America's unique landscapes were one (of its most distinguishing features)] both had a hand (in the desire) (to set aside) western lands. [■] Interestingly, business interests also encouraged the conservation movement. It may seem antithetical, but business leaders, (such as railroad barons) pushed for and supported these national parks, [since they would encourage rich easterners (to take) long trips (on their lines) and stay) (in the hotel) [they set up (on the outskirts) (of the parks)]]. Their desire (for profits) also led them (to heavily advertise) the majesty (of western parks and features), (such as the Grand Canyon, Yellowstone, and Yosemite), [which greatly raised awareness (of the parks) (amongst the general public)].

03. Surprisingly, the adoption (of the automobile) (by American's) (in the early 20th century) also bolstered the national parks movement. [As the number (of cars) rose (from 0.11) (per 1,000 citizens) (in 1900) (to 86.78/K (in 1920) and 217.34/K) (in 1930)], drivers began calling (for investment) (in better roads and highways), especially those (in the west). 1916's Federal Aid Road Act paid states (to construct or improve) rural roadways, (including those) (near parkland). This encouraged people (to not only drive) more, but also (to visit) the increasing number (of national parks). (At around the same time), business magnate Stephen

Mather was pushing (for an independent agency) (to oversee) the national parks and barely a month (after passing) the Road Act, President Woodrow Wilson signed a bill setting up (such an agency) and named Mather its first director. He worked (to protect) these pristine lands (from the business interests) [that were attempting (to have) them opened (for logging and other business ventures)].

04. (By the middle) (of the 20th century), cross-country road trips had become quite popular (with families) [who visited national parks, newly founded amusement parks, and ski resorts]. They made the need (for better roadways) evident. This increased recreational travel helped ensure the passage (of 1956's Interstate and Defense Highway Act), [which authorized the construction (of nearly 66,000 Km) (of roads) (around the country)]. This $25B project was the largest public works project (in the country's history) and increased mobility (by linking) urban centers (through wide divided highways). A direct side effect (of this) was easier access (to national parks) (for urban inhabitants), [which caused a dramatic increase (in park usage)]. (In 1920) only 1M people visited the national parks, but (by 1950) that number had risen (to 33M). (After the completion) (of the new highways) the nation's parks welcomed 172M visitors. This increase vastly outpaced the increase (in the nation's population), [which had only doubled (during that time)].

05. The increased number (of visitors) quickly caused degradation (in the national parks), causing activists, (like Sierra Club founder John Muir), (to argue) [that the parks should be preserved (as pristine wilderness) and protected (from further human destruction)]. This was important, [since early parks, (like Yellowstone) had been set up (as recreational areas)]. His impassioned writing helped (to convince) Americans, especially the eastern elite, (of the importance or preservation) (of these unique areas).

06. This movement had a great impact (on the national park system). Not only did the park system begin working (to preserve) the wilderness, but it also greatly expanded the amount (of protected land). Today, more than 277M people visit the 210,000 Km2 (of land) protected (by the 59 national parks), an area larger (than 109 current countries), each year. The beauty, geological features, ecosystems, and recreational opportunities (of the land) (in these parks) are now permanently preserved (for all American citizens) both now and (in the future).

[■] The fact [that America was a relatively young nation interacting (with other nations)] also had a large influence (on the establishment) (of parks).

TEST 6-1   The Role of Dress in Africa

01. [When most people think (about the concept) (of dressing)], they automatically think (of only clothing and accessories) and [whether they are (in the right style)]. However, dress can actually be a much more complex concept, [which can be used (to communicate) both simple ideas and complex information (about the wearer)]. The type (of dress) [that a person chooses] can communicate immediate information (about their gender, ethnic group, religion, age or even occupation). A few common examples (of these) are the burka worn (by Muslim women) and the yarmulke worn (by Jewish men). Both (of these items) point (to the age, religion, and gender) (of their wearers). This complexity and symbolism is a key feature (of African dress), [which has fascinated outside viewers (with its striking range) (of styles) [since Arabic writers first described it (in the fourteenth century)]].

02. African dress, (like most forms), is intimately connected (to the identity) (of its wearers and observers), [since it acts (as a signifier) (of so many aspects) (of the societies)]. (Despite the neutrality) (of the adornment), the way [(in which) it is worn], or simply the fact [that it is worn], can become symbolically important (to a society). There may be importance assigned (to the form, type, adornment, and materials) used (to form) the dress worn and this can cause it (to become) a sensitive aspect (of the society). [Since many aspects (of dress) are tied (to tribal or religious identity)], their use denotes inclusion (with the society), but can also draw the ire or derision (of society members) [if they are inappropriately worn or displayed].

03. (In addition to denoting) societal and religious identity, African dress can also be seen (as an indicator) (of the wearer's sociopolitical standing) (in the society). (In many African societies) leaders wear some sort (of insignia or symbolic aspect) (of dress) (to denote) their leadership. (In fact), some (of these) are made (of highly prized materials), (such as ivory, gold, or decorative beading), [that are only worn (by the leaders)]. One example (of this) is the Oba, or leader, (of the Benin people) (in present-day Nigeria). His official dress includes a coral-beaded smock and crown (with coral necklaces and ivory pendants and amulets). Further, he carries a flywhisk made (of red coral beads) [that signify his divine rule]. (In other societies), other flywhisk materials were used (to denote) the regal nature (of the bearer). Two examples (of this) are the Fare-Fare and Ashanti people (of Ghana), [whose respective use (of horsehair and elephant tail hair) denoted kings or

chiefs (of the highest importance)]. These flywhisks are such a strong symbol (of power and leadership) [that they have come (to be used) (by rulers) (across the continent), (including by Jomo Kenyatta), the first leader (of the modern state) (of Kenya)].

04. The use (of these flywhisks) (as a symbol) (of leadership) brings up another interesting aspect (of "dress"). Contrary (to the common, narrow interpretation) (of the term dress), the true definition is much broader and includes more (than just the clothing) worn. It includes accessories, (such as the flywhisks), and other methods (of beautifying and adorning) the body. Items (such as cosmetics, jewelry, and accessories) (like staffs, parasols, and fans), are all considered aspects (of dress). However, not all (of these aspects) can be easily removed. Some societies use permanent bodily modification (to perform) the same functions. Tattooing may be the most common form (of these) (in modern day western society), but there are a profusion (of other forms), (such as scarring, piercings and the use) (of lip plates).

05. [■] (In most) (of sub-Saharan Africa), the use (of purposefully inflicted scars, or cicatrization), is the most common type (of permanent body modification). [■] They signify membership and status (in the society), but can act (as protective devices), (in addition to simply being) beautiful bodily adornment. [■] These scars are placed (on different parts) (of the body), (including the face, abdomen and extremities), and can sometimes take the form (of elaborate patterns) [that cover most (of the body)]. [■] Oftentimes, the lengthy scarification acts (as an initiation process), (with the aesthetics) (of the scars) correlating (to other important figurative aspects) (of the society), (such as pottery and sculpture).

06. Farther north, (along the Nile River), tattooing was the main form (of permanent body adornment). Researchers have found evidence (of tattoos) being used (as fertility signals) (in female Egyptian mummies) (from 2000 B.C.). (In addition), the adjacent Nubian civilization appears (to have utilized) tattoos (to adorn) their bodies, as well. The tattoos (in both) (of these civilizations) served the same purpose (as scarification, apparel and accessories) (in other African tribes, and elsewhere). They were symbols (of inclusion, protection and identification) (for their bearers).

[■] The permanent scars are culturally important and hold important information (for those) (in the society) [who know their relevance].

TEST 6-2 Evidence of an Asteroid Impact

01. Throughout Earth's history, there have been mass extinctions that permanently altered its biodiversity. The most recent of these occurred at the boundary between the Cretaceous and Paleogene periods, around 65 million years ago. During this time, scientists estimate that 75% of all species perished. By the end of the extinction, all non-avian dinosaurs had died off, allowing mammals to rise to the dominant position in most ecosystems.

02. Since discovering this dramatic change in species diversity in the late 19th century, geologists have attempted to explain why so many species died off concurrently. Some posited that dinosaurs could not adapt to climate change or the lowered sea level, while others thought that a more catastrophic event precipitated the disappearance of so many species. They point to such catastrophes as a massive volcanic eruption, an extraterrestrial body striking Earth's surface (which geologists refer to as a bolide), or the effects of cosmic radiation as possible explanations. Unfortunately, they could not produce concrete evidence to support these theories.

03. This changed in 1977 when geologist Walter Alvarez was studying the strata of the soil near Gubbio, Italy and discovered a layer of unique clay from the Cretaceous–Paleogene boundary. Upon sending it for analysis by his father's physics laboratory, he found that it contained nearly 30 times more iridium than is normally found in the rocks of Earth's crust. This was surprising, because, despite the fact that the earth's core and mantle are believed to contain this metallic element, it is rare in the crust. This led him to question the source of the mineral. [■] While a volcanic eruption could have deposited iridium in Earth's crust, he pointed out that it was more likely that a large (10+ Km in diameter) extraterrestrial body containing iridium forcefully struck the earth and sent up a dense cloud of iridium-filled dust across the atmosphere. [■] He proposed that when this dust mixed with other atmospheric matter, atmospheric circulation pushed it throughout the atmosphere and blocked the sun's rays, thereby causing the extinction of the plants that formed the base of the food chain for most other life forms. [■] Eventually, this dust settled on the ground and entered the soil column. [■] This theory was bolstered when high iridium levels were found in soil from the Cretaceous-Paleogene boundary in locations as distant as Russia, Haiti, and New Zealand, and in layers of sediment under the Pacific and Atlantic Oceans.

04. The theory was further strengthened [when geologists studying the Cretaceous-Paleogene Boundary found materials common (in proven meteoric impact sites) (such as the Barringer Crater) (in Arizona)]. The first (of these), shocked quartz, displays a unique planar pattern [that is only created (by shockwaves) traveling (through quartz-filled rock) (after an intense impact)], so it indicates [that there was some massive impact (at the time)]. They also found stichovite, a dense compressed silicate uncommon (in Earth's crust) [that is formed only (in high-pressure situations)], (in samples) (from the period). (In addition), the existence (of tektites, or tiny glasslike droplets) formed [when terrestrial material is super-heated and thrown (into the air) (during a meteor's impact)], (in the Cretaceous-Paleogene layer samples) (from distant locations) further supported the theory. The presence (of soot) (in this stratum) also points (to a meteoric impact), [since such an impact would have likely caused widespread wildfires].

05. The missing piece (of the puzzle) was the lack (of a bolide impact site), but the lack (of one) does not necessarily negate the theory, [since Earth's atmosphere can weather and erode geological features (over time)]. However, (in 1978), [while working (for Petróleos Mexicanos)], geophysicist Glen Penfield found evidence (of an impact crater) just (off the Yucatan Peninsula), (near the town) (of Chicxulub), [that was 180 Km (in diameter) and 20 km (in depth)]. This find, [although under-reported and appreciated (at the time)], would make it the impact site (of the largest bolide) (to ever strike) Earth, [which (at 10+ Km) (in diameter), matched Alvarez's estimate perfectly]. Further research (by geoscientist Alan Hildebrand) used core samples, magnetic and gravity surveys (to reveal) other telltale signs (of a bolide) (at the supposed impact site), (such as the existence) (of andesitic rocks), [which have isotopic and chemical compositions similar (to tektites) found (in the Cretaceous-Paleogene boundary) (across the Caribbean region)].

06. Today, Alvarez's theory is the most widely accepted explanation (for the mass extinction). Further testing (of the event) (by the Berkeley Geochronology Center) dated the bolide impact (to 66-65 million years ago), (with the extinction) occurring (within 33,000 years), thereby confirming Alvarez's time line. Even more convincingly, (in 2010) a group (of scientists) published the results (of their two decade long study) (of the Cretaceous-Paleogene boundary layer) and concluded [that debris (from the Chicxulub bolide) would have caused the environmental disturbances required (to prompt) the mass extinction].

[■] The two best explanations would be the result (of volcanism or a major bolide collision).

TEST 6-3 Native Americans and European Trade Goods

01. (Prior to their exploration and settlement) (by Europeans), the United States and Canada hosted a thriving trade network administered (by the various native tribes) found there. These Pre-Colombian tribes developed extensive trade routes (between themselves) [that allowed them (to trade) pelts, shells, pottery and other handicrafts (from the Great Lakes) (to the Gulf of Mexico) and as far west (as the Rocky Mountains)]. These interactions changed the individual tribes, (by providing) them not only new material goods and revenue, but also differing ideas and ways (of thinking). These changes would, however, pale (in comparison) (to the changes) brought about (by the introduction) (of Europeans) (into the North American economy).

02. [Although native tribes had encountered Europeans as early (as the 11th Century), [when Norse explorers tried (to create) a settlement (in eastern Canada)]], true economic interactions did not occur (until the early 1500s). (At this time), French fishermen and Basque whalers were regularly travelling (to the Grand Banks) (off of Newfoundland) and began trading (with the locals) [they met [when they came ashore (to process) their catches]]. The native inhabitants [they met] were eager (to trade) their goods (for European products), (such as metal tools, glassware and cloth), and allowed European explorers and traders (to establish) settlements and trading posts (throughout New England), (along the St. Lawrence River), and as far south (as Virginia). This situation provided European explorers a beneficial new trading source, but perhaps the biggest draw (for them) was the trade (in fur), especially that (of beaver pelts), [which had become a phenomenally popular status symbol (in Europe) (at the time)].

03. The fur trade dominated early European-Native American trade and had a profound impact (on many aspects) (of the native societies) (including their organization, relationships (with one another), and even their art and handicrafts). (Prior to their interactions) (with European explorers and products), these tribes had spent thousands (of years) procuring and trading materials and refined products [that were both precious and symbolically important (to their cultures' ideals) (of leadership, influence, wealth and spirituality)]. The products [they received (from trading) (with the Europeans)] offered them these same opportunities and were incorporated (into the indigenous communities values, crafts, and understanding) (of the world) early on.

04. (With the permanent settlements), the native tribes had more interaction (with European products) and became even more influenced (by them). (Over time), long held traditions (such as pottery and tool making) were abandoned (in favor) (of European products) (such as brass kettles and durable steel and iron tools). This became more pronounced [as European settlements spread westward and encroached (on tribal lands), [which allowed them (to trade) directly (with the local tribes)]]. This can be seen (in the early 17th century Dutch settlements) (in the upper Hudson area) (of present day New York). [■] (Prior to these settlements), the powerful Iroquois tribe used beaver tooth blades (to carve) moose antlers (into rudimentary three or four tine combs), but (after the introduction) (of steel blades) (by their Dutch neighbors) these ornaments became much more ornate. [■] (In fact), archaeologists excavated one (from a Cayuga village) (with many narrow tines and an intricate carving) (of two European's) (on horseback). [■] It is assumed [this was (to commemorate) the visit (of an English dignitary), Wentworth Greenhalgh, (in 1699)]. [■]

05. [Although many (of the European goods) [that found their way (into the society)] provided increased productivity and security – guns, metal blades, and brass kettles –] their longevity led (to market saturation), eventually causing a shift (in trading). (Over time), native tribes began (to favor) raw materials and the trade (in cloth, wool, glass beads) and decorative silver became more important. Native tribes incorporated items (like glass beads) (into their practices and costumes) (in place) (of ornaments) made (of pipestone, copper, and shell). Some local artisans, usually tribeswomen, used these replacement materials (to create) elaborate formal attire and regalia. The new products offered the native tribes the correct look and symbolism (for their practices), but the 'luxurious' imported products also gave the bearer an air (of power, wealth, and success).

06. Unfortunately (for the native tribes), these positive trade interactions (with European settlers) did not last forever. (Over time), [as the number (of settlers and traders) (in the region) increased], they brought (with them corporatization) (of the industry) and European diseases). The native population was not immune (to the ill effects) (of either) (of these) and soon began (to suffer). (By the 1850s), beaver fur had fallen (out of favor) (in Europe) and the native tribes lost a major source (of income). This, combined (with oppression) (by the settlers), threw them (into a state) (of poverty) [(from which) many (of the tribes) have still not recovered].

[■] Others found (in the region) seem (to indicate) [that the natives felt [that their new neighbors possessed great wealth and power]].

usherin.usher.co.kr

USHER

iBT TOEFL
INTERMEDIATE READING 02
구문 외우고 열번 읽기

단계별
1. 정확히 구문 암기!
2. 하나하나 철저히 적용!
3. 확실히 적용할 줄 알면 7분내 지문 읽기!

Costs of Quitting a Job

1 High job mobility has long been ⁽⁰¹⁾**held as** a hallmark of the American economy. ⁽⁰²⁾**In contrast to** employees in Japan and Europe, American employees ⁽⁰³⁾**appear to switch** jobs much more readily. ⁽⁰⁴⁾**On average**, American workers ⁽⁰⁵⁾**have been with** their current employer for a shorter period and have had ⁽⁰⁶⁾**a larger number of** employers than those in other regions. This ⁽⁰⁷⁾**has been blamed**, ⁽⁰⁸⁾**in part**, by the lower levels of training provided by American companies for their workers, but this is likely an oversimplified explanation. ⁽⁰⁹⁾**In reality**, many diverse factors influence American employees' ⁽¹⁰⁾**decisions to switch** jobs more frequently than their counterparts in Europe and Japan.

2 While economic theories posit that mobility is most likely in prosperous times, when the costs and risks of changing jobs are low, ⁽¹¹⁾**a number of** logistical differences make it more likely. One of the most surprising of these is the location of the job. Those employed in urban areas **are** more ⁽¹²⁾**likely to change** jobs, likely ⁽¹³⁾**due to** the easy availability of other jobs in the city, which means that the employee will not ⁽¹⁴⁾**have to relocate** his or her home to ⁽¹⁵⁾**take another job**. Those who live in non-urban areas who quit their jobs will ⁽¹⁶⁾**have more difficulty in finding** another job due to the limited number available in the region.

3 ⁽¹⁷⁾**In addition to** logistical and monetary factors, psychological factors also ⁽¹⁸⁾**play a large role in** job mobility. Individuals with more adventurous personalities and fewer familial responsibilities are more likely to switch jobs easily, as they can overcome ⁽¹⁹⁾**the fear of the unknown** and ⁽²⁰⁾**are more willing to risk** the consequences of job change. In fact, studies have shown that 13% of workers who have switched jobs ⁽²¹⁾**more than 3 times** ⁽²²⁾**are responsible for** about half of all permanent employment separations. On the other hand, fear and cultural norms can keep employees in their current positions. One of these, the Japanese "lifetime employment" system, has made job switching almost ⁽²³⁾**unheard of** in Japanese society. This system, which ⁽²⁴⁾**was meant to limit the** ⁽²⁵⁾**ability of** companies **to** ⁽²⁶⁾**lay off** employees, has also built a strong sense of employee loyalty, which ⁽²⁷⁾**makes it societally undesirable for** employees **to switch** jobs without good reason.

4 Interestingly, real estate prices have also been ⁽²⁸⁾**linked to** the incidence of job change. Housing policies in Japan and Europe often ⁽²⁹⁾**make** residential relocation an expensive prospect, which discourages job mobility ⁽³⁰⁾**in much the same way that** non-urban locations do. In many of these countries, rental subsidies are more widely available than in the United States, which makes workers ⁽³¹⁾**loath to** relocate for a job change. In addition, ⁽³²⁾**rent control** schemes that limit ⁽³³⁾**the increase in** rent between consecutive rental contracts reduce job and residential mobility, because landlords can negotiate any rental amount for new contracts. This means that any job move that requires relocation could ⁽³⁴⁾**result in** an astronomical increase in housing cost.

5 Some researchers also ⁽³⁵⁾**point to** history as ⁽³⁶⁾**an indicator of** the ⁽³⁷⁾**propensity for** job change. The United States, Canada, and Australia are all large, rather sparsely populated countries that show much lower job tenures than most European countries and Japan. They hypothesize that these country's long history of attracting international immigration and their citizens' ⁽³⁸⁾**willingness to undertake** long-distance relocation have made job change much less unusual. In a country where people have previously moved thousands of miles from their homeland, ⁽³⁹⁾**pulling up stakes** and moving for another job is much less of an event than in countries with more stable populations.

6 With all of these possible explanations for the ⁽⁴⁰⁾**differences in** job mobility rates, another question arises: what is the societal impact of increased job mobility? Some believe that increased job mobility has a positive impact because it increases worker satisfaction and worker-job matches. Economists also ⁽⁴¹⁾**point to** larger numbers of workers and employers seeking matches as ⁽⁴²⁾**a sign of** the economic flexibility that makes economic adaptation possible. Conversely, higher mobility with lower costs can ⁽⁴³⁾**cause** employers **to** ⁽⁴⁴⁾**skimp on** training for employees who they constantly fear will ⁽⁴⁵⁾**jump ship**. Whatever the societal cost of job mobility, employers must ⁽⁴⁶⁾**try to balance** job mobility and its associated costs ⁽⁴⁷⁾**in order to succeed**.

Costs of Quitting a Job

1   High job mobility has long been held as a hallmark of the American economy. In contrast to employees in Japan and Europe, American employees appear to switch jobs much more readily. On average, American workers have been with their current employer for a shorter period and have had a larger number of employers than those in other regions. This has been blamed, in part, by the lower levels of training provided by American companies for their workers, but this is likely an oversimplified explanation. In reality, many diverse factors influence American employees' decisions to switch jobs more frequently than their counterparts in Europe and Japan.

2   While economic theories posit that mobility is most likely in prosperous times, when the costs and risks of changing jobs are low, a number of logistical differences make it more likely. One of the most surprising of these is the location of the job. Those employed in urban areas are more likely to change jobs, likely due to the easy availability of other jobs in the city, which means that the employee will not have to relocate his or her home to take another job. Those who live in non-urban areas who quit their jobs will have more difficulty in finding another job due to the limited number available in the region.

3   In addition to logistical and monetary factors, psychological factors also play a large role in job mobility. Individuals with more adventurous personalities and fewer familial responsibilities are more likely to switch jobs easily, as they can overcome the fear of the unknown and are more willing to risk the consequences of job change. In fact, studies have shown that 13% of workers who have switched jobs more than 3 times are responsible for about half of all permanent employment separations. On the other hand, fear and cultural norms can keep employees in their current positions. One of these, the Japanese "lifetime employment" system, has made job switching almost unheard of in Japanese society. This system, which was meant to limit the ability of companies to lay off employees, has also built a strong sense of employee loyalty, which makes it societally undesirable for employees to switch jobs without good reason.

4   Interestingly, real estate prices have also been linked to the incidence of job change. Housing policies in Japan and Europe often make residential relocation an expensive prospect, which discourages job mobility in much the same way that non-urban locations do. In many of these countries, rental subsidies are more widely available than in the United States, which makes workers loath to relocate for a job change. In addition, rent control schemes that limit the increase in rent between consecutive rental contracts reduce job and residential mobility, because landlords can negotiate any rental amount for new contracts. This means that any job move that requires relocation could result in an astronomical increase in housing cost.

5   Some researchers also point to history as an indicator of the propensity for job change. The United States, Canada, and Australia are all large, rather sparsely populated countries that show much lower job tenures than most European countries and Japan. They hypothesize that these country's long history of attracting international immigration and their citizens' willingness to undertake long-distance relocation have made job change much less unusual. In a country where people have previously moved thousands of miles from their homeland, pulling up stakes and moving for another job is much less of an event than in countries with more stable populations.

6   With all of these possible explanations for the differences in job mobility rates, another question arises: what is the societal impact of increased job mobility? Some believe that increased job mobility has a positive impact because it increases worker satisfaction and worker-job matches. Economists also point to larger numbers of workers and employers seeking matches as a sign of the economic flexibility that makes economic adaptation possible. Conversely, higher mobility with lower costs can cause employers to skimp on training for employees who they constantly fear will jump ship. Whatever the societal cost of job mobility, employers must try to balance job mobility and its associated costs in order to succeed.

Cell Theory

1 The three main tenets of cell theory, that cells are the basic unit of life, that all organisms (01)**are composed of** cells, and that cells (02)**arise** only **from** other cells, are some of the most basic principles (03)**in the field of** biology. From this theory scientists (04)**have been able to** extrapolate (05)**a great deal of** other scientific knowledge. (06)**In fact**, our understanding of the role of cells in sexual reproduction and the discovery of our genetic building blocks, DNA, are direct results of this. Cell theory has also (07)**allowed** medical researchers **to better** understand illnesses, such as cancer, as well as the cause of viral and bacterial infections. While the theory is now commonly accepted, and may seem like (08)**common sense**, its development took hundreds of years.

2 In fact, the earliest discoveries in the field (09)**took place** (10)**in the middle of** the 17th century when light microscopy (11)**began to be regularly used** on living creatures. It was during this time that physicist Robert Hooke (12)**melted glass into** lenses with which he could study fish scales, feathers, and the bodies of various insects, however his greatest discovery was that he noticed (13)**a series of** chambers in a sample of cork oak, which he felt resembled cubicles and named "cells". Antoine van Leeuwenhoek who created even stronger lenses would later trump this discovery. Using his microscopes he studied the tartar from his teeth and noticed that it contained microscopic organisms he called "aminalcules". Over time he was able to view microorganisms, such as bacteria, that were previously unknown. Leeuwenhoek was able to accurately describe microorganisms and microscopic parts of larger organisms, including the red blood cell. He did not, unfortunately, observe the reproduction of these animalcules or organisms, so he erroneously believed, as did most others of the time, that they simply spontaneously generated.

3 Over the next two centuries a great deal of additional observations would accumulate, but a true cell theory would not emerge until the middle of the 19th century. Today scientists (14)**blame** this great delay **on** the inferior scientific equipment, such as microscopes, and techniques, such as preserving samples of living material without destroying it, of 17th & 18th century researchers, which hindered their discoveries. In addition, the early observations of Hooke and Leeuwenhook did not (15)**address larger issues**, such as cells (16)**making up** all larger organisms. Hooke had simply noticed the cellular imprint, not the actual cell itself, while Leeuwenhook observed the actual cell, but (17)**failed to provide** an accurate description or categorization of its common structures.

4 As the 19th century progressed, these problems were solved through the invention of stronger microscopes, more diligent recording of findings, and increased cooperation by scientists. One of (18)**the first to** (19)**take advantage of** these was Scottish surgeon Robert Brown, who noted in 1831 that a circular object (20)**was present in** all of the orchid cells he studied. Using this finding, he researched other types of cells and found the same structure, which he then posited was a common cellular feature that he named the nucleus. Today, we know that the nucleus is the carrier of our genetic material.

5 By the late 1830s these discoveries only (21)**increased in** frequency and the cell theory truly began to (22)**take hold**. In 1838 and 1839, German biologists Matthias Schleiden and Theodor Schwann respectively discovered that all plants and animals were composed of cells. The discovery of cells with nuclei in both types of organisms allowed them to (23)**conclude that** the cell was the basic unit of life. It also helped them understand that microscopic bacteria (24)**had something in common** with larger organisms; they were both (25)**made up of** cells, which were the building blocks of all organisms. These two discoveries were the basic premises for the cell theory.

6 Later, other cellular biologists (26)**expanded on** these findings. Perhaps the most important of these was German pathologist Rudolf Virchow who contributed the third tenet of the cell theory in 1855: All cells (27)**come from** other living cells. This contradicted most common understanding (28)**of the time**, as it was thought that cells could spontaneously generate when a nucleus was able to form and grow the remainder of the cell body around itself. His explanation allowed later scientists to observe and describe cell division in the late 1880s. His theories also (29)**acted as** the basic (30)**principle behind** Pasteur's germ theory of disease, despite Virchow's personal (31)**objection to** such a theory. He felt that diseases were caused by internal cellular abnormalities and not outside pathogens, which he thought (32)**were** simply **attracted to** the abnormal cells as a habitat. While germ theory discounts this for most diseases, he did correctly suggest that abnormal cells could cause some diseases that affect the rest of the body, such as leukemia.

Cell Theory

1 The three main tenets of cell theory, that cells are the basic unit of life, that all organisms are composed of cells, and that cells arise only from other cells, are some of the most basic principles in the field of biology. From this theory scientists have been able to extrapolate a great deal of other scientific knowledge. In fact, our understanding of the role of cells in sexual reproduction and the discovery of our genetic building blocks, DNA, are direct results of this. Cell theory has also allowed medical researchers to better understand illnesses, such as cancer, as well as the cause of viral and bacterial infections. While the theory is now commonly accepted, and may seem like common sense, its development took hundreds of years.

2 In fact, the earliest discoveries in the field took place in the middle of the 17th century when light microscopy began to be regularly used on living creatures. It was during this time that physicist Robert Hooke melted glass into lenses with which he could study fish scales, feathers, and the bodies of various insects, however his greatest discovery was that he noticed a series of chambers in a sample of cork oak, which he felt resembled cubicles and named "cells". Antoine van Leeuwenhoek who created even stronger lenses would later trump this discovery. Using his microscopes he studied the tartar from his teeth and noticed that it contained microscopic organisms he called "aminalcules". Over time he was able to view microorganisms, such as bacteria, that were previously unknown. Leeuwenhoek was able to accurately describe microorganisms and microscopic parts of larger organisms, including the red blood cell. He did not, unfortunately, observe the reproduction of these animalcules or organisms, so he erroneously believed, as did most others of the time, that they simply spontaneously generated.

3 Over the next two centuries a great deal of additional observations would accumulate, but a true cell theory would not emerge until the middle of the 19th century. Today scientists blame this great delay on the inferior scientific equipment, such as microscopes, and techniques, such as preserving samples of living material without destroying it, of 17th & 18th century researchers, which hindered their discoveries. In addition, the early observations of Hooke and Leeuwenhook did not address larger issues, such as cells making up all larger organisms. Hooke had simply noticed the cellular imprint, not the actual cell itself, while Leeuwenhoek observed the actual cell, but failed to provide an accurate description or categorization of its common structures.

4 As the 19th century progressed, these problems were solved through the invention of stronger microscopes, more diligent recording of findings, and increased cooperation by scientists. One of the first to take advantage of these was Scottish surgeon Robert Brown, who noted in 1831 that a circular object was present in all of the orchid cells he studied. Using this finding, he researched other types of cells and found the same structure, which he then posited was a common cellular feature that he named the nucleus. Today, we know that the nucleus is the carrier of our genetic material.

5 By the late 1830s these discoveries only increased in frequency and the cell theory truly began to take hold. In 1838 and 1839, German biologists Matthias Schleiden and Theodor Schwann respectively discovered that all plants and animals were composed of cells. The discovery of cells with nuclei in both types of organisms allowed them to conclude that the cell was the basic unit of life. It also helped them understand that microscopic bacteria had something in common with larger organisms; they were both made up of cells, which were the building blocks of all organisms. These two discoveries were the basic premises for the cell theory.

6 Later, other cellular biologists expanded on these findings. Perhaps the most important of these was German pathologist Rudolf Virchow who contributed the third tenet of the cell theory in 1855: All cells come from other living cells. This contradicted most common understanding of the time, as it was thought that cells could spontaneously generate when a nucleus was able to form and grow the remainder of the cell body around itself. His explanation allowed later scientists to observe and describe cell division in the late 1880s. His theories also acted as the basic principle behind Pasteur's germ theory of disease, despite Virchow's personal objection to such a theory. He felt that diseases were caused by internal cellular abnormalities and not outside pathogens, which he thought were simply attracted to the abnormal cells as a habitat. While germ theory discounts this for most diseases, he did correctly suggest that abnormal cells could cause some diseases that affect the rest of the body, such as leukemia.

Mating Songs of Frogs

1 Most species of frogs (01)**rely upon** auditory signals to (02)**communicate with** (03)**one another**. This occurs because auditory communication is much more efficient than visual forms of communication. This is because auditory signaling, unlike visual communication, does not require a specific orientation to receive a message. The recipient need not be facing the sender to receive the signal. They also allow signals to be sent over greater distances than visual communication methods. (04)**Instead of** being blocked by physical barriers, the auditory signal can be transmitted. (05)**In fact**, auditory communication (06)**allows** frogs **to broadcast** their messages through the air, underwater, and even through the substrate. Further, since most frog and toad species are nocturnal, auditory messages have the advantage of being usable even in complete darkness. (07)**Due to** these advantages, male frogs have developed a complex system of communication that allows them to attract potential mates.

2 Male frogs (08)**are able to produce** these signs due to a series of adaptations, the most notable being the vocal sacs located beneath the floor of the mouth. To create their distinctive croaking sounds, frogs (09)**seal off** their nostrils and mouths and use the muscles along their body wall to (10)**force air** (11)**back-and-forth** from the lungs through the larynx and into the vocal sac. This air movement across the larynx (12)**causes** the vocal cords **to vibrate** and the sound is then amplified by the vocal sacs to produce a loud, clear croaking sound. These sounds attract females, which may respond by approaching the male or even by (13)**calling back to** the male. This can even (14)**lead to** duets between receptive couples. Unfortunately, they can also increase the mortality risk, since predators can also recognize the croaking.

3 To human ears these croaks may all (15)**sound the same**, but they are actually a complex system that allows frogs to learn (16)**a great deal** about the croaking frog. Perhaps the most important information that a female frog can discern from the croaking is the temporal pattern and frequency, both of which are species specific. Although some frog species can interbreed, hybridization usually produces non-viable offspring; therefore female frogs (17)**are attracted to** the call of males from their species. Frogs are (18)**so** (19)**attuned to** differentiating calls **that** they can even determine if the caller is from the same region. (20)**In much the same way that** human languages have developed dialects, frog calls vary slightly amongst different geographic populations and can be (21)**used to determine** whether the call is from a male in a neighboring territory, or if an intruder has appeared.

4 Another key piece of information that females (22)**glean from** the croaking is the relative size and age of the croaker. Many frog species undergo indeterminate growth, meaning they continuously grow larger as they age. This (23)**provides** them **with** larger vocal sacs and larynxes that produce louder and lower tones as they age. Females, which are generally attracted to older frogs, recognize the (24)**differences in** amplitude and pitch of the caller and are attracted to them. This inherent (25)**bias of** female frogs toward older males is a method of selecting genetically superior mates, since their age and size indicate that the male frogs have survived environmental and predatory hazards, two traits that would be (26)**beneficial for** her offspring. However, these two aspects can be ambiguous, as both temperature and distance can cause the calls of younger males to seem louder and lower than older specimens.

5 Female frogs can determine the relative health and territorial safety of the male though his calls (27)**as well**. Because of the continuous muscle contractions required to push air through the vocal mechanisms, some of which (28)**make up** 15% of the frogs overall mass, croaking requires a considerable energy expenditure of part of the male. Some studies show tree frog croaking is the most energy intensive activity of any vertebrate. Therefore, it can only be performed by males that are healthy (29)**enough to** eschew feeding (30)**in order to** (31)**search for** a mate. Further, the (32)**ability to** continually croak (33)**indicates to** the female **that** the male has a secure territory in which he is safe from predation, since he is calling so much attention to himself.

6 Interestingly, male-female interaction is not the only use of auditory communication in frogs. Male frogs also communicate with one another to establish a territory. This is especially important because during the mating season when the males form large 'choruses,' they learn the croaking of their direct neighbors. When they hear these croaks they are (34)**not alarmed, but** when they hear an unfamiliar call they croak aggressively to (35)**warn** the intruder **that** they are (36)**encroaching** upon another frog's territory.

Mating Songs of Frogs

1 Most species of frogs rely upon auditory signals to communicate with one another. This occurs because auditory communication is much more efficient than visual forms of communication. This is because auditory signaling, unlike visual communication, does not require a specific orientation to receive a message. The recipient need not be facing the sender to receive the signal. They also allow signals to be sent over greater distances than visual communication methods. Instead of being blocked by physical barriers, the auditory signal can be transmitted. In fact, auditory communication allows frogs to broadcast their messages through the air, underwater, and even through the substrate. Further, since most frog and toad species are nocturnal, auditory messages have the advantage of being usable even in complete darkness. Due to these advantages, male frogs have developed a complex system of communication that allows them to attract potential mates.

2 Male frogs are able to produce these signs due to a series of adaptations, the most notable being the vocal sacs located beneath the floor of the mouth. To create their distinctive croaking sounds, frogs seal off their nostrils and mouths and use the muscles along their body wall to force air back-and-forth from the lungs through the larynx and into the vocal sac. This air movement across the larynx causes the vocal cords to vibrate and the sound is then amplified by the vocal sacs to produce a loud, clear croaking sound. These sounds attract females, which may respond by approaching the male or even by calling back to the male. This can even lead to duets between receptive couples. Unfortunately, they can also increase the mortality risk, since predators can also recognize the croaking.

3 To human ears these croaks may all sound the same, but they are actually a complex system that allows frogs to learn a great deal about the croaking frog. Perhaps the most important information that a female frog can discern from the croaking is the temporal pattern and frequency, both of which are species specific. Although some frog species can interbreed, hybridization usually produces non-viable offspring; therefore female frogs are attracted to the call of males from their species. Frogs are so attuned to differentiating calls that they can even determine if the caller is from the same region. In much the same way that human languages have developed dialects, frog calls vary slightly amongst different geographic populations and can be used to determine whether the call is from a male in a neighboring territory, or if an intruder has appeared.

4 Another key piece of information that females glean from the croaking is the relative size and age of the croaker. Many frog species undergo indeterminate growth, meaning they continuously grow larger as they age. This provides them with larger vocal sacs and larynxes that produce louder and lower tones as they age. Females, which are generally attracted to older frogs, recognize the differences in amplitude and pitch of the caller and are attracted to them. This inherent bias of female frogs toward older males is a method of selecting genetically superior mates, since their age and size indicate that the male frogs have survived environmental and predatory hazards, two traits that would be beneficial for her offspring. However, these two aspects can be ambiguous, as both temperature and distance can cause the calls of younger males to seem louder and lower than older specimens.

5 Female frogs can determine the relative health and territorial safety of the male though his calls as well. Because of the continuous muscle contractions required to push air through the vocal mechanisms, some of which make up 15% of the frogs overall mass, croaking requires a considerable energy expenditure of part of the male. Some studies show tree frog croaking is the most energy intensive activity of any vertebrate. Therefore, it can only be performed by males that are healthy enough to eschew feeding in order to search for a mate. Further, the ability to continually croak indicates to the female that the male has a secure territory in which he is safe from predation, since he is calling so much attention to himself.

6 Interestingly, male-female interaction is not the only use of auditory communication in frogs. Male frogs also communicate with one another to establish a territory. This is especially important because during the mating season when the males form large 'choruses,' they learn the croaking of their direct neighbors. When they hear these croaks they are not alarmed, but when they hear an unfamiliar call they croak aggressively to warn the intruder that they are encroaching upon another frog's territory.

Milankovitch Cycles and Glaciation

1 Scientists have [01]**pieced together** a relatively detailed timeline of the twenty glacial cycles that [02]**took place** during the Pleistocene Epoch (10,000-2,000,000 years ago). During these frigid periods, glaciers up to 3,900m thick covered 30% of Earth's surface. These were most prevalent in the higher-latitude regions of both hemispheres, which [03]**were covered by** glaciers as far south as Germany in the Northern Hemisphere and as far north as the Andes in the Southern Hemisphere. However, despite 100+ years of [04]**research into** these periods, researchers [05]**are unable to explain** their cause.

2 Over the years, diverse factors, such as continental location, oceanic circulation and solar energy fluctuation, have been cited as possible causes of these glaciations. One of the most interesting was [06]**put forth** by Scottish scientist James Croll who [07]**used** the previously known fact that cyclic [08]**changes in** Earth's orbit affect how solar radiation impacts Earth's surface **to deduce** that they could also affect the global climate. Using this theory, Yugoslavian mathematician Milutin Milankovitch developed an equation that showed how these cyclic changes in Earth's orbit, now known as Milankovitch cycles, could cause climatic changes and [09]**lead to** continental glaciations.

3 Milankovitch [10]**based** his equation on three cyclic changes in Earth's position [11]**relative to** the Sun that he thought could collectively [12]**have an effect on** the solar radiation that is incident on Earth's surface: eccentricity, obliquity, and precession. The first of these, eccentricity, is the elliptical variation in the Earth's orbit that sometimes [13]**brings** it **closer to** the Sun and slightly changes every revolution in a 96,000-year cycle. The second of these, obliquity, [14]**is concerned with** the annual changes in the tilt of Earth's axis that causes seasonal variation. As this tilt changes, in a 41,000-year cycle, the temperature difference between winter and summer becomes extreme and more mild as the tilt is respectively higher or lower. The final of the Milankovitch cycles, precession, is the circular wobble that Earth performs on its axis every 12,700 years, in a movement that resembles the wobble of a slowly moving top. Although these three cycles do not affect the amount of solar radiation that reaches the Earth, they greatly affect its distribution. Milankovitch's equation showed that every 40,000 years these three cycles would perfectly synchronize [15]**in a way that** would greatly reduce the difference between winter and summer temperatures and [16]**prevent** the winter ice **from** melting during the summer, thereby [17]**allowing** it **to build up**, and causing an overall glacial growth.

4 Despite developing this theory in the 1920s, Milankovitch was limited in his [18]**ability to test** it extensively, since the timeline of the Pleistocene Epoch temperature changes [19]**necessary for** testing it was not developed until the 1970s. After the development of this new chronology, a [20]**correlation between** Milankovitch cycles **and** the major climatic changes of the last 65 million years became clearer. Further, core samples [21]**taken from** the deep-sea floor proved that Milankovitch's equation was incredibly [22]**accurate in** predicting climate changes over the last few hundred thousand years, including the end of the Pleistocene Epoch.

5 Unfortunately, this accuracy and correlation does not fully explain the cause of glaciation throughout history. If Milankovitch's explanation was accurate, it would [23]**require** glaciations **to have occurred** regularly throughout Earth's history, yet they [24]**appear to have occurred** only rarely. This has [25]**led** scientists **to determine** that there must be another factor that [26]**works with** the Milankovitch cycles to cause glaciations. When this mystery factor has sufficiently lowered the average temperature, the cyclic variations of solar radiation caused by the Milankovitch Cycles can [27]**throw** Earth **into and out of** glacial periods [28]**with the regularity** predicted by the Milankovitch equation.

6 [29]**In the quest to discover** this mystery-cooling factor, [30]**a number of** possibilities have been suggested. One of these is that changes in the Sun's luminosity have allowed fluctuations in the solar energy that reaches Earth. However, this is highly unlikely, since [31]**it is now believed that** the Sun has steadily become stronger over time. Another possible cause of lower temperatures was volcanic dust in the atmosphere [32]**shielding** Earth **from** solar radiation and [33]**causing** temperatures **to drop**. This is also rather unlikely, since the beginning of the last glaciation does not [34]**correspond with** known major eruptions. A more recent theory states that [35]**differences in** atmospheric carbon dioxide (CO_2) have caused temperature fluctuations on Earth. Since CO_2 traps radiation in the atmosphere, periods of decreased atmospheric CO_2 [36]**results in** lower temperatures on Earth's surface, allowing solar radiation to escape. This [37]**is especially attractive to** researchers, because studies of the Greenland ice cap show that [38]**the number of** CO_2 bubbles found in the different strata changes [39]**depending on** when the ice formed. Samples from periods [40]**known to be** warmer show higher CO_2 levels, while colder periods have significantly less, thereby confirming the correlation between CO_2 levels and Earth's temperature.

Milankovitch Cycles and Glaciation

1 Scientists have pieced together a relatively detailed timeline of the twenty glacial cycles that took place during the Pleistocene Epoch (10,000-2,000,000 years ago). During these frigid periods, glaciers up to 3,900m thick covered 30% of Earth's surface. These were most prevalent in the higher-latitude regions of both hemispheres, which were covered by glaciers as far south as Germany in the Northern Hemisphere and as far north as the Andes in the Southern Hemisphere. However, despite 100+ years of research into these periods, researchers are unable to explain their cause.

2 Over the years, diverse factors, such as continental location, oceanic circulation and solar energy fluctuation, have been cited as possible causes of these glaciations. One of the most interesting was put forth by Scottish scientist James Croll who used the previously known fact that cyclic changes in Earth's orbit affect how solar radiation impacts Earth's surface to deduce that they could also affect the global climate. Using this theory, Yugoslavian mathematician Milutin Milankovitch developed an equation that showed how these cyclic changes in Earth's orbit, now known as Milankovitch cycles, could cause climatic changes and lead to continental glaciations.

3 Milankovitch based his equation on three cyclic changes in Earth's position relative to the Sun that he thought could collectively have an effect on the solar radiation that is incident on Earth's surface: eccentricity, obliquity, and precession. The first of these, eccentricity, is the elliptical variation in the Earth's orbit that sometimes brings it closer to the Sun and slightly changes every revolution in a 96,000-year cycle. The second of these, obliquity, is concerned with the annual changes in the tilt of Earth's axis that causes seasonal variation. As this tilt changes, in a 41,000-year cycle, the temperature difference between winter and summer becomes extreme and more mild as the tilt is respectively higher or lower. The final of the Milankovitch cycles, precession, is the circular wobble that Earth performs on its axis every 12,700 years, in a movement that resembles the wobble of a slowly moving top. Although these three cycles do not affect the amount of solar radiation that reaches the Earth, they greatly affect its distribution. Milankovitch's equation showed that every 40,000 years these three cycles would perfectly synchronize in a way that would greatly reduce the difference between winter and summer temperatures and prevent the winter ice from melting during the summer, thereby allowing it to build up, and causing an overall glacial growth.

4 Despite developing this theory in the 1920s, Milankovitch was limited in his ability to test it extensively, since the timeline of the Pleistocene Epoch temperature changes necessary for testing it was not developed until the 1970s. After the development of this new chronology, a correlation between Milankovitch cycles and the major climatic changes of the last 65 million years became clearer. Further, core samples taken from the deep-sea floor proved that Milankovitch's equation was incredibly accurate in predicting climate changes over the last few hundred thousand years, including the end of the Pleistocene Epoch.

5 Unfortunately, this accuracy and correlation does not fully explain the cause of glaciation throughout history. If Milankovitch's explanation was accurate, it would require glaciations to have occurred regularly throughout Earth's history, yet they appear to have occurred only rarely. This has led scientists to determine that there must be another factor that works with the Milankovitch cycles to cause glaciations. When this mystery factor has sufficiently lowered the average temperature, the cyclic variations of solar radiation caused by the Milankovitch Cycles can throw Earth into and out of glacial periods with the regularity predicted by the Milankovitch equation.

6 In the quest to discover this mystery-cooling factor, a number of possibilities have been suggested. One of these is that changes in the Sun's luminosity have allowed fluctuations in the solar energy that reaches Earth. However, this is highly unlikely, since it is now believed that the Sun has steadily become stronger over time. Another possible cause of lower temperatures was volcanic dust in the atmosphere shielding Earth from solar radiation and causing temperatures to drop. This is also rather unlikely, since the beginning of the last glaciation does not correspond with known major eruptions. A more recent theory states that differences in atmospheric carbon dioxide (CO_2) have caused temperature fluctuations on Earth. Since CO_2 traps radiation in the atmosphere, periods of decreased atmospheric CO_2 results in lower temperatures on Earth's surface, allowing solar radiation to escape. This is especially attractive to researchers, because studies of the Greenland ice cap show that the number of CO_2 bubbles found in the different strata changes depending on when the ice formed. Samples from periods known to be warmer show higher CO_2 levels, while colder periods have significantly less, thereby confirming the correlation between CO_2 levels and Earth's temperature.

The Making of Calendars

1 Even before the invention of the modern calendar, people were (01)**able to** (02)**keep track of** events in their lives using the phases of the moon and the seasons. (03)**In this way**, one could explain that something would occur two days after the next full moon or that one was born 25 winters ago. This (04)**reliance upon** the moon may seem quite rudimentary, but it also (05)**allowed** them **to** count the days between the moons phases and the equinoxes (when the duration of the days and nights are approximately equal) and the solstices (the longest and shortest days of the year), which mark the traditional beginning of each of the seasons. As knowledge and understanding of these events increased, calendars as we now know them (06)**began to** (07)**come together**.

2 As these empirical lunar- and solar-based calendars became more popular, their flaws became more evident. For one, they (08)**were** extremely **dependent upon** the weather. While it does not affect the actual movement of either of the celestial bodies, it can obscure them and cause inaccuracies in the calendar. The calendars were also dependent upon the location, since the timing of the moon's phases and the solstices and equinoxes change over distances. For instance, the timing of the rise of the new moon would be earlier in eastern locations. It may not even occur on the same day if the second observer is far enough west. This is also problematic for observers in extreme northern latitudes where the sun remains below the horizon for 4.5 months during winter and remains overhead (09)**for an equal amount of time** in the summer.

3 Secondary problems arose due to the fact that the basic unit of the calendar, the day, does not evenly fit in the calendric concept of either the month or the year. Over time, this (10)**causes** the calendar day **to fall** (11)**out of line with** (12)**both** the lunar **and** solar cycle. This basic inaccuracy required that days or months be intercalated, or added to the calendar. Unfortunately, this process was overseen by government officials or holy men who could be corrupt, inept, or both. This problem (13)**came to a head** during the reign of Julius Caesar, when the intercalation cycle was (14)**thrown off** by war and were observed in some consecutive years and forgotten in others, causing the calendar year to fall (15)**out of sync**. To solve this problem, the Julian calendar was introduced around 50 BCE and the Roman Empire's year was officially (16)**lengthened to** 365.25 days.

4 The new Julian calendar could be easily calculated and remained better (17)**synchronized with** the cycles of the sun and moon over time. This removed the chance for abuse by (18)**laying out** a systematic method for intercalations. Surprisingly, calendars in the East and West diverged (19)**at this time**. Those in the East, namely China and India, (20)**depended upon** the exact timing of lunar and solar events, because of the importance of these in the society's religions and traditions. But those in the West and Middle East followed rigid arithmetical rules that kept them synchronized with the natural world without (21)**the need for** constant observations and calculations of astronomical events.

5 Both lunisolar and arithmetic calendar systems still (22)**suffered from** the problem mentioned earlier, the impossibility of the larger units of time to be divided evenly by the basic unit of measure, the day. Calendars based on lunation, or the period between new moons, are inherently self-adjusting and will synchronize with the cycles, but arithmetical calendars will only remain synchronized (23)**on average**. However, this does not mean that the lunar calendar is more accurate, because the cycles of the moon are still not easily divisible by days as each lunation takes approximately 29.53 days.

6 Today, (24)**all but a handful of** countries have (25)**settled on** the use of one civil arithmetically based calendar, the Gregorian calendar, which Pope Gregory XIII introduced in 1582. Under the Gregorian calendar, the problem with the uneven number of days in the year was solved through the use of leap years, which contain an extra day, every four years, except those that are divisible by 100, but not by 400. This means that 1700, 1800, and 1900 would be common (non-leap) years, but 2000 would be a leap year. This new calculation effectively (26)**brought** the average length of the year **to** 365.2425 years, more (27)**in line with** the actual (28)**time it takes for** earth **to** (29)**revolve around** the sun. The new calendar system also dropped 10 days to realign the yearly equinoxes, since the accumulated errors in the calendar over the previous 1000-1200 years had (30)**moved** them **forward** by 10 days. This does not, however, mean that the Gregorian calendar is without its flaws. The system is (31)**estimated to** have an error of one day every 3,300 years.

The Making of Calendars

1 Even before the invention of the modern calendar, people were able to keep track of events in their lives using the phases of the moon and the seasons. In this way, one could explain that something would occur two days after the next full moon or that one was born 25 winters ago. This reliance upon the moon may seem quite rudimentary, but it also allowed them to count the days between the moons phases and the equinoxes (when the duration of the days and nights are approximately equal) and the solstices (the longest and shortest days of the year), which mark the traditional beginning of each of the seasons. As knowledge and understanding of these events increased, calendars as we now know them began to come together.

2 As these empirical lunar- and solar-based calendars became more popular, their flaws became more evident. For one, they were extremely dependent upon the weather. While it does not affect the actual movement of either of the celestial bodies, it can obscure them and cause inaccuracies in the calendar. The calendars were also dependent upon the location, since the timing of the moon's phases and the solstices and equinoxes change over distances. For instance, the timing of the rise of the new moon would be earlier in eastern locations. It may not even occur on the same day if the second observer is far enough west. This is also problematic for observers in extreme northern latitudes where the sun remains below the horizon for 4.5 months during winter and remains overhead for an equal amount of time in the summer.

3 Secondary problems arose due to the fact that the basic unit of the calendar, the day, does not evenly fit in the calendric concept of either the month or the year. Over time, this causes the calendar day to fall out of line with both the lunar and solar cycle. This basic inaccuracy required that days or months be intercalated, or added to the calendar. Unfortunately, this process was overseen by government officials or holy men who could be corrupt, inept, or both. This problem came to a head during the reign of Julius Caesar, when the intercalation cycle was thrown off by war and were observed in some consecutive years and forgotten in others, causing the calendar year to fall out of sync. To solve this problem, the Julian calendar was introduced around 50 BCE and the Roman Empire's year was officially lengthened to 365.25 days.

4 The new Julian calendar could be easily calculated and remained better synchronized with the cycles of the sun and moon over time. This removed the chance for abuse by laying out a systematic method for intercalations. Surprisingly, calendars in the East and West diverged at this time. Those in the East, namely China and India, depended upon the exact timing of lunar and solar events, because of the importance of these in the society's religions and traditions. But those in the West and Middle East followed rigid arithmetical rules that kept them synchronized with the natural world without the need for constant observations and calculations of astronomical events.

5 Both lunisolar and arithmetic calendar systems still suffered from the problem mentioned earlier, the impossibility of the larger units of time to be divided evenly by the basic unit of measure, the day. Calendar's based on lunation, or the period between new moons, are inherently self-adjusting and will synchronize with the cycles, but arithmetical calendars will only remain synchronized on average. However, this does not mean that the lunar calendar is more accurate, because the cycles of the moon are still not easily divisible by days as each lunation takes approximately 29.53 days.

6 Today, all but a handful of countries have settled on the use of one civil arithmetically based calendar, the Gregorian calendar, which Pope Gregory XIII introduced in 1582. Under the Gregorian calendar, the problem with the uneven number of days in the year was solved through the use of leap years, which contain an extra day, every four years, except those that are divisible by 100, but not by 400. This means that 1700, 1800, and 1900 would be common (non-leap) years, but 2000 would be a leap year. This new calculation effectively brought the average length of the year to 365.2425 years, more in line with the actual time it takes for earth to revolve around the sun. The new calendar system also dropped 10 days to realign the yearly equinoxes, since the accumulated errors in the calendar over the previous 1000-1200 years had moved them forward by 10 days. This does not, however, mean that the Gregorian calendar is without its flaws. The system is estimated to have an error of one day every 3,300 years.

The Decline of the Ottoman Empire

1 After its foundation in 1299, Anatolia's Ottoman Empire enjoyed extensive success and expansion under ⁽⁰¹⁾**a series of** very powerful leaders. Many agree that the empire reached its apex during the reign of its 10th, and longest serving, sultan, Suleyman the Magnificent. Although his predecessors were ⁽⁰²⁾**known for** their wisdom, savage conquests, and administrative ability, Suleyman ⁽⁰³⁾**took** this **to another level** and ⁽⁰⁴⁾**expanded** the empire **into** central Europe, Persia, to the southern coast of the Arabian Peninsula, and across northern Africa. This gave the Ottoman Empire near total ⁽⁰⁵⁾**hegemony over** Mediterranean trade and this period ⁽⁰⁶⁾**is considered** the "Golden Age" of the empire. Unfortunately, Suleyman's successors lacked initiative and competence and under their leadership the empire suffered. Luckily, some of these incompetent leaders ⁽⁰⁷⁾**relied upon** "viziers," or executive officers, who kept the empire in tact for nearly 400 more years.

2 Unfortunately for the Ottoman Sultans, the end of the 16th century ⁽⁰⁸⁾**marked** ⁽⁰⁹⁾**not only** the end of their territorial expansion and regional dominance, **but also** the beginning of the empire's slow decline. However, this cannot ⁽¹⁰⁾**be** completely **blamed on** the incompetence of the leaders. Changes within the empire and the rise of other regional powers, especially those neighboring the empire's European territories, both ⁽¹¹⁾**played a** large **role in** the decline of the empire. These changes ⁽¹²⁾**caused** the role of the Sultan **to change** dramatically. ⁽¹³⁾**Instead of** ⁽¹⁴⁾**being dedicated to** leading armies into ⁽¹⁵⁾**battle for** territorial expansion, bureaucracy and diplomacy became more ⁽¹⁶⁾**important to** the Sultans ⁽¹⁷⁾**so that** they could administer the enormous territory of the empire and to ⁽¹⁸⁾**deal with** its increasingly powerful neighbors. In addition, large army units ⁽¹⁹⁾**needed to be** permanently **positioned, funded, and controlled to** ⁽²⁰⁾**fend off** the Russian's in the Crimea, the Persians to the west, and other powers around the Mediterranean region.

3 These were new roles that would have been difficult for the empire's early successful sultans, but with the ⁽²¹⁾**lack of** skill and experience of those who followed Suleyman the empire ⁽²²⁾**fell behind in** military and administrative technology and suffered military defeats, such as the empire's ⁽²³⁾**loss to** Phillip II of Spain and the stunning loss to the Habsburgs and the Holy League when ⁽²⁴⁾**attempting to** capture Vienna. The large territory covered ⁽²⁵⁾**too** much area **for** one person **to** ⁽²⁶⁾**rule over**, ⁽²⁷⁾**forcing** the sultans **to** ⁽²⁸⁾**reply upon** the Divan, a group of trusted officers, ministers, and a Grand Vizier. These Viziers and their bureaucratic organizations became very powerful ⁽²⁹⁾**in their own right** and later sultans, such as Selim II, ⁽³⁰⁾**began to rely upon** them to administer the territory.

4 Surprisingly, another group that greatly reduced the power of the Sultan and increased that of the Grand Vizier was the imperial harem. These women, who ⁽³¹⁾**were connected to** the sultan, became more powerful ⁽³²⁾**as time went on**. Since the Grand Vizier was generally ⁽³³⁾**related to** the sultan through marriage, he was directly connected to the harem as well and could use these powerful women to increase his power and affect the Sultan. This was probably most easily accomplished through the most powerful member of the harem, the Valide Sultan, who was the Sultan's mother. These women were ⁽³⁴⁾**so** powerful **that** for over 130 years during the 16th and 17th century they were de facto rulers of the empire due to their ⁽³⁵⁾**influence over** their sons, many of who were minors.

5 All of these factors weakened the power of the sultan, and ⁽³⁶⁾**in turn** the empire, but perhaps the most detrimental change was the major ⁽³⁷⁾**shift in** trade from the Mediterranean to the Atlantic Ocean. The European "Age of Discovery" sent explorers and settlers around the world ⁽³⁸⁾**looking for** ⁽³⁹⁾**both** colonies **and** trade routes. When they ⁽⁴⁰⁾**began sailing** around Africa to reach the markets of Asia, they effectively removed the Ottoman Empire's great source of wealth and power, it's ⁽⁴¹⁾**ability to** ⁽⁴²⁾**act as** an intermediary for trade between Europe and Asia. This was ⁽⁴³⁾**not an immediate loss, but** ⁽⁴⁴⁾**over time** it became more ⁽⁴⁵⁾**detrimental for** the Ottoman Empire and without strong leadership and a fractured social and political structure, the empire began to decline more rapidly.

6 Over the next 200 years, these problems continued and the Ottoman Empire ⁽⁴⁶⁾**continued to fade** from its previous ⁽⁴⁷⁾**position as** a world super power. By the late 1800s the empire had lost so much territory and was so dominated by European powers that Tsar Nicholas ⁽⁴⁸⁾**referred to** it **as** the "sick man of Europe," which needed help from its neighbors. Unfortunately, for the empire, this help would not come fast enough. Despite a ⁽⁴⁹⁾**push for** modernization that moved it in a more secular direction to match the European powers, the empire was doomed. After a series of revolutions and wars, the empire joined WWI's Central Powers. This decision ultimately ⁽⁵⁰⁾**resulted in** the final dissolution of the empire.

The Decline of the Ottoman Empire

1 After its foundation in 1299, Anatolia's Ottoman Empire enjoyed extensive success and expansion under a series of very powerful leaders. Many agree that the empire reached its apex during the reign of its 10th, and longest serving, sultan, Suleyman the Magnificent. Although his predecessors were known for their wisdom, savage conquests, and administrative ability, Suleyman took this to another level and expanded the empire into central Europe, Persia, to the southern coast of the Arabian Peninsula, and across northern Africa. This gave the Ottoman Empire near total hegemony over Mediterranean trade and this period is considered the "Golden Age" of the empire. Unfortunately, Suleyman's successors lacked initiative and competence and under their leadership the empire suffered. Luckily, some of these incompetent leaders relied upon "viziers," or executive officers, who kept the empire in tact for nearly 400 more years.

2 Unfortunately for the Ottoman Sultans, the end of the 16th century marked not only the end of their territorial expansion and regional dominance, but also the beginning of the empire's slow decline. However, this cannot be completely blamed on the incompetence of the leaders. Changes within the empire and the rise of other regional powers, especially those neighboring the empire's European territories, both played a large role in the decline of the empire. These changes caused the role of the Sultan to change dramatically. Instead of being dedicated to leading armies into battle for territorial expansion, bureaucracy and diplomacy became more important to the Sultans so that they could administer the enormous territory of the empire and to deal with its increasingly powerful neighbors. In addition, large army units needed to be permanently positioned, funded, and controlled to fend off the Russian's in the Crimea, the Persians to the west, and other powers around the Mediterranean region.

3 These were new roles that would have been difficult for the empire's early successful sultans, but with the lack of skill and experience of those who followed Suleyman the empire fell behind in military and administrative technology and suffered military defeats, such as the empire's loss to Phillip II of Spain and the stunning loss to the Habsburgs and the Holy League when attempting to capture Vienna. The large territory covered too much area for one person to rule over, forcing the sultans to reply upon the Divan, a group of trusted officers, ministers, and a Grand Vizier. These Viziers and their bureaucratic organizations became very powerful in their own right and later sultans, such as Selim II, began to rely upon them to administer the territory.

4 Surprisingly, another group that greatly reduced the power of the Sultan and increased that of the Grand Vizier was the imperial harem. These women, who were connected to the sultan, became more powerful as time went on. Since the Grand Vizier was generally related to the sultan through marriage, he was directly connected to the harem as well and could use these powerful women to increase his power and affect the Sultan. This was probably most easily accomplished through the most powerful member of the harem, the Valide Sultan, who was the Sultan's mother. These women were so powerful that for over 130 years during the 16th and 17th century they were de facto rulers of the empire due to their influence over their sons, many of who were minors.

5 All of these factors weakened the power of the sultan, and in turn the empire, but perhaps the most detrimental change was the major shift in trade from the Mediterranean to the Atlantic Ocean. The European "Age of Discovery" sent explorers and settlers around the world looking for both colonies and trade routes. When they began sailing around Africa to reach the markets of Asia, they effectively removed the Ottoman Empire's great source of wealth and power, it's ability to act as an intermediary for trade between Europe and Asia. This was not an immediate loss, but over time it became more detrimental for the Ottoman Empire and without strong leadership and a fractured social and political structure, the empire began to decline more rapidly.

6 Over the next 200 years, these problems continued and the Ottoman Empire continued to fade from its previous position as a world super power. By the late 1800s the empire had lost so much territory and was so dominated by European powers that Tsar Nicholas referred to it as the "sick man of Europe," which needed help from its neighbors. Unfortunately, for the empire, this help would not come fast enough. Despite a push for modernization that moved it in a more secular direction to match the European powers, the empire was doomed. After a series of revolutions and wars, the empire joined WWI's Central Powers. This decision ultimately resulted in the final dissolution of the empire.

Geographic Isolation of Species

1 One of the most popular definitions of the word species was provided by renowned evolutionary biologist Ernest Mayr, who (01)**described** a species **as** a population with the (02)**ability to** interbreed, which does not (03)**interbreed with** other such populations. Today, we (04)**are unsure of** exactly how many species exist in the world, but we have (05)**learned of** several ways that new species develop. One of the major discoveries has been that the most common method of speciation, called allopatric or geographic speciation, occurs when a population becomes geographically separated. When the two species are separated, they can (06)**no longer** interbreed. This allows the two populations to (07)**follow** separate evolutionary **courses** due to different selective pressures, genetic drift, and mutations within the isolated populations.

2 (08)**It may seem illogical that** one population could be (09)**split into** two or more by geography, but there are actually several methods through which this can occur. A quick (10)**look at** Earth's topography will give several clues (11)**as to** how this can occur. The first things one notices is that the continents (12)**separated by** oceans, but knowing about continental drift (13)**tells us that** these were not always in their current positions. This movement (14)**caused** populations **to be separated**. Further, the rise of towering mountain ranges can also divide populations when they become too much of an obstacle for a population to cross. The formation of the Isthmus of Panama would (15)**have had the same effect** when it formed 3 million years ago. Before this time, populations of organisms swam freely (16)**between** the Caribbean Sea **and** the Pacific Ocean, but as the landmass developed it became (17)**a barrier to** this and the populations were effectively divided between the two great bodies of water.

3 It may seem that these geographical barriers must be quite formidable to cause speciation, but the size of the required barrier (18)**depends upon** the population (19)**in question**. Animals like birds can easily cross mountain ranges, rivers and large distances, so speciation in bird populations requires rather large barriers. Animals that cannot fly (20)**require** much smaller barriers **to split** the populations. This can be seen when a river changes course and small animal populations that cannot swim are divided. An example of this occurred when the Grand Canyon formed and the population of antelope squirrels was separated. Despite being only a few miles apart, the antelope squirrel population (21)**evolved into** two separate species, the white-tailed antelope squirrel north of the canyon and the Harris' antelope squirrel in the deserts south of the canyon.

4 Geographic separation does not necessarily cause speciation, but it creates the (22)**opportunity for** it when a gene pool changes (23)**enough to form** a reproductive barrier between the two parts of the population. Interestingly, this is much more likely in a small isolated population than it is in larger populations because their genetic pools can undergo considerable change. This can be seen in the remote Galapagos Islands, which are over 900 Km from the nearest landmass. In 2 million years, a relatively short period (24)**in geographical terms**, organisms from the South American mainland reached the islands and colonized them.

5 The distance of the Galapagos from the mainland, but the relatively close proximity of the islands to one another, (25)**allows them to** (26)**serve as** an outdoor evolutionary laboratory. Marine volcanism formed the archipelago's 18 main islands, which (27)**were** eventually **colonized by** organisms that floated there along oceanic currents or winds and (28)**founded** new **populations** on the islands. Some were even brought there by other organisms, such as seeds that were carried in the guts, fur and feathers of animals that (29)**made** their **way to** the islands.

6 Today, (30)**due to** the founder effect, the descendants of these original colonizers have evolved into (31)**a variety of** species, most of which are (32)**unique to** the island. The 13 finch species that Charles Darwin discovered on the island are a prime example of this. Research has shown that they (33)**descended from** the same early colonizers, yet they have differing feeding habits and beak types. This likely occurred because the small population that colonized the island underwent genetic changes that (34)**set** them **apart**. This continued when some of these individuals somehow (35)**found** their **way to** one of the other islands and founded a second new population. As these populations (36)**filled niches** in the ecosystem and became (37)**reliant upon** a particular type of food, their bodies became (38)**adapted to** it. This (39)**led to** differences in the shapes of beaks of the various types of finches. Eventually, these isolated populations developed an (40)**affinity for** only their own population and (41)**began breeding** with only their own kind. This effectively set them apart as separate species.

Geographic Isolation of Species

1 One of the most popular definitions of the word species was provided by renowned evolutionary biologist Ernest Mayr, who described a species as a population with the ability to interbreed, which does not interbreed with other such populations. Today, we are unsure of exactly how many species exist in the world, but we have learned of several ways that new species develop. One of the major discoveries has been that the most common method of speciation, called allopatric or geographic speciation, occurs when a population becomes geographically separated. When the two species are separated, they can no longer interbreed. This allows the two populations to follow separate evolutionary courses due to different selective pressures, genetic drift, and mutations within the isolated populations.

2 It may seem illogical that one population could be split into two or more by geography, but there are actually several methods through which this can occur. A quick look at Earth's topography will give several clues as to how this can occur. The first things one notices is that the continents separated by oceans, but knowing about continental drift tells us that these were not always in their current positions. This movement caused populations to be separated. Further, the rise of towering mountain ranges can also divide populations when they become too much of an obstacle for a population to cross. The formation of the Isthmus of Panama would have had the same effect when it formed 3 million years ago. Before this time, populations of organisms swam freely between the Caribbean Sea and the Pacific Ocean, but as the landmass developed it became a barrier to this and the populations were effectively divided between the two great bodies of water.

3 It may seem that these geographical barriers must be quite formidable to cause speciation, but the size of the required barrier depends upon the population in question. Animals like birds can easily cross mountain ranges, rivers and large distances, so speciation in bird populations requires rather large barriers. Animals that cannot fly require much smaller barriers to split the populations. This can be seen when a river changes course and small animal populations that cannot swim are divided. An example of this occurred when the Grand Canyon formed and the population of antelope squirrels was separated. Despite being only a few miles apart, the antelope squirrel population evolved into two separate species, the white-tailed antelope squirrel north of the canyon and the Harris' antelope squirrel in the deserts south of the canyon.

4 Geographic separation does not necessarily cause speciation, but it creates the opportunity for it when a gene pool changes enough to form a reproductive barrier between the two parts of the population. Interestingly, this is much more likely in a small isolated population than it is in larger populations because their genetic pools can undergo considerable change. This can be seen in the remote Galapagos Islands, which are over 900 Km from the nearest landmass. In 2 million years, a relatively short period in geographical terms, organisms from the South American mainland reached the islands and colonized them.

5 The distance of the Galapagos from the mainland, but the relatively close proximity of the islands to one another, allows them to serve as an outdoor evolutionary laboratory. Marine volcanism formed the archipelago's 18 main islands, which were eventually colonized by organisms that floated there along oceanic currents or winds and founded new populations on the islands. Some were even brought there by other organisms, such as seeds that were carried in the guts, fur and feathers of animals that made their way to the islands.

6 Today, due to the founder effect, the descendants of these original colonizers have evolved into a variety of species, most of which are unique to the island. The 13 finch species that Charles Darwin discovered on the island are a prime example of this. Research has shown that they descended from the same early colonizers, yet they have differing feeding habits and beak types. This likely occurred because the small population that colonized the island underwent genetic changes that set them apart. This continued when some of these individuals somehow found their way to one of the other islands and founded a second new population. As these populations filled niches in the ecosystem and became reliant upon a particular type of food, their bodies became adapted to it. This led to differences in the shapes of beaks of the various types of finches. Eventually, these isolated populations developed an affinity for only their own population and began breeding with only their own kind. This effectively set them apart as separate species.

The Empire of Alexander the Great

1 Despite their centuries long ⁽⁰¹⁾**fight against** Persian domination, the Classical Greek city-states were not unified ⁽⁰²⁾**in any meaningful way**. In fact, squabbling and infighting for power between the city-states marked the period, with power switching between them at different times. By the end of the Classical Period, Philip II of Macedon, in northern Greece, began an expansion of his territory, conquering the other city-states and uniting them ⁽⁰³⁾**under his** Macedonian **rule**. However, this expansion would eventually seem trivial ⁽⁰⁴⁾**when compared to** the expansion that was accomplished by his son, Alexander III, who ⁽⁰⁵⁾**ascended the throne** in 336 BCE upon his assassination. This brash new king, who was only 20 years old at the time, would continue his father's planned invasion of the Persian Empire and eventually control a larger empire than any ruler before him, ⁽⁰⁶⁾**leading to** great ⁽⁰⁷⁾**changes in** the regions he conquered.

2 Within two years of ⁽⁰⁸⁾**taking the throne**, Alexander had begun his campaign of international expansion and by 331 BCE the Macedonian ruler had overtaken the Persian Empire in the Levant, including the ancient city of Babylon, and had established a foothold in Egypt ⁽⁰⁹⁾**as well**. After consolidating this great empire, he continued eastward and reached as far east as modern-day India. The great extent of this empire, along with the strong central control that was exerted by Alexander, caused ⁽¹⁰⁾**a great number of** changes in the movement of goods, capital and people throughout the empire. The removal of trade barriers and movement restrictions, as well as interconnected markets, ⁽¹¹⁾**made it easier for** people **to travel** and ⁽¹²⁾**trade with** ⁽¹³⁾**one another**, and ⁽¹⁴⁾**allowed** Greek artisans and traders **to** ⁽¹⁵⁾**seek** their **fortunes** in a greatly expanded region. This expansion of trade and territory had several important consequences for ⁽¹⁶⁾**both** Classical Greece **and** the regions conquered ⁽¹⁷⁾**in its name**.

3 One of the most obvious of these changes in the newly unified empire was the expansion of Greek culture and influence. This occurred because Alexander founded ⁽¹⁸⁾**at least** 70 new urban centers, many of them ⁽¹⁹⁾**named after** himself, ⁽²⁰⁾**not so much** for military control **as** for cultural expansion. One of the most important ways that this was done was through the propagation of Greek literature and language through the establishment of Greek libraries, such as those established in Antioch (modern-day Turkey) and Alexandria, Egypt, which was the largest and most significant library in the ancient world.

4 Another major change caused by the empire's expansion was the demise of the Greek city-state. ⁽²¹⁾**Prior to** the imperial period the Greek city-states were sparsely populated and centered around the agoras, marketplaces where the population ⁽²²⁾**came together** to discuss the important issues of society and ⁽²³⁾**make decisions** ⁽²⁴⁾**in person**. Greek philosophers such as Plato and Aristotle, who had been the teenaged Alexander's tutor, felt that this form of government required a small population (less than 5,000) ⁽²⁵⁾**in order to** ⁽²⁶⁾**insure that** all citizens knew one another and could share their knowledge to make the best decisions. Further, prior to expansion these city-states lacked specialization, which allowed citizens to ⁽²⁷⁾**engage in** various civil and personal activities. After trade and commerce developed across the empire citizens ⁽²⁸⁾**had to develop** specializations, which ⁽²⁹⁾**brought about** professionalism. This meant that the small populations and "jack-of-all-trades" nature of the city-states' residents were ⁽³⁰⁾**no longer** sufficient and Greek cities changed dramatically.

5 Imperial expansion also ⁽³¹⁾**brought** the Greeks **into contact with** eastern philosophy and religion, which affected their previous belief in human-like gods with superhuman powers who could be ⁽³²⁾**counted on** to intercede ⁽³³⁾**on behalf of** the city-states citizens and provided protection and good luck during life's milestones. However, these beliefs had ⁽³⁴⁾**begun to** wane even before Alexander's time as Greek's no longer ⁽³⁵⁾**seemed interested in** only serving the city-state. In fact, the Athenian philosopher Socrates had previously been executed for suggesting a new morality ⁽³⁶⁾**based upon** personal conscience rather than the traditional gods. This new philosophy, however, did not ⁽³⁷⁾**take the place of** religion, but instead made the Classical Greeks ⁽³⁸⁾**receptive to** new ideas that allowed the religions of the Middle East to mix with Greek philosophy. This new combined system spread across the world after Alexander's death in 323 BCE, forever intertwining the cultures of Greece and the Levant.

6 This dramatic territorial expansion ⁽³⁹⁾**had** ⁽⁴⁰⁾**such** a profound **effect on** the world **that** Alexander's death ushered in ⁽⁴¹⁾**what is known as** the Hellenistic period in Greek history, when its influence ⁽⁴²⁾**was at** its **peak** in Europe, Africa, and Asia. During this period the Greeks ⁽⁴³⁾**made great strides in** art, literature, architecture, mathematics, governance, philosophy, and science. Without the influence of Alexander the Great's territorial expansion, these advances may have remained ⁽⁴⁴⁾**confined to** the borders of Classical Greece.

The Empire of Alexander the Great

1 Despite their centuries long fight against Persian domination, the Classical Greek city-states were not unified in any meaningful way. In fact, squabbling and infighting for power between the city-states marked the period, with power switching between them at different times. By the end of the Classical Period, Philip II of Macedon, in northern Greece, began an expansion of his territory, conquering the other city-states and uniting them under his Macedonian rule. However, this expansion would eventually seem trivial when compared to the expansion that was accomplished by his son, Alexander III, who ascended the throne in 336 BCE upon his assassination. This brash new king, who was only 20 years old at the time, would continue his father's planned invasion of the Persian Empire and eventually control a larger empire than any ruler before him, leading to great changes in the regions he conquered.

2 Within two years of taking the throne, Alexander had begun his campaign of international expansion and by 331 BCE the Macedonian ruler had overtaken the Persian Empire in the Levant, including the ancient city of Babylon, and had established a foothold in Egypt as well. After consolidating this great empire, he continued eastward and reached as far east as modern-day India. The great extent of this empire, along with the strong central control that was exerted by Alexander, caused a great number of changes in the movement of goods, capital and people throughout the empire. The removal of trade barriers and movement restrictions, as well as interconnected markets, made it easier for people to travel and trade with one another, and allowed Greek artisans and traders to seek their fortunes in a greatly expanded region. This expansion of trade and territory had several important consequences for both Classical Greece and the regions conquered in its name.

3 One of the most obvious of these changes in the newly unified empire was the expansion of Greek culture and influence. This occurred because Alexander founded at least 70 new urban centers, many of them named after himself, not so much for military control as for cultural expansion. One of the most important ways that this was done was through the propagation of Greek literature and language through the establishment of Greek libraries, such as those established in Antioch (modern-day Turkey) and Alexandria, Egypt, which was the largest and most significant library in the ancient world.

4 Another major change caused by the empire's expansion was the demise of the Greek city-state. Prior to the imperial period the Greek city-states were sparsely populated and centered around the agoras, marketplaces where the population came together to discuss the important issues of society and make decisions in person. Greek philosophers such as Plato and Aristotle, who had been the teenaged Alexander's tutor, felt that this form of government required a small population (less than 5,000) in order to insure that all citizens knew one another and could share their knowledge to make the best decisions. Further, prior to expansion these city-states lacked specialization, which allowed citizens to engage in various civil and personal activities. After trade and commerce developed across the empire citizens had to develop specializations, which brought about professionalism. This meant that the small populations and "jack-of-all-trades" nature of the city-states' residents were no longer sufficient and Greek cities changed dramatically.

5 Imperial expansion also brought the Greeks into contact with eastern philosophy and religion, which affected their previous belief in human-like gods with superhuman powers who could be counted on to intercede on behalf of the city-states citizens and provided protection and good luck during life's milestones. However, these beliefs had begun to wane even before Alexander's time as Greek's no longer seemed interested in only serving the city-state. In fact, the Athenian philosopher Socrates had previously been executed for suggesting a new morality based upon personal conscience rather than the traditional gods. This new philosophy, however, did not take the place of religion, but instead made the Classical Greeks receptive to new ideas that allowed the religions of the Middle East to mix with Greek philosophy. This new combined system spread across the world after Alexander's death in 323 BCE, forever intertwining the cultures of Greece and the Levant.

6 This dramatic territorial expansion had such a profound effect on the world that Alexander's death ushered in what is known as the Hellenistic period in Greek history, when its influence was at its peak in Europe, Africa, and Asia. During this period the Greeks made great strides in art, literature, architecture, mathematics, governance, philosophy, and science. Without the influence of Alexander the Great's territorial expansion, these advances may have remained confined to the borders of Classical Greece.

Early Maize Cultivation in the American Southwest

1 The North American continent ⁽⁰¹⁾**has been blessed with** vast areas of arable land that allow extensive agricultural output; yet not all areas are ⁽⁰²⁾**conducive to** farming. The American southwest is one of these areas. The region's extremely dry conditions and high temperatures make it ⁽⁰³⁾**unfavorable for** most farming. In fact, the largest agricultural crop produced across the region today is hay, which is ⁽⁰⁴⁾**used to feed** livestock. However, this was not always the case. It is believed that the climate was much more stable and less arid from around 2500 to 100 B.C.E. It was during this period that certain food crops ⁽⁰⁵⁾**were introduced to** the area from northern Mexico. ⁽⁰⁶⁾**Around this time**, the native inhabitants ⁽⁰⁷⁾**began** farm**ing** crops such as beans, squash, and most importantly maize, which, although not highly productive, ⁽⁰⁸⁾**enjoyed an advantage over** the others, its production was very predictable.

2 Early inhabitants practiced ⁽⁰⁹⁾**hunting and gathering**, which was particularly risky due to their ⁽¹⁰⁾**reliance upon** weather patterns, such as rainfall and sunlight. Although the populations were generally low and could sustain themselves this way, they may sometimes have grown larger and ⁽¹¹⁾**had trouble** do**ing** so. This would be particularly true during the leaner times before the spring rains. The coincidence of larger populations and less available food stock may have been the ⁽¹²⁾**impetus for** the inhabitants **to begin** growing reliable crops such as maize. Despite its low yield, growing such a crop would have ⁽¹³⁾**allowed** them **to** ⁽¹⁴⁾**have** greater **control over** their food supply ⁽¹⁵⁾**even if** it did not fully satisfy the populations' nutritional needs.

3 Researchers performing radiocarbon dating on maize cobs and seeds believe their introduction occurred between 2000-1500 B.C.E. and then ⁽¹⁶⁾**spread to** other areas. While maize eventually becomes the most well known of these, the others ⁽¹⁷⁾**played** great **roles** ⁽¹⁸⁾**not only in** the diet of the southwestern people, **but also** in the success of their maize crops. Beans and legumes were especially important during this time, because they replenish the nitrogen that maize depletes from the soil. By planting these crops together, early farmers ⁽¹⁹⁾**were able to** ⁽²⁰⁾**ensure that** their soil ⁽²¹⁾**stayed fertile** ⁽²²⁾**enough to produce** crops ⁽²³⁾**year after year**.

4 The first maize species successfully introduced to the region from northern Mexico was most likely a small, brown kernelled variety called chapalote. This species was important because it matures quickly and requires little irrigation after its initial planting, so it is highly drought resistant. Eventually this species ⁽²⁴⁾**was hybridized with** an indigenous grass, teosinte, to produce a more fruitful species with more kernel rows and larger cobs. It is believed that the regions inhabitants ⁽²⁵⁾**continued to crossbreed** maize species until they ⁽²⁶⁾**came up with** the more productive maiz de ocho. This is likely the result of using selection to produce a maize variety with larger kernels for grinding and an earlier flowering season, since growing seasons are highly unpredictable in the region. The short growing season of maiz de ocho and its ⁽²⁷⁾**adaptability to** assorted climates made it particularly ⁽²⁸⁾**valuable to** the region's inhabitants.

5 This hybridization was particularly important because maize eventually became a staple across the Americas, including in places that pushed the boundaries of its production. By selective breeding of different varieties of maize, early farmers were able to develop varieties that could be planted in regions with poor soil, short growing seasons, and adverse weather. In fact, the maiz de ocho variety allowed maize production to spread from the arid southwest to regions as far north as Canada, which has temperatures too low for most earlier species to survive. This ⁽²⁹⁾**attention to** maize cultivation allowed the local inhabitants to become more ⁽³⁰⁾**adept at** farming. They ⁽³¹⁾**learned to** ⁽³²⁾**favor soil** that held water better and received adequate sunlight. They also ⁽³³⁾**realized that** the flood plains and canyon mouths contained better soil because of the water that they ⁽³⁴⁾**were exposed to**. However, one of the most important farming skills they developed was irrigation. This allowed them to farm in more locations, which ensured their crops even if one area experienced a poor growing season.

6 Surprisingly, the introduction of maize and the early farming attempts did not spark a great ⁽³⁵⁾**shift in** the regions' inhabitants' lifestyles. Since early maize was rather unproductive and required little work, it was planted casually. ⁽³⁶⁾**In fact**, most of the area tribes continued to lead nomadic lives for nearly 1000 years after maize was introduced north of the Rio Grande. This could also ⁽³⁷⁾**be attributed to** the fact that maize is not a complete grain and lacks certain amino acids. It could only become a staple product when consumed alongside other agricultural products. Luckily, two of those were introduced ⁽³⁸⁾**around the same time**, squash and beans.

Early Maize Cultivation in the American Southwest

1 The North American continent has been blessed with vast areas of arable land that allow extensive agricultural output; yet not all areas are conducive to farming. The American southwest is one of these areas. The region's extremely dry conditions and high temperatures make it unfavorable for most farming. In fact, the largest agricultural crop produced across the region today is hay, which is used to feed livestock. However, this was not always the case. It is believed that the climate was much more stable and less arid from around 2500 to 100 B.C.E. It was during this period that certain food crops were introduced to the area from northern Mexico. Around this time, the native inhabitants began farming crops such as beans, squash, and most importantly maize, which, although not highly productive, enjoyed an advantage over the others, its production was very predictable.

2 Early inhabitants practiced hunting and gathering, which was particularly risky due to their reliance upon weather patterns, such as rainfall and sunlight. Although the populations were generally low and could sustain themselves this way, they may sometimes have grown larger and had trouble doing so. This would be particularly true during the leaner times before the spring rains. The coincidence of larger populations and less available food stock may have been the impetus for the inhabitants to begin growing reliable crops such as maize. Despite its low yield, growing such a crop would have allowed them to have greater control over their food supply even if it did not fully satisfy the populations' nutritional needs.

3 Researchers performing radiocarbon dating on maize cobs and seeds believe their introduction occurred between 2000-1500 B.C.E. and then spread to other areas. While maize eventually becomes the most well known of these, the others played great roles not only in the diet of the southwestern people, but also in the success of their maize crops. Beans and legumes were especially important during this time, because they replenish the nitrogen that maize depletes from the soil. By planting these crops together, early farmers were able to ensure that their soil stayed fertile enough to produce crops year after year.

4 The first maize species successfully introduced to the region from northern Mexico was most likely a small, brown kernelled variety called chapalote. This species was important because it matures quickly and requires little irrigation after its initial planting, so it is highly drought resistant. Eventually this species was hybridized with an indigenous grass, teosinte, to produce a more fruitful species with more kernel rows and larger cobs. It is believed that the regions inhabitants continued to crossbreed maize species until they came up with the more productive maiz de ocho. This is likely the result of using selection to produce a maize variety with larger kernels for grinding and an earlier flowering season, since growing seasons are highly unpredictable in the region. The short growing season of maiz de ocho and its adaptability to assorted climates made it particularly valuable to the region's inhabitants.

5 This hybridization was particularly important because maize eventually became a staple across the Americas, including in places that pushed the boundaries of its production. By selective breeding of different varieties of maize, early farmers were able to develop varieties that could be planted in regions with poor soil, short growing seasons, and adverse weather. In fact, the maiz de ocho variety allowed maize production to spread from the arid southwest to regions as far north as Canada, which has temperatures too low for most earlier species to survive. This attention to maize cultivation allowed the local inhabitants to become more adept at farming. They learned to favor soil that held water better and received adequate sunlight. They also realized that the flood plains and canyon mouths contained better soil because of the water that they were exposed to. However, one of the most important farming skills they developed was irrigation. This allowed them to farm in more locations, which ensured their crops even if one area experienced a poor growing season.

6 Surprisingly, the introduction of maize and the early farming attempts did not spark a great shift in the regions' inhabitants' lifestyles. Since early maize was rather unproductive and required little work, it was planted casually. In fact, most of the area tribes continued to lead nomadic lives for nearly 1000 years after maize was introduced north of the Rio Grande. This could also be attributed to the fact that maize is not a complete grain and lacks certain amino acids. It could only become a staple product when consumed alongside other agricultural products. Luckily, two of those were introduced around the same time, squash and beans.

Temperature Regulation in Marine Organisms

1   For most organisms maintaining thermal homeostasis, or keeping the body temperature within a certain range, is **(01)necessary for** proper metabolic functioning. If the internal temperature of these organisms leaves the preferred range, which differs **(02)based on** the species, for extended periods, enzyme degradation and tissue/organ destruction may occur, which can **(03)make it difficult** or impossible **for** their bodies **to** properly **function**. This **(04)makes it** extremely **important that** these organisms find some **(05)way to maintain** their temperature within these ranges, especially in marine environments.

2   Most organisms that do this can be classified in one of two categories. The first of these, the homeotherms, can **(06)be thought of as** thermoregulators, since they maintain a near constant temperature **(07)regardless of** ambient temperatures. This group includes mammals and birds, both of which have developed specialized features and functions to harness heat released through the metabolic process to maintain their relatively high average temperatures of 34-40°C. Poikilotherms, such as reptiles, amphibians, and most fish, on the other hand, can be considered thermoconformers, since their body temperatures **(08)are dependent upon** the ambient temperature. Having a body temperature that fluctuates with the external temperature does not, however, mean that these organisms **(09)are protected from** temperature changes. However, higher temperatures generally produce higher metabolic rates. This means that they must find ways to maintain their temperatures within a certain range. This is done **(10)in (11)a host of ways** such as moving, finding areas with appropriate temperatures or basking in the sun's warming rays.

3   Interestingly, not all animals **(12)fall into** these two categories. Several species fall somewhere in the middle of the two. Some of the most well known examples of this are fast-swimming fish, such as the yellowfin tuna, which has an internal temperature that is several degrees warmer than the relatively cold seawater it inhabits. This occurs because they possess a heat retention mechanism that harnesses the heat produced by their **(13)muscular activity** while swimming. Scientists believe this is necessary because of their **(14)reliance upon** heat dependent biochemical reactions for their constant physical exertion. An entirely opposite example can be found in the intertidal zone. Some species in this area maintain their bodies at several degrees cooler than the ambient temperature by harnessing the powers of evaporation and circulation of bodily fluids. This **(15)allows** them **to live** in areas where the shallow waters reach high temperatures due to the effects of the suns rays and reflection from the light colored substrate. By absorbing and **(16)losing** heat directly **to** the air they **(17)are able to** remain much cooler than non-living objects with corresponding sizes and shapes.

4   In marine environments, homeotherms **(18)have** the most **difficulty** maintain**ing** their internal body temperature, since most oceans average between 1.9 and 27°C. **(19)Exposure to** these cold water temperatures can cause lower internal temperatures due to heat loss through the skin faster than in air. However, several other factors **(20)lead to** lower temperatures. One of the biggest is the fact that these animals have closed circulatory systems that pump blood around the body, causing heat loss as it approaches the colder peripheral areas of the body. Further, the body's natural radiation of heat and respiration also lower the temperature, since the evaporation of water from the nasal cavities during exhalation **(21)has a** natural cooling **effect on** their bodies.

5   Marine animals have developed **(22)an assortment of** ways to counteract this heat loss. The most common way is by developing a layer of insulation, but even this can **(23)take** different **forms**. Most cetaceans, such as whales and porpoises, and seals **(24)build up** a thick layer of fat under the skin, known as blubber. However, this does not work for smaller marine mammals such as sea otters. These nimble, weasel-like sea creatures do not store great fat reserves, but instead constantly preen and fluff their thick dual-layer fur. This allows the outer hairs to **(25)prevent** water **from** reach**ing** the softer undercoat and traps warm, dry air around the otter. This process is also used by marine birds, which have waterproof outer feathers covering softer down that traps air and body heat. These methods are enhanced by the fact that marine mammals have higher body temperatures than their terrestrial counterparts.

6   Interestingly, the circulatory systems of some marine species also help conserve body heat by **(26)acting as** countercurrent heat exchangers. In species, like porpoises, the veins that return the used blood surround the arteries, which **(27)pump** blood **from** the warm core. This allows the warmer arteries to heat the blood as it **(28)returns from** relatively colder areas such as the skin surface and flippers, which are not protected by thick blubber layers. This reduces the amount of heat lost to the water and can even be found in some fish, **(29)such as** skipjack tuna.

Temperature Regulation in Marine Organisms

1 For most organisms maintaining thermal homeostasis, or keeping the body temperature within a certain range, is necessary for proper metabolic functioning. If the internal temperature of these organisms leaves the preferred range, which differs based on the species, for extended periods, enzyme degradation and tissue/organ destruction may occur, which can make it difficult or impossible for their bodies to properly function. This makes it extremely important that these organisms find some way to maintain their temperature within these ranges, especially in marine environments.

2 Most organisms that do this can be classified in one of two categories. The first of these, the homeotherms, can be thought of as thermoregulators, since they maintain a near constant temperature regardless of ambient temperatures. This group includes mammals and birds, both of which have developed specialized features and functions to harness heat released through the metabolic process to maintain their relatively high average temperatures of 34-40°C. Poikilotherms, such as reptiles, amphibians, and most fish, on the other hand, can be considered thermoconformers, since their body temperatures are dependent upon the ambient temperature. Having a body temperature that fluctuates with the external temperature does not, however, mean that these organisms are protected from temperature changes. However, higher temperatures generally produce higher metabolic rates. This means that they must find ways to maintain their temperatures within a certain range. This is done in a host of ways such as moving, finding areas with appropriate temperatures or basking in the sun's warming rays.

3 Interestingly, not all animals fall into these two categories. Several species fall somewhere in the middle of the two. Some of the most well known examples of this are fast-swimming fish, such as the yellowfin tuna, which has an internal temperature that is several degrees warmer than the relatively cold seawater it inhabits. This occurs because they possess a heat retention mechanism that harnesses the heat produced by their muscular activity while swimming. Scientists believe this is necessary because of their reliance upon heat dependent biochemical reactions for their constant physical exertion. An entirely opposite example can be found in the intertidal zone. Some species in this area maintain their bodies at several degrees cooler than the ambient temperature by harnessing the powers of evaporation and circulation of bodily fluids. This allows them to live in areas where the shallow waters reach high temperatures due to the effects of the suns rays and reflection from the light colored substrate. By absorbing and losing heat directly to the air they are able to remain much cooler than non-living objects with corresponding sizes and shapes.

4 In marine environments, homeotherms have the most difficulty maintaining their internal body temperature, since most oceans average between 1.9 and 27°C. Exposure to these cold water temperatures can cause lower internal temperatures due to heat loss through the skin faster than in air. However, several other factors lead to lower temperatures. One of the biggest is the fact that these animals have closed circulatory systems that pump blood around the body, causing heat loss as it approaches the colder peripheral areas of the body. Further, the body's natural radiation of heat and respiration also lower the temperature, since the evaporation of water from the nasal cavities during exhalation has a natural cooling effect on their bodies.

5 Marine animals have developed an assortment of ways to counteract this heat loss. The most common way is by developing a layer of insulation, but even this can take different forms. Most cetaceans, such as whales and porpoises, and seals build up a thick layer of fat under the skin, known as blubber. However, this does not work for smaller marine mammals such as sea otters. These nimble, weasel-like sea creatures do not store great fat reserves, but instead constantly preen and fluff their thick dual-layer fur. This allows the outer hairs to prevent water from reaching the softer undercoat and traps warm, dry air around the otter. This process is also used by marine birds, which have waterproof outer feathers covering softer down that traps air and body heat. These methods are enhanced by the fact that marine mammals have higher body temperatures than their terrestrial counterparts.

6 Interestingly, the circulatory systems of some marine species also help conserve body heat by acting as countercurrent heat exchangers. In species, like porpoises, the veins that return the used blood surround the arteries, which pump blood from the warm core. This allows the warmer arteries to heat the blood as it returns from relatively colder areas such as the skin surface and flippers, which are not protected by thick blubber layers. This reduces the amount of heat lost to the water and can even be found in some fish, such as skipjack tuna.

The Upper Paleolithic Revolution

1 Around 35 to 40 KYA (thousands of years ago), there was a dramatic (01)**change in** the archaeological record in Europe that (02)**marked the change** from the Middle to Upper Paleolithic periods. During this transition, anatomically modern humans (AMH) replaced Neanderthal populations in Europe and (03)**brought about** great changes in humanity. The rise of the AMH population can be seen through a dramatic (04)**increase in** the use of tools and the invention of several purely human activities. The changes that occurred during the Upper Paleolithic era are (05)**so dramatic that** they have been (06)**referred to as** the Upper Paleolithic Revolution.

2 Archaeological finds in many areas across Europe have supported this revolutionary change. The new population (07)**used** much more versatile stone implements and animal products, such as bone and antler, **to produce** much more advanced tools. Barbed reindeer harpoons and spear throwers, (08)**known as** atlatl, have been discovered in European caves indicating a great (09)**leap forward** in the understanding of hunting, and even rudimentary concepts in physics, such as torque. Interestingly, this also (10)**appears to be** the period when humans developed art forms, such as figurative art. However, swan bone pipes with worn finger holes (11)**similar to** flutes and primitive tattooing kits have been found in other European archaeological sites, indicating that figurative cave art was not the AMH's only artistic endeavor.

3 An interesting aspect of these discoveries is that they were all found in Europe, (12)**leading** researchers **to believe** that the advances of early AMH were a purely European occurrence around 40 KYA that eventually spread elsewhere. However, the later discovery of decorated ochre and shell beads, as well as evidence of AMH's (13)**ability to fish**, in South Africa's Blombos Cave (14)**dating to** 77 KYA and contemporary bone tools found in other African sites indicate that this "revolution" was simply an example of human behavioral evolution that had been occurring for much longer. This led researchers to question why the discovery of modern tools from this period were concentrated in Europe and whether the European discoveries were the start of a new form of human behavior, or if they were simply built upon earlier innovations in other parts of the world.

4 Anthropologists Sally McBrearty and Alison Brooks (15)**point to** Eurocentric bias and (16)**disregard for** the extent of the African archaeological record **as** the most likely causes for the discovery of more tools in Europe. They (17)**hold that** evidence of more modern tools in Africa, such as blades and microlithic technology, higher geographic ranges, art, and long distance trade networks, predates its appearance in Europe by (18)**at least** 10,000 years and can be found in archaeological sites separated by both geographical area and time frame, thus suggesting a natural evolution, rather than an immediate revolution such as in Europe. This indicates that AMH behavior was likely formed in Africa and (19)**exported to** other regions. The myriad forms of early rock art found in Australia further support this idea. Since people arrived in Australia around 60 KYA and were (20)**isolated from** the "revolution" in Europe 40 KYA, their rock art can be (21)**seen to show** that creativity was already a part of human cognition when early AMH (22)**began** (23)**migrating out of** Africa around 70 KYA.

5 This type of scrutiny has (24)**caused** theories of a sudden advent of modern behavior and tool making during an "Upper Paleolithic Revolution" in Europe **to falter**. The most logical (25)**reason for** its supposed sudden occurrence would be, as McBrearty and Brooks (26)**pointed out**, deficiencies in the archaeological record in Africa and other regions, while those in Europe are rather well preserved. (27)**It may** simply (28)**turn out that** artifacts elsewhere have been lost, or (29)**have yet to be found**. This can be seen by the recent discovery of pierced shells dating from 43 KYA in Lebanon, suggesting the modernization had occurred (30)**prior to** the date of the "revolution," but (31)**went undetected** until recently.

6 However, the presence of tools in other areas does not explain the sudden appearance of tools in the European archaeological record. One theory for this is climate change. Prior to the suggested dates of the Upper Paleolithic Revolution, Europe underwent a major climate change that caused the disappearance of the previous glaciers and an overall warming, which made the continent more (32)**hospitable for** early AMH. This could have allowed a (33)**migration** of early AMH **to** the previously uninhabited area. This sudden appearance of AMH in Europe would have led to an increase in more modern tools in the archaeological record, which could explain why they suddenly appeared around 35 KYA.

The Upper Paleolithic Revolution

1 Around 35 to 40 KYA (thousands of years ago), there was a dramatic change in the archaeological record in Europe that marked the change from the Middle to Upper Paleolithic periods. During this transition, anatomically modern humans (AMH) replaced Neanderthal populations in Europe and brought about great changes in humanity. The rise of the AMH population can be seen through a dramatic increase in the use of tools and the invention of several purely human activities. The changes that occurred during the Upper Paleolithic era are so dramatic that they have been referred to as the Upper Paleolithic Revolution.

2 Archaeological finds in many areas across Europe have supported this revolutionary change. The new population used much more versatile stone implements and animal products, such as bone and antler, to produce much more advanced tools. Barbed reindeer harpoons and spear throwers, known as atlatl, have been discovered in European caves indicating a great leap forward in the understanding of hunting, and even rudimentary concepts in physics, such as torque. Interestingly, this also appears to be the period when humans developed art forms, such as figurative art. However, swan bone pipes with worn finger holes similar to flutes and primitive tattooing kits have been found in other European archaeological sites, indicating that figurative cave art was not the AMH's only artistic endeavor.

3 An interesting aspect of these discoveries is that they were all found in Europe, leading researchers to believe that the advances of early AMH were a purely European occurrence around 40 KYA that eventually spread elsewhere. However, the later discovery of decorated ochre and shell beads, as well as evidence of AMH's ability to fish, in South Africa's Blombos Cave dating to 77 KYA and contemporary bone tools found in other African sites indicate that this "revolution" was simply an example of human behavioral evolution that had been occurring for much longer. This led researchers to question why the discovery of modern tools from this period were concentrated in Europe and whether the European discoveries were the start of a new form of human behavior, or if they were simply built upon earlier innovations in other parts of the world.

4 Anthropologists Sally McBrearty and Alison Brooks point to Eurocentric bias and disregard for the extent of the African archaeological record as the most likely causes for the discovery of more tools in Europe. They hold that evidence of more modern tools in Africa, such as blades and microlithic technology, higher geographic ranges, art, and long distance trade networks, predates its appearance in Europe by at least 10,000 years and can be found in archaeological sites separated by both geographical area and time frame, thus suggesting a natural evolution, rather than an immediate revolution such as in Europe. This indicates that AMH behavior was likely formed in Africa and exported to other regions. The myriad forms of early rock art found in Australia further support this idea. Since people arrived in Australia around 60 KYA and were isolated from the "revolution" in Europe 40 KYA, their rock art can be seen to show that creativity was already a part of human cognition when early AMH began migrating out of Africa around 70 KYA.

5 This type of scrutiny has caused theories of a sudden advent of modern behavior and tool making during an "Upper Paleolithic Revolution" in Europe to falter. The most logical reason for its supposed sudden occurrence would be, as McBrearty and Brooks pointed out, deficiencies in the archaeological record in Africa and other regions, while those in Europe are rather well preserved. It may simply turn out that artifacts elsewhere have been lost, or have yet to be found. This can be seen by the recent discovery of pierced shells dating from 43 KYA in Lebanon, suggesting the modernization had occurred prior to the date of the "revolution," but went undetected until recently.

6 However, the presence of tools in other areas does not explain the sudden appearance of tools in the European archaeological record. One theory for this is climate change. Prior to the suggested dates of the Upper Paleolithic Revolution, Europe underwent a major climate change that caused the disappearance of the previous glaciers and an overall warming, which made the continent more hospitable for early AMH. This could have allowed a migration of early AMH to the previously uninhabited area. This sudden appearance of AMH in Europe would have led to an increase in more modern tools in the archaeological record, which could explain why they suddenly appeared around 35 KYA.

Nineteenth-Century Theories of Mountain Formation

1 Due to several major misconceptions, our understanding of mountain formation is relatively new. (01)**As recently as** the early 19th century, most geological findings were (02)**viewed as** (03)**a series of** catastrophic events that (04)**allowed** geological knowledge **to corroborate** a short Earth history that (05)**corresponded to** biblical narratives. However, during the 19th century, scientists (06)**began to offer** other explanations for geological features, (07)**such as** mountain formation. Unfortunately, most of the theories they developed were (08)**based upon** the idea that Earth had been formed as a superheated mass and had steadily cooled through time. This (09)**led** them **to postulate** that Earth's core must be shrinking as it cools, as most objects do. From this, they extrapolated that Earth's crust would be deformed by the shrinkage and mountains would form.

2 One of (10)**the first** geologists **to** (11)**try to** explain this was Eduard Suess. He explained that Earth's crust wrinkled as it contracted, just as a drying apple's peel does. His theory assumed that Earth's crust had begun as a single layer, but separated as the "wrinkles" formed. This (12)**led to** great depressions that became ocean basins and higher areas that formed the continents. Further, he thought that continued contraction would lead to instability and the two features could alternate, meaning that oceans would become continental land and (13)**vice versa**. Using this theory, he incorrectly postulated that the Alps had once been (14)**at the bottom of** a massive ocean, but had risen and (15)**left** the Mediterranean **as** its only remnant.

3 This alternation was an important point in his theory, because it (16)**helped to explain** other geological features that scientists, even the great Leonardo da Vinci, (17)**had been unable to interpret**, such as the discovery of marine fossils on dry land and the interspersed marine and terrestrial sediment found in the stratigraphic column. It also helped to explain a problem (18)**brought about** by Darwin's contemporaneous theory of evolution. By the mid-1800s, scientists had noticed similar, or even identical, fossils in distant places, such as South America and Africa. Darwin's theory (19)**made** this identical evolution of two distant species highly unlikely, but Suess countered this with the theory that (20)**changes in** Earth's landmasses and oceans made it possible. He developed the theory of an ancient, giant landmass connected by land bridges that he (21)**referred to as** Gondwanaland.

4 Ironically, acceptance of Suess's theory was geographically split; it gained a greater acceptance in Europe than in North America. On the other side of the Atlantic, geologists like James Dwight Dana developed their own explanations for mountain formation. Dana's theory, (22)**known as** permanence, was based on the continents and oceans remaining as they are. He theorized that as Earth cooled and contracted, minerals with low melting points, like feldspar and quartz, solidified (23)**early on** and those with higher melting points, like pyroxene and olivine, became solid later, thereby creating ocean basins. As the contraction continued it (24)**put** immense **pressures on** Earth's surface, especially along the oceanic/continental boundaries, which caused the creation of the mountain ranges found along continental edges, such as those on the west coast of both North & South America.

5 Dana's theory led fellow American geologist James Hall to theorize that subsidence, or sinking, of sediment from a former shallow sea formed the Appalachian Mountains. Hall felt that these materials were produced by continental erosion and accumulated in linear troughs along the mountain's edge, called geosynclines. As these troughs filled and began to subside, they became deeper and Earth's inner heat (25)**turned** the sediment **into** stone. Eventually, it was uplifted to form mountains. Dana slightly modified this theory to explain that sediment had (26)**not** caused subsidence, **but** was actually the result of it. Unfortunately for both, their explanations of how shallow-water sediment (27)**built up** (28)**did nothing to** accurately **explain** how these thick layers of sediment were uplifted.

6 By the early 1900s, the flaws in these theories became evident. Through the discovery of certain features in the earth's crust, such as unexplainable strata shortening and the theory of isostasy that explained that the crust and its mountains were actually floating on Earth's mantle, and not (29)**held in place** (30)**on their own**, scientists were able to disprove Suess's theory of oceanic/continental changeability. However, the most important discovery was radiogenic heating, which definitively negated the theory of contraction, and all theories based on it. All of this (31)**caused** scientists **to** (32)**look for** more accurate explanations of mountain formation. The best of these was Alfred Wegener's theory of continental drift. Unfortunately, this theory was not accepted until the existence of tectonic plates was confirmed nearly 50 years later. Today, we know that the actions of these tectonic plates created Earth's various mountain ranges.

Nineteenth-Century Theories of Mountain Formation

1 Due to several major misconceptions, our understanding of mountain formation is relatively new. As recently as the early 19th century, most geological findings were viewed as a series of catastrophic events that allowed geological knowledge to corroborate a short Earth history that corresponded to biblical narratives. However, during the 19th century, scientists began to offer other explanations for geological features, such as mountain formation. Unfortunately, most of the theories they developed were based upon the idea that Earth had been formed as a superheated mass and had steadily cooled through time. This led them to postulate that Earth's core must be shrinking as it cools, as most objects do. From this, they extrapolated that Earth's crust would be deformed by the shrinkage and mountains would form.

2 One of the first geologists to try to explain this was Eduard Suess. He explained that Earth's crust wrinkled as it contracted, just as a drying apple's peel does. His theory assumed that Earth's crust had begun as a single layer, but separated as the "wrinkles" formed. This led to great depressions that became ocean basins and higher areas that formed the continents. Further, he thought that continued contraction would lead to instability and the two features could alternate, meaning that oceans would become continental land and vice versa. Using this theory, he incorrectly postulated that the Alps had once been at the bottom of a massive ocean, but had risen and left the Mediterranean as its only remnant.

3 This alternation was an important point in his theory, because it helped to explain other geological features that scientists, even the great Leonardo da Vinci, had been unable to interpret, such as the discovery of marine fossils on dry land and the interspersed marine and terrestrial sediment found in the stratigraphic column. It also helped to explain a problem brought about by Darwin's contemporaneous theory of evolution. By the mid-1800s, scientists had noticed similar, or even identical, fossils in distant places, such as South America and Africa. Darwin's theory made this identical evolution of two distant species highly unlikely, but Suess countered this with the theory that changes in Earth's landmasses and oceans made it possible. He developed the theory of an ancient, giant landmass connected by land bridges that he referred to as Gondwanaland.

4 Ironically, acceptance of Suess's theory was geographically split; it gained a greater acceptance in Europe than in North America. On the other side of the Atlantic, geologists like James Dwight Dana developed their own explanations for mountain formation. Dana's theory, known as permanence, was based on the continents and oceans remaining as they are. He theorized that as Earth cooled and contracted, minerals with low melting points, like feldspar and quartz, solidified early on and those with higher melting points, like pyroxene and olivine, became solid later, thereby creating ocean basins. As the contraction continued it put immense pressures on Earth's surface, especially along the oceanic/continental boundaries, which caused the creation of the mountain ranges found along continental edges, such as those on the west coast of both North & South America.

5 Dana's theory led fellow American geologist James Hall to theorize that subsidence, or sinking, of sediment from a former shallow sea formed the Appalachian Mountains. Hall felt that these materials were produced by continental erosion and accumulated in linear troughs along the mountain's edge, called geosynclines. As these troughs filled and began to subside, they became deeper and Earth's inner heat turned the sediment into stone. Eventually, it was uplifted to form mountains. Dana slightly modified this theory to explain that sediment had not caused subsidence, but was actually the result of it. Unfortunately for both, their explanations of how shallow-water sediment built up did nothing to accurately explain how these thick layers of sediment were uplifted.

6 By the early 1900s, the flaws in these theories became evident. Through the discovery of certain features in the earth's crust, such as unexplainable strata shortening and the theory of isostasy that explained that the crust and its mountains were actually floating on Earth's mantle, and not held in place on their own, scientists were able to disprove Suess's theory of oceanic/continental changeability. However, the most important discovery was radiogenic heating, which definitively negated the theory of contraction, and all theories based on it. All of this caused scientists to look for more accurate explanations of mountain formation. The best of these was Alfred Wegener's theory of continental drift. Unfortunately, this theory was not accepted until the existence of tectonic plates was confirmed nearly 50 years later. Today, we know that the actions of these tectonic plates created Earth's various mountain ranges.

Colonial America and the Navigation Acts

1 Mercantilism swept across Europe in the sixteenth century. Under this system governments (01)**attempted to regulate and protect** their economies by ensuring a positive balance of trade using high tariffs and protective import laws. This was especially true in the British Empire, which was threatened by the rising power of Dutch traders after the (02)**Eighty Years' War** and the (03)**lifting** of Spanish **embargoes on** trade with them. After this time, Dutch traders overwhelmed British trade on the Iberian Peninsula, around the Mediterranean Sea, and into the Levant; however, the most troubling development was their rising power in the British colonies, especially those in the New World. (04)**In order to protect** its trade power, Parliament passed (05)**a series of** trade laws (06)**known** collectively **as** the Navigation Acts, which effectively controlled all imperial commerce.

2 One of the first of the Navigation Acts was the Navigation Ordinance of 1651. This new ordinance (07)**limited** imports into the British Empire **to** those brought by British ships or those from the country in which the product had been manufactured. This severely limited Dutch imports, since they (08)**specialized in** carry**ing** products from other regions, and mainly exported (09)**locally made** dairy products. (10)**As time went by**, more of these types of acts were passed, further increasing (11)**restrictions on** trade, which greatly affected the colonies. In fact, the passage of the Navigation Acts of 1660 and 1663, (12)**forced** British colonies **to export** commodities, like sugar and tobacco, only to England aboard British-flagged vessels. They were not, however, all (13)**detrimental to** the colonies. For instance, the Molasses Act of 1733 (14)**added** an import tariff **to** molasses entering the colonies from outside the empire. This basically created a molasses monopoly for plantation owners in the British West Indies, since it was cheaper than that produced on French Caribbean islands. By the 1750s, the economic impact of these laws had become clear in the North American colonies.

3 The first major condition (15)**set forth** by the Navigation Acts was the use of only British ships with crews that were 75% British, which included colonists and their slaves. This dramatically reduced imports and foreign shipping into the Empire, which (16)**allowed** the British fleet **to become** the world's most powerful. Interestingly, it also encouraged shipbuilding in North America, since the colonists could freely (17)**trade within** the Empire. This (18)**brought about** the foundation of an American merchant marine fleet and, by the 1750s, one-third of the British fleet (19)**was composed of** American ships. The concentration of the shipbuilding and export industries in the northeast (20)**led to** rapid urbanization in the region as more warehouses, docks, and maintenance firms were built there. By the late 18th century, New York City and Philadelphia had become (21)**not only** the two largest cities in the colonies, **but also** two of the busiest ports in the entire empire.

4 Another major stipulation of the Navigation Acts was that certain "enumerated goods," (22)**such as** tobacco, rice, hides, sugar, and naval supplies, could only be (23)**shipped** directly **to** England or Scotland, thus giving the British government control over the respective markets. However, the Navigation Acts did not kill the trade in the enumerated goods. In fact, Parliament blocked the import of foreign tobacco and rice, the two commodities most affected by the Acts. This proved burdensome to British citizens, but helped the tobacco farmers. They also (24)**agreed to** (25)**refund** import **duties on** products that were eventually shipped (26)**out of** the empire, which (27)**accounted for** 85% of the North American exports. These measures meant that tobacco and rice producers suffered a (28)**less than** 3% reduction in their income.

5 Eventually, the Navigation Acts led to economic diversification and increased trade in the colonies, since Parliament (29)**paid** subsidies **to** colonists for producing raw materials that would have otherwise have been imported from trade rivals, such as silk, iron, dye, and lumber. They did not, however, allow the large-scale production of manufactured goods, such as clothing, that could affect Britain's large-scale factories. This meant that tailors, milliners, and other clothing manufacturers (30)**were restricted to** producing their products in small shops. These restrictions allowed British clothing to be sold (31)**at much lower prices** than locally manufactured goods. Surprisingly, the production of ironworks was not limited by the acts and it became a major industry.

6 The last major effect of these acts was that they created a protected market for lower-priced British goods. (32)**Demand for** colonial materials (33)**remained high** and led to prosperity in the colonies. This led to an increased demand for British manufactured goods, such as dishware, tea, and furniture, (34)**in addition to** clothing. This allowed (35)**exports to** the American colonies to rise from 5% of all British exports in 1700 to nearly 40% by 1760. The influx of these manufactured goods allowed middle-class colonists to live as comfortably as their British counterparts.

Colonial America and the Navigation Acts

1 Mercantilism swept across Europe in the sixteenth century. Under this system governments attempted to regulate and protect their economies by ensuring a positive balance of trade using high tariffs and protective import laws. This was especially true in the British Empire, which was threatened by the rising power of Dutch traders after the Eighty Years' War and the lifting of Spanish embargoes on trade with them. After this time, Dutch traders overwhelmed British trade on the Iberian Peninsula, around the Mediterranean Sea, and into the Levant; however, the most troubling development was their rising power in the British colonies, especially those in the New World. In order to protect its trade power, Parliament passed a series of trade laws known collectively as the Navigation Acts, which effectively controlled all imperial commerce.

2 One of the first of the Navigation Acts was the Navigation Ordinance of 1651. This new ordinance limited imports into the British Empire to those brought by British ships or those from the country in which the product had been manufactured. This severely limited Dutch imports, since they specialized in carrying products from other regions, and mainly exported locally made dairy products. As time went by, more of these types of acts were passed, further increasing restrictions on trade, which greatly affected the colonies. In fact, the passage of the Navigation Acts of 1660 and 1663, forced British colonies to export commodities, like sugar and tobacco, only to England aboard British-flagged vessels. They were not, however, all detrimental to the colonies. For instance, the Molasses Act of 1733 added an import tariff to molasses entering the colonies from outside the empire. This basically created a molasses monopoly for plantation owners in the British West Indies, since it was cheaper than that produced on French Caribbean islands. By the 1750s, the economic impact of these laws had become clear in the North American colonies.

3 The first major condition set forth by the Navigation Acts was the use of only British ships with crews that were 75% British, which included colonists and their slaves. This dramatically reduced imports and foreign shipping into the Empire, which allowed the British fleet to become the world's most powerful. Interestingly, it also encouraged shipbuilding in North America, since the colonists could freely trade within the Empire. This brought about the foundation of an American merchant marine fleet and, by the 1750s, one-third of the British fleet was composed of American ships. The concentration of the shipbuilding and export industries in the northeast led to rapid urbanization in the region as more warehouses, docks, and maintenance firms were built there. By the late 18th century, New York City and Philadelphia had become not only the two largest cities in the colonies, but also two of the busiest ports in the entire empire.

4 Another major stipulation of the Navigation Acts was that certain "enumerated goods," such as tobacco, rice, hides, sugar, and naval supplies, could only be shipped directly to England or Scotland, thus giving the British government control over the respective markets. However, the Navigation Acts did not kill the trade in the enumerated goods. In fact, Parliament blocked the import of foreign tobacco and rice, the two commodities most affected by the Acts. This proved burdensome to British citizens, but helped the tobacco farmers. They also agreed to refund import duties on products that were eventually shipped out of the empire, which accounted for 85% of the North American exports. These measures meant that tobacco and rice producers suffered a less than 3% reduction in their income.

5 Eventually, the Navigation Acts led to economic diversification and increased trade in the colonies, since Parliament paid subsidies to colonists for producing raw materials that would have otherwise have been imported from trade rivals, such as silk, iron, dye, and lumber. They did not, however, allow the large-scale production of manufactured goods, such as clothing, that could affect Britain's large-scale factories. This meant that tailors, milliners, and other clothing manufacturers were restricted to producing their products in small shops. These restrictions allowed British clothing to be sold at much lower prices than locally manufactured goods. Surprisingly, the production of ironworks was not limited by the acts and it became a major industry.

6 The last major effect of these acts was that they created a protected market for lower-priced British goods. Demand for colonial materials remained high and led to prosperity in the colonies. This led to an increased demand for British manufactured goods, such as dishware, tea, and furniture, in addition to clothing. This allowed exports to the American colonies to rise from 5% of all British exports in 1700 to nearly 40% by 1760. The influx of these manufactured goods allowed middle-class colonists to live as comfortably as their British counterparts.

The Most Common Bird on Earth

1 Most people ⁽⁰¹⁾**outside of** Africa have never ⁽⁰²⁾**heard of** the red-billed quelea, but these small African birds are the most common bird species on Earth. A member of the weaver family, they live on the grasslands of sub-Saharan Africa in extremely large colonies that contain up to 30 million individuals. Conservative estimates ⁽⁰³⁾**put** the total population of the birds across Africa **at** more than 1.5 billion breeding pairs, with some saying there may be up to 10 billion of the birds.

2 It may seem illogical that these small birds survive in such a harsh environment, but their extreme success is even more remarkable when one considers that they survive nearly entirely on the annual grasses in the region. Although researchers have noted that they eat some insects, mainly beetles, and a few non-grass seeds, these ⁽⁰⁴⁾**accounted for** ⁽⁰⁵⁾**less than** two percent of their overall diet. One might expect that this great ⁽⁰⁶⁾**dependence upon** annual grasses would ⁽⁰⁷⁾**lead to** regular reduction or extinction of the populations, but, much like early humans ⁽⁰⁸⁾**learned to hoard** wheat and barley seeds to ⁽⁰⁹⁾**deal with** lean times, the red-billed quelea have developed certain behaviors that help them ⁽¹⁰⁾**cope with** the feast or famine nature of the grass crops.

3 One of the most advantageous adaptations made by the red-billed quelea has been the development of variable annual weather-dependent cycles. During the dry season the bird population must ⁽¹¹⁾**sustain itself** with the seeds produced at the end of the rainy season. To do this, they ⁽¹²⁾**gorge** themselves **on** seeds to gain ⁽¹³⁾**enough** wait **to sustain** them while they ⁽¹⁴⁾**migrate to** more productive places. This must be done during the dry season, since monsoon rains ⁽¹⁵⁾**cause** the remaining seeds **to germinate**, thereby interrupting the food supply for weeks and instigating the move. Luckily, this does not occur simultaneously across the entire savanna and dry seeds, young grasses, and mature ripe grasses are available in different areas. To ⁽¹⁶⁾**take advantage of** this the quelea make 50-200 km migrations across the savannas, which ⁽¹⁷⁾**allows** them **to survive** in such a forbidding environment.

4 ⁽¹⁸⁾**By the time** the rains have germinated and fresh seeds become available, these early-rain migrations end and the quelea ⁽¹⁹⁾**return to** the previously abandoned areas. ⁽²⁰⁾**Access to** these new seeds ⁽²¹⁾**stimulates** the population's males **to weave** ovoid grass and straw nests in acacia trees. The females who help them complete the nest and who then lay two to four eggs later join them. These colonies can cover up to 100 hectares with 500 nests in each acacia. With an average of 100,000 fledglings per hectare, up to 10 million offspring are produced by each successful colony. Surprisingly, the entire process of nest weaving, mating, brooding and fledging of the juveniles takes only six weeks, which is much shorter than in other birds, and is incredibly synchronized, as the eggs all hatch ⁽²²⁾**on the same day**. However, this process ⁽²³⁾**is dependent upon** weather patterns, as an earlier dry season can cause the quelea to abandon their colony, while an extended green season with abundant seed stock can allow them to produce multiple broods in the same region.

5 Since they ⁽²⁴⁾**rely upon** seeds, these large colonies can cause problems for the region's farmers. As more and more grains are planted across sub-Saharan Africa, the birds have ⁽²⁵⁾**turned to** the crops for nourishment. This has allowed their numbers to explode in the region. It is estimated that the population of these "feathered locusts" has increased by 10-100 times since the 1970s. With each bird eating its own weight in seeds per day this ⁽²⁶⁾**leaves** fields within 30 Km. of the breeding **sites** highly **susceptible**. Researchers have estimated that flocks can consume upwards of 50 tons of seeds per day, which allows them to ⁽²⁷⁾**wipe out** entire small crops and approximately 20% of the annual production of large commercial farms. Annual losses directly ⁽²⁸⁾**attributable to** these small birds have been calculated at $70m, in a region where agricultural production is already ⁽²⁹⁾**in a** precarious **state**.

6 Their easy adaptability and ⁽³⁰⁾**propensity to migrate** in large flocks has made the red-billed quelea a cause for concern in areas where their introduction could allow them to become entrenched as an invasive species. One such region is Australia's northwestern state of Queensland, where the climate resembles the quelea's native habitat. Queensland's $440m annual cereal grain harvest would be devastated if large colonies of quelea became established. Colony establishment would also ⁽³¹⁾**wreak havoc on** the region's native species, such as the endangered Gouldian finch, which could not compete with such massive flocks. This has caused the Australian government to ban the import of the world's most common and destructive bird.

The Most Common Bird on Earth

1 Most people outside of Africa have never heard of the red-billed quelea, but these small African birds are the most common bird species on Earth. A member of the weaver family, they live on the grasslands of sub-Saharan Africa in extremely large colonies that contain up to 30 million individuals. Conservative estimates put the total population of the birds across Africa at more than 1.5 billion breeding pairs, with some saying there may be up to 10 billion of the birds.

2 It may seem illogical that these small birds survive in such a harsh environment, but their extreme success is even more remarkable when one considers that they survive nearly entirely on the annual grasses in the region. Although researchers have noted that they eat some insects, mainly beetles, and a few non-grass seeds, these accounted for less than two percent of their overall diet. One might expect that this great dependence upon annual grasses would lead to regular reduction or extinction of the populations, but, much like early humans learned to hoard wheat and barley seeds to deal with lean times, the red-billed quelea have developed certain behaviors that help them cope with the feast or famine nature of the grass crops.

3 One of the most advantageous adaptations made by the red-billed quelea has been the development of variable annual weather-dependent cycles. During the dry season the bird population must sustain itself with the seeds produced at the end of the rainy season. To do this, they gorge themselves on seeds to gain enough wait to sustain them while they migrate to more productive places. This must be done during the dry season, since monsoon rains cause the remaining seeds to germinate, thereby interrupting the food supply for weeks and instigating the move. Luckily, this does not occur simultaneously across the entire savanna and dry seeds, young grasses, and mature ripe grasses are available in different areas. To take advantage of this the quelea make 50-200 km migrations across the savannas, which allows them to survive in such a forbidding environment.

4 By the time the rains have germinated and fresh seeds become available, these early-rain migrations end and the quelea return to the previously abandoned areas. Access to these new seeds stimulates the population's males to weave ovoid grass and straw nests in acacia trees. The females who help them complete the nest and who then lay two to four eggs later join them. These colonies can cover up to 100 hectares with 500 nests in each acacia. With an average of 100,000 fledglings per hectare, up to 10 million offspring are produced by each successful colony. Surprisingly, the entire process of nest weaving, mating, brooding and fledging of the juveniles takes only six weeks, which is much shorter than in other birds, and is incredibly synchronized, as the eggs all hatch on the same day. However, this process is dependent upon weather patterns, as an earlier dry season can cause the quelea to abandon their colony, while an extended green season with abundant seed stock can allow them to produce multiple broods in the same region.

5 Since they rely upon seeds, these large colonies can cause problems for the region's farmers. As more and more grains are planted across sub-Saharan Africa, the birds have turned to the crops for nourishment. This has allowed their numbers to explode in the region. It is estimated that the population of these "feathered locusts" has increased by 10-100 times since the 1970s. With each bird eating its own weight in seeds per day this leaves fields within 30 Km. of the breeding sites highly susceptible. Researchers have estimated that flocks can consume upwards of 50 tons of seeds per day, which allows them to wipe out entire small crops and approximately 20% of the annual production of large commercial farms. Annual losses directly attributable to these small birds have been calculated at $70m, in a region where agricultural production is already in a precarious state.

6 Their easy adaptability and propensity to migrate in large flocks has made the red-billed quelea a cause for concern in areas where their introduction could allow them to become entrenched as an invasive species. One such region is Australia's northwestern state of Queensland, where the climate resembles the quelea's native habitat. Queensland's $440m annual cereal grain harvest would be devastated if large colonies of quelea became established. Colony establishment would also wreak havoc on the region's native species, such as the endangered Gouldian finch, which could not compete with such massive flocks. This has caused the Australian government to ban the import of the world's most common and destructive bird.

National Parks in the Western United States

1 The Treaty of Paris, which ended the revolutionary war (01)**between** Great Britain **and** its former colonies in the United States, (02)**more than doubled** the territory of the (03)**13 original colonies** as the crown (04)**ceded** all lands east of the Mississippi River **to** the newly formed nation. However, the new country's expansion would not stop there. (05)**By the middle of** the next century, cessations, purchases and treaties would (06)**expand** the nation's contiguous territory **to** its current state. This dramatically increased the amount of land owned by the nation and, before (07)**mass immigration** and westward movement; much of this land was pristine wilderness with (08)**a plethora of** different geological formations and ecosystems. With so much vacant land, the theory of "landscape democracy," the idea that scenic landscapes (09)**belong to** all people, (10)**came into play** and a movement was (11)**put forth** to preserve this land (12)**in perpetuity** as national parkland.

2 This theory was revolutionary for the time, as (13)**prior to** the establishment of Yellowstone National Park in 1872, no national government had ever (14)**set aside** large swaths of undeveloped land. However, this was not only done for preservation. (15)**A sense of inferiority** (16)**with regards to** old world monuments and the belief that America's unique landscapes were one of its most distinguishing features both (17)**had a hand in** (18)**the desire to** set aside western lands. Interestingly, (19)**business interests** also encouraged the conservation movement. It may seem antithetical, but business leaders, such as railroad barons (20)**pushed for** and supported these national parks, since they would (21)**encourage** rich easterners **to** (22)**take** long **trips** on their lines and stay in the hotel they (23)**set up** (24)**on the outskirts** of the parks. Their desire for profits also led them to heavily advertise the majesty of western parks and features, such as the Grand Canyon, Yellowstone, and Yosemite, which greatly (25)**raised awareness** of the parks amongst the (26)**general public**.

3 Surprisingly, the adoption of the automobile by American's in the early 20th century also bolstered the national parks movement. As the number of cars (27)**rose from** 0.11 per 1,000 citizens in 1900 **to** 86.78/K in 1920 and 217.34/K in 1930, drivers (28)**began** (29)**calling for** investment in better roads and highways, especially those in the west. 1916's (30)**Federal Aid Road Act** paid states to construct or improve rural roadways, including those near parkland. This encouraged people to (31)**not only** drive more, **but also** to visit the increasing number of national parks. (32)**At around the same time**, (33)**business magnate** Stephen Mather was pushing for an (34)**independent agency** to oversee the national parks and (35)**barely a month after** passing the Road Act, President Woodrow Wilson (36)**signed a bill** setting up such an agency and (37)**named** Mather its first director. He worked to (38)**protect** these pristine lands **from** the (39)**business interests** that were (40)**attempting to** (41)**have** them opened for logging and other business ventures.

4 By the middle of the 20th century, (42)**cross-country** road trips had become quite (43)**popular with** families who visited national parks, newly founded amusement parks, and ski resorts. They made (44)**the need for** better roadways evident. This increased recreational travel helped ensure the passage of 1956's Interstate and Defense Highway Act, which authorized the construction of nearly 66,000 Km of roads around the country. This $25B project was the largest public works project in the country's history and increased mobility by linking urban centers through wide divided highways. A direct (45)**side effect** of this was easier (46)**access to** national parks for urban inhabitants, which caused a dramatic (47)**increase in** park usage. In 1920 only 1M people visited the national parks, but by 1950 that number had risen to 33M. After the completion of the new highways the nation's parks welcomed 172M visitors. This increase vastly outpaced the increase in the nation's population, which had only doubled during that time.

5 The increased number of visitors quickly caused degradation in the national parks, causing activists, like Sierra Club founder John Muir, to (48)**argue that** the parks should be preserved as pristine wilderness and protected from further human destruction. This was important, since early parks, like Yellowstone had been set up as recreational areas. His impassioned writing (49)**helped to** (50)**convince** Americans, especially the eastern elite, **of** the importance or preservation of these unique areas.

6 This movement (51)**had** a great **impact on** the national park system. Not only did the park system begin working to preserve the wilderness, but it also greatly expanded the amount of protected land. Today, more than 277M people visit the 210,000 Km2 of land protected by the 59 national parks, an area larger than 109 current countries, each year. The beauty, geological features, ecosystems, and recreational opportunities of the land in these parks are now permanently preserved for all American citizens (52)**both** now **and** in the future.

National Parks in the Western United States

1 The Treaty of Paris, which ended the revolutionary war between Great Britain and its former colonies in the United States, more than doubled the territory of the 13 original colonies as the crown ceded all lands east of the Mississippi River to the newly formed nation. However, the new country's expansion would not stop there. By the middle of the next century, cessations, purchases and treaties would expand the nation's contiguous territory to its current state. This dramatically increased the amount of land owned by the nation and, before mass immigration and westward movement; much of this land was pristine wilderness with a plethora of different geological formations and ecosystems. With so much vacant land, the theory of "landscape democracy," the idea that scenic landscapes belong to all people, came into play and a movement was put forth to preserve this land in perpetuity as national parkland.

2 This theory was revolutionary for the time, as prior to the establishment of Yellowstone National Park in 1872, no national government had ever set aside large swaths of undeveloped land. However, this was not only done for preservation. A sense of inferiority with regards to old world monuments and the belief that America's unique landscapes were one of its most distinguishing features both had a hand in the desire to set aside western lands. Interestingly, business interests also encouraged the conservation movement. It may seem antithetical, but business leaders, such as railroad barons pushed for and supported these national parks, since they would encourage rich easterners to take long trips on their lines and stay in the hotel they set up on the outskirts of the parks. Their desire for profits also led them to heavily advertise the majesty of western parks and features, such as the Grand Canyon, Yellowstone, and Yosemite, which greatly raised awareness of the parks amongst the general public.

3 Surprisingly, the adoption of the automobile by American's in the early 20th century also bolstered the national parks movement. As the number of cars rose from 0.11 per 1,000 citizens in 1900 to 86.78/K in 1920 and 217.34/K in 1930, drivers began calling for investment in better roads and highways, especially those in the west. 1916's Federal Aid Road Act paid states to construct or improve rural roadways, including those near parkland. This encouraged people to not only drive more, but also to visit the increasing number of national parks. At around the same time, business magnate Stephen Mather was pushing for an independent agency to oversee the national parks and barely a month after passing the Road Act, President Woodrow Wilson signed a bill setting up such an agency and named Mather its first director. He worked to protect these pristine lands from the business interests that were attempting to have them opened for logging and other business ventures.

4 By the middle of the 20th century, cross-country road trips had become quite popular with families who visited national parks, newly founded amusement parks, and ski resorts. They made the need for better roadways evident. This increased recreational travel helped ensure the passage of 1956's Interstate and Defense Highway Act, which authorized the construction of nearly 66,000 Km of roads around the country. This $25B project was the largest public works project in the country's history and increased mobility by linking urban centers through wide divided highways. A direct side effect of this was easier access to national parks for urban inhabitants, which caused a dramatic increase in park usage. In 1920 only 1M people visited the national parks, but by 1950 that number had risen to 33M. After the completion of the new highways the nation's parks welcomed 172M visitors. This increase vastly outpaced the increase in the nation's population, which had only doubled during that time.

5 The increased number of visitors quickly caused degradation in the national parks, causing activists, like Sierra Club founder John Muir, to argue that the parks should be preserved as pristine wilderness and protected from further human destruction. This was important, since early parks, like Yellowstone had been set up as recreational areas. His impassioned writing helped to convince Americans, especially the eastern elite, of the importance or preservation of these unique areas.

6 This movement had a great impact on the national park system. Not only did the park system begin working to preserve the wilderness, but it also greatly expanded the amount of protected land. Today, more than 277M people visit the 210,000 Km2 of land protected by the 59 national parks, an area larger than 109 current countries, each year. The beauty, geological features, ecosystems, and recreational opportunities of the land in these parks are now permanently preserved for all American citizens both now and in the future.

The Role of Dress in Africa

1 When most people think about the concept of dressing, they automatically ⁽⁰¹⁾**think of** only clothing and accessories and whether they ⁽⁰²⁾**are in the right** style. However, dress can actually be a much more complex concept, which can be ⁽⁰³⁾**used to communicate** ⁽⁰⁴⁾**both** simple ideas **and** complex information about the wearer. The type of dress that a person chooses can communicate immediate information about their gender, ethnic group, religion, age or even occupation. A few common examples of these are the burka ⁽⁰⁵⁾**worn by** Muslim women and the yarmulke worn by Jewish men. Both of these items ⁽⁰⁶⁾**point to** the age, religion, and gender of their wearers. This complexity and symbolism is a key feature of African dress, which has fascinated outside viewers with its striking range of styles since Arabic writers first described it in the fourteenth century.

2 African dress, like most forms, is intimately ⁽⁰⁷⁾**connected to** the identity of its wearers and observers, since it ⁽⁰⁸⁾**acts as** a signifier of so many aspects of the societies. Despite the neutrality of the adornment, the way in which it is worn, or simply the fact that it is worn, can become symbolically ⁽⁰⁹⁾**important to** a society. There may be importance ⁽¹⁰⁾**assigned to** the form, type, adornment, and materials used to form the dress worn and this can ⁽¹¹⁾**cause** it **to** become a sensitive aspect of the society. Since many aspects of dress are ⁽¹²⁾**tied to** tribal or religious identity, their use denotes inclusion with the society, but can also draw the ire or derision of society members if they are inappropriately worn or displayed.

3 ⁽¹³⁾**In addition to** denoting societal and religious identity, African dress can also be ⁽¹⁴⁾**seen as** an indicator of the wearer's sociopolitical standing in the society. In many African societies leaders wear some sort of insignia or symbolic aspect of dress to denote their leadership. ⁽¹⁵⁾**In fact**, some of these are ⁽¹⁶⁾**made of** ⁽¹⁷⁾**highly prized** materials, such as ivory, gold, or decorative beading, that are only worn by the leaders. One example of this is the Oba, or leader, of the Benin people in present-day Nigeria. His official dress includes a coral-beaded smock and crown with coral necklaces and ivory pendants and amulets. Further, he carries a flywhisk made of red coral beads that signify his divine rule. In other societies, other flywhisk materials were used to denote the regal nature of the bearer. Two examples of this are the Fare-Fare and Ashanti people of Ghana, whose respective use of horsehair and elephant tail hair denoted kings or chiefs ⁽¹⁸⁾**of the highest importance**. These flywhisks are ⁽¹⁹⁾**such** a strong symbol of power and leadership **that** they have ⁽²⁰⁾**come to be used** by rulers across the continent, including by Jomo Kenyatta, the first leader of the modern state of Kenya.

4 The use of these flywhisks as a symbol of leadership ⁽²¹⁾**brings up** another interesting aspect of "dress." ⁽²²⁾**Contrary to** the common, narrow interpretation of the term dress, the true definition is much broader and includes more than just the clothing worn. It includes accessories, such as the flywhisks, and other methods of beautifying and adorning the body. Items such as cosmetics, jewelry, and accessories like staffs, parasols, and fans, are all ⁽²³⁾**considered** aspects of dress. However, not all of these aspects can be easily removed. Some societies use permanent bodily modification to perform the same functions. Tattooing may be the most common form of these in modern day western society, but there are ⁽²⁴⁾**a profusion of** other forms, such as scarring, piercings and ⁽²⁵⁾**the use of** lip plates.

5 In most of sub-Saharan Africa, the use of purposefully inflicted scars, or cicatrization, is the most common type of permanent body modification. They signify membership and status in the society, but can act as protective devices, in addition to simply being beautiful bodily adornment. These scars are ⁽²⁶⁾**placed on** different parts of the body, including the face, abdomen and extremities, and can sometimes ⁽²⁷⁾**take the form** of elaborate patterns that cover most of the body. Oftentimes, the lengthy scarification acts as an initiation process, with the aesthetics of the scars ⁽²⁸⁾**correlating to** other important figurative aspects of the society, such as pottery and sculpture.

6 Farther north, along the Nile River, tattooing was the main form of permanent body adornment. Researchers have found evidence of tattoos being used as fertility signals in female Egyptian mummies from 2000 B.C. ⁽²⁹⁾**In addition**, the adjacent Nubian civilization ⁽³⁰⁾**appears to have** ⁽³¹⁾**utilized** tattoos **to adorn** their bodies, ⁽³²⁾**as well**. The tattoos in both of these civilizations ⁽³³⁾**served** ⁽³⁴⁾**the same purpose as** scarification, apparel and accessories in other African tribes, and elsewhere. They were symbols of inclusion, protection and identification for their bearers.

The Role of Dress in Africa

1 When most people think about the concept of dressing, they automatically think of only clothing and accessories and whether they are in the right style. However, dress can actually be a much more complex concept, which can be used to communicate both simple ideas and complex information about the wearer. The type of dress that a person chooses can communicate immediate information about their gender, ethnic group, religion, age or even occupation. A few common examples of these are the burka worn by Muslim women and the yarmulke worn by Jewish men. Both of these items point to the age, religion, and gender of their wearers. This complexity and symbolism is a key feature of African dress, which has fascinated outside viewers with its striking range of styles since Arabic writers first described it in the fourteenth century.

2 African dress, like most forms, is intimately connected to the identity of its wearers and observers, since it acts as a signifier of so many aspects of the societies. Despite the neutrality of the adornment, the way in which it is worn, or simply the fact that it is worn, can become symbolically important to a society. There may be importance assigned to the form, type, adornment, and materials used to form the dress worn and this can cause it to become a sensitive aspect of the society. Since many aspects of dress are tied to tribal or religious identity, their use denotes inclusion with the society, but can also draw the ire or derision of society members if they are inappropriately worn or displayed.

3 In addition to denoting societal and religious identity, African dress can also be seen as an indicator of the wearer's sociopolitical standing in the society. In many African societies leaders wear some sort of insignia or symbolic aspect of dress to denote their leadership. In fact, some of these are made of highly prized materials, such as ivory, gold, or decorative beading, that are only worn by the leaders. One example of this is the Oba, or leader, of the Benin people in present-day Nigeria. His official dress includes a coral-beaded smock and crown with coral necklaces and ivory pendants and amulets. Further, he carries a flywhisk made of red coral beads that signify his divine rule. In other societies, other flywhisk materials were used to denote the regal nature of the bearer. Two examples of this are the Fare-Fare and Ashanti people of Ghana, whose respective use of horsehair and elephant tail hair denoted kings or chiefs of the highest importance. These flywhisks are such a strong symbol of power and leadership that they have come to be used by rulers across the continent, including by Jomo Kenyatta, the first leader of the modern state of Kenya.

4 The use of these flywhisks as a symbol of leadership brings up another interesting aspect of "dress." Contrary to the common, narrow interpretation of the term dress, the true definition is much broader and includes more than just the clothing worn. It includes accessories, such as the flywhisks, and other methods of beautifying and adorning the body. Items such as cosmetics, jewelry, and accessories like staffs, parasols, and fans, are all considered aspects of dress. However, not all of these aspects can be easily removed. Some societies use permanent bodily modification to perform the same functions. Tattooing may be the most common form of these in modern day western society, but there are a profusion of other forms, such as scarring, piercings and the use of lip plates.

5 In most of sub-Saharan Africa, the use of purposefully inflicted scars, or cicatrization, is the most common type of permanent body modification. They signify membership and status in the society, but can act as protective devices, in addition to simply being beautiful bodily adornment. These scars are placed on different parts of the body, including the face, abdomen and extremities, and can sometimes take the form of elaborate patterns that cover most of the body. Oftentimes, the lengthy scarification acts as an initiation process, with the aesthetics of the scars correlating to other important figurative aspects of the society, such as pottery and sculpture.

6 Farther north, along the Nile River, tattooing was the main form of permanent body adornment. Researchers have found evidence of tattoos being used as fertility signals in female Egyptian mummies from 2000 B.C. In addition, the adjacent Nubian civilization appears to have utilized tattoos to adorn their bodies, as well. The tattoos in both of these civilizations served the same purpose as scarification, apparel and accessories in other African tribes, and elsewhere. They were symbols of inclusion, protection and identification for their bearers.

Evidence of an Asteroid Impact

1 Throughout Earth's history, there have been mass extinctions that permanently altered its biodiversity. The most recent of these occurred at (01)**the boundary between** the Cretaceous and Paleogene periods, around 65 million years ago. During this time, scientists estimate that 75% of all species perished. By the end of the extinction, all non-avian dinosaurs had (02)**died off**, (03)**allowing** mammals **to** (04)**rise to the** dominant **position** in most ecosystems.

2 Since discovering this dramatic change in species diversity in the late 19th century, geologists have (05)**attempted to explain** why so many species died off concurrently. Some posited that dinosaurs could not (06)**adapt to** climate change or the lowered sea level, while others thought that a more catastrophic event precipitated the disappearance of so many species. They (07)**point to** such catastrophes as a massive volcanic eruption, an extraterrestrial body striking Earth's surface (which geologists (08)**refer to as** a bolide), or the effects of cosmic radiation as possible explanations. Unfortunately, they could not produce concrete evidence to support these theories.

3 This changed in 1977 when geologist Walter Alvarez was studying the strata of the soil near Gubbio, Italy and discovered a layer of unique clay from the Cretaceous–Paleogene boundary. (09)**Upon send**ing it for analysis by his father's physics laboratory, he found that it contained nearly 30 times more iridium than is normally found in the rocks of Earth's crust. This was surprising, because, despite the fact that the earth's core and mantle are (10)**believed to contain** this metallic element, it is rare in the crust. This led him to question the source of the mineral. While a volcanic eruption could have deposited iridium in Earth's crust, he (11)**pointed out** that (12)**it was** more **likely that** a large (10+ Km (13)**in diameter**) extraterrestrial body containing iridium forcefully struck the earth and (14)**sent up** a dense cloud of iridium-filled dust across the atmosphere. He proposed that when this dust (15)**mixed with** other atmospheric matter, atmospheric circulation pushed it throughout the atmosphere and blocked the sun's rays, thereby causing the extinction of the plants that formed the base of the food chain for most other life forms. Eventually, this dust (16)**settled on** the ground and entered the soil column. This theory was bolstered when high iridium levels were found in soil from the Cretaceous-Paleogene boundary in locations as distant as Russia, Haiti, and New Zealand, and in layers of sediment under the Pacific and Atlantic Oceans.

4 The theory was further strengthened when geologists studying the Cretaceous-Paleogene Boundary found materials (17)**common in** proven meteoric impact sites such as the Barringer Crater in Arizona. The first of these, shocked quartz, displays a unique planar pattern that is only created by shockwaves (18)**traveling through** quartz-filled rock after an intense impact, so it indicates that there was some massive impact at the time. They also found stichovite, a dense compressed silicate uncommon in Earth's crust that is formed only in high-pressure situations, in samples from the period. In addition, the existence of tektites, or tiny glasslike droplets formed when terrestrial material is super heated and (19)**thrown into** the air during a meteor's impact, in the Cretaceous-Paleogene layer samples from distant locations further supported the theory. The presence of soot in this stratum also points to a meteoric impact, since such an impact would have likely caused widespread wildfires.

5 The missing piece of the puzzle was (20)**the lack of** a bolide impact site, but the lack of one does not necessarily negate the theory, since Earth's atmosphere can weather and erode geological features over time. However, in 1978, while (21)**working for** Petróleos Mexicanos, geophysicist Glen Penfield found evidence of an impact crater (22)**just off** the Yucatan Peninsula, near the town of Chicxulub, that was 180 Km in diameter and 20 km in depth. This find, although under-reported and appreciated at the time, would make it the impact site of the largest bolide to ever strike Earth, which at 10+ Km in diameter, matched Alvarez's estimate perfectly. Further research by geoscientist Alan Hildebrand (23)**used** core samples, magnetic and gravity surveys **to reveal** other telltale signs of a bolide at the supposed impact site, such as the existence of andesitic rocks, which have isotopic and chemical compositions (24)**similar to** tektites found in the Cretaceous-Paleogene boundary across the Caribbean region.

6 Today, Alvarez's theory is the most widely accepted explanation for the mass extinction. Further testing of the event by the Berkeley Geochronology Center (25)**dated** the bolide impact **to** 66-65 million years ago, with the extinction occurring within 33,000 years, thereby confirming Alvarez's time line. Even more convincingly, in 2010 a group of scientists published the results of their two decade long study of the Cretaceous-Paleogene boundary layer and (26)**concluded that** debris from the Chicxulub bolide would have caused the environmental disturbances (27)**required to prompt** the mass extinction.

Evidence of an Asteroid Impact

1 Throughout Earth's history, there have been mass extinctions that permanently altered its biodiversity. The most recent of these occurred at the boundary between the Cretaceous and Paleogene periods, around 65 million years ago. During this time, scientists estimate that 75% of all species perished. By the end of the extinction, all non-avian dinosaurs had died off, allowing mammals to rise to the dominant position in most ecosystems.

2 Since discovering this dramatic change in species diversity in the late 19th century, geologists have attempted to explain why so many species died off concurrently. Some posited that dinosaurs could not adapt to climate change or the lowered sea level, while others thought that a more catastrophic event precipitated the disappearance of so many species. They point to such catastrophes as a massive volcanic eruption, an extraterrestrial body striking Earth's surface (which geologists refer to as a bolide), or the effects of cosmic radiation as possible explanations. Unfortunately, they could not produce concrete evidence to support these theories.

3 This changed in 1977 when geologist Walter Alvarez was studying the strata of the soil near Gubbio, Italy and discovered a layer of unique clay from the Cretaceous–Paleogene boundary. Upon sending it for analysis by his father's physics laboratory, he found that it contained nearly 30 times more iridium than is normally found in the rocks of Earth's crust. This was surprising, because, despite the fact that the earth's core and mantle are believed to contain this metallic element, it is rare in the crust. This led him to question the source of the mineral. While a volcanic eruption could have deposited iridium in Earth's crust, he pointed out that it was more likely that a large (10+ Km in diameter) extraterrestrial body containing iridium forcefully struck the earth and sent up a dense cloud of iridium-filled dust across the atmosphere. He proposed that when this dust mixed with other atmospheric matter, atmospheric circulation pushed it throughout the atmosphere and blocked the sun's rays, thereby causing the extinction of the plants that formed the base of the food chain for most other life forms. Eventually, this dust settled on the ground and entered the soil column. This theory was bolstered when high iridium levels were found in soil from the Cretaceous-Paleogene boundary in locations as distant as Russia, Haiti, and New Zealand, and in layers of sediment under the Pacific and Atlantic Oceans.

4 The theory was further strengthened when geologists studying the Cretaceous-Paleogene Boundary found materials common in proven meteoric impact sites such as the Barringer Crater in Arizona. The first of these, shocked quartz, displays a unique planar pattern that is only created by shockwaves traveling through quartz-filled rock after an intense impact, so it indicates that there was some massive impact at the time. They also found stichovite, a dense compressed silicate uncommon in Earth's crust that is formed only in high-pressure situations, in samples from the period. In addition, the existence of tektites, or tiny glasslike droplets formed when terrestrial material is super heated and thrown into the air during a meteor's impact, in the Cretaceous-Paleogene layer samples from distant locations further supported the theory. The presence of soot in this stratum also points to a meteoric impact, since such an impact would have likely caused widespread wildfires.

5 The missing piece of the puzzle was the lack of a bolide impact site, but the lack of one does not necessarily negate the theory, since Earth's atmosphere can weather and erode geological features over time. However, in 1078, while working for Petróleos Mexicanos, geophysicist Glen Penfield found evidence of an impact crater just off the Yucatan Peninsula, near the town of Chicxulub, that was 180 Km in diameter and 20 km in depth. This find, although under-reported and appreciated at the time, would make it the impact site of the largest bolide to ever strike Earth, which at 10+ Km in diameter, matched Alvarez's estimate perfectly. Further research by geoscientist Alan Hildebrand used core samples, magnetic and gravity surveys to reveal other telltale signs of a bolide at the supposed impact site, such as the existence of andesitic rocks, which have isotopic and chemical compositions similar to tektites found in the Cretaceous-Paleogene boundary across the Caribbean region.

6 Today, Alvarez's theory is the most widely accepted explanation for the mass extinction. Further testing of the event by the Berkeley Geochronology Center dated the bolide impact to 66-65 million years ago, with the extinction occurring within 33,000 years, thereby confirming Alvarez's time line. Even more convincingly, in 2010 a group of scientists published the results of their two decade long study of the Cretaceous-Paleogene boundary layer and concluded that debris from the Chicxulub bolide would have caused the environmental disturbances required to prompt the mass extinction.

Native Americans and European Trade Goods

1 ⁽⁰¹⁾**Prior to** their exploration and settlement by Europeans, the United States and Canada hosted a thriving trade network administered by the various native tribes found there. These Pre-Colombian tribes developed extensive trade routes between themselves that ⁽⁰²⁾**allowed** them **to trade** pelts, shells, pottery and other handicrafts from the Great Lakes to the Gulf of Mexico and as far west as the Rocky Mountains. These interactions changed the individual tribes, by providing them ⁽⁰³⁾**not only** new material goods and revenue, **but also** differing ideas and ⁽⁰⁴⁾**ways of thinking**. These changes would, however, ⁽⁰⁵⁾**pale in comparison to** the changes ⁽⁰⁶⁾**brought about** by the introduction of Europeans into the North American economy.

2 Although native tribes had encountered Europeans as early as the 11th Century, when Norse explorers ⁽⁰⁷⁾**tried to** create a settlement in eastern Canada, true economic interactions did not occur until the early 1500s. ⁽⁰⁸⁾**At this time**, French fishermen and Basque whalers were regularly ⁽⁰⁹⁾**travelling to** the Grand Banks ⁽¹⁰⁾**off of** Newfoundland and ⁽¹¹⁾**began** ⁽¹²⁾**trading with** the locals they met when they came ashore to process their catches. The native inhabitants they met ⁽¹³⁾**were eager to trade** their goods for European products, such as metal tools, glassware and cloth, and allowed European explorers and traders to establish settlements and trading posts throughout New England, along the St. Lawrence River, and as far south as Virginia. This situation provided European explorers a beneficial new trading source, but perhaps the biggest draw for them was the ⁽¹⁴⁾**trade in fur**, especially that of beaver pelts, which had become a phenomenally popular status symbol in Europe at the time.

3 The fur trade dominated early European-Native American trade and ⁽¹⁵⁾**had a** profound **impact on** many aspects of the native societies including their organization, relationships with ⁽¹⁶⁾**one another**, and even their art and handicrafts. Prior to their ⁽¹⁷⁾**interactions with** European explorers and products, these tribes had ⁽¹⁸⁾**spent** thousands of years procur**ing** and trad**ing** materials and refined products that were ⁽¹⁹⁾**both** precious **and** symbolically important to their cultures' ideals of leadership, influence, wealth and spirituality. The products they received from trading with the Europeans ⁽²⁰⁾**offered** them these same opportunities and were ⁽²¹⁾**incorporated into** the indigenous communities values, crafts, and understanding of the world ⁽²²⁾**early on**.

4 With the permanent settlements, the native tribes had more interaction with European products and became even more influenced by them. Over time, long held traditions such as pottery and tool making were abandoned ⁽²³⁾**in favor of** European products such as brass kettles and durable steel and iron tools. This became more pronounced as European settlements spread westward and ⁽²⁴⁾**encroached on** tribal lands, which allowed them to trade directly with the local tribes. This can be seen in the early 17th century Dutch settlements in the upper Hudson area of present day New York. Prior to these settlements, the powerful Iroquois tribe ⁽²⁵⁾**used** beaver tooth blades **to** ⁽²⁶⁾**carve** moose antlers **into** rudimentary three or four tine combs, but after the introduction of steel blades by their Dutch neighbors these ornaments became much more ornate. In fact, archaeologists excavated one from a Cayuga village with many narrow tines and an intricate carving of two European's ⁽²⁷⁾**on horseback**. It is assumed this was to commemorate the visit of an English dignitary, Wentworth Greenhalgh, in 1699.

5 Although many of the European goods that ⁽²⁸⁾**found** their **way into** the society provided increased productivity and security – guns, metal blades, and brass kettles – their longevity ⁽²⁹⁾**led to** market saturation, eventually causing a ⁽³⁰⁾**shift in** trading. Over time, native tribes ⁽³¹⁾**began to** favor raw materials and ⁽³²⁾**the trade in** cloth, wool, glass beads and decorative silver became more important. Native tribes ⁽³³⁾**incorporated** items like glass beads **into** their practices and costumes ⁽³⁴⁾**in place of** ornaments ⁽³⁵⁾**made of** pipestone, copper, and shell. Some local artisans, usually tribeswomen, used these replacement materials to create elaborate formal attire and regalia. The new products offered the native tribes the correct look and symbolism for their practices, but the 'luxurious' imported products also ⁽³⁶⁾**gave** the bearer an air of power, wealth, and success.

6 Unfortunately for the native tribes, these positive trade interactions with European settlers did not last forever. Over time, as the number of settlers and traders in the region increased, they ⁽³⁷⁾**brought with** them corporatization of the industry and European diseases. The native population ⁽³⁸⁾**was not immune to** the ⁽³⁹⁾**ill effects** of either of these and soon began to suffer. By the 1850s, beaver fur had ⁽⁴⁰⁾**fallen out of favor** in Europe and the native tribes lost a major source of income. This, ⁽⁴¹⁾**combined with** oppression by the settlers, ⁽⁴²⁾**threw** them **into** a state of poverty from which many of the tribes have still not recovered.

Native Americans and European Trade Goods

1 Prior to their exploration and settlement by Europeans, the United States and Canada hosted a thriving trade network administered by the various native tribes found there. These Pre-Colombian tribes developed extensive trade routes between themselves that allowed them to trade pelts, shells, pottery and other handicrafts from the Great Lakes to the Gulf of Mexico and as far west as the Rocky Mountains. These interactions changed the individual tribes, by providing them not only new material goods and revenue, but also differing ideas and ways of thinking. These changes would, however, pale in comparison to the changes brought about by the introduction of Europeans into the North American economy.

2 Although native tribes had encountered Europeans as early as the 11th Century, when Norse explorers tried to create a settlement in eastern Canada, true economic interactions did not occur until the early 1500s. At this time, French fishermen and Basque whalers were regularly travelling to the Grand Banks off of Newfoundland and began trading with the locals they met when they came ashore to process their catches. The native inhabitants they met were eager to trade their goods for European products, such as metal tools, glassware and cloth, and allowed European explorers and traders to establish settlements and trading posts throughout New England, along the St. Lawrence River, and as far south as Virginia. This situation provided European explorers a beneficial new trading source, but perhaps the biggest draw for them was the trade in fur, especially that of beaver pelts, which had become a phenomenally popular status symbol in Europe at the time.

3 The fur trade dominated early European-Native American trade and had a profound impact on many aspects of the native societies including their organization, relationships with one another, and even their art and handicrafts. Prior to their interactions with European explorers and products, these tribes had spent thousands of years procuring and trading materials and refined products that were both precious and symbolically important to their cultures' ideals of leadership, influence, wealth and spirituality. The products they received from trading with the Europeans offered them these same opportunities and were incorporated into the indigenous communities values, crafts, and understanding of the world early on.

4 With the permanent settlements, the native tribes had more interaction with European products and became even more influenced by them. Over time, long held traditions such as pottery and tool making were abandoned in favor of European products such as brass kettles and durable steel and iron tools. This became more pronounced as European settlements spread westward and encroached on tribal lands, which allowed them to trade directly with the local tribes. This can be seen in the early 17th century Dutch settlements in the upper Hudson area of present day New York. Prior to these settlements, the powerful Iroquois tribe used beaver tooth blades to carve moose antlers into rudimentary three or four tine combs, but after the introduction of steel blades by their Dutch neighbors these ornaments became much more ornate. In fact, archaeologists excavated one from a Cayuga village with many narrow tines and an intricate carving of two European's on horseback. It is assumed this was to commemorate the visit of an English dignitary, Wentworth Greenhalgh, in 1699.

5 Although many of the European goods that found their way into the society provided increased productivity and security – guns, metal blades, and brass kettles – their longevity led to market saturation, eventually causing a shift in trading. Over time, native tribes began to favor raw materials and the trade in cloth, wool, glass beads and decorative silver became more important. Native tribes incorporated items like glass beads into their practices and costumes in place of ornaments made of pipestone, copper, and shell. Some local artisans, usually tribeswomen, used these replacement materials to create elaborate formal attire and regalia. The new products offered the native tribes the correct look and symbolism for their practices, but the 'luxurious' imported products also gave the bearer an air of power, wealth, and success.

6 Unfortunately for the native tribes, these positive trade interactions with European settlers did not last forever. Over time, as the number of settlers and traders in the region increased, they brought with them corporatization of the industry and European diseases. The native population was not immune to the ill effects of either of these and soon began to suffer. By the 1850s, beaver fur had fallen out of favor in Europe and the native tribes lost a major source of income. This, combined with oppression by the settlers, threw them into a state of poverty from which many of the tribes have still not recovered.

usherin.usher.co.kr

USHER
iBT TOEFL
INTERMEDIATE READING 02
TEST 해설지

USHER

iBT TOEFL
INTERMEDIATE READING 02

TEST 1

답안 및 취약 유형 분석표

해석·해설

답안 및 문제 유형 분석표

TEST 1-1

01 (A) Inference
02 (A) Fact
03 (C) Inference
04 (B) Fact
05 (C) Vocabulary
06 (C) Fact
07 (B) Fact
08 (B) Purpose
09 4th ■ Insertion
10 (B), (C), (E) Summary

TEST 1-2

11 (B) Purpose
12 (C) Fact
13 (D) Highlight
14 (C) Fact
15 (A) Fact
16 (B) Vocabulary
17 (B) Fact
18 (A) Fact
19 3rd ■ Insertion
20 (A), (E), (F) Summary

TEST 1-3

21 (C) Fact
22 (D) Purpose
23 (D) Fact
24 (B) Highlight
25 (B) Inference
26 (C) Vocabulary
27 (A) Fact
28 (C) Inference
29 3rd ■ Insertion
30 (A), (C), (F) Summary

각 문제 유형별 맞춘 개수를 아래에 적어 보세요.

유형	맞춘 답의 개수	정답률
단어 (Vocabulary)	/ 3	정답률: %
사실 확인 문제 (Fact)	/ 12	정답률: %
지시어 찾기 (Reference)	/ 0	정답률: %
끼워 넣기 (Insertion)	/ 3	정답률: %
문장 변환문제 (Highlight)	/ 2	정답률: %
목적 (Purpose)	/ 3	정답률: %
추론 (Inference)	/ 4	정답률: %
단락 요약 (Summary / Category Chart)	/ 3	정답률: %
전체	/ 30	정답률: %

※ 자신이 취약한 유형은 READING STRATEGIES를 통해 다시 한번 점검하시기 바랍니다. (p.44)

TEST 1-1　Costs of Quitting a Job　퇴사 비용

Introduction	단락 1	미국인들의 높은 직업 이동성
Point	단락 2	직업의 지리적 위치
Point	단락 3	심리적 요소
Point	단락 4	부동산 가격과 정책
Point	단락 5	이주 역사와의 관계
Point	단락 6	높은 직업 유동성의 사회적 영향

단락 1 — 미국인들의 높은 직업 이동성

1　High job mobility has long been held as a hallmark of the American economy. In contrast to employees in Japan and Europe, American employees appear to switch jobs much more readily. On average, American workers have been with their current employer for a shorter period and have had a larger number of employers than those in other regions. This has been blamed, in part, by the lower levels of training provided by American companies for their workers, but this is likely an oversimplified explanation. In reality, many diverse factors influence American employees' decisions to switch jobs more frequently than their counterparts in Europe and Japan.

해석: 높은 직업 유동성은 오랫동안 미국 경제의 특징으로 유지되어 왔다. 일본과 유럽의 근로자들과는 대조적으로, 미국의 근로자들은 직업을 훨씬 더 쉽게 바꾸는 것처럼 보인다. 평균적으로, 미국 고용인들은 짧은 기간 동안 현재의 고용주와 함께 이어왔고 다른 지역의 근로자들보다 더 많은 수의 고용주들 가졌었다. 이것은 부분적으로 그들의 근로자들을 위해 미국 회사에서 제공되는 낮은 수준의 훈련에 의해 비난 받아왔지만 이것은 아마 과도하게 단순화 된 설명일 것이다. 실제로, 많은 다양한 요소들이 유럽과 일본에 있는 고용인들보다 미국의 고용인들의 직업을 더 자주 바꾸는 결정에 영향을 끼친다.

단락 2 — 직업의 지리적 위치

2　While economic theories posit that mobility is most likely in prosperous times, when the costs and risks of changing jobs are low, a number of logistical differences make it more likely. [■] One of the most surprising of these is the location of the job. [■] Those employed in urban areas are more likely to change jobs, likely due to the easy availability of other jobs in the city, which means that the employee will not have to relocate his or her home to take another job. [■] Those who live in non-urban areas who quit their jobs will have more difficulty in finding another job due to the limited number available in the region. [■]

해석: 경제적 이론들이 유동성이 번성의 시기에 발생할 가능성이 가장 높다고 상정하는 반면에, 직업을 바꾸는 위험과 비용이 낮을 때, 수 많은 수송의 차이들이 이것을 더 그럴듯하게 만든다. 이것들 중 가장 놀라운 것 중 하나는 직업의 위치이다. 도시지역에서 고용된 사람들은 도시에서의 다른 직업의 쉬운 이용가능성때문에 직업을 바꿀 가능성이 더 높고, 이것은 근로자가 직업을 구하기 위해 그 또는 그녀의 집을 이전하지 않아도 되는 것을 의미한다. 직업을 그만 둔 비 도시지역에 사는 사람들은 그 지역에 이용 가능한 제한된 직업의 수 때문에 다른 직업을 찾는 데 더 많은 어려움을 갖는다.

단락 3 — 심리적 요소

3　In addition to logistical and monetary factors, psychological factors also play a large role in job mobility. Individuals with more adventurous personalities and fewer familial responsibilities are more likely to switch jobs easily, as they can overcome the fear of the unknown and are more willing to risk the consequences of job change. In fact, studies have shown that 13% of workers who have

해석: 수송과 금전적 요소 뿐만 아니라, 정신적 요소들이 또한 직업 유동성에 큰 역할을 한다. 더욱 모험적인 성격과 적은 가족에 대한 책임감을 가진 개인들은 직업을 쉽게 바꿀 가능성이 높고, 이것은 그들이 미지의 것의 두려움을 극복할 수 있고 직업 변화의 결과에 기꺼이 위험을 무릅쓰기 때문이다. 실제로, 연구들은 3배더 자주 직업을 바꾼

switched jobs more than 3 times are responsible for about half of all permanent employment separations. On the other hand, fear and cultural norms can keep employees in their current positions. One of these, the Japanese "lifetime employment" system, has made job switching almost unheard of in Japanese society. ==This system, which was meant to limit the ability of companies to layoff employees, has also built a strong sense of employee loyalty, which makes it societally undesirable for employees to switch jobs without good reason.==

4 Interestingly, real estate prices have also been linked to the incidence of job change. Housing policies in Japan and Europe often make residential relocation an expensive prospect, which discourages job mobility in much the same way that non-urban locations do. In many of these countries, rental subsidies are more widely available than in the United States, which makes workers **loath** to relocate for a job change. In addition, rent control schemes that limit the increase in rent between consecutive rental contracts reduce job and residential mobility, because landlords can negotiate any rental amount for new contracts. This means that any job move that requires relocation could result in an astronomical increase in housing cost.

5 Some researchers also point to history as an indicator of the **propensity** for job change. The United States, Canada, and Australia are all large, rather sparsely populated countries that show much lower job tenures than most European countries and Japan. They hypothesize that these country's long history of attracting international immigration and their citizens' willingness to undertake long-distance relocation have made job change much less unusual. In a country where people have previously moved thousands of miles from their homeland, pulling up stakes and moving for another job is much less of an event than in countries with more stable populations.

6 With all of these possible explanations for the differences in job mobility rates, another question arises: what is the societal impact of increased job mobility? Some believe that increased job mobility has a positive impact because it increases worker satisfaction and worker-job matches. Economists also point to larger numbers of workers and employers seeking matches as a sign of the economic flexibility that makes economic adaptation possible. Conversely, higher mobility with lower costs can cause employers to skimp on training for employees who they constantly fear will jump ship. Whatever the societal cost of job mobility, employers must try to balance job mobility and its associated costs in order to succeed.

두려워하는 떠나버리는 근로자들을 위한 훈련의 비용을 절약하도록 만든다. 직업 유동성의 사회적 비용이 어떻게 되든지 간에, 고용주들은 성공을 하기 위해 직업 유동성과 이것의 관련된 비용의 균형을 맞추도록 노력해야 한다.

01

What can be inferred from paragraph 1 about job mobility and on-the-job training? ★★

(A) Companies that offer extensive training are less likely to have high employee turnover.
(B) The American government doesn't allow on-the-job training, in order to keep job mobility rates high.
(C) Workers remain at their jobs longer in Europe and Japan because it takes them longer to complete their training.
(D) Most on-the-job training is meant to entice employees to remain at their current job for a longer period.

직업 이동성과 현장 교육에 대해 1문단에서 추론할 수 있는 것은 무엇인가? ★★

(A) 광범위한 교육을 제공하는 기업은 직원 이직률이 높을 가능성이 적다.
(B) 미국 정부는 높은 직업 이동률을 유지하기 위해 현장 교육을 허용하지 않는다.
(C) 유럽과 일본에서는 교육을 마치는데 더 오랜 시간이 걸리기 때문에 근로자들이 더 오래 직장에 남아 있게 된다.
(D) 대부분의 현장실습은 직원들이 현 직장에 더 오래 머물도록 유인하기 위한 것이다.

Inference **(A)** - This has been blamed, (in part), (by the lower levels) (of training) provided (by American companies) (for their workers), 문장에서 낮은 훈련 수준 때문이라고 나와 있기 때문에 **(B)**는 정부가 주체가 지문에 나오지 않았고, **(C)**는 훈련 완성의 기간이 오래 걸린다는 내용, **(D)**는 훈련의 목적이 현재 직업을 오랜 기간동안 유지하도록 유도하는 것 이라는 내용이 틀렸기 때문에 오답이다.

02

According to paragraph 2, which of the following is **NOT** true about the location of a job? ★

(A) The site of a job has little bearing on job mobility.
(B) Those who work in urban areas have higher rates of job mobility.
(C) Having to relocate for a job discourages job mobility.
(D) There are limited job opportunities in rural areas.

다음 중 직업의 위치에 대한 설명으로 옳지 않은 것은? ★

(A) 직업의 현장은 직업 이동성과 거의 관련이 없다.
(B) 도시 지역에서 일하는 사람들은 직업 이동률이 더 높다.
(C) 일자리를 위해 이전해야 하는 것은 직업 이동성을 저해한다.
(D) 농촌 지역에는 취업 기회가 제한되어 있다.

Fact **(B)** -Those employed (in urban areas) are more likely to change jobs. **(C)** – the employee will not have (to relocate) his or her home (to take) another job. **(D)** - Those [who live (in non-urban areas) [who quit their jobs]] will have more difficulty (in finding) another job (due to the limited number available in the region.

03

Which of the sentences below best expresses the essential information in the highlighted sentence in the passage? Incorrect choices change the meaning in important ways or leave out essential information.

This system, which was meant to [01]limit the ability of companies to layoff employees, has also built [02]a strong sense of employee loyalty, which [03]makes it societally undesirable for employees to switch jobs without good reason.

(A) Increasing employee loyalty was ~~the main goal of the Japanese~~ "lifetime employment," which discourages companies from laying off employees.
(B) The Japanese employment loyalty scheme had ~~the unintended impact~~ of complicating the process of changing jobs and causing workers to remain in one job.
(C) [01]The Japanese scheme for ensuring that employers didn't fire employees built such [02]a strong sense of allegiance in employees that [03]job mobility began to be frowned upon.
(D) ~~Japanese companies that layoff workers violate~~ the country's "lifetime employment" system for maintaining loyal employees.

아래의 문장 중 지문 속의 음영 표시된 문장의 핵심 정보를 가장 잘 표현하고 있는 것은 무엇인가? 오답은 문장의 의미를 현저하게 바꾸거나 핵심 정보를 빠트리고 있다.

이 제도는 회사들이 직원을 해고할 수 있는 능력을 제한하기 위한 것이었으며, 직원에 대한 강한 충성심을 구축해서 사원들이 정당한 이유 없이 직장을 옮기는 것을 사회적으로 바람직하지 않게 만들었다.

(A) 직원들의 충성도를 높이는 것이 ~~일본인들의~~ '평생 고용'의 ~~주요 목표~~였는데, 이는 기업들이 직원들을 해고하는 것을 단념하게 한다.
(B) 일본인들의 일자리 충성 제도는 이직 과정을 복잡하게 만들고 노동자들이 한 직장에 남도록 하는 ~~의도치 않은 영향~~을 끼쳤다.
(C) 고용주가 종업원을 해고하지 않도록 확실히 하려는 일본의 계획은 직업 이동성을 막기 시작 할 정도로 종업원에 대한 강한 충성심을 구축했다.
(D) 근로자들을 ~~해고하는~~ 일본 기업들은 충실한 근로자들을 유지하기 위한 일본의 "평생 고용" 제도를 ~~위반한다~~.

Inference 표시된 문장에서 ⅰ) 해고를 하지 못하게 하는 제도 ⅱ) 충성심의 형성 ⅲ) 이직을 하기 어렵게 만든다는 내용이 있으므로 **(C)**에 모두 알맞게 들어가 있고 **(A)**에서는 직원들의 충성심이 주요한 요인이다. **(B)**는 의도치 않은 영향을 끼친다. **(D)**는 일본의 직원을 해고하는 회사가 평생 고용을 훼손한다는 내용 때문에 오답이다.

04

According to paragraph 3 which of the following is most likely to change jobs?

(A) ~~A married father~~ with several children.
(B) A young, single recent college graduate.
(C) A ~~Japanese~~ office worker.
(D) Someone who ~~has never left~~ a previous job.

다음 중 직업을 바꿀 가능성이 가장 높은 것은?

(A) ~~결혼해서~~ 여러 명의 자녀를 둔 ~~아버지~~
(B) 최근에 대학을 졸업한 젊은 미혼
(C) ~~일본인~~ 사무근로자
(D) 이전 직장을 ~~떠난 적이 없는~~ 사람

Fact **(A)** - familial responsibilities **(C)**- cultural norms can keep employees **(D)** - studies have shown [that 13% (of workers) [who have switched jobs more than 3 times] are responsible (for about half) (of all permanent employment separations)

05

The term "loath" in the passage is closest in meaning to:

(A) Overjoyed
(B) Likely
(C) Unwilling
(D) Unable

이 글에서 "~하기를 꺼리는"이라는 단어의 뜻과 가장 가까운 것은?

(A) 매우 기뻐하는
(B) 있을 법한
(C) 마음이 내키지 않는
(D) 할 수 없는

06 According to paragraph 4, all of the following are mentioned regarding real estate's impact on job mobility EXCEPT

(A) Rent controls have a negative effect on the job mobility rate.
(B) People receiving rental subsidies are less likely to take jobs that require them to move.
(C) High rents are ~~only common~~ in areas with ~~high average salaries~~.
(D) Hefty relocation expenses discourage people from changing jobs.

4문단에 따르면 직업 이동성에 대한 부동산의 영향과 관련하여 언급하는 것이 아닌 것은?

(A) 임대료 통제는 직업 이동률에 부정적인 영향을 미친다.
(B) 임대료 지원금을 받는 사람들은 이사해야 하는 직업을 가질 가능성이 적다.
(C) 높은 임대료는 평균 급여가 높은 지역에서만 ~~흔하다~~.
(D) 거액의 이전 비용 때문에 사람들이 직장을 옮기는 것을 단념하게 된다.

Fact **(A)** - Housing policies (in Japan and Europe) often make residential relocation an expensive prospect **(B)** - rental subsidies are more widely available [than (in the United States)], [which makes workers loath (to relocate) (for a job change)]. **(D)** - This means [that any job move [that requires relocation] could result (in an astronomical increase) (in housing cost)].

---

07 According to paragraph 5, which of the following is true regarding the effect of history on job mobility rates?

(A) ~~Younger nations~~ tend to have high job mobility than countries established long ago.
(B) Countries that were founded by immigrant populations display higher job mobility rates.
(C) ~~Former British colonies~~ have some of the ~~highest~~ job mobility rates in the world.
(D) Nations that were set up in ~~rather isolated locations~~ have lower job mobility.

5문단에 따르면, 역사가 직업 이동률에 미치는 영향에 관한 설명으로 옳은 것은?

(A) ~~젊은 국가들은~~ 오래 전에 설립된 국가들보다 직업 이동성이 높은 경향이 있다.
(B) 이민자 인구에 의해 설립된 국가들은 더 높은 직업 이동률을 보인다.
(C) ~~이전의 영국 식민지들은~~ 세계에서 ~~가장 높은~~ 직업 이동률을 가지고 있다.
(D) ~~다소 고립된 지역에~~ 세워진 국가들은 직업 이동성이 낮다.

Fact **(B)** - (In a country) [where people have previously moved thousands (of miles) (from their homeland)], pulling up stakes and moving (for another job) is much less (of an event) [than (in countries) (with more stable populations)].

---

08 Why does the author mention "employees who they constantly fear will jump ship"?

(A) To show that job mobility makes ~~overseas immigration~~ more likely.
(B) To explain the reason for one of the detriments of high job mobility.
(C) To point out that ~~the shipping industry~~ has the highest rate of job mobility.
(D) To give an example of ~~what happens when companies skimp on training~~.

글쓴이가 "계속 두려워하는 직원들이 배에서 뛰어내릴 것"을 언급하는 이유는 무엇인가?

(A) 직업 이동성이 ~~해외 이민을~~ 더 쉽게 만든다는 것을 보여주기 위해.
(B) 높은 직업의 이동성을 저해하는 요소 중 하나에 대한 이유를 설명하기 위해.
(C) ~~해운업이~~ 일자리 이동률이 가장 높다는 점을 지적하기 위해.
(D) ~~기업들이 훈련을 게을리 할 때 어떤 일이 일어나는지~~ 예를 들기 위해.

Purpose **(B)** - higher mobility (with lower costs) can cause employers (to skimp) (on training).

09

Look at the four squares [■] that indicate where the following sentence could be added to the passage.

This could cause them to need to make a costly, life-altering move to another region.

Where would the sentence best fit?

4th

네 개의 네모[■]는 다음 문장이 삽입될 수 있는 부분을 나타내고 있다.

이것은 그들이 다른 지역으로 비용이 많이 들고 생명을 바꾸는 이사를 하게 만들 수 있다.

이 문장은 어느 자리에 들어가는 것이 적절한가?

네 번째

Insertion insertion문장에서의 This가 나타내는 것이 네 번째 [■] 앞에 있는 문장의 limited number of other jobs 이기 때문에 답은 [D] 이다.

10

Directions: An introductory sentence for a brief summary of the passage is provided below. Complete the summary by selecting the THREE answer choices that express the most important ideas in the passage. Some sentences do not belong in the summary because they express ideas that are not presented in the passage or are minor ideas in the passage. **This question is worth 2 points.**

지시: 지문 요약을 위한 도입 문장이 아래에 주어져 있다. 지문의 가장 중요한 내용을 나타내는 보기 3개를 골라 요약을 완성하시오. 어떤 문장은 지문에 언급되지 않은 내용이나 사소한 정보를 담고 있으므로 요약에 포함되지 않는다. 이 문제는 2점이다.

A number of factors influence mobility in today's job market.

(B) Countries with large immigrant numbers are more likely to have higher job mobility because the population is less averse to major changes and movements. – paragraph 5

(C) It is believed that expensive real estate markets can make job changes more unlikely. – paragraph 4

(E) Personality and culture are both factors that can make job changes more or less likely depending on the individual and where they are from. – paragraph 3

오늘날 고용 시장의 이동성에 영향을 미치는 요인에는 여러 가지가 있다.

(B) 이민자 수가 많은 국가는 인구가 주요 변화와 이동을 덜 싫어하기 때문에 직업 이동성이 더 높을 가능성이 있다.

(C) 비싼 부동산 시장은 직업을 바꿀 가능성을 더 낮게 만들 수 있다고 여겨진다.

(E) 성격과 문화는 모두 개인과 출신지에 따라 직업을 바꿀 가능성이 다소 높아질 수 있는 요인이다.

(A) American job mobility has traditionally been much higher than that of other industrialized countries such as those in Europe and Japan.

(D) Japan's "lifetime employment" system guarantees workers a job ~~if they decide to leave the company~~ they have been working for.

(F) Businesses encourage job mobility because it reduces their training costs, ~~since employees that have been trained by other companies can easily be hired.~~

(A) 미국의 직업 이동성은 전통적으로 유럽과 일본과 같은 다른 선진국의 직업 이동성보다 훨씬 높았다.

(D) 일본의 "평생 고용" 제도는 근로자들이 ~~근무하던~~ 회사를 ~~떠나기로 결정하면~~ 일자리를 보장한다.

(F) 기업은 다른 회사에서 교육을 받은 직원을 쉽게 고용할 수 있기 때문에, 그들의 교육 비용을 줄이기 때문에 직업 이동성을 장려한다.

TEST 1-2   Cell Theory 셀 이론

Introduction	단락 1	세포이론 소개와 이해 시기
Point	단락 2	Cell의 유래와 현미경의 발전
Point	단락 3	세포 연구의 지연
Point	단락 4	19세기의 기술 진전
Point	단락 5	세포내의 핵의 발견
Point	단락 6	Virchow와 Pasteur의 배종설

문단주제 / 본문내용 / 해석

단락 1 — 세포이론 소개와 이해 시기

1   The three main tenets of cell theory, that cells are the basic unit of life, that all organisms are composed of cells, and that cells arise only from other cells, are some of the most basic principles in the field of biology. From this theory scientists have been able to extrapolate a great deal of other scientific knowledge. In fact, our understanding of the role of cells in sexual reproduction and the discovery of our genetic building blocks, DNA, are direct results of this. Cell theory has also allowed medical researchers to better understand illnesses, such as cancer, as well as the cause of viral and bacterial infections. While the theory is now commonly accepted, and may seem like common sense, its development took hundreds of years.

세포가 생명의 기본적인 구성 단위라는 것과 모든 생물은 세포로 구성되어져 있다는, 그리고 세포는 오직 다른 세포들로부터 발생한다는 세포 이론의 세가지 주된 이론들은 생물학의 분야에서 가장 기본적인 원리들 중 몇몇이다. 이러한 이론으로부터, 과학자들은 다른 과학적 지식의 많은 것들을 추론할 수 있어왔다. 실제로, 유성생식에서의 세포의 역할에 대한 우리의 이해와 DNA와 같은 우리의 유전적 구성 요소들의 발견은 이것의 직접적인 결과이다. 세포 이론은 의학 연구진들이 바이러스성 감염과 박테리아 세균성 감염의 원인 뿐만 아니라 암과 같은 질병을 더 잘 이해하도록 해주어 왔다. 이론이 현재는 흔히 받아들여지고 상식처럼 보일지도 모르지만, 이것의 발전은 수백년이 걸렸다.

단락 2 — Cell의 유래와 현미경의 발전

2   In fact, the earliest discoveries in the field took place in the middle of the 17th century when light microscopy began to be regularly used on living creatures. It was during this time that physicist Robert Hooke melted glass into lenses with which he could study fish scales, feathers, and the bodies of various insects, however his greatest discovery was that he noticed a series of chambers in a sample of cork oak, which he felt resembled cubicles and named "cells". Antoine van Leeuwenhoek who created even stronger lenses would later trump this discovery. Using his microscopes he studied the tartar from his teeth and noticed that it contained microscopic organisms he called "aminalcules". Over time he was able to view microorganisms, such as bacteria, that were previously unknown. Leeuwenhoek was able to accurately describe microorganisms and microscopic parts of larger organisms, including the red blood cell. He did not, unfortunately, observe the reproduction of these animalcules or

사실상, 이 분야의 가장 초기의 발견물은 광학 현미경 기법이 살아있는 생물에 정기적으로 사용되기 시작했던 17세기 중반에 나타났다. 물리학자인 Rober Hooke가 유리를 그가 물고기 비늘과, 깃털, 그리고 다양한 곤충들의 몸을 연구할 수 있었던 렌즈로 바꿨던 시기가 바로 이 시기동안 있었다. 하지만, 그의 가장 대단한 발견은 그가 좁은 방과 닮다고 느껴서 "cells"라고 칭했던 코르크 오크 나무 샘플의 일련의 공간을 알아차린 것이었다. 훨씬 더 강력한 렌즈를 만들었던 Antoine van Leeuwenhoek는 이 발견을 나중에 뛰어넘었다. 그의 현미경을 사용하여, 그는 그의 치아에 있는 치석을 연구 했고 이것이 그가 "극미 동물"라고 불렀던 미생물을 포함했다는것을 알았다. Leeuwenhoek는 적혈구 세포를 포함하여 큰 생물들의 미세한 부분과 미생물들을 정확하게 묘사할 수 있었다. 불행히도 그는 이러한 극미 동물과 생물의 번식을 관찰하지는 못했고, 따라서 그는 다른 그 당시의 사람들이 믿는것처럼 그것들이 단순히 자발적으로

organisms, so he erroneously believed, as did most others of the time, that they simply spontaneously generated.

3   Over the next two centuries a great deal of additional observations would accumulate, but a true cell theory would not emerge until the middle of the 19th century. Today scientists blame this great delay on the inferior scientific equipment, such as microscopes, and techniques, such as preserving samples of living material without destroying it, of 17th & 18th century researchers, which hindered their discoveries. In addition, the early observations of Hooke and Leeuwenhook did not address larger issues, such as cells making up all larger organisms. Hooke had simply noticed the cellular imprint, not the actual cell itself, while Leeuwenhoek observed the actual cell, but failed to provide an accurate description or categorization of its common structures.

4   As the 19th century progressed, these problems were solved through the invention of stronger microscopes, more diligent recording of findings, and increased cooperation by scientists. [■] One of the first to take advantage of these was Scottish surgeon Robert Brown, who noted in 1831 that a circular object was present in all of the orchid cells he studied. [■] Using this finding, he researched other types of cells and found the same structure, which he then posited was a common cellular feature that he named the nucleus. [■] Today, we know that the nucleus is the carrier of our genetic material. [■]

5   By the late 1830s these discoveries only increased in frequency and the cell theory truly began to take hold. In 1838 and 1839, German biologists Matthias Schleiden and Theodor Schwann respectively discovered that all plants and animals were composed of cells. The discovery of cells with nuclei in both types of organisms allowed them to conclude that the cell was the basic unit of life. It also helped them understand that microscopic bacteria had something in common with larger organisms; they were both made up of cells, which were the building blocks of all organisms. These two discoveries were the basic premises for the cell theory.

6   Later, other cellular biologists expanded on these findings. Perhaps the most important of these was German pathologist Rudolf Virchow who contributed the third tenet of the cell theory in 1855: All cells come from other living cells. This contradicted

most common understanding of the time, as it was thought that cells could spontaneously generate when a nucleus was able to form and grow the remainder of the cell body around itself. His explanation allowed later scientists to observe and describe cell division in the late 1880s. His theories also acted as the basic principle behind Pasteur's germ theory of disease, despite Virchow's personal objection to such a theory. He felt that diseases were caused by internal cellular abnormalities and not outside pathogens, which he thought were simply attracted to the abnormal cells as a habitat. While germ theory discounts this for most diseases, he did correctly suggest that abnormal cells could cause some diseases that affect the rest of the body, such as leukemia.

11 Why does the author mention "the role of cells in sexual reproduction and the discovery of our genetic building blocks, DNA"?

(A) To show two of the main points of the cell theory.
(B) To give examples of discoveries made because of cell theory.
(C) To explain how scientists discovered the basic tenets of cell theory.
(D) To offer later discoveries that validated the cell theory.

Purpose (B) - (In fact), our understanding (of the role) (of cells) (in sexual reproduction) and the discovery (of our genetic building blocks), DNA, are direct results (of this)

12 According to paragraph 1, which of the following is **NOT** a major facet of cell theory?

(A) Complex organisms are composed of cells.
(B) The basic unit of all life is the cell.
(C) All biological discoveries are cell-based.
(D) Cells are produced by previous living cells.

1문단에 따르면, 다음 중 세포 이론의 주요 측면이 아닌 것은?

(A) 복잡한 유기체는 세포로 구성되어 있다.
(B) 모든 생명체의 기본 단위는 세포이다.
(C) 모든 생물학적 발견은 세포를 기반으로 한다.
(D) 세포는 이전의 살아있는 세포에 의해 생산된다.

Fact (A) - that all organisms are composed (of cells). (B) - that cells are the basic unit (of life). (D) - that cells arise only (from other cells).

---

13 Which of the sentences below best expresses the essential information in the highlighted sentence in the passage? Incorrect choices change the meaning in important ways or leave out essential information.

It was (during this time) [that physicist (01)Robert Hooke (02)melted glass (into lenses) [(with which) he could study fish scales, feathers, and the bodies (of various insects)], (03)however his greatest discovery was [that he noticed a series (of chambers) (in a (04)sample) (of cork oak), [which he felt (05)resembled cubicles and (06)named "cells"].

(A) Cells were first discovered by a physicist who used melted glass to study the minute cellular structures of living material such as the small features of insects and fish, as well as material froms some plants, such as the cork oak.
　　<MISSING INFO>　　　　　　　　resembled 정보 ✗
(B) Robert Hooke made many important discoveries about insects, fish, and birds, however, he is best known for his botanical discoveries, such as the discovery that they also contained small chambers called cells.
　　　　　　　– made glass lenses 정보 ✗
(C) The discovery of celslular structures occurred when Robert Hooke used homemade magnifying glasses to note that scales, feathers, and insect samples all had structures that resembled the chambers of the cork oak, which he called "cells".
(D) Robert Hooke called the compartmentalized structures "cells" found in plants because he thought they bore small rooms when using the glass lenses he made to scrutinize small objects.

아래의 문장 중 지문 속의 음영 표시된 문장의 핵심 정보를 가장 잘 표현하고 있는 것은 무엇인가? 오답은 문장의 의미를 현저하게 바꾸거나 핵심 정보를 빠트리고 있다.

Cells 물리학자 Robert Hooke이 물고기의 비늘, 깃털, 그리고 다양한 곤충의 몸을 연구할 수 있는 렌즈에 유리를 녹인 것이 이 시기였다. 그러나 그의 가장 위대한 발견은 코르크 오크 표본에서 일련의 방을 발견했다는 것인데, 그는 이것이 좁은 방과 비슷하다고 느꼈고 "cell"라고 이름 붙여졌다.

(A) 녹은 유리를 사용하여 곤충과 물고기의 작은 특징과 코르크 참나무와 같은 일부 식물의 물질과 같은 살아있는 물질의 미세한 세포 구조를 연구한 물리학자에 의해 처음 발견되었다.

(B) Robert Hooke은 곤충, 물고기, 그리고 조류에 대한 많은 중요한 발견을 했지만, 세포라고 불리는 작은 방도 포함하고 있다는 발견과 같은 그의 식물학적 발견으로 가장 잘 알려져 있다.

(C) 세포 구조의 발견은 로버트 훅이 집에서 만든 확대경을 사용하여 비늘, 깃털, 곤충 표본이 모두 코르크 참나무의 방과 비슷한 구조를 가지고 있다는 것을 지적했을 때 발생했다.

(D) 로버트 훅은 작은 물체를 면밀히 살펴보기 위해 그가 만든 유리 렌즈를 사용했을 때 작은 공간을 가지고 있다고 생각했기 때문에 식물에서 발견되는 구획화된 구조를 "세포"라고 불렀다.

Highlight ⅰ)Hooke가 렌즈를 만들었던 시기 ⅱ)렌즈를 통해 다른 생물들 관찰 ⅲ)식물에서의 공간의 발견 ⅳ) 공간발견 후 cell 이라고 명명한 내용을 바탕으로 (A)에서는 ⅳ) 정보가 (B)에서는 ⅰ) 정보가 빠져 있고 (C) 에서는 생물들의 구조가 식물의 공간 구조와 닮았다는 내용이 본문에 없기 때문에 오답이다.

14 According to paragraph 3, which of the following is **NOT** a reason for the slow progress on the cell theory from the 17th-19th centuries?

(A) The equipment of the time was rudimentary and did not provide researchers enough data.
(B) It was nearly impossible to collect and store samples of living material in a way that did not damage it.
(C) ~~Most early biologists did not believe that~~ the cell was the basic building block of living organisms.
(D) Researchers did not perform enough research into, or documentation of, the cells that they were studying.

3문단에 따르면, 다음 중 17-19세기 세포이론의 발전이 더딘 이유가 아닌 것은?

(A) 그 당시의 장비는 초보적이었고 연구자들에게 충분한 데이터를 제공하지 못했다.
(B) 파손되지 않는 방법으로 살아있는 물질의 샘플을 수집하고 보관하는 것은 거의 불가능했다.
(C) ~~대부분의 초기 생물학자들은~~ 세포가 살아 있는 유기체의 기본적인 구성 요소라고 ~~믿지 않았다.~~
(D) 연구자들은 연구 중인 세포에 대한 충분한 연구나 기록을 수행하지 않았다.

Fact **(A)** - scientists blame this great delay (on the inferior scientific equipment), **(B)** - scientists blame this great delay (on the inferior techniques), (such as preserving) samples (of living material) (without destroying) it. **(D)** - the early observations (of Hooke and Leeuwenhook) did not address larger issues.

---

15 What can be inferred about Robert Brown's 1831 discovery of the cellular nucleus from paragraph 4?

(A) His discovery was possible because of scientific advances that took over the previous two centuries.
(B) Brown was ~~the first~~ researcher ~~to use a microscope to view~~ the nucleus of a cell.
(C) The discovery of the nucleus ~~disproved the earlier theory~~ of spontaneous generation of cells.
(D) Brown was the first researcher ~~to identify DNA~~ as the central component of cells that allows them to reproduce.

4문단에서 로버트 브라운이 1831년 세포핵을 발견한 것에 대해 추론할 수 있는 것은?

(A) 그의 발견은 지난 2세기를 차지했던 과학적 진보가 있었기에 가능했다.
(B) 브라운은 세포의 핵을 ~~보기 위해 현미경을 사용한 최초의~~ 연구자였다.
(C) 핵의 발견은 세포의 자발적 생성에 대한 ~~초기 이론을 반증했다.~~
(D) 브라운은 ~~DNA가~~ 세포의 번식을 가능하게 하는 중심 구성 요소라는 것을 알아낸 최초의 연구자였다.

Fact **(A)** - [As the 19th century progressed], these problems were solved (through the invention) (of stronger microscopes, more diligent recording) (of findings), and increased cooperation) (by scientists).

---

16 The term "frequency" in the passage is closest in meaning to:

(A) Irregularity
(B) Number
(C) Density
(D) Rhythm

문단의 "빈도수"라는 단어의 뜻과 가장 가까운 것은?

(A) 불규칙성
(B) 횟수
(C) 밀도
(D) 운율

17 According to paragraph 5, which of the following is true regarding the cell theory?

(A) Robert Brown developed it ~~prior to~~ the discovery of the nucleus.
(B) Researchers who found that plants and animals had similarities at the microscopic level developed it.
(C) Schleiden and Schwann proved that microscopic ~~bacteria could form larger organisms~~.
(D) ~~The three tenets of the theory were developed at the same time~~.

5문단에 따르면, 다음 중 세포 이론에 관한 설명으로 옳은 것은?

(A) 로버트 브라운은 핵의 발견 ~~이전에~~ 이론을 발전시켰다.
(B) 식물과 동물이 미시적인 수준에서 유사성을 가지고 있다는 것을 발견한 연구원들이 이론을 발전시켰다.
(C) 슐라이덴과 슈반은 미세한 ~~박테리아가 더 큰 유기체를 형성할 수 있다는 것을~~ 증명했다.
(D) ~~이론의 세 가지 교리가 동시에 발전되었다~~.

Fact (B) - It also helped them understand [that microscopic bacteria had something (in common) (with larger organisms)]; they were both made up (of cells), [which were the building blocks (of all organisms)].

---

18 According to paragraph 6, which of the following can be inferred regarding the theories of Rudolph Virchow?

(A) They were so groundbreaking that they contributed to scientific discoveries by other, later scientists in a variety of fields.
(B) They were opposed by later scientists, such as Pasteur, who ~~believed that~~ Virchow did not understand the true cause of human illnesses.
(C) They ~~caused scientists to change the main rules of theory~~, since he had proven that they were inaccurate.
(D) They proved that cells came into being when a nucleus forms in a cell body, not when a cell body forms around a nucleus, ~~as was previously believed~~.

6문단에 따르면, 다음 중 루돌프 비르쵸의 이론과 관련하여 추론할 수 있는 것은?

(A) 그것들은 매우 획기적이어서 나중에 다양한 분야의 다른 과학자들에 의한 과학적 발견에 기여했다.
(B) 그것들은 피르코가 인간의 질병의 진짜 원인을 이해하지 못한다고 믿었던 파스퇴르와 같은 후대의 과학자들에 의해 반대되었다.
(C) 그가 이론이 부정확하다는 것을 증명했기 때문에, 그들은 ~~과학자들이 이론의 주요 규칙을 바꾸도록~~ 만들었다.
(D) 그들은 ~~이전에 믿었던 것처럼~~ 핵 주위에 세포체가 형성될 때가 아니라 세포체 안에서 핵이 형성될 때 세포가 발생한다는 것을 증명했다.

Fact (A) - His explanation allowed later scientists (to observe and describe) cell division (in the late 1880s). His theories also acted (as the basic principle) (behind Pasteur's germ theory) (of disease).

---

19 Look at the four squares [■] that indicate where the following sentence could be added to the passage.

Although Brown discovered this core component of the cell, he did not know the true significance of his discovery.

Where would the sentence best fit?

3rd

네 개의 네모[■]는 다음 문장이 삽입될 수 있는 부분을 나타내고 있다.

브라운은 이 세포의 핵심 성분을 발견했지만, 자신의 발견이 갖는 진정한 의미를 알지 못했다.

이 문장은 어느 자리에 들어가는 것이 적절한가?

세 번째

Insesrtion [C] – 문장에서의 his discovery 와 관련된 문장은 세번째 [■] 앞에 있는 Using this finding, he researched other types (of cells) and found the same structure 이다.

20

Directions: An introductory sentence for a brief summary of the passage is provided below. Complete the summary by selecting the THREE answer choices that express the most important ideas in the passage. Some sentences do not belong in the summary because they express ideas that are not presented in the passage or are minor ideas in the passage. **This question is worth 2 points.**

Cells were discovered in the 1600s, but it took over 200 years before the cell theory explained their true importance and nature.

(A) Robert Hooke first described the cell during the 17th century after viewing a series of chambers in a magnified sample of the cork oak. – paragraph 2

(E) Refinements in tools and practices by the 19th century allowed scientists to more accurately and systematically study cells. – paragraph 4

(F) Our current understanding of cells states that they are the basic biological units, which make up larger organisms, and that they must propagate through division. – paragraph 5, 6

(B) Leeuwenhook ~~developed more powerful microscopes~~ so that he could confirm the earlier discoveries of Robert Hooke.   - INCORRECT

(C) Robert Brown was the first researcher to identify the central portion of the cell, which he named the nucleus.
   - MINOR

(D) Delays in developing the cell theory were caused by the rudimentary tools used in the 17th and 18th centuries and scientists' ~~insistence upon hiding their discoveries~~ - ½, ½

지시: 지문 요약을 위한 도입 문장이 아래에 주어져 있다. 지문의 가장 중요한 내용을 나타내는 보기 3개를 골라 요약을 완성하시오. 어떤 문장은 지문에 언급되지 않은 내용이나 사소한 정보를 담고 있으므로 요약에 포함되지 않는다. 이 문제는 2점이다.

세포는 1600년대에 발견되었지만, 세포 이론이 세포들의 진정한 중요성과 본질을 설명하는데 200년이 넘는 시간이 걸렸다.

(A) 로버트 훅은 코르크 오크의 확대 표본에서 일련의 방을 본 후 17세기에 처음으로 세포를 묘사했다.

(E) 19세기까지 도구와 실습의 개선은 과학자들이 세포를 더 정확하고 체계적으로 연구할 수 있게 해주었다.

(F) 세포에 대한 우리의 현재 이해는 세포들이 더 큰 유기체를 구성하는 기본적인 생물학적 단위이며 분열을 통해 번식해야 한다는 것이다.

(B) 레벤후크는 로버트 훅의 초기 발견을 확인하기 위해 ~~더 강력한 현미경을 개발했다.~~

(C) 로버트 브라운은 세포의 중심 부분을 식별한 최초의 연구자로, 그는 세포핵의 이름을 지었다.

(D) 세포이론의 발전 지연은 17세기와 18세기에 사용된 기초적인 도구들과 ~~크들의 발견을 숨기려는~~ 과학자들의 주장에 의해 야기되었다.

usherin.usher.co.kr

TEST 1-3 Mating Songs of Frogs 개구리의 짝짓기 노래

Introduction	단락 1	청각 신호의 이점
Point	단락 2	노래주머니와 암컷을 이끄는 울음소리
Point	단락 3	울음소리의 특성과 구별
Point	단락 4	울음소리에서 알 수 있는 개구리의 나이와 크기
Point	단락 5	건강과 영역 안전 정보전달
Point	단락 6	영토 설립의 수단

단락 1 — 청각 신호의 이점

1 Most species of frogs rely upon auditory signals to communicate with one another. This occurs because auditory communication is much more efficient than visual forms of communication. This is because auditory signaling, unlike visual communication, does not require a specific orientation to receive a message. The recipient need not be facing the sender to receive the signal. [■] They also allow signals to be sent over greater distances than visual communication methods. [■] Instead of being blocked by physical barriers, the auditory signal can be transmitted. [■] In fact, auditory communication allows frogs to broadcast their messages through the air, underwater, and even through the substrate. [■] Further, since most frog and toad species are nocturnal, auditory messages have the advantage of being usable even in complete darkness. Due to these advantages, male frogs have developed a complex system of communication that allows them to attract potential mates.

대부분의 개구리 종들은 서로 의사소통하기위해 청각 신호에 의존한다. 이것은 청각 소통이 시각형태의 의사소통보다 훨씬 더 효율적이기 때문에 발생한다. 이것은 시각 신호와 달리 청각 신호는 메세지를 받기 위해 특정한 방향을 요구하지 않기 때문이다. 받는 대상은 신호를 받기 위해 보내는 대상을 바라볼 필요가 없다. 그것들은 또한 시각 소통보다 더 먼 거리에 걸쳐 신호가 전송되는 것을 가능케한다. 물리적인 장`벽에 의해 막히지 않고, 청각 신호는 전달 될 수 있다. 실제로, 청각 소통은 개구리들이 공기와 수중, 심지어 기저층을 통해 그들의 메세지를 알리도록 해준다. 게다가, 대부분의 개구리와 두꺼비 종들은 야행성이기 때문에 청각 메세지는 완전한 어둠에서도 이용가능한 이점을 가진다. 이러한 장점들 때문에, 수컷 개구리들은 그들이 잠재적인 짝을 이끌 수 있는 의사소통의 복잡한 체계를 발전시켜왔다.

단락 2 — 노래주머니와 암컷을 이끄는 울음소리

2 Male frogs are able to produce these signs due to a series of adaptations, the most notable being the vocal sacs located beneath the floor of the mouth. To create their distinctive croaking sounds, frogs seal off their nostrils and mouths and use the muscles along their body wall to force air back-and-forth from the lungs through the larynx and into the vocal sac. This air movement across the larynx causes the vocal cords to vibrate and the sound is then amplified by the vocal sacs to produce a loud, clear croaking sound. These sounds attract females, which may respond by approaching the male or even by calling back to the male. This can even lead to duets between receptive couples. Unfortunately, they can also increase the mortality risk, since predators can also recognize the croaking.

수컷 개구리는 일련의 적응력 때문에 이러한 신호를 생산할 수 있는데 그중 가장 두드러진 것은 입의 바닥 아래에 위치해있는 노래주머니이다. 그들의 독특한 개굴개굴 우는 소리를 만들기 위해서 개구리는 그들의 콧구멍과 입을 봉쇄하고 그들의 체벽을 따라 있는 근육을 사용해서 폐로부터 공기를 노래주머니까지 앞뒤로 이동하게 만든다. 이러한 후두를 가로지르는 공기의 이동은 성대가 떨리는 것을 야기하고 그 소리는 그런다음 노래주머니에 의해 증폭되어서 더 크고 선명한 울음소리를 만들어 낸다. 이러한 소리는 수컷에게 접근하거나 수컷에 소리에 반응할지도 모르는 암컷을 이끈다. 이것은 심지어 수용적인 짝들 사이에서의 이중주를 이끌어 낼 수도 있다. 불행하게도, 그것들은 또한 사망의 위험을 증가시키는데, 포식자도 울음소리를 인지할 수 있기 때문이다.

3   To human ears these croaks may all sound the same, but they are actually a complex system that allows frogs to learn a great deal about the croaking frog. Perhaps the most important information that a female frog can discern from the croaking is the temporal pattern and frequency, both of which are species specific. Although some frog species can interbreed, hybridization usually produces non-viable offspring; therefore female frogs are attracted to the call of males from their species. Frogs are so attuned to differentiating calls that they can even determine if the caller is from the same region. In much the same way that human languages have developed dialects, frog calls vary slightly amongst different geographic populations and can be used to determine whether the call is from a male in a neighboring territory, or if an intruder has appeared.

4   Another key piece of information that females glean from the croaking is the relative size and age of the croaker. Many frog species undergo indeterminate growth, meaning they continuously grow larger as they age. This provides them with larger vocal sacs and larynxes that produce louder and lower tones as they age. Females, which are generally attracted to older frogs, recognize the differences in amplitude and pitch of the caller and are attracted to them. This inherent bias of female frogs toward older males is a method of selecting genetically superior mates, since their age and size indicate that the male frogs have survived environmental and predatory hazards, two traits that would be beneficial for her offspring. However, these two aspects can be ambiguous, as both temperature and distance can cause the calls of younger males to seem louder and lower than older specimens.

5   Female frogs can determine the relative health and territorial safety of the male though his calls as well. Because of the continuous muscle contractions required to push air through the vocal mechanisms, some of which make up 15% of the frogs overall mass, croaking requires a considerable energy expenditure of part of the male. Some studies show tree frog croaking is the most energy intensive activity of any vertebrate. Therefore, it can only be performed by males that are healthy enough to eschew feeding in order to search for a mate. Further, the ability to continually croak indicates to the female that the male has a secure territory in which he is safe from predation, since he is calling so much attention to himself.

USHER

단락 6
영토 설립의 수단

6 Interestingly, male-female interaction is not the only use of auditory communication in frogs. Male frogs also communicate with one another to establish a territory. This is especially important because during the mating season when the males form large 'choruses,' they learn the croaking of their direct neighbors. When they hear these croaks they are not alarmed, but when they hear an unfamiliar call they croak aggressively to warn the intruder that they are encroaching upon another frog's territory.

흥미롭게도, 수컷과 암컷의 상호작용은 개구리의 청각 의사소통의 유일한 사용은 아니다. 수컷 개구리는 또한 영토를 확립하기 위해 서로 의사소통을 한다. 이것은 수컷들이 많은 '후렴'을 형성하는 짝짓기 기간동안 그들이 직접적인 이웃의 울음소리를 배우기때문에 특히 중요하다. 그들이 이러한 울음소리를 들을 때, 그들은 불안해지지 않고 그들이 친숙한 울음소리를 들었을 때, 침입자에게 다른 개구리의 영토에 침입했다는 것을 경고하기 위해 공격적으로 울음소리를 낸다.

---

21 According to paragraph 1, which of the following is **NOT** a benefit of auditory communication?

(A) It makes communication over long distances easier.
(B) It allows communication between physically separated individuals
(C) It reduces the importance of the sense of vision.
(D) It can be used in low light situations.

1문단에 따르면, 다음 중 청각 의사소통의 이점이 아닌 것은?

(A) 장거리 통신을 더 쉽게 해준다.
(B) 그것은 신체적으로 분리된 개인들 간의 의사소통을 가능하게 한다.
(C) 시각의 중요성을 감소시킨다.
(D) 조도가 낮은 상황에서 사용될 수 있다.

Fact (A) - They also allow signals (to be sent) (over greater distances) (than visual communication methods). (B) - (Instead of being blocked) (by physical barriers), the auditory signal can be transmitted. (D) - auditory messages have the advantage (of being) usable even (in complete darkness).

---

22 Why does the author mention that "hybridization usually produces non-viable offspring"?

(A) To give an example of a reason that male frogs croak in order to attract females.
(B) To show the reader that there is a biological reason that female frogs only understand croaks from their own species.
(C) To help readers understand why female frogs are attracted to the croaking of males.
(D) To explain why recognizing the species is the most important aspect of discerning the male's croaking.

저자가 "혼성화는 보통 생존할 수 없는 새끼를 낳는다"를 언급한 이유는?

(A) 수컷 개구리가 암컷을 유혹하기 위해 우는 이유를 예로 들기 위해
(B) 암컷 개구리가 자신의 종에서 나는 울음소리만 이해하는 생물학적인 이유가 있다는 것을 독자들에게 보여주기 위해
(C) 암컷 개구리가 수컷의 울음소리에 끌리는 이유를 독자들이 이해할 수 있도록 돕기 위해
(D) 왜 종을 인식하는 것이 수컷의 울음소리를 구별하는 가장 중요한 측면인지 설명하기 위해

Purpose Perhaps the most important information although some frog species can interbreed], hybridization usually produces non-viable offspring; therefore female frogs are attracted (to the call) (of males) (from their species).

23 According to paragraph 3, which of the following is true regarding the pattern of croaks made by male frogs?

(A) Species of related frogs have similar patterns, which ~~leads to interbreeding~~.
(B) Frogs ~~use~~ different patterns ~~to communicate with frogs from other areas~~.
(C) Female frogs ~~do not seem to be able to recognize~~ patterns in the croaking.
(D) Distinctive patterns increase the reproductive efficiency of the frog species.

3문단에 따르면, 다음 중 수컷 개구리가 짖는 패턴에 대한 설명으로 옳은 것은?

(A) 근연종 개구리들은 비슷한 패턴을 가지고 있어서 ~~아종교배를 하게 된다~~.
(B) 개구리는 다른 지역에서 온 개구리들과 ~~의사소통하기 위해~~ 다른 패턴을 사용한다
(C) 암컷 개구리들은 울음소리의 패턴을 인식하지 ~~못하는 것 같아 보인다~~.
(D) 독특한 패턴은 개구리 종의 생식 효율을 높인다.

> **Fact** Although some frog species can interbreed], hybridization usually produces non-viable offspring; therefore female frogs are attracted (to the call) (of males) (from their species).

---

24 Which of the sentences below best expresses the essential information in the highlighted sentence in the passage? Incorrect choices change the meaning in important ways or leave out essential information.

This inherent $^{(01)}$bias of female frogs toward older males is a $^{(02)}$method of selecting genetically superior mates, since their $^{(03)}$age and size indicate that the male frogs have survived environmental and predatory hazards, two $^{(04)}$traits that would be beneficial for her offspring

(A) Female frogs select older male partners because they ~~produce larger offspring~~ that will be more able to endure risks and predators in the natural environment.
(B) To ensure that her brood has genetic advantages, female frogs are innately attracted to older males whose ages denote that they have survived danger in the ecosystem.
(C) Older ~~male frogs have been~~ able to withstand environmental hazards, which ~~gives them an inherent genetic advantage~~ that attracts female frogs to them.
(D) To have stronger offspring, ~~avoiding~~ predators and other threats in the natural environment ~~makes~~ males more attractive to females.

아래의 문장 중 지문 속의 음영 표시된 문장의 핵심 정보를 가장 잘 표현하고 있는 것은 무엇인가? 오답은 문장의 의미를 현저하게 바꾸거나 핵심 정보를 빠트리고 있다.

암컷 개구리의 나이와 크기가 수컷 개구리가 환경적, 포식적 위험에서 살아남았다는 것을 나타내기 때문에 나이든 수컷 개구리는 유전적으로 우월한 짝을 고르는 방법이다.

(A) 암컷 개구리들은 자연환경에서 위험과 포식자를 더 잘 견딜 수 있는 ~~더 큰 새끼를 낳기~~ 때문에 나이 든 수컷 파트너를 선택한다.
(B) 암컷 개구리들이 유전적 이점을 갖도록 하기 위해, 암컷 개구리들은 나이가 많은 수컷들에게 선천적으로 끌린다.
(C) 나이든 수컷 개구리는 환경적 위험에도 견딜 수 있으며, 이는 암컷 개구리를 유혹하는 ~~유전적 이점을 부여한다~~.
(D) 자연환경에서 포식자와 다른 위협을 ~~피하는 것은~~ 수컷이 암컷에게 더 ~~매력적이게 만든다~~.

> **Highlight** ⅰ) 나이든 수컷을 선택하는 암컷의 내재된 성향 ⅱ) 수컷의 나이가 크기가 위험으로부터 살아남았다는 표시 ⅲ) 두 가지 특성이 자손에게 이로울 수 있다 총 세가지 정보 중 **(A), (C), (D)** 모두 틀린 내용과 ⅰ)의 정보가 누락되어 있어서 오답이다.

25
What can be inferred about the croaks of young frogs from paragraph 4?

(A) They are generally higher than older frogs because ~~they need to travel longer~~, since younger frog territories are generally farther from the population center.
(B) They can sometime confuse female frogs and lead them to mate with younger males.
(C) They sometimes ~~mimic those of older frogs~~ in order to disguise their relative youth and inexperience.
(D) They do not initially sound like those of older males since it ~~takes time~~ for them to learn ~~the most productive amplitude and pitch~~.

4문단에 나오는 어린 개구리들의 울음소리에 대해 추론될 수 있는 것은?

(A) 어린 개구리의 영역이 개체수 중심에서 일반적으로 더 멀어서 ~~그들은 더 오래 이동해야~~ 하기 때문에, 일반적으로 나이가 든 개구리보다 높다.
(B) 그들은 때때로 암컷 개구리를 혼란스럽게 할 수 있고 어린 수컷과 짝짓기를 하도록 이끌 수 있다.
(C) 상대적으로 젊고 경험이 없는 개구리를 감추기 위해 ~~나이 든 개구리의 흉내를 내기도~~ 한다.
(D) 가장 생산적인 진폭과 음높이를 배우는 데 ~~시간이 걸려서~~ 때문에 처음에는 나이 든 남성의 소리처럼 들리지 않는다.

Inference However, these two aspects can be ambiguous, [as both temperature and distance can cause the calls (of younger males) (to seem) louder and lower (than older specimens)].

26
The term "eschew" in the passage is closest in meaning to:

(A) Embrace
(B) Postpone
(C) Forgo
(D) Dislike

문단의 "피하다, 삼가다"라는 단어의 뜻과 가장 가까운 것은?

(A) 포용하다, 받아들이다.
(B) 미루다, 연기하다.
(C) 포기하다.
(D) 싫어하다.

27
According to paragraph 5, which of the following is **NOT** true regarding frogs that croak during mating season?

(A) They ~~wander around the area croaking until they find a receptive female~~.
(B) Their continued croaking is a sign that they are relatively safe.
(C) They expend a great deal of energy to produce the noises.
(D) They do not hunt for food while they are croaking.

5문단에 따르면, 다음 중 짝짓기 철에 울부짖는 개구리에 대한 설명으로 옳지 않은 것은?

(A) 그들은 ~~수용적인 암컷을 찾을 때까지 개굴거리며 주변을 배회한다~~.
(B) 그들이 계속해서 울부짖는 것은 그들이 상대적으로 안전하다는 신호이다.
(C) 그들은 소음을 내기 위해 많은 에너지를 소비한다.
(D) 그들은 울음소리를 내는 동안 먹이를 사냥하지 않는다.

Fact (B)-Female frogs can determine the relative health and territorial safety (of the male) (through his calls as well. (C)- Some studies show [tree frog croaking is the most energy intensive activity (of any vertebrate)] (D)- Therefore, it can only be performed (by males) [that are healthy enough (to eschew) feeding (in order to search) (for a mate)].

28
According to paragraph 6, which of the following can be inferred regarding the frog chorus?

(A) ~~Female frogs join the chorus~~ when they have found a suitable mate.
(B) ~~Members of the chorus~~ learn to croak from the ~~other males~~ in adjacent territories.
(C) They do not display aggressive behavior to other frogs within the chorus.
(D) The chorus is generally set up ~~to protect the territory of the local males~~.

다음 중 개구리 합창과 관련하여 추론할 수 있는 것은?

(A) ~~암컷 개구리들은~~ 적당한 짝을 찾으면 ~~합창단에 합류한다~~.
(B) ~~합창단의 단원들은~~ 인접한 지역에 있는 ~~다른 남성들~~로부터 울음소리를 배운다.
(C) 그들은 합창단 내의 다른 개구리들에게 공격적인 행동을 보이지 않는다.
(D) 합창단은 일반적으로 ~~지역 남성의 영역을 보호하기 위해~~ 구성된다.

Inference [When they hear these croaks] they are not alarmed, but [when they hear an unfamiliar call] they croak aggressively (to warn) the intruder [that they are encroaching (upon another frog's territory)].
This is especially important [because (during the mating season) [when the males form large 'choruses],' they learn the croaking (of their direct neighbors)].

---

29 Look at the four squares [■] that indicate where the following sentence could be added to the passage.

This ability allows frogs to broadcast their messages no matter where they are located.

Where would the sentence best fit?

3rd

네 개의 네모[■]는 다음 문장이 삽입될 수 있는 부분을 나타내고 있다.

이 능력은 개구리가 어디에 있든 그들의 메시지를 방송할 수 있게 해준다.

이 문장은 어느 자리에 들어가는 것이 적절한가?

세 번째

Insertion This ability가 나타내는 것은 청각 신호의 이점이고 위치의 제약이 없다는 내용의 부연설명으로 in fact, 예시 문장의 공기와 물, 기저층에 대한 내용이 나오기 때문에 정답은 **[C]** 이다.

---

30 Directions: An introductory sentence for a brief summary of the passage is provided below. Complete the summary by selecting the THREE answer choices that express the most important ideas in the passage. Some sentences do not belong in the summary because they express ideas that are not presented in the passage or are minor ideas in the passage. **This question is worth 2 points.**

지시: 지문 요약을 위한 도입 문장이 아래에 주어져 있다. 지문의 가장 중요한 내용을 나타내는 보기 3개를 골라 요약을 완성하시오. 어떤 문장은 지문에 언급되지 않은 내용이나 사소한 정보를 담고 있으므로 요약에 포함되지 않는다. 이 문제는 2점이다.

> **Although frog croaking seems basic to our ears, it is a complex communication system.**
>
> (A) Frogs utilize a system of auditory communication due to its ability to be transmitted over long distances, through barriers, and in the darkness. - paragraph 1
> (C) Croaking transmits information regarding the size and age of the frog croaking, both of which are important factors in mate selection for female frogs.
>   - paragraph 3, 4
> (F) Differences in croaks allow frogs to identify members of their chorus and outsiders that may be attempting to horn in to their territory. - paragraph 6

> **개구리 울음소리는 우리 귀에 기본처럼 보이지만, 복잡한 의사소통 체계이다.**
>
> (A) 개구리는 먼 거리, 장벽, 어둠 속에서 전달되는 능력 때문에 청각 의사소통 체계를 이용한다.
>
> (C) 울음소리는 개구리 울음소리의 크기와 나이에 관한 정보를 전달하는데, 둘 다 암컷 개구리의 짝을 선택하는 데 중요한 요소이다.
>
> (F) 울음소리의 차이로 인해 개구리들은 그들의 영역에 들어오려고 하는 합창단원과 외부인을 식별할 수 있다.

(B) Despite auditory communication requiring great energy expenditure, male frogs cannot forage for good while they are engaged in croaking. - MINOR - 5
(D) Female frogs are naturally attracted to older males because they ~~tend to have larger territories~~ that can support more offspring. - ½, ½
(E) ~~Most frog~~ species ~~cannot recognize~~ the croaking patterns of other species, so they often interbreed, which causes hybridization and lower reproductive efficiency.
                                                - INCORRECT

(B) 청각적 의사소통이 많은 에너지를 소모함에도 불구하고, 수컷 개구리는 개굴개굴 울면서 먹이를 영원히 구할 수 없다.
(D) 암컷 개구리는 더 많은 새끼를 낳을 수 있는 ~~더 큰 영역을 가진 경향이 있기~~ 때문에 자연스럽게 나이든 수컷에게 끌린다.
(E) 대부분의 개구리 종은 다른 종의 곡예 패턴을 인식할 ~~수 없기 때문에~~ 잡종 교배와 생식능력 저하의 원인이 된다.

USHER

iBT TOEFL
INTERMEDIATE READING 02
TEST 2

답안 및 취약 유형 분석표

해석·해설

답안 및 문제 유형 분석표

TEST 2-1

01 (A) Inference
02 (D) Vocabulary
03 (B) Purpose
04 (C) Highlight
05 (D) Fact
06 (A) Fact
07 (B) Inference
08 (D) Fact
09 2nd ■ Insertion
10 (B), (C), (F) Summary

TEST 2-2

11 (A) Inference
12 (B) Fact
13 (D) Vocabulary
14 (C) Highlight
15 (C) Fact
16 (D) Fact
17 (A) Inference
18 (B) Purpose
19 3rd ■ Insertion
20 (B), (E), (F) Summary

TEST 2-3

21 (C) Purpose
22 (A) Highlight
23 (C) Fact
24 (B) Inference
25 (B) Vocabulary
26 (D) Fact
27 (B) Fact
28 (D) Inference
29 4th ■ Insertion
30 (B), (C), (F) Summary

각 문제 유형별 맞춘 개수를 아래에 적어 보세요.

유형	맞춘 답의 개수	정답률
단어 (Vocabulary)	/ 3	정답률: %
사실 확인 문제 (Fact)	/ 9	정답률: %
지시어 찾기 (Reference)	/ 0	정답률: %
끼워 넣기 (Insertion)	/ 3	정답률: %
문장 변환문제 (Highlight)	/ 3	정답률: %
목적 (Purpose)	/ 3	정답률: %
추론 (Inference)	/ 6	정답률: %
단락 요약 (Summary / Category Chart)	/ 3	정답률: %
전체	/ 30	정답률: %

※ 자신이 취약한 유형은 READING STRATEGIES를 통해 다시 한번 점검하시기 바랍니다. (p.44)

TEST 2-1 Milankovitch Cycles and Glaciation
밀란코비치 사이클스 앤 빙하화

Introduction	단락 1	최신세 기간의 빙결과 원인 분석 불가
Point	단락 2	James Croll의 연구와 Milankovitch의 방정식
Point	단락 3	Milankovitch 주기의 세 가지 기반
Point	단락 4	연대기의 발전과 표본 채취 이후 정확도 증명
Point	단락 5	원인 규명의 불확실과 다른 요인
Point	단락 6	냉각 요소의 탐색과 CO_2 수준과의 상관 관계 확인

문단주제	본문내용	해석
단락 1 최신세 기간의 빙결과 원인 분석 불가	**1** Scientists have pieced together a relatively detailed timeline of the twenty glacial cycles that took place during the Pleistocene Epoch (10,000-2,000,000 years ago). During these frigid periods, glaciers up to 3,900m thick covered 30% of Earth's surface. These were most prevalent in the higher-latitude regions of both hemispheres, which were covered by glaciers as far south as Germany in the Northern Hemisphere and as far north as the Andes in the Southern Hemisphere. However, despite 100+ years of research into these periods, researchers are unable to explain their cause.	과학자들은 대략 만년에서 20만년 전인 최신세 동안 발생했던 스무 번의 빙하 주기의 상대적으로 상세한 연대표를 종합해왔다. 이러한 추운 기간 동안, 최대 3,900미터만큼 두꺼운 빙하는 지구 표면의 30%를 덮었다. 이러한 현상들은 남반구의 안데스와 같은 먼 북쪽과 남반구의 독일만큼 먼 남쪽까지 빙하로 덮여 있는 두 반구의 높은 위도 지역에서 가장 만연했다. 그러나, 이러한 기간의 100년 이상에 걸친 연구에도 불구하고, 연구자들은 그들의 원인을 설명할 수 없었다.
단락 2 James Croll의 연구와 Milankovitch의 방정식	**2** Over the years, diverse factors, such as continental location, oceanic circulation and solar energy fluctuation, have been cited as possible causes of these glaciations. One of the most interesting was put forth by Scottish scientist James Croll who used the previously known fact that cyclic changes in Earth's orbit affect how solar radiation impacts Earth's surface to deduce that they could also affect the global climate. Using this theory, Yugoslavian mathematician Milutin Milankovitch developed an equation that showed how these cyclic changes in Earth's orbit, now known as Milankovitch cycles, could cause climatic changes and lead to continental glaciations.	수 년간, 대륙의 위치와 해수의 순환, 그리고 태양 에너지의 변동과 같은 다양한 요소들이 이러한 빙결의 가능한 원인들로 언급되어왔다. 가장 흥미로운 것들 중 하나는 스코틀랜드 과학자인 James Croll에 의해서 제시되었는데, 지구의 주기적 변화가 어떻게 태양 복사열이 지구의 표면에 영향을 끼치는지에 대한 이전에 알려진 사실을 그것들이 또한 지구 기후에 영향을 끼친다는 것을 추론하는데 사용했다. 이러한 이론을 사용하여 유고슬라비아의 수학자인 Milutin Milankovitch는 밀란코비치 주기라고 알려진 이러한 주기적인 지구 궤도의 변화가 기후변화와 대륙의 빙결을 어떻게 야기할 수 있는지를 보여주는 방정식을 발전시켰다.
단락 3 Milankovitch 주기의 세 가지 기반	**3** Milankovitch based his equation on three cyclic changes in Earth's position relative to the Sun that he thought could collectively have an effect on the solar radiation that is incident on Earth's surface: eccentricity, obliquity, and precession. The first of these, eccentricity, is the elliptical variation in the Earth's orbit that sometimes brings it closer to the Sun and slightly changes every	Milankovitch는 그의 방정식을 지구 표면의 사건인 태양 복사열에 집합적으로 영향을 끼친다고 그가 생각한 태양과 상대적인 지구의 위치에서의 세 가지 주기적인 변화에 기반을 두었고 그것은 이심률, 황도 경사각 그리고 세차 운동이었다. 그 중 첫번째인 이심률은 가끔씩 태양과 가깝게 만드는 지구의 궤도의 타원형의 변화이고 그것은 9만 6천년의 매

revolution in a 96,000-year cycle. The second of these, obliquity, is concerned with the annual changes in the tilt of Earth's axis that causes seasonal variation. As this tilt changes, in a 41,000-year cycle, the temperature difference between winter and summer becomes extreme and more mild as the tilt is respectively higher or lower. The final of the Milankovitch cycles, precession, is the circular wobble that Earth performs on its axis every 12,700 years, in a movement that resembles the wobble of a slowly moving top. Although these three cycles do not affect the amount of solar radiation that reaches the Earth, they greatly affect its distribution. Milankovitch's equation showed that every 40,000 years these three cycles would perfectly synchronize in a way that would greatly reduce the difference between winter and summer temperatures and prevent the winter ice from melting during the summer, thereby allowing it to build up, and causing an overall glacial growth.

4   Despite developing this theory in the 1920s, Milankovitch was limited in his ability to test it extensively, since the timeline of the Pleistocene Epoch temperature changes necessary for testing it was not developed until the 1970s. After the development of this new chronology, a correlation between Milankovitch cycles and the major climatic changes of the last 65 million years became clearer. Further, core samples taken from the deep-sea floor proved that Milankovitch's equation was incredibly accurate in predicting climate changes over the last few hundred thousand years, including the end of the Pleistocene Epoch.

5   [■] Unfortunately, this accuracy and correlation does not fully explain the cause of glaciation throughout history. [■] If Milankovitch's explanation was accurate, it would require glaciations to have occurred regularly throughout Earth's history, yet they appear to have occurred only rarely. [■] This has led scientists to determine that there must be another factor that works with the Milankovitch cycles to cause glaciations. [■] When this mystery factor has sufficiently lowered the average temperature, the cyclic variations of solar radiation caused by the Milankovitch Cycles can throw Earth into and out of glacial periods with the regularity predicted by the Milankovitch equation.

6   In the quest to discover this mystery-cooling factor, a number of possibilities have been suggested. One of these is that changes in the Sun's luminosity have allowed fluctuations in the solar energy that reaches Earth. However, this is highly unlikely, since

it is now believed that the Sun has steadily become stronger over time. Another possible cause of lower temperatures was volcanic dust in the atmosphere shielding Earth from solar radiation and causing temperatures to drop. This is also rather unlikely, since the beginning of the last glaciation does not correspond with known major eruptions. A more recent theory states that differences in atmospheric carbon dioxide (CO_2) have caused temperature fluctuations on Earth. Since CO_2 traps radiation in the atmosphere, periods of decreased atmospheric CO_2 results in lower temperatures on Earth's surface, allowing solar radiation to escape. This is especially attractive to researchers, because studies of the Greenland ice cap show that the number of CO_2 bubbles found in the different strata changes depending on when the ice formed. Samples from periods known to be warmer show higher CO_2 levels, while colder periods have significantly less, thereby confirming the correlation between CO_2 levels and Earth's temperature.

01
What can be inferred from paragraph 1 about the glaciations of the Pleistocene Epoch?

(A) The frigid temperatures of the last glaciation had relatively little effect on the regions surrounding Earth's equator.
(B) During the glaciations, the entire Earth was exposed to frigid temperatures that formed large glaciers.
(C) Geologists and climatologists have pieced together a great deal of information related to the causes of glaciations.
(D) The glaciers that covered the Northern Hemisphere were much thicker than those in the Southern Hemisphere.

Inference These were most prevalent (in the higher-latitude regions) (of both hemispheres).

02
The term "incident" in the passage is closest in meaning to:

(A) Concentrated
(B) Insinuated
(C) Burning
(D) Striking

03

Why does the author mention "a slowly moving top"?

(A) To help ~~children understand~~ the theory by explaining it with a toy.
(B) To give the reader a common image that can help them understand an abstract idea.
(C) To show that ~~Earth's rotation~~ is slowing as it continues to wobble on its axis.
(D) To imply that Earth will eventually ~~stop wobbling and fall to one side~~.

저자가 "천천히 움직이는 팽이"를 언급한 이유는?

(A) 장난감으로 이론을 설명함으로써 ~~아이들의 이해를~~ 돕기 위해서
(B) 추상적인 생각을 이해하는 데 도움을 줄 수 있는 공통의 이미지를 독자에게 주기 위해서
(C) 지구가 축에서 계속 흔들리면서 ~~자전~~ 속도가 느려지고 있다는 것을 보여주기 위해서
(D) 지구가 결국 흔들림을 멈추고 한쪽으로 떨어진다는 것을 암시하기 위해서

Purpose The final (of the Milankovitch cycles), precession, is the circular wobble [that Earth performs (on its axis) every 12,700 years, (in a movement) [that resembles the wobble (of a slowly moving top)].

04

Which of the sentences below best expresses the essential information in the highlighted sentence in the passage? Incorrect choices change the meaning in important ways or leave out essential information.

(01)Milankovitch's equation showed [that (02)every 40,000 years these (03)three cycles would perfectly synchronize (in a way) [that would greatly (04)reduce the difference (between winter and summer temperatures) and prevent the winter ice (from melting) (during the summer)], thereby (05)allowing it (to build up), and causing an overall glacial growth.

(A) The glaciations that occur every 40,000 years were shown by the Milankovitch equation which showed how the temperature differential between summer and winter allowed more ice growth ~~because of higher winter temperatures~~.
(B) Lower overall temperatures prevented ice from melting during the summer 40,000 years ago, which allowed increased glacial growth to occur, just as ~~was predicted by~~ the equation Milankovitch ~~developed to explain~~ changes in the three aspects of Earth's orbit.
(C) Milankovitch developed an equation showing that glaciations occurred when the glaciers grew as the seasonal temperature gradient decreased and they remained intact through the summer when the three cycles of Earth's orbit line up every 40,000 years.
(D) The three Milankovitch cycles equalize every 40,000 years in such a way that allows glacial growth ~~because~~ the summer temperatures are closer to the winter temperatures, so the glaciers do not melt during the summer.

아래의 문장 중 지문 속의 음영 표시된 문장의 핵심 정보를 가장 잘 표현하고 있는 것은 무엇인가? 오답은 문장의 의미를 현저하게 바꾸거나 핵심 정보를 빠트리고 있다.

밀란코비치의 방정식은 매 4만 년마다 이 세 번의 순환이 완전히 동기화되어 겨울과 여름의 온도 차이를 크게 줄이고, 여름 동안 얼음이 녹는 것을 방지하여, 빙하가 축적되고, 전반적인 빙하의 성장을 야기한다는 것을 보여주었다.

(A) 매 4만 년마다 일어나는 빙하는 밀란코비치 방정식으로 예측되었는데, 밀란코비치 방정식은 여름과 겨울의 온도 차이가 ~~겨울의 높은 기온으로~~ 인해 얼음 성장이 어떻게 가능했는지를 보여주었다.
(B) 전반적인 낮은 온도가 4만년 전 여름 동안 얼음이 녹지 않도록 막아서 빙하의 성장이 증가하도록 만들었는데, 이것은 밀란코비치가 지구 궤도의 세 가지 ~~변화를 설명하기 위해 개발한~~ 방정식으로 인해 예상이 되었다.
(C) 밀란코비치는 매 4만년 마다 지구 궤도의 3주기가 일치할 때 계절적 기온 변화도 감소함에 따라, 얼음이 여름까지 온전하게 남아서 빙하가 커지면서 빙결이 일어난다는 것을 보여주는 방정식을 개발하였다.
(D) 밀란코비치 3주기는 여름 기온이 겨울 온도에 가까워져 여름에 빙하가 녹지 않기 ~~때문에~~ 빙하의 성장이 가능하도록 4만년마다 균일화된다.

Highlight i) 밀란코비치 방정식이 이러한 세 가지 주기가 완벽히 동시에 발생한다는 것을 증명 ii) 겨울과 여름사이의 온도차를 줄이고 겨울기간의 얼음이 여름에 녹지 않게 된 것과 iii) 얼음이 쌓이게 되어 전반적인 빙결을 야기했다는 정보를 기반으로 **(A), (B), (D)** 모두 틀린 내용이 포함되어 있어서 오답이다.

05

According to paragraph 3, which of the following is NOT true about the Milankovitch Cycles?

(A) Eccentricity in Earth's orbit can cause it to be closer to the Sun during some of its annual orbits.
(B) The reduction in the obliquity of Earth's axis causes fewer extreme temperatures in winter and summer.
(C) Precession is the most rapid of the Milankovitch cycles that affect Earth's orientation with regard to the sun during its orbit.
(D) Variations in certain aspects of Earth's orbit ~~cause differences in the amount~~ of solar radiation that reaches Earth's surface.

3문단에 따르면, 밀란코비치 사이클에 대한 설명으로 옳지 않은 것은?

(A) 지구 궤도의 이심률로 인해 이 별은 태양과 가까워질 수 있다.
(B) 지구 축의 경사도의 감소는 겨울과 여름에 더 적은 극단적 온도를 야기한다.
(C) 세차운동은 밀란코비치 주기 중 가장 빠른 주기이며, 공전 중 태양과 관련하여 지구의 방향에 영향을 미친다.
(D) 지구 궤도의 특정 측면에서의 변화는 지구 표면에 도달하는 태양 복사량의 ~~차이를 야기한다~~.

Fact **(A)** - The first (of these), eccentricity, is the elliptical variation (in the Earth's orbit) [that sometimes brings it closer (to the Sun). **(B)** - The second (of these), obliquity, is concerned (with the annual changes) (in the tilt) (of Earth's axis) [that causes seasonal variation]. [As this tilt changes], (in a 41,000-year cycle), the temperature difference (between winter and summer) becomes extreme. **(C)** The final of the Milankovitch cycles, precession, is the circular wobble that Earth performs on its axis every 12,700 years, in a movement that resembles the wobble of a slowly moving top. **(D)** [Although these three cycles do not affect the amount (of solar radiation) [that reaches the Earth]], they greatly affect its distribution.

06

According to paragraph 4, which of the following is true regarding the timeline of the Pleistocene Epoch?

(A) Milankovitch was never able to verify his theory because he did not have enough information about the climate of the Pleistocene Epoch.
(B) ~~Scientists were unaware of existence of glaciations~~ during the Pleistocene Epoch until the 1970s.
(C) ~~The dawn~~ of the Pleistocene Epoch 65 million years ago ~~was verified~~ by Milankovitch's equation.
(D) ~~Core samples~~ from the sea floor ~~confirmed the timeline~~ of the Pleistocene Epoch that Milankovitch had put forth.

4문단에 따르면, 최신세의 연대표에 관해 다음 중 옳은 것은?

(A) 밀란코비치는 플라이스토세 시대의 기후에 대한 충분한 정보를 가지고 있지 않았기 때문에 그의 이론을 증명할 수 없었다.
(B) ~~과학자들은~~ 1970년대까지 최신세 기간동안 ~~빙하의 존재를 알지 못했다~~.
(C) 6500만년 전의 최신세의 ~~여명은~~ 밀란코비치 방정식에 의해 ~~증명되었다~~.
(D) 해저에서 채취한 ~~핵심 샘플은~~ 밀란코비치가 제시한 최신세의 ~~연대표를 확인시켜~~ 주었다.

Fact (Despite developing) this theory (in the 1920s), Milankovitch was limited (in his ability) (to test) it extensively, [since the timeline (of the Pleistocene Epoch temperature changes) necessary (for testing) it was not developed (until the 1970s)].

07

What can be inferred about the accuracy of the Milankovitch equation from paragraph 5?

(A) Inaccuracies in the Milankovitch equation caused more recent scientists ~~to disregard his findings~~.
(B) The equation that Milankovitch developed overestimated the frequency of large scale glaciations throughout history.
(C) ~~The mystery-cooling feature~~ Milankovitch included in his equation ~~caused~~ inaccuracies in the prediction of past glacial periods.
(D) Milankovitch's equation was ~~only accurate for recent glaciations~~ and could not be used to predict glaciations before the Pleistocene Epoch.

5문단에서 밀란코비치 방정식의 정확성에 대해 추론할 수 있는 것은?

(A) 밀란코비치 방정식의 부정확성은 더 최근의 과학자들이 ~~그의 발견을 무시하도록~~ 만들었다.
(B) 밀란코비치가 개발한 방정식은 역사상 대규모 빙하의 빈도를 과대평가했다.
(C) 밀란코비치 방정식에 포함된 ~~미스터리한 냉각 특성~~ 은 과거 빙하기의 예측에 부정확함을 ~~야기했다~~.
(D) 밀란코비치의 방정식은 ~~최근의 빙하에서만 정확했으며~~ 최신세 이전에는 빙하를 예측하는 데 사용할 수 없었다.

Inference If Milankovitch's explanation was accurate, it would require glaciations (to have occurred) regularly (throughout Earth's history), yet they appear (to have occurred) only rarely.

08

According to paragraph 6, which of the following is true regarding the search for the mystery-cooling factor?

(A) Scientists have determined that ~~an increase in CO_2 levels~~ in the environment caused the ~~glaciations~~ of the Pleistocene Epoch.
(B) ~~Volcanic eruptions~~ likely clouded the environment and trapped colder temperatures in Earth's environment.
(C) Earth's surface has become warmer since the last glaciation due to an increase in the ~~Sun's luminosity~~ over time.
(D) Scientists have found a correspondence between the fluctuations in environmental CO_2 levels and the temperatures of the Earth's surface.

6문단에 따르면, 다음 중 미스터리한 냉각 요소 탐구에 관한 설명 중 옳은 것은?

(A) 과학자들은 환경의 ~~CO_2 수치의 증가가~~ 최신세의 빙하를 일으켰다고 결론내렸다.
(B) ~~화산 폭발은~~ 환경을 흐리게 하고 지구의 환경에 더 추운 온도를 가두었을 것이다.
(C) 지구의 표면은 시간이 지남에 따라 ~~밝기가 증가하여~~ 마지막 빙하 이후 따뜻해졌다.
(D) 과학자들은 환경의 이산화탄소 수치의 변동과 지구 표면의 온도 사이의 관련성을 발견했다.

Fact Samples (from periods) known (to be) warmer show higher CO_2 levels, [while colder periods have significantly less], thereby confirming the correlation (between CO_2 levels and Earth's temperature).

09

Look at the four squares [■] that indicate where the following sentence could be added to the passage.

This can be understood if one looks back **at Earth's climate since its formation** approximately 4.5 billion years ago.

Where would the sentence best fit?

2nd

네 개의 네모[■]는 다음 문장이 삽입될 수 있는 부분을 나타내고 있다.

이것은 약 45억년 전 지구의 기후를 되돌아보면 이해될 수 있다.

이 문장은 어느 자리에 들어가는 것이 적절한가?

두번째

Insertion insertion문장에서의 This의 주장이 앞에 나와야 하고 뒷 문장에는 Earth's climate since its formation이 언급되어야 하기 때문에 시작점부터 발생해온 순서를 나열한 **[B]**의 공간이 적절하다.

Directions: An introductory sentence for a brief summary of the passage is provided below. Complete the summary by selecting the THREE answer choices that express the most important ideas in the passage. Some sentences do not belong in the summary because they express ideas that are not presented in the passage or are minor ideas in the passage. **This question is worth 2 points.**

Scientists such as Milankovitch have long tried to explain the glaciations of the Pleistocene Epoch.

(B) Milankovitch furthered claims by James Croll that cyclical changes in Earth's orbit led to environmental changes that allowed Pleistocene Glaciations to occur. – paragraph 2

(C) Milankovitch used variations in Earth's orbit, which bring it closer to the sun, and the wobble and tilt of its axis to determine that at certain times Earth's seasons are milder, making glaciations more likely. – paragraph 3

(F) Modern scientists believe that Milankovitch Cycles do not cause glaciations, but they coincide with another factor that lowers overall temperatures and together they cause them. – paragraph 6

(A) Scientists previously ~~believed that dust~~ produced by volcanic eruptions blocked out the sun's solar energy and led to a rapid cooling of the planet, resulting in glaciations.

(D) Milankovitch lacked the scientific knowledge and tools to test his theory, so it remained unconfirmed for more than fifty years. – MINOR

(E) The theory proposed by Milankovitch showed that the Earth has undergone a period of glaciation every 40,000 years since the end of the Pleistocene Epoch. – MINOR

usherin.usher.co.kr

TEST 2-2 The Making of Calendars 달력 만들기

Introduction	단락 1	달력 발명 이전의 기록
Point	단락 2	날씨에 따른 결함
Point	단락 3	단위의 불일치와 Julian calendar 도입
Point	단락 4	동서양의 달력 분기
Point	단락 5	태음태양력과 산술력의 공통된 문제
Point	단락 6	그레고리력으로 통합

문단주제	본문내용	해석
단락 1 달력 발명 이전의 기록	**1** Even before the invention of the modern calendar, people were able to keep track of events in their lives using the phases of the moon and the seasons. In this way, one could explain that something would occur two days after the next full moon or that one was born 25 winters ago. This reliance upon the moon may seem quite rudimentary, but it also allowed them to count the days between the moons phases and the equinoxes (when the duration of the days and nights are approximately equal) and the solstices (the longest and shortest days of the year), which mark the traditional beginning of each of the seasons. As knowledge and understanding of these events increased, calendars as we now know them began to come together.	현대 달력이 발명되기 전에도, 사람들은 달의 위상과 계절을 이용하여 그들의 삶에서 일어나는 일들을 기록할 수 있었다. 이러한 방식으로, 다음 보름달이 뜨고 이틀 후에 어떤 일이 일어나거나 25년 전에 어떤 달이 태어났다고 설명할 수 있다. 달에 대한 이러한 의존은 매우 초보적인 것처럼 보일 수도 있지만, 그것은 또한 그들이 각 계절의 전통적인 시작을 나타내는 달 단계와 분점 사이의 날들을 셀 수 있게 해주었다. 이러한 사건들에 대한 지식과 이해가 증가함에 따라, 우리가 지금 알고 있는 달력들이 함께 만들어지기 시작했다.
단락 2 날씨에 따른 결함	**2** As these empirical lunar- and solar-based calendars became more popular, their flaws became more evident. [■] For one, they were extremely dependent upon the weather. [■] While it does not affect the actual movement of either of the celestial bodies, it can obscure them and cause inaccuracies in the calendar. [■] The calendars were also dependent upon the location, since the timing of the moon's phases and the solstices and equinoxes change over distances. [■] For instance, the timing of the rise of the new moon would be earlier in eastern locations. It may not even occur on the same day if the second observer is far enough west. This is also problematic for observers in extreme northern latitudes where the sun remains below the horizon for 4.5 months during winter and remains overhead for an equal amount of time in the summer.	이러한 경험에 의거한 음력과 태양을 기반으로 한 달력이 알려지게 되면서, 그들의 결점은 더욱 분명해졌다. 우선, 그들은 날씨에 극도로 의존했다. 그것이 두 천체의 실제 움직임에 영향을 미치지는 않지만, 그것은 천체를 가리고 달력에 부정확한 결과를 초래할 수 있다. 달력은 또한 달의 위상과 용암과 분점의 타이밍이 거리에 따라 변하기 때문에 위치에 따라 달라졌다. 예를 들어, 새로운 달이 뜨는 시기는 동쪽 지역에서 더 빨라질 것이다. 두 번째 관찰자가 서쪽으로 충분히 멀리 떨어져 있으면 같은 날에도 일어나지 않을 수 있다. 이것은 또한 태양이 겨울에는 4.5개월 동안 지평선 아래에 있고 여름에는 같은 시간 동안 머리 위에 있는 극북위도 관측자들에게도 문제가 된다.
단락 3 단위의 불일치와 Julian calendar 도입	**3** Secondary problems arose due to the fact that the basic unit of the calendar, the day, does not evenly fit in the calendric	이차적인 문제는 달력의 기본 단위인 날이 달이나 연도의 달력 개념에 고르게 들어맞지 않기 때문에 발생했다. 시간이 지남에 따라,

concept of either the month or the year. Over time, this causes the calendar day to fall out of line with both the lunar and solar cycle. This basic inaccuracy required that days or months be intercalated, or added to the calendar. Unfortunately, this process was overseen by government officials or holy men who could be corrupt, inept, or both. This problem came to a head during the reign of Julius Caesar, when the intercalation cycle was thrown off by war and were observed in some consecutive years and forgotten in others, causing the calendar year to fall out of sync. To solve this problem, the Julian calendar was introduced around 50 BCE and the Roman Empire's year was officially lengthened to 365.25 days.

4 The new Julian calendar could be easily calculated and remained better synchronized with the cycles of the sun and moon over time. This removed the chance for abuse by laying out a systematic method for intercalations. Surprisingly, calendars in the East and West diverged at this time. Those in the East, namely China and India, depended upon the exact timing of lunar and solar events, because of the importance of these in the society's religions and traditions. But those in the West and Middle East followed rigid arithmetical rules that kept them synchronized with the natural world without the need for constant observations and calculations of astronomical events.

5 Both lunisolar and arithmetic calendar systems still suffered from the problem mentioned earlier, the impossibility of the larger units of time to be divided evenly by the basic unit of measure, the day. Calendar's based on lunation, or the period between new moons, are inherently self-adjusting and will synchronize with the cycles, but arithmetical calendars will only remain synchronized on average. However, this does not mean that the lunar calendar is more accurate, because the cycles of the moon are still not easily divisible by days as each lunation takes approximately 29.53 days.

6 Today, all but a handful of countries have settled on the use of one civil arithmetically based calendar, the Gregorian calendar, which Pope Gregory XIII introduced in 1582. Under the Gregorian calendar, the problem with the uneven number of days in the year was solved through the use of leap years, which contain an extra day, every four years, except those that are divisible by 100, but not by 400. This means that 1700, 1800, and 1900 would be common (non-leap) years, but 2000 would be a leap year. This new calculation effectively brought the average length of the year to 365.2425 years, more in line with the actual time it takes for earth to revolve around the sun. The new calendar system also dropped 10 days to realign the yearly equinoxes, since the accumulated errors in the calendar over the previous 1000-1200 years had moved them forward by 10 days. This does not, however, mean that the Gregorian calendar is without its flaws. The system is estimated to have an error of one day every 3,300 years.

11 What can be inferred from paragraph 1 about calendars?

(A) They evolved from earlier systems that involved memorizing celestial occurrences.
(B) They were developed because moon phases were ~~unreliable time markers~~.
(C) They were initially used to ~~predict the upcoming seasonal changes~~.
(D) They allowed people to keep track of ~~past events for the first time~~.

Inference [As knowledge and understanding (of these events) increased], calendars [as we now know them] began (to come together).

12 According to paragraph 2, which of the following is **NOT** true about early calendars based upon lunar and solar data?

(A) They were based on actual observations of the sun and moon.
(B) They contained errors due to ~~misunderstandings of the lunisolar cycle~~.
(C) They could be thrown off by the weather.
(D) They were only accurate in the location where they were developed.

Fact (A) - (For one), they were extremely dependent (upon the weather). (C) - The calendars were also dependent (upon the location). (D) - This is also problematic (for observers).

13 The term "inept" in the passage is closest in meaning to:

(A) Dishonest
(B) Unreasonable
(C) Competent
(D) Unskilled

14

Which of the sentences below best expresses the essential information in the highlighted sentence in the passage? Incorrect choices change the meaning in important ways or leave out essential information.

This⁽⁰¹⁾ problem came (to a head) (during the reign) (of Julius Caesar), [when the ⁽⁰²⁾intercalation cycle was thrown off (⁽⁰³⁾by war) and ⁽⁰⁴⁾were observed (in some consecutive years) and forgotten (in others), causing the ⁽⁰⁵⁾calendar year (to fall) (out of sync)].

(A) ~~The reign~~ of Julius Caesar ~~was responsible for~~ inaccuracies in the calendar because cycles of interluding wars were not aligned by the calendar year during his time, causing a disturbance with the natural world.

(B) Intercalation cycle became a problem when people forgot to add days under the reign of Julius Caesars so that wars ~~could throw off~~ the annual calendar's ~~synchronization~~ with the natural world.

(C) The calendar and natural world were out of an agreement under the rule of Julius Caesar on account of ongoing wars as the incorrect sequences for a time in the calendar were made out.

(D) Many leaders, like Julius Caesar, felt that was more important than intercalations, so they ~~refused to perform them~~, which led to widespread inaccuracies in the calendar.

아래의 문장 중 지문 속의 음영 표시된 문장의 핵심 정보를 가장 잘 표현하고 있는 것은 무엇인가? 오답은 문장의 의미를 현저하게 바꾸거나 핵심 정보를 빠트리고 있다.

이 문제는 율리우스 카이사르의 통치 기간 동안 정점에 도달했고, 전쟁에 의해 몇 년 연속해서 관찰되고 어떤 해에는 잊혀져서 일치되지 않는 역년을 야기시켰다.

(A) 율리우스 시저의 ~~통치는~~ 달력의 부정확성에 ~~책임이 있었다~~. 왜냐하면 그의 시대 동안 전쟁의 순환이 달력 연도에 의해 정렬되지 않아서 자연계에 혼란을 야기했기 때문이다.

(B) 삽입 주기는 사람들이 율리우스 시저의 통치 기간 동안 일수를 추가하는 것을 잊었을 때 문제가 ~~되어서 그 결과~~ 전쟁은 자연 세계와의 연간 달력의 동기화를 ~~없앨 수 있었다~~.

(C) 달력과 자연계는 율리우스 시저의 통치하에서 일정 기간 동안 부정확한 순서가 만들어지면서 계속되는 전쟁으로 인해 일치를 벗어났다.

(D) 율리우스 카이사르와 같은 많은 지도자들은 그것이 중간 휴식보다 더 중요하다고 생각했고, 그래서 그들은 ~~그것을 수행하는 것을 거부했고~~, 이것은 달력에서 광범위한 부정확함으로 이어졌다.

Highlight   i) 문제가 정점에 이르렀다 ii) 전쟁에 의해서 주기가 일치하지 않게 되었다 iii) 그 다음 몇해에 관찰되다가 다른 년도 때는 잊혀졌다. iv) 결국 안 맞게 되었다 총 4가지 정보 중 **(A), (B), (D)**는 모두 틀린 내용이 있어서 오답이다.

15

What can be inferred about intercalation during Julius Caesar's reign from paragraph 3?

(A) It ~~was abandoned~~ during the period because of the constant warfare.
(B) It ~~was rendered unnecessary~~ by the lengthening of the year.
(C) It caused great inaccuracies in the calendar of the time.
(D) It could not be done some years ~~because of the changes in the lunisolar patterns~~.

율리우스 카이사르의 통치 기간 동안의 윤일에 대해 3문단으로부터 추론될 수 있는 것은?

(A) 이것은 끊임없는 전쟁으로 인해 그 기간 동안 ~~버려졌다~~.
(B) 그것은 년도의 연장에 의해 ~~불필요하다고 여겨졌다~~.
(C) 그것은 당시의 달력에서 큰 부정확성을 야기했다.
(D) 그것은 ~~태음 태양 패턴의 변화 때문에~~ 몇 년 동안 행해질 수 없었다.

Fact   This problem came (to a head) (during the reign) (of Julius Caesar), [when the intercalation cycle was thrown off (by war) and were observed (in some consecutive years) and forgotten (in others), causing the calendar year (to fall) (out of sync)].

16 According to paragraph 4, which of the following is **NOT** true about the new Julian calendar?

(A) It remained synchronized with lunisolar events better than previous calendars.
(B) It contained systematic intercalations that made their misapplication less likely.
(C) It became widely used across Europe and the Middle East.
(D) It made it ~~easier to determine the dates of Eastern religious and cultural events~~.

4문단에 따르면, 다음 중 새로운 율리우스력에 대해 사실이 아닌 것은?

(A) 이전의 달력보다 태음 태양의 사건과 동기화된 상태를 유지했다.
(B) 그것은 잘못 적용할 가능성을 낮게 만드는 체계적인 조정을 포함했다.
(C) 그것은 유럽과 중동 전역에서 널리 사용되었다.
(D) 그것은 ~~동양의 종교와 문화 행사의 날짜를 결정하는~~ 것을 쉽게 만들었다.

> **Fact** (A) - This problem came (to a head) (during the reign) (of Julius Caesar), [when the intercalation cycle was thrown off (by war) and were observed (in some consecutive years) and forgotten (in others), causing the calendar year (to fall) (out of sync)]. (B) - This removed the chance (for abuse) (by laying out) a systematic method (for intercalations). (C) - those (in the West and Middle East) followed rigid arithmetical rules.

17 According to paragraph 5, which of the following can be inferred regarding lunisolar calendars?

(A) The problems inherent in lunisolar calendars are very similar to those that exist in calendars based on calculations.
(B) They are ~~less accurate~~ than arithmetic calendars because their months all have 29 days.
(C) Inappropriate manipulation is ~~more difficult with lunisolar calendars~~ because they are self-syncing.
(D) The year is ~~shorter~~ under this system ~~because of the lower number of days~~ in each lunar cycle.

5문단에 따르면, 다음 중 태양력과 관련하여 추론될 수 있는 것은?

(A) 태양력에 내재된 문제들은 계산에 근거한 달력들에 존재하는 문제들과 매우 유사하다.
(B) 그들의 달은 모두 29일이기 때문에 산술 달력보다 ~~정확하지 않다~~.
(C) 달력은 자가 동기가 되기 때문에 부적절한 조작이 ~~더 어렵다~~.
(D) 태음 주기에서는 각 달의 주기에 있는 ~~일수가 적어서~~ 한 해가 짧다.

> **Inference** Both lunisolar and arithmetic calendar systems still suffered (from the problem) mentioned earlier, the impossibility (of the larger units) (of time) (to be divided) evenly (by the basic unit) (of measure), the day.

18 Why does the author mention that "1700, 1800, and 1900 would be common (non-leap) years, but 2000 would be a leap year"?

(A) To help the reader understand that the Gregorian calendar ~~adds leap years every 400 years~~.
(B) To clarify the intercalation system that was used under the Gregorian calendar.
(C) To show that most leap years occur in years ~~that are divisible by 400~~.
(D) To provide an explanation of ~~why~~ the Gregorian calendar ~~was adopted globally~~.

저자는 왜 "1700년, 1800년, 1900년은 보통(비-윤)년이겠지만 2000년은 윤년이 될 것"이라고 언급하는가?

(A) 그레고리력이 ~~400년마다 윤년을 더한다~~는 것을 독자들이 이해하는 것을 돕기 위해.
(B) 그레고리력 하에서 사용된 윤일 체계를 명확히 하기 위해.
(C) 대부분의 윤년이 ~~400으로 나누어진~~ 해에 발생한다는 것을 보여주기 위해.
(D) 그레고리력이 ~~세계적으로 채택된 이유~~를 설명하기 위해.

> **Purpose** (Under the Gregorian calendar), the problem (with the uneven number) (of days) (in the year) was solved (through the use) (of leap years), [which contain an extra day, every four years, (except those) [that are divisible (by 100), but not (by 400)]].

19

Look at the four squares [■] that indicate where the following sentence could be added to the passage.

This was not likely to cause problems in the desert regions of Egypt or Mesopotamia, but it could easily throw off the calendar in regions prone to large storm systems.

Where would the sentence best fit?

3rd

네 개의 네모[■]는 다음 문장이 삽입될 수 있는 부분을 나타내고 있다.

이것은 이집트나 메소포타미아의 사막 지역에서 문제를 일으킬 것 같진 않지만, 큰 폭풍전선이 발생하기 쉬운 지역에서는 달력을 쉽게 버릴 수 있다.

이 문장은 어느 자리에 들어가는 것이 적절한가?

세 번째

Insertion 문장 맨 앞의 This와 맨 뒤의 large storm 으로 봤을 때 날씨의 영향을 언급하고 있으므로 시야를 가릴 수 있다는 내용의 뒤이자 위치의 영향이 나오기 전 위치인 [C]가 적절하다.

20

Directions: An introductory sentence for a brief summary of the passage is provided below. Complete the summary by selecting the THREE answer choices that express the most important ideas in the passage. Some sentences do not belong in the summary because they express ideas that are not presented in the passage or are minor ideas in the passage. **This question is worth 2 points.**

지시: 지문 요약을 위한 도입 문장이 아래에 주어져 있다. 지문의 가장 중요한 내용을 나타내는 보기 3개를 골라 요약을 완성하시오. 어떤 문장은 지문에 언급되지 않은 내용이나 사소한 정보를 담고 있으므로 요약에 포함되지 않는다. 이 문제는 2점이다.

Since their invention, calendars have undergone a number of changes.

(B) Because months and years are not evenly divided by days, early calendars required periodic adjustments to stay in line with lunisolar events.　– paragraph 3

(E) After the introduction of arithmetical calendars, the types of calendars used in different regions split as Eastern societies held on to the lunisolar calendar and Western societies followed the newer form.　– paragraph 4

(F) The present-day Gregorian calendar more accurately accounts for time differences using an arithmetical formula and is the most widely used calendar in the modern era.　– paragraph 6

(A) Prior to the invention of the modern calendar, people relied upon lunar and solar events in order to keep track of time.　– MINOR 1

(C) Intercalations, or adding days to the calendar, were used to synchronize lunar and solar events such as the full moon and the solstices.　– MINOR 3

(D) The Julian calendar was particularly problematic, ~~because~~ its intercalations were decided ~~by politicians~~ and priest who could be inept or corrupt.

달력이 발명된 이후, 달력은 많은 변화를 겪어왔다.

(B) 월과 연도가 일수로 고르게 나뉘지 않기 때문에, 초기 달력은 태음태양의 사건과 일치시키기 위해 주기적인 조정이 필요했다.

(E) 산술적 달력의 도입 이후, 동양 사회가 태음태양력을 고수하고 서구 사회가 새로운 형태를 따름에 따라 다른 지역에서 사용되는 달력의 종류가 분리되었다.

(F) 오늘날의 그레고리력은 산술 공식을 사용하여 시차를 더 정확하게 설명하며 현대에서 가장 널리 사용되는 달력이다.

(A) 현대 달력이 발명되기 전에, 사람들은 시간을 기록하기 위해 달과 태양에 의존했다.

(C) 중간 또는 달력에 날짜를 추가하는 것은 보름달과 동지,하지와 같은 달과 태양의 사건을 동시에 일치시키기 위해 사용되었다.

(D) 율리우스력은 특히 문제가 많았는데, 그 이유는 율리우스력이 서투르거나 타락할 수 있는 ~~정치인들과~~ 성직자들~~에 의해 축약되었기~~ ~~때문이다~~.

TEST 2-3 The Decline of the Ottoman Empire 오스만 제국의 쇠퇴

Introduction	단락 1	술레이만 아래에서의 오스만 제국의 번영
Point	단락 2	제국의 쇠퇴와 술탄의 역할
Point	단락 3	추밀원 집단과 행정 기술 의존
Point	단락 4	하렘과 제국에 끼친 영향력
Point	단락 5	무역의 변화와 중개 무역 역할 손실로 인한 쇠퇴
Point	단락 6	유럽에 의한 지배와 전쟁 이후 해체

단락 1
술레이만 아래에서의 오스만 제국의 번영

1 After its foundation in 1299, Anatolia's Ottoman Empire enjoyed extensive success and expansion under a series of very powerful leaders. Many agree that the empire reached its apex during the reign of its 10th, and longest serving, sultan, Suleyman the Magnificent. Although his predecessors were known for their wisdom, savage conquests, and administrative ability, Suleyman took this to another level and expanded the empire into central Europe, Persia, to the southern coast of the Arabian Peninsula, and across northern Africa. This gave the Ottoman Empire near total hegemony over Mediterranean trade and this period is considered the "Golden Age" of the empire. Unfortunately, Suleyman's successors lacked initiative and competence and under their leadership the empire suffered. Luckily, some of these incompetent leaders relied upon "viziers," or executive officers, who kept the empire in tact for nearly 400 more years.

1299년에 건국된 이후, 아나톨리아의 오스만 제국은 일련의 매우 강력한 지도자들 아래서 광범위한 성공과 확장을 누렸다. 많은 사람들은 이 제국이 10대 술탄인 술레이만 대제의 통치 기간 동안 정점에 이르렀다는 것에 동의한다. 비록 그의 전임자들은 지혜와 야만적인 정복, 그리고 행정적인 능력으로 유명했지만, 술레이만은 이것을 한 단계 더 끌어올렸고 제국을 중부 유럽, 페르시아, 아라비아 반도의 남쪽 해안, 그리고 북아프리카 전역으로 확장시켰다. 이것은 오스만 제국에 지중해 무역에 대한 거의 완전한 패권을 주었고 이 시기는 제국의 "황금 시대"로 여겨진다. 불행하게도 술레이만의 후계자들은 진취성과 역량이 부족했고 그들의 지도력 아래 제국은 고통받았다. 운 좋게도, 이 무능한 지도자들 중 일부는 거의 400년 동안 제국을 온전하게 유지시켜주는 "재능가" 즉 행정관들에게 의존했다.

단락 2
제국의 쇠퇴와 술탄의 역할

2 Unfortunately for the Ottoman Sultans, the end of the 16th century marked not only the end of their territorial expansion and regional dominance, but also the beginning of the empire's slow decline. However, this cannot be completely blamed on the incompetence of the leaders. Changes within the empire and the rise of other regional powers, especially those neighboring the empire's European territories, both played a large role in the decline of the empire. These changes caused the role of the Sultan to change dramatically. Instead of being dedicated to leading armies into battle for territorial expansion, bureaucracy and diplomacy became more important to the Sultans so that they could administer the enormous territory of the empire and to deal with its increasingly powerful neighbors. In addition, large army

오스만 술탄들에게는 불행하게도, 16세기의 끝은 그들의 영토 확장과 지역 지배의 종말을 의미했을 뿐만 아니라 제국의 느린 쇠퇴의 시작을 의미했다. 그렇다고 해서 지도자들의 무능 탓만 할 수는 없다. 제국 내에서의 변화와 다른 지역 강대국들, 특히 제국의 유럽 영토와 인접한 국가들의 부상은 모두 제국의 쇠퇴에 큰 역할을 했다. 이러한 변화는 술탄의 역할을 극적으로 변화시켰다. 영토 확장을 위해 군대를 이끄는 대신, 관료주의와 외교가 술탄들에게 더욱 중요해졌다. 또한 크림 반도에 있는 러시아군, 서쪽에 있는 페르시아군, 지중해 지역 주변의 다른 세력들을 막기 위해 대규모 부대가 영구적으로 배치, 자금 지원 및 통제되어야 했다.

units needed to be permanently positioned, funded, and controlled to fend off the Russian's in the Crimea, the Persians to the west, and other powers around the Mediterranean region.

3   These were new roles that would have been difficult for the empire's early successful sultans, but with the lack of skill and experience of those who followed Suleyman the empire fell behind in military and administrative technology and suffered military defeats, such as the empire's loss to Phillip II of Spain and the stunning loss to the Habsburgs and the Holy League when attempting to capture Vienna. The large territory covered too much area for one person to rule over, forcing the sultans to reply upon the Divan, a group of trusted officers, ministers, and a Grand Vizier. These Viziers and their bureaucratic organizations became very powerful in their own right and later sultans, such as Selim II, began to rely upon them to administer the territory.

4   Surprisingly, another group that greatly reduced the power of the Sultan and increased that of the Grand Vizier was the imperial harem. These women, who were connected to the sultan, became more powerful as time went on. Since the Grand Vizier was generally related to the sultan through marriage, he was directly connected to the harem as well and could use these powerful women to increase his power and affect the Sultan. This was probably most easily accomplished through the most powerful member of the harem, the Valide Sultan, who was the Sultan's mother. These women were so powerful that for over 130 years during the 16th and 17th century they were de facto rulers of the empire due to their influence over their sons, many of who were minors.

5   All of these factors weakened the power of the sultan, and in turn the empire, but perhaps the most detrimental change was the major shift in trade from the Mediterranean to the Atlantic Ocean. The European "Age of Discovery" sent explorers and settlers around the world looking for both colonies and trade routes. When they began sailing around Africa to reach the markets of Asia, they effectively removed the Ottoman Empire's great source of wealth and power, it's ability to act as an intermediary for trade between Europe and Asia. This was not an immediate loss, but over time it became more detrimental for the Ottoman Empire and without strong leadership and a fractured social and political structure, the empire began to decline more rapidly.

USHER

단락 6
유럽에 의한 지배와 전쟁 이후 해체

6 Over the next 200 years, these problems continued and the Ottoman Empire continued to fade from its previous position as a world super power. By the late 1800s the empire had lost so much territory and was so dominated by European powers that Tsar Nicholas referred to it as the "sick man of Europe," which needed help from its neighbors. Unfortunately, for the empire, this help would not come fast enough. [■] Despite a push for modernization that moved it in a more secular direction to match the European powers, the empire was doomed. [■] After a series of revolutions and wars, the empire joined WWI's Central Powers. [■] This decision ultimately resulted in the final dissolution of the empire. [■]

그 후 200년 동안, 이러한 문제들이 계속되었고 오스만 제국은 세계 초강대국으로서의 이전의 위치에서 계속 사라지게 되었다. 1800년대 후반까지 제국은 너무 많은 영토를 잃었고, 차르 니콜라스는 이웃 국가들로부터 도움이 필요한 "유럽의 환자"라고 언급할 정도로 유럽의 강대국들에 의해 지배되었다. 불행하게도, 제국에게 이것의 도움은 충분히 빨리 오지 않을 것이다. 근대화에 대한 추진으로 유럽 열강과 맞먹는 세속적인 방향으로 나아가게 되었음에도 불구하고, 제국은 멸망했다. 일련의 혁명과 전쟁 후에, 제국은 제1차 세계 대전의 동맹국들에 가입했다. 이 결정은 궁극적으로 제국의 해체로 귀결되었다.

---

21 Why does the author mention that Suleyman "took this to another level"?

(A) To indicate that Suleyman declared himself above his predecessors.
(B) To give the reader an impression of how Suleyman expanded the Ottoman territory.
(C) To indicate that Suleyman was wiser, more savage and a better administrator than earlier sultans.
(D) To show that the sultans after Suleyman were quite ineffective comparatively.

저자는 왜 슐레이만이 "이 문제를 다른 차원으로 끌어올렸다"고 언급하는가?

(A) 슐레이만이 전임자들보다 자신을 더 우월하다고 선언했다는 것을 나타내기 위해.
(B) 슐레이만이 어떻게 오스만 영토를 확장했는지 독자들에게 인상을 주기 위해.
(C) 술리만이 이전의 술탄들보다 더 현명하고, 더 야만적이며, 더 나은 행정가였다는 것을 나타내기 위해.
(D) 슐레만 이후의 술탄이 비교적 효과가 없다는 것을 보여주기 위해.

Purpose [Although his predecessors were known (for their wisdom, savage conquests, and administrative ability)], Suleyman took this (to another level) and expanded the empire (into central Europe, Persia)

---

22 Which of the sentences below best expresses the essential information in the highlighted sentence in the passage? Incorrect choices change the meaning in important ways or leave out essential information.

(01)(Instead of being dedicated) (to leading) armies (into battle) (for territorial expansion), (02)bureaucracy and diplomacy became more important (to the Sultans) (03)[so that they could administer the enormous territory (of the empire)] (04)and (to deal) (with its increasingly powerful neighbors).

아래의 문장 중 지문 속의 음영 표시된 문장의 핵심 정보를 가장 잘 표현하고 있는 것은 무엇인가? 오답은 문장의 의미를 현저하게 바꾸거나 핵심 정보를 빠트리고 있다.

술탄 제국의 거대한 규모는 군사력과 성장이 거대한 제국을 통치하고 강력한 이웃 국가들과 평화적인 교류를 하는 부차적인 것이 되었다는 것을 의미했다.

(A) To govern the massive empire and to concern its mighty neighbors, military strength and growth became secondary and administration and foreign affairs arose its importance.

(B) Once it reached ~~its largest size~~ by leading armies into battle, the Ottoman Empire shifted its focus to managing the vast territory and defending itself from its neighbors.

(C) Because of the increasingly powerful nations that encircled the Ottoman Empire, its armies ~~were tasked with~~ administrative and diplomatic duties, instead of expansion.

(D) Ottoman Sultan's gave up expanding the Empire because they though that proper governance was more important that increasing territory, ~~which made their neighbors more powerful.~~

(A) 거대한 제국을 통치하고 그 강력한 이웃들을 염려해서, 군사력과 성장은 부차적인 것이 되었고 행정과 외교는 그것의 중요성을 증가시켰다.

(B) 오스만 제국은 군대를 이끌고 전투를 벌여 ~~최대 규모에 도달하자~~ 광대한 영토를 관리하고 이웃 국가들로부터 스스로를 방어하는 데 초점을 맞췄다.

(C) 오스만 제국을 둘러싼 강대국들 때문에 오스만 제국의 군대는 확장 대신 행정 및 외교 ~~임무를 맡았다.~~

(D) 오스만 술탄은 영토 확장보다 적절한 통치가 더 중요하여 ~~이웃 국가들을 더 강하게 만들었기~~ 때문에 제국의 확장을 포기했다.

Highlight i) 군대를 이끌고 영토를 확장하는것에 헌신하는 대신에 ii) 그들의 넓은 영역을 통치하는데 있어서 관료제와 외교가 더욱 중요해졌다 iii) 인접한 나라들의 커지는 세력에 대처하기 위해서 까지의 내용을 모두 다 담고 있는 보기는 **(A)**이다.

---

23 According to paragraph 2, which of the following is **NOT** a reason for the decline of the Ottoman Empire?

(A) Internal changes within the empire
(B) Incompetent leadership
(C) ~~Expansion into hostile territory~~
(D) The increasing power of European countries

다음 중 오스만 제국의 쇠퇴의 원인이 아닌 것은?

(A) 제국 내부의 변화
(B) 무능한 리더쉽
(C) ~~적대적 영토로의 확장~~
(D) 유럽 국가들의 증가하는 힘

Fact **(A), (D)** - Changes (within the empire) and the rise (of other regional powers), especially those neighboring the empire's European territories, both played a large role (in the decline) (of the empire). **(B)** - However, this cannot be completely blamed (on the incompetence) (of the leaders).

---

24 What can be inferred about Ottoman leadership from paragraph 3? ★

(A) ~~The emperor became less important~~ than the Grand Viziers.
(B) If earlier powerful Sultans ruled during this time they would have needed to rely upon advisors as well.
(C) Sultans delegated administrative duties to the Vizier so they could ~~focus on the military.~~
(D) The defeat by the Habsburgs ~~led to the rise of the Vizier and the Divan.~~

3문단에서 오스만 지도력에 대해 추론할 수 있는 것은? ★

(A) ~~황제는 수상들보다 덜 중요해졌다.~~
(B) 만약 이전의 강력한 술탄들이 이 시기에 통치했다면, 그들은 조언자들에게도 의존할 필요가 있었을 것이다.
(C) 술탄들은 ~~군대에 집중할~~ 수 있도록 고관들에게 행정 업무를 위임했다.
(D) 합스부르크에 의한 패배는 ~~군관과 추밀원의 부흥을 이끌었다.~~

Inference These were new roles [that would have been difficult (for the empire's early successful sultans)], but (with the lack) (of skill and experience) (of those) [who followed Suleyman] the empire fell behind (in military and administrative technology).

25

The term "de facto" in the passage is closest in meaning to:

(A) Figurative
(B) Effective
(C) Fictional
(D) Essential

문단의 "사실상의"라는 단어의 뜻과 가장 가까운 것은?

(A) 비유적인
(B) 실질적인
(C) 허구적인
(D) 필수적인

26

According to paragraph 4, which of the following is **NOT** true about the imperial harem in the Ottoman Empire?

(A) It was a powerful group of women connected to the Sultan.
(B) It could be used by the Grand Vizier to increase his power.
(C) It included the female members of the Sultan's family.
(D) ~~It ran the Ottoman Empire during the time of the inept Sultans.~~

4문단에 따르면, 다음 중 오스만 제국의 제국 하렘에 대한 사실이 아닌 것은?

(A) 술탄과 연관된 강력한 여성 집단이었다.
(B) 권력을 강화하기 위해 수상들에 의해 사용될 수 있었다.
(C) 술탄 가문의 여성 구성원도 포함되었다.
(D) ~~술탄이 서투르던 시기에 오스만 제국을 통치했다.~~

Fact **(A)** - These women, [who were connected (to the sultan)], became more powerful [as time went on]. **(B)** - [Since the Grand Vizier was generally related (to the sultan) (through marriage)], he was directly connected (to the harem) as well and could use these powerful women (to increase) his power and affect) the Sultan. **(C)** - This was probably most easily accomplished (through the most powerful member) (of the harem), the Valide Sultan, [who was the Sultan's mother].

27

According to paragraph 5, which of the following is true regarding the Age of Discovery?

(A) ~~It was begun by the Ottomans in the Atlantic Ocean.~~
(B) It allowed traders to bypass Ottoman outposts when trading.
(C) It made it ~~more expensive for Ottoman goods to reach~~ new markets.
(D) It caused ~~the rapid collapse~~ of the Ottoman Empire.

5문단에 따르면, 다음 중 Discovery 시대에 관한 설명으로 옳은 것은?

(A) ~~그것은 대서양에서 오스만인에 의해 시작되었다.~~
(B) 무역상들이 무역을 할 때 오스만 전초기지를 우회할 수 있도록 했다.
(C) 그것은 ~~오스만의 상품들이 새로운 시장에 도달하~~ 것을 더 비싸게 만들었다.
(D) 그것은 오스만 제국의 ~~급속한 붕괴~~를 야기했다.

Fact [When they began sailing (around Africa) (to reach) the markets (of Asia)], they effectively removed the Ottoman Empire's great source (of wealth and power), it's ability (to act) (as an intermediary) (for trade) (between Europe and Asia).

28

According to paragraph 6, which of the following can be inferred regarding the collapse of the Ottoman Empire?

(A) ~~200 years of wars caused instability~~ in the empire and it collapsed in the late 1800s.
(B) The Ottoman Empire ~~remained a powerful~~, modern nation until it was eventually destroyed by war.
(C) ~~Large scale illnesses weakened~~ the empire and allowed it to easily be overtaken during World War I.
(D) Its collapse was brought about by joining the losing side during World War I.

6문단에 따르면, 다음 중 오스만 제국의 붕괴와 관련하여 추론할 수 있는 것은?

(A) ~~200년간의 전쟁은~~ 제국의 불안을 ~~야기했고~~ 1800년대 후반에 멸망했다.
(B) 오스만 제국은 결국 전쟁으로 멸망할 때까지 ~~강력하고 현대적인 국가로 남아있었다.~~
(C) ~~대규모 질병은~~ 제국을 약화시켰고 제1차 세계 대전 동안 제국을 쉽게 정복할 수 있게 했다.
(D) 그것의 붕괴는 제1차 세계 대전 동안 패배한 쪽에 합류함으로써 야기되었다.

Inference (After a series) (of revolutions and wars), the empire joined WWI's Central Powers. This decision ultimately resulted (in the final dissolution) (of the empire).

29

Look at the four squares [■] that indicate where the following sentence could be added to the passage.

Its territories were divided up by the European powers and the modern country of Turkey rose to replace it on the Anatolian peninsula.

Where would the sentence best fit?

4th

네 개의 네모[■]는 다음 문장이 삽입될 수 있는 부분을 나타내고 있다.

이곳의 영토는 유럽 열강들에 의해 분할되었고 현재의 터키가 아나톨리아 반도를 대체하기 위해 일어났다.

이 문장은 어느 자리에 들어가는 것이 적절한가?

네 번째

Insertion 최종적으로 영토가 나눠지고 오늘날의 터키가 그 지역을 대체했다는 내용은 1차 세계대전 이후 종말 다음의 내용이므로 [D]가 적절하다.

30

Directions: An introductory sentence for a brief summary of the passage is provided below. Complete the summary by selecting the THREE answer choices that express the most important ideas in the passage. Some sentences do not belong in the summary because they express ideas that are not presented in the passage or are minor ideas in the passage. **This question is worth 2 points.**

지시: 지문 요약을 위한 도입 문장이 아래에 주어져 있다. 지문의 가장 중요한 내용을 나타내는 보기 3개를 골라 요약을 완성하시오. 어떤 문장은 지문에 언급되지 않은 내용이나 사소한 정보를 담고 있으므로 요약에 포함되지 않는다. **이 문제는 2점이다.**

After the rule of Suleyman the Magnificent, the Ottoman Empire began a slow decline until it was eventually dissolved.

술레이만 1세의 통치 이후, 오스만 제국은 마침내 해산될 때까지 서서히 쇠퇴하기 시작했다.

(B) Early expansion left the empire too large to be efficiently ruled, especially by the later inept rulers, and the reliance upon advisors led to a weakening of the Sultan and the Empire. – paragraph 2

(C) Economic changes brought about by the exploration of the increasingly powerful European nations caused a great weakening of the Empire and its economy. – paragraph 5

(F) A series of conflict greatly reduced the empire's territory, but its decision to participate in WWI led to its eventual total destruction. – paragraph 6

(B) 초기의 팽창으로 제국은 특히 미숙한 후대의 통치자들에 의해 효율적으로 통치되기에는 너무 커졌고, 조언자들에 대한 의존은 술탄과 제국의 약화로 이어졌다.

(C) 점점 더 강력해지는 유럽 국가들의 탐험에 의해 초래된 경제적 변화는 제국과 그 경제의 큰 약화를 야기했다.

(F) 일련의 분쟁으로 제국의 영토가 크게 줄어들었지만, 1차 세계대전에 참여하기로 한 결정은 결국 제국의 완전한 파괴로 이어졌다.

(A) Under Suleyman the Magnificent, the Ottoman Empire reached its peak and ~~was in control of most of the Middle East and the Mediterranean coastal region~~.

(D) Defeat at the hands of Spain, the Hapsburgs, and the Holy league ~~caused the Empire to shrink as it lost important territories, such as Vienna~~.

(E) By the late 1800s the Empire had weakened greatly and it was eventually ~~absorbed by the Central Powers during World War I~~.

(A) 술레이만 1세 치하에서 오스만 제국은 절정에 달했고 중동과 지중해 연안 지역의 ~~대부분을 장악했다~~.

(D) 스페인, 합스부르크, 신성 동맹의 패배는 ~~비엔나와 같은 중요한 영토를 잃으면서 제국이 위축되는 원인이 되었다~~.

(E) 1800년대 후반에 이르러 제국은 크게 약화되었고 결국 제1차 세계 대전 동안 ~~동맹국들에 흡수되었다~~.

USHER

iBT TOEFL
INTERMEDIATE READING 02

TEST 3

답안 및 취약 유형 분석표

해석·해설

답안 및 문제 유형 분석표

TEST 3-1

01 (B) Purpose
02 (C) Vocabulary
03 (B) Fact
04 (A) Inference
05 (C) Highlight
06 (C) Inference
07 (D) Fact
08 (A) Fact
09 4th ■ Insertion
10 (A), (B), (F) Summary

TEST 3-2

11 (A) Fact
12 (C) Fact
13 (D) Fact
14 (A) Fact
15 (A) Highlight
16 (D) Purpose
17 (C) Vocabulary
18 (B) Fact
19 3rd ■ Insertion
20 (A), (B), (D) Summary

TEST 3-3

21 (A) Fact
22 (C) Highlight
23 (B) Fact
24 (C) Fact
25 (C) Vocabulary
26 (C) Fact
27 (D) Fact
28 (D) Purpose
29 4th ■ Insertion
30 (C), (E), (F) Summary

각 문제 유형별 맞춘 개수를 아래에 적어 보세요.

유형	맞춘 답의 개수	정답률	
단어 (Vocabulary)	/ 3	정답률:	%
사실 확인 문제 (Fact)	/ 13	정답률:	%
지시어 찾기 (Reference)	/ 0	정답률:	%
끼워 넣기 (Insertion)	/ 3	정답률:	%
문장 변환문제 (Highlight)	/ 3	정답률:	%
목적 (Purpose)	/ 3	정답률:	%
추론 (Inference)	/ 2	정답률:	%
단락 요약(Summary / Category Chart)	/ 3	정답률:	%
전체	/ 30	정답률:	%

※ 자신이 취약한 유형은 READING STRATEGIES를 통해 다시 한번 점검하시기 바랍니다. (p.44)

TEST 3-1 Geographic Isolation of Species 종의 지리적 고립

Introduction	단락 1	이종 교배와 이지역 종분화
Point	단락 2	대륙이동으로 인한 개체 분리
Point	단락 3	개체의 이동 능력에 따른 지리적 분리
Point	단락 4	유전자 집단 변화와 번식 장벽
Point	단락 5	군도 형성과 개체군 형성
Point	단락 6	설립자 효과와 틈새 적응에 따른 번식

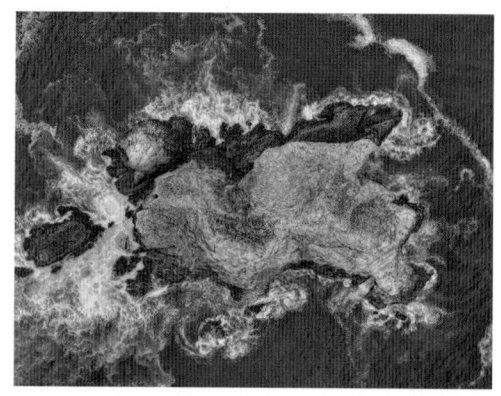

단락 1
이종 교배와 이지역 종분화

1 One of the most popular definitions of the word species was provided by renowned evolutionary biologist Ernest Mayr, who described a species as a population with the ability to interbreed, which does not interbreed with other such populations. Today, we are unsure of exactly how many species exist in the world, but we have learned of several ways that new species develop. One of the major discoveries has been that the most common method of speciation, called allopatric or geographic speciation, occurs when a population becomes geographically separated. When the two species are separated, they can no longer interbreed. This allows the two populations to follow separate evolutionary courses due to different selective pressures, genetic drift, and mutations within the isolated populations.

단락 2
대륙이동으로 인한 개체 분리

2 It may seem illogical that one population could be split into two or more by geography, but there are actually several methods through which this can occur. A quick look at Earth's topography will give several clues as to how this can occur. The first things one notices is that the continents separated by oceans, but knowing about continental drift tells us that these were not always in their current positions. This movement caused populations to be separated. Further, the rise of towering mountain ranges can also divide populations when they become too much of an obstacle for a population to cross. The formation of the Isthmus of Panama would have had the same effect when it formed 3 million years ago. Before this time, populations of organisms swam freely between the Caribbean Sea and the Pacific Ocean, but as the landmass developed it became a barrier to this and the populations were effectively divided between the two great bodies of water.

3 It may seem that these geographical barriers must be quite formidable to cause speciation, but the size of the required barrier depends upon the population in question. Animals like birds can easily cross mountain ranges, rivers and large distances, so speciation in bird populations requires rather large barriers. Animals that cannot fly require much smaller barriers to split the populations. This can be seen when a river changes course and small animal populations that cannot swim are divided. An example of this occurred when the Grand Canyon formed and the population of antelope squirrels was separated. Despite being only a few miles apart, the antelope squirrel population evolved into two separate species, the white-tailed antelope squirrel north of the canyon and the Harris' antelope squirrel in the deserts south of the canyon.

4 Geographic separation does not necessarily cause speciation, but it creates the opportunity for it when a gene pool changes enough to form a reproductive barrier between the two parts of the population. Interestingly, this is much more likely in a small isolated population than it is in larger populations because their genetic pools can undergo considerable change. This can be seen in the remote Galapagos Islands, which are over 900 Km from the nearest landmass. In 2 million years, a relatively short period in geographical terms, organisms from the South American mainland reached the islands and colonized them.

5 The distance of the Galapagos from the mainland, but the relatively close proximity of the islands to one another, allows them to serve as an outdoor evolutionary laboratory. Marine volcanism formed the archipelago's 18 main islands, which were eventually colonized by organisms that floated there along oceanic currents or winds and founded new populations on the islands. Some were even brought there by other organisms, such as seeds that were carried in the guts, fur and feathers of animals that made their way to the islands.

6 Today, due to the founder effect, the descendants of these original colonizers have evolved into a variety of species, most of which are unique to the island. The 13 finch species that Charles Darwin discovered on the island are a prime example of this. Research has shown that they descended from the same early colonizers, yet they have differing feeding habits and beak types. This likely occurred because the small population that colonized the island underwent genetic changes that set them apart. This continued when some of these individuals somehow found their way to one of the other islands and founded a second new population. As these populations filled niches in the ecosystem and became reliant upon a particular type of food, their bodies became adapted to it. [■] This led to differences in the shapes of beaks of the various types of finches. [■] Eventually, these isolated populations developed an affinity for only their own population and began breeding with only their own kind. [■] This effectively set them apart as separate species. [■]

일어난 것 같다. 이러한 현상은 이 개체들 중 일부가 어떻게든 다른 섬들 중 한 곳으로 가서 두 번째 새로운 인구를 만들었을 때 계속되었다. 이 개체들이 생태계의 틈새를 채우고 특정한 종류의 음식에 의존하게 되면서, 그들의 몸은 그것에 적응하게 되었다. 이것은 다양한 종류의 finch의 부리 모양에 차이를 가져왔다. 결국, 이 고립된 개체군은 그들 자신의 개체군에 대해서만 친밀감을 갖게 되었고, 그들 종들과만 교배하기 시작했다. 이것은 실질적으로 그들을 별개의 종으로 구분한다.

01

Why does the author mention "selective pressures, genetic drift, and mutations"?

(A) To show how populations become isolated from one another.
(B) To explain how populations diverge after a geographic separation.
(C) To give examples of alternative evolutionary processes.
(D) To point out some of the reasons that isolated populations avoid interbreeding.

저자가 왜 "선택압, 유전자 이동, 돌연변이"를 언급하였을까?

(A) 어떻게 객체들이 서로 고립시키는지를 보여주기 위해
(B) 어떻게 객체들이 지리적 분리 이후에 퍼져나가는지 설명하기 위해
(C) 대안적 진화 과정의 예시를 주기 위해
(D) 고립된 객체들이 이종교배를 피하는 이유중 몇가지를 지적하기 위해

Purpose [When the two species are separated], they can no longer interbreed.

02

The term "towering" in the passage is closest in meaning to:

(A) Transient
(B) Newly formed
(C) Lofty
(D) Preeminent

문단의 "우뚝 솟은"이라는 단어의 뜻과 가장 가까운 것은?

(A) 일시적인
(B) 새롭게 형성된
(C) 높은
(D) 특출난

03

According to paragraph 2, which of the following is **NOT** a cause of allopatric speciation?

(A) The movement of tectonic plates that rearranged Earth's landmasses.
(B) An earthquake wiping out an entire population.
(C) The formation of new mountain ranges.
(D) The appearance of a land bridge between two landmasses.

2문단에 따르면 다음중 이원적 분화의 원인이 아닌 것은?

(A) 지구의 대륙을 재배치하는 지각판의 움직임
(B) 전 객체를 쓸어버린 지진
(C) 새로운 산맥의 형성
(D) 두 대륙을 잇는 육교의 출현

Fact **(A)** - knowing (about continental drift) tells us [that these were not always (in their current positions)]] **(C)** - the rise (of towering mountain ranges) can also divide populations [when they become too much (of an obstacle) (for a population) (to cross)]. **(D)** - [as the landmass developed] it became a barrier (to this) and the populations were effectively divided (between the two great bodies) (of water).

04
What can be inferred about geographical barriers from paragraph 3?

(A) Small physical barriers can cause speciation just as easily as large ones.
(B) Geographic barriers arise when ~~niches go unfilled~~ in ecosystems.
(C) Animals that can fly are ~~unaffected~~ by the development of physical geographical barriers.
(D) River changes are the cause of ~~most~~ geographical barriers in the natural world.

3문단에서 지리적 장벽에 대해 추론할 수 있는 것은?

(A) 작은 물리적 장벽은 큰 물리적 장벽만큼이나 쉽게 종 분화를 야기할 수 있다.
(B) 생태계에서 ~~틈새를 채우지 않으면~~ 지리학적 장벽이 생긴다.
(C) 날 수 있는 동물은 발달에 ~~영향을 받지 않는다~~.
(D) 자연에서 강의 변화는 ~~대부분의~~ 지리학적 변화를 야기하는 주된 원인이다.

Inference the size (of the required barrier) depends (upon the population) (in question).

05
Which of the sentences below best expresses the essential information in the highlighted sentence in the passage? Incorrect choices change the meaning in important ways or leave out essential information.

(01)Geographic separation does not necessarily cause speciation, but it creates the (02)opportunity for it when a (03)gene pool changes enough to (04)form a reproductive barrier between the two parts of the population

(A) Genetic changes can cause a reproductive barrier within a population that ~~leads them to separate geographically~~ when the opportunity arises and brings about the evolution of new species.
(D) Speciation ~~is brought about by geographic separation~~ because reproductive barriers arise when genetic changes occur in a population that has had the chance to interbreed.
(C) The division of a population by geography does not cause the formation of new species; rather it allows the two genetic groups to diverge enough that interbreeding becomes impossible.
(D) Genetic changes arise due to reproductive barriers that disallow the breeding of two species that ~~are located within a close proximity to one another~~, leading to the creation of a new population.

단락에 밑줄친 부분을 가장 잘 표현한 문장은 어떤 문장인가요? 오답은 중요한 정보의 의미를 바꾸거나 필수 정보를 생략했다.

지리적 분리가 반드시 종분화를 일으키는 것은 아니지만, 유전자 공급원이 개체군의 두 부분 사이에 번식 장벽을 형성하기에 충분할 정도로 변화할 때 그 기회를 만들어낸다.

(A) 유전적 변화는 기회가 생기고 새로운 종의 진화를 겪어 올 때 ~~큰들어 지리학적 분리를 야기할수 있는~~ 개체 내에서 생식 장벽을 야기할수 있다.
(B) 종의 분화는 면 이종 교배 기회가 있었던 개체군에서 유전적 변화가 일어날 때 생식 장벽이 발생하기 때문에 ~~지리적 분리에 의해 야기된다~~.
(C) 지질학에 의한 객체의 분할은 다른 종들의 형성의 야기하지 않는데; 그대신 그것은 두개의 유전 집단이 이종교배가 불가능 해 지기에 충분할 분리를 허락한다.
(D) 유전적 변화는 ~~인접한 장소에 위치한 두 종 사이의~~ 교배를 허락하지 않는 생식의 장벽때문에 발생한고 새로운 개체의 탄생을 야기한다.

Highlight ⅰ) 지리적 분리가 반드시 종 분화를 야기하지는 않는다 ⅱ) 유전자 공급원이 변화할 때 ⅲ) 번식 장벽을 형성하기에 충분할 때 ⅳ) 발생의 기회를 제공한다. 총 4가지 정보를 확인했을 때, **(A), (B), (D)** 에서는 언급되지 않은 내용이 있기 때문에 **(C)** 가 답이다.

06

According to paragraph 4, which of the following can be inferred regarding the Galapagos Islands? ★

(A) The islands are filled with animal species that were previously found on the South American mainland.
(B) Geographic separation is required for speciation, as can be seen in Galapagos.
(C) A small isolated population is more likely to go through speciation than larger one with relatively unchanged gene pool.
(D) The organisms that live in the Galapagos do not travel between the islands.

4문단에 따르면, 갈라파고스 섬들에 관하여 추론할 수 있는것은? ★

(A) 그 섬들은 이전에 남미 본토에서 발견되던 종들로 차있다.
(B) 지리적 분리는 종 분리를 위해 요구된다, 갈라파고스 섬에서 볼 수 있는 것처럼
(C) 하나의 작은 고립된 객체는 상대적으로 변하지 않는 유전자 풀을 가진 큰 종보다 종 변화를 겪을 가능성이 더 높다.
(D) 갈라파고스에 사는 유기물들은 섬들 사이를 이동하지 않는다.

Inference Interestingly, this is much more likely (in a small isolated population) [than it is (in larger populations)] [because their genetic pools can undergo considerable change]]. This can be seen (in the remote Galapagos Islands), [which are over 900 Km (from the nearest landmass)].

07

According to paragraph 5, which of the following is **NOT** an example of a way that new species arrived in the Galapagos Islands?

(A) Floating over the ocean
(B) Being blown there by winds
(C) Other organisms carry them
(D) Volcanic eruptions placed them there

5문단에 따르면, 갈라파고스 섬들에 새로운 종들이 도달했던 방법의 예시가 아닌 것은?

(A) 바다 위에 떠서
(B) 바람에 의해 날아서
(C) 다른 유기체가 그들을 옮겼다.
(D) 화산의 폭팔이 그들을 그곳에 위치 시켰었다.

Fact (A), (B) – Marine volcanism formed the archipelago's 18 main islands, [which were eventually colonized (by organisms) [that floated there (along oceanic currents or winds)]]. (C) – Some were even brought there (by other organisms).

08

According to paragraph 6, which of the following is true regarding the different finch species found in the Galapagos Islands?

(A) They all evolved from the initial colonizers that arrived from South America.
(B) They were created by the interbreeding of different finch species on the islands.
(C) They live on separate islands because of competition over food sources.
(D) They were introduced to the islands by Charles Darwin.

6문단에 따르면 갈라파고스 섬에서 발견되는 다른 핀치 종들에 대하여 사실인 것은?

(A) 그들은 모두 남미에서 처음 도달해온 서식지에서 부터 진화됐다.
(B) 그들은 섬들에서 다른 핀치 종들의 이종교배에 의하여 만들어졌다.
(C) 그들은 음식 자원에 의한 경쟁 때문에 다른 섬에 살고 있다.
(D) 그들은 찰스 다윈에 의해 섬에 도입되었다.

Fact Research has shown [that they descended (from the same early colonizers), yet they have differing feeding habits and beak types].

09

Look at the four squares [■] that indicate where the following sentence could be added to the passage.

Today, each island has distinct species, with some of them having up to 10 separate finch species.

Where would the sentence best fit?

4th

> **Insertion** insertion 문장에서 각각의 섬이 개별적인 종을 가지고 그 종이 최대 10개까지 분리가 된다는 내용을 중심으로 분리가 된 이후의 예시로 숫자가 나온것이기 때문에 **[D]**가 정답이다.

10

Directions: An introductory sentence for a brief summary of the passage is provided below. Complete the summary by selecting the THREE answer choices that express the most important ideas in the passage. Some sentences do not belong in the summary because they express ideas that are not presented in the passage or are minor ideas in the passage. **This question is worth 2 points.**

지시: 지문 요약을 위한 도입 문장이 아래에 주어져 있다. 지문의 가장 중요한 내용을 내타내는 보기 3개를 골라 요약을 완성하시오. 어떤 문장은 지문에 언급되지 않은 내용이나 사소한 정보를 담고 있으므로 요약에 포함되지 않는다. 이 문제는 2점이다.

Allopatric speciation occurs when geographic isolation causes the development of new species.

(A) The introduction of a geographic barrier that divides a population allows the two smaller populations to evolve separately and can eventually lead to two discrete species.   – paragraph 3

(B) Geographic isolation does not cause speciation on its own, but it sets the scene for evolutionary processes that can lead to major differences between the two populations.   – paragraph 4

(F) The evolution of a multitude of finch species on the different Galapagos islands from the original founding population occurred because of their isolation.
  – paragraph 6

이원적 분화는 지리적 고립이 새로운 종의 개발을 야기할 때 발생한다.

(A) 개체를 나누는 지리적 장벽의 도입은 두개의 작은 개체가 분리되어 진화되는 것을 가능하게 하였고 결과적으로 두개의 다른 종을 야기했다.

(B) 지리적 장벽은 그자체로 종의 분화를 야기하지는 않지만, 두개의 개체들 사이에 주요한 차이를 이끌수 있는 진화적 과정의 초석이다.

(F) 다른 갈라파고스 섬에서 시초의 개체로부터 많은 핀치 종의 진화는 섬들의 고립 때문에 일어났다.

(C) The size of the barrier required to divide and isolate a population is dependent upon the size of the organisms and the number of individuals involved.   – INCORRECT

(D) Continental drift after the split-up of Pangaea separated early landmasses and allowed different species to evolve from early species.   – MINOR

(E) The Galapagos Islands acts as a natural evolutionary laboratory due to the large number of islands and the many species that inhabit them.   – ½, ½

(C) 개체를 분리시키고 고립시키기 위해 필요한 장벽의 크기는 유기체의 크기와 포함된 개체 수에 달려있다.

(D) 판게아의 분할 이후 대륙의 이동은 초기 대륙을 분리시키고 초기의 종들로부터 다른 종의 진화를 가능하게 했다.

(E) 갈라포고스 섬들은 많은 수의 섬들과 거기에 살고 있던 많은 종들 때문에 자연 진화 실험식의 역활을 했다.

TEST 3-2 The Empire of Alexander the Great 알렉산더 대왕 제국

Introduction	단락 1	마케도니아 Philip 2세와 Alexander 3세의 도시국가 정복
Point	단락 2	통합 이후의 무역 활성화
Point	단락 3	그리스 문화의 영향력
Point	단락 4	그리스 도시 국가의 적은 인구와 전문화 촉진
Point	단락 5	제국주의 팽창과 새로운 결합 체계
Point	단락 6	영토확장으로 인한 그리스의 영향력

문단주제	본문내용	해석
단락 1 마케도니아 Philip 2세와 Alexander 3세의 도시국가 정복	**1** Despite their centuries long fight against Persian domination, the Classical Greek city-states were not unified in any meaningful way. In fact, squabbling and infighting for power between the city-states marked the period, with power switching between them at different times. By the end of the Classical Period, Philip II of Macedon, in northern Greece, began an expansion of his territory, conquering the other city-states and uniting them under his Macedonian rule. However, this expansion would eventually seem trivial when compared to the expansion that was accomplished by his son, Alexander III, who ascended the throne in 336 BCE upon his assassination. This brash new king, who was only 20 years old at the time, would continue his father's planned invasion of the Persian Empire and eventually control a larger empire than any ruler before him, leading to great changes in the regions he conquered.	페르시아의 지배에 대항하여 수세기 동안 싸워왔음에도 불구하고, 고대 그리스 도시국가들은 어떤 의미 있는 방법으로도 통합되지 않았다. 사실, 도시 국가들 간의 권력 다툼과 내분은 서로 다른 시기에 그들 사이의 권력 교환과 함께 그 시기를 나타냈다. 고대 말기, 그리스 북부에 있는 마케도니아의 Philip 2세는 그의 영토를 확장하기 시작했고, 다른 도시국가들을 정복하고 그것들을 마케도니아의 지배하에 통합시켰다. 그러나, 기원전 336년 그가 암살당하고 그의 아들 알렉산더 3세가 왕위에 오른 것에 비하면 이러한 팽창은 결국 사소한 것으로 보일 것이다. 그 당시에 겨우 20살이었던 이 용감한 새 왕은 그의 아버지가 계획한 페르시아 제국 침략을 계속했고 결국 그 이전의 어떤 통치자보다 더 큰 제국을 지배했고, 그가 정복한 지역에 큰 변화를 이끌었다.
단락 2 통합 이후의 무역 활성화	**2** Within two years of taking the throne, Alexander had begun his campaign of international expansion and by 331 BCE the Macedonian ruler had overtaken the Persian Empire in the Levant, including the ancient city of Babylon, and had established a foothold in Egypt as well. After consolidating this great empire, he continued eastward and reached as far east as modern-day India. The great extent of this empire, along with the strong central control that was exerted by Alexander, caused a great number of changes in the movement of goods, capital and people throughout the empire. The removal of trade barriers and movement restrictions, as well as interconnected markets, made it easier for people to travel and trade with one another, and allowed Greek artisans and traders to seek their fortunes in a greatly expanded region. This expansion	왕위에 오른 지 2년 만에 알렉산더는 국제적인 정복 활동을 시작했고 기원전 331년에 마케도니아 통치자는 고대 도시 바빌론을 포함한 레반트에서 페르시아 제국을 능가했고 이집트에도 기반을 마련했다. 이 위대한 제국을 통합한 후에, 그는 동쪽으로 계속 나아갔고 오늘날의 인도지역인 동쪽에 도달했다. 알렉산더 대왕에 의해 발휘된 강력한 중앙 통제와 함께, 이 제국의 대부분은 제국 전체에 상품, 자본, 그리고 사람들의 이동에 많은 변화를 일으켰다. 상호 연결된 시장뿐만 아니라 무역 장벽과 이동 제한의 철폐는 사람들이 여행하고 서로 거래하는 것을 더 쉽게 해주었고, 그리스 장인들과 무역상들이 엄청나게 확장된 지역에서 그들의 부를 추구할 수 있게 해주었다. 무역과 영토의 확장은 고대 그리스와 그 이름으로 정복된 지역 모두에게 몇 가지 중요한 결과를

of trade and territory had several important consequences for both Classical Greece and the regions conquered in its name.

3 [■] One of the most obvious of these changes in the newly unified empire was the expansion of Greek culture and influence. [■] This occurred because Alexander founded at least 70 new urban centers, many of them named after himself, not so much for military control as for cultural expansion. [■] One of the most important ways that this was done was through the propagation of Greek literature and language through the establishment of Greek libraries, such as those established in Antioch (modern-day Turkey) and Alexandria, Egypt, which was the largest and most significant library in the ancient world. [■]

4 Another major change caused by the empire's expansion was the demise of the Greek city-state. Prior to the imperial period the Greek city-states were sparsely populated and centered around the agoras, marketplaces where the population came together to discuss the important issues of society and make decisions in person. Greek philosophers such as Plato and Aristotle, who had been the teenaged Alexander's tutor, felt that this form of government required a small population (less than 5,000) in order to insure that all citizens knew one another and could share their knowledge to make the best decisions. Further, prior to expansion these city-states lacked specialization, which allowed citizens to engage in various civil and personal activities. After trade and commerce developed across the empire citizens had to develop specializations, which brought about professionalism. This meant that the small populations and "jack-of-all-trades" nature of the city-states' residents were no longer sufficient and Greek cities changed dramatically.

5 Imperial expansion also brought the Greeks into contact with eastern philosophy and religion, which affected their previous belief in human-like gods with superhuman powers who could be counted on to intercede on behalf of the city-states citizens and provided protection and good luck during life's milestones. However, these beliefs had begun to wane even before Alexander's time as Greek's no longer seemed interested in only serving the city-state. In fact, the Athenian philosopher Socrates had previously been executed for suggesting a new morality based upon personal conscience rather than the traditional gods. This new philosophy, however, did not take the place of religion, but instead made the Classical Greeks receptive to new ideas that allowed the religions of the Middle East to mix with Greek philosophy. This new combined system spread across the world after Alexander's death in 323 BCE, forever intertwining the cultures of Greece and the Levant.

체계는 기원전 323년 알렉산더의 죽음 이후 그리스와 레반트의 문화를 영원히 뒤엉키며 전 세계로 퍼져나갔다.

단락 6
영토확장으로 인한 그리스의 영향력

6 This dramatic territorial expansion had such a profound effect on the world that Alexander's death ushered in what is known as the Hellenistic period in Greek history, when its influence was at its peak in Europe, Africa, and Asia. During this period the Greeks made great strides in art, literature, architecture, mathematics, governance, philosophy, and science. Without the influence of Alexander the Great's territorial expansion, these advances may have remained confined to the borders of Classical Greece.

극적인 영토 확장은 세계에 너무나 깊은 영향을 끼쳐서 알렉산더의 죽음은 그리스 역사에서 헬레니즘 시대로 알려졌는데, 그 시대는 유럽, 아프리카, 그리고 아시아에서 그것의 영향력이 최고조에 달했을 때였다. 이 기간 동안 그리스인들은 예술, 문학, 건축, 수학, 통치, 철학, 과학에서 큰 발전을 이루었다. 알렉산드로스 대왕의 영토 확장의 영향 없이, 이러한 발전은 고전 그리스의 국경에 한정되어 있었을지도 모른다.

11 What can be inferred from paragraph 1 about Philip II's expansion of Macedonian territory?

(A) He was unable to successfully take over the Persian territories.
(B) He expanded the territory to make Macedon less susceptible to Persian control.
(C) He united the Greek city-states and Persian territory to increase his power.
(D) He created the largest empire that the world had ever known.

단락1에서 필리포스 2세의 마케도니아 영토 확장에 대해 추론할 수 있는 것은 무엇인가?

(A) 그는 성공적으로 페르시아의 영토를 점령할 수 없었다.
(B) 그는 마케도니아를 페르시아의 영향력 덜 받게 만들커 위해 영토를 확장시켰다.
(C) 그는 그리스 도시 국가와 페르시아 영토를 그의 힘을 늘리기 위해 통합했다.
(D) 그는 지금까지 세계에서 알려진 가장 큰 제국을 만들었다.

Fact This brash new king, [who was only 20 years old (at the time)], would continue his father's planned invasion (of the Persian Empire) and eventually control a larger empire (than any ruler) (before him), leading (to great changes) (in the regions) [he conquered].

12 According to paragraph 2, which of the following is NOT true regarding Greece under Alexander the Great?

(A) It overtook the territory formerly controlled by the Persians.
(B) It expanded its territory as far east as India.
(C) It became ~~the largest power in the Western Mediterranean region~~.
(D) It experienced increased trade and movement due to the unification of new territories.

단락 2에 따르면, 알렉산더 대왕 치하의 그리스에 대해 사실이 아닌 것은 다음 중 무엇인가?

(A) 이것은 이전에 페르시아인들이 지배하던 영토를 뺏았었다.
(B) 이것은 영토를 동쪽의 인도까지 확장시켰다.
(C) 이것은 서부 지중해에서 가장 큰 영향력을 가지게 되었다.
(D) 이것은 새로운 영토들의 통일 때문에 증가한 무역과 이동을 경험했다.

Fact **(A)** - (by 331 BCE) the Macedonian ruler had overtaken the Persian Empire (in the Levant), (including the ancient city) (of Babylon). **(B)** - (After consolidating) this great empire, he continued eastward and reached as far east (as modern-day India). **(D)** - The removal (of trade barriers) and movement restrictions, as well as interconnected markets, made it easier (for people) (to travel and trade) (with one another).

13 According to paragraph 3, which of the following is true about the new cities in Alexander the Great's empire?

(A) Intellectual leaders ~~rather than military generals~~ ruled them.
(B) They ~~were built around central libraries~~.
(C) Many Greek citizens settled in them ~~because they were looking for Greek literature~~.
(D) They acted as sources of Greek culture and influence in the expanded territory.

단락3에 따르면, 알렉산더 대왕의 제국의 신도시들에 대한 다음 중 옳은 것은 무엇인가?

(A) ~~군장성보다는~~ 지식인 지도자가 그들을 통치했다.
(B) 많은 그리스 시민들은 ~~크리스 문학을 찾고 있었기 때문에~~ 그곳에 정착했다.
(C) 많은 그리스 시민들은 ~~크리스의 문학을 찾고 있었기~~ 에 그곳에 거주했다.
(D) 그들은 확장된 영토에서 그리스 문화와 영향력의 원천으로 작용했다.

Fact One (of the most obvious) (of these changes) (in the newly unified empire) was the expansion (of Greek culture and influence).

14 What can be inferred about urban centers in Greece from paragraph 4?

(A) Their populations increased greatly after the expansion of the empire.
(B) The demise of the city-state ~~led to greater expansion of the empire~~.
(C) Urban centers on the Greek mainland ~~fell apart as citizens moved into the new territory~~.
(D) Their ~~specialization allowed~~ Greece ~~to expand it s trade network~~.

4문단으로부터 그리스의 도심에 대해 추론 할수 있는 것은?

(A) 그들의 인구는 제국의 확장 이후에 크게 증가했다.
(B) 도시 국가의 멸망은 ~~제국의 확장을 더욱 이끌었다~~.
(C) 그리스 본토의 도시 중심지는 시민들이 ~~새로운 영토~~ 로 이주하면서 무너졌다.
(D) 그들의 ~~전문화는~~ 그리스가 ~~그들의 무역로를 확장하는 것을 가능하게 했다~~.

Fact This meant [that the small populations and "jack-of-all-trades" nature (of the city-states' residents) were no longer sufficient and Greek cities changed dramatically.

15 Which of the sentences below best expresses the essential information in the highlighted sentence in the passage? Incorrect choices change the meaning in important ways or leave out essential information.

(01)Imperial expansion also brought the Greeks (into contact) (with eastern philosophy and religion), (02)[which affected their previous belief (in human-like gods) (with superhuman powers) [who could be counted on (to intercede) (on behalf) (of the city-states citizens) and (03)provided protection and good luck (during life's milestones)]].

(A) Although the Greeks previously relied upon their super-humanoid gods for help and prosperity their faith changed as the territorial grew and eastern ways of thinking had taken hold.
(B) The Eastern Greek religions were greatly changed by the new philosophies that were brought about by Alexander the Great's expansion of the empire and caused the citizens to change their impression of the gods.
(C) After the expansion of the Greek city-state, citizens prayed to human-like gods for good luck on important dates and for protection, so that as they expanded eastern religions and philosophy changed the previous beliefs.
(D) The Greek religion had a great impact on eastern philosophy and religion as they brought their ideas about human-like gods, who helped the citizenry and passed on good luck, as the empire expanded eastward.

아래 문장 중 지문 속의 음영된 문장의 핵심 정보를 가장 잘 표현하고 있는 것은 무엇인가? 오답은 문장의 의미를 현저히 왜곡하거나 핵심 정보를 빠뜨리고 있다.

제국주의 팽창은 또한 그리스인들이 도시 국가 시민들을 대신해서 중재하고 인생의 중요한 기간동안 보호와 행운을 제공하는 초인적인 힘을 가진 인간과 비슷한 신들에 대한 이전의 믿음에 영향을 끼쳤다.

(A) 비록 그리스인들은 이전에 그들의 초인적인 신들에게 도움과 번영을 의존했지만, 영토의 성장에 따라 그들이 동양의 사고방식과 상호작용하게 되면서 그들의 믿음이 바뀌었다.
(B) 동그리스 종교는 알렉산더 대왕의 제국 확장에 의해 야기된 새로운 철학에 의해 크게 변화하였고, 시민들로 하여금 신들에 대한 그들의 인상을 바꾸게 하였다.
(C) 그리스 도시국가 확장 이후 시민들은 인간과 같은 신들에게 중요한 날짜에 행운을 빌고 그 결과, 그들이 동양의 종교와 철학을 확장하면서 이전의 신앙을 변화시켰다.
(D) 그리스 종교는 제국이 동쪽으로 확장되면서 시민들을 돕고 행운을 물려준 인간과 같은 신들에 대한 생각을 가져왔기 때문에 동양 철학과 종교에 큰 영향을 미쳤다.

16 Why does the author mention "Socrates had previously been executed"?

(A) To emphasize that the imperial expansion had the greatest influence on change in Greek's previous beliefs.
(B) To give an indication of the flourishment of his new philosophy in Greece.
(C) To exemplify the type of new philosophies that came from the East.
(D) To insinuate that expansion is not the only cause for changing their belief.

왜 저자는 "소크라테스는 이전에 이 일을 겪었었다"고 언급하는가?

(A) 제국의 팽창이 그리스의 이전 믿음의 변화에 가장 큰 영향을 미쳤다는 것을 강조하기 위해.
(B) 그리스에서 그의 새로운 철학의 번영을 나타내기 위해서.
(C) 동양에서 유래한 새로운 철학의 본보기다.
(D) 그 확장이 그들의 믿음을 바꾸는 유일한 원인은 아니라는 것을 암시하는 것이다.

Purpose However, these beliefs had begun (to wane) even (before Alexander's time) [as Greek's no longer seemed interested (in only serving) the city-state].

17 The term "intertwining" in the passage is closest in meaning to:

(A) Untangling
(B) Comparing
(C) Connecting
(D) Destroying

지문의 단어 "연결하는"의 의미와 가장 유사한 것은?

(A) 얽히지 않는
(B) 비교하는
(C) 연결하는
(D) 파괴하는

18 According to paragraph 6, which of the following can be inferred regarding the influence of the period?

(A) Alexander's rapid expansion of the Greek territory caused his rule to be known as the Hellenistic Period.
(B) Greek philosophy and advances expanded beyond the territory due to the influence of the large empire.
(C) The advances made during the Hellenistic period were a result of the interactions the Greeks had with other cultures in Asia, Europe and Africa.
(D) The influence of the Greeks allowed other cultures to make great strides in arts, literature and governance.

단락 6에서 다음 중 기간의 영향과 관련하여 추론할 수 있는 것은 무엇인가?

(A) 알렉산더의 그리스 영토의 급속한 확장은 그의 통치를 헬레니즘 시대로 알려지게 했다.
(B) 대제국의 영향으로 그리스 철학과 진보는 영토를 넘어 확장되었다.
(C) 헬레니즘 시대에 이루어진 발전은 그리스인이 아시아, 유럽 및 아프리카의 다른 문화와 교류한 결과였다.
(D) 그리스인들의 영향은 다른 문화들이 예술, 문학 그리고 통치에서 큰 발전을 이루도록 허락했다.

Fact This dramatic territorial expansion had such a profound effect (on the world) [that Alexander's death ushered (in [what is known (as the Hellenistic period) (in Greek history).

19 Look at the four squares [■] that indicate where the following sentence could be added to the passage.

The new cities were meant to turn the "barbaric" subjects into civilized subjects of the empire.

Where would the sentence best fit?

3rd

네 개의 네모[■]는 다음 문장이 삽입될 수 있는 부분을 나타내고 있다.

새로운 도시들은 "야만적인" 시민들은 제국의 문명화된 시민들로 바꾸는 것을 의미했다.

이 문장은 어느 자리에 들어가는 것이 가장 적합한가?

세 번째

Insertion 새로운 도시에 대한 설명이 앞 문장에 나오고 새로운 이방인을 문명화된 시민으로 만드는 방법이 뒤에 나와야 하기 때문에 [C]가 적절하다.

Directions: An introductory sentence for a brief summary of the passage is provided below. Complete the summary by selecting the THREE answer choices that express the most important ideas in the passage. Some sentences do not belong in the summary because they express ideas that are not presented in the passage or are minor ideas in the passage. **This question is worth 2 points.**

지시: 지문 요약을 위한 도입 문장이 아래에 주어져 있다. 지문의 가장 중요한 내용을 나타내는 보기 3개를 골라 요약을 완성하시오. 어떤 문장은 지문에 언급되지 않은 내용이나 사소한 정보를 담고 있으므로 요약에 포함되지 않는다. 이 문제는 2점이다.

Alexander the Great's territorial expansion had great consequences for Classical Greece and the conquered lands.

(A) The vast territorial expansion removed barriers to trade and movement that allowed people to cover longer distances and trade in interconnected markets through the empire. – paragraph 2

(B) The increased trade and commerce of the larger empire led to a need for specialization and larger urban populations, which marked the end of the classical Greek city-state. – paragraph 4

(D) Expansion of the empire allowed an interchange of ideas that spread Greek culture, while causing changes in Greek philosophy and religion in the motherland. – paragraph 5

알렉산더 대왕의 영토 확장은 고전 그리스와 정복지에 큰 결과를 가져왔다.

(A) 거대한 영토 확장으로 무역과 이동의 장벽이 제거되어 사람들은 더 먼 거리를 여행하고 제국을 통해 상호 연결된 시장에서 무역을 할 수 있게 되었다.

(B) 더 큰 제국의 무역과 상업의 증가는 전문화와 더 큰 도시 인구의 필요성으로 이어졌고, 이것은 고전적인 그리스 도시 국가의 종말을 알렸다.

(D) 제국의 팽창은 그리스 문화를 전파하는 사상 교환을 가능하게 했고, 모국에서 그리스 철학과 종교에 변화를 일으켰다.

(C) Alexander expanded Greek territory from his home region of Macedon by overtaking the Persian Empire and continuing eastward towards India. – MINOR

(E) Eventually, the religions from the eastern section of the empire ~~supplanted~~ the traditional Greek religion based on human-like gods with superhuman abilities.

(F) The expansion of Alexander's empire ~~increased the number of Greek citizens~~ and allowed them to make many strides in science and math.

(C) 알렉산더는 페르시아 제국을 추월하고 동쪽으로 인도를 향해 나아감으로써 그의 고향인 마케도니아에서 그리스 영토를 확장했다.

(E) 결국, 제국의 동쪽 지역에서 온 종교들은 초인적인 능력을 가진 인간과 같은 신들에 기반을 둔 전통적인 그리스 종교를 ~~대체했다~~.

(F) 알렉산더의 제국의 확장은 ~~그리스 시민의 수를 증가시켰고~~ 과학과 수학에서 많은 발전을 이루게 했다.

usherin.usher.co.kr

Early Maize Cultivation in the American Southwest

1   The North American continent has been blessed with vast areas of arable land that allow extensive agricultural output; yet not all areas are conducive to farming. The American southwest is one of these areas. The region's extremely dry conditions and high temperatures make it unfavorable for most farming. In fact, the largest agricultural crop produced across the region today is hay, which is used to feed livestock. However, this was not always the case. It is believed that the climate was much more stable and less arid from around 2500 to 100 B.C.E. It was during this period that certain food crops were introduced to the area from northern Mexico. Around this time, the native inhabitants began farming crops such as beans, squash, and most importantly maize, which, although not highly productive, enjoyed an advantage over the others, its production was very predictable.

2   Early inhabitants practiced hunting and gathering, which was particularly risky due to their reliance upon weather patterns, such as rainfall and sunlight. Although the populations were generally low and could sustain themselves this way, they may sometimes have grown larger and had trouble doing so. [■] This would be particularly true during the leaner times before the spring rains. [■] The coincidence of larger populations and less available food stock may have been the impetus for the inhabitants to begin growing reliable crops such as maize. [■] Despite its low yield, growing such a crop would have allowed them to have greater control over their food supply even if it did not fully satisfy the populations' nutritional needs. [■]

3   Researchers performing radiocarbon dating on maize cobs and seeds believe their introduction occurred between 2000-1500 B.C.E. and then spread to other areas. While maize eventually becomes the most well known of these, the others played great roles not only in the diet of the southwestern people, but also in the success of their maize crops. Beans and legumes were especially important during this time, because they replenish the nitrogen that maize depletes from the soil. By planting these crops together, early farmers were able to ensure that their soil stayed fertile enough to produce crops year after year.

4   The first maize species successfully introduced to the region from northern Mexico was most likely a small, brown kernelled variety called chapalote. This species was important because it matures quickly and requires little irrigation after its initial planting, so it is highly drought resistant. Eventually this species was hybridized with an indigenous grass, teosinte, to produce a more fruitful species with more kernel rows and larger cobs. It is believed that the regions inhabitants continued to crossbreed maize species until they came up with the more productive maiz de ocho. This is likely the result of using selection to produce a maize variety with larger kernels for grinding and an earlier flowering season, since growing seasons are highly unpredictable in the region. The short growing season of maiz de ocho and its adaptability to assorted climates made it particularly valuable to the region's inhabitants.

5   This hybridization was particularly important because maize eventually became a staple across the Americas, including in places that pushed the boundaries of its production. By selective breeding of different varieties of maize, early farmers were able to develop varieties that could be planted in regions with poor soil, short growing seasons, and adverse weather. In fact, the maiz de ocho variety allowed maize production to spread from the arid southwest to regions as far north as Canada, which has temperatures too low for most earlier species to survive. This attention to maize cultivation allowed the local inhabitants to become more adept at farming. They learned to favor soil that held water better and received adequate sunlight. They also realized that the flood plains and canyon mouths contained better soil because of the water that they were exposed to. However, one of the most important farming skills they developed was irrigation. This allowed them to farm in more locations, which ensured their crops even if one area experienced a poor growing season.

USHER

단락 6
호박과 콩의
도입 이후의
생활방식 변화

6 Surprisingly, the introduction of maize and the early farming attempts did not spark a great shift in the regions' inhabitants' lifestyles. Since early maize was rather unproductive and required little work, it was planted casually. In fact, most of the area tribes continued to lead nomadic lives for nearly 1000 years after maize was introduced north of the Rio Grande. This could also be attributed to the fact that maize is not a complete grain and lacks certain amino acids. It could only become a staple product when consumed alongside other agricultural products. Luckily, two of those were introduced around the same time, squash and beans.

놀랍게도, 옥수수의 도입과 초기 농업 시도는 그 지역 주민들의 생활 방식에 큰 변화를 일으키지 않았다. 초기 옥수수는 다소 비생산적이고 일손이 거의 필요하지 않았기 때문에, 그것은 가끔씩 심어졌다. 사실, 대부분의 지역 부족들은 옥수수가 Rio Grande 강 북쪽에 유입된 이후 거의 1000년 동안 유목 생활을 계속했다. 이것은 또한 옥수수가 완전한 곡물이 아니며 특정한 아미노산이 부족하다는 사실에 기인할 수 있다. 그것은 다른 농산물과 함께 소비될 때에만 주산물이 될 수 있었다. 다행히도, 그 중 두 가지가 비슷한 시기에 도입되었는데 그것은 호박과 콩이었다.

21

Which of the sentences below best expresses the essential information in the highlighted sentence in the passage? Incorrect choices change the meaning in important ways or leave out essential information.

(01)Around this time, the native inhabitants began farming crops (such as beans, squash, and most importantly maize), (02)[which, [although not highly productive], (03)enjoyed an advantage (over the others)], its production was very predictable.

(A) Nearly assured crop yields gave an edge over the other tribes that existed during the contemporary period, despite its relatively low productivity.
(B) Southwestern tribes began planting crops like beans and squash ~~to make up for the predictably low yields~~ that maize plants returned at the time.
(C) Squash, beans and maize had a major benefit over other farmed food sources in that their harvests, although small, were very predictable over time.
  – native began framing crop 언급 ✗
(D) Because crops were predictable, they gave the native farmers an advantage in times ~~when the others were not productive~~ of the plants they farmed.

아래 문장 중 지문 속의 음영된 문장의 핵심 정보를 가장 잘 표현하고 있는 것은 무엇인가? 오답은 문장의 의미를 현저히 왜곡하거나 핵심 정보를 빠뜨리고 있다.

이 무렵, 원주민들은 콩, 호박, 그리고 가장 중요한 옥수수와 같은 농작물을 재배하기 시작했는데, 옥수수는 생산성이 높지는 않지만 다른 농작물들에 비해 이점을 누렸기 때문에 생산량은 매우 예측이 가능했다.

(A) 거의 확실한 농작물 수확량은 상대적으로 낮은 생산성에도 불구하고 당대에 존재했던 다른 부족들보다 우위를 점했다.
(B) 남서부 부족들은 당시 옥수수가 수확한 ~~예상대로 낮은 수확량을 보충하기~~ 위해 콩과 호박 같은 작물을 심기 시작했다.
(C) 호박, 콩, 옥수수는 비록 작기는 하지만 시간이 지남에 따라 수확이 매우 예측 가능하다는 점에서 다른 양식원들에 비해 큰 이점이 있었다.
(D) 농작물이 예측 가능했기 때문에, 그들은 ~~다른 농부들이 그들이 경작한 식물들을 생산하지 못할~~ 때 원주민 농부들에게 이점을 주었다.

Fact ⅰ) 토착민들이 작물재배를 하기 시작 ⅱ) 그 중 옥수수는 생산성이 매우 높지는 않았다 ⅲ) 생산이 예측가능하다는 점에서 다른 작물보다 이점이 있었다 의 정보 중 **(B), (D)** 는 틀린 내용이 있고 **(C)**는 ⅰ)의 정보가 누락 되어서 오답이다.

22 What can be inferred from paragraph 1 about the American southwest?

(A) It is the ~~major livestock-producing region~~ of the United States.
(B) The region's inhabitants ~~have less livestock diversity~~ due to the environment.
(C) It has undergone a major climate change over the past two millennia.
(D) Early inhabitants of the area were ~~the first farmers on the North American continent~~.

미국 남서부에 대해 단락 1에서 추론할 수 있는 것은 무엇인가?

(A) 이곳은 미국의 ~~주요 축산지~~이다.
(B) 이 지역의 주민들은 환경 때문에 ~~가축의 다양성이 떨어진다~~.
(C) 그것은 지난 2천년 동안 큰 기후 변화를 겪어왔다.
(D) 그 지역의 초기 거주자들은 ~~북미 대륙의 첫 번째 농부들이었다~~.

Highlight The American southwest is one (of these areas). The region's extremely dry conditions and high temperatures make it unfavorable (for most farming). (In fact), the largest agricultural crop produced (across the region) today is hay.

23 According to paragraph 2, which of the following is **NOT** true about early inhabitants of the American southwest?

(A) They were traditionally hunters and gatherers.
(B) Maize ~~made up the majority of their diets~~.
(C) Their populations were not very large.
(D) The weather controlled their ability to provide for themselves.

문단3에 따라서, 미국 남서부의 초기 거주자들에 대해 사실이 아닌 것은 다음 중 무엇인가?

(A) 그들은 전통적으로 사냥꾼과 채집인이었다.
(B) 옥수수는 ~~그들의 식단의 대부분을 차지했다~~.
(C) 그들의 인구는 그리 많지 않았다.
(D) 날씨는 그들의 자급자족 능력을 통제했다.

Fact (A) - Early inhabitants practiced hunting and gathering **(C)** - [Although the populations were generally low and could sustain themselves this way], they may sometimes have grown larger and had trouble doing so. **(D)** - [Although the populations were generally low and could sustain themselves this way], they may sometimes have grown larger and had trouble doing so.

24 What can be inferred about the introduction of maize from paragraph 3?

(A) Maize's spread to the other areas ~~didn't play a part in the southwest people~~.
(B) Had it not been for beans and legumes, Maize ~~would become the most well known crops~~.
(C) Beans and legumes were concerned with the success of maize crops.
(D) It was ~~the first time a new plant species had been planted~~ in the southwest.

문단3에서 옥수수의 도입에 대해 추론할 수 있는 것은?

(A) 옥수수의 다른 지역으로의 확산은 ~~남서부 사람들에게는 영향을 미치지 않았다~~.
(B) 콩과 콩과 식물들이 없었다면 옥수수는 ~~가장 잘 알려진 작물이 되었을 것이다~~.
(C) 콩과 콩과식물들 옥수수 작물의 성공과 관련이 있었다.
(D) 남서쪽에 ~~새로운 식물 종이 심어진 것은 이번이 처음이었다~~.

Fact [While maize eventually becomes the most well known (of these)], the others played great roles not only (in the diet) (of the southwestern people), but also (in the success) (of their maize crops).

25 The term "fruitful" in the passage is closest in meaning to:

(A) Hardy
(B) Valuable
(C) Productive
(D) Impotent

지문의 단어 "생산성 있는"의 의미와 가장 유사한 것은?

(A) 거의
(B) 가치 있는
(C) 생산성 있는
(D) 무력한

26

According to paragraph 4, which of the following is **NOT** true about chapalote?

(A) It was the first maize species to be purposefully cultivated in the American southwest.
(B) It needs little water to produce an edible product.
(C) It remains ~~the most popular species of maize in the United States~~.
(D) It was crossbred to form hybrids with even more advantageous characteristics.

문단4에 따르면 다음 중 chapalote에 대해 사실이 아닌 것은 무엇인가?

(A) 그것은 미국 남서부에서 의도적으로 재배된 최초의 옥수수 종이었다.
(B) 그것은 먹을 수 있는 제품을 만들기 위해 물을 거의 필요로 하지 않는다.
(C) 그것은 미국에서 가장 일반적인 옥수수 종으로 남아 있다.
(D) 교배하여 더욱 유리한 특성을 가진 하이브리드를 형성했다.

Fact **(A)** - The first maize species successfully introduced (to the region) (from northern Mexico) was most likely a small, brown kernelled variety called chapalote. **(B)** - This species was important [because it matures quickly and requires little irrigation (after its initial planting)], so it is highly drought resistant. **(D)** - This is likely the result (of using) selection (to produce) a maize variety (with larger kernels) (for grinding and an earlier flowering season), [since growing seasons are highly unpredictable (in the region)].

27

According to paragraph 5, how did early inhabitants of the American southwest guarantee they would have enough food?

(A) By ~~developing maize~~ that could be grown in ~~regions with lower temperatures~~.
(B) Selecting areas where the soil was able ~~to drain water more effectively~~.
(C) Bringing ~~water to areas like the canyon mouths~~.
(D) Planting crops in multiple locations.

문단5에 따르면, 미국 남서부의 초기 거주자들은 어떻게 충분한 식량을 가지고 있을 것이라고 보장했는가?

(A) ~~기온이 낮은~~ 지역에서 재배할 수 있는 ~~옥수수를 개발했다~~.
(B) 토양이 물을 ~~더 효과적으로 배출할 수 있는~~ 지역을 선정했다.
(C) 협곡 입구와 같은 곳에 물을 가져다주었다.
(D) 여러 곳에 작물을 심었다.

Fact This allowed them (to farm) (in more locations), [which ensured their crops [even if one area experienced a poor growing season]].

28

Why does the author mention that "tribes continued to lead nomadic lives for nearly 1000 years"?

(A) To help the reader understand ~~how long it took~~ before maize was introduced to the region.
(B) To show that hunting and gathering were ~~much more important~~ than farming for early inhabitants of the southwestern United States.
(C) To explain ~~how~~ maize production ~~expanded~~ from the American southwest to other regions of the continent.
(D) To reinforce the notion that maize production did not have an immediate effect on the lifestyles of the region's inhabitants.

저자는 왜 "부족이 1000년 가까이 유목생활을 이어왔다"고 말했을까?

(A) 옥수수가 그 지역에 소개되기까지 ~~얼마나 오래 걸렸는~~지 독자들이 이해할 수 있도록 돕기 위해서.
(B) 사냥과 채집이 미국 남서부의 초기 거주자들에게는 농사보다 ~~훨씬 더 중요하다~~는 것을 보여주기 위해서였다.
(C) 옥수수 생산량이 미국 남서부에서 대륙의 다른 지역으로 ~~어떻게 확장되었는~~지를 설명하기 위해.
(D) 옥수수 생산이 그 지역 주민들의 생활양식에 즉각적인 영향을 미치지 않았다는 생각을 강화한다.

Purpose Surprisingly, the introduction (of maize) and the early farming attempts did not spark a great shift (in the regions' inhabitants' lifestyles).

29

Look at the four squares [■] that indicate where the following sentence could be added to the passage.

It could be said that planting crops did not turn the hunters and gatherers into farmers, but rather allowed them to be better at foraging because they had a supplemental food supply.

Where would the sentence best fit?

4th

네 개의 네모[■]는 다음 문장이 삽입될 수 있는 부분을 나타내고 있다.

작물을 심는 것은 사냥꾼과 채집인을 (농민이) 되게 한 것이 아니라, 오히려 그들이 (식량 공급을) 더 잘 할 수 있게 해 주었다]고 말해 질 수 있다.

이 문장은 어느 자리에 들어가는 것이 가장 적합한가?

네 번째

> **Insesrtion** 주어진 문장에서 추가적인 음식공급을 가지기 때문에 채집을 더 잘 할 수 있게 되었다는 내용이 have greater control over their food supply 에 대한 부연설명으로 [D] 가 적절하다.

30

Directions: An introductory sentence for a brief summary of the passage is provided below. Complete the summary by selecting the THREE answer choices that express the most important ideas in the passage. Some sentences do not belong in the summary because they express ideas that are not presented in the passage or are minor ideas in the passage. **This question is worth 2 points.**

지시: 지문 요약을 위한 도입 문장이 아래에 주어져 있다. 지문의 가장 중요한 내용을 내타내는 보기 3개를 골라 요약을 완성하시오. 어떤 문장은 지문에 언급되지 않은 내용이나 사소한 정보를 담고 있으므로 요약에 포함되지 않는다. 이 문제는 2점이다.

The introduction of maize into the American southwest between 2000 BCE and 1500 BCE spurred the regions agricultural development.

(C) Maize allowed it easier for the larger tribes of the region to feed themselves as their populations increased since it supplemented their previous methods of food acquisition. – paragraph 2

(E) Hybridization made maize more drought resistant, productive, and quicker to bloom, however it still lacked an essential nutrient, which could be attained through other agricultural products. – paragraph 4

(F) The region's inhabitants became more adept at farming and developed techniques that increased their yield, as maize became an important part of their diets. – paragraph 5

기원전 2000년과 1500년 사이에 옥수수가 미국 남서부로 유입되면서 그 지역의 농업 발전이 촉진되었다.

(C) 옥수수는 그 지역의 더 큰 부족들이 그들의 이전 식량 획득 방법을 보완했기 때문에 그들의 인구가 증가함에 따라 그들 스스로 더 쉽게 먹을 수 있게 해주었다.

(E) 잡종은 옥수수를 가뭄에 강하고, 생산적이며, 꽃을 빨리 피울 수 있게 만들었지만, 다른 농산물을 통해 얻을 수 있는 필수 영양소가 여전히 부족했다.

(F) 이 지역 주민들은 옥수수가 그들의 식난의 중요한 부분이 되면서 농사에 더 능숙해졌고 수확량을 늘리는 기술을 개발했다.

(A) The climate of the American southwest from 2500 BCE to 100 BCE was much more stable than it is now and had more rainfall. – MINOR

(B) Due to the region's erratic weather patterns reliance upon farming was risky, so the native tribes ~~continued their hunting and gathering activities as well~~. – INCORRECT

(D) ~~Maiz de ocho~~ was introduced to the southwestern region from Mexico and eventually hybridized to form more tolerant maize that could be grown in other regions. – ½, ½

(A) 기원전 2500년부터 기원전 100년까지 미국 남서부의 기후는 지금보다 훨씬 안정적이고 더 많은 비가 내렸다.

(B) 그 지역의 변덕스러운 날씨 패턴 때문에 농사에 의존하는 것은 위험했고, 그래서 원주민 부족들도 사냥과 채집 활동을 계속했다.

(D) Maiz de ocho는 멕시코에서 남서부 지역으로 유입되어 결국 잡종되어 다른 지역에서 재배할 수 있는 보다 내성 있는 옥수수를 형성했다.

USHER

iBT TOEFL
INTERMEDIATE READING 02

TEST 4

답안 및 취약 유형 분석표

해석·해설

답안 및 문제 유형 분석표

TEST 4-1

01 (D) Highlight

02 (A) Fact

03 (C) Fact

04 (C) Vocabulary

05 (A) Inference

06 (D) Fact

07 (B) Purpose

08 (A) Fact

09 3rd ■ Insertion

10 (A), (D), (E) Summary

TEST 4-2

11 (A) Inference

12 (C) Purpose

13 (D) Fact

14 (A) Highlight

15 (C) Inference

16 (B) Fact

17 (D) Fact

18 (B) Inference

19 3rd ■ Insertion

20 (A), (D), (F) Summary

TEST 4-3

21 (A) Inference

22 (C) Fact

23 (D) Highlight

24 (D) Inference

25 (A) Fact

26 (C) Inference

27 (B) Purpose

28 (A) Vocabulary

29 2nd ■ Insertion

30 (B), (E), (F) Summary

각 문제 유형별 맞춘 개수를 아래에 적어 보세요.

유형	맞춘 답의 개수	정답률
단어 (Vocabulary)	/ 2	정답률: %
사실 확인 문제 (Fact)	/ 9	정답률: %
지시어 찾기 (Reference)	/ 0	정답률: %
끼워 넣기 (Insertion)	/ 3	정답률: %
문장 변환문제 (Highlight)	/ 3	정답률: %
목적 (Purpose)	/ 3	정답률: %
추론 (Inference)	/ 7	정답률: %
단락 요약(Summary / Category Chart)	/ 3	정답률: %
전체	/ 30	정답률: %

※ 자신이 취약한 유형은 READING STRATEGIES를 통해 다시 한번 점검하시기 바랍니다. (p.44)

TEST 4-1 — Temperature Regulation in Marine Organisms
해양생물의 온도조절

Introduction	단락 1	생물의 체온 유지와 범위
Point	단락 2	온혈동물과 냉혈동물의 2가지 분류
Point	단락 3	그 외의 범주의 생물과 체계
Point	단락 4	해양온혈동물의 열 손실
Point	단락 5	열 손실 대응 방법
Point	단락 6	역류 열 교환기 체계

단락 1 — 생물의 체온 유지와 범위

1 [■] For most organisms maintaining thermal homeostasis, or keeping the body temperature within a certain range, is necessary for proper metabolic functioning. [■] If the internal temperature of these organisms leaves the preferred range, which differs based on the species, for extended periods, enzyme degradation and tissue/organ destruction may occur, which can make it difficult or impossible for their bodies to properly function. [■] This makes it extremely important that these organisms find some way to maintain their temperature within these ranges, especially in marine environments. [■]

대부분의 생물의 경우, 열 항상성을 유지하거나 체온을 일정 범위 이내로 유지하는 것은 적절한 대사 기능을 위해 필요하다. 이러한 생물의 내부 온도가 종에 따라 다른 바람직한 범위를 장기간 벗어날 경우 효소 분해와 조직/장기 파괴가 발생할 수 있으며, 이는 그들의 몸이 제대로 기능하기 어렵거나 불가능하게 만들 수 있다. 이것은 이 유기체들이 이 범위 내에서, 특히 해양 환경에서 그들의 온도를 유지하는 방법을 찾는 것을 매우 중요하게 만든다.

단락 2 — 온혈동물과 냉혈동물의 2가지 분류

2 Most organisms that do this can be classified in one of two categories. The first of these, the homeotherms, can be thought of as thermoregulators, since they maintain a near constant temperature regardless of ambient temperatures. This group includes mammals and birds, both of which have developed specialized features and functions to harness heat released through the metabolic process to maintain their relatively high average temperatures of 34-40°C. Poikilotherms, such as reptiles, amphibians, and most fish, on the other hand, can be considered thermoconformers, since their body temperatures are dependent upon the ambient temperature. Having a body temperature that fluctuates with the external temperature does not, however, mean that these organisms are protected from temperature changes. However, higher temperatures generally produce higher metabolic rates. This means that they must find ways to maintain their temperatures within a certain range. This is done in a host of ways such as moving, finding areas with appropriate temperatures or basking in the sun's warming rays.

대부분의 온도를 유지하는 생물은 2가지 범주 중 하나로 분류할 수 있다. 이들 중 첫 번째인 온혈동물은 주변 온도에 관계없이 거의 일정한 온도를 유지하기 때문에 체온조절기라 할 수 있다. 이 그룹에는 포유류 및 조류들이 포함되는데, 이들은 대사 과정을 통해 방출되는 열을 이용하여 34-40°C의 비교적 높은 평균 온도를 유지하는 특화된 특징과 기능을 발전시켜왔다. 반면에 파충류, 양서류, 그리고 대부분의 물고기와 같은 냉혈동물들은 그들의 체온이 주변 온도에 의존하기 때문에 열적응자로 간주될 수 있다. 하지만 외부 온도에 따라 변화하는 체온을 갖는다고 해서 이 유기체들이 온도 변화로부터 보호받는 것은 아니다. 그러나 온도가 높으면 일반적으로 대사율이 높아진다. 이것은 그들이 일정한 범위 내에서 온도를 유지하는 방법을 찾아야 한다는 것을 의미한다. 이것은 이동, 적절한 온도가 있는 지역을 찾거나 따뜻한 태양광선을 쬐는 것과 같은 많은 방법으로 행해진다.

단락3 그 외의 범주의 생물과 체계

3   Interestingly, not all animals fall into these two categories. Several species fall somewhere in the middle of the two. Some of the most well known examples of this are fast-swimming fish, such as the yellowfin tuna, which has an internal temperature that is several degrees warmer than the relatively cold seawater it inhabits. This occurs because they possess a heat retention mechanism that harnesses the heat produced by their muscular activity while swimming. Scientists believe this is necessary because of their reliance upon heat dependent biochemical reactions for their constant physical exertion. An entirely opposite example can be found in the intertidal zone. Some species in this area maintain their bodies at several degrees cooler than the ambient temperature by harnessing the powers of evaporation and circulation of bodily fluids. This allows them to live in areas where the shallow waters reach high temperatures due to the effects of the suns rays and reflection from the light colored substrate. By absorbing and losing heat directly to the air they are able to remain much cooler than non-living objects with corresponding sizes and shapes.

단락4 해양온혈동물의 열 손실

4   In marine environments, homeotherms have the most difficulty maintaining their internal body temperature, since most oceans average between 1.9 and 27°C. Exposure to these cold water temperatures can cause lower internal temperatures due to heat loss through the skin faster than in air. However, several other factors lead to lower temperatures. One of the biggest is the fact that these animals have closed circulatory systems that pump blood around the body, causing heat loss as it approaches the colder peripheral areas of the body. Further, the body's natural radiation of heat and respiration also lower the temperature, since the evaporation of water from the nasal cavities during exhalation has a natural cooling effect on their bodies.

단락5 열 손실 대응 방법

5   Marine animals have developed an assortment of ways to counteract this heat loss. The most common way is by developing a layer of insulation, but even this can take different forms. Most cetaceans, such as whales and porpoises, and seals build up a thick layer of fat under the skin, known as blubber. However, this does not work for smaller marine mammals such as sea otters. These nimble, weasel-like sea creatures do not store great fat reserves, but instead constantly preen and fluff their thick dual-layer fur. This allows the outer hairs to prevent water from reaching the softer undercoat and traps warm, dry air around the otter. This

USHER

단락6
역류 열 교환기 체계

process is also used by marine birds, which have waterproof outer feathers covering softer down that traps air and body heat. These methods are enhanced by the fact that marine mammals have higher body temperatures than their terrestrial counterparts.

6 Interestingly, the circulatory systems of some marine species also help conserve body heat by acting as countercurrent heat exchangers. In species, like porpoises, the veins that return the used blood surround the arteries, which pump blood from the warm core. This allows the warmer arteries to heat the blood as it returns from relatively colder areas such as the skin surface and flippers, which are not protected by thick blubber layers. This reduces the amount of heat lost to the water and can even be found in some fish, such as skipjack tuna.

열을 가두는 부드러운 표면을 덮는 방수 외피의 깃털을 가진 해양 조류들에게도 사용된다. 이러한 방법들은 해양 포유류가 육지 포유류보다 더 높은 체온을 가지고 있다는 사실에 의해 강화된다.

흥미롭게도 일부 해양생물의 순환계도 역류 열교환기 역할을 하여 체열을 보존하는데 도움을 준다. 알락돌고래처럼, 종에서 사용된 피를 되돌려주는 정맥은 동맥을 둘러싸고 있는데, 동맥은 따뜻한 중심부에서 혈액을 펌프질한다. 이것은 따뜻한 동맥이 두꺼운 지방층에 의해 보호되지 않는 피부 표면과 지느러미 같은 상대적으로 차가운 지역에서 돌아올 때 혈액을 가열할 수 있게 해준다. 이것은 물로 손실되는 열의 양을 줄이고 심지어 가다랭이와 같은 일부 생선에서도 발견될 수 있다.

---

01 Which of the sentences below best expresses the essential information in the highlighted sentence in the passage? Incorrect choices change the meaning in important ways or leave out essential information.

If the $^{(01)}$internal temperature of these organisms leaves the preferred range, which differs $^{(02)}$based on the species, for extended periods, $^{(03)}$enzyme degradation and tissue/ organ destruction may occur, which can $^{(04)}$make it difficult or impossible for their bodies to properly function.

(A) Animals must ensure that their bodies' enzymes and tissues remain within a specific range to ensure that their internal temperatures do not fluctuate too wildly that it destroys themselves. – 인과관계 ✗

(B) Species must be in the range of the average internal temperatures, which makes it impossible for their bodies to adapt to the temperatures when it is out of specific ranges, causing malfunction. – iii) 내용 ✗

(C) When the body temperatures change too drastically, many species cannot function properly because their enzymes, organs, and tissues are designed to function only with a certain range.

(D) Proper functioning can become unfeasible when temperatures of intramural species have become out of range, depending on its average range, causing internal damage by enzymes and tissues.

아래 문장 중 지문 속의 음영된 문장의 핵심 정보를 가장 잘 표현하고 있는 것은 무엇인가? 오답은 문장의 의미를 현저히 왜곡하거나 핵심 정보를 빠뜨리고 있다.

이러한 생물의 내부 온도가 종에 따라 다른 바람직한 범위를 장기간 벗어날 경우 효소 분해와 조직/장기 파괴가 발생할 수 있으며, 이는 그들의 몸이 제대로 기능하기 어렵거나 불가능하게 만들 수 있다.

(A) 동물들은 몸의 효소와 조직이 특정 범위 내에 있도록 해야 하며, 내부 온도가 너무 심하게 변동하여 스스로를 파괴하지 않도록 해야 한다.

(B) 종들은 반드시 평균 내부 온도 범위에 있어야 하는데, 이것은 특정한 범위를 벗어나면 그들의 몸이 온도에 적응하는 것을 불가능하게 만들어 오작동을 일으킨다.

(C) 체온이 너무 급격하게 변할 때, 많은 종들은 그들의 효소, 장기, 그리고 조직이 특정한 범위에서만 가능하도록 설계되었기 때문에 제대로 기능할 수 없다.

(D) 평균 범위에 따라 교내 종의 온도가 범위를 벗어나 효소와 조직에 의해 내부 손상을 일으킬 때 적절한 기능이 불가능해질 수 있다..

Highlight i) 생물이 적합한 온도 범위를 벗어날 경우 ii) 온도범위는 생물마다 다르다 iii) 효소저하와 조직/장기의 파괴가 발생한다.
iv) 몸이 적절히 기능할 수 없게된다는 정보를 가장 잘 담고 있는 **(D)**를 제외한 나머지 보기들은 틀린 부분 또는 정보가 부족해서 오답이다

02
According to paragraph 2, which of the following is NOT true regarding poikilotherms?

(A) Their internal temperatures change very quickly and often.
(B) They maintain their temperature within certain ranges.
(C) Their metabolic rates are temperature dependent.
(D) They use external mechanisms for temperature control.

2문단에 따르면, 다음 중 포이킬로온증에 관한 사실이 아닌 것은?

(A) 그들의 내부 온도는 매우 빠르고 자주 변한다.
(B) 그들은 일정한 범위 내에서 온도를 유지한다.
(C) 그들의 신진대사 속도는 온도에 따라 다르다.
(D) 그들은 온도 조절을 위해 외부 메커니즘을 사용한다.

Fact **(B)** - This means [that they must find ways (to maintain) their temperatures (within a certain range)]. **(C)** - higher temperatures generally produce higher metabolic rates. **(D)** - This is done (in a host of ways) (such as moving, finding) areas (with appropriate temperatures) or basking) (in the sun's warming rays).

03
According to paragraph 3, which of the following is true regarding animals that display traits of both homeotherms and poikilotherms?

(A) Their metabolisms are not dependent upon their temperature.
(B) They are only found in marine environments.
(C) They can be warmer or cooler than their environments.
(D) They do not regulate their temperatures

3문단에 따르면, 다음 중 가정온증과 포이킬로온증의 특징을 모두 보여주는 동물에 관한 설명으로 옳은 것은?

(A) 그들의 신진대사는 온도에 의존하지 않는다.
(B) 그들은 해양 환경에서만 발견된다.
(C) 그들은 환경보다 따뜻할 수도 있고 시원할 수도 있다.
(D) 그들은 온도를 조절하지 않는다.

Fact Some (of the most well known examples) (of this) are fast-swimming fish, (such as the yellowfin tuna), [which has an internal temperature [that is several degrees warmer (than the relatively cold seawater) [it inhabits]]]. Some species (in this area) maintain their bodies (at several degrees) cooler (than the ambient temperature) (by harnessing) the powers (of evaporation and circulation) (of bodily fluids).

04
The term "peripheral" in the passage is closest in meaning to:

(A) Central
(B) Thinner
(C) Outlying
(D) Auxiliary

지문의 단어 "주변적인"의 의미와 가장 유사한 것은?

(A) 중심의
(B) 얇은
(C) 외진
(D) 보조의

05
According to paragraph 4, which of the following can be inferred regarding air and water?

(A) Water is a better conductor of heat than air.
(B) Air and water can be used to maintain thermal homeostasis
(C) Only air breathing species need to worry about lower water temperatures.
(D) Water reduces internal temperatures, while air increases them

4문단에 따르면, 다음 중 공기와 물과 관련하여 추론할 수 있는 것은 무엇인가?

(A) 물은 공기보다 열의 전도성이 더 좋다.
(B) 공기와 물은 열 항상성을 유지하는 데 사용될 수 있다.
(C) 오직 공기 호흡 종만이 낮은 수온에 대해 신경쓰면 된다.
(D) 물은 내부 온도를 낮추는 반면 공기는 온도를 높인다.

Inference Exposure (to these cold water temperatures) can cause lower internal temperatures (due to heat loss) (through the skin) faster [than (in air)].

06 Which of the following is NOT mentioned as a means of maintaining body temperature in paragraph 5?

(A) Thick layers of subcutaneous fat.
(B) Dual-layered coats of fur that trap heat.
(C) Waterproof feathers over soft, warm down.
(D) ~~Increased activity~~ to create more heat than land animals.

5문단에 따르면, 체온을 유지하는 수단으로 언급되지 않은 것은?

(A) 피하지방의 두꺼운 층
(B) 열을 보호하는 두겹의 모피 가죽들
(C) 부드럽고 따뜻한 깃털 위에 방수성의 깃털
(D) 육지 동물보다 더 많은 열을 생성하기 위한 활동량 증가.

Fact **(A)** - Most cetaceans, (such as whales and porpoises), and seals build up a thick layer (of fat) (under the skin), known (as blubber). **(B)** - These nimble, weasel-like sea creatures do not store great fat reserves, but instead constantly preen and fluff their thick dual-layer fur. **(C)** - This process is also used (by marine birds), [which have waterproof outer feathers covering softer down [that traps air and body heat]].

---

07 Why does the author mention "fish, such as skipjack tuna"?

(A) To denote that ~~some fish are actually mammals~~.
(B) To give an idea of the wide variety of species that use this method.
(C) To explain ~~how countercurrent exchange systems work~~.
(D) To show that circulatory systems are ~~common in various animal species~~.

왜 저자는 "가다랑어와 같은 물고기"를 언급하는가?

(A) 어떤 물고기들은 실제로 포유동물이라는 것을 나타내기 위해.
(B) 이 방법을 사용하는 다양한 종의 아이디어를 제공하기 위해.
(C) 역전류 교환 시스템의 작동 방식을 설명하기 위해.
(D) 다양한 동물 종에서 순환계가 흔하다는 것을 보여주기 위해.

Purpose This reduces the amount (of heat) lost (to the water) and can even be found (in some fish), (such as skipjack tuna).

---

08 What can be inferred about countercurrent circulation from paragraph 6?

(A) It maintains internal temperatures more than surface temperatures.
(B) It is ~~the most common circulatory system in fish species~~.
(C) It allows ~~more blood to be exchanged~~ than would normally occur.
(D) It can also ~~help cool~~ marine species when the water becomes too hot.

6문단에서 역류 순환에 대해 추론할 수 있는 것은?

(A) 표면 온도보다 내부 온도를 더 유지한다.
(B) 그것은 어중에서 가장 흔한 순환계이다.
(C) 그것은 보통 일어나는 것보다 더 많은 혈액을 교환할 수 있게 해준다.
(D) 그것은 또한 물이 너무 뜨거워질 때 해양 생물의 온도를 낮추는 데 도움을 줄 수 있다.

Fact (In species), (like porpoises), the veins [that return the used blood (surround the arteries), [which pump blood (from the warm core)]].

09

Look at the four squares [■] that indicate where the following sentence could be added to the passage.

In extreme cases this can lead to permanent damage, or even death, for the organism.

Where would the sentence best fit?

3rd

네 개의 네모[■]는 다음 문장이 삽입될 수 있는 부분을 나타내고 있다.

극단적인 경우, 이것은 유기체에 영구적인 손상이나 심지어 죽음을 초래할 수 있다.

이 문장은 어느 자리에 들어가는 것이 가장 적합한가?

세 번째

> **Insertion** 몸이 적절하게 기능하지 못한다는 내용이 문장 앞에 나온 다음 극단적인 경우, 심지어 죽음까지 야기할 수 있다는 내용으로 이어지는 내용이기 때문에 **[C]**가 적절하다.

10

Directions: An introductory sentence for a brief summary of the passage is provided below. Complete the summary by selecting the THREE answer choices that express the most important ideas in the passage. Some sentences do not belong in the summary because they express ideas that are not presented in the passage or are minor ideas in the passage. **This question is worth 2 points.**

지시: 지문 요약을 위한 도입 문장이 아래에 주어져 있다. 지문의 가장 중요한 내용을 나타내는 보기 3개를 골라 요약을 완성하시오. 어떤 문장은 지문에 언급되지 않은 내용이나 사소한 정보를 담고 있으므로 요약에 포함되지 않는다. 이 문제는 2점이다.

Maintaining body temperature within a certain range is important for many animal species, especially those in marine environments.

(A) Hometherms have near constant internal temperatures, while poikilotherms internal temperatures fluctuate depending on the environment; however, some species display aspects of both. — paragraph 2, 3

(D) Marine homeotherms can easily lose their inner warmth due to respiration, circulation, and heat conduction by the cold waters of the marine environments. — paragraph 4

(E) Most animals that live in water have developed adaptations such as layered feathers and fur, thick layers of fat, and specially adapted circulatory systems to prevent heat loss. — paragraph 5, 6

(B) Most animals have internal body temperatures that remain between 34 and 40°C, which allows them to survive ~~in frigid oceanic waters~~. — INCORRECT

(C) Animal species can be categorized into either homeotherms or poikilotherms depending on the way in which they can maintain thermal homeostasis. — MINOR 2

(F) Fast-swimming fish are able to cope with increased water temperatures because of the way in which their circulatory systems ~~react to changing water temperatures~~. — ½, ½

체온을 일정 범위 내에서 유지하는 것은 많은 동물 종, 특히 해양 환경에 있는 동물들에게 중요하다.

(A) homeotherms은 내부 온도가 거의 일정한 반면, 포이킬라온류의 내부 온도는 환경에 따라 변동한다. 그러나 일부 종은 두 가지 측면을 모두 보여준다.

(D) 해양 homeotherms은 해양 환경의 차가운 물에 의한 호흡, 순환, 열전도 때문에 내면의 온기를 쉽게 잃을 수 있다.

(E) 물에 사는 대부분의 동물들은 층이 있는 깃털과 털, 두꺼운 지방층, 그리고 열 손실을 막기 위해 특별히 적응된 순환 시스템과 같은 적응 시스템을 발달시켰다.

(B) 대부분의 동물들은 34도에서 40도 사이의 내부 체온을 가지고 있어서 차가운 바닷물에서도 생존할 수 있다.

(C) 동물 종은 열적 항상성을 유지하는 방법에 따라 항상성 또는 포이킬성 중 하나로 분류될 수 있다.

(F) 빠르게 헤엄치는 물고기는 그들의 순환 시스템이 변화하는 수온에 반응하는 방식 때문에 높아진 수온에 대처할 수 있다.

TEST 4-2 The Upper Paleolithic Revolution 구석기 시대 후기 혁명

Introduction	단락 1	상부 구석기 시대의 극적인 변화 소개
Point	단락 2	도구와 예술형태의 고고학적 발견물
Point	단락 3	아프리카 유적지의 발견물과 유럽과 연관된 의문점
Point	단락 4	아프리카에서 시작된 자연적인 진화 주장
Point	단락 5	두 지역에서의 유물의 보존과 발견의 차이
Point	단락 6	기후변화로 인한 유럽으로의 이주

단락 1 — 상부 구석기 시대의 극적인 변화 소개

1 Around 35 to 40 KYA (thousands of years ago), there was a dramatic change in the archaeological record in Europe that marked the change from the Middle to Upper Paleolithic periods. During this transition, anatomically modern humans (AMH) replaced Neanderthal populations in Europe and brought about great changes in humanity. The rise of the AMH population can be seen through a dramatic increase in the use of tools and the invention of several purely human activities. The changes that occurred during the Upper Paleolithic era are so dramatic that they have been referred to as the Upper Paleolithic Revolution.

약 35~40 KYA (수천년 전)에 유럽의 고고학 기록에는 중기에서 상부 구석기 시대로의 변화를 나타내는 극적인 변화가 있었다. 이 전환기 동안, 해부학적으로 현생인류는 유럽의 네안데르탈인을 대체했고 인류에 큰 변화를 가져왔다. AMH 인구의 증가는 도구의 사용과 순수 인간 활동의 발명을 통해 확인할 수 있다. 상부 구석기 시대 동안에 일어났던 변화는 매우 극적이어서 '상부 구석기 혁명'이라고 일컬어 왔다.

단락 2 — 도구와 예술형태의 고고학적 발견물

2 Archaeological finds in many areas across Europe have supported this revolutionary change. The new population used much more versatile stone implements and animal products, such as bone and antler, to produce much more advanced tools. [■] Barbed reindeer harpoons and spear throwers, known as atlatl, have been discovered in European caves indicating a great leap forward in the understanding of hunting, and even rudimentary concepts in physics, such as torque. [■] Interestingly, this also appears to be the period when humans developed art forms, such as figurative art. [■] However, swan bone pipes with worn finger holes similar to flutes and primitive tattooing kits have been found in other European archaeological sites, indicating that figurative cave art was not the AMH's only artistic endeavor. [■]

유럽 전역의 많은 지역에서 발견된 고고학적 발견물들이 이러한 혁명적인 변화를 뒷받침하고 있다. 새로운 개체군은 훨씬 더 발전된 도구를 생산하기 위해 더 다용도 석기와 뼈와 뿔과 같은 동물 제품을 사용했다. 사냥에 대한 이해와 심지어 토크와 같은 물리학의 기초적인 개념에 큰 도약을 나타내는 Atlatl로 알려진 가시 돋친 순록 작살과 창들이 유럽의 동굴에서 발견되었다. 흥미롭게도, 이 시기는 또한 인간이 조형 예술과 같은 예술 형태를 발전시킨 시기로 보인다. 그러나 플룻과 유사한 손가락 구멍이 마모된 백조 뼈 관과 원시적인 문신도구가 유럽의 다른 고고학적 유적지에서 발견되었는데, 이는 동굴 예술이 AMH의 유일한 예술적 노력이 아니었음을 나타낸다.

단락 3 — 아프리카 유적지의 발견물과 유럽과 연관된 의문점

3 An interesting aspect of these discoveries is that they were all found in Europe, leading researchers to believe that the advances of early AMH were a purely European occurrence around 40 KYA that eventually spread elsewhere. However, the later discovery

이러한 발견의 흥미로운 측면은 모두 유럽에서 발견되었고, 연구자들은 초기 AMH의 발전이 결국 다른 곳으로 확산된 40 KYA 즈음에 순수하게 유럽에서 발생했다고 믿게 만들었다. 그러나, 남아프리카 공화국의 Blombos

of decorated ochre and shell beads, as well as evidence of AMH's ability to fish, in South Africa's Blombos Cave dating to 77 KYA and contemporary bone tools found in other African sites indicate that this "revolution" was simply an example of human behavioral evolution that had been occurring for much longer. This led researchers to question why the discovery of modern tools from this period were concentrated in Europe and whether the European discoveries were the start of a new form of human behavior, or if they were simply built upon earlier innovations in other parts of the world.

4   Anthropologists Sally McBrearty and Alison Brooks point to Eurocentric bias and disregard for the extent of the African archaeological record as the most likely causes for the discovery of more tools in Europe. They hold that evidence of more modern tools in Africa, such as blades and microlithic technology, higher geographic ranges, art, and long distance trade networks, predates its appearance in Europe by at least 10,000 years and can be found in archaeological sites separated by both geographical area and time frame, thus suggesting a natural evolution, rather than an immediate revolution such as in Europe. This indicates that AMH behavior was likely formed in Africa and exported to other regions. The myriad forms of early rock art found in Australia further support this idea. Since people arrived in Australia around 60 KYA and were isolated from the "revolution" in Europe 40 KYA, their rock art can be seen to show that creativity was already a part of human cognition when early AMH began migrating out of Africa around 70 KYA.

5   This type of scrutiny has caused theories of a sudden advent of modern behavior and tool making during an "Upper Paleolithic Revolution" in Europe to falter. The most logical reason for its supposed sudden occurrence would be, as McBrearty and Brooks pointed out, deficiencies in the archaeological record in Africa and other regions, while those in Europe are rather well preserved. It may simply turn out that artifacts elsewhere have been lost, or have yet to be found. This can be seen by the recent discovery of pierced shells dating from 43 KYA in Lebanon, suggesting the modernization had occurred prior to the date of the "revolution" but went undetected until recently.

6   However, the presence of tools in other areas does not explain the sudden appearance of tools in the European

archaeological record. One theory for this is climate change. Prior to the suggested dates of the Upper Paleolithic Revolution, Europe underwent a major climate change that caused the disappearance of the previous glaciers and an overall warming, which made the continent more hospitable for early AMH. This could have allowed a migration of early AMH to the previously uninhabited area. This sudden appearance of AMH in Europe would have led to an increase in more modern tools in the archaeological record, which could explain why they suddenly appeared around 35 KYA.

변화이다. 구석기 시대 이전에 유럽은 이전 빙하의 소멸과 전반적인 온난화를 야기한 큰 기후 변화를 겪었고, 이로 인해 초기 AMH는 더 잘 적응할 수 있었다. 유럽에서 AMH의 갑작스러운 출현은 고고학적 기록에서 더 현대적인 도구의 증가로 이어졌을 것이며, 이것은 왜 35 KYA에 갑자기 나타났는지를 설명할 수 있다.

11 What can be inferred from paragraph 1 about changes that occurred during the Upper Paleolithic?

(A) They were a result of the population of AMH that replaced the Neanderthal.
(B) They remain ~~the most fundamental technological changes~~ that have ever occurred.
(C) They ~~caused~~ the Neanderthal population ~~to evolve into~~ AMH.
(D) They allowed AMH to ~~overpower~~ the Neanderthal and conquer their territory.

후기 구석기의 변화에 대해 문단1에서 추론할 수 있는 것은?

(A) 그들은 네안데르탈인을 대체한 AMH의 개체수의 결과였다.
(B) 그들은 지금까지 일어난 것 중 ~~가장 근본적인 기술 변화로~~ 남아있다.
(C) 그들은 네안데르탈인을 ~~AMH로의 진화를 야기시켰~~ 다.
(D) 그들은 AMH가 네안데르탈인을 제압하고 그들의 영토를 ~~정복하도록~~ 허락했다.

Inference (During this transition), anatomically modern humans (AMH) replaced Neanderthal populations (in Europe) and brought about great changes (in humanity).

12 Why does the author mention "rudimentary concepts in physics, such as torque"?

(A) To indicate that tools were ~~not the only advances made by AMH in Europe~~.
(B) To give an example of ~~the new fields of study initiated~~ by AMH in Europe.
(C) To show a form of higher knowledge exemplified by the new tools found in Europe.
(D) To explain that the Upper Paleolithic Revolution also ~~led to great strides in science~~.

저자는 왜 "토크 등 물리학의 초보적 개념"을 언급하는가?

(A) 도구만이 ~~유럽에서 AMH에 의해 만들어진 것이 아~~ 님을 나타내기 위해.
(B) 유럽에서 AMH에 의해 ~~시작된 새로운 연구 분야의~~ 예를 제시하기 위해.
(C) 유럽에서 발견된 새로운 도구에 의해 예시되는 고급 지식의 형태를 보여주기 위해
(D) 후기 구석기 혁명이 과학에도 ~~큰 발전을 가져왔다는~~ 것을 설명하기 위해

13 According to paragraph 2, which of the following is **NOT** included amongst the archaeological finds from the Upper Paleolithic?

(A) Advanced tools
(B) Cave art
(C) Musical instruments
(D) Early tattoos

2문단에 따르면, 다음 중 후기 구석기 시대의 고고학적 발견물에 포함되지 않은 것은?

(A) 발전된 도구
(B) 동굴 벽화
(C) 악기
(D) 초기 문신

Fact **(A)** - The new population used much more versatile stone implements and animal products, (such as bone and antler), (to produce) much more advanced tools. **(B)** - Barbed reindeer harpoons and spear throwers, known (as atlatl), have been discovered (in European caves) **(C)** - However, swan bone pipes (with worn finger holes) similar (to flutes and primitive tattooing kits) have been found (in other European archaeological sites), indicating [that figurative cave art was not the AMH's only artistic endeavor].

14 Which of the sentences below best expresses the essential information in the highlighted sentence in the passage? Incorrect choices change the meaning in important ways or leave out essential information.

However, the (01)later discovery of decorated ochre and shell beads, as well as evidence of AMH's ability to fish, in (02) South Africa's Blombos Cave (03)dating to 77 KYA and (04) contemporary bone tools found in other African sites indicate that (05)this "revolution" was simply an example of human behavioral evolution that had been occurring for much longer.

(A) Many forms of artifacts that human activities evolved before the "revolution" was found in several sites in Africa, indicating that the "revolution" is all but an example of human behavioral evolution.
(B) ~~Decoration of~~ ochre and shells beads in the Blombos Cave and other African sites in 77 Kya, which indicated that the evolution of human behavior is simply the revolution.
(C) Artifacts from the Blombos Cave showed that many types of human activity had evolved before the "revolution" ~~in Europe~~ 77 KYA, such as decorative beads and evidence of fishing in Africa.
(D) Tools that predate the European "revolution" were found in various archaeological sites in Africa, corroborating that the African people ~~were competent in making tools~~ even before the Europeans.

아래 문장 중 지문 속의 음영된 문장의 핵심 정보를 가장 잘 표현하고 있는 것은 무엇인가? 오답은 문장의 의미를 현저히 왜곡하거나 핵심 정보를 빠뜨리고 있다.

그러나, 남아프리카 공화국의 Blombos 동굴에서 77 KYA의 연대를 거슬러 올라가는 장식된 황토와 조개구슬이 발견된 이후, 그리고 다른 아프리카 유적지에서 발견된 동시대의 뼈 도구들은 이 "혁명"이 훨씬 더 오랜 기간 동안 일어났던 인간의 행동 진화의 한 예였다는 것을 보여준다.

(A) "혁명" 이전에 인간의 활동이 진화한 많은 형태의 유물이 아프리카의 여러 곳에서 발견되었는데, 이는 "혁명"이 거의 인간의 행동 진화의 예시라는 것을 보여준다.
(B) 77 Kya의 Blombos 동굴과 다른 아프리카 유적지에 황토와 조개구슬을 ~~장식~~했는데, 이것은 인간의 행동의 진화가 단순히 혁명임을 나타냈다.
(C) 블롬보스 동굴에서 나온 유물들은 장식용 구슬과 아프리카에서 낚시를 했다는 증거와 같은 많은 종류의 인간 활동이 ~~유럽~~ 77 KYA에서 "혁명" 이전에 진화 했음을 보여주었다.
(D) 유럽의 "혁명" 이전의 도구들이 아프리카의 여러 고고학 유적지에서 발견되었는데, 이는 ~~아프리카 사람들이 유럽인들보다도 도구를 만드는 데 능숙했~~다는 것을 증명했다.

Highlight ⅰ) 아프리카 동굴에서 발견된 증거들과 ⅱ) 이러한 혁명이 오랜 기간동안 발생해왔다는 것을 보여준다는 2 가지 정보를 그대로 가지고 있는 답은 **(A)**가 적절하다.

15 What can be inferred about the tools found in Africa from paragraph 3?

(A) They were ~~superior~~ to the ones ~~believed to be from the Upper Paleolithic Revolution~~.
(B) Early African populations ~~could not have made them before Europeans visited~~.
(C) They were as advanced as those from the Upper Paleolithic Revolution.
(D) Modern researchers believe ~~that they are from the Upper Paleolithic Revolution~~.

3문단에서, 아프리카에서 발견된 도구에 대해 추론할 수 있는 것은?

(A) 그것들은 후기 구석기 혁명으로 추정되는 것들보다 ~~우수했다~~.
(B) 초기 아프리카 인구는 유럽인들이 방문하기 전에는 ~~그것을 만들 수 없었을 것이다~~.
(C) 그들은 후기 구석기 혁명의 그것들과 같이 발전했다.
(D) 현대의 연구자들은 ~~그들이 구석기시대 후기 혁명에서 왔다고 믿는다~~.

Inference However, the later discovery (of decorated ochre and shell beads), as well as evidence (of AMH's ability) (to fish), (in South Africa's Blombos Cave) dating (to 77 KYA) and contemporary bone tools) found (in other African sites) indicate [that this "revolution" was simply an example (of human behavioral evolution) [that had been occurring (for much longer)]].

16 According to paragraph 4, which of the following is **NOT** true about the discovery of advanced tools in Africa?

(A) It contradicts the theory of the Upper Paleolithic Revolution in Europe.
(B) The tools ~~were discovered before~~ the Upper Paleolithic Revolution in Europe.
(C) The discoveries were ignored by, or unknown to, the Europeans who developed the Upper Paleolithic Revolution theory.
(D) The tools were likely the precursors for the tools attributed to the Upper Paleolithic Revolution in Europe.

4문단에 따르면, 아프리카에서 첨단 도구의 발견에 대해 사실이 아닌 것은 다음 중 무엇인가?

(A) 그것은 유럽의 후기 구석기 혁명의 이론과 모순된다.
(B) 이 도구들은 유럽의 구석기시대 후기 혁명 ~~이전에 발견되었다~~.
(C) 그 발견은 후기 구석기 혁명 이론을 발전시킨 유럽인들에게 무시당하거나 알려지지 않았다.
(D) 그 도구들은 아마도 유럽의 후기 구석기 혁명에 기인한 도구들의 전조였을 것이다.

Fact **(A),(D)** - They hold [that evidence (of more modern tools) (in Africa), (such as blades and microlithic technology, higher geographic ranges, art, and long distance trade networks), predates its appearance (in Europe) (by at least) 10,000 years) and can be found (in archaeological sites) separated (by both geographical area and time frame), thus suggesting a natural evolution, rather (than an immediate revolution) (such as in Europe). **(C)** - Anthropologists Sally McBrearty and Alison Brooks point (to Eurocentric bias and disregard) (for the extent) (of the African archaeological record) (as the most likely causes) (for the discovery) (of more tools) (in Europe).

17 According to paragraph 5, which of the following is true regarding the Upper Paleolithic Revolution?

(A) It is the best explanation for the discovery of advanced tools in other regions that date to this period.
(B) Recent discoveries make it likely that it occurred in Lebanon and not Europe, as was previously thought.
(C) It is the most likely explanation for gaps in the archaeological record in other regions that made European advances seem groundbreaking.
(D) The Upper Paleolithic Revolution has been largely disproven by the discovery of advanced tools elsewhere.

5문단에 따르면, 다음 중 상부 구석기 혁명에 대한 올바른 설명은 무엇인가?

(A) 이는 이 기간까지 거슬러 올라가는 다른 지역의 고급 도구 발견에 대한 가장 좋은 설명이다.
(B) 최근의 발견으로 인해, 이전에 생각했던 것처럼 유럽이 아니라 레바논에서 일어났을 가능성이 높아졌다.
(C) 그것은 유럽의 발전을 획기적으로 보이게 한 다른 지역의 고고학적 기록의 격차에 대한 가장 유력한 설명이다.
(D) 후기 구석기 혁명은 다른 곳에서 진보된 도구들이 발견됨으로써 반증되었다.

Fact The most logical reason (for its supposed sudden occurrence) would be, [as McBrearty and Brooks pointed out], deficiencies (in the archaeological record) (in Africa and other regions), [while those (in Europe) are rather well preserved].

18 According to paragraph 6, which of the following can be inferred about the role of climate change in the Upper Paleolithic Revolution?

(A) Climate change caused great changes around the world, and forced early AMH to migrate to Europe, which had the world's most hospitable climate at the time.
(B) Deglaciation of Europe caused people with contemporary tools of Africa to move to inhabitable lands of Europe, causing the sudden appearance of tools in the area.
(C) Glaciation in Europe preserved the tools of the early AMH, causing it to be the source of most examples of advanced tools from the era.
(D) The effect of the changing weather patterns caused early AMH to adapt to a new environment and forced them to develop new tools.

6문단에 따르면, 다음 중 상부 구석기 혁명의 기후 변화의 역할에 대해 추론할 수 있는 것은 무엇인가?

(A) 기후 변화는 전 세계에 큰 변화를 일으켰고, 초기 AMH는 당시 세계에서 가장 쾌적한 기후를 가지고 있던 유럽으로 이주하도록 강요했다.
(B) 유럽의 해빙은 아프리카의 현대 도구를 가진 사람들을 유럽의 거주 가능한 땅으로 이동하게 했고, 그 지역에 도구의 갑작스러운 출현을 야기했다.
(C) 유럽의 빙하화는 초기 AMH의 도구를 보존했고, 그 시대의 고급 도구의 대부분 사례의 원천이 되었다.
(D) 변화하는 날씨 패턴의 영향으로 인해 초기 AMH는 새로운 환경에 적응하게 되었고 새로운 도구를 개발하게 되었다.

Inference This could have allowed a migration (of early AMH) (to the previously uninhabited area). This sudden appearance (of AMH) (in Europe) would have led (to an increase) (in more modern tools) (in the archaeological record), [which could explain [why they suddenly appeared around 35 KYA]].

19

Look at the four squares [■] that indicate where the following sentence could be added to the passage.

The most famous of these are, doubtlessly, cave paintings, such as those found in the Lascaux caves outside Montignac, France.

Where would the sentence best fit?

3rd

네 개의 네모[■]는 다음 문장이 삽입될 수 있는 부분을 나타내고 있다.

이들 중 가장 유명한 것은 의심할 여지 없이 프랑스 몽티냑 외곽의 라스코 동굴에서 발견된 것과 같은 동굴 벽화이다.

이 문장은 어느 자리에 들어가는 것이 가장 적합한가?

세 번째

Insertion 주어진 문장에서의 these 가 가리키는 것이 art forms이고 cave paintings와 연결이 되고 있기 때문에 [C]가 적절하다.

20

Directions: An introductory sentence for a brief summary of the passage is provided below. Complete the summary by selecting the THREE answer choices that express the most important ideas in the passage. Some sentences do not belong in the summary because they express ideas that are not presented in the passage or are minor ideas in the passage. **This question is worth 2 points.**

지시: 지문 요약을 위한 도입 문장이 아래에 주어져 있다. 지문의 가장 중요한 내용을 나타내는 보기 3개를 골라 요약을 완성하시오. 어떤 문장은 지문에 언급되지 않은 내용이나 사소한 정보를 담고 있으므로 요약에 포함되지 않는다. 이 문제는 2점이다.

Researchers have noted a great leap forward in human behavior and knowledge in Europe's archaeological record called the "Upper Paleolithic Revolution"

(A) The Upper Paleolithic Revolution theory was formed when archaeologists found uses of tools more dramatic than any of the previous record.
— paragraph 1

(D) Anthropologists believe that the behavioral and technological changes found in Europe likely occurred elsewhere and made their way to Europe.
— paragraph 4

(F) Climate change allowed a migration to Europe after the ice age, which caused the sudden appearance of tools and art forms there.
— paragraph 6

연구자들은 "후기 구석기 혁명"이라고 불리는 유럽의 고고학 기록에서 인간의 행동과 지식에 있어 큰 도약에 주목했다.

(A) 후기 구석기 혁명 이론은 고고학자들이 도구의 사용이 이전의 어떤 기록보다 더 극적인 것을 발견했을 때 형성되었다.

(D) 인류학자들은 유럽에서 발견된 행동과 기술적 변화가 다른 곳에서 일어났을 가능성이 있고 유럽으로 옮겨갔을 것으로 믿고 있다.

(F) 기후 변화는 빙하기 이후 유럽으로의 이주를 가능하게 했고, 그것은 그곳에 갑자기 도구와 예술 형태가 출현하게 만들었다.

(B) The tools found in Europe indicate great changes in human evolution, because they are ~~the oldest tools that archaeologists have ever unearthed~~.

(C) Artifacts found in the Blombos Cave resembled those found at European archaeological sites allowing scientist to determine ~~that they were created by AMH before they migrated~~.

(E) Aboriginal Australian artwork indicates that the AMH in Europe were ~~much more advanced than those~~ who dispersed to other areas.

(B) 유럽에서 발견된 도구들은 고고학자들이 ~~발굴한 가장 오래된 도구이기~~ 때문에 인류 진화의 큰 변화를 보여준다.

(C) 블롬보스 동굴에서 발견된 유물은 유럽 고고학 유적지에서 발견된 유물과 흡사해 과학자들은 ~~그들이 이주하기 전에 AMH에 의해 만들어졌다는~~ 것을 확인할 수 있었다.

(E) 호주 원주민의 예술작품은 유럽의 AMH가 ~~다른 지역으로 흩어진 사람들보다 훨씬 더 발전했음을~~ 보여준다.

usherin.usher.co.kr

Nineteenth-Century Theories of Mountain Formation

1 Due to several major misconceptions, our understanding of mountain formation is relatively new. As recently as the early 19th century, most geological findings were viewed as a series of catastrophic events that allowed geological knowledge to corroborate a short Earth history that corresponded to biblical narratives. However, during the 19th century, scientists began to offer other explanations for geological features, such as mountain formation. Unfortunately, most of the theories they developed were based upon the idea that Earth had been formed as a superheated mass and had steadily cooled through time. This led them to postulate that Earth's core must be shrinking as it cools, as most objects do. From this, they extrapolated that Earth's crust would be deformed by the shrinkage and mountains would form.

2 One of the first geologists to try to explain this was Eduard Suess. He explained that Earth's crust wrinkled as it contracted, just as a drying apple's peel does. His theory assumed that Earth's crust had begun as a single layer, but separated as the "wrinkles" formed. This led to great depressions that became ocean basins and higher areas that formed the continents. Further, he thought that continued contraction would lead to instability and the two features could alternate, meaning that oceans would become continental land and vice versa. Using this theory, he incorrectly postulated that the Alps had once been at the bottom of a massive ocean, but had risen and left the Mediterranean as its only remnant.

3 This alternation was an important point in his theory, because it helped to explain other geological features that scientists, even the great Leonardo da Vinci, had been unable to interpret, such as the discovery of marine fossils on dry land and the interspersed marine and terrestrial sediment found in the stratigraphic column. It also helped to explain a problem brought about by Darwin's contemporaneous theory of evolution. By the mid-1800s, scientists had noticed similar, or even identical, fossils in distant places, such as South America and Africa. Darwin's theory made this identical evolution of two distant species highly unlikely, but Suess countered this with the theory that changes in Earth's landmasses and oceans made it possible. He developed the theory of an ancient, giant landmass connected by land bridges that he referred to as Gondwanaland.

4 Ironically, acceptance of Suess's theory was geographically split; it gained a greater acceptance in Europe than in North America. On the other side of the Atlantic, geologists like James Dwight Dana developed their own explanations for mountain formation. Dana's theory, known as permanence, was based on the continents and oceans remaining as they are. He theorized that as Earth cooled and contracted, minerals with low melting points, like feldspar and quartz, solidified early on and those with higher melting points, like pyroxene and olivine, became solid later, thereby creating ocean basins. As the contraction continued it put immense pressures on Earth's surface, especially along the oceanic/continental boundaries, which caused the creation of the mountain ranges found along continental edges, such as those on the west coast of both North & South America.

5 [■] Dana's theory led fellow American geologist James Hall to theorize that subsidence, or sinking, of sediment from a former shallow sea formed the Appalachian Mountains. [■] Hall felt that these materials were produced by continental erosion and accumulated in linear troughs along the mountain's edge, called geosynclines. [■] As these troughs filled and began to subside, they became deeper and Earth's inner heat turned the sediment into stone. [■] Eventually, it was uplifted to form mountains. Dana slightly modified this theory to explain that sediment had not caused subsidence, but was actually the result of it. Unfortunately for both, their explanations of how shallow-water sediment built up did nothing to accurately explain how these thick layers of sediment were uplifted.

USHER

단락 6
지각균형설로
인한 반증과
대륙이동설

6 By the early 1900s, the flaws in these theories became evident. Through the discovery of certain features in the earth's crust, such as unexplainable strata shortening and the theory of isostasy that explained that the crust and its mountains were actually floating on Earth's mantle, and not held in place on their own, scientists were able to disprove Suess's theory of oceanic/continental changeability. However, the most important discovery was radiogenic heating, which definitively negated the theory of contraction, and all theories based on it. All of this caused scientists to look for more accurate explanations of mountain formation. The best of these was Alfred Wegener's theory of continental drift. Unfortunately, this theory was not accepted until the existence of tectonic plates was confirmed nearly 50 years later. Today, we know that the actions of these tectonic plates created Earth's various mountain ranges.

1900년대 초까지, 이 이론들의 결함은 명백해졌다. 설명할 수 없는 지층 단축과 지각과 산이 실제로 지구의 맨틀 위에 떠 있고 스스로 제자리에 고정되지 않았다는 등 지각균형설과 같은 지각의 특정 특징들을 발견함으로써 과학자들은 Suess의 해양/대륙 변화 이론을 반증할 수 있었다. 그러나 가장 중요한 발견은 복사열이었으며, 이는 수축 이론과 그에 기초한 모든 이론을 부정하는 것이었다. 이 모든 것은 과학자들이 산 형성에 대한 더 정확한 설명을 찾도록 만들었다. 그 중 최고는 Alfred Wegener의 대륙 이동 이론이었다. 불행하게도, 이 이론은 지각판의 존재가 거의 50년 후에 확인될 때까지 받아들여지지 않았다. 오늘날, 우리는 이러한 지각판의 작용이 지구의 다양한 산맥을 만들었다는 것을 알고 있다..

---

21 What can be inferred from paragraph 1 about Earth's formation and composition?

(A) The theory that the super-heated core being [had been] gradually cooled since Earth's formation was proven inaccurate.
(B) Scientists have been unable to explain the formation of landmasses because they do not understand how Earth was formed.
(C) Earth was a much larger planet at the time of its formation due to the great heat that it contained before the cooling process started.
(D) Compared to 19th century, before that time, the Christian bible was the main source of scientific discovery and exploration.

지구의 형성과 구성에 대해 문단 1에서 추론할 수 있는 것은 무엇인가?

(A) 과열된 핵이 지구의 형성 이후 점차 식어갔다는 이론은 부정확한 것으로 입증되었다.
(B) 과학자들은 지구가 어떻게 형성되었는지 이해하지 못하기 때문에 육지의 형성을 설명할 수 없었다.
(C) 지구는 냉각 과정이 시작되기 전에 포함된 엄청난 열 때문에 형성 당시 훨씬 더 큰 행성이었다.
(D) 그 이전인 19세기에 비해 기독교 성경은 과학적 발견과 탐구의 주요 원천이었다.

Inference Unfortunately, most (of the theories) [they developed] were based (upon the idea) [that Earth had been formed (as a superheated mass) and had steadily cooled (through time)].

22 According to paragraph 2, which of the following is **NOT** true regarding Suess's theory about differences in the Earth's crust?

(A) It was based on the contraction of Earth's core due to its gradual cooling over time.
(B) It attempted to explain the different geological features, such as ocean basins and mountains.
(C) It held that the geological features that we know today are ~~permanent~~ since contraction slows over time.
(D) It inaccurately explained the formation of both the Alps in Southern Europe and the nearby Mediterranean Sea.

2 문단에 따르면, 다음 중 지구 지각의 차이에 대한 수에스의 이론에 대해 사실이 아닌 것은?

(A) 그것은 시간이 지남에 따라 서서히 식어가는 지구핵의 수축에 기초했다.
(B) 그것은 해양 분지와 산과 같은 다른 지질학적 특징들을 설명하려고 시도했다.
(C) 그것은 시간이 지남에 따라 수축이 느려지기 때문에 오늘날 우리가 알고 있는 지질학적 특징들은 ~~영구적이라고~~ 주장했다.
(D) 그것은 남유럽의 알프스 산맥과 인근 지중해의 형성을 부정확하게 설명했다.

Fact (A) - He explained [that Earth's crust wrinkled [as it contracted], [just as a drying apple's peel does]]. (B) - Further, he thought [that continued contraction would lead (to instability) and the two features could alternate, meaning [that oceans would become continental land and vice versa]]. (D) - Using this theory, he incorrectly postulated [that the Alps had once been (at the bottom) (of a massive ocean), but had risen and left the Mediterranean (as its only remnant)].

23 Which of the sentences below best expresses the essential information in the highlighted sentence in the passage? Incorrect choices change the meaning in important ways or leave out essential information.

This (01)alternation was an important point (in his theory), [because it helped (to (02)explain) other geological features [that (03)scientists, even the great Leonardo da Vinci, had been unable (to interpret)], (such as the (04)discovery) (of marine fossils) (on dry land) and (05)the interspersed marine and terrestrial sediment) found (in the stratigraphic column)].

(A) The theory of alternation ~~was developed to answer the questions~~ posed by scientists, such as da Vinci, who questioned why terrestrial fossils were found in the stratigraphic column along with marine fossils.
(B) ~~Leonardo da Vinci was unable to understand~~ the presence of marine fossils in ~~terrestrial~~ regions before a theory of alteration was developed that explained why marine and terrestrial fossils are found in the same places.
(C) The discovery of marine fossils in terrestrial regions, and the appearance of the two types of fossils in one region was a mystery until the theory of land alteration definitively proved that the lands and seas shifted location over time.   – da Vinci 언급 ✗
(D) Finding fossils from sea life on dry land had confused scientists, such as Leonardo, for many years, but the theory or alternation helped to explain it along with other geological conundrums like the mix of land and sea fossils in the soil strata.

아래 문장 중 지문 속의 음영된 문장의 핵심 정보를 가장 잘 표현하고 있는 것은 무엇인가? 오답은 문장의 의미를 현저히 왜곡하거나 핵심 정보를 빠뜨리고 있다.

이 변화는 그의 이론에서 중요한 점이었는데, 이는 과학자들이, 심지어 위대한 레오나르도 다빈치조차도 해석할 수 없었던, 지층서 기둥에서 발견된 해양과 육지 사이의 퇴적물과 같은 다른 지질학적 특징들을 설명하는 데 도움이 되었기 때문이다.

(A) 대체 이론은 다빈치와 같은 과학자들이 제기한 질문에 답하기 위해 개발되었는데, 다빈치는 왜 해양 화석과 함께 지상 화석이 지층학 기둥에서 ~~발견되는지 의문을 제기했다~~.
(B) ~~레오나르도 다빈치는~~ 왜 해양과 육지 화석이 같은 장소에서 발견되는지를 설명하는 변형이론이 개발되기 전에는 육지 지역에 해양 화석이 존재한다는 것을 ~~이해할 수 없었다~~.
(C) 육지에서의 해양 화석의 발견과 한 지역에서 두 종류의 화석이 출현한 것은 육지변화 이론이 시간이 지남에 따라 육지와 바다의 위치가 바뀌었다는 것을 확실히 증명하기 전까지 미스터리였다. - 다빈치 ✗
(D) 건조한 육지에서 바다 생물로부터 화석을 발견하는 것은 레오나르도와 같은 과학자들을 오랫동안 혼란스럽게 했지만, 그 이론이나 대안은 토양 지층에서 육지와 바다 화석이 섞인 것과 같은 다른 지질학적 난제와 함께 그것을 설명하는데 도움을 주었다.

Highlight ⅰ) 이러한 변화가 중요했다 ⅱ) 여러 지질학적 특징들을 설명하는 것을 도와주었다 ⅲ) 심지어 다빈치도 설명하지 못했던 것을, 각 정보들 중 **(A)**는 목적이 틀렸고, **(B)**는 다빈치가 중심이고 **(C)**는 ⅲ) 정보가 누락되어 **(D)**가 적절하다.

24 What can be inferred about Darwin's theory of evolution from paragraph 3?

(A) It ~~was greatly influenced by the concept of contraction~~ that Suess was working on.
(B) Although it was concerned mainly with the evolution of animals ~~it also included theories about geological formation.~~
(C) Darwin ~~developed the theory after~~ Suess had announced his theory of mountain formation and landmass changes.
(D) It could have posed a great problem for Suess's theory if he had not included the interchangeability of oceanic/continental landmasses.

3문단에서 다윈의 진화론에 대해 추론할 수 있는 것은 무엇인가?

(A) 그것은 수에스가 연구하던 ~~수축의 개념에 큰 영향을 받았다.~~
(B) 그것은 주로 동물의 진화에 관한 것이었지만 ~~지질 형성에 관한 이론도 포함하고 있었다.~~
(C) 다윈은 수에스가 산악 형성과 대륙 변화에 대한 이론을 발표한 후 ~~아~~ 이론을 발전시켰다.
(D) 만약 그가 해양/대륙 육지의 교환성을 포함하지 않았다면, 그것은 수에스의 이론에 큰 문제를 제기했을 것이다.

Inference but Suess countered this (with the theory) [that changes (in Earth's landmasses and oceans) made it possible]

---

25 According to paragraph 4, which of the following is **NOT** true about J.D. Dana's theory of permanence?

(A) Its acceptance in North America led it to ~~overtake Suess's theory in Europe as well.~~
(B) It did not allow for changes in the location or position of the continents and oceans.
(C) It was based on the physical properties of the different components of Earth's interior.
(D) It attributed geological changes to the same basic force as Suess's theory.

4문단에 따르면, J.D. 다나의 영속성 이론에 대한것 중 사실이 아닌 것은?

(A) 북미에서 그것이 받아들여지면서 ~~유럽에서도 수에스의 이론을 추월하게 되었다.~~
(B) 그것은 대륙과 해양의 위치나 위치의 변화를 허용하지 않았다.
(C) 그것은 지구 내부의 여러 구성 요소들의 물리적 특성에 기초했다.
(D) 그것은 지질학적 변화를 수에스의 이론과 같은 기본적인 힘 때문이라고 보았다.

Fact **(B)** - Dana's theory, known (as permanence), was based (on the continents and oceans) remaining [as they are]. **(C)** - He theorized [that [as Earth cooled and contracted], minerals (with low melting points), (like feldspar and quartz), solidified early on and those (with higher melting points), (like pyroxene and olivine), became solid later, thereby creating ocean basins]. **(D)** - [As the contraction continued] it put immense pressures (on Earth's surface), especially (along the oceanic/continental boundaries)

---

26 According to paragraph 5, which of the following can be inferred regarding the theory of subsidence?

(A) Subsidence ~~failed to gain widespread acceptance~~ in the scientific community because it could only be applied to one mountain range.
(B) There was ~~not enough evidence~~ to prove the occurrence of subsidence in geosyncline troughs near the Appalachian mountains.
(C) Subsidence can be used to explain the composition of some mountains, but not their actual formation.
(D) Dana realized the importance of the subsidence theory and ~~abandoned his previous theory to work on the new one.~~

5문단에 따르면, 침하 이론에 관해 다음 중 추론할 수 있는 것은 무엇인가?

(A) 침하가 한 산맥에만 적용되기 때문에 과학계에서 ~~널리 받아들여지지 못했다.~~
(B) 애팔래치아 산맥 근처의 지압골에서 침하 발생을 증명할 ~~충분한 증거가 없었다.~~
(C) 침하를 사용하여 일부 산의 구성을 설명할 수 있지만 실제 형성은 설명할 수 없다.
(D) 다나는 침하 이론의 중요성을 깨닫고 이전의 이론을 ~~버리고 새로운 이론을 연구했다.~~

Inference Unfortunately (for both), their explanations (of [how shallow-water sediment built up]) did nothing (to accurately explain) [how these thick layers (of sediment) were uplifted].

27

Why does the author mention "unexplainable strata shortening and the theory of isostasy"?

(A) To offer two theories for the creation of mountains that were developed in the early 20th century.
(B) To give examples of two discoveries that allowed scientists to invalidate earlier theories about changes in Earth's crust and mountain formation.
(C) To show two new theories that were developed as a result of the discoveries made by scientists in the 19th century, such as Suess.
(D) To allow the reader to understand how earlier theories of mountain formation led to the development of the theory of continental drift.

왜 작가가 "설명할 수 없는 지층의 단축과 지각균형설"을 언급하였을까?

(A) 20세기 초에 개발된 산의 생성에 대한 두 가지 이론을 제시하기 위해.
(B) 과학자들이 지구의 지각과 산의 형성에 관한 이전의 이론을 무효화 할 수 있게 해준 두 가지 발견의 예를 들기 위해.
(C) 19세기 과학자들의 발견의 결과로 개발된 두 가지 새로운 이론을 보여주기 위해.
(D) 초기 산 형성 이론이 어떻게 대륙 이동 이론의 발전으로 이어졌는지를 독자들이 이해할 수 있도록 하기 위해.

Purpose (Through the discovery) (of certain features) (in the earth's crust), (such as unexplainable strata shortening) and the theory) (of isostasy) [that explained [that the crust and its mountains were actually floating (on Earth's mantle), and not held (in place) (on their own)]], scientists were able (to disprove) Suess's theory (of oceanic/continental changeability).

28

The term "definitively" in the passage is closest in meaning to:

(A) Conclusively
(B) Accurately
(C) Conditionally
(D) Belatedly

지문의 단어 "확실하게"의 의미와 가장 유사한 것은?

(A) 결론적으로
(B) 정확하게
(C) 조건부로
(D) 뒤늦게

29

Look at the four squares [■] that indicate where the following sentence could be added to the passage.

He based this idea on the fact that the mountains were made up of layers of shallow-water sedimentary rocks several thousands of feet thick.

Where would the sentence best fit?

2nd

네 개의 네모[■]는 다음 문장이 삽입될 수 있는 부분을 나타내고 있다.

그는 산이 수천 피트 두께의 얕은 물의 퇴적암 층으로 이루어져 있다는 사실에 이 아이디어를 기초했다.

이 문장은 어느 자리에 들어가는 것이 가장 적합한가?

두 번째

Insertion 문장에서 He 와 this idea 부분이 앞에 나와야 하기 때문에 이론을 주장한 다음 문장인 **[B]**가 적절하다.

30

Directions: An introductory sentence for a brief summary of the passage is provided below. Complete the summary by selecting the THREE answer choices that express the most important ideas in the passage. Some sentences do not belong in the summary because they express ideas that are not presented in the passage or are minor ideas in the passage. **This question is worth 2 points.**

Nineteenth Century Scientists Developed Contrasting Theories Regarding the Formation of Mountains.

(B) In Europe, Eduard Suess developed the most accepted theories of mountain formation which said that Earth's crust buckled in various ways as Earth cooled after its formation. — paragraph 4

(E) American geologists disputed the changeability of oceanic/continental lands and explained mountain formation through mineral differences and sediment accretion. — paragraph 5

(F) Discoveries in the twentieth century disproved the contraction theory upon which the earlier theories had been based and revealed the more accurate theory of plate tectonics. — paragraph 6

(A) Nineteenth century geologists found that after the radiogenic heating that caused Earth's formation ceased, the planet ~~gradually cooled~~ and as it did the size shrunk. — ½, ½

(C) Eduard Suess discovered that the Alps had once been located under a nearby sea, which eventually shrunk and formed the Mediterranean Basin. — MINOR 2

(D) Darwin's theory of evolution caused problems for geologists because similar fossils were found in various distant locations around the world. — MINOR

지시: 지문 요약을 위한 도입 문장이 아래에 주어져 있다. 지문의 가장 중요한 내용을 내타내는 보기 3개를 골라 요약을 완성하시오. 어떤 문장은 지문에 언급되지 않은 내용이나 사소한 정보를 담고 있으므로 요약에 포함되지 않는다. 이 **문제는 2점이다.**

19세기 과학자들은 산의 형성과 관련하여 대조적인 이론을 개발했다.

(B) 유럽에서 에두아르트 수에스는 지구의 지각이 형성된 후 식으면서 다양한 방식으로 무너진다는 산악 형성 이론을 개발했다.

(E) 미국 지질학자들은 해양/대륙 땅의 변화 가능성에 대해 이의를 제기하고 광물 차이와 퇴적물 침전을 통해 산의 형성을 설명했다.

(F) 20세기의 발견은 초기 이론들이 근거를 두고 있던 수축 이론을 반증했고 판구조론의 더 정확한 이론을 밝혀냈다.

(A) 19세기 지질학자들은 지구의 형성을 야기한 방사능 발생 가열이 멈춘 후, 행성이 점차 식어갔고 크기가 줄어들었다는 것을 발견했다.

(C) Eduard Suess는 알프스 산맥이 한때 가까운 바다 밑에 있었고, 그것은 결국 줄어들어 지중해 분지를 형성했다는 것을 발견했다.

(D) 다윈의 진화론은 지질학자들에게 문제를 일으켰다. 왜냐하면 비슷한 화석이 세계의 여러 먼 곳에서 발견됐기 때문이다.

usherin.usher.co.kr

USHER

iBT TOEFL
INTERMEDIATE READING 02

TEST 5

답안 및 취약 유형 분석표

해석·해설

답안 및 문제 유형 분석표

TEST 5-1

01 (D) Purpose
02 (C) Fact
03 (D) Inference
04 (C) Fact
05 (C) Fact
06 (B) Highlight
07 (A) Fact
08 (A) Inference
09 1st ■ Insertion
10 (B), (E), (F) Summary

TEST 5-2

11 (C) Fact
12 (D) Highlight
13 (D) Vocabulary
14 (C) Fact
15 (A) Inference
16 (B) Purpose
17 (A) Fact
18 (D) Fact
19 1st ■ Insertion
20 (A), (C), (E) Summary

TEST 5-3

21 (B) Fact
22 (A) Highlight
23 (D) Fact
24 (A) Inference
25 (C) Vocabulary
26 (B) Fact
27 (D) Fact
28 (C) Purpose
29 3rd ■ Insertion
30 (B), (E), (F) Summary

각 문제 유형별 맞춘 개수를 아래에 적어 보세요.

유형	맞춘 답의 개수	정답률	
단어 (Vocabulary)	/ 2	정답률:	%
사실 확인 문제 (Fact)	/ 12	정답률:	%
지시어 찾기 (Reference)	/ 0	정답률:	%
끼워 넣기 (Insertion)	/ 3	정답률:	%
문장 변환문제 (Highlight)	/ 3	정답률:	%
목적 (Purpose)	/ 3	정답률:	%
추론 (Inference)	/ 4	정답률:	%
단락 요약 (Summary / Category Chart)	/ 3	정답률:	%
전체	/ 30	정답률:	%

※ 자신이 취약한 유형은 READING STRATEGIES를 통해 다시 한번 점검하시기 바랍니다. (p.44)

TEST 5-1 — Colonial America and the Navigation Acts
식민지와 항해에 관한 법률

Introduction	단락 1	16세기 유럽의 중상주의와 영국의 무역법 시행
Point	단락 2	항해 조례와 영국의 무역 독점
Point	단락 3	영국인 중심의 선박과 조선업 발달 이후 미국의 도시화
Point	단락 4	진열상품의 거래 제한과 관세 환급
Point	단락 5	식민지 내 무역 증가와 소규모 의류 생산
Point	단락 6	저가 상품에 대한 보호로 인한 식민지 번영

단락 1 — 16세기 유럽의 중상주의와 영국의 무역법 시행

1 Mercantilism swept across Europe in the sixteenth century. Under this system governments attempted to regulate and protect their economies by ensuring a positive balance of trade using high tariffs and protective import laws. This was especially true in the British Empire, which was threatened by the rising power of Dutch traders after the Eighty Years' War and the lifting of Spanish embargoes on trade with them. After this time, Dutch traders overwhelmed British trade on the Iberian Peninsula, around the Mediterranean Sea, and into the Levant; however, the most troubling development was their rising power in the British colonies, especially those in the New World. In order to protect its trade power, Parliament passed a series of trade laws known collectively as the Navigation Acts, which effectively controlled all imperial commerce.

중상주의는 16세기에 유럽 전역을 휩쓸었다. 이 제도 하에서 정부는 높은 관세와 보호 수입법을 사용하여 무역의 균형을 유지함으로써 경제를 규제하고 보호하려고 시도했다. 특히 대영제국은 80년 전쟁 이후 네덜란드 무역상들의 세력이 커지고 스페인 무역 금수조치가 해제되면서 위협을 받았다. 이 시기 이후 네덜란드 상인들은 이베리아 반도, 지중해, 레반트 등지에서 영국의 무역을 압도했다. 그러나 가장 문제를 일으키는 발전은 특히 신대륙에서와 같이 영국 식민지에서의 그들의 증가하는 힘이었다. 무역력을 보호하기 위해 의회는 항해법으로 알려진 일련의 무역법을 통과시켰고, 이 법은 제국 무역을 효과적으로 통제했다.

단락 2 — 항해 조례와 영국의 무역 독점

2 One of the first of the Navigation Acts was the Navigation Ordinance of 1651. This new ordinance limited imports into the British Empire to those brought by British ships or those from the country in which the product had been manufactured. This severely limited Dutch imports, since they specialized in carrying products from other regions, and mainly exported locally made dairy products. As time went by, more of these types of acts were passed, further increasing restrictions on trade, which greatly affected the colonies. In fact, the passage of the Navigation Acts of 1660 and 1663, forced British colonies to export commodities, like sugar and tobacco, only to England aboard British-flagged vessels. They were not, however, all detrimental to the colonies. For instance, the Molasses Act of 1733 added an import tariff to molasses entering the colonies from outside the empire. This

항해법의 첫 번째 중 하나는 1651년의 항해 조례였다. 이 새로운 법령은 대영제국에 대한 수입을 영국 선박이나 제품이 제조된 국가에서 가져온 것으로 제한했다. 이는 네덜란드가 다른 지역으로부터 제품을 운반하는 것을 전문화했기 때문에 수입에 심각한 제약을 주었고 그래서 현지생산한 유제품을 주로 수출했다. 시간이 지남에 따라, 이러한 종류의 행위들이 더 많이 행해졌고, 무역에 대한 제약이 더욱 증가하면서 이는 식민지에 큰 영향을 미쳤다. 사실상, 1660년과 1663년의 항해법의 통과는 영국 식민지들로 하여금 설탕과 담배와 같은 상품들을 영국 국적의 선박을 타고 영국으로만 수출하도록 강요했다. 그러나 그들이 모두 식민지에 해로운 것은 아니었다. 예를 들어, 1733년의 당밀법은 제국 외부에서 식민지로 들어오는 당밀에 수입 관세를 추가했다. 이로 인해 당밀은 프랑스령 카리브 제도에서 생산되는 당밀보다 비쌌기 때문에 영국령

basically created a molasses monopoly for plantation owners in the British West Indies, since it was cheaper than that produced on French Caribbean islands. By the 1750s, the economic impact of these laws had become clear in the North American colonies.

3   The first major condition set forth by the Navigation Acts was the use of only British ships with crews that were 75% British, which included colonists and their slaves. This dramatically reduced imports and foreign shipping into the Empire, which allowed the British fleet to become the world's most powerful. Interestingly, it also encouraged shipbuilding in North America, since the colonists could freely trade within the Empire. This brought about the foundation of an American merchant marine fleet and, by the 1750s, one-third of the British fleet was composed of American ships. The concentration of the shipbuilding and export industries in the northeast led to rapid urbanization in the region as more warehouses, docks, and maintenance firms were built there. By the late 18th century, New York City and Philadelphia had become not only the two largest cities in the colonies, but also two of the busiest ports in the entire empire.

4   Another major stipulation of the Navigation Acts was that certain "enumerated goods," such as tobacco, rice, hides, sugar, and naval supplies, could only be shipped directly to England or Scotland, thus giving the British government control over the respective markets. [■] However, the Navigation Acts did not kill the trade in the enumerated goods. [■] In fact, Parliament blocked the import of foreign tobacco and rice, the two commodities most affected by the Acts. [■] This proved burdensome to British citizens, but helped the tobacco farmers. [■] They also agreed to refund import duties on products that were eventually shipped out of the empire, which accounted for 85% of the North American exports. These measures meant that tobacco and rice producers suffered a less than 3% reduction in their income.

5   Eventually, the Navigation Acts led to economic diversification and increased trade in the colonies, since Parliament paid subsidies to colonists for producing raw materials that would have otherwise have been imported from trade rivals, such as silk, iron, dye, and lumber. They did not, however, allow the large-scale production of manufactured goods, such as clothing, that could affect Britain's large-scale factories. This meant that tailors, milliners, and other clothing manufacturers were restricted to producing their products in small shops. These restrictions allowed British clothing to be sold at much lower prices than locally manufactured goods. Surprisingly, the production of ironworks was not limited by the acts and it became a major industry.

생산된 상품보다 훨씬 낮은 가격에 판매할 수 있게 했다. 놀랍게도, 제철소의 생산은 법에 의해 제한되지 않았고 그것은 주요 산업이 되었다.

단락 6
저가 상품에 대한 보호로 인한 식민지 번영

6   The last major effect of these acts was that they created a protected market for lower-priced British goods. Demand for colonial materials remained high and led to prosperity in the colonies. This led to an increased demand for British manufactured goods, such as dishware, tea, and furniture, in addition to clothing. This allowed exports to the American colonies to rise from 5% of all British exports in 1700 to nearly 40% by 1760. The influx of these manufactured goods allowed middle-class colonists to live as comfortably as their British counterparts.

이 법들의 마지막 주요 효과는 그들이 저가의 영국 상품에 대한 보호 시장을 만들었다는 것이다. 식민지 물자에 대한 수요는 여전히 높았고 식민지의 번영을 이끌었다. 이로 인해 의류 외에도 식기, 차, 가구와 같은 영국 공산품에 대한 수요가 증가했다. 이로 인해 미국 식민지에 대한 수출은 1700년 영국 전체 수출의 5%에서 1760년 40%로 증가했다. 이러한 공산품의 유입은 중산층 식민지 개척자들이 영국 식민지 개척자들처럼 편안하게 살 수 있도록 해주었다.

---

01   Why does the author mention that the Dutch "mainly exported locally-made dairy products"?

(A) To show that Dutch products were everyday staple products required by the British.
(B) To give the reader an understanding of the weakness of the Dutch economy.
(C) To point out some products that the Dutch could export to the British Empire.
(D) To explain why the Navigation Acts were particularly detrimental to Dutch traders.

저자는 왜 "mainly exported locally-made dairy products"를 언급했는가?

(A) 네덜란드산 제품이 영국인들이 매일 필요로 하는 주요 제품임을 보여주기 위해.
(B) 독자들에게 네덜란드 경제의 약점을 이해시키기 위해.
(C) 네덜란드인들이 대영제국에 수출할 수 있는 제품들을 지적하기 위해.
(D) 항해법이 네덜란드 무역상들에게 특히 해로운 이유를 설명하기 위해.

Purpose   This severely limited Dutch imports, [since they specialized (in carrying) products (from other regions)], and mainly exported locally-made dairy products.

02

According to paragraph 2, which of the following is **NOT** true about the Navigation Acts?

(A) They effectively limited the import of products from outside the British Empire.
(B) They increased the central governments regulation of colonial trade systems.
(C) They encouraged more trade between colonies located far from Great Britain.
(D) They created monopolies for some products within the empire.

2문단에 따르면, 다음 중 항해법에 대해 사실이 아닌 것은?

(A) 그들은 사실상 대영제국 외부로부터의 제품 수입을 제한했다.
(B) 그들은 식민지 무역 시스템에 대한 중앙 정부의 규제를 강화했다.
(C) 그들은 영국으로부터 멀리 떨어진 식민지들 사이의 더 많은 무역을 장려했다.
(D) 그들은 제국 내에서 일부 제품에 대한 독점권을 만들었다.

Fact **(A)** - This new ordinance limited imports (into the British Empire) (to those) brought (by British ships) or those) (from the country) [(in which) the product had been manufactured]. **(B)** - [As time went by], more (of these types) (of acts) were passed, further increasing restrictions (on trade), [which greatly affected the colonies]. **(D)** - (In fact), the passage (of the Navigation Acts) (of 1660 and 1663), forced British colonies (to export) commodities, (like sugar and tobacco), only (to England) (aboard British-flagged vessels).

03

What can be inferred about the Navigation Acts' regulations on ships and their crews from paragraph 3?

(A) They were seen as a way of providing jobs to more British subjects in the colonies, where the economy was previously faltering.
(B) They inadvertently encouraged the use of slaves since they were considered British under the regulations.
(C) They led to a reduction in the export of products from the Empire, which caused a general downturn in the global economy.
(D) They established the northern colonies as economic powerhouses and greatly altered the population dispersion of early America.

3문단에 따르면 선박과 그 승무원들에 대한 항해법의 규정에 대해 추론할 수 있는 것은 무엇인가?

(A) 그들은 이전에 경제가 휘청거렸던 식민지에서 더 많은 영국인들에게 일자리를 제공하는 방법으로 여겨졌다.
(B) 그들은 규정상 영국인으로 간주되었기 때문에 의도치 않게 노예의 사용을 장려했다.
(C) 그들은 제국으로부터의 상품 수출 감소로 이어져 세계 경제의 전반적인 침체를 초래했다.
(D) 그들은 북부 식민지를 경제 강국으로 설립했고 초기 미국의 인구 분포를 크게 변화시켰다.

Inference The concentration (of the shipbuilding and export industries) (in the northeast) led (to rapid urbanization) (in the region) [as more warehouses, docks, and maintenance firms were built there].

04

The term "stipulation" in the passage is closest in meaning to:

(A) Implication
(B) Suggestion
(C) Condition
(D) Association

지문의 단어 "조건, 조항"의 의미와 가장 유사한 것은?

(A) 영향
(B) 제안
(C) 조건
(D) 연관

05

According to paragraph 4, which of the following is true regarding the enumeration of goods by the Navigation Acts?

(A) It ~~caused the collapse of several important industries~~ in the colonies.
(B) ~~Most colonists became richer because of the higher prices~~ that could be charged for the products.
(C) The regulations had only a negligible effect on trade in the enumerated goods due to concessions made by Parliament.
(D) It was meant to ~~ensure that~~ the Empire had sufficient supplies of products like tobacco and rice.

4문단에 따르면, 항해법에 의한 상품 일람표시에 관한 다음 중 올바른 것은 무엇인가?

(A) 그것은 식민지의 ~~몇몇 중요한 산업의 붕괴를 야기했~~다.
(B) ~~대부분의 식민지 주민들은~~ 제품에 부과될 수 있는 ~~높은 가격 때문에 부자가 되었다.~~
(C) 그 규제는 의회의 양보로 인해 열거된 물품의 무역에 무시해도 될 정도의 효과만 가져왔다.
(D) 그것은 제국이 담배와 쌀과 같은 충분한 물자를 공급하도록 ~~하기 위한~~ 것이었다.

06

Which of the sentences below best expresses the essential information in the highlighted sentence in the passage? Incorrect choices change the meaning in important ways or leave out essential information.

⁽⁰¹⁾Eventually, the ⁽⁰²⁾Navigation Acts led (to economic diversification) and increased trade (in the colonies), [since ⁽⁰³⁾ Parliament paid subsidies (to colonists) (for producing) ⁽⁰⁴⁾raw materials [that would have ⁽⁰⁵⁾otherwise have been imported (from trade rivals), ⁽⁰⁶⁾(such as silk, iron, dye, and lumber)]]

(A) Parliament provided the colonists money to add additional elements to their economy that were eventually used ~~to increase the raw materials that were exported to other countries~~ that had signed the Navigation Acts.
(B) Over time, Parliament's payments to colonists for providing unprocessed materials that were previously imported from outside the empire under the Navigation Acts brought about more trade and expanded the colonial economy.
(C) The Navigation Acts were written to increase trade to the colonies and allow them to diversify their economy in such a way that would ~~allow them to produce materials that were not available in the Empire at the time.~~
(D) The imperial government paid a premium for certain products, since the economic expansion of the Navigation Acts ~~made raw materials, like lumber and metals, more expensive to import from rivals~~ in the mercantile system.

아래 문장 중 지문 속의 음영된 문장의 핵심 정보를 가장 잘 표현하고 있는 것은 무엇인가? 오답은 문장의 의미를 현저히 왜곡하거나 핵심 정보를 빠뜨리고 있다.

결국, 항해법은 비단과 철, 염료, 목재와 같은 무역 경쟁국들로부터 수입되었을 원자재를 생산하기 위해 식민지 주민들에게 보조금을 지급한 이후, 경제적 다양화와 식민지 내 무역을 증가시켰다.

(A) 의회는 식민지 주민들에게 그들의 경제에 추가적인 요소들을 추가하기 위해 돈을 제공했고, 이는 결국 항해법에 서명한 ~~다른 나라들로 수출되는 원자재를 증가시키는데 사용되었다.~~
(B) 시간이 흐르면서, 의회가 과거 항해법에 따라 제국 외부에서 수입된 가공되지 않은 재료를 제공한 식민지 주민에게 지급한 돈은 더 많은 무역을 초래했고 식민지 경제를 확장시켰다.
(C) 항해법은 식민지에 대한 무역을 늘리고 ~~당시 제국에서 구할 수 없었던 자재를 생산할 수 있는~~ 방식으로 그들의 경제를 다각화할 수 있도록 하기 위해 제정되었다.
(D) 항해법의 경제 팽창으로 ~~목재와 금속과 같은 원자재가 상업 시스템의 경쟁자들로부터 수입하는 데 더 비싸졌기 때문에,~~ 제국 정부는 특정 상품에 할증료를 지불했다.

Highlight i) 항해법으로 인한 경제 다양화와 식민지내 무역 증가 ii) 의회가 원자재 생산하는 식민지에게 보조금 지급 iii) 무역 경재자들로부터 수입되어졌을 원자재 총 세 가지의 정보를 담고 있는 보기는 B가 적절하다.

07

According to paragraph 5, which of the following was **NOT** a change in the colonial economy brought about by the Navigation Acts?

(A) Colonial products ~~were supplanted by those made by the British~~.
(B) Colonists increased their production of raw materials.
(C) Most American finished goods were produced through cottage industries.
(D) The production of ironworks became a major industry.

5문단에 따르면, 다음 중 항해법에 의해 초래된 식민지 경제의 변화가 아닌 것은?

(A) 식민지 제품은 영국제 제품으로 ~~대체되었다~~.
(B) 식민지 주민들은 원자재 생산을 늘렸다.
(C) 대부분의 미국 완제품은 가내공업을 통해 생산되었다.
(D) 제철소 생산은 주요 산업이 되었다.

Fact **(B)** - the Navigation Acts led (to economic diversification) and increased trade (in the colonies) **(C)** - This meant [that tailors, milliners, and other clothing manufacturers were restricted (to producing) their products (in small shops)]. **(D)** - the production (of ironworks) was not limited (by the acts) and it became a major industry.

08

According to paragraph 6, which of the following can be inferred regarding the effects of the mercantile system in the North American colonies?

(A) Mercantilism greatly changed the lifestyle of the colonists.
(B) American colonists ~~surpassed~~ the British middle-class in terms of personal wealth.
(C) British manufactured goods ~~replaced American made products~~ causing America to develop a trade imbalance.
(D) Colonists became ~~dependent upon~~ the British Empire ~~for finished goods~~.

6문단에 따르면, 다음 중 북미 식민지에서의 상업체제의 영향에 대해 추론할 수 있는 것은?

(A) 상업주의는 식민지 주민들의 생활 방식을 크게 변화시켰다.
(B) 미국의 식민지 개척자들은 개인 재산 면에서 영국 중산층을 ~~앞질렀다~~.
(C) 영국의 공산품은 미국의 무역 불균형을 초래하는 ~~미국산 제품을 대체했다~~.
(D) 식민지 주민들은 ~~완제품을~~ 대영제국에 ~~의존하게 되었다~~.

Inference This allowed exports (to the American colonies) (to rise) (from 5%) (of all British exports) (in 1700) (to nearly 40%) (by 1760).

09

Look at the four squares [■] that indicate where the following sentence could be added to the passage.

Luckily for the colonists, the list of enumerated goods did not include livestock, lumber, rum, fish, or grains, which made up 60% of their exports.

Where would the sentence best fit?

1st

네 개의 네모[■]는 다음 문장이 삽입될 수 있는 부분을 나타내고 있다.

식민지 주민들에게는 다행스럽게도, 가축, 목재, 럼주, 생선, 곡물은 수출의 60%를 차지하지 않았다.

이 문장은 어느 자리에 들어가는 것이 가장 적합한가?

첫 번째

Insertion 조항에 포함되지 않은 다른 상품들의 리스트를 언급하고 있기 때문에 물품 자체에 대한 설명을 하고 있는 **[A]**가 적절하다

Directions: An introductory sentence for a brief summary of the passage is provided below. Complete the summary by selecting the THREE answer choices that express the most important ideas in the passage. Some sentences do not belong in the summary because they express ideas that are not presented in the passage or are minor ideas in the passage. **This question is worth 2 points.**

The American colonies were greatly affected by the passage of the Navigation Acts by the British imperial government.

(B) Restrictions in the legislation limited the type of goods colonists could export and the types of industries that could be set up in the colonies. — paragraph 4, 5

(E) The colonial economy was diversified to meet the needs of the empire, since tariffs in the Navigation Acts made importing raw materials expensive and benefitted rivals. — paragraph 5

(F) Colonists migrated to urban areas to support the growing shipping industry, while the standard of living increased as the colonists became wealthier from trade with Britain. — paragraph 3

(A) The American Parliament passed the Navigation Acts in an effort to control trade within the empire and ~~reduce the influence of foreign powers~~ under mercantilism. — ½, ½

(C) ~~The Navigation Acts required that~~ the crew of all American ships be British citizens or their slaves. — INCORRECT

(D) Because of the Molasses Act of 1733, American colonists could freely import cheap molasses from other British colonies in the West Indies. — MINOR

usherin.usher.co.kr

TEST 5-2 The Most Common Bird on Earth — 지구상에서 가장 흔한 새

Introduction	단락 1	붉은부리 쿠엘레아 소개와 개체 수
Point	단락 2	식단 종류와 생존을 위한 행동
Point	단락 3	날씨기반의 적응력을 이용한 섭식과 이동
Point	단락 4	계절에 따른 군락의 형성 과정
Point	단락 5	곡물섭식으로 인한 농업 생산 문제
Point	단락 6	지역파괴의 우려 원인과 호주의 도입 금지

문단주제 / 본문내용 / 해석

단락 1 — 붉은부리 쿠엘레아 소개와 개체 수

1 Most people outside of Africa have never heard of the red-billed quelea, but these small African birds are the most common bird species on Earth. A member of the weaver family, they live on the grasslands of sub-Saharan Africa in extremely large colonies that contain up to 30 million individuals. Conservative estimates put the total population of the birds across Africa at more than 1.5 billion breeding pairs, with some saying there may be up to 10 billion of the birds.

아프리카 밖의 대부분의 사람들은 붉은부리 쿠엘레아에 대해 들어본 적이 없지만, 이 작은 아프리카 새들은 지구상에서 가장 흔한 조류 종이다. 직물과에 속하는 그들은 사하라 이남 아프리카의 초원에서 3천만 마리까지 서식하는 아주 큰 군락에서 산다. 보수적인 추정에 의하면 아프리카 전역의 총 개체수는 15억쌍이 넘으며 일부는 최대 100억쌍이 될 수도 있다고 한다.

단락 2 — 식단 종류와 생존을 위한 행동

2 It may seem illogical that these small birds survive in such a harsh environment, but their extreme success is even more remarkable when one considers that they survive nearly entirely on the annual grasses in the region. Although researchers have noted that they eat some insects, mainly beetles, and a few non-grass seeds, these accounted for less than two percent of their overall diet. One might expect that this great dependence upon annual grasses would lead to regular reduction or extinction of the populations, but, much like early humans learned to hoard wheat and barley seeds to deal with lean times, the red-billed quelea have developed certain behaviors that help them cope with the feast or famine nature of the grass crops.

이 작은 새들이 열악한 환경에서 살아남는 것이 비논리적으로 보일 수 있지만, 이 지역의 거의 모든 연초들을 먹고 산다는 것을 고려할 때 이들의 극단적인 성공은 더욱 놀랍다. 비록 연구자들은 그들이 주로 딱정벌레와 몇몇 풀뿌리가 아닌 씨앗을 먹는다는 것에 주목했지만, 이 씨앗들은 그들의 전체 식단의 2%도 차지하지 않는다. 해마다 풀밭에 크게 의존하는 것이 개체수의 정기적인 감소나 멸종으로 이어질 것이라고 예상할 수 있지만, 초기 인간들이 기근에 대처하기 위해 밀과 보리의 씨앗을 저장해두는 것을 배운 것처럼 붉은부리 쿠엘레아는 풀밭 작물의 성찬이나 기근에 대처하는 데 도움이 되는 특정한 행동을 발달시켰다.

단락 3 — 날씨기반의 적응력을 이용한 섭식과 이동

3 One of the most advantageous adaptations made by the red-billed quelea has been the development of variable annual weather-dependent cycles. [■] During the dry season the bird population must sustain itself with the seeds produced at the end of the rainy season. [■] To do this, they gorge themselves on seeds to gain enough wait to sustain them while they migrate to more productive places. [■] This must be done during the

붉은부리 쿠엘레아에 의해 만들어진 가장 유리한 적응 중 하나는 가변적인 연간 날씨를 기반으로 주기의 발달이다. 건기 동안 쿠엘레아 개체는 우기 말에 생성된 씨앗으로 스스로를 지탱해야 한다. 그러기 위해, 그들은 씨앗을 먹고 더 생산적인 장소로 이동하는 동안 씨앗을 지탱하기 위한 충분한 무게를 얻는다. 건기때는 장마로 인해 남은 씨앗이 발아하여 먹이 공급이 몇 주 동안 중단되고 이동을 부추기기 때문에

dry season, since monsoon rains cause the remaining seeds to germinate, thereby interrupting the food supply for weeks and instigating the move. [■] Luckily, this does not occur simultaneously across the entire savanna and dry seeds, young grasses, and mature ripe grasses are available in different areas. To take advantage of this the quelea make 50-200 km migrations across the savannas, which allows them to survive in such a forbidding environment.

4   By the time the rains have germinated and fresh seeds become available, these early-rain migrations end and the quelea return to the previously abandoned areas. Access to these new seeds stimulates the population's males to weave ovoid grass and straw nests in acacia trees. The females who help them complete the nest and who then lay two to four eggs later join them. These colonies can cover up to 100 hectares with 500 nests in each acacia. With an average of 100,000 fledglings per hectare, up to 10 million offspring are produced by each successful colony. Surprisingly, the entire process of nest weaving, mating, brooding and fledging of the juveniles takes only six weeks, which is much shorter than in other birds, and is incredibly synchronized, as the eggs all hatch on the same day. However, this process is dependent upon weather patterns, as an earlier dry season can cause the quelea to abandon their colony, while an extended green season with abundant seed stock can allow them to produce multiple broods in the same region.

5   Since they rely upon seeds, these large colonies can cause problems for the region's farmers. As more and more grains are planted across sub-Saharan Africa, the birds have turned to the crops for nourishment. This has allowed their numbers to explode in the region. It is estimated that the population of these "feathered locusts" has increased by 10-100 times since the 1970s. With each bird eating its own weight in seeds per day this leaves fields within 30 Km. of the breeding sites highly susceptible. Researchers have estimated that flocks can consume upwards of 50 tons of seeds per day, which allows them to wipe out entire small crops and approximately 20% of the annual production of large commercial farms. Annual losses directly attributable to these small birds have been calculated at $70m, in a region where agricultural production is already in a precarious state.

USHER

단락 6
지역파괴의 우려 원인과 호주의 도입 금지

6 Their easy adaptability and propensity to migrate in large flocks has made the red-billed quelea a cause for concern in areas where their introduction could allow them to become entrenched as an invasive species. One such region is Australia's northwestern state of Queensland, where the climate resembles the quelea's native habitat. Queensland's $440m annual cereal grain harvest would be devastated if large colonies of quelea became established. Colony establishment would also wreak havoc on the region's native species, such as the endangered Gouldian finch, which could not compete with such massive flocks. This has caused the Australian government to ban the import of the world's most common and destructive bird.

그들의 쉬운 적응력과 큰 무리를 지어 이동하는 성향은 붉은부리 쿠엘레아를 침입종으로서 정착하게 할 수 있는 지역에서 우려의 원인으로 만들었다. 이러한 지역 중 하나는 호주의 북서부 퀸즐랜드주이며, 기후는 쿠엘레아의 토착 서식지와 유사하다. 퀸즐랜드의 연간 4억4천만 달러 규모의 곡물 수확은 퀸즐랜드의 대규모 쿠엘레아 군집체가 세워질 경우 엄청난 타격을 입을 것이다. 군집의 형성은 또한 멸종위기에 처한 굴드 핀치와 같은 이 지역의 토착종들에게 큰 피해를 입힐 것이다. 이것은 호주 정부가 이러한 세계에서 가장 흔하고 파괴적인 새의 도입을 금지하도록 만들었다.

---

11 What can be inferred from paragraph 1 about the red-billed quelea?

(A) They are ~~difficult to spot~~ in their natural environment.
(B) They inhabit remote areas ~~far from human settlements.~~
(C) They are rarely found outside of their native habitats.
(D) They are ~~the largest species of animals~~ in the world.

붉은부리 쿠엘레아에 대해 단락 1에서 추론할 수 있는 것은?

(A) 그들은 자연환경에서 ~~발견하기 어렵다~~.
(B) 그들은 인간의 ~~거주지~~에서 멀리 떨어진 외딴 지역에 산다.
(C) 그들은 그들의 서식지 밖에서 거의 발견되지 않는다.
(D) 그들은 세계에서 ~~가장 큰~~ 동물 종이다.

Fact Most people (outside of Africa) have never heard (of the red-billed quelea), but these small African birds are the most common bird species (on Earth).

---

12 Which of the sentences below best expresses the essential information in the highlighted sentence in the passage? Incorrect choices change the meaning in important ways or leave out essential information.

$^{(01)}$One might expect that this great $^{(02)}$dependence upon annual grasses would lead to $^{(03)}$regular reduction or extinction of the populations, but, $^{(04)}$much like early humans learned to hoard wheat and barley seeds to deal with lean times, $^{(05)}$the red-billed quelea have developed certain behaviors that help them cope with the feast or famine nature of the grass crops.

(A) ~~From watching Human's saving seeds~~ for poor harvest seasons, the red-billed quelea developed behaviors to cope with famine of grass crops.
(B) The red-billed quelea ~~learned to have~~ special traits because of survival in a famine of cereals, as pre-historic humans hoarded grains of wheat and seeds.

아래 문장 중 지문 속의 음영된 문장의 핵심 정보를 가장 잘 표현하고 있는 것은 무엇인가? 오답은 문장의 의미를 현저히 왜곡하거나 핵심 정보를 빠뜨리고 있다.

해마다 풀밭에 크게 의존하는 것이 개체수의 정기적인 감소나 멸종으로 이어질 것이라고 예상할 수 있지만, 초기 인간들이 기근에 대처하기 위해 밀과 보리의 씨앗을 저장해두는 것을 배운 것처럼 붉은부리 쿠엘레아는 풀밭 작물의 성찬이나 기근에 대처하는 데 도움이 되는 특정한 행동을 발달시켰다.

(A) 수확이 적은 계절을 위해 ~~씨앗을 아끼는 인간의 모습을 지켜보면서~~ 붉은부리 쿠엘레아는 풀 작물의 기근에 대처하는 행동을 발달시켰다.
(B) 붉은부리 쿠엘레아는 선사시대 인류가 밀과 씨앗의 곡식을 저장한 것처럼 곡물의 기근에서 살아남기 때문에 특별한 특징을 ~~갖는 것을 배웠다~~.

(C) The red-billed quelea developed certain feeding traits that helped them avoid population reduction when crops were bad, much like prehistoric people.   – cope with 정보 누락

(D) The red-billed quelea has evolved behaviors to allow them to deal with crop fluctuations in the way that prehistoric people stockpiled grain crops for food shortages.

(C) 붉은부리 쿠엘레아는 선사시대 사람들과 마찬가지로 농작물이 흉작일 때 개체수 감소를 피하도록 돕는 특정한 먹이 특성을 발달시켰다.

(D) 붉은부리 쿠엘레아는 선사시대 사람들이 식량 부족을 위해 곡물을 비축하는 방식과 같이 농작물의 변동에 대처할 수 있도록 행동을 진화시켜 왔다.

13 The term "forbidding" in the passage is closest in meaning to:

(A) Off-limits
(B) Barren
(C) Volatile
(D) Inhospitable

지문의 단어 "무서운, 험악한"의 의미와 가장 유사한 것은?

(A) 출입 금지의
(B) 메마른
(C) 휘발성의
(D) 불친절한

14 According to paragraph 3, which of the following is **NOT** an adaptation made by the red-billed quelea?★

(A) Stuffing themselves with seeds during the dry season.
(B) Searching for regions where food sources are more abundant.
(C) Establishing colonies 50-200 Km from the grasslands.
(D) Relocating to new areas when the rainy season begins.

3문단에 따르면, 다음 중 붉은부리 쿠엘레아가 각색한 것이 아닌 것은?★

(A) 건기에 씨앗으로 속을 채우는 것.
(B) 식량원이 풍부한 지역을 찾다.
(C) 초원에서 50~200km 떨어진 곳에 식민자를 건설하는 것
(D) 장마철이 시작되면 새로운 지역으로 이전하는 것.

Fact **(A)** - (During the dry season) the bird population must sustain itself (with the seeds) produced (at the end) (of the rainy season). **(B)** - this does not occur simultaneously (across the entire savanna) and dry seeds, young grasses, and mature ripe grasses are available (in different areas). **(D)** - This must be done (during the dry season), [since monsoon rains cause the remaining seeds (to germinate), thereby interrupting the food supply (for weeks) and instigating the move.

15 According to paragraph 4, which of the following can be inferred regarding the red-billed quelea's brooding cycle?

(A) Extended periods of favorable weather can cause large increases in the bird's population.
(B) The queleas build their nests during the rainy season when they are waiting for seeds to ripen once again.
(C) The male and female quelea forms a strong pair bond that lasts until the brooding season has ended.
(D) When the dry season approaches, the adult quelea abandon their offspring who form a large, new colony.

4문단에 따르면, 붉은부리 쿠엘레아의 부화 주기와 관련하여 다음 중 어떤 것을 추론할 수 있는가?

(A) 날씨가 좋아지면 새 개체수가 크게 늘어날 수 있다.
(B) 쿠엘레아는 씨앗이 다시 익기를 기다리는 장마철에 둥지를 튼다.
(C) 수컷과 암컷은 알을 낳는 계절이 끝날 때까지 지속되는 강한 짝을 형성한다.
(D) 건기가 다가오면, 성충 쿠엘레아는 크고 새로운 군락을 형성하는 그들의 새끼를 버린다.

Inference an extended green season (with abundant seed stock) can allow them (to produce) multiple broods (in the same region).

16 Why does the author mention "feathered locusts"?

(A) To describe a new pest species that competes with the red-billed quelea.
(B) To indicate that the birds are thought of in a similar way to common pests.
(C) To introduce a new species that evolved after the quelea became more common.
(D) To explain that queleas have replaced the local insect populations through competition.

저자는 왜 "깃털이 있는 메뚜기"를 언급하는가?

(A) 붉은부리 쿠엘레아와 경쟁하는 새로운 해충 종을 묘사하기 위해.
(B) 새들이 일반적인 해충과 비슷한 방식으로 생각된다는 것을 나타낸다.
(C) 쿠엘레아가 보편화된 이후 진화한 새로운 종을 소개하기 위해서.
(D) 쿠엘레아가 경쟁을 통해 지역 곤충 수를 대체했다는 것을 설명하는 것.

Purpose With each bird) eating its own weight (in seeds) (per day) this leaves fields (within 30 Km) (of the breeding sites) highly susceptible.

---

17 According to paragraph 5, which of the following is true regarding the large red-billed quelea populations?

(A) They threaten the region's farmers ability to produce staple crops.
(B) Local farmers are actively looking for ways to eradicate them.
(C) There are now fewer species of other animals to compete with them.
(D) Their populations have reached a plateau and are likely to decline.

5문단에, 큰 붉은부리 쿠엘레아 개체군에 관한 다음 중 올바른 것은?

(A) 그들은 그 지역의 농부들이 주요 작물을 생산할 수 있는 능력을 위협하고 있다.
(B) 지역 농부들은 그들을 근절할 방법을 적극적으로 찾고 있다.
(C) 이제 그들과 경쟁할 수 있는 다른 종의 동물들이 더 적다.
(D) 그들의 개체수는 안정기에 이르렀고 감소할 것 같다.

Fact Annual losses directly attributable (to these small birds) have been calculated (at $70m), (in a region) [where agricultural production is already (in a precarious state)].

---

18 According to paragraph 6, which of the following is NOT a reason for concern about the introduction of the red-billed quelea to Australia?

(A) Some regions of the country have climates similar to the quelea's native habitat.
(B) Australian farmers plant large amounts of grain crops that could support a quelea population.
(C) The quelea's large colonies would out-compete native species.
(D) Their import has been banned by the Australian national government.   - 관련성 없음

6문단에 따르면, 붉은부리 쿠엘레아의 호주로의 도입에 대한 염려의 이유가 아닌 것은?

(A) 그 나라의 일부 지역은 쿠엘레아의 서식지와 비슷한 기후를 가지고 있다.
(B) 호주 농부들은 이는 쿠엘레아의 수를 유지할 수 있게하는 많은 양의 곡물 작물을 심는다.
(C) 쿠엘레아의 큰 군집은 토종보다 더 경쟁력이 있을 것이다.
(D) 그들의 수입은 호주 정부에 의해 금지되었다.

Fact **(A)**- One such region is Australia's northwestern state (of Queensland), [where the climate resembles the quelea's native habitat]. **(B)**- Queensland's $440m annual cereal grain harvest would be devastated [if large colonies (of quelea) became established]. **(C)**- Colony establishment would also wreak havoc (on the region's native species), (such as the endangered Gouldian finch), [which could not compete (with such massive flocks)].

19

Look at the four squares [■] that indicate where the following sentence could be added to the passage.

Although the grasslands of sub-Saharan Africa do not undergo major temperature changes, the weather patterns do change dramatically as part of the year is characterized by arid conditions until the monsoon winds bring heavy rains to the region.

Where would the sentence best fit?

1st

네 개의 네모[■]는 다음 문장이 삽입될 수 있는 부분을 나타내고 있다.

사하라 사막 이남의 아프리카 초원이 그렇긴 하지만 큰 기온 변화를 겪지 않고, 계절풍이 그 지역에 폭우를 몰고 올 때까지 한 해의 일부가 건조한 상태로 특징지어지기 때문에 날씨 패턴은 극적으로 변화한다.

이 문장은 어느 자리에 들어가는 것이 가장 적합한가?

첫 번째

Insertion weather pattern에 대한 전반적인 설명이 나올 수 있는 부분은 계절적 변화에 따른 행동변화가 나오기 전인 **[A]**가 적절하다.

20

Directions: An introductory sentence for a brief summary of the passage is provided below. Complete the summary by selecting the THREE answer choices that express the most important ideas in the passage. Some sentences do not belong in the summary because they express ideas that are not presented in the passage or are minor ideas in the passage. **This question is worth 2 points.**

지시: 지문 요약을 위한 도입 문장이 아래에 주어져 있다. 지문의 가장 중요한 내용을 내타내는 보기 3개를 골라 요약을 완성하시오. 어떤 문장은 지문에 언급되지 않은 내용이나 사소한 정보를 담고 있으므로 요약에 포함되지 않는다. 이 문제는 2점이다.

The Tiny Seed-eating Red-billed Quelea is the World's Most Common Bird.

(A) Populations of the quelea on the African savanna can reach up to 10 million individuals and the species population ranges from 1.5 billion breeding pairs to 10 billion individuals. – paragraph 1

(C) Despite being dependent upon grass seeds, they have developed migratory and breeding patterns that allow them to flourish in their harsh ecosystems. – paragraph 3

(E) Their massive colonies can devastate human farming efforts and are feared in places with similar climates, where they could thrive as an invasive species, such as Australia. – paragraph 5

작은 씨앗을 먹는 붉은부리 쿠엘레아는 세계에서 가장 흔한 새이다.

(A) 아프리카 사바나에 있는 쿠엘레아 개체수는 최대 1000만 마리에 달하며, 개체수는 15억 마리에서 100억 마리에 이른다.

(C) 씨앗에 의존함에도 불구하고, 그들은 가혹한 생태계에서 번성할 수 있도록 하는 이동과 번식 패턴을 발달시켰다.

(E) 그들의 거대한 군락은 인간의 농사 노력을 파괴할 수 있고, 호주와 같은 침략적인 종으로 번성할 수 있는 비슷한 기후의 장소에서 두려움에 떨고 있다.

(B) Although the quelea's diet is composed mainly of wild grass seeds, they have been known to eat other seeds and insects. – MINOR

(D) Most of the bird population migrates during the rainy season when more seeds are available ~~to replenish the energy they loose during the journey~~.

(F) Red-billed quelea ~~have been blamed~~ for destroying more than $70m of grain fields in Australia and ~~for causing~~ native species like the Gouldian finch to be endangered. – paragraph 6

(B) 퀴레아의 먹이는 주로 야생 풀의 씨로 구성되어 있지만, 그들은 다른 씨앗과 곤충을 먹는 것으로 알려져 있다.

(D) 조류 개체군의 대부분은 이동 중에 소비하는 에너지를 보충할 수 있는 더 많은 씨앗이 있는 장마철에 이동한다.

(F) 붉은부리 쿠엘레아는 호주의 7천만 달러 이상의 곡물밭을 파괴하고 굴디안 핀치와 같은 토착종들을 멸종 위기에 처하게 한 것으로 비난 받아왔다.

TEST 5-3 National Parks in the Western United States
미국 서부의 국립공원

Introduction	단락 1	파리조약과 영토 확장으로 인한 국토 보존
Point	단락 2	국립공원 추진과 사업 이익
Point	단락 3	자동차의 도입과 감독 독립 기관 설립
Point	단락 4	고속도로 건설로 인한 공원 방문 증가
Point	단락 5	국립공원 보호를 위한 노력
Point	단락 6	보호 운동으로 인한 보호 토지 확장

문단 주제	본문 내용	해석
단락 1 파리조약과 영토 확장으로 인한 국토 보존	**1** The Treaty of Paris, which ended the revolutionary war between Great Britain and its former colonies in the United States, more than doubled the territory of the 13 original colonies as the crown ceded all lands east of the Mississippi River to the newly formed nation. However, the new country's expansion would not stop there. By the middle of the next century, cessations, purchases and treaties would expand the nation's contiguous territory to its current state. This dramatically increased the amount of land owned by the nation and, before mass immigration and westward movement; much of this land was pristine wilderness with a plethora of different geological formations and ecosystems. With so much vacant land, the theory of "landscape democracy," the idea that scenic landscapes belong to all people, came into play and a movement was put forth to preserve this land in perpetuity as national parkland.	영국과 미국의 이전 식민지들 사이의 혁명 전쟁을 끝낸 파리 조약은 미시시피 강 동쪽의 모든 영토를 새로 형성된 국가에 양도하면서 13개의 원래 식민지들의 영토를 두 배 이상 늘렸다. 하지만, 새로운 나라의 팽창은 거기서 멈추지 않았다. 다음 세기 중반까지, 분할, 구매, 조약은 국가의 인접한 영토를 현재의 상태로 확장시켰다. 이로 인해 국토의 소유 면적이 급격히 증가하였고, 대규모 이민과 서부로의 이동 전에는 많은 지질학적 형태와 생태계가 있었던 자연 그대로의 황무지였다. 이렇게 많은 빈 땅이 생기면서 경치가 만인의 것이라는 생각인 '경관민주주의' 이론이 작용해 이 땅을 국립공원으로 영구 보존하자는 운동이 일어났다.
단락 2 국립공원 추진과 사업 이익	**2** [■] This theory was revolutionary for the time, as prior to the establishment of Yellowstone National Park in 1872, no national government had ever set aside large swaths of undeveloped land. [■] However, this was not only done for preservation. [■] A sense of inferiority with regards to old world monuments and the belief that America's unique landscapes were one of its most distinguishing features both had a hand in the desire to set aside western lands. [■] Interestingly, business interests also encouraged the conservation movement. It may seem antithetical, but business leaders, such as railroad barons pushed for and supported these national parks, since they would encourage rich easterners to take long trips on their lines and stay in the hotel they set up on the outskirts of the parks. Their desire for profits also	1872년 Yellowstone 국립공원이 설립되기 전에는 어떤 국가 정부도 개발되지 않은 넓은 땅을 따로 떼어 놓은 적이 없었기 때문에 이 이론은 당시로서는 혁명적이었다. 그러나 이것은 단지 보존을 위해서만 이루어진 것은 아니다. 옛 세계 기념물에 대한 열등감과 미국의 독특한 풍경이 가장 두드러진 특징 중 하나라는 믿음은 둘 다 서부의 땅을 분리해 두고자 하는 열망에 영향을 미쳤다. 흥미롭게도, 대사업가들 또한 보존 운동을 장려했다. 반대되는 것처럼 보일 수도 있지만, 철도 부호와 같은 사업 지도자들은 부유한 동부인들이 그들의 노선으로 긴 여행을 하고 그들이 공원 외곽에 설치한 호텔에 머물도록 장려할 것이기 때문에 이러한 국립공원을 추진하고 지지했다. 그들의 이익에 대한 열망은 또한 Grand Canyon, Yellowstone, and Yosemite 같은 서부 공원의 장엄함과

led them to heavily advertise the majesty of western parks and features, such as the Grand Canyon, Yellowstone, and Yosemite, which greatly raised awareness of the parks amongst the general public.

3   Surprisingly, the adoption of the automobile by American's in the early 20th century also bolstered the national parks movement. As the number of cars rose from 0.11 per 1,000 citizens in 1900 to 86.78/K in 1920 and 217.34/K in 1930, drivers began calling for investment in better roads and highways, especially those in the west. 1916's Federal Aid Road Act paid states to construct or improve rural roadways, including those near parkland. This encouraged people to not only drive more, but also to visit the increasing number of national parks. At around the same time, business magnate Stephen Mather was pushing for an independent agency to oversee the national parks and barely a month after passing the Road Act, President Woodrow Wilson signed a bill setting up such an agency and named Mather its first director. He worked to protect these pristine lands from the business interests that were attempting to have them opened for logging and other business ventures.

4   By the middle of the 20th century, cross-country road trips had become quite popular with families who visited national parks, newly founded amusement parks, and ski resorts. They made the need for better roadways evident. This increased recreational travel helped ensure the passage of 1956's Interstate and Defense Highway Act, which authorized the construction of nearly 66,000 Km of roads around the country. This $25B project was the largest public works project in the country's history and increased mobility by linking urban centers through wide divided highways. A direct side effect of this was easier access to national parks for urban inhabitants, which caused a dramatic increase in park usage. In 1920 only 1M people visited the national parks, but by 1950 that number had risen to 33M. After the completion of the new highways the nation's parks welcomed 172M visitors. This increase vastly outpaced the increase in the nation's population, which had only doubled during that time.

5   The increased number of visitors quickly caused degradation in the national parks, causing activists, like Sierra Club founder John Muir, to argue that the parks should be preserved as pristine wilderness and protected from further human destruction. This was important, since early parks, like Yellowstone had been set up as recreational areas. His impassioned writing helped to convince Americans, especially the eastern elite, of the importance or preservation of these unique areas.

단락 6
보호 운동으로 인한 보호 토지 확장

6 This movement had a great impact on the national park system. Not only did the park system begin working to preserve the wilderness, but it also greatly expanded the amount of protected land. Today, more than 277M people visit the 210,000 Km2 of land protected by the 59 national parks, an area larger than 109 current countries, each year. The beauty, geological features, ecosystems, and recreational opportunities of the land in these parks are now permanently preserved for all American citizens both now and in the future.

만들었다. Yellowstone과 같은 초기 공원이 휴양 지역으로 설립되었을 때부터 이것은 중요했다. 그의 열정적인 글은 미국인들, 특히 동부 엘리트들에게 이러한 독특한 지역의 중요성과 보존을 납득시키는 데 도움을 주었다.

이 운동은 국립공원 체계에 큰 영향을 미쳤다. 공원 시스템은 황야를 보존하기 위해 작동하기 시작했을 뿐만 아니라, 보호 토지의 양을 크게 확장시켰다. 오늘날, 2억 7천 7백만 명 이상의 사람들이 59개의 국립공원으로 보호되는 21만 km2의 땅을 매년 방문하는데, 이는 현재 109개국보다 더 큰 면적이다. 이 공원에 있는 땅의 아름다움, 지질학적 특징, 생태계, 그리고 휴양의 기회들은 현재와 미래의 모든 미국 시민들을 위해 영구적으로 보존된다.

---

21 What can be inferred from paragraph 1 about the American west prior to the 1850s?

(A) It was ~~being exploited by new settlers~~.
(B) It was relatively uninhabited.
(C) It was ~~the subject of many disputes~~.
(D) It was ~~used mainly as farmland~~.

1850년대 이전의 미국 서부에 대해 1문단에서 추론할 수 있는 것은 무엇인가?

(A) 그것은 ~~새로운 정착민들에 의해 이용되고 있었다~~.
(B) 그곳은 비교적 사람이 살지 않았다.
(C) 그것은 ~~많은 논쟁의 주제였다~~.
(D) 그것은 ~~주로 농지로 사용되었다~~.

Fact much (of this land) was pristine wilderness (with a plethora) (of different geological formations and ecosystems).

---

22 Which of the sentences below best expresses the essential information in the highlighted sentence in the passage? Incorrect choices change the meaning in important ways or leave out essential information.

(01)With so much vacant land, the theory of (02)"landscape democracy," the idea that scenic (03)landscapes belong to all people, came into play and a (04)movement was put forth to preserve this land in perpetuity as national parkland.

아래 문장 중 지문 속의 음영된 문장의 핵심 정보를 가장 잘 표현하고 있는 것은 무엇인가? 오답은 문장의 의미를 현저히 왜곡하거나 핵심 정보를 빠뜨리고 있다.

이로 인해 국토의 소유 면적이 급격히 증가하였고, 대규모 이민과 서부로의 이동 전에는 많은 지질학적 형태와 생태계가 있었던 자연 그대로의 황무지였다. 이렇게 많은 빈 땅이 생기면서 경치가 만인의 것이라는 생각인 '경관민주주의' 이론이 작용해 이 땅을 국립공원으로 영구 보존하자는 운동이 일어났다.

(A) The eternal preservation of America's abundant uninhabited lands to be in the hands of all people came about because of the idea of landscape democracy.
(B) Landscape democracy led to the acquisition of America's land because the idea that people have rights to any vacant land they could claim was put forth.
— preservation 정보 없음
(C) Because America is a democracy, all vacant national parkland is considered to belong to all people and ~~people can move there freely if~~ they agree to preserve it.
(D) ~~Many early settlers who moved west preserved~~ the vacant lands they came across because they believed in landscape democracy and thought the land should be protected forever.

(A) 미국의 풍부한 무인지대가 모든 사람들의 손에 들어갈 수 있도록 영원히 보존된 것은 풍경 민주주의의 개념 때문에 발생했다.
(B) 풍경 민주주의는 사람들이 그들이 주장할 수 있는 빈 땅에 대한 권리를 가지고 있다는 생각이 제시되었기 때문에 미국의 땅을 획득하는 것으로 이어졌다.
(C) 미국은 민주주의 국가이기 때문에, 모든 공원은 모든 사람들의 것으로 간주되고, 만약 그들이 그것을 보존하는 것에 동의한다면 ~~사람들은 자유롭게 그곳으로 이동할 수 있다.~~
(D) ~~서부로 이주한 많은 초기 정착민들은~~ 풍경 민주주의를 믿고 이 땅은 영원히 보호되어야 한다고 생각했기 때문에 그들이 건너온 빈 땅을 보존했다.

Highlight i) 많은 빈 토지와 ii) 자연 경관이 대중의 것이라는 내용 iii) 국립공원으로서 이 토지를 영구적으로 보존하기 위한 운동이 제기된 내용까지 모두 다 담고 있는 보기는 **(A)**이다.

---

23 According to paragraph 2, which of the following is **NOT** true regarding the establishment of national parks in the United States?

(A) It was the first time a country had reserved large plots of land for preservation.
(B) It included an aspect of competition with European powers.
(C) It was supported by business concerns.
(D) It was ~~designed through the meeting hled by business leaders~~.

2문단에 따르면, 다음 중 미국 국립공원의 설립과 관련하여 사실이 아닌 것은?

(A) 한 나라가 보존을 위해 큰 땅을 남겨둔 것은 이번이 처음이었다.
(B) 그것은 유럽 강대국들과의 경쟁 양상을 포함하고 있었다.
(C) 그것은 사업상의 우려로 뒷받침되었다
(D) ~~그것은 비즈니스 리더들이 주최한 회의를 통해 고안되었다.~~

Fact **(A)** - prior to the establishment) (of Yellowstone National Park) (in 1872), no national government had ever set aside large swaths (of undeveloped land)]. **(B)** - A sense (of inferiority) (with regards to old world monuments and the belief) [that America's unique landscapes were one (of its most distinguishing features)] both had a hand (in the desire) (to set aside) western lands. **(C)** - business interests also encouraged the conservation movement.

---

24 What can be inferred about Stephen Mather from paragraph 3?

(A) He underwent a major career change.
(B) He ~~wanted to open the parks to business interests~~.
(C) He ~~was involved in logging~~.
(D) He was a ~~lifelong politician~~.

3문단에서 스티븐 매더에 대해 추론할 수 있는 것은?

(A) 그는 커다란 직업의 변화를 겪었다.
(B) 그는 ~~사업상의 이익을 위해 공원을 개방하기를 원했다.~~
(C) 그는 ~~벌채에 관여했다.~~
(D) 그는 ~~평생 정치인이었다.~~

Inference (At around the same time), business magnate Stephen Mather was pushing (for an independent agency) (to oversee) the national parks and barely a month (after passing) the Road Act, President Woodrow Wilson signed a bill setting up (such an agency) and named Mather its first director.

25
The term "magnate" in the passage is closest in meaning to:

(A) Leader
(B) Representative
(C) Tycoon
(D) Advocate

지문의 단어 "거물"의 의미와 가장 유사한 것은?

(A) 리더
(B) 대표자
(C) 거물
(D) 옹호자

26
According to paragraph 4, which of the following is NOT true about cross-country trips?

(A) They were often undertaken by families in their automobiles.
(B) They began after the completion of new interstate highways.
(C) They showed the need for a new, improved roadway system.
(D) They often ended at recreational facilities, national parks and resorts.

4문단에 따르면, 다음 중 국가-횡단 여행에 대해 사실이 아닌 것은?

(A) 그들은 종종 자동차로 가족들이 맡았다.
(B) 그들은 새로운 주간 고속도로가 완공된 후에 시작되었다.
(C) 그들은 새롭고 개선된 도로 시스템의 필요성을 보여주었다.
(D) 그들은 종종 레크리에이션 시설, 국립공원, 리조트에서 끝이 났다.

Fact (A) - cross-country road trips had become quite popular (with families). (C) - They made the need (for better roadways) evident. (D) - popular (with families) [who visited national parks, newly founded amusement parks, and ski resorts]

27
According to paragraph 5, which of the following is true regarding John Muir?

(A) He thought people should be banned from the national parks.
(B) He wanted the national park system to be closed down.
(C) He was employed by the National Park System.
(D) He played a large role in changing people's minds about national parks.

5문단에 따르면, 다음 중 존 뮤어에 관한 설명으로 옳은 것은?

(A) 그는 사람들이 국립공원에서 금지되어야 한다고 생각했다.
(B) 그는 국립공원 시스템이 폐쇄되기를 원했다.
(C) 그는 국립공원 시스템에 고용되었다.
(D) 그는 국립공원에 대한 사람들의 생각을 바꾸는데 큰 역할을 했다.

Fact His impassioned writing helped (to convince) Americans, especially the eastern elite, (of the importance or preservation) (of these unique areas).

28
Why does the author mention "109 current countries"?

(A) To help the reader understand how American national parks influenced the world.
(B) To reinforce the fact that the United States was the first country with national parks.
(C) To give the reader an idea of the great expanse of the American national parks.
(D) To suggest that the American national parks should be a separate country.

저자는 왜 "현재 109개국"을 언급하는가?

(A) 미국 국립공원이 세계에 어떤 영향을 미쳤는지 독자들이 이해할 수 있도록 돕기 위해서다.
(B) 미국이 국립공원을 가진 첫 번째 나라라는 사실을 강조하기 위해서.
(C) 미국 국립공원의 광대한 광활한 모습을 독자들에게 알려주기 위해.
(D) 미국 국립공원이 독립된 국가가 되어야 한다고 제안하는 것.

Purpose Not only did the park system begin working (to preserve) the wilderness, but it also greatly expanded the amount (of protected land).

29

Look at the four squares [■] that indicate where the following sentence could be added to the passage.

The fact that America was a relatively young nation interacting with other nations also had a large influence on the establishment of parks.

Where would the sentence best fit?

3rd

네 개의 네모[■]는 다음 문장이 삽입될 수 있는 부분을 나타내고 있다.

미국이 다른 나라와 교류하는 비교적 젊은 나라였다는 사실 또한 공원 설립에 큰 영향을 미쳤다.

이 문장은 어느 자리에 들어가는 것이 가장 적합한가?

세 번째

Insertion   주어진 문장에서 공원의 설립에 대한 설명과 also를 근거로 앞에서 한 내용의 부연설명이 나와있는 부분으로 [C]가 적절하다.

30

Directions: An introductory sentence for a brief summary of the passage is provided below. Complete the summary by selecting the THREE answer choices that express the most important ideas in the passage. Some sentences do not belong in the summary because they express ideas that are not presented in the passage or are minor ideas in the passage. **This question is worth 2 points.**

지시: 지문 요약을 위한 도입 문장이 아래에 주어져 있다. 지문의 가장 중요한 내용을 나타내는 보기 3개를 골라 요약을 완성하시오. 어떤 문장은 지문에 언급되지 않은 내용이나 사소한 정보를 담고 있으므로 요약에 포함되지 않는다. 이 문제는 2점이다.

Territorial expansion in the United States led to the establishment of the world's first national parks.

(B) National parks were set up in America as a means of showcasing the unique geological and environmental characteristics of the land and were promoted by business interests.   – paragraph 2

(E) Automobile ownership and the vast road network of the country greatly increased the number of visitors to the US's national parks.   – paragraph 3

(F) Conservationists like John Muir helped convince the national park system that preservation was more important than recreation in the protected lands.   – paragraph 5

미국의 영토 확장은 세계 최초의 국립공원 설립으로 이어졌다.

(B) 국립공원은 토지의 독특한 지질학적, 환경적 특성을 보여주는 수단으로 미국에 설치되었고 사업적 이해관계에 의해 촉진되었다.

(E) 자동차 소유권과 미국의 광대한 도로망으로 인해 미국 국립공원의 방문객 수가 크게 증가하였다.

(F) 존 뮤어와 같은 자연보호론자들은 보호지역에서의 휴양보다 보존이 더 중요하다고 국립공원 시스템을 설득하는 데 도움을 주었다.

(A) Early national parks were established to allow American citizens ~~more recreational opportunities~~ as they moved to the rural western regions.   – MINOR/INACCURATE

(C) The establishment of national parks encouraged people to visit the areas, which led to ~~overall degradation of the natural environment.~~   – MINOR/SLIGHTLY INACCURATE

(D) 1916's Federal Aid Road Act ~~was meant to increase the amount of rural roads~~ near national parks to allow more people to visit them.   – ½, ½

(A) 초기 국립공원은 미국 시민들이 시골 서부 지역으로 이주하면서 더 많은 오락적 기회를 주기 위해 설립되었다.

(C) 국립공원의 설립은 사람들이 그 지역을 방문하도록 장려했고, 이것은 전반적인 자연 환경의 악화로 이어졌다.

(D) 1916년의 연방원조도로법은 더 많은 사람들이 국립공원을 방문하도록 하기 위해 국립공원 근처의 시골길의 양을 늘리기 위한 것이었다.

USHER

iBT TOEFL

INTERMEDIATE READING 02

TEST 6

답안 및 취약 유형 분석표

해석·해설

답안 및 문제 유형 분석표

TEST 6-1

01 (B) Inference
02 (D) Fact
03 (C) Highlight
04 (B) Purpose
05 (C) Vocabulary
06 (D) Fact
07 (C) Fact
08 (D) Inference
09 2nd ■ Insertion
10 (A), (D), (E) Summary

TEST 6-2

11 (D) Fact
12 (A) Fact
13 (B) Inference
14 (C) Purpose
15 (D) Fact
16 (D) Vocabulary
17 (A) Highlight
18 (C) Fact
19 1st ■ Insertion
20 (C), (D), (F) Summary

TEST 6-3

21 (C) Purpose
22 (A) Highlight
23 (B) Fact
24 (C) Fact
25 (B) Vocabulary
26 (C) Inference
27 (D) Fact
28 (A) Inference
29 4th ■ Insertion
30 (B), (D), (F) Summary

각 문제 유형별 맞춘 개수를 아래에 적어 보세요.

유형	맞춘 답의 개수	정답률	
단어 (Vocabulary)	/ 3	정답률:	%
사실 확인 문제 (Fact)	/ 10	정답률:	%
지시어 찾기 (Reference)	/ 0	정답률:	%
끼워 넣기 (Insertion)	/ 3	정답률:	%
문장 변환문제 (Highlight)	/ 3	정답률:	%
목적 (Purpose)	/ 3	정답률:	%
추론 (Inference)	/ 5	정답률:	%
단락 요약 (Summary / Category Chart)	/ 3	정답률:	%
전체	/ 30	정답률:	%

※ 자신이 취약한 유형은 READING STRATEGIES를 통해 다시 한번 점검하시기 바랍니다. (p.44)

TEST 6-1 The Role of Dress in Africa 아프리카에서 드레스의 역할

Introduction	단락 1	옷차림의 정보전달과 아프리카 드레스의 특징
Point	단락 2	아프리카 의상의 사회적 측면
Point	단락 3	사회정치적 지위의 지표
Point	단락 4	장신구와 문신과 같은 광범위한 복장
Point	단락 5	반흔 형성과 역할
Point	단락 6	문신의 상징성

문단 주제	본문 내용	해 석
단락 1 옷차림의 정보전달과 아프리카 드레스의 특징	**1** When most people think about the concept of dressing, they automatically think of only clothing and accessories and whether they are in the right style. However, dress can actually be a much more complex concept, which can be used to communicate both simple ideas and complex information about the wearer. The type of dress that a person chooses can communicate immediate information about their gender, ethnic group, religion, age or even occupation. A few common examples of these are the burka worn by Muslim women and the yarmulke worn by Jewish men. Both of these items point to the age, religion, and gender of their wearers. This complexity and symbolism is a key feature of African dress, which has fascinated outside viewers with its striking range of styles since Arabic writers first described it in the fourteenth century.	대부분의 사람들이 옷차림에 대한 개념을 생각할 때, 자동적으로 옷과 악세사리들, 그리고 스타일이 맞는지를 생각한다. 하지만, 드레스는 사실 훨씬 더 복잡한 개념일 수 있는데, 이것은 착용자에 대한 간단한 생각과 복잡한 정보 모두를 전달하는데 사용될 수 있다. 한 사람이 선택하는 드레스의 종류는 성별, 인종, 종교, 나이, 심지어 직업에 대한 즉각적인 정보를 전달할 수 있다. 이슬람 여성들이 착용한 Burka와 유대 남성들이 착용한 Yarmulke를 예로 들 수 있다. 이 두 품목 모두 착용자의 나이, 종교, 성별을 가리킨다. 이러한 복잡성과 상징성은 아프리카 드레스의 주요 특징인데, 아프리카 드레스는 아랍 작가들이 14세기에 처음으로 묘사한 이후 눈에 띄는 다양한 스타일로 외부 관찰자들을 매료시켰다.
단락 2 아프리카 의상의 사회적 측면	**2** African dress, like most forms, is intimately connected to the identity of its wearers and observers, since it acts as a signifier of so many aspects of the societies. Despite the neutrality of the adornment, the way in which it is worn, or simply the fact that it is worn, can become symbolically important to a society. There may be importance assigned to the form, type, adornment, and materials used to form the dress worn and this can cause it to become a sensitive aspect of the society. Since many aspects of dress are tied to tribal or religious identity, their use denotes inclusion with the society, but can also draw the ire or derision of society members if they are inappropriately worn or displayed.	대부분의 형태와 마찬가지로, 아프리카 의상은 사회의 많은 측면을 나타내는 징표로 작용하기 때문에, 착용자와 관찰자의 정체성과 밀접하게 연관되어 있다. 장식의 중립성에도 불구하고, 이것의 착용 방식, 또는 단순히 착용하고 있다는 사실이 사회에 상징적으로 중요해질 수 있다. 입는 옷의 형태, 종류, 장식, 재료에 부여된 중요성이 있을 수 있으며, 이것이 사회의 민감한 측면이 될 수 있다. 복장의 많은 측면들이 부족이나 종교적 정체성에 얽매여 있기 때문에, 복장의 사용은 사회에 포함된다는 것을 의미하지만, 만약 그들이 부적절하게 입거나 전시된다면 사회 구성원의 분노나 조롱을 받을 수도 있다.
단락 3 사회정치적 지위의 지표	**3** In addition to denoting societal and religious identity, African dress can also be seen as an indicator of the wearer's sociopolitical standing in the society. In many African societies	사회적, 종교적 정체성을 나타내는 것 외에도, 아프리카 의상은 착용자의 사회정치적 지위를 나타내는 지표로 볼 수 있다. 많은 아프리카 사회에서 지도자들은 그들의 지도력을

leaders wear some sort of insignia or symbolic aspect of dress to denote their leadership. In fact, some of these are made of highly prized materials, such as ivory, gold, or decorative beading, that are only worn by the leaders. One example of this is the Oba, or leader, of the Benin people in present-day Nigeria. His official dress includes a coral-beaded smock and crown with coral necklaces and ivory pendants and amulets. Further, he carries a flywhisk made of red coral beads that signify his divine rule. In other societies, other flywhisk materials were used to denote the regal nature of the bearer. Two examples of this are the Fare-Fare and Ashanti people of Ghana, whose respective use of horsehair and elephant tail hair denoted kings or chiefs of the highest importance. These flywhisks are such a strong symbol of power and leadership that they have come to be used by rulers across the continent, including by Jomo Kenyatta, the first leader of the modern state of Kenya.

4   The use of these flywhisks as a symbol of leadership brings up another interesting aspect of "dress." Contrary to the common, narrow interpretation of the term dress, the true definition is much broader and includes more than just the clothing worn. It includes accessories, such as the flywhisks, and other methods of beautifying and adorning the body. Items such as cosmetics, jewelry, and accessories like staffs, parasols, and fans, are all considered aspects of dress. However, not all of these aspects can be easily removed. Some societies use permanent bodily modification to perform the same functions. Tattooing may be the most common form of these in modern day western society, but there are a profusion of other forms, such as scarring, piercings and the use of lip plates.

5   [■] In most of sub-Saharan Africa, the use of purposefully inflicted scars, or cicatrization, is the most common type of permanent body modification. [■] They signify membership and status in the society, but can act as protective devices, in addition to simply being beautiful bodily adornment. [■] These scars are placed on different parts of the body, including the face, abdomen and extremities, and can sometimes take the form of elaborate patterns that cover most of the body. [■] Oftentimes, the lengthy scarification acts as an initiation process, with the aesthetics of the scars correlating to other important figurative aspects of the society, such as pottery and sculpture.

USHER

단락 6 문신의 상징성

6 Farther north, along the Nile River, tattooing was the main form of permanent body adornment. Researchers have found evidence of tattoos being used as fertility signals in female Egyptian mummies from 2000 B.C. In addition, the adjacent Nubian civilization appears to have utilized tattoos to adorn their bodies, as well. The tattoos in both of these civilizations served the same purpose as scarification, apparel and accessories in other African tribes, and elsewhere. They were symbols of inclusion, protection and identification for their bearers.

나일강을 따라 있는 먼 북쪽에는, 문신이 영구적인 신체 장식의 주요 형태였다. 연구자들은 문신이 기원전 2000년부터 이집트 여성 미라에서 다산의 상징으로 사용된 증거를 발견했다. 게다가, 인접한 누비아 문명은 그들의 몸을 장식하기 위해 문신을 사용한 것으로 보인다. 이 두 문명의 문신은 다른 아프리카 부족과 다른 곳에서 흉터화, 의복, 액세서리와 같은 목적으로 사용되었다. 그것들은 그들의 소유자를 위한 포함, 보호, 신분의 상징이었다.

---

01 What can be inferred from paragraph 1 about the concept of "dressing"?

(A) It is only concerned with the symbolic aspects of clothing used by people in similar religious groups.
(B) It is a complex concept that has different meaning for people of different cultures.
(C) It has nothing to do with the donning of clothes that the wearer thinks are fashionable.
(D) It limits the ability of society members to express themselves because of religious rules.

1문단에서 "옷 입는 것"의 개념에 대해 추론할 수 있는 것은 무엇인가?

(A) 그것은 비슷한 종교 집단에 속한 사람들이 사용하는 옷의 상징적인 측면에만 관심이 있다.
(B) 그것은 다른 문화권의 사람들에게 다른 의미를 갖는 복잡한 개념이다.
(C) 그것은 입는 사람이 멋있다고 생각하는 옷을 입는 것과는 아무 상관이 없다.
(D) 그것은 종교적 규칙 때문에 사회 구성원들이 자신을 표현할 수 있는 능력을 제한한다.

Inference However, dress can actually be a much more complex concept, [which can be used (to communicate) both simple ideas and complex information (about the wearer)].

---

02 According to paragraph 2, which of the following is **NOT** true regarding the correlation between dress and identity?

(A) The materials used to adorn the body have no natural importance on their own.
(B) The wearing of certain items, or the way in which they are worn, can denote inclusion in certain social or religious groups.
(C) Certain religions and civil societies can assign importance to some materials or forms of adornment.
(D) Due to their religious and cultural significance, members of certain groups cannot wear some items of dress.

2문단에 따르면, 다음 중 드레스와 정체성의 상관관계에 대해 사실이 아닌 것은?

(A) 몸을 장식하는 데 사용되는 재료는 그 자체로는 자연적인 중요성이 없다.
(B) 특정 아이템의 착용 또는 착용 방식은 특정 사회 또는 종교 집단에 포함되는 것을 나타낼 수 있다.
(C) 특정 종교와 시민사회는 어떤 재료나 장식의 형태에 중요성을 부여할 수 있다.
(D) 그들의 종교적, 문화적 중요성 때문에, 특정 집단의 구성원들은 몇몇 옷들을 입을 수 없다.

Fact **(A)** - (Despite the neutrality) (of the adornment), **(B)** - [Since many aspects (of dress) are tied (to tribal or religious identity)], their use denotes inclusion (with the society) **(C)** - There may be importance assigned (to the form, type, adornment, and materials) used (to form) the dress worn and this can cause it (to become) a sensitive aspect (of the society).

03

Which of the sentences below best expresses the essential information in the highlighted sentence in the passage? Incorrect choices change the meaning in important ways or leave out essential information.

Since many (01)aspects of dress are tied to tribal or religious identity, their use (02)denotes inclusion with the society, (03)but can also draw the ire or derision of society members if (04)they are inappropriately worn or displayed.

(A) Because tribal dress is so religiously important, the inappropriate uses of the elements can cause anger amongst society members. – inclusion 언급 ✗
(B) The use of particular items of dress can indicate membership in a certain group and their misuse can lead to societal anger and ridicule of them. - i) 정보 누락.
(C) Societal members can be upset by inappropriately used items of dress ~~because they signify membership~~ in a tribally or religiously united group.
(D) Anger often occurs when items of dress are worn that do not connote an allegiance to the social groups tribal and religious affiliations. – inclusion 언급 ✗

아래 문장 중 지문 속의 음영된 문장의 핵심 정보를 가장 잘 표현하고 있는 것은 무엇인가? 오답은 문장의 의미를 현저히 왜곡하거나 핵심 정보를 빠뜨리고 있다.

복장의 많은 측면들이 부족이나 종교적 정체성에 얽매여 있기 때문에, 복장의 사용은 사회에 포함된다는 것을 의미하지만, 만약 그들이 부적절하게 입거나 전시된다면 사회 구성원의 분노나 조롱을 받을 수도 있다.

(A) 부족 복장은 매우 종교적으로 중요하기 때문에, 부적절한 요소들의 사용은 사회 구성원들 사이에서 분노를 야기할 수 있다.
(B) 복장의 특정 아이템을 사용하는 것은 특정 그룹의 멤버십을 나타낼 수 있고 그들의 오용은 사회적 분노와 조롱으로 이어질 수 있다.
(C) 사회 구성원들은 부적절하게 사용된 옷 아이템이 부족하거나 종교적으로 통합된 그룹의 멤버십을 의미하기 때문에 화가 날 수 있다.
(D) 분노는 종종 사회 집단 부족과 종교적 관계에 대한 충성을 나타내지 않는 옷을 입을 때 발생한다.

Highlight i) 의상의 많은 측면들이 부족과 종교적 정체성과 연결된다 ii) 그들의 사용은 사회의 포함을 나타낸다 iii) 만약 적절하게 입혀지지 않을 경우 사회구성원들의 분노를 자아낼 수 있다는 3가지 정보를 모두 담고 있는 보기는 **(C)**가 적절하다.

04

Why does the author mention "horsehair and elephant tail hair"?

(A) To emphasize ~~the number of materials~~ that can be used in flywhisks.
(B) To give examples of materials that were culturally significant.
(C) To illustrate ~~the variety of fibers~~ used in African dress.
(D) To show that ~~even cheap materials~~ could be used to signify royalty.

저자는 왜 "말털과 코끼리 꼬리털"을 언급하는가?

(A) 플라이위스키에 사용할 수 있는 ~~소재의 수~~를 강조한다.
(B) 문화적으로 중요한 소재의 예를 들겠다.
(C) 아프리카 드레스에 사용되는 ~~다양한 섬유~~를 묘사하기 위해.
(D) ~~값싼 재료~~도 로열티를 나타내는 데 사용될 수 있다는 것을 보여주기 위해.

Purpose African dress can also be seen (as an indicator) (of the wearer's sociopolitical standing) (in the society)

05

The term "profusion" in the passage is closest in meaning to:

(A) Scarcity
(B) Number
(C) Abundance
(D) Amount

지문의 단어 "풍부함"의 의미와 가장 유사한 것은?

(A) 희소성
(B) 수
(C) 풍부
(D) 총액

06
According to paragraph 4, which of the following is NOT true about the definition of dress?

(A) Used to denote the garments that people place on their bodies for both bodily coverage and adornment.
(B) It includes both temporary and permanent adornments of the body.
(C) Accessories that are both worn and held, such as flywhisks and umbrellas, are included in the definition of dress.
(D) Tattooing and scarification ~~are not considered~~ part of dress in most western societies.

4문단에 따르면, 다음 중 드레스의 정의에 대해 사실이 아닌 것은?

(A) 몸을 가리고 장식하기 위해 몸에 착용하는 의류를 나타내는 데 사용된다.
(B) 그것은 몸의 일시적인 장식과 영구적인 장식 모두를 포함한다.
(C) 플라이 휘스크(flywhisk) 및 우산과 같이 착용하고 보유하는 액세서리는 드레스의 정의에 포함된다.
(D) 문신과 흉터는 대부분의 서구 사회에서 옷의 일부로 ~~여겨지지 않는다~~.

Fact Tattooing may be the most common form (of these) (in modern day western society), but there are a profusion (of other forms), (such as scarring, piercings and the use) (of lip plates)

07
According to paragraph 5, which of the following is true regarding cicatrization in sub-Saharan Africa?

(A) It is ~~so common that many societies have designed pottery to mimic the patterns~~ used on their members.
(B) It is used ~~to quickly identify individual members~~ of a society ~~because~~ their clothing styles are very similar.
(C) It is the most prevalent form of permanent bodily adornment used in most of Southern Africa.
(D) It has different meanings and uses ~~based on the location of the scarification~~.

5문단에 따르면 사하라 이남 아프리카에서의 반흔 형성에 관한 다음 내용 중 올바른 것은?

(A) 그것은 매우 흔한 일이어서 많은 사회가 그들의 구성원들에게 ~~사용되는 무늬를 모방하여 도자기를 디자인해 왔다~~.
(B) 그것은 그들의 옷 스타일이 매우 비슷하기 ~~때문에~~ 사회의 개별 구성원을 ~~빠르게 식별하기 위해~~ 사용된다.
(C) 그것은 대부분의 남아프리카에서 사용되는 영구적인 신체 장식의 가장 일반적인 형태이다.
(D) ~~흉터의 위치에 따라~~ 의미와 용도가 다르다.

Fact (In most) (of sub-Saharan Africa), the use (of purposefully inflicted scars, or cicatrization), is the most common type (of permanent body modification).

08
According to paragraph 6, which of the following can be inferred regarding about tattooing in Africa?

(A) The Ancient Egyptians who resided along the Nile River in northern Africa ~~invented the art form.~~
(B) Scarification ~~was not widely used in Ancient Egypt~~ because the process was developed much later than tattooing.
(C) The Nubians and the Egyptians ~~shared their knowledge of tattooing with one another.~~
(D) Tattooing the skin served the same purposes as clothing and scarification in other regions.

6문단에 따르면, 다음 중 아프리카에서 문신에 대해 추론할 수 있는 것은 무엇인가?

(A) 북아프리카 나일강을 따라 살았던 고대 이집트인들이 ~~예술 형태를 발명했다~~.
(B) ~~고대 이집트에서는~~ 문신보다 훨씬 늦게 개발되었기 때문에 스카리피케이션이 ~~널리 사용되지 않았다~~.
(C) 누비아인들과 이집트인들은 ~~문신에 대한 그들의 지식을 서로 공유했다~~.
(D) 피부에 문신을 새기는 것은 다른 지역의 옷과 같은 목적을 수행했다.

Inference (In addition), the adjacent Nubian civilization appears (to have utilized) tattoos (to adorn) their bodies, as well.

09

Look at the four squares [■] that indicate where the following sentence could be added to the passage.

The permanent scars are culturally important and hold important information for those in the society who know their relevance.

Where would the sentence best fit?

2nd

네 개의 네모[■]는 다음 문장이 삽입될 수 있는 부분을 나타내고 있다.

영구적인 상처는 문화적으로 중요하고, 그 관련성을 알고 있는 사람들에게 중요한 정보를 가지고 있다.

이 문장은 어느 자리에 들어가는 것이 가장 적합한가?

두 번째

Insertion 주어진 문장에서 영구적인 반흔이 중요한 정보를 함유하고 있다는 내용 다음 구성원과 직위가 나오는 흐름으로 **[B]**가 적절하다.

10

Directions: An introductory sentence for a brief summary of the passage is provided below. Complete the summary by selecting the THREE answer choices that express the most important ideas in the passage. Some sentences do not belong in the summary because they express ideas that are not presented in the passage or are minor ideas in the passage. **This question is worth 2 points.**

지시: 지문 요약을 위한 도입 문장이 아래에 주어져 있다. 지문의 가장 중요한 내용을 나타내는 보기 3개를 골라 요약을 완성하시오. 어떤 문장은 지문에 언급되지 않은 내용이나 사소한 정보를 담고 있으므로 요약에 포함되지 않는다. 이 문제는 2점이다.

African dress comes in many forms and serves many purposes

(A) Dress has been used by many African societies to communicate information, such as tribal membership and religious beliefs. — paragraph 2

(D) Some aspects of tribal dress are meant to denote a higher sociopolitical status of the bearer, such as elaborate clothing, flywhisks, and crowns. — paragraph 3

(E) Permanent body modifications, such as scarification, perform the same roles as clothing and accessories and are considered an aspect of African dress. — paragraph 6

아프리카 드레스는 다양한 형태로 제공되며 다양한 용도로 사용된다.

(A) 복장은 부족원이나 종교적 신념과 같은 정보를 전달하기 위해 많은 아프리카 사회에 의해 사용되어 왔다.

(D) 부족 복장의 일부 측면은 정교한 옷, 플라이위스키, 왕관과 같은 소지자의 더 높은 사회적 정치적 지위를 나타내기 위한 것이다.

(E) 흉터와 같은 영구적인 신체 변형은 의류 및 액세서리와 동일한 역할을 수행하며 아프리카 복장의 한 측면으로 간주된다.

(B) Flywhisks can be found in many African tribes, as well as in modern society, and are made of a variety of different materials. — MINOR

(C) African tribes developed elaborate costumes and body modifications that allowed them to differentiate themselves from and show power ~~to the colonialists.~~

(F) Tattooing is used in fertility in some regions of Africa, but it is much more common in western cultures as a decorative element. — MINOR

(B) 플라이위스는 현대 사회뿐만 아니라 많은 아프리카 부족에서 발견될 수 있고 다양한 다른 물질로 만들어진다.

(C) 아프리카 부족들은 자신들을 식민주의자들과 차별화하고 힘을 보여줄 수 있는 정교한 의상과 신체 개조품을 개발했다.

(F) 문신은 아프리카의 일부 지역에서 다산성으로 사용되지만, 서양 문화에서는 장식적인 요소로 훨씬 더 흔하다.

TEST 6-2 Evidence of an Asteroid Impact 소행성 충돌의 증거

Introduction	단락 1	대멸종과 생물 다양성 변화
Point	단락 2	원인 분석과 재앙
Point	단락 3	토양층 분석과 이리듐 수치
Point	단락 4	석영의 발견과 유성 충돌의 흔적
Point	단락 5	충돌 분화구의 발견과 추가 연구
Point	단락 6	유성의 연대 추정과 잔해로 인한 멸종 확인

단락 1 — 대멸종과 생물 다양성 변화

1 Throughout Earth's history, there have been mass extinctions that permanently altered its biodiversity. The most recent of these occurred at the boundary between the Cretaceous and Paleogene periods, around 65 million years ago. During this time, scientists estimate that 75% of all species perished. By the end of the extinction, all non-avian dinosaurs had died off, allowing mammals to rise to the dominant position in most ecosystems.

지구의 역사를 통틀어, 지구의 생물 다양성을 영구적으로 변화시킨 대량 멸종이 있었다. 이들 중 가장 최근의 것은 약 6천 5백만 년 전 백악기와 고제3기 사이의 경계에서 발생했다. 이 기간 동안, 과학자들은 모든 종의 75%가 죽었다고 추정한다. 멸종이 끝날 무렵, 모든 비-조류 공룡들은 멸종했고, 포유류가 대부분의 생태계에서 지배적인 위치에 오를 수 있게 되었다.

단락 2 — 원인 분석과 재앙

2 Since discovering this dramatic change in species diversity in the late 19th century, geologists have attempted to explain why so many species died off concurrently. Some posited that dinosaurs could not adapt to climate change or the lowered sea level, while others thought that a more catastrophic event precipitated the disappearance of so many species. They point to such catastrophes as a massive volcanic eruption, an extraterrestrial body striking Earth's surface (which geologists refer to as a bolide), or the effects of cosmic radiation as possible explanations. Unfortunately, they could not produce concrete evidence to support these theories.

19세기 말, 종 다양성에서의 이러한 극적인 변화를 발견한 이후, 지질학자들은 왜 그렇게 많은 종이 동시에 멸종했는지 설명하려고 노력해 왔다. 어떤 사람들은 공룡들이 기후 변화나 낮아진 해수면에 적응할 수 없다고 가정한 반면, 다른 사람들은 더 치명적인 사건이 그렇게 많은 종의 멸종을 촉발시켰다고 생각했다. 그들은 거대한 화산 폭발, 지구 표면에 충돌하는 외계 물체, 또는 우주 방사선의 영향과 같은 재앙들을 가능한 설명으로 가리킨다. 불행하게도, 그들은 이러한 이론을 뒷받침할 구체적인 증거를 제시하지 못했다.

단락 3 — 토양층 분석과 이리듐 수치

3 This changed in 1977 when geologist Walter Alvarez was studying the strata of the soil near Gubbio, Italy and discovered a layer of unique clay from the Cretaceous–Paleogene boundary. Upon sending it for analysis by his father's physics laboratory, he found that it contained nearly 30 times more iridium than is normally found in the rocks of Earth's crust. This was surprising, because, despite the fact that the earth's core and mantle are believed to contain this metallic element, it is rare in the crust. This led him to question the source of the mineral. [■] While a

이것은 1977년 지질학자 Walter Alvarez가 이탈리아 Gubbio 근처의 토양 지층을 연구하고 백악기-고제3기 경계에서 독특한 점토 층을 발견했을 때 바뀌었다. 그의 아버지의 물리학 실험실에서 분석을 하기 위해 그것을 보낸 후, 그는 그것이 지각의 암석에서 보통 발견되는 것보다 거의 30배나 더 많은 이리듐을 함유하고 있다는 것을 발견했다. 지구의 핵과 맨틀이 이 금속성 원소를 포함하고 있다고 믿어졌던 사실에도 불구하고, 이것이 지각에서는 드물기 때문에, 놀라운 일이었다. 이로 인해 그는 광물의 출처에 대해 의문을 품게 되었다. 화산

volcanic eruption could have deposited iridium in Earth's crust, he pointed out that it was more likely that a large (10+ Km in diameter) extraterrestrial body containing iridium forcefully struck the earth and sent up a dense cloud of iridium-filled dust across the atmosphere. [■] He proposed that when this dust mixed with other atmospheric matter, atmospheric circulation pushed it throughout the atmosphere and blocked the sun's rays, thereby causing the extinction of the plants that formed the base of the food chain for most other life forms. [■] Eventually, this dust settled on the ground and entered the soil column. [■] This theory was bolstered when high iridium levels were found in soil from the Cretaceous-Paleogene boundary in locations as distant as Russia, Haiti, and New Zealand, and in layers of sediment under the Pacific and Atlantic Oceans.

4 The theory was further strengthened when geologists studying the Cretaceous-Paleogene Boundary found materials common in proven meteoric impact sites such as the Barringer Crater in Arizona. The first of these, shocked quartz, displays a unique planar pattern that is only created by shockwaves traveling through quartz-filled rock after an intense impact, so it indicates that there was some massive impact at the time. They also found stichovite, a dense compressed silicate uncommon in Earth's crust that is formed only in high-pressure situations, in samples from the period. In addition, the existence of tektites, or tiny glasslike droplets formed when terrestrial material is super heated and thrown into the air during a meteor's impact, in the Cretaceous-Paleogene layer samples from distant locations further supported the theory. The presence of soot in this stratum also points to a meteoric impact, since such an impact would have likely caused widespread wildfires.

5 The missing piece of the puzzle was the lack of a bolide impact site, but the lack of one does not necessarily negate the theory, since Earth's atmosphere can weather and erode geological features over time. However, in 1978, while working for Petróleos Mexicanos, geophysicist Glen Penfield found evidence of an impact crater just off the Yucatan Peninsula, near the town of Chicxulub, that was 180 Km in diameter and 20 km in depth. This find, although under-reported and appreciated at the time, would make it the impact site of the largest bolide to ever strike Earth, which at 10+ Km in diameter, matched Alvarez's estimate perfectly. Further research by geoscientist Alan Hildebrand used core samples, magnetic and gravity surveys to reveal other telltale signs of a bolide at the supposed impact site, such as the existence of andesitic rocks, which have isotopic and chemical compositions similar to tektites found in the Cretaceous-Paleogene boundary across the Caribbean region.

6 Today, Alvarez's theory is the most widely accepted explanation for the mass extinction. Further testing of the event by the Berkeley Geochronology Center dated the bolide impact to 66-65 million years ago, with the extinction occurring within 33,000 years, thereby confirming Alvarez's time line. Even more convincingly, in 2010 a group of scientists published the results of their two decade long study of the Cretaceous-Paleogene boundary layer and concluded that debris from the Chicxulub bolide would have caused the environmental disturbances required to prompt the mass extinction.

---

11 What can be inferred from paragraph 1 about the five major mass extinctions?

(A) Without the mass extinction at the end of the Cretaceous Period the existence of mammals would be unlikely.

(B) Although they were quite rare, mass extinctions have occurred with regularity throughout Earth's history.

(C) Mass extinctions have allowed Earth to support a larger number of species because they reduced competition.

(D) Without the effects of the final mass extinction, mammals would not likely have evolved into the apex predators in their habitats.

Fact (By the end) (of the extinction), all non-avian dinosaurs had died off, allowing mammals (to rise) (to the dominant position) (in most ecosystems).

12 According to paragraph 2, which of the following is **NOT** true regarding scientists' understanding of the extinction of dinosaurs?

(A) There was ~~little research~~ into the topic before the late 1900s.
(B) Some scientists attributed it to climate change and an inability to adapt.
(C) Several theories blaming the extinction on catastrophes emerged.
(D) The evidence that scientists presented for their theories was disputable.

2문단에 따르면, 다음 중 공룡의 멸종에 대한 과학자들의 이해와 관련하여 사실이 아닌 것은?

(A) 1900년대 후반 이전에는 이 주제에 대한 연구가 거의 없었다.
(B) 일부 과학자들은 기후 변화와 적응할 수 없는 탓으로 돌렸다.
(C) 대재앙을 원인으로 하는 몇 가지 이론이 나왔다.
(D) 과학자들이 그들의 이론을 위해 제시한 증거는 논란의 여지가 있었다.

Fact **(B)** - Some posited [that dinosaurs could not adapt (to climate change or the lowered sea level), [while others thought [that a more catastrophic event precipitated the disappearance (of so many species)]]]. **(C)** - They point (to such catastrophes) (as a massive volcanic eruption), an extraterrestrial body striking Earth's surface (which geologists refer to as a bolide), or the effects) (of cosmic radiation) (as possible explanations). **(D)** - Unfortunately, they could not produce concrete evidence (to support) these theories.

13 What can be inferred about Walter Alvarez from paragraph 3?★

(A) He ~~was looking for a pattern~~ in the soil layers that could explain why mass extinctions historically occurred.
(B) His discovery of the iridium-filled layer of clay was the first incontrovertible evidence to support the theory of a bolide impact causing the dinosaur's extinction.
(C) He ~~was unaware of the presence of iridium in Earth's mantle~~ when he came up with his theory about the cause of the Cretaceous–Paleogene boundary.
(D) He was ~~the first scientist to come up with~~ the theory that the dinosaurs went extinct after a major extraterrestrial body collided with Earth's surface.

3문단에 월터 알바레즈에 대해 추론할 수 있는 것은?★

(A) 그는 역사적으로 대멸종이 일어난 이유를 설명할 수 있는 토양층의 패턴을 찾고 있었다.
(B) 이리듐으로 가득 찬 점토층을 발견한 것은 공룡의 멸종을 야기하는 볼라이드 충돌 이론을 뒷받침하는 최초의 명백한 증거였다.
(C) 그는 백악기-팔레오진 경계의 원인에 대한 이론을 제시했을 때 지구 맨틀에 이리듐이 있다는 것을 알지 못했다.
(D) 그는 공룡이 지구 표면과 충돌하면서 멸종했다는 이론을 내놓은 최초의 과학자였다.

Inference [While a volcanic eruption could have deposited iridium (in Earth's crust)], he pointed out [that it was more likely [that a large (10+ Km in diameter) extraterrestrial body containing iridium forcefully struck the earth and sent up a dense cloud (of iridium-filled dust) (across the atmosphere)]].

14 Why does the author mention the "Barringer Crater in Arizona"?

(A) To propose ~~the location of the impact that caused the extinction at the end of the Cretaceous period.~~
(B) To inform the reader that bolide impacts have occurred ~~in many regions of the world~~.
(C) To give an example of a documented impact site where the materials in question were found.
(D) To suggest another source for ~~the materials~~ that were found in the layer of soil ~~corresponding to the Cretaceous–Paleogene boundary~~.

저자는 왜 "애리조나의 배링거 크레이터"를 언급하는가?

(A) 백악기 말 멸종의 원인이 된 충격의 위치를 제안하기 위해.
(B) 독자들에게 폭발 충격이 세계의 많은 지역에서 발생했음을 알리기 위해.
(C) 문제의 물질이 발견된 문서화된 충격 현장의 예를 제시하기 위해.
(D) 백악기-팔레오겐 경계에 해당하는 토양층에서 발견된 물질에 대한 또 다른 출처를 제시하기 위해.

Purpose The theory was further strengthened [when geologists studying the Cretaceous-Paleogene Boundary found materials common (in proven meteoric impact sites) (such as the Barringer Crater) (in Arizona)].

15 According to paragraph 4, which of the following is true about the materials found in the Cretaceous–Paleogene boundary?

(A) They have ~~not been found in any other soil layers~~.
(B) They are ~~only found in bolide impact sites~~.
(C) They can be used to ~~determine the age~~ of the impact site.
(D) They are only formed by the extreme pressure of a bolide impact.

Fact They also found stichovite, a dense compressed silicate uncommon (in Earth's crust) [that is formed only (in high-pressure situations)].

---

16 The term "telltale" in the passage is closest in meaning to:

(A) Satisfactory
(B) Detracting
(C) Destructive
(D) Indicative

---

17 Which of the sentences below best expresses the essential information in the highlighted sentence in the passage? Incorrect choices change the meaning in important ways or leave out essential information.

(01)Further research by geoscientist Alan Hildebrand used (02)core samples, magnetic and gravity surveys to (03)reveal other telltale signs of a bolide at the supposed impact site, such as (04)the existence of andesitic rocks, which (05)have isotopic and chemical compositions similar to tektites, found in the Cretaceous-Paleogene boundary (06)across the Caribbean region.

(A) Andesitic rocks similar to tektites from the Cretaceous-Paleogene Boundary in other areas of the Caribbean, which are indicative of an extraterrestrial impact, were discovered at the impact site by researcher Alan Hildebrand as he surveyed the site's soil layers, magnetism and gravitation.

(B) Alan Hildebrand used scientific testing to reveal Andesitic rocks, which are a form of tektite, thereby ~~indicating that~~ a bolide impact had occurred somewhere in the Caribbean.

(C) Scientist Alan Hildebrand used core samples as well as magnetic and gravity surveys ~~to locate the impact site~~ by searching for andesitic rocks, which have a composition like tektites. – reveal other telltale signs of a bolide.   — 언급 X

(D) The presence of Andesitic rocks in the Caribbean region ~~convinced Alan Hildebrand to conduct~~ further testing on the Cretaceous-Paleogene boundary using core samples and magnetic and gravity surveys to search for the similarly composed tektites which indicated the location of the impact site.

(D) 카리브해 지역에 안데스암 암석이 존재함에 따라 앨런 칠데브란드는 충돌 지점의 위치를 나타내는 유사한 합성 텍타이트를 찾기 위해 코어 샘플과 자기 및 중력 조사를 사용하여 백악기-팔레오진 경계에서 추가 테스트를 수행하도록 설득했다.

Highlight i) Hildebrand가 추정되는 충돌지점에서 명확한 유성의 흔적을 찾기 위해서 여러 조사를 시행했다 ii) 안데스 암석은 백악기와 고제3기의 물질과 비슷한 동위원소 및 화학성분을 갖는다는 정보에서 **(B)**와 **(D)**는 틀린 정보가 있고 **(C)**는 연구의 목적이 틀렸음으로 오답이다.

18 According to paragraph 6, which of the following is **NOT** true regarding Alvarez's explanation for the mass extinction?

(A) It is currently the most commonly accepted explanation for the disappearance of the dinosaurs.
(B) The timing of the impact was confirmed by testing by researchers and coincided with the mass extinction.
(C) ~~It was validated by other scientists~~ and is now accepted as the cause of the extinctions, instead of simply a theory.
(D) It was corroborated by research into the bolide impact at Chicxulub.

6문단에 따르면, 대멸종에 대한 알바레즈의 설명과 관련하여 다음 중 사실이 아닌 것은?

(A) 그것은 현재 공룡의 실종에 대해 가장 일반적으로 받아들여지고 있는 설명이다.
(B) 충돌의 시기는 연구자들에 의한 실험으로 확인되었고 대멸종과 동시에 일어났다.
(C) 그것은 다른 과학자들에 의해 검증되었고 지금은 단순한 이론이 아닌 멸종 원인으로 받아들여지고 있다.
(D) 칙술루브에서 일어난 볼라이드 충격에 대한 연구를 통해 입증되었다.

Fact **(A)** - Today, Alvarez's theory is the most widely accepted explanation (for the mass extinction). **(B)**- Further testing (of the event) (by the Berkeley Geochronology Center) dated the bolide impact (to 66-65 million years ago), (with the extinction) occurring (within 33,000 years), thereby confirming Alvarez's time line. **(D)** - Even more convincingly, (in 2010) a group (of scientists) published the results (of their two decade long study) (of the Cretaceous-Paleogene boundary layer) and concluded [that debris (from the Chicxulub bolide) would have caused the environmental disturbances required (to prompt) the mass extinction].

19 Look at the four squares [■] that indicate where the following sentence could be added to the passage.

The two best explanations would be the result of volcanism or a major bolide collision.

Where would the sentence best fit?

1st

네 개의 네모[■]는 다음 문장이 삽입될 수 있는 부분을 나타내고 있다.

가장 좋은 두 가지 설명은 화산활동의 결과이거나 대형 화산 폭발의 결과일 것이다.

이 문장은 어느 자리에 들어가는 것이 가장 적합한가?

첫 번째

Insertion The two best explanation 을 단서로 앞에는 의문점이 뒤쪽에는 volcanism과 bolide collision의 내용이 나와야 하기 때문에 **[A]**가 적절하다.

20

Directions: An introductory sentence for a brief summary of the passage is provided below. Complete the summary by selecting the THREE answer choices that express the most important ideas in the passage. Some sentences do not belong in the summary because they express ideas that are not presented in the passage or are minor ideas in the passage. **This question is worth 2 points.**

> **Geologists have produced evidence that explains Earth's most recent mass extinction.**
>
> (C) Walter Alvarez found a layer of iridium-rich clay that led him to theorize that the mass extinction was caused by the impact of an extraterrestrial mass on Earth's surface. – paragraph 3
>
> (D) Later scientists found indicators of a bolide impact, such as soot, tektites, and shocked quartz, in the Cretaceous-Paleogene boundary in locations around the world, bolstering the theory of a massive asteroid impact. – paragraph 5
>
> (F) Extensive scientific research has confirmed that Alvarez's theory and time frame accurately describe the event that caused the mass extinction and the Chicxulub crater is the most likely location of the impact. – paragraph 6

(A) Scientists did not discover the existence of a mass extinction after the cretaceous period until the end of the 19th century – MINOR

(B) Geologists and researchers thought that the extinction of the dinosaurs was caused by the effects of solar radiation, a volcanic eruption, or the inability of dinosaurs to adapt to change. – MINOR

(E) Alan Hildebrand's proposed ~~a competing theory~~ of an asteroid impact at Chicxulub after he conducted extensive testing and found indicators of a large meteor impact just off the coast of the Yucatan Peninsula.

지시: 지문 요약을 위한 도입 문장이 아래에 주어져 있다. 지문의 가장 중요한 내용을 나타내는 보기 3개를 골라 요약을 완성하시오. 어떤 문장은 지문에 언급되지 않은 내용이나 사소한 정보를 담고 있으므로 요약에 포함되지 않는다. **이 문제는 2점이다.**

> **지질학자들은 지구의 가장 최근의 대멸종을 설명하는 증거를 만들어냈다.**
>
> (C) 월터 알바레즈는 이리듐이 풍부한 점토층을 발견하여 대멸종이 지구 표면에 있는 외계 질량의 충격에 의해 발생했다는 이론을 세웠다.
>
> (D) 후에 과학자들은 거대한 소행성 충돌 이론을 뒷받침하면서 백악기와 팔레진 경계에서 그을음, 철광석, 충격 석영과 같은 볼라이드 충돌의 징후를 발견했다.
>
> (F) 광범위한 과학적 연구는 알바레즈의 이론과 시간대가 대멸종을 일으킨 사건을 정확하게 묘사하고 있으며 칙술루브 분화구가 충돌의 가장 유력한 장소라는 것을 확인시켜 주었다.

(A) 과학자들은 백악기 이후 19세기 말까지 대멸종의 존재를 발견하지 못했다.

(B) 지질학자들과 연구원들은 공룡들의 멸종이 태양 복사, 화산 폭발, 또는 공룡들이 변화에 적응하지 못했기 때문에 일어났다고 생각했다.

(E) 앨런 힐데브란드는 광범위한 실험을 통해 유카탄 반도 바로 앞바다에서 대규모 운석 충돌 징후를 발견한 후 칙술루브에서 소행성 충돌에 대한 경쟁 이론을 제안했다.

usherin.usher.co.kr

TEST 6-3 Native Americans and European Trade Goods
아메리카 원주민 및 유럽 무역 상품

Introduction	단락 1	유럽인들의 정착 이전의 무역로와 변화
Point	단락 2	진정한 경제적 교류와 교역소 설립
Point	단락 3	모피 무역의 활성화와 문화적 이해
Point	단락 4	유럽 생산품들과의 직접 무역과 환대
Point	단락 5	시장 포화로 인한 무역 상품의 변화
Point	단락 6	무역 증가로 인한 부작용과 무역 중단

단락 1 유럽인들의 정착 이전의 무역로와 변화

1 Prior to their exploration and settlement by Europeans, the United States and Canada hosted a thriving trade network administered by the various native tribes found there. These Pre-Colombian tribes developed extensive trade routes between themselves that allowed them to trade pelts, shells, pottery and other handicrafts from the Great Lakes to the Gulf of Mexico and as far west as the Rocky Mountains. These interactions changed the individual tribes, by providing them not only new material goods and revenue, but also differing ideas and ways of thinking. These changes would, however, pale in comparison to the changes brought about by the introduction of Europeans into the North American economy.

유럽인들에 의한 탐험과 정착 이전에, 미국과 캐나다는 그곳에서 발견된 다양한 토착 부족들에 의해 관리된 번영하는 무역 네트워크를 관리했다. 콜럼버스가 미 대륙을 발견하기 이전의 이러한 부족들은 오대호에서 멕시코 만까지, 그리고 서쪽으로 록키 산맥까지 가죽, 조개껍데기, 도자기 등 수공예품을 거래할 수 있는 광범위한 무역로를 개발했다. 이러한 상호작용은 새로운 물질적 상품과 수익뿐만 아니라 다양한 생각과 사고방식을 제공함으로써 개별 부족들을 변화시켰다. 그러나 이러한 변화는 유럽인들이 북미 경제에 유입되면서 야기된 변화에 비하면 미미할 것이다.

단락 2 진정한 경제적 교류와 교역소 설립

2 Although native tribes had encountered Europeans as early as the 11th Century, when Norse explorers tried to create a settlement in eastern Canada, true economic interactions did not occur until the early 1500s. At this time, French fishermen and Basque whalers were regularly travelling to the Grand Banks off of Newfoundland and began trading with the locals they met when they came ashore to process their catches. The native inhabitants they met were eager to trade their goods for European products, such as metal tools, glassware and cloth, and allowed European explorers and traders to establish settlements and trading posts throughout New England, along the St. Lawrence River, and as far south as Virginia. This situation provided European explorers a beneficial new trading source, but perhaps the biggest draw for them was the trade in fur, especially that of beaver pelts, which had become a phenomenally popular status symbol in Europe at the time.

비록 토착 부족들이 11세기 초에 유럽인들을 만났지만, 노르드 탐험가들이 동부 캐나다에 정착지를 만들려고 했을 때, 진정한 경제적 교류는 1500년대 초까지 일어나지 않았다. 이 시기에 프랑스 어부들과 바스크의 포경선들은 정기적으로 뉴펀들랜드에서 떨어진 그랜드 뱅크(Grand Bank)로 이동하고 있었으며, 그들이 해안으로 와서 잡은 어획물을 처리하기 위해 만난 현지인들과 거래를 시작했다. 그들이 만난 원주민들은 그들의 상품을 금속 도구, 유리제품, 옷과 같은 유럽 상품과 교환하기를 열망했고, 유럽 탐험가들과 무역상들이 뉴잉글랜드 전역, 세인트 로렌스 강변, 그리고 먼 남쪽 버지니아에 걸쳐 정착지와 교역소를 설립할 수 있도록 허락했다. 이러한 상황은 유럽 탐험가들에게 유익한 새로운 무역원을 제공했지만, 아마도 그들에게 가장 큰 끌림은 모피 무역, 특히 그 당시 유럽에서 경이적으로 인기 있는 지위의 상징이 된 비버 가죽 무역이었을 것이다.

3 The fur trade dominated early European-Native American trade and had a profound impact on many aspects of the native societies including their organization, relationships with one another, and even their art and handicrafts. Prior to their interactions with European explorers and products, these tribes had spent thousands of years procuring and trading materials and refined products that were both precious and symbolically important to their cultures' ideals of leadership, influence, wealth and spirituality. The products they received from trading with the Europeans offered them these same opportunities and were incorporated into the indigenous communities values, crafts, and understanding of the world early on.

4 With the permanent settlements, the native tribes had more interaction with European products and became even more influenced by them. Over time, long held traditions such as pottery and tool making were abandoned in favor of European products such as brass kettles and durable steel and iron tools. This became more pronounced as European settlements spread westward and encroached on tribal lands, which allowed them to trade directly with the local tribes. This can be seen in the early 17th century Dutch settlements in the upper Hudson area of present day New York. [■] Prior to these settlements, the powerful Iroquois tribe used beaver tooth blades to carve moose antlers into rudimentary three or four tine combs, but after the introduction of steel blades by their Dutch neighbors these ornaments became much more ornate. [■] In fact, archaeologists excavated one from a Cayuga village with many narrow tines and an intricate carving of two European's on horseback. [■] It is assumed this was to commemorate the visit of an English dignitary, Wentworth Greenhalgh, in 1699. [■]

5 Although many of the European goods that found their way into the society provided increased productivity and security – guns, metal blades, and brass kettles – their longevity led to market saturation, eventually causing a shift in trading. Over time, native tribes began to favor raw materials and the trade in cloth, wool, glass beads and decorative silver became more important. Native tribes incorporated items like glass beads into their practices and costumes in place of ornaments made of pipestone, copper, and shell. Some local artisans, usually tribeswomen, used these replacement materials to create elaborate formal attire and regalia. The new products offered the native tribes the correct look and symbolism for their practices, but the 'luxurious' imported products also gave the bearer an air of power, wealth, and success.

분위기를 주었다.

단락 6
무역 증가로 인한 부작용과 무역 중단

6   Unfortunately for the native tribes, these positive trade interactions with European settlers did not last forever. Over time, as the number of settlers and traders in the region increased, they brought with them corporatization of the industry and European diseases. The native population was not immune to the ill effects of either of these and soon began to suffer. By the 1850s, beaver fur had fallen out of favor in Europe and the native tribes lost a major source of income. This, combined with oppression by the settlers, threw them into a state of poverty from which many of the tribes have still not recovered.

원주민들에게 불행하게도, 유럽 정착민들과의 이러한 긍정적인 무역 상호작용은 영원히 지속되지 않았다. 시간이 지남에 따라, 이 지역의 정착민들과 무역상들의 수가 증가하면서, 그들은 그 산업의 민영화와 유럽의 질병들을 가지고 왔다. 원주민들은 이 둘 중 어느 것의 부작용도 견뎌내지 못했고 곧 고통을 받기 시작했다. 1850년대까지 비버의 털은 유럽에서 인기가 떨어졌고 원주민들은 주요 수입원을 잃었다. 이것은 정착민들에 의한 억압과 결합되어 많은 부족들이 아직도 회복하지 못한 빈곤의 상태로 내몰게 되었다.

---

21   Why does the author say that tribal changes will "pale in comparison to the changes brought about by the introduction of Europeans"?

(A) Because the European settlers would ~~offer a greater diversity of trade goods~~.
(B) Because ~~early native tribes~~ were very ~~similar and underwent few changes~~.
(C) Because trade with Europeans would profoundly change life for the native tribes.
(D) Because European settlers ~~had much lighter skin~~ than the members of the native tribes.

저자는 왜 부족의 변화가 "유럽인의 유입에 의해 초래된 변화와 비교될 것"이라고 말하는가?

(A) 왜냐하면 유럽 정착민들은 ~~더 다양한 무역 상품을 제공할 것이기 때문이다~~.
(B) 왜냐하면 ~~초기 원주민 부족들은 매우 비슷했고 거의 변화를 겪지 않았기 때문이다~~.
(C) 왜냐하면 유럽인과의 무역은 원주민 부족의 삶을 크게 바꿀 것이기 때문이다.
(D) 왜냐하면 유럽 정착민들은 원주민 부족들보다 ~~훨씬 더 하얀 피부를~~ 가지고 있었기 때문이다.

Purpose   These interactions changed the individual tribes, (by providing) them not only new material goods and revenue, but also differing ideas and ways (of thinking).

22. Which of the sentences below best expresses the essential information in the highlighted sentence in the passage? Incorrect choices change the meaning in important ways or leave out essential information.

(01)This situation provided European explorers a beneficial new trading source, but perhaps the (02)biggest draw (for them) was the trade (in fur), especially that (of (03)beaver pelts), [which had become a (04)phenomenally popular status symbol (in Europe) (at the time)].

(A) Extended trade networks, especially those involved in animal hides, like beaver, which was considered a signifier of wealth, were an advantage of European settlements.
(B) European explorers first went to America to find a new source of beaver pelts, which had become important fashion accessories in Europe.
(C) Early native traders provided European settlers with beaver fur, which had religious significance in Europe, thereby starting a new trade network in North America.
(D) Explorers introduced the beaver to Europe, because they were attempting to introduce a new trade source for their settlements in North America, where they were very popular.

아래 문장 중 지문 속의 음영된 문장의 핵심 정보를 가장 잘 표현하고 있는 것은 무엇인가? 오답은 문장의 의미를 현저히 왜곡하거나 핵심 정보를 빠뜨리고 있다.

이러한 상황은 유럽 탐험가들에게 유익한 새로운 무역원을 제공했지만, 아마도 그들에게 가장 큰 끌림은 모피 무역, 특히 그 당시 유럽에서 경이적으로 인기 있는 지위의 상징이 된 비버 가죽 무역이었을 것이다.

(A) 확장된 무역 네트워크, 특히 부의 상징으로 여겨졌던 비버와 같은 동물 가죽과 관련된 것은 유럽 정착지의 이점이었다.
(B) 유럽 탐험가들은 유럽에서 중요한 패션 액세서리가 된 비버 가죽의 새로운 공급원을 찾기 위해 처음으로 미국으로 갔다.
(C) 초기 원주민 무역업자들은 유럽 정착민들에게 비버 모피를 제공했는데, 이것은 유럽에서 종교적인 의미가 있었고, 따라서 북미에서 새로운 무역망을 시작했다.
(D) 탐험가들은 비버를 유럽에 소개했는데, 이는 그들이 매우 인기가 있었던 북미에 정착하기 위해 새로운 무역원을 소개하려고 시도했기 때문이다.

Highlight   i) 유럽탐험가들에게 도움이되는 자원을 주었다 ii) 가장 특별한 것은 비버의 가죽과 같은 모피였다 iii) 그때 당시에 유럽에서 굉장히 인기가 좋았다 의 정보를 다 담고 있는 보기는 A이다.

23. According to paragraph 2, which of the following is **NOT** true regarding early Europeans in North America?

(A) The first Europeans reached North America during the 11th century.
(B) French fishermen and Basque whalers visited Newfoundland to trade with the natives there.
(C) The goods they brought to N. America were highly sought after by the native inhabitants.
(D) Early European settlers benefited greatly from trading with the N. American natives.

2문단에 따르면, 북미의 초기 유럽인들과 관련하여 사실이 아닌 것은 다음 중 무엇인가?

(A) 최초의 유럽인들은 11세기 동안 북아메리카에 도착했다.
(B) 프랑스 어부들과 바스크 고래잡이들은 뉴펀들랜드를 방문하여 원주민들과 무역을 했다.
(C) 그들이 북미로 가져온 상품은 원주민들이 많이 찾는 상품이었다.
(D) 초기 유럽 정착민들은 북미 원주민과의 무역으로 많은 혜택을 받았다.

Fact   **(A)** - Although native tribes had encountered Europeans as early (as the 11th Century   **(C)** - The native inhabitants [they met] were eager (to trade) their goods (for European products), (such as metal tools, glassware and cloth).   **(D)** - This situation provided European explorers a beneficial new trading source.

24

According to paragraph 3, which of the following is true regarding early North American trade?

(A) European explorers and settlers ~~introduced trade to the native tribes~~ they found in North America.
(B) ~~Europeans brought furs to trade with the natives~~ they came across because they were considered valuable in Europe at the time.
(C) The native inhabitants were well versed in long distance travel long before the appearance of Europeans.
(D) Products from the Europeans ~~were revered~~ in the native communities because of their ~~novelty~~.

3문단에 따르면, 북미 초기 무역에 관한 다음 중 올바른 것은?

(A) 유럽 탐험가들과 정착민들은 그들이 북미에서 발견한 원주민 부족들에게 무역을 ~~소개했다~~.
(B) 유럽인들은 모피들이 그 당시 유럽에서 가치 있는 것으로 여겨졌기 때문에 그들이 마주친 ~~원주민들과 무역하기 위해 모피를 가져왔다~~.
(C) 원주민들은 유럽인들이 등장하기 훨씬 전부터 장거리 여행에 익숙했다.
(D) 유럽산 제품은 그 참신함 때문에 원주민 사회에서 존경을 받았다.

> **Fact** The products [they received (from trading) (with the Europeans)] offered them these same opportunities and were incorporated (into the indigenous communities values, crafts, and understanding) (of the world) early on.

25

The term "commemorate" in the passage is closest in meaning to:

(A) Assemble
(B) Remember
(C) Invite
(D) Tell of

지문의 단어 "기념하다"의 의미와 가장 유사한 것은?

(A) 조립하다
(B) 기억하다
(C) 초대하다
(D) 에 대해 말하다

26

What can be inferred about the native tribes from paragraph 4? ★

(A) The Iroquois tribes were ~~the most welcoming~~ of European settlers and created decoratice artwork in their honor.
(B) Interaction with new settlers was ~~so positive that~~ they spread westward to trade with them.
(C) European settlements and the products they brought with them changed the convention of the sedentary tribes.
(D) The introduction of metal tools ~~caused~~ the native tribes ~~to admire the European settlers for their advanced technology~~.

4단락에서 원주민 부족에 대해 추론할 수 있는 것은? ★

(A) 이로쿼이 부족은 유럽 정착민들을 ~~가장 환영했고~~ 그들의 명예를 위해 장식 미술품을 만들었다.
(B) 새로운 정착민들과의 상호작용은 ~~매우 긍정적이어서~~ 그들은 그들과 무역하기 위해 서쪽으로 퍼져나갔다.
(C) 유럽의 정착지와 그들이 가져온 상품들은 정착한 부족들의 관습을 바꾸었다.
(D) 금속 도구의 도입은 원주민 부족들로 ~~하여금 그들의 진보된 기술에 대해 유럽 정착민들을 존경하게 만들었다~~.

> **Inference** This became more pronounced [as European settlements spread westward and encroached (on tribal lands), [which allowed them (to trade) directly (with the local tribes)]]

27

According to paragraph 5, which of the following is **NOT** true about the European products that were traded with the natives?

(A) Initially the natives favored products that provided them protection and the ability to produce more.
(B) The type of goods traded changed over time.
(C) Tribespeople incorporated European goods into their traditional customs and practices.
(D) European products were chosen because they ~~had a symbolic value not found in traditional products.~~

문단5에 따르면, 다음 중 현지인들과 거래된 유럽 제품에 대해 사실이 아닌 것은?

(A) 처음에 원주민들은 보호와 더 많은 생산 능력을 제공하는 제품을 선호했다.
(B) 거래되는 상품의 종류는 시간이 지남에 따라 변화했다.
(C) 부족 사람들은 그들의 전통적인 관습과 관행에 유럽 상품을 포함시켰다.
(D) 유럽산 제품은 전통적인 제품에는 없는 상징적인 가치가 있기 때문에 선택되었다.

Fact **(A)** - [Although many (of the European goods) [that found their way (into the society)] provided increased productivity and security – guns, metal blades, and brass kettles –] **(B)** - (Over time), native tribes began (to favor) raw materials and the trade (in cloth, wool, glass beads) and decorative silver became more important. **(C)** - Native tribes incorporated items (like glass beads) (into their practices and costumes) (in place) (of ornaments) made (of pipestone, copper, and shell).

28

According to paragraph 6, which of the following can be inferred regarding the native tribes after European settlement?

(A) New diseases killed many of the native inhabitants of North America.
(B) European ~~settlers purposefully killed off the natives~~ in order to take their lands.
(C) The fur trade made the tribes very wealthy, but they ~~were unable to compete when commercial fur companies entered the market.~~
(D) ~~Tribes that avoided trading with the Europeans remained powerful~~ because their economies were not dependent upon the fur trade.

6항에 따르면, 다음 중 유럽 정착 후 원주민 부족에 대해 추론할 수 있는 것은?

(A) 새로운 질병은 북미 원주민들의 많은 목숨을 앗아갔다.
(B) 유럽 ~~정착민들은 그들의 땅을 차지하기 위해 의도적으로 원주민들을 죽였다.~~
(C) 모피 무역은 부족들을 매우 부유하게 만들었지만, ~~상업적인 모피 회사들이 시장에 들어왔을 때 그들은 경쟁할 수 없었다.~~
(D) ~~유럽과의 무역을 거부하는 부족들은~~ 그들의 경제가 모피 무역에 의존하지 않았기 때문에 ~~여전히 강력했다.~~

Inference The native population was not immune (to the ill effects) (of either) (of these) and soon began (to suffer).

29

Look at the four squares [■] that indicate where the following sentence could be added to the passage.

Others found in the region seem to indicate that the natives felt that their new neighbors possessed great wealth and power.

Where would the sentence best fit?

4th

네 개의 네모[■]는 다음 문장이 삽입될 수 있는 부분을 나타내고 있다.

이 지역에서 발견된 다른 것들은 원주민들이 그들의 새로운 이웃들이 엄청난 부와 권력을 가지고 있다고 느꼈다는 것을 보여주는 것으로 보인다.

이 문장은 어느 자리에 들어가는 것이 가장 적합한가?

네 번째

30

Directions: An introductory sentence for a brief summary of the passage is provided below. Complete the summary by selecting the THREE answer choices that express the most important ideas in the passage. Some sentences do not belong in the summary because they express ideas that are not presented in the passage or are minor ideas in the passage. **This question is worth 2 points.**

From the early 1500s to the mid 1800s Native North American tribes traded extensively with European settlers and traders.

(B) The tribes that inhabited North America before it was colonized allowed European's to settle the land because they wanted access to their goods.
　　　　　　　　　　　　　　　　　　　　– paragraph 2

(D) European products were adopted by the native inhabitants and eventually began to replace traditional products in both everyday life and in spiritual practices.　　　– paragraph 5

(F) Trade between European settlers and native tribes eventually had a detrimental effect on the tribespeople.　　　　　　　– paragraph 6

(A) Norse settlers set up the first permanent settlements in North America, but the did not trade with the native inhabitants until the fifteenth century.

(C) North American beaver pelts were in high demand ~~because~~ the native tribes were unaware of their value ~~and sold them cheaper~~ than their European counterparts.

(E) Native tribes adopted the usage of European goods such as brass kettles and glass beads ~~to more quickly assimilate with the new settlers.~~

1500년대 초반부터 1800년대 중반까지 북미 원주민 부족들은 유럽 정착민들과 무역상들과 광범위하게 무역을 했다.

(B) 식민지화되기 전에 북아메리카에 거주했던 부족들은 유럽인들이 그들의 물품에 접근하기를 원했기 때문에 그 땅에 정착하는 것을 허락했다.

(D) 유럽 제품들은 원주민들에 의해 채택되었고 결국 일상과 영적 실천 모두에서 전통적인 제품들을 대체하기 시작했다.

(F) 유럽 정착민과 토착 부족 간의 무역은 결국 부족 사람들에게 해로운 영향을 미쳤다.

(A) 북유럽 정착민들은 북미에 최초의 영구 정착촌을 세웠지만, 15세기까지 원주민들과 무역을 하지 않았다.

(C) 북미의 비버 가죽은 원주민 부족들이 그들의 가치를 모르고 유럽보다 ~~싸게 팔았기 때문에~~ 수요가 많았다.

(E) 원주민 부족들은 ~~새로운 정착민들과 더 빨리 동화되기 위해~~ 놋쇠 주전자와 유리구슬과 같은 유럽 상품들의 사용을 채택했다.

첨삭권 소개

01 스피킹/라이팅 첨삭이 필요한 이유?

대체로 독학을 할 수 있다고 생각하는 리딩, 리스닝과는 달리 스피킹 라이팅은 독학이 힘듭니다.

이유는? "내가 뭘 틀렸는지 모르니까!!!"
대안은?? 독학이라고 했으니, 과외나, 학원은 빼고, 남는 건 첨삭이나, 그냥 혼자 틀린 걸 계속 보거나….

그런데, 첨삭을 받으러 검색을 해보면 가격이 라이팅 한편당 23000…원…?
한편만 첨삭 받으면 끝날 것 같진 않은 내 실력을 봐서는…
비용 감당 안됨. 어쩌지?

02 학원 다니면 첨삭도 해결되나요?

단과반 (2020.10.05 현재)

학원명		첨삭 횟수	실전 프로그램 사용 여부	수업일수	수업시간	가격(D.C적용가)	
어셔어학원	단과 스피킹	월5회	O	주5일	50분	최저가	160,000
	단과 라이팅	월5회	O	주5일	50분	최저가	160,000
해**어학원	단과 스피킹	월2회	×	주5일	50분		165,000
	단과 라이팅	월2회	×	주5일	50분		165,000
영**어학원	단과 스피킹 (2020.06 이후 단과 수업 진행×)	폐강	O				
	단과 라이팅 (2020.06 이후 단과 수업 진행×)	폐강	O				

03 학원까지 다니고 싶진 않은데 스피킹/라이팅 첨삭만 받을 순 없나요?

라이팅 첨삭
30회권은 어셔수강생에게만 제공됩니다
(2020.10.05 현재)

1회권	어셔	1회 첨삭권 25,000원	최저가 1회당 25,000원
	해**	1회권 없음	1회권 없음
	영**	1회 첨삭(1일 소요)권 28,000원	1회당(1일 소요)권 28,000원
5회권	어셔	5회 첨삭권 75,000원	최저가 1회당 15,000원
	해**	5회 첨삭권 120,000원	1회당 24,000원
	영**	5회 첨삭(1일 소요)권 119,000원	1회당(1일소요)권 23,800원
10회권	어셔	10회 첨삭권 100,000원	최저가 1회당 10,000원
	해**	10회권 없음	10회권 없음
	영**	10회권 없음	10회권 없음
30회권 어셔수강생 한정	어셔	30회 첨삭권 220,000원	최저가 1회당 7,330원 *어셔수강생 한정
	해**	30회권 없음	30회권 없음
	영**	30회권 없음	30회권 없음

스피팅 첨삭
(2020.10.05 현재)

1회권	어셔	1회 첨삭권 15,000원	최저가 1회당 15,000원
	해**	1회권 없음	1회권 없음
	영**	1회 첨삭(1일 소요)권 16,000원	1회당(1일 소요)권 16,000원
5회권	어셔	5회 첨삭권 56,000원	최저가 1회당 11,200원
	해**	5회 첨삭권 139,000원	1회당 27,800원
	영**	5회 첨삭(1일 소요)권 68,000원	1회당(1일소요)권 13,600원
10회권	어셔	10회 첨삭권 80,000원	최저가 1회당 8,000원
	해**	10회권 없음	10회권 없음
	영**	10회권 없음	10회권 없음
30회권 어셔수강생 한정	어셔	30회 첨삭권 144,000원	최저가 1회당 4,800원(1회당) *어셔수강생 한정
	해**	30회권 없음	30회권 없음
	영**	30회권 없음	30회권 없음

04 첨삭 구성은 어떻게 되나요?

스피킹 첨삭

1. 토픽 제공
2. 학생 음성 녹음(홈페이지 자체 기능 제공)
3. 학생 self 자가 첨삭
4. 첨삭 전문가 음성 녹음 지원+채점
5. 채점을 출제 기관인 ETS와 같은 기준으로 구체적 채점

라이팅 첨삭

1. 토픽 제공
2. 학생 1차 답변
3. 학생 self 자가 첨삭
4. 첨삭
5. 채점을 출제 기관인 ETS와 같은 기준으로 구체적 채점

05 첨삭 신청하기

라이팅 첨삭권

1회 첨삭권	5회 첨삭권	10회 첨삭권	30회 첨삭권
사용기간 15일	사용기간 30일	사용기간 60일	사용기간 90일
25,000원	~~110,000원~~ → 75,000원	~~220,000원~~ → 100,000원	~~660,000원~~ → 220,000원

*30회권은 어셔수강생에게만 제공됩니다

스피킹 첨삭권

1회 첨삭권	5회 첨삭권	10회 첨삭권	30회 첨삭권
사용기간 15일	사용기간 30일	사용기간 60일	사용기간 90일
15,000원	~~80,000원~~ → 56,000원	~~160,000원~~ → 160,000원	~~480,000원~~ → 144,000원

*30회권은 어셔수강생에게만 제공됩니다

첨삭은 근무일 기준(평일)으로 진행되며, 주말 또는 휴일은 익일 평일에 진행됩니다.

강의대상

1. 책으로 토플을 공부해왔지만 컴퓨터로 실전 대비가 필요한 학생
2. 단기간 실전과 같은 형식의 문제풀이를 통한 실전감각이 필요한 학생
3. 토플 공부를 제대로 해본 적은 없지만 급하게 제출할 점수가 필요한 학생
4. 영어 실력이 어느정도 있고 실전 연습을 통해 빠르게 점수를 만들고 싶은 학생

강의목표

종이로 공부하고 시험보는 것이 아닌,
컴퓨터로 보는 실제 시험 환경에서,
시험당일 시험보는 스케줄대로 시험을 보고
시험 당일엔 확인할 수 없는 답안들을 확인하는
Reading과 Listening 수업을 듣고,
점수만 주는 Speaking & Writing 시험이 아닌,
점수와, 점수의 근거, 점수를 올리기 위한 첨삭까지
모든 걸 포함하는 풀 케어 서비스

별도 구매 가능

모의토플
시장 최저가로 준비된 시험가격

~~50,000원~~

50% 추가 할인가
25,000원

가격소개
*시중에 나와있는 3사를 비교한 표입니다.

시장구성	USHER	D사	H사
구성	Half and Full (new 토플 반영)	Half and Full (new 토플 반영)	자체시험 (4가지 영역중 하나선택)
가격	27,000원/50,000원	27,000원/52,000원	66,000원
응시날짜	언제든지 응시가능	언제든지 응시가능	매주 토요일
첨삭	있음	없음	있음

등록하기

25% off
3일 등록
~~600,000원~~
450,000원
하루 15만원

50% off
5일 등록
~~1,000,000원~~
500,000원
하루 10만원

50% off
7일 등록
~~1,400,000원~~
700,000원
하루 10만원

가격구성

모의토플 + 첨삭 + 수업

06 모의토플
시장 최저가로 준비된 시험가격

~~50,000원~~

50% 추가 할인가
25,000원

가격소개
*시중에 나와있는 3사를 비교한 표입니다.

시장구성	USHER	D사	H사
구성	Half and Full (new 토플 반영)	Half and Full (new 토플 반영)	자체시험 (4가지 영역중 하나선택)
가격	27,000원/50,000원	27,000원/52,000원	66,000원
응시날짜	언제든지 응시가능	언제든지 응시가능	매주 토요일
첨삭	있음	없음	있음

07 스피킹 첨삭
시장 최저가 첨삭 가격!!!

스피킹 1일 4문제
~~60,000원~~

50% 추가 할인가
30,000원

01 스피킹 첨삭
2020. 10. 05

1회권	어셔	1회 첨삭권 15,000원	최저가 1회당 15,000원
	해**	1회권 없음	1회권 없음
	영**	1회 첨삭(1일소요)권 16,000원	1회당(1일소요)권 16,000원
5회권	어셔	5회 첨삭권 56,000원	최저가 1회당 11,200원
	해**	5회 첨삭권 139,000원	1회당 27,800원
	영**	5회 첨삭(1일소요)권 68,000원	1회당(1일소요)권 13,600원
10회권	어셔	10회 첨삭권 80,000원	최저가 1회당 8,000원
	해**	10회권 없음	10회권 없음
	영**	10회권 없음	10회권 없음
10회권 *어셔 수강생 한정	어셔	30회 첨삭권 144,000원	최저가 1회당 4,800원 *어셔수강생 한정
	해**	30회권 없음	30회권 없음
	영**	30회권 없음	30회권 없음

08 라이팅 첨삭
시장 최저가 첨삭 가격!!!

라이팅 1일 2문제
~~50,000원~~

50% 추가 할인가
25,000원

02 라이팅 첨삭
2020. 10. 05

1회권	어셔	1회 첨삭권 25,000원	최저가 1회당 25,000원
	해**	1회권 없음	1회권 없음
	영**	1회 첨삭(1일소요)권 28,000원	1회당(1일소요)권 28,000원
5회권	어셔	5회 첨삭권 75,000원	최저가 1회당 15,000원
	해**	5회 첨삭권 120,000원	1회당 24,000원
	영**	5회 첨삭(1일소요)권 119,000원	1회당(1일소요)권 23,000원
10회권	어셔	10회 첨삭권 100,000원	최저가 1회당 10,000원
	해**	10회권 없음	10회권 없음
	영**	10회권 없음	10회권 없음
10회권 *어셔 수강생 한정	어셔	30회 첨삭권 220,000원	최저가 1회당 7,330원 *어셔수강생 한정
	해**	30회권 없음	30회권 없음
	영**	30회권 없음	30회권 없음

09 수업
국내 유일 수업!

수업 1일 4시간
~~40,000원~~

50% 추가 할인가
20,000원

국내유일
비교대상이 없음

usherin.usher.co.kr

usherin.usher.co.kr